W9-DFY-947

POST–COLD WAR POLICY

The Social and Domestic Context

Published in conjunction with the
Policy Studies Organization

Advisory board: J. Edwin Benton, *University of South Florida;* Roger
Handberg, *Central Florida University;* Christina Jeffrey, *Kennesaw College;*
Jonathan Morell, *Industrial Technology Institute;* Marian Palley, *University
of Delaware;* Austin Ranney, *University of California at Berkeley;* Warren
Samuels, *Michigan State University;* Frank Scioli, *National Science
Foundation;* and William Waugh, *Georgia State University*

HN
57
.P58
1995

POST–COLD WAR POLICY

The Social and Domestic Context

Edited by

William Crotty
Northwestern University

GOSHEN COLLEGE LIBRARY
GOSHEN, INDIANA

Nelson-Hall Publishers
Chicago

Project Editor: Dorothy Anderson
Typesetter: Alexander Graphics
Printer: Capital City Press
Cover Painting: "Linoleum" by Victoria J. Ness

Library of Congress Cataloging-in-Publication Data

Post-cold war policy : the social and domestic context / edited by
  William Crotty.
      p. cm.
    Includes bibliographical references and index.
    ISBN 0-8304-1361-8
    1. United States--Social policy. 2. United States--Economic
policy. 3. World politics--1985-1995. 4. United States--Foreign
economic relations. I. Crotty, William J.
    HN57.P58 1995
    306'.0973'09049--dc20   94-34114
                                                                    CIP

Copyright © 1995 by Nelson-Hall Inc.

All rights reserved. No part of this book may be reproduced in any form without permission in
writing from the publisher, except by a reviewer who wishes to quote brief passages in
connection with a review written for broadcast or for inclusion in a magazine or newspaper. For
information address Nelson-Hall Publishers, 111 North Canal Street, Chicago, Ilinois 60606.

Manufactured in the United States of America

10 9 8 7 6 5 4 3 2 1

 The paper used in this book meets the minimum requirements of American National Standard for Information Sciences—Permanence of Paper for Printed Library Materials, ANSI Z39.48-1984.

Dedicated to the
memory of the late
Miriam K. Mills,
who was a major
part of this project.

Contents

Introduction

The Cold War has come to an end. The denouement was quick, too quick and unexpected for any serious long-range planning to have taken place.

The earliest phases of the newly dawned post–Cold War era have been unsettling. In the short period since the Cold War's abrupt end, it has already begun to dim in memory, an artifact of historical conditions and a curiosity of a particular phase in America's, and the world's, political evolution. Such perceptions carry a price; they can serve to diminish an appreciation of the overwhelming influence Cold War animosities had in determining national priorities, absorbing a country's resources and framing its national psyche. The potential for a cataclysmic, worldwide conflagration was always present. The Cold War with its constant threat of mutual nuclear annihilation, determined a state's policies, governmental objectives (national survival, the triumph of democracy) and international and domestic commitments during the last half of the twentieth century. Above all, Cold War concerns took precedence in defining who we were, what we hoped to achieve, and what we could reasonably expect to accomplish as a nation and a people.

Then it ended. And curiously, the removal of a bipolar super-power contest for world supremacy has brought in its wake its own anxieties and uncertainties. The ramifications of the Cold War's demise are just beginning to be appreciated. The world's economies are in various states of recession and contraction, with the promise of more of the same. International economic competition among the world's great producers has replaced military strength and the potential for overwhelming force as the new standard for power, status, and influence. It is a change that many nations, including the United States, have proven poorly prepared to meet. Internally, domestic options in a shrinking economy have to be rethought. What programs and which groups should the government support? What best serves a reformulated conception of the national interest and national strength, and what is best left to private initiatives and a restyled free enterprise economy?

Internationally, the now former Soviet Union has surrendered its role as one of the two undisputed super powers, in the process giving up parts of its former national territory as well as its control over Eastern Europe. Efforts at democratization and the attempts to modernize its economy and institute free market assumptions have placed extraordinary strains on the newly defined nation's social fabric. As with most of the former Communist world, its future remains uncertain.

The rest of Eastern Europe is undergoing much the same political and economic metamorphosis. Poland, the first of the former Soviet-dominated nations to begin the transformation, is experimenting with forms of democratic representation (with some recent indications of successes). Turnover in its leadership has destabilized but not halted its efforts to survive the dislocations inherent in a move to a free market economy. Czechoslovakia, following a period of self-examination, has divided into two separate nations. Hungary has celebrated its return to free nation status with a more comfortable, although still stressful, embrace of the new political and economic commitments. Yugoslavia has disappeared into a brutal civil war that has revived ancient hostilities and pitted Muslims, Croats, and Serbs against each other, a form of ethnic conflict that has surfaced in parts of the old Soviet Union, Turkey, Iran, Iraq, and the Middle East, among other places. It is a form of warfare that many fear may prove to be the major international challenge to future peace. The Balkan nations have yet to settle upon any clear conception of their future direction. And, as challenging as any, the former East Germany has merged with the former West Germany, placing enormous strain on the reunified nation's economy but establishing the groundwork for the emergence of the new Germany as the dominant force in a restructured, and more interdependent, Western Europe. And to add more to the previously unimaginable, the new Russia and the countries it formerly dominated, until recently seen as the principal threat to world order and democratic development, have turned to the United States and its European allies for the economic help and political guidance necessary in the evolution to a new society.

The Western democracies are experiencing their own problems. The consequence and future course of policy in the United States is uncertain. Seemingly, the collapse of communism and the triumph of western democratic and economic values would be welcomed, as it has been in an understated way. Seemingly also these developments should lead to a new era of national prosperity produced by an economy freed from the demands of heavy defense expenditures and periodic, and potentially world-encompassing, confrontations (Korea, Viet Nam, and any number of other lesser involvements from Afghanistan to Nicaragua). The prospects of committing to an inclusive domestic agenda that would lead to better social contributions and improved life opportunities would appear to be enhanced by the removal of the Soviet empire as a world threat. This may all come, but not at present. The American economy has been in recession; the decline of defense and science-related spending and the increases in and commitments needed by the former Soviet Union and its allies have been viewed in economic terms as negatives—further drains on an already troubled economy. The future appears as clouded and unpredictable as it did a decade or two ago.

The structural changes needed to meet the problems posed by a post-industrial order—a service and information-based economy; the demand of expanding populations for social services, from schools and housing to health care needs; the decline in an industrial base and in entry-level industrial jobs; the transition from a quasi-war to a peacetime economy; the retraining of a work force; the loss of low-level jobs to third world countries; the protection of a living environment; the remedying of the inequities of race, gender, and class; and the need to effectively compete in international markets—have yet to be agreed upon, much less implemented. To date, the policy process of meeting such needs has been piecemeal and crisis-driven, not unlike most political decision-making.

The United States is not alone in its problems. Economic uncertainty has replaced the international insecurity of the Cold War years. The world's economies have been experiencing recession or worse. A degree of certainty, however fearful, was associated with a bipolarized world struggle. It resulted in a type of Cold War thinking, an "us against them" mentality, that provided a clarity to international perceptions and a sense of national purpose that has yet to be replaced. The demands of the Cold War have set policy priorities since the end of World War II. Concerns over national security determined international commitments and, in a very basic sense, established the parameters as to what could be achieved domestically. The Cold War defined American politics and policy directions for two generations.

This commitment to a sense of mission has disappeared with the end of Cold War hostilities. The aftereffects can be unsettling. What will come to fill the void is presently unknown: A renewed sense of national identification?; a realignment of American politics and political parties around a yet-to-be-determined set of post–Cold War issues?; a reasserted dedication to social and economic equity? What is certain is that there will be a period of prolonged change as national priorities are reevaluated, resources redirected, and societal objectives reaffirmed. The restructuring of a social order, whether recognized or not, has begun.

Such a rethinking of national commitments is, of course, to be welcomed. A very bad (but quite real) national nightmare is over. The world community appears to be opening up, to be accepting universal standards of human rights and democratic decision-making. The opportunities as to what America can or should become appears to be as limited as the nation's collective imagination and as realizable as the strength of its political will.

A national debate has begun to emerge over how the nation will define itself; what it should become; and, not incidentally, how best to achieve the goals it sets for itself. This debate is likely to be coupled in national politics with a period of governmental activism and policy exploration. The present generation has an unusual, and most rare, opportunity to commit to, and then create, the type of society it envisions best represents what the nation stands for.

This is what this book is all about. It identifies problem areas to be encountered and policy alternatives of relevance to the nation in achieving its goals. Our objective is to contribute to the national debate by outlining policy options and tracing the significant developments, including identifying the unfinished agendas, in the areas most relevant to contemporary post–Cold War concerns. We do this, first, by providing a comprehensive framework for assessing policy initiatives, one that builds on and expands the welfare state model that provides the intellectual foundations for policy direction in the advanced industrial democracies. This model of government has never been fully implemented in the United States, due in part to the pragmatic and piecemeal approach of the New Deal—characteristics that define policy-making in America—and the demands occasioned by the onset of the Second World War. A return to the fulfillment of promise implicit in the welfare state embodiment of governmental objectives was further stunted by the commitment to national security and military preparedness that began in the late 1940s and that came to characterize the just-ended Cold War era.

There is no one conception of the welfare state. Each country has followed its own path, as the first chapter makes clear. Still, a broadened and resculptured version of the welfare state, suited to the economic climate and changing social demands of a new century, may well provide the broad policy guidelines and sense of direction needed during a period of transition.

The first chapter provides such a framework by reviewing the evolution of the welfare state, offering comparisons with other nations, and then tracing in broad strokes recent policy trends—all of which helps set the stage for the more intensive discussion of individual policy concerns in the chapters to follow. The introductory chapter also provides an overview and guide to the analyses in the essays on the specific areas of policy development, and it highlights their major contributions. Each of the chapters that follows focuses on the principal historic marking points in the evolution of policy concerns in the substantive area, the significant intellectual questions and social concerns relevant to policy enactment, and the major policy alternatives meant to address the social needs identified. The objective in each chapter, and of the volume more generally, is to make the relevant policy alternatives more understandable and, secondly, to contribute to a reasoned national debate as to options available and the courses open for future development.

No one point of view or ideological or political commitment guides the contributors. This was intentional. The objective was to tap into the best available knowledge. Each of the essays is by an acknowledged expert in the field with a record of scholarly achievement. Each of the authors has made a contribution to the thinking in the policy area. In developing their contributions, authors were requested to provide a broad perspective on the issues involved and the manner in which policy has evolved and then to identify the proposals that deserved particular consideration. It was up to each author to determine what was most relevant and useful in addressing the social needs of a society in transition.

The opportunities then are extraordinary. But the society will first have to identify its priorities and commit its resources to both unresolved problems of long-run duration and to those specifically associated with the economic and social dislocations of a nation moving into a new historical era. The essays in this volume should help in focusing on some of the more absorbing challenges facing the nation as well as point the way to some of the potential solutions.

This volume and its companion, *Post–Cold War Policy: The International Context*, have been sponsored by the Policy Studies Organization. The royalties from these volumes go to the Policy Studies Organization. Consequently, it is with particular gratitude that we thank the authors of the individual chapters who have contributed their time, energy, and ideas to this project. As editor, I would like to express my thanks to Stuart S. Nagel, Secretary-Treasurer of the Policy Studies Organization, for his encouragement and support of this effort; Stephen A. Ferrara, President, and Richard Meade, General Manager, of Nelson-Hall, Inc. for their continued assistance in the publication of these volumes; Dorothy J. Anderson, senior editor at Nelson-Hall, for significant contributions to the published text; Nan Williams Crotty for her editorial work in developing both volumes; and, for specific contributions at individual stages of research and publication, Jurgen Kohl and Antonia Maioni.

WILLIAM CROTTY

The Role of the State in a Post–Cold War Society

WILLIAM CROTTY

Expanding the Conception of the Welfare State

The welfare state is one answer—in reality, a series of different answers building on a few common assumptions—of how society can move to meet the needs of its citizenry. Basically, like much of government, welfare states arose as ad hoc and largely experimental reactions to the social conditions and political issues raised in specific historic eras. Little theorizing, at least initially, underlay this evolution. The role of society, as directed through its political branch, the government, was restructured to address the worst excesses of the Industrial Revolution.

There are many explanations for the turn toward a more activist government role in mitigating the abuses of capitalist systems, expanding the availability of social maintenance networks, and moderately redistributing wealth among classes through more progressive tax codes, all characteristics of a welfare state society. The dominant motivations varied by society. In some nations, it was to insure social stability and to allow the nation's economy to compete effectively with others (Bismarck's Germany, for example). Other countries also recognized the need for stability and legitimation. This was coupled with a fear of the sporadic violence and civil disorder, most often associated with the developing trade union movement, that occurred. For some, it was a matter of social conscience as well as a rejection of the alternatives, from creating a Marxist, socialist, or Communist society to continuing with conditions as they existed. In all societies to some degree, the evolution of the welfare state was associated with the extension of the franchise and democratic rights and the rise of political parties (and especially political parties tied to a working-class base and determined to achieve workers' rights).

The adoption of a welfare state in its various forms proved beneficial to all concerned. The capitalist system, while modified, retained its dominance. Society remained reasonably stable, and the governing framework was accepted as legitimate. Those who profited most directly from the Industrial Revolution continued to prosper, and the working class was rewarded with access to the essentials of life—some form of job security and occupational safety protections, basic housing, and health care and at least a rudimentary education.

Nonetheless, the welfare states that evolved in various countries exhibited significant differences. For example, the systems developed in Sweden and the other Scandinavian countries and among the major European nations and, for that matter, in North America between neighbors, the United States and Canada, appeared to have few similarities.

The following introduces a working definition for the welfare state, one relevant to contemporary political concerns; indicates the variety of approaches to welfare statism and speculates on the reasons for the differences and what these might hold for future policy developments; examines both the attacks on the welfare state and the concept of a broad range of government-initiated social services and the support for such a social delivery system; posits an extension of social rights as rights of citizenship as the next stage for the advancement of a more encompassing social service network; and, within this context, introduces the policy issues and proposals examined in depth in the chapters that follow.

Identifying the Welfare State

There have been two basic thrusts in the academic treatments of the welfare state. First and more familiar are the policy-oriented assessments. These are primarily descriptive, charting the unfolding of policy in specific areas or nations, or comparatively assessing these within a cross-national context. The second approach is of more recent vintage: theoretical justifications for welfare state activities (or, less common, a rejection or minimalization of these) and the promotion of broad criteria to judge their effectiveness, impact, and stage of development. The more theoretical explorations develop assumptions that encourage the expansion of state social policy commitments that might well serve a broader conception of the welfare state's relevance in the post–Cold War world.

The welfare state can be defined in many ways. One possibility is to list the core programs included and the extent of their coverage. This is a familiar but fairly mechanical approach, useful in determining the comprehensiveness of coverage in a given country or for assessing the expenditures by program or the proportion of the population reached comparatively by nation. Such measures are common and help isolate the limits and different workings of individual programs.

A more useful definition for our purposes, one inclusive in design and encompassing in application, calls on assumptions found in the broadly theoretical interpretations of welfare state objectives. Christopher Pierson points the way. What Pierson refers to as the "welfare state under capitalism" he defines as "a society in which the state intervenes within the processes of economic reproduction and distribution *to reallocate life chances* between individuals and/or classes" (Pierson, 1991, 7; italics added). Such a definition moves beyond the enumeration and measurement of a variety of individual programs to set goals to which a society might aspire. It assures a wide variety of government-sponsored programs; an activist role for the state; a philosophic and ideological commitment to a greater equalization of resources and greater social and economic opportunities for all segments of the population; and policies designed, at least in part, to redistribute social resources and better equalize life opportunities through government action. If the definition is amended to refer to "a liberal democratic society," already implied in the discussion, then it can be taken as assuring a democratic state under rule of law, with limits on the state's authority and a recognition of the inherent rights of the individual. This posits a government responsive to the views and needs of the citizenry as determined through elections. These qualifications in turn distinguish the welfare state from any type of nondemocratic, authoritarian form of governing.

A society's commitment to extensive redistributive economic and social programs is not, as some conservative critics might charge, a synonym for or the initiation of steps toward a repressive and undemocratic state apparatus. Such an outcome is no more likely than the assertions that an unrepentant and free-form capitalism is the best guarantor of pure democracy.

There then are broad goals as well as an ideological component implicit in this type of definitional approach that relate to the quality of life and a variety of programs a state might enact in moving toward the long-run objectives of an equalization of life chances. It also implies a form of social democratic government but one with possibilities of growth and adaptation along well specified policy lines. And finally, of course, this is all built on a basic capitalist economic structure.

Consequently, and building on Pierson's approach, a workable definition of the welfare state that serves our purposes would be: a liberal democratic state in which the government actively intervenes in economic matters with the objective of better equalizing life opportunities through income redistribution and the provision of an extensive network of basic social services.

Models of the Welfare State

The welfare state has many variations. Theoretically, the extremes could be placed on a continuum, ranging from situations in which society assumes no responsibility for individual social needs—we are dealing here with domestic social policy; all nations recognize their internal police functions and international security demands—to where a society attempts to provide most or all of the citizens' fundamental needs on a reasonably equitable basis (figure 1.1). Neither is practical.

On the one hand, the industrial democracies could not continue to ignore the basic social and occupational problems associated with a primitive capitalism that threatened the very stability of the state—through strikes, lockouts, shutdowns, mass demonstrations, and other forms of collective violence. The emerging industrial countries had to act, and they had to adapt, at times reluctantly and with minimal provision of programs (as will be shown).

The communist countries, as much products of their own history as the industrialized Western nations, took matters to the other extreme. The effort to provide for all equally, theoretically within a classless society, through a government-managed economic system is as visionary and unrealizeable as any unreconstructed "survival of the fittest" capitalist system. In the former Union of Soviet Socialist Republics, Eastern Europe, and China, among other nations, the centralization of economic power became synonymous with the centralization of political power in the government and the restriction of basic individual freedoms. While advocates of such a system might argue that it represented a purer form of democracy than found in the West—"economic democratcy" as it was called—it was the denial of basic political rights westerners found most unacceptable. The economic contradictions build into a centralized, bureaucratized, and government-run economic system, not attuned to market forces, weakened the national economic systems and damaged their political viability. Eventually, a failure to respond to demand and an emphasis on production and job security rather than consumer need and market forces, over-bureaucratization and heavy security costs, and poor decision making would prove fatal. Most dramatically, in 1989 the former Soviet Union declared an end to the old system and embraced free enterprise economics.

This is not to argue that some type of centralized economic system, less the political restrictions, might be both acceptable for, and in fact needed in, some developing nations. Such may be the case. Our concern, however, is with the advanced democratic nations and the types of private enterprise/public sphere trade-offs that have evolved there.

In this context, the economic development of the welfare state *directly* correlates with the political expansion of the liberal democratic state. The begrudging recognition of the evils of an unremitting capitalism in Germany, England, and Western Europe more generally (and later in the United States)

FIGURE 1.1

Hypothetical Range of State Responsibilities to Individual (Social Policy)

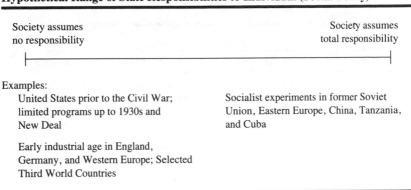

Society assumes
no responsibility

Society assumes
total responsibility

Examples:
United States prior to the Civil War;
limited programs up to 1930s and
New Deal

Socialist experiments in former Soviet
Union, Eastern Europe, China, Tanzania,
and Cuba

Early industrial age in England,
Germany, and Western Europe; Selected
Third World Countries

coincided with the organization of interests by workers, primariy through the trade union movement and political parties—basically the Socialist and Social Democratic parties in Europe and, again at a later stage, the Democratic party in the United States. More inclusive local definitions of citizenship; the expansion of the franchise; the rise of a competitive political party system with, as noted, at least one party representing working class interests are preconditions for the operation of a welfare state (Stephens, 1979). These developments gave increased visibility and importance on the political agenda to social questions. In this scenario, welfare state social and economic policies are ultimately tied to the evolution and fulfillment of the citizens political rights within the liberal state. "The welfare state is found in democratic nations only" (Ringen, 1989, 95).

The adoption of social, health, and welfare measures in various countries at different points in time can be seen as responses to the demands of organized constituencies and the strength of its political advocates. In more specific terms and among the historical firsts: Germany was the first to introduce industrial accident insurance (1871), health (1883), and pension programs (1889), policies Chancellor Otto Bismarck felt would help in stabilizing the emerging nation and its working force and allow it to compete as a major European economic and military power. France provided employment insurance in 1905, and Austria was the leader in establishing family allowance programs, a relative late-comer (1921) to the stable of welfare policies (Pierson, 1991, 107–11; Flora and Heidenheimer, eds., 1990; Jones, 1985). Table 1.1 provides an idea of the sweep and chronology of program adoptions by both substantive area and in relation to country.[1] Industrial accident insurance came first, followed by government sponsored health and pension plans and unem-

TABLE 1.1

Government Assumption of Basic Social Programs by Category and Date of Adoption

Program category	Country and Date of Adoption		
	A. 1870–1900	B. 1901–1920	C. 1929–
I. Industrial accident	Germany 1871	Netherlands 1901	Canada 1930
	Switzerland 1881	Sweden 1901	United States 1930
	Austria 1887	Australia 1902	
	Norway 1894	Belgium 1903	
	Finland 1895		
	Ireland 1897		
	United Kingdom 1897		
	France 1898		
	Italy 1898		
	Denmark 1898		
	New Zealand 1900		
II. Health insurance	Germany 1883	Norway 1909	Netherlands 1929
	Italy 1886	Ireland 1911	New Zealand 1938
	Austria 1888	United Kingdom 1911	Australia 1945
	Sweden 1891	Switzerland 1911	Finland 1963
	Denmark 1892		Canada 1971
	Belgium 1894		United States (NA)
	France 1898		
III. Pension insurance	Germany 1889	Ireland 1908	Austria 1927
	Denmark 1891	United Kingdom 1908	Canada 1927
	France 1895	Australia 1909	United States 1935
	Italy 1898	Netherlands 1913	Norway 1936
	New Zealand 1898	Sweden 1913	Finland 1937
	Belgium 1900		Switzerland 1946
IV. Unemployment insurance		France 1905	Switzerland 1924
		Norway 1906	Germany 1927
		Denmark 1907	Sweden 1934
		Ireland 1911	United States 1935
		United Kingdom 1911	New Zealand 1938
		Netherlands 1916	Canada 1940
		Finland 1917	Australia 1945
		Italy 1919	
		Belgium 1920	
		Austria 1920	
V. Family allowance			Austria 1921
			New Zealand 1926
			Belgium 1930
			France 1932

TABLE 1.1

Continued

	Country and Date of Adoption		
Program category	A. 1870–1900	B. 1901–1920	C. 1929–
			Italy 1936
			Netherlands 1940
			Australia 1941
			Ireland 1944
			Canada 1944
			United Kingdom 1945
			Norway 1946
			Sweden 1947
			Finland 1948
			Denmark 1952
			Switzerland 1952
			Germany 1954
			United States (NA)

*NA: Not adopted
Source: Developed from data in Christopher Pierson, *Beyond the Welfare State*? (University Park: Pennsylvania State University Press, 1991), table 4.1, p. 108, and Peter Flora and Arnold J. Heidenheimer, eds., *The Development of Welfare States in Europe and America* (New Brunswick, NJ: Transaction, 1990), table 3.1. p. 83.

ployment insurance. More recent (although all of the programs were adopted between 1921 and 1954) have been provisions for family allowance.

During the period from 1880 to the beginning of the First World War, of the seventeen European and former British Commonwealth democracies (Australia, New Zealand, and Canada), all (excepting the United States and Canada) had some form of government-based workers' compensation insurance and the majority had health insurance and old age pensions and, by 1920, unemployment insurance (see table 1.1). Social welfare programs from 1920 on enjoyed a sustained growth in virtually all of the nations. Among the slowest to adopt such policies, however, has been the United States, and in two of the five areas examined (health and family allowance) it has yet to adopt programs.

In the related area of political rights and representation, early leaders in establishing universal male suffrage—Germany (1871), France (1848), Denmark (1849), and New Zealand (1878)—were early entrants in developing a range of welfare state programs. Another nine of the seventeen nations followed suit between 1890 and 1920. By 1928, all but four—Belgium (1948),

France (1945), Italy (1946), and Switzerland (1971)—had universal adult suffrage.

At present, there is a wide variation in types of welfare states, the comprehensiveness of their programs, the way in which they operate, and how they are perceived by the citizenry. In a large part, it is a product of the manner in which they were conceived and the differences relate to the government's, and the society's, basic commitment to social and economic equity. On the one hand, there could be a belief in the need of the state to actively intervene in the economy to meet social needs and redistribute income. Or, the society could allow the maximum feasible play for unrestricted market forces (within a welfare state framework) in meeting social needs and rely on the state to guarantee only the most pressing demands of its citizenry and then only in as limited a manner as possible. There are many ways to address the distinctions. Stein Ringen refers to them as the "marginal" and "institutionalized" welfare state (1989, 11).

Both approaches can be found in current practices. The United States favors something closer to the second conception: a limited welfare state with government sponsored program allocations only as necessary, or politically feasible, to meet pronounced needs (Berkowitz, 1991; Berkowitz and McQuaid, 1992; Gutman, ed., 1988). Most European nations take a different, more inclusive approach (Jones, 1985; Flora and Heidenheimer, eds., 1990; Esping-Andersen, 1990, 1985; Rueschemeyer et al., 1992).

The differences in approach are elaborated by Ringen: "The marginal welfare state [has] . . . [redistributive] goals of limited ambition . . . and [uses] . . . mainly selective and income-tested anti-poverty policies. The institutionalized type has more ambitious [redistributive] goals . . . and tends to use universal programmes, by which is meant that all citizens with the same needs are treated equally, irrespective of 'irrelevant' differences between them, as, for example, in income" (1989, 11-12). In the marginal approach, the groups targeted for attention may "suffer stigmatization"; they are singled out from others and are the object of resentment, thus dividing the society and serving as scapegoats. The services received by the target groups are given with reservation, restricted in scope and inferior in quality.

The institutionalized welfare state treats all groups and social classes equally in the provision of services ("the clients are the majority"), and the distinction between those who pay and those who receive, the basis for the antagonism in other systems, is minimized ("clients with the same needs have the same right to the best available services irrespective of income") (Ringen, 1989, 12; Esping-Andersen, 1990).

One approach is believed to divide a population (in the process making the social programs more controversial and politically vulnerable), the other to promote unity. Whether this is true or not, the distinctions do allow for a convenient categorization of types of welfare states and allow a judgment as to what they do and how well they perform comparatively. Employing this approach, the United States could be said to be a reluctant provider, one that falls closest to the marginal category, and Sweden and the other Scandinavian countries, more generous in their social programming, a better fit with the institutionalized model (Tilton, 1991; Stephens 1979; Esping-Andersen, 1985; Rueschemeyer et al 1992; Flora and Heidenheimer, eds., 1990).

Other welfare state models or categorizations can serve for comparative valuative purposes. In line with the definition put forward earlier, all in the modern era would have these characteristics:

1. a mixed economic system,
2. a liberal democratic political order, and
3. some kind of government-sponsored social welfare redistributive policies.

Within these parameters, each state can be judged in relation (and comparatively) according to:

1. the level of expenditures on social programs (for some observers, the defining criteria for welfare states).
2. the organization of groups and the nature and effectiveness of their mobilization tactics, class-based appeal and political impact. The groups would include, in rough priority ordering, trade unions, political parties (and, of particular importance, the presence of a socialist and/or a social democratic party).
3. the type of programs included under the social welfare umbrella (health, retirement, unemployment, family leave, education).
4. the delivery of programs: How are they structured? Who controls services and entitlements? How centralized are the operations? How open to non-governmental group or political pressure is the management of the programs?
5. funding and specifically in relation to how well-funded the programs are: Which programs are better funded than others (and why)? What proportion of the Gross National Product (GNP) or, what some believe to be a better indicator, the Gross Domestic Product (GDP), is invested in social programming? What are the main policy competitors for government financing? And comparatively, in terms of the availability of funding, how progressive is the nation's tax structure?
6. the impact of the programs: What proportion of the targeted groups do they reach? Do they have the results intended? What are some of the unanticipated consequences of policies (inherent by-products of even the best designed of programs)? How comprehensive are the programs and what is the quality of services? Are the policies divisive—aligning

the interests of one group in society against another, taxpayers against recipients or are they unifying, available to all regardless of class or income and financially supported by all through taxation?

These are some of the questions that can be asked. They help to differentiate states, and they provide a basis for comparison both in specific policy areas (health care, for example) and in terms of the network of social services provided by governments. While each of the dimensions would apply in selected substantive areas and to the offerings of individual governments, the differences among states are significant, resulting in a range of social programming among the major democracies. We will look to these considerations when we compare the social policies found in the United States with other advanced industrial nations.

Considerations in the Development of the Stages of Welfare State in the United States

The birth of the American welfare state dates to Franklin Roosevelt's presidency and the New Deal. More specifically, it is associated with the Social Security Act of 1935, an imperfect beginning, to be sure (Lubove, 1986; Margaret Weir et al., ed., 1988, Robertson and Judd, 1989). This piece of legislation was the first of many enacted during the mid to late 1930s in a variety of areas, from old-age pensions and welfare benefits to expanded agricultural subsidies, intended to modify the harshest aspects of the Great Depression (Berkowitz and McQuaid, 1992; McElvane, 1984).

In the United States, the programs enacted were primarily reactive and individualized, an ad hoc series of responses to the economic crisis confronting the nation. Their adoption was conditioned both by what the administration felt it could get from the Congress and the strength of the various constituencies affected—from social workers and labor union members to bankers, doctors, manufacturers—in shaping, or negotiating, the programs that applied directly to them. The policies were devised with little systematic theorizing or concern with ideological coherence. In American politics, crisis management has been the order of the day, and the New Deal was no different. The result was that not all social demands were met or that necessarily the best of policies put forth. The programs enacted represented the attainable. The hope was that they would prove reasonably useful in alleviating the immediate situation. And, by any standard, they were considerable improvements over what preceded them.

Much was left undone. The newness of the programs; the uncertainty as to their public reception; the inexperience of the United States in extending federally sponsored social programs to a national constituency; concern over their operations, delivery and impact, the intense reaction of conservatives and proponents of the traditional limited role of government to the new policy departures; political gaffes by the Roosevelt administration (its plan to expand the Supreme Court to permit the appointment of judges favorable to its conception of government, for example), and a general lessening of the intensity of support for the New Deal; and, most pronouncedly and most decisively, the advent of World War II and a refocusing of attention on international concerns and national survival all played their part. Whatever its shortcomings, the New Deal was the most effective period of social policy exploration and implementation in American history. Efforts would be made, most notably in Lyndon Johnson's "Great Society" and potentially in the present era, to expand and complete the New Deal's welfare state agenda.

The United States does experience periodic efforts at social reform. The Progressive Era of the period 1890–1920, in addition to the New Deal and Johnson's "Great Society" of the years 1963–1968 and its immediate aftermath, come to mind. Each era made its contribution. But with the exception of the New Deal and not to discount advances made in individual policy such as civil rights and poverty (a more contentious assertion) under Lyndon Johnson, the impact of the programs adopted has been limited.

One school of social enquiry believes that the outcomes, and the differences found between the United States and European democracies are best explained by the institutional structures that process political representation.

> Throughout the history of American social policy, the possibilities for reform have been constrained by the legacies of state-building as well as by the characteristics of the American state structure. The fragmentation of authority encouraged by federalism and the division of powers has consistently undermined coordinated national welfare initiatives, even in the periods most hospitable to reform. The patronage practices initially encouraged by early mass democracy and the lack of bureaucratic state-building in America deprived reformers of readily available institutional capacities for carrying out new social-spending activities. Successful reforms have had to work around the obstacles represented by America's institutional and policy legacies, and they have built the bureaucratic capacity for social intervention slowly when it has been possible to build it at all. (Orloff, 1988, 80)

Ann Shola Orloff concludes that the prospects "for more generous public social provisions in America" are limited: "Policy options are always constrained by the legacies of existing policy, politics, and administration, and our choices today are burdened by our past—not the least by the legacies of the initial incomplete welfare state . . . and we will do well to understand the limits to our alternatives" (1988, 80).

A key to the successful enactment of social programs in this country and Europe appears to be their inclusiveness, their concern for the needs of the middle class, their failure to distinguish among (or target for condemnation and retribution) segments of the citizenry (minority groups), the equity of their funding, and a belief in the value or deservedness of the programs for the society. Theda Skocpol found that such concerns were met in the programs for Civil War veterans and their families in an era of reputedly limited government. "These policies signaled the potential for honorable, cross-class and cross-racial social provision to flourish in American democracy" (1992, 531). Those who received the benefits were believed to have "earned" them and were "worthy"; they were not considered "charity" cases. When the relevant generations died, the benefits stopped.

It is questionable how much of a precedent the post-Civil War pension programs provided for the adoption of later progressive social legislation. And, in fact, Skocpol indicated that the attacks by reformers "against democratic patronage parties and the 'horrors' of social spending for the masses helped to ensure that [the] Civil War benefits would become an obstacle rather than an entering wedge for more general old-age pensions and workingmen's insurance in the United States" (1992, 532). Nonetheless, the identification of the approaches that lead to the embrace of social legislation appear well-founded, as relevant, for example, to the Scandinavian countries or elsewhere as they are to United States (Helco and Madsen, 1987).

The "new institutionalism" of Skocpol, Orloff, and their associates makes its contributions to understanding the stunted evolution and restrictive nature of the American welfare state. It also has its limits. For one thing, it is not much different from the old institutionalism of the pre–behavioral period in political science in its reliance on formal government structure and, supplementarily, the history of policy implementation to explain outcomes. It deemphasizes the impact of social forces and demographic change and, to a lesser extent, the politics of mass mobilization in pushing to have its demands met, the role of political leadership in setting agendas and its skill in pursuing its goals and the political resources and strategizing of those groups impacted by the policy shifts—in short, the less formalized aspects of government policy-making—in shaping program adoption or neglect. Given the often vague criteria as to what to include (or exclude) from explorations, it is difficult to refute or fully embrace the explanations offered.

As an example, the United States of the 1930s was not the America of the post–Civil War period or, for that matter, of the turn-of-the-century Progressive Era. Society had changed and changed dramatically. It made new demands on its governing institutions; to continue to function, these had to respond with some degree of effectiveness. In the process of attuning itself to the needs of a changing society, the governing system itself was fundamentally altered.

Statistics help tell the story (Robertson and Judd, 1989). During the fifty-year period from 1870 to 1920, the U.S. population increased from 39.8 to 105.7 million; America was on its way to being a dominantly urban nation with the doubling of the number of people living in cities (from 25.7 percent to 51.2 percent). The proportion of those working in agriculture about halved (from 50.8 percent, the dominant employment in 1870 and previously, to 27.6 percent), and industrial employment rose from 30.9 to 44.8 percent (with an additional 27.6 percent in services). The stage was set for the modern era and, little noticed at the time, the emergence of the social and economic demands that would find a response in the New Deal.

For comparison, by the time of the 1990 Census the U.S. population had increased to 248.7 million, and farm occupations accounted for but 2.4 percent of the total work force.

There were other precursors to policy explosion of the 1930s. As one indicator, the tax base needed to support an expanded network of government-financed social programs had been undergoing a restructuring. David B. Robertson and Dennis R. Judd report that from 1902 to 1932 per capita federal taxes rose from $6.48/individual to $14.51 and state and local taxes from $10.06 to $49.33. Correspondingly, direct federal government expenditures (education, highways, welfare, hospitals, health, police) increased from $7.14/capita to $31.88 and state and local outlays from $12.80/capita to $62.15 (1989, 41).

As a point of comparison and an indicator of the fundamental changes introduced during the New Deal, for the period 1934–1940, federal taxes increased from $23.26 to 36.92/capita (with better than a doubling of both the individual income and corporate taxes). State and local taxes went from $46.74/per capita to $59.11. Federal expenditures also increased dramatically in the space of a few years, and by the beginning of the 1940s about equalled those of the state and local governments, the traditional providers of government services. Direct federal expenditures per capita went from $38.78 to $67.33 and, less dramatically, state and local expenditures from $56.77 to $69.85. The national government basically equalled state and local governments in service outlays, a marked revision in historic patterns. Finally, between 1933 and 1939, federal grants-in-aid rose from $125 million to approximately $543 million, a further measure of the extension of social services through the national government (vocational training, old-age assistance, aid to dependent children, unemployment benefits, services for the disabled) (Robertson and Judd, 1989, 90–168, 202–248).

Major changes in the society create new social constituencies and different government responses. Such changes preceded the New Deal, as they have the entire modern era of welfare services, and go a long way in explaining what has evolved.

A few points in conclusion. There was, as indicated, the necessity to respond to changing social conditions and priorities. This preceded the New Deal, as did the fiscal policies that led to the increasing taxing power of the federal government. When the Great Depression demonstrated for all the failures of the old economic policies, the federal government was in a position to act. Such considerations must be taken into account in explaining the bursts of social policy development in the United States.

It is also true that governing structures and the forces that affect political representation have much to do with the policies that result and the differences found among nations. Social policy in a democratic system sooner or later must reflect social need. The state's legitimacy and, eventually, survival depend on it. Social change produces social concerns that the government must address. What is open to debate is the direction that the government should move; the quality and comprehensiveness of the services to be offered; the manner in which the programs should be financed; and the groups targeted to receive the benefits. Implicit in such decisions is the extent to which government should become involved in the economy in redistributing wealth.

It may well be that the United States will never have a welfare state along the lines of many European nations. This point has been made by Margaret Weir and associates, who go on to say "that social policy choices in the United States are best understood in the context of changes in the polity and [the] society" (Weir et al., 1988, xi). This is correct. This is the best context for understanding what has been done, its strength and its weakness, and conceivably what is likely to be accomplished in the future. The social agenda of the American welfare state remains incomplete.

Comparing Welfare State Services in the United States and Other Nations

America ranks at the bottom, or close to it, among the industrial democracies on virtually all measures relating to its commitment to providing social services to its citizenry. "The United States, along with Japan, comes closest to having only a level of spending which is functionally necessary for the maintenance of a capitalist society" (Stephens, 1979, 149). These are the words of John D. Stephens in comparing welfare state development in Sweden, France, Great Britain, and the United States.

A few figures can illustrate the differences among industrial nations and the relative ranking of the United States. As shown earlier (table 1.1), America does not place among the top three countries in the early, and therefore pioneering, introduction of social benefit programs in any of the core areas of industrial accident insurance, health policy, pensions, unemployment benefits, or family allowances (Pierson, 1991, 100). Compared with seventeen

European and former British Commonwealth democracies, it is the only one that still does not offer universal national health and family allowance plans (Pierson, 1991, 108–11; Kudrle and Marmor, 1990, 81–121).

Looking at the comparative social expenditures of eighteen democracies, even prior to the Reagan-Bush era (1980), the United States ranked first in its reliance on means-tested poor relief (18.2 percent against an average of 5.9 percent); first in *private* individual (nongovernmental) spending for health (57 percent of total health care expenditures came from private sources as against an average for all 18 nations of 22 percent; see below); just above the bottom (Australia and New Zealand tied for last) in proportion of the population aged sixteen to sixty-four eligible for sickness, employment, and pension benefits; and last in the average ratio of social benefits provided to the maximum allowable under law. Gosta Esping-Andersen, who compiled these data, positions the United States above only Australia (and well below Japan, as an example) in relation to benefits provided as a matter of social right unrelated to performance in the labor market. By this gauge, including those who opt out of the labor market, recipients automatically receive benefits roughly equal to normal earnings (1990, 69).

This is a different, and advanced, conception of welfare state (see below); it strives to extend substantial benefits and control over their own economic destiny to members of the working class and to a large proportion of population in general by right rather than tying these to position in the work force (Esping-Andersen, 1990, 52–53). It may not be as radical as it sounds. Some countries come close to this position at present (the Scandinavian countries and, on a lesser scale, many of the European democracies and Japan), and such types of benefits are available to those in selected white collar occupations now (higher level business and professional people, government employees, academicians).

Old-age assistance, the first and oldest of the social welfare measures in the United States and in many other nations, offers another gauge as to the comparative impact of social service measures. Comparing the effectiveness of old-age support through poverty rates of the elderly in 1982 in five nations again finds the United States ranking last. A quarter of those over seventy-five years of age and just under one-fifth of those in the sixty-five to seventy-four age group had levels of disposable income below half of the median for all families, the measure used in the study. The average for the two age groups for the other four nations was 10 and 12 percent, respectively (and Sweden, in contrast to the United States, had zero percent among the aged qualifying for inclusion in the poverty category) (Myles, 1988, 269).

There are many approaches to measuring such effects. Indices can be constructed in a variety of ways. It is the relative positioning of the nations' social service systems in terms of the provisions and delivery of benefits that sheds light on the extent of America's national commitment. What is clear is

TABLE 1.2

Comparative Indications of Comparative Health Care Expenditures

I. Per Capita and Longitudinal Costs

A. Per capita as percent of U.S. total	B. Per capita outlays (dollars)	C. Changes in health care expenditures 1970–1987	D. Costs as percent of GDP
United States 100%	$2,051	4.2%	11.2%
Other Nations 46.3%	$948	6.6%	7.5%
U.S. Rank 19	19	1	19
Total Number of Countries 19	19	8	19

1. Expenditures as percent of 1987 Gross National Product (GNP).
Source: Columns A, B, and D are calculated from data in Henry J. Aaron, *Serious and Unstable Condition: Financing America's Health Care* (Washington, DC: Brookings Insitution, 1991), Table 4-1 p. 80; and column C from data in Henry J. Aaron, "A Prescription for Health Care," in H. Aaron, ed., *Setting National Priorities: Policy for the Nineties* (Washington, DC: Brookings Institution, 1990), table 8-2, p. 253. Data are for the year 1987.

II. Hospital and Ambulatory Costs

A. Total health care expenditures	B. Hospital care costs	C. Ambulatory care costs
United States 41%	52%	24%
Other nations 70%	81%	66%
US rank 23	16	16
Total number of countries 23	18	16

Source: Calculated from data in Henry J. Aaron, *Serious and Unstable Condition: Financing America's Health Care* (Washington, DC: Brookings Institution, 1991), table 4-6, p. 93.

that they all show basically the same thing: in relation to social policy, the United States does poorly.

Perhaps the most fundamental, and controversial, comparative indicator of social expenditures in the contemporary political climate relates to health care. Table 1.2 contrasts the per capita expenditures for health care in the United States with other nations (Aaron, 1991, 1990; Marmor and Barr, 1992; Rosner, 1993; Meyer and Moon, 1988; Reinhardt, 1992). Americans pay more per capita in health costs than the citizens in any of nineteen nations surveyed, and a greater proportion of the nation's wealth, measured in relation to the Gross Domestic Product (GDP), goes into health costs than in other countries. In addition, public funds pay substantially less (the United States again ranks last) of the health costs than in any of twenty-three countries studied (Aaron, 1991, 80).

The U.S. government also puts less into the cost of hospital care, the single biggest consumer of the health care dollar, than most other nations (sixteenth among the eighteen nations for which data are available). It puts even significantly less of its public funds into ambulatory care (outpatient servicing; primary care; and preventive health measures), where it ranks last among the sixteen countries examined. Health care costs overall have increased faster, and government support slower, than in other systems.

While the United States invests more individually and collectively in health care and while its costs have increased faster, the results are not always satisfactory. Henry J. Aaron writes: "Although the United States spends more on health care than other countries do, the health of its citizens is no better, and by some indicators worse, than that in other countries. Among [the twenty-three] countries in the Organization for Economic Cooperation and Development, U.S. life expectancy is about average and infant mortality is slightly below average. The coincidence of mediocre health outcomes and high outlays has led some observers to conclude that the United States misdirects health care spending" (1990, 251–53). He goes on to say that "persuasive evidence suggests that the well-being of the American population could be improved in important ways if health services were redistributed or increased for those who are underserved" (1990, 253).

Comparatively, then, the United States does not do well. Health care costs are higher, delivery is primarily contingent on ability to pay, and the individual subsidizes more of the costs and the government less than in any other major nation in the world. It is little wonder that health care and talk of some form of national health insurance, issues left over from the New Deal, have emerged as the principal social concern of the contemporary period.

Nonetheless, efforts to fundamentally change the health care system can be explosive politically. The last major drive to introduce a national medical insurance program was initiated by the Truman administration in the immediate aftermath to the Second World War. The plan was strongly opposed by the American Medical Association, whose journal editorialized: "The movement for placing of American medicine under control of the Federal Government through a system of federal compulsory sickness insurance is the first step toward a regimentation of utilities, of industries, of finance, and eventually of labor itself. This is the kind of regimentation that led to totalitarianism in Germany and the downfall of that nation" (Meyer, 1993). This was the official voice of American medicine speaking.

Health care may be the most glaring example, but overall in relation to comparative social expenditures among the major nations of the world, America ranks among the weakest of investors. On none of the major indicators does the country compare favorably to other nations in the range or munificence of government-sponsored, public-financed social services. The American government is not overly generous towards its own citizens (Kohl, 1990; Kelley, 1987; Katz, 1986, 1989; Rossi, 1989; Howe, ed., 1982; Jencks and Peterson, 1991; Piven and Cloward, 1971).

Finally, the political rhetoric concerning social programs usually centers on the cost to the taxpayer, accompanied by assertions that Americans are already overtaxed as it is. The arguments can become heated, and they have been effective. Anyone who has followed the debates in a campaign for public office or a legislative battle over a proposed social policy should be familiar with the contentions.

Are Americans overtaxed? Do they pay more to their government in taxes than the citizens of other countries? Quite the contrary is actually the case (table 1.3). Compared to six other democratic nations, the United States collects the lowest proportion of taxes (as measured against the Gross Domestic Product) of any of the countries. It has by far the lowest tax rate for high income individuals and equals the average for the rate on lowest income categories. The personal income tax is the highest tax producer, a situation true in three of the other countries, although the proportion of funds collected is well above the average for the other six nations. Its corporate taxes are below the mean, and its levies on goods and services well below the mean for the other nations. It is above average in placing the responsibility for social security on the individual employee, and the contribution it receives from employees in this regard fits in with the average found elsewhere. Overall, in a comparative context, Americans are significantly undertaxed; in fact among the twenty-three nations in the study issued by the Organization for Economic Cooperation and Development, only Turkey collected less of its GDP in taxes than the United States (America's 30 percent compared with the twenty-three other nation's 40 percent). The report contended that the United States "would remain among the least taxed [of nations] even if taxes were raised sufficiently to balance the federal budget" (Greenhouse, 1992). Taxation is not the problem. Political will is. If anything, taxes should be increased significantly to place federal revenues proportionately in line with those available to other industrialized countries, in the process providing the financial resources to fund an expanded network of social programs.

The Reagan-Bush Years and the Reaction Against the Welfare State

Much has been written about the efforts of the Reagan (and later Bush) administration(s) to dismantle the welfare state and return the United States to a purer form of laissez-faire market economics, one not dissimilar to the pre–New Deal 1920s. The effort was serious, and it enjoyed some successes (Salamon

TABLE 1.3

Tax Rates for Various Countries, 1989 (in percent)

Category	Britain	Canada	France	Germany	Italy	Japan	United States	Average for six nations (excluding the United States)
General:								
Highest and lowest personal income tax rates	25/40	17/29	5/56.8	22/56	10/50	10/50	15/28	14.8/46.9
All taxes as percentage of GDP	36.5	35.3	43.8	38.1	37.8	30.6	30.1	37.0
Sources of tax revenue:								
Personal income	26.6	38.4	11.8	29.5	26.7	24.7	35.7	26.2
Corporate	12.3	8.5	5.5	5.5	10.1	24.4	8.5	11.0
Social Security (employee)	7.5	4.4	13.0	15.6	6.4	10.1	11.5	9.5
Social Security (employer)	9.5	8.4	27.2	18.5	23.8	14.5	16.5	16.9
Goods and services	30.9	29.5	28.7	25.6	26.9	12.6	16.2	25.7
Other	13.2	10.8	13.7	5.3	6.1	13.7	11.5	10.4

Source: Organization for Economic Cooperation and Development, as reported in Steven Greenhouse, ''A Foreign Nation in Washington: U.S. Needs Higher Taxes,'' *New York Times*, Nov. 29, 1992, p. 2E. Note: 1989 is the most recent year for which information is available.

and Lund, 1984; Palmer and Sawhill, 1984; Burt and Pittman, 1985; Berman, ed., 1990; Blumenthal and Edsall, 1988; Jones, ed., 1988; Campbell and Rockman, 1991).

The Reagan agenda was clear; he had been promoting it since his pre-politics days as a spokesperson for the General Electric Corporation in the 1950s. It included:

1. Tax reduction: major cuts in corporate and upper-income personal taxes, justified as a means of stimulating the economy (the "supply side" packaging of trickle-down economics).
2. Redistribution of wealth: employing the tax code to substantially reduce upper income taxes while retaining the rate on the middle class at basically the same or slightly higher levels; the result would be to place the burden of financing government funding more substantially on the middle class.
3. Reduction of social services: to quote David Stockman, Reagan's first budget director, the administration planned an "all-out assault" on social spending (Stockman, 1987). Welfare was to be eliminated, if at all possible ("workfare" and related ideas came to be the catchwords), and social programs were to be reduced to the minimum level of political feasibility (the "safety net") (Gueron and Pauly, 1991; Burt and Pittman, 1985).
4. Increase in defense spending: make America strong again and respected (a reaction to President Jimmy Carter's handling of the Iran hostage situation and the more general desire "to put Viet Nam behind us") and fight communism, the Soviet Union, and its world ambitions ("the evil empire") through a renewed commitment to defense preparedness. The emphasis, in turn, would favor a quick reliance on force," a rejection of diplomacy "as one observer labeled it (Ignatius, 1988). The use of military force, or the subsidization of proxies emphasizing military means, occurred during the Reagan-Bush presidencies in such countries as Grenada, Nicaragua, Salvador, Afghanistan, Angola, Honduras, and, under Bush, Panama (Rice, 1990; Pastor, 1990; Lieber, 1990; Berman and Jentleson, 1991).

   The consuming effort to halt communism, wherever found, could go too far, inviting charges of extremism and nearly precipitating a constitutional crisis. In the "Iran-Contra Affair," as it came to be referred to, the Reagan administration sold arms to Iran through Israel in pursuit of hostages held by Iranian sympathizers in Lebanon. These transactions were, in themselves, direct repudiations of the administration's antiterrorist campaign and its public rhetoric. The profits were then laundered and used to support the Contra's aggression in Nicaragua, a clear violation of congressional prohibitions (the Boland Amendment of 1984).

The president claimed not to remember whether he knew and sanctioned the dealings or not. Eventually, a number of key administration officials were indicted (Oliver North, John Poindexter, Elliot Abrams, Robert McFarlane, and Caspar W. Weinberger being the most prominent), and several were judged guilty, but the administration was able to ride the crisis out (Draper, 1991).[2]

5. Deregulation: eliminate or minimize government regulation of business; corporate takeovers, airlines, trucking and transportation, occupational health and safety guidelines, security exchanges, banks, savings and loans institutions, environmental standards, doctors and hospitals, real estate transactions, and so on. The expressed intention was to serve the ends of economic development, in the phrase of the time, freeing business from government red tape in order for it to compete more effectively.

6. Balanced budget: candidate Reagan vowed to balance the budget and reduce (actually eliminate) the national debt. His contribution was in "creating fiscal deficits unprecedented in size" (Peterson and Rom, 1988, 238). The failures in this area are glaring obvious to conservatives and liberals alike and leave a legacy that other administrations will have to deal with.

7. Rejection of affirmative action: during the Reagan-Bush years, the government opposed civil rights, affirmative action, and gender equalization proposals and became an advocate (as, for example, through such agencies as the Department of Justice, the U.S. Commission on Civil Rights, the Fair Employment Practices Commission, and the administrative interpretation of laws) for the other side (a concept of fairness and equal opportunity not based on racial, gender, ethnic, or minority considerations), rolling back or not enforcing much of what had been accepted practice and opposing—legislatively, administratively, and judicially—any new efforts to achieve such ends.

8. Commitment to the New Right's social and cultural agenda: this meant, among other things, a strong antiabortion position to serve as a litmus test for the appointment of Supreme Court and federal judges; antipornography campaigns, including a commission chaired by the attorney general on the subject and sustained efforts to reduce or eliminate federal support for the arts, particularly any deemed pornographic or irreverent (through appointments to and grants funded by the National Endowment for the Arts and the National Endowment for the Humanities and through legislative restrictions); and an emphasis on religious and family values in contemporary life (although Reagan himself was not particularly a religious person). These were concerns of the fundamentalist Right, a vocal and effective part of Reagan's electoral coalition. The issues were of intense concern to them. They were also ones

Reagan repeatedly identified with publicly and ones that his administration supported.

Much was expected and attempted. "At the center of Reagan's economic package was $700 billion in program cuts, $50 billion in tax cuts, and a three-year, 27 percent increase in defense spending. The premise of the administration's supply-side economics was that reducing federal spending and cutting taxes would stimulate the economy. The supply-side theory argued that added tax savings would be invested by upper-income people, who benefitted most from the tax act. This investment would trigger productivity, increase employment, decrease welfare, and lead to an increased income base for taxation and, somewhere down the road, a balanced budget with reduced interest and inflation rates" (Berman, 1990, 10).

It was an ambitious agenda. It was trumpeted by the administration as *America's New Beginning* and introduced to the public in Reagan's initial Inaugural Address in 1981. "Not since 1932 has there been such a redirection of public purpose"(quoted in Berman, 1990, 11). This judgment by two researchers at the Urban Institute is one Reagan would have welcomed.

The approach was ideological. Translating it into political reality presented problems. Did it work? Politically, yes. Reagan was reelected overwhelmingly and a spirit of optimism and pride ("Morning in America") permeated the Reagan years. In economic and social terms, it was another matter. Stockman again: "None of us really understand what's going on with these numbers" (quoted in Berman, 1990, 10).

How successful was the Reagan administration?

Social and Economic Policy

It all depended where you were on the economic ladder. Under Reagan, the wealthy prospered, the poor suffered, and the middle classes were required to take over more of the tax burden. The largest federal tax cut in history (the top rate was reduced from 70 percent to below 30 percent) and a business climate favoring investment and speculation did lead to a redistribution of wealth. An economist at the Massachusetts Institute of Technology contended that the richest 1 percent in the country accounted for 70 percent of the growth in average family increases between 1977 and 1988. According to Barry Bosworth of the Brookings Institution: "People at the top in America had huge capital gains. . . . America in the 1980s became a country of [a] widening inequality of wealth" (unlike the 1970s when the richest 1 percent had close to the smallest share of wealth in American history). Another evaluation of the years 1977–1986 showed an increase of 65 percent for the top quartile (highest 20 percent) in terms of earnings.

A Federal Reserve Bank analysis of the Reagan policies (1983–1989) supported the assessment of critics. Accepted as impartial, the Federal Reserve Board periodically surveyed families between 1983 and 1989. Overall, average real family income, accounting for inflation, rose from $33,400 to $35,700. Most of the increase, however, was accounted for by the wealthiest, who benefitted from a bullish stock market, high interest rates, and increased real estate values. The better-off did well; the poor, blacks, and Latinos did not. And according to the report, the middle class was basically unaffected. As an example, for the six year period, a family earning more than $50,000 saw its net worth increase from $176,100 to $185,600; a family earning less than $10,000 had its net worth decline from $3,800 to $2,300 (Risen, 1992).

In terms of budgetary policy, the Reagan message of responsible fiscal conservatism had been well received. Once in office, Reagan promised to balance the budget and eliminate the national debt, positions he had championed for decades. This would all be done within his first term. In actuality, the Reagan administration doubled the national debt, increasing it by more than that of all of his predecessors combined. During the Reagan-Bush years, the deficit (the difference between what the government takes in through taxes and what it spends) grew by $200 to $300 billion per fiscal year. By 1993, it had reached an estimated $327 billion.

The Reagan and Bush administrations borrowed to cover the difference, adding $3 trillion to a national debt that had been $1 trillion when Reagan took office (for a total debt of $4 trillion by 1993) (Mills, 1984; Schick, 1984; Weatherford and McDonnell, 1990; McIntyre, 1992; Schultze, 1990; Shapiro, 1993; Stockman, 1989).

All of this had consequences that were especially severe for the less well-off in society. A report by the Children's Defense Fund, an organization critical of the Reagan-Bush policies, found that the income of poorer families fell over a seventeen year period from an average of $27,765 to $18,844 in constant 1990 dollars. The decrease in income impacted the hardest on blacks, Hispanics, the young, and those with the least formal education (Goldsmith and Blakely, 1992; Hacker, 1992; Jencks and Peterson, eds, 1991; Moon and Sawhill, 1984). Cutbacks in government welfare and unemployment programs contributed to 40 percent of children living in poverty. "Poverty rates rose to 23.8 percent for the children in young white families, 43.5 percent for those in Hispanic families and 57.9 for those in black families" (DeParle, 1992; see also: Edelman, 1992; Palmer et al., 1988; Burt and Pittman, 1985, 1–56; Kozol, 1992).

A report by the U.S. Census Bureau also showed a deterioration in family structure. The number of children living in one-parent households increased over a period of two decades from 15 percent to 28 percent. There was a particularly notable change in the family conditions of black children with an increase in the proportion living in one-parent homes from 31.3 percent in 1970 to 45.8 percent in 1980 and 57.5 percent in 1991. Such figures "reflect the deterioration of the American family structure" according to one social analyst. They do indicate the growing acceptance of unmarried women having children, a trend that contributes to the greater number of children being brought up in poverty. "The child's chances [in a one-parent household] of living in poverty are six times as high as they would be in a two-parent family" (Associated Press, 1992b).

Clearly, many of these social trends indicate long-term problems. Rather than being arrested or slowed during the Reagan-Bush years, they were accelerated.

The contrasting perspectives on the problem, and the polarization over social issues that marked the Reagan-Bush presidencies, are clear in the contrasting assessment of such data. Marian Wright Edelman, president of the Children's Fund, saw the results as "tragic" because they occurred during a period when the nation was becoming more prosperous and because they reflected "a conscious political or community choice." A former domestic policy advisor to Reagan believed the Children's Defense Fund "has the causes of this problem upside down"; child poverty increased because more children were born out of wedlock "and as long as the number of single-parent families is going up, we are stuck with this problem" (Associated Press, 1992a).

The expression of views can be taken as indicative of the different approaches to social problems. One camp sees the problem in social and economic terms and responsive to government initiatives, the other in moral and ethical terms and a matter of individual responsibility. One holds the government accountable for social problems; the other sees no role for the government and emphasizes a change in moral and family values. The ideological and social polarization of the Reagan years could not be better illustrated.

The changes in the distribution of wealth, the worsened condition of minorities and the poor, and the attacks on welfare state policies more generally did not go unnoticed. Critics existed, as committed and determined as the architects of the Reagan policies. Two of the more vocal were Frances Fox Piven and Richard A. Cloward. They accused Reagan and his associates of directing their, and the public's, hostility towards the less organized, more vulnerable groups in the society, and in particular those receiving Aid to Families with Dependent Children (AFDC). It is one of the more limited of government social programs: "*Before* the Reagan cuts, about $14 billion (*including* state and local shares) was spent to provide for slightly more than 11 million AFDC recipients, of whom more than 7 million were children" (1985, 3; italics added). Public anger "is not directed against . . . programs that support the aged, . . . by far the most costly of the social welfare programs; nor . . . programs that support the disabled, or . . . that support the temporarily unemployed" (1985, 3). These account for most of the welfare dollar but, and unlike AFDC, benefit adults primarily and include more politically powerful voting blocs.

Their indictment of the Reagan administration's social policies is inclusive: a rewriting of tax codes to reward the wealthy and large corporations—"80 percent of the benefits go to the 1,700 largest corporations (which have generated only 4 percent of all new employment over the last twenty years)"; personal income and estate tax cuts with "85 percent of the benefits [going] to those with annual incomes exceeding $50,000," and the loss of an estimated $750 billion over a five year period through such changes in the tax laws. Social programs are then reduced to partially make up the difference. They continue:

> The budgets and powers of agencies responsible for controlling the polluting effects of industry, enforcing health and safety standards in the work-place, overseeing guidelines for the hiring of women and minorities, prosecuting anti-trust suits, and limiting the exploitation of mineral resources on federal lands, to mention a few, were all reduced or abolished. Directives were promulgated that explicitly relaxed enforcement standards and lowered the penalties for violations. The agencies were internally reorganized to remove stubborn bureaucrats from the scene of enforcement, and a new crop of officials was recruited, usually from the regulated industries. (1985, 7–8)

Piven and Cloward attribute the Reagan approach to a class theory of politics, "the archaic idea that people in different social classes have different human natures and thus different basic motivations . . . the affluent . . . [respond] to rewards . . . working people to punishments" (1985, 38–39). And finally in this vein, Piven and Cloward and their co-authors find the "New Right" emphasis embraced by Reagan frightening in a democracy in that "it represents a kind of moral authoritarianism that is reminiscent of European fascism" (Block et al., 1985, 163).

Strong stuff certainly. Again, it gives some idea of the intensity of the social and ideological divisions during the Reagan years.

Writing from a different perspective but with similar conclusions as to the impact of the Reagan administration's economic and social policies was Republican strategist and commentator, Kevin Phillips. Initially, Phillips had gained attention by predicting the dissolution of the New Deal's electoral coalition and the beginning of a period of conservative Republican ascendancy (*The Emerging Republican Majority*, 1969). In several more recent works, Phillips has cautioned that the Reagan economic policies have undercut America's industrial base, redistributed its wealth upwards, and weakened its position in the highly competitive international marketplace. In the process, gains enjoyed by the middle class have eroded (1993). As summarized by a reviewer: "In the years of the Reagan and Bush Presidencies, the middle classes of America declined precipitously. No group has been hurt more by rising taxes, declining real income, escalating expenses, a shrinking job market, deteriorating public services, falling home values, growing health costs, weakening safety nets, the loss of savings, and the threat of collapsing pension and insurance funds" (Lehmann-Haupt, 1993).

Phillips himself has indicated that a change in direction was due: "The 1980s were the triumph of upper [income] America—an ostentatious celebration of wealth, the political ascendancy of the richest third of the population and a glorification of capitalism, free markets, and finance." (1991, xvii). This "second Gilded Age" had resulted in "too many stretch limousines, too many enormous incomes, and too much high fashion [and] foreshadowed a significant shift of mood. A new plutocracy—some critics were even using the word 'oligarchy'—had created a new target for populist reaction" (1991, xviii). The themes and results of the 1992 presidential election would appear to prove Phillips right again. The Clinton campaign ran on the economy and with a decidedly populist and middle-class tenor to its campaign, later carried over into the Clinton presidency (Crotty, ed., 1993).

Military and Foreign Policy

The defense budget grew during the Reagan years, in line with the administration's ideology, its ardent anticommunism, and its emphasis on national security. Two commentaries on defense spending: As Paul E. Peterson and Mark Rom report: "Reagan gained the largest increase in peace-time defense spending" (1989). When Reagan entered office, and despite yearly incremental increases under Carter, defense spending was 5 percent of the GNP, the lowest it had been since 1968 at the height of the Vietnam war. "Real spending on defense increased by 17 percent in Reagan's first year in office. . . . As a percentage of GNP, defense costs rose to only 7 percent, still short of the 10 percent level of the Vietnam era . . . but in real dollar terms, defense expenditures climbed well above their Vietnam war high" (Peterson and Rom, 1988, 233–34; see also Korb, 1990).

The results could be a little overwhelming. One example, and potentially the most breathtaking: in 1983, the Reagan administration promoted what it called the "Strategic Defense Initiative" (SDI or, as it was more popularly known, "Star Wars"), a kind of futuristic high-tech umbrella or shield that was intended to protect against nuclear attack. An aspect of the plan called for missiles to be launched from space in any purported enemy attack to destroy their opposite numbers on their pads or shortly after their launching.

The program was extraordinarily ambitious. And, as I. M. Destler says, it was "an idea had never before been taken seriously by a president or anyone close to him" (1988, 250). It soon became "a centerpiece, often *the* centerpiece, of the president's nuclear arms policies and the arms control debate"

(1988, 250) and, despite opposition from some conservatives and Republicans, "joined the list of cherished right-wing causes" (1988, 251). It was also extraordinarily expensive (costing an estimated $33 billion over the next ten years with, according to congressional critics, "nothing to show for it") (Evans, 1993a, 1993b).[3]

There were ramifications to the increased spending on defense, both policy based and political (although the two are often hard to separate). Phillips develops the point: "Increased spending for defense was a prime factor in shifting dollars away from human resources. . . . [Spending on] human resources [went] *down* from 28 percent of all federal outlays to just 22 percent; defense [went] *up* from 23 percent to 28 percent. . . . If many . . . dependent on housing, urban and social services outlays suffered, other[s] . . . gained" (1991, 87–88). An exact inverse ratio, in fact, exists between increased military spending and decreased social service expenditures for the years 1980–1987. Phillips continues: "Accelerating military expenditures brought new contracts, plants and jobs to the prime contract regions. . . . Pentagon consultants and think tanks also prospered . . . By 1989 federal spending increases in the Reagan era had clearly benefited Republican constituencies (military producers and defense installations, farmers and agribusiness, bondholders and the elderly), while decreases in federal social programs served to defund Democratic interests and constituencies (the poor, the big cities, subsidized housing, education and many other federal services" (1991, 88–89).

The end of the Cold War and the installation of a new administration in January 1993, with the Democrats taking over the White House, meant a shift in priorities and the beginning of what promises to be severe reductions in military appropriations, with substantial consequences for the areas of the country, sectors of the population, and industries that have been dependent on high levels of defense spending. The halting efforts to defund the SDI program shows how difficult the process of reallocating resources can be (Evans, 1993a, 1993b; Jouzatis, 1993; Andrews, 1993; Johnson, 1993; Prokesch, 1993; Associated Press, 1993; Pear, 1993).

A New Era

Once in office, the Clinton administration began to dismantle the Reagan programs and roll back Reagan policies. Clinton's press secretary explained to reporters the administration's first set of proposals to the Congress as "a reversal of Reaganomics, a reversal of the last twelve years" (Stein, 1993). The *New York Times* described the first formal Clinton message to the Congress and the nation as portraying "government as a powerful engine of social change, a catalyst for economic growth, an incubator for new technology, [and] a partner of private industry" (Pear, 1993). The package of policy and budget proposals was entitled *A Vision of Change for America*, in itself a label not dissimilar to what the Reagan administration might have used. But the thrust and consequences of the program were quite different. What that means, in short,'' wrote one observer, ''is an end to twelve years of laissez-faire social policy''(Pear, 1993; see also Nasar, 1993).

A new era of government activism may be upon us (Clinton and Gore, 1992, Aaron and Schultze, eds., 1992). Less clear is the specific policy directions this new era will take.

Support for the Welfare State

The antagonism the Reagan administration directed towards the social policies of the welfare state was not unique. Many of the European democracies were facing the prospects of retrenchment in their social programs. The welfare state worked best in periods of economic expansion. As the industrial economies stagnated and contracted and the need for a restructuring to meet postindustrial conditions became increasingly apparent, social programs became a target for budget-cutters.[4] And, as Hugh Helco indicates, ''complacency about the momentum of the welfare state gave way to doom-mongering by many in the intellectual elite, people who were once the strongest champions of activist social policies'' (Helco, 1990, 399). The pessimism concerning social programs was not confined to the most vocal of intellectuals; it appeared to be shared by the media, opinion-makers of various convictions, government officials, and the public. Ronald Reagan and his supporters acted on their concerns.

The major objections heard concerning the welfare state were as follows[5]:

1. The programs cost too much; the costs had expanded to ''run-away'' proportions; and the middle class was being asked to shoulder excessive tax burdens to fund them, financial demands that were likely to become even greater in the future.
2. The programs were ineffective. They did not reach the groups in need with the services promised; the delivery capabilities of the government were limited and inefficient; and the programs failed to achieve their intended objectives.
3. The governmental bureaucracy designed to administer the programs was growing at an excessive rate and in the process becoming more removed and unaccountable to the constituencies it was meant to service. For some, this raised fears of the seeds of an authoritarian state. For others, the illogical requirements and complexity of eligibility provisions raised the specter of public agencies increasingly distancing themselves from their client groups to the point of undercutting whatever success the programs might have enjoyed and in the process imposing solutions essentially out of bureaucratic convenience.

Such views were expressed with greater frequency during the 1970s as economic conditions worsened. Lyndon Johnson's "Great Society" (1963–1968) had exhausted itself, fueling increasing skepticism that its overly ambitious goals (oversold to begin with) were beyond society's reach. By the end of the decade, and for the twelve years of the Reagan-Bush presidencies, such arguments dominated the public discourse (Pierson, 1991, 123–26; Murray, 1984).

Yet, whatever their problems and however intense the criticism, the welfare state policies consistently enjoyed a strong base of support. Evidence from the pre–New Deal period as to their appeal is limited and indirect. Still, there is reason to believe that such social policies did prove attractive to segments of the electorate. As an example, the vote cost for Progressive candidates Woodrow Wilson, the winner of a three-way presidential race in 1912, and runner-up Theodore Roosevelt well exceeded that for third-place finisher and candidate of the regular Republicans, William Howard Taft (they outpolled Taft 3 to 1).

The Progressives ran on a platform that called for "the protection of home life against the hazards of sickness, irregular employment, and old age through the adoption of a system of social insurance adapted to American use." Citing this, Ann Shola Orloff contends that "turn of the century American popular support for new welfare measures has been underestimated in conventional historical accounts" (Orloff, 1988, 55). The interpretation is arguable of course: elections and voting decisions turn on many factors. Less debatable is the force of the New Deal's appeal since the electoral realignment of the 1930s (Anderson, 1979; Petrocik, 1981; Burnham, 1970; Sundquist, 1983).

The popularity of the New Deal social programs and Roosevelt's administration established the Democrats as the majority party in the electorate, and the division between the parties along class and economic lines constituted the fundamental structuring force in creating the contending electoral coalitions. The "New Deal Party System" has persisted to this day as the basic fault line of American politics. Stanley Kelley, Jr., after analyzing national survey returns for presidential elections between 1952 and 1984, a period that includes the two decisive Reagan victories, concludes that the New Deal policy divisions still fuel party politics. "In this period, about three-quarters of all voters mentioned one or more New Deal issues as something to like or dislike about the major parties and their candidates. The salience of New Deal issues stood at 85 percent in 1952, dropped about ten points in 1956, held steady for the next quarter of a century, and then rose in 1984 almost to its 1952 level. . . . The issues arising out of the New Deal retained their hold on voters into the 1980s" (1988, 191; see also Sundquist, 1983).

Further, and contrary to its interpretation by the media, Congress, and politicians of both political parties at the time, Ronald Reagan's 1980 and

1984 victories did not constitute a conservative mandate. "References to deregulation, reductions in federal spending, changes in welfare programs, or the lowering of taxes were not prominent in voters' evaluations of the parties and candidates either in absolute terms or relative to their frequency in other elections" (Kelley, 1988, 197). Reagan's monetary and fiscal proposals, his tax program, and his attacks on government services and their cost were not the decisive factors in his electoral success.

Kelley concluded that "these data . . . provide almost no support for the view that the Reagan administration came to power as a result of an increasing insistent popular demand for the economic and welfare policies Reagan had proposed. . . . Opposition to New Deal-like policies won some support for Reagan, but *it had won support in roughly equal measure for all Republican candidates for president since 1952*" (1988, 197; italics added). Kelley's analysis is as sound and definitive as any available, and its message is clear (see also Abramson et al., 1982, 1986). What did appear to be decisive was the public's apparent loss of confidence in the Democrats, and in the 1980 election, incumbent Jimmy Carter's ability to govern effectively. The voters preferred to entrust their security and well-being to the Republicans.

Taking a different approach, Herbert McClosky and John Zaller focused on explaining citizens' ideological commitments to democracy and capitalism. Looking at those most likely to embrace the government's social role and those most likely to oppose it, the authors write:

> Such ideological conflict as exists in America is confined within a broad framework of almost universal public support for the basic values of capitalism and democracy. . . . People who are convinced of the need for social change, who are strongly motivated to alleviate distress, and who take an optimistic view of human nature tend . . . to be enthusiastic about democracy and wary of capitalism. . . . In contrast, people who value order and stability, who are tough-minded about the prospects for alleviating social distress, and who take an essentially pessimistic view of human nature tend to be strongly procapitalist and cautiously democratic. (1984, 232–33)

Liberals, or optimists, attempt to reform capitalism and extend democratic and economic rights through government to wider publics. These are the reformers. The conservatives, or pessimists, see their role as protecting a free market capitalist system and limiting and slowing any changes that might alter it. The two sets of forces contend in American politics, alternatingly holding political power.

The matter can be carried further. A related study by Stanley Feldman and John Zaller (1992), conducted at the height of the Reagan era (1986–1987), found that Americans may not be totally comfortable with an ideological *conception* of the welfare state; it contrasts sharply with a cultural emphasis on individualism and the desirability of limited government, values dominant in the United States since at least the time of Thomas Jefferson. Consequently, liberals who support the welfare state are more conflicted in their value commitments than the conservatives who oppose it. Conservatives can claim an ideological consistency built on a societal emphasis on the individual's responsibility for his or her own well-being, arguments basic to the opposition to the welfare state. For liberals, and Americans more generally, an ambivalence exists between support for specific social policies and the need for a larger and more powerful state to enact the egalitarian and redistributive programs they endorse. The broader values of the national culture emphasize the dangers inherent in a government of the size necessary to administer a broad range of social services. As a consequence, the anti–welfare statists begin with an advantage in debates over social policy (although not one of sufficient magnitude to halt the creation of the welfare state).

Theda Skocpol approaches the same type of issue with a reference to "the vunerability of social policies without collective justification" (1988, 307). Such a policy rationale would include both a coherent theory of legitimation and broad public support based on acceptance of the policies and a belief they serve the best ends of the society. Others have made basically the same point. This casts the problem in the relevant context. As Skocpol maintains: "The New Deal made direct federal governmental activities an immediate reality for all Americans, *and the justification and portrayal of the new economic and social programs in New Deal rhetoric was a portentous ideological development in U.S. history* (1988, 308; italics in original).

Fay Lomax Cook and Edith J. Barrett conducted a national survey of 1,200 residents of the United States in 1986 to measure their support for welfare state programs. Their findings assume practical political relevance in explaining what took place during the 1980s.

> The Reagan administration . . . appears to have misunderstood public opinion. . . . There is no such program called "welfare" and no reason to assume that because one dislikes "welfare" one therefore dislikes individual programs within the welfare system. . . . Misinterpretation arose from extrapolating assessments of low support from the complaints of citizens, policymakers, and the media about program ineffectiveness. . . . [To conclude] that Americans are critical and would like to eliminate programs or are unwilling to finance them through their tax dollars . . . the misinterpretation of public sentiments can probably be attributed in part to the media . . . [which has] a tendency to paint dramatically and with broad brushstrokes policy issues as policy crises. . . . Criticisms of social welfare programs may have been so dominant that proponents of social welfare may have felt outnumbered and retreated to silence (1992, 237–38)

The Reagan people also misjudged the Congress and its willingness to cut social service programs. "Despite the widespread rhetoric about a crisis of support for the welfare state, members of Congress supported social welfare programs. . . . In so doing and in refusing to follow the president's proposals, they represented the views of the public" (Cook and Barrett, 1992, 236–37; see also 58-73). As was to be expected, Democrats in the Congress fought more strenuously for the social programs, although Republicans, in response to their constituents, supported their retention to a greater degree than the Reagan administration anticipated.

Cook and Barrett demonstrate the broad support among the citizenry for the welfare state's social policies. They interpret the Reagan administration's efforts to reduce or eliminate these as a misreading of public opinion. Another interpretation is possible: the Reagan administration's antipathy to the welfare state was fundamentally ideological. It was not based on calculations of popular support or media endorsement and did not require such reinforcement to sustain it. Quite the contrary, it sprang from deep-seated ideological beliefs and was marketed, with considerable popular success, to the public and the media. Ronald Reagan had been making much the same arguments for decades. He was chosen to run for governor of California by a small group of wealthy businessmen who shared his views and believed he represented a creditable spokesperson for their conservative ideology (Cannon, 1982; Dugger, 1983; Johnson, 1991; Rogin, 1987).

The failure of the Reagan and Bush administrations to fundamentally alter the welfare state policies bears witness to the strength and intensity of the public's commitment to their continuation. As Cook and Barrett conclude, "the welfare state suffers from no generalized crisis of legitimacy" (1992, 93). The major accomplishment of the Reagan-Bush presidencies may have been to limit the growth of the welfare state. Then again, the basic contribution of these years may have been to demonstrate the welfare state's resiliency and its popularity with the American public.

The matter can be put in broader perspective. Nicholas Barr has given a persuasive argument for the resiliency of the welfare state under Margaret Thatcher in Britain and Ronald Reagan in the United States. Barr approaches the historical evolution of the welfare state within an economic theoretical context with attention to the developments of the 1980s. He concluded:

> The welfare state has two purposes: one is redistributive, or compensatory, to enhance social justice, the other functional, e.g., to deal with varying forms of market failure, thereby increasing economic efficiency. Virtually all parts of the welfare state display both aspects. . . .
> Once the welfare state's efficiency role is understood, it is no longer surprising that neither in Britain nor in the USA, despite determined efforts during the 1980s, was government able to roll back the frontiers of the state in these areas.

. . . The major efficiency role of social institutions makes them relevant to the population at large, not just to the poor. The welfare state is much more than a safety net: it is justified not simply by any redistributive aims one may (or may not) have, but because it does things which private markets for technical reasons either would not do at all, or would do inefficiently. We need a welfare state of some sort for efficiency reasons, and would continue to do so even if all distributional problems had been solved. (Barr, 1993, 432–33)

In short, the welfare state serves societal needs better (more economically and more efficiently) than any alternative method yet devised and with a robustness that private markets can not duplicate. Its resiliency is not accidental.

Social Rights in a Post–Cold War World

The evolution of the welfare state, and especially its expansion in the post–World War II period, is more than an accident of history or a fortuitous conjunction of social demands and political will. For proponents and critics alike it has come to symbolize a larger meaning: a statement of the government's obligation to meet the social needs of its citizenry.What does the state owe its citizens? What types and levels of social service support can the individual expect as a matter of right from the state?

These are the nature of the questions likely to frame debate in the post–Cold War political world. The presumption here is that the state is obligated to meet the basic needs of its citizens and to provide them with the opportunities necessary for a reasonably full and productive life. In this conception of the obligations of government, individuals have a social right, analogous to any political right now held uncontestedly, to such support from their government. Further, there is a presumption to a moral justification of government built on how well it serves the members of society. It is within these bounds that the future justification for social programs will be fought. This approach can be considered the post–Cold War conception of governmental responsibility; it moves beyond the present level of services provided in the United States to develop a rationale for the universal availability of a comprehensive range of programs to meet the society's social needs.

Such a conception of government is not universally accepted; clearly, and, as indicated, it is in marked contrast to what is currently conceived as society's responsibility. It also conflicts with long-held American values (although these may not be as relevant or as limiting as they were once thought to be) relating to individual responsibility, limited government, and free-market capitalism. A broadened concept of social *rights* is the issue on which future theoretical arguments will center. The resolution of the debate will have enormous real-world political consequences.

As has been argued, the expansion of social services represented the state's response to the social problems created by industrialization and an early and overly exploitive capitalism. The philosophic justification as to the value and necessity for such state action was utilitarian, a necessary accommodation to social dislocations within a democratic political culture. More specifically, it reflected an acceptance of the class demands of an organized and politically mobilized working population (Stephens, 1979; Rueschemeyer et al., 1992).

The age of industrialization is well past. Global concerns now focus on the demands of a post-industrial economic order. Questions arise as to how adequate governmental social and economic policies forged to meet the challenge of industrialism will prove in satisfying the demands of a new age. The belief here is that the state is likely to expand its social functions and provide greater support services for all citizens. In time, these will come to be accepted by the majority of the public, much as the basic social programs brought on by the New Deal are now. Eventually such a broadened concentration of state social obligations will become part of the value structure of the nation, judging how adequately given administration's perform. This is the argument. It is open to dispute, and quite clearly the realization of such a society is far off.

Systematic, coherent, and comprehensive intellectual and philosophic justifications for the operations of a welfare state emerged well after the government had assumed its more active social role. This is not unusual. A society responds to social demands in order to maintain stability and retain its legitimacy. In a democracy, and the welfare state is very much a creature of democracy and an extension of the thinking as to political rights to the social arena, there are built-in mechanisms (elections being the most significant) that, if operating properly, assure the state's adjustment to significant social pressures. Normally, the theorizing that justifies an expanded set of governmental responsibilities comes later. Nonetheless, such a theoretical legitimation is essential to the long-run acceptance and survival of the new state practices.

Within recent years, there has been a development of thinking in this area and a willingness to wrestle with questions relating to the social rights of citizens in a post-industrial welfare state. Gosta Esping-Andersen for one has argued that academic concerns must "move from the black box of [state] expenditures to the content of welfare states: targeted versus universalistic programs, the conditions of eligibility, the quality of benefits and services, and, perhaps most importantly, the extent to which employment and working life are encompassed in the state's extension of citizen rights" (1990, 20). Esping-Andersen accepts the idea "that social citizenship constitutes the core idea of a welfare state" which should "involve the granting of social rights" (1990, 21). Such social rights should be "given the legal and practical status of property rights"; they should be "inviolable"; and they should be "granted on the basis of citizenship rather than performance" (1990, 21). Such an approach rejects the notion of the individual's labor as a bargaining commodity in a capitalist economy: "a [social] service is rendered as a matter of right. . . . A person can maintain a livelihood without reliance on the market" (1990, 22). Such an approach is yet to be widely debated much less accepted.

T. H. Marshall (1964, 1977) was one of the first to argue for the "social rights of citizenship," rights he saw as extensions of the process of political democratization. While not alone in developing the lines of exploration (see Wolfe, 1984), his work and the influential theorizing of John Rawls (1971, 1993) have proven decisive in establishing the early context of the debate and should frame its future course.

The ideological battle is just beginning. Its outcome will serve to determine the state's obligations and its future social role. The intellectual challenge is to develop a compellingly acceptable theoretical argument for social rights, one that provides an appealing philosophic justification for a broadened conception of the social commitments of the state in a post–Cold War society. "We may conclude that the most paramount human rights, derived from basic human needs, will establish both crucial individual freedoms—notably personal security—and an essential level of well-being" (Okin, 1981, 250).

The conception is enticing. Perhaps we can leave it at that. Its full implications have yet to be thought through and its realization, which may be stipulated as desirable, is at best problematical.

Assessing the Policy Areas and Options

The foregoing provides a broader context for considering and evaluating the proposals and analyses put forward in the individual policy areas. We begin with a brief overview of the issues and policy recommendations that serves to introduce the discussions to be found in the chapters that follow. First, appropriately, is old age assistance, the oldest of the welfare state programs and the one that set in motion the New Deal.

Aging Policy

The United States has been called the "Old Age Welfare State." The Social Security Act of 1935, the first of the major New Deal social legislation and the initiator of Franklin Roosevelt's domestic program, established the concept of older people (defined in the act and thereafter as those sixty-five or older) as needing government assistance. From this point to late in the decade of the seventies, the American people were generous (in comparison with other social programs) in the scope of programs and services provided the elderly. This period of "compassionate agism" was generally beneficial. The following decades saw the enactment of 134 federal programs, frequently with state-level supplemental efforts, consisting of everything from publicly insured private pensions, energy and transportation assistance, and protection against job discrimination to the creation of a separate National Institute on Aging.

The old-age programs have been successful. Over a three decade period, as an example, the proportion of the elderly living in poverty declined from 35 percent to 11 percent. It would seem that such programs might serve as a model for the extension of social services in other areas and to all categories of the public. This decidedly did not happen.

One questionable consequence of the 1935 Social Security Act was to create in the public consciousness and to establish a legislative precedent for a category, "the aged," that was to be viewed as basically homogenous in terms of needs, economic status, and social characteristics, a proposition that masks the realities. The depiction of a group with monolithic needs and views has had negative political consequences in more recent years. The elderly are not socially, economically, or politically likeminded. Their political attitudes vary, and their voting behavior roughly splits along the same lines as that of the rest of the population. In addition, the economic conditions and the social service requirements of subpopulations within the aged differ significantly. For example, the "oldest of the oldest," a group growing in numbers, has considerable more claim on financial assistance and medical care than the younger old. Life-style is important. Low-income people and minorities have inferior health care throughout their lives and thus a greater need for financial and medical assistance in later life than the middle- and upper-income people. The aged are not all the same, and their requirements are not necessarily similar.

This fact of life has been conveniently overlooked by those who would pit the aged against the rest of society in the quest for scarce federal dollars. In recent years, the once sympathetic depiction in the media and among the public has turned increasingly hostile. "Greedy geezers" who demand much from government and who in return live off the sweat of younger generations has become the new stereotype.

In large part, the changing depiction is a product of competition for government funds. Thirty percent of the national budget is invested in benefits for the elderly, and one-third of all health care costs are paid on behalf of older people (who account for only 12.5 percent of the population). The health care budget rivals defense allocations in size. In addition, the numbers of older people are increasing, and the elderly population is expected to double to 69 million by mid twenty-first century. It is projected to rise to 20 percent of the total population by the year 2030. The controversy over funding for medical attention for the aged (the vast majority of which are accounted for by increases in hospital care and other provider costs) and other benefits has been used in political rhetoric to position older citizens and their benefits in direct conflict with the social service funding requirements of the rest of society.

Robert A. Binstock develops these trends in detail and offers a more realistic, nuanced view of the aged, who they are and what their needs are. He makes the point that older people still require help: 27 percent fall under the "near-poverty" line at present; health costs tripled in a little over a decade (1977–1988); and 41 percent of medical costs are financed directly by the elderly. As life is prolonged, such trends are likely to become more acute.

Policy on the aging is at a crossroads. For the most part, those supporting aid programs for the elderly are on the defensive. Yet the future may see, in fact, an expansion of medical programs relevant to the population in general; an acceptance of intragenerational and intragroup class and economic differences; and revised eligibility standards based more on need than categorical age.

Health Care Policy

The United States does not have a national health care plan, the only one of the industrial democracies not to provide such a social service for its citizens. A significant proportion of the population is without health care insurance (an estimated 37 million people); health care in the United States on a per capita average is the most expensive in the world, and the costs keep rising; and the aging of the population has focused increased concern on health issues. These factors have helped make health care one of the most debated and controversial issues in contemporary American politics. Virtually everyone agrees that something has to be done. Severe disagreements exist, however, over what to do; how to finance it; who the major beneficiaries will be; whether significant controls over hospitals, doctors, and medical plans will be instituted; and what the government's role in any new program should be. Health care reform will be a major issue of the 1990s.

Robert H. Blank reviews the rapid expansion of research and funding, the breakthroughs in antibiotic and vaccines development, and the generous public funding for hospital construction in the post–World War II years. In the 1960s, concern shifted to questions of access and supplemental insurance for the poor and elderly. The Great Society years also saw the introduction of Medicare and Medicaid. On a different track, there were breakthroughs in life-prolonging technologies, such as organ transplants and intensive care provisions.

The 1970s and, in particular, the 1980s saw a shift in the health care debate to concerns over cost containment. Costs increased while access to adequate care decreased. Late in the 1980s and into the 1990s, a number of programs to reform health care were debated. Efforts to introduce some form of national health care restructuring, with a prominent role played by the government, promises to be a dominating concern of contemporary politics.

Blank reviews the options and the peculiarly American value context in which the debate will take place. Americans value a freedom of choice in lifestyles; a right to medical aid; a fascination with high-technology medicine; a personal relationship with physicians; third-pariy payment systems that hide the real costs of health care; and an emphasis on prolonging life seemingly at any cost. Blank indicates that each of these positions affects how people will respond to the present need for swift and comprehensive action on the part of the federal government. He also points out some directions the government might take in making health care more affordable and more accessible to the members of society.

Child Care Policy

The debate over child care presents a microcosm of the major issues that divide proponents and opponents of social welfare policy, with one exception. By the 1990s, liberals and conservatives, Democrats and Republicans agreed it had come to the center of the political stage: child care concerns would become a defining issue for social welfare policy as the nation approached the twenty-first century.

The intense interest actually began late in the Reagan years with the recognition that children had suffered grievously from the neglect of social concerns. The Bush and Dukakis campaigns of 1988 became something of a watershed, with both candidates and political parties committing to proposals that would place the concern over the fate of children and, relatedly, the family at the center of the policy debate. As a consequence of the growing recognition during the 1980s of the problem and the politics of the 1988 presidential election, a variety of bills were introduced into the Congress. The legislation that emerged in 1990 may well set the parameters for policy development in the area for the rest of the 1990s. The passage of the bill also illustrates the issues of controversy in child care policy.

Jennifer Mezey, Michael L. Mezey, and Susan Gluck Mezey explore in detail the differing positions and legislative conflicts over child care policy during the most recent period of intensive congressional concern. They also develop the evolution of policy in the area from the initial programs in the New Deal, most notably what is now called Aid to Families with Dependent Children (AFDC), up through the Head Start programs of the Johnson years to the contemporary debate over tax policy designed to benefit mostly middle and higher income families with children (earned income tax credits; increased personal tax exemptions; provisions for low-income families). The strengthening of family, seen in quite different terms by liberals and conservatives, and the improvement of child care program delivery systems are also issues that have received considerable rhetorical, if not actual legislative, attention in the contemporary political climate.

All factions agree that the condition of children, as assessed by virtually any measure, has worsened over the last several decades. The questions as to what social policies to adopt involve a range of questions as to political ideology; the obligation of government in preserving traditional family structure;

the changing role of women in society; racial and minority beneficiaries, the major recipients of aid; and an entitlement strategy versus an appropriations strategy (which basically involves the necessity of seeking renewed annual support). Entitlements result in more generous and more consistent funding.

These are among the issues that have to be addressed and ones that will dominate the debate for several decades to come. They are inclusive and take the controversy well beyond the needs of children into assessments of, and reactions to, a changing societal structure and a redefining of social and family roles. The programmatic battles to date with their ideological and class overtones indicate that no consensus exists over the proper approach to child care policy.

Hunger Policy

The focus on malnutrition, hunger, and supplemental food programs is a comparatively recent extension of social concerns and social consciousness. In the 1960s, the federal government introduced a series of major programs intended to alleviate hunger in the United States. The efforts have been substantial, and they have had some success. The Food Stamp program is one example. New groups were targeted for assistance, and old programs (the National School Lunch Program) were expanded. Not unreasonably, it was expected that with sufficient infusion of energy, aid, and time, the problem of hunger would be eliminated.

In actuality, during the last decade there has been a renewed concern about hunger. Groups not previously believed to be vulnerable were included in programs (the underemployed and unemployed, the homeless, children, farmers). In addition, the traditional constituencies (the old, the ill, and single-parent families) continued to be cause for concern. Similar to other areas of social policy, the demand for an expansion of service came at a time when there was a call for retrenchment and a reduction in the funds available and a redirecting of financial resources toward other ends (the national debt, as an example).

This particular area also serves as a lightning rod for controversy, one that evokes intense ideological debate. There appears to be little middle ground. Proponents feel the government has a duty to supply food as needed; and hunger in America for them is something that is intolerable. Opponents believe the very same policies worsen the situation, encouraging a dependency on government aid, and waste money. To the extent it exists, the problem should be a matter of individual concern best served through private agencies. The "social responsibility" controversy, as this may be called, can be intense.

Peter A. Manning reviews these arguments and assesses the operation and the future of government-sponsored food assistance programs. He looks at the ways in which such programs have been conceived; the quality of information on the prevalence of hunger and the targeting of the populations most requiring relief; the manner in which hunger programs are administered; and the debate over responsibility (who should be expected to service such needs).

Manning recommends improved approaches to measuring hunger and identifying the types of food programs most likely to bring the best results; an emphasis on nutritional issues, which broadens the coalition supporting such programs to three major clientele sectors of the economy (in addition to agriculture and welfare, the traditional constituent base, health care advocates would be included). He suggests more economical and efficient approaches to implementing and administering programs.

The focus of hunger policy needs clearer definition in light of present conditions and more innovative programs in addressing the problem—for example, through combining private and public initiatives in "hunger entrepreneurship" ventures.

The goals and operations of the hunger program are being rethought. Basic questions arise, such as, Who will pay? Who is best equipped to do the job? And how best can the available resources be used? While a broad public consensus on such concerns is not likely to emerge, the present efforts can be supplemented and improved.

Housing Policy

The term "housing crisis" has been over-used for far too long to create much reaction. Yet it is an accurate description of the problems faced in the United States. The need is particularly acute among low-income and poverty families. Costs are absorbing an increasingly higher proportion of personal incomes, a trend that has been in progress for decades and one that shows little sign of abating.

In making these points, R. Allen Hays goes on to examine trends, and nontrends (what has not happened in federal housing policy), the federal programs enacted to subsidize the housing market, and the options available and likely future directions in housing policy.

Government interacts at virtually every stage of the housing market. Its policies have much to do with the approaches taken by private builders and the availability of housing stock. Present trends are not encouraging: the cost of housing continues to increase; there is a decline in the rate of home ownership; first-time home buyers are at a particular disadvantage in the contemporary market; rents have risen substantially; and the construction of rental units has declined as the investment return has decreased. The result is that there is a scarcity of new housing and an increasing inadequacy in both numbers and in the maintenance condition of what is available. In addition, homelessness has become a major social problem. While the conditions that have created the homeless are complex, the restricted availability of adequate housing is a contributing factor.

The 1960s saw the birth of a number of new housing initiatives, the most since the New Deal. The programs funded the development of public housing units and stimulated private construction. The Nixon administration suspended these in 1973 in reaction to a series of scandals, segregation suits, tenant strikes, maintenance problems, and foreclosures. Its own preference was for policies of cash allowances paid directly to tenants dependent on public housing. Housing starts increased in the late 1970s, but the problems encountered in a sluggish economy restricted the scope of what could be attempted and set the stage for the Reagan administration's efforts to minimize or eliminate governmental support for new housing. Cuts of about 70 percent followed in the early Reagan years, although the full impact was not immediately felt due to units then under construction.

The Bush administration proved to be more sympathetic to housing issues and attempted to encourage the sale of public units to tenants. The program was small and underfunded and had only a modest impact.

One consequence of the Reagan policies was the efforts of many local and state governments to fill the void through creative public financing and encourage community nonprofit groups to enter the field. The costs of such programs, however, exceeded the financial capabilities of local governments.

What has not happened in relation to housing policy is as important as what has happened. Housing subsidies are not considered entitlements. Rather, they are categorized as discretionary funding and therefore represent an easier target for budget-cutters. Federal subsidies, through the deductibility of mortgage payments or property taxes on federal income tax returns, have benefitted the middle and upper classes more than the lower classes or the poor. Politically popular, these deductions are likely to be continued. The provision of housing has never been considered as an integral part of the welfare state's core social commitment in the United States, resulting in extensive fluctuations in program development and funding and the lack of a strong public base for a comprehensive set of programs.

The future does not look promising. The trends indicated are likely to continue with increasingly severe consequences for the poor as well as for working- and middle-class families. A redefinition of housing as an entitlement would help significantly as would a doubling of the housing budget (to approximately $30 billion a year, a relatively small sum in an annual federal budget of $1 trillion in a nation with a $5 trillion GNP). Neither is likely to occur in the foreseeable future.

Urban Policy

From the 1930s to the early 1980s, the federal government operated on the assumption that it had an obligation to help the cities and that its aid was needed to fight urban ills and mitigate the problems brought on by social and economic change. As a consequence, the package of what was labelled ''urban policies'' was comprehensive: transportation, education, nutritional programs, crime, racial segregation, job training, housing, economic development, and supplemental health care were all areas of federal concern. In turn, the federal commitment to contribute funds to urban areas was reinforced by political and intergovernmental developments. The New Deal, which initiated the urban programs, and the Democratic party, which sustained them over the decades, benefitted from strong urban minority support in elections. As Dennis R. Judd indicates in tracing these developments, comprehensive urban programs were in their political interests.

Second, from the 1930s on, the federal government developed a grant program for cities that made local governments partners in administering policy. As a consequence, an "iron triangle" was built over the years uniting bureaucrats, local politicians, and congressional committees in a coalition that successfully promoted urban legislative interests. This continued up to the early 1980s.

Judd indicates that at this point things began to change, in large part in reaction to a declining domestic economy and the demands of international economic competition. Much of what had been the cities' industrial base was siphoned off to other, more rural areas or to countries offering cheap labor and attractive tax incentives. The shift of significant proportions of the urban populations to the suburbs and both the economic and population growth of the Sunbelt states contributed to a weakening of the political power of the older Frostbelt cities.

Jimmy Carter was not especially responsive to urban needs and, as president, Ronald Reagan was actively hostile. Beginning in the early 1980s, and by design, a systematic reduction in aid for urban areas took place. It took many forms. Funding was reduced; grant programs were bundled together and then reduced in size or, when possible eliminated; new fiscal policies were initiated in the 1981 and 1986 revisions of the tax code that reduced the funding available for urban aid; and many programs were transferred to state governments with financing dependent on state legislatures. The state governments were not capable of administering the volume of programs demanded of them and historically state legislatures have been hostile to urban interests. The broad coalition that had supported urban aid had been effectively undone.

The major policy innovation of the Reagan and Bush presidencies was the emphasis on urban enterprise zones. In actuality, while they might benefit certain types of businesses, they stood to lose cities an estimated $1 billion in income from tax concessions. For whatever reasons, plans for enterprise zones never progressed far.

Ronald Reagan sought to eliminate urban aid. As Judd shows, he succeeded in restructuring urban policy to refocus almost exclusively on economic development. It is unlikely that either the Clinton or that future administrations can revert to the old approaches. Future urban aid may well come in the form of broader social policies that impact all citizens regardless of residence. And the cities may prove more skillfiil in advancing their interests within a new economic order, a point the next chapter develops in detail.

Urban Policy in a Global Context

There is some good news for the cities. Federal domestic support may be considerably lessened and more indirect than at any time since the 1930s. Yet the restructuring of world economies and the necessity of all countries to open their borders to trade will serve to reemphasize the importance of metropolitan areas as centers of international economic operations. It will be up to the urban communities to develop competitive economic policies that will reinforce their importance in the emerging global economy. These are problems that city governments have only begun to deal with.

Traditional assumptions that dictated business fortunes—notably the proximity of markets and suppliers—are considerably less relevant in an age of accessible air transportation and the revolution in information technology and telecommunications. Consequently, the locations that can supply human skills, a culturally challenging environment, and a high quality of life are likely to profit most from the emerging economic developments. The American cities that are able to adjust and restructure to meet the complex economic changes in progress and the demands of the growing international knowledge industries will prosper. This is the argument of Jack N. Behrman and Dennis A. Rondinelli.

It is a far cry from the politics and economic dependency of an old urban order built to meet the requirements of an industrial economy. And, in fact, the transformation of urban economies from a heavy manufacturing base to a "knowledge" and service industry base has already begun. The cities that adapt the best to their role as international information centers and are able to supply the technicians, white-collar work force, and knowledge specialists required in the globalized world market should do well. The changes needed will not be easy. For example, given the urban decay that plagues many cities, the development of a rich cultural life and a healthy and safe living environment pose enormous challenges.

The new global economy will be characterized by economic integration; accelerated technological change; growing similarities in consumer behavior and market demand; the spread of international corporations; an increased reliance on intercorporate networks; the internationalization of finance; and, for what many may seem unthinkable, the decline in importance of the nation-state.

The short-term, consumer-oriented, immediate-gratification culture dominant in many American cities (and the nation more generally) may make difficult the substantial investments in public institutions—specifically, the quality school systems and the physical infrastructure (sewers, streets, bridges, water systems)—required to attract business.

A number of American cities have started to make the commitments necessary to adapt successfully to a new age. A stronger competitive position will be linked in the increasingly globalized economy to a better quality of life. There just might be good news for all concerned in this.

Education Policy

America is a "Nation at Risk," as the title of a report on the nation's education system in the early 1980s stated. Education training and the levels of achievement are not of a sufficient quality to sustain the country during a time of increased international economic competition. The charges are serious, and there is good reason to believe the depiction of education in the United States is reasonably accurate.

There is a tension here. By virtually all measures, as Barry Keating and Maryann Keating indicate, American education has been in a freefall for decades. Yet the American public consistently supports more rigorous standards of achievement, and they do not appear willing to accept the low level of performance the school system is accused of delivering. Seemingly, a strong level of public support would lead to an improved educational environment. This has not been the case; measures of educational performance indicate a continued worsening.

Financial aid for a range of educational programs increased substantially during the 1960s. This growth in both funding and scope of programs slowed during the 1970s and was reversed in the 1980s, experiencing a modest decline during the Reagan years. Funding for education has always been primarily a local (property tax) and state function with the federal government playing a lesser role. Little of the public expenditures goes to private schools. Over the last several decades, the states have been forced to shoulder more of the schools' financing, potentially leading to an equalization and homogenization of educational efforts that offer consumers—the families and students—less of a range of choice. Current expenditures on education are about 4 percent of the nation's GNP.

The report "Nation at Risk" recommended: greater emphasis on basic English, math, and science course offerings; more demanding standards of student achievement; a lengthened school year; and more financial support for teachers with more attention paid to the evaluation of their performance. The Clinton administration has publicly supported the tenor of these recommendations as has other administrations. The problem has been to move in the policy arena to improve the situation.

Recent studies have reviewed the quality of the educational experience in the United States and recommended a variety of changes. A major debate has been joined, one that promises to question the foundations of public educational policy in the United States. The Keatings frame the debate in terms of educational production, an economists' approach that defines and uses technical and economic (outlays) concepts of performance. In reviewing the research conducted, they show that many measures expected to relate to better performance (small class size and higher teacher salaries, as examples) do not necessarily do so (there is some variation among studies, although the broader outlines are clear). Teacher quality and the learning context or environment do appear to be important. The Keatings suggest employing a ''value added'' approach as potentially depictive of educational impact; has a given teacher added something of substance to a student's knowledge.

Schools have been funded regardless of their performance; good, mediocre, and bad schools all receive public money. The Keatings argue that in effect a cartel has developed, enforced by the state and federal governments; an ''American OPEC'' (a reference to the Organization of the Petroleum Exporting Countries, which sets production quotas and prices for the major oil producing nations). Their preferred solution is to increase incentives to promote school competition, resulting in better performance and more educational alternatives.

Private schools, as an example, are subject to market forces. The parents' commitment is substantial. The schools are more likely to be responsive to their governing boards and are more sensitive to their constituencies; dissatisfied clients (parents) can ''vote with their feet'' (that is, take their business elsewhere).

This type of example may show the importance of incentives in education and the value of a free market emphasis in education. The approach would allow incentives to be used to permit options and to reward efforts to achieve educational superiority. Good schools would prosper; poor schools would be weeded out.

The debate has been engaged. There is little disagreement that the American educational system is underachieving or that educational performance needs to be considerably improved in the post–Cold War period if the United States is to compete economically. The issues that arise involve which road to travel and, as significant, the necessity of a fundamental political commitment to achieve educational excellence.

Environmental Policy

Unlike many other areas, the concern with environmental issues, and the need to do something about these, is receiving increasing public and governmental attention. The reasons are many. The consequences of pollution and toxic waste and the necessity for protecting national resources are widely recognized and policies to deal with them broadly endorsed. Rapid industrializa-

GOSHEN COLLEGE LIBRARY
GOSHEN, INDIANA

tion and unregulated economic growth have increased the seriousness of the threats to health and environment. A sense of urgency concerning the ecological deterioration of the earth has produced international cooperation, a practice that will likely be expanded with the termination of the Cold War.

Within this context, Sheldon Kamieniecki, Anthony Kandel, and Louis Shubert analyze American policy in three areas: air pollution abatement; toxic waste; and natural resource conservation. The development of public policy in each of these areas is examined as are the problems of greatest significance at present and the issues and alternatives most likely to command attention in the post–Cold War era. Environmental issues have international implications, and they bring together a variety of political and economic forces attempting to influence the manner in which they are to be attacked.

Toxic and hazardous waste is the most serious environmental threat facing the nation and the one about which the least has been done. The continued generation of waste coupled with an increasingly sophisticated appreciation of how wastes affect human health has brought such concerns to the front of the political agenda. Congress has enacted significant legislation in the area and the Environmental Protection Agency (EPA) has attempted to introduce controls over the disposal of toxic substances. In general, however, industry has been uncooperative and minimally responsive. The slow implementation of the "Superfund" intended to clean up toxic waste dumps is a case in point. The politically sensitive administration of the program in the EPA during the Reagan years did little to improve matters.

Air pollution has often been accepted as inevitable in an industrial society. Tolerance for air pollution by the public has decreased and calls for government control of industrial polluters have increased. Toxins emitted into the air from plants and cars damage health and contribute to such environmental dangers as global warming and the desertification of the land.

The Clean Air Act and its successors have had an impact. It is estimated that America's smoggiest cities experienced a 10 percent drop in air pollution during the 1980s. In general, the signs—on both the federal and state levels— are encouraging, although serious air pollution problems are likely to plague the nation for years to come.

In relation to wildlife management and the protection of natural resources, the battle is between preservationists who argue the long-term good and developers who emphasize jobs and immediate economic need. It is a battle that has been played out over and over again. The Reagan administration's (and to a lesser extent, the Bush administration's) policies favored developers over environmentalists, a reversal of the resource and wildlife conservation movement that had been dominant in U.S. policy since the 1960s. The Clinton administration appears more attuned to the interests of preservationists in attempting to balance these concerns with those favoring economic development.

In general, Kamieniecki, Kandel, and Schubert are, with exceptions, critical of the United States' environmental policies. While America has more laws and regulations than any other nation, their enforcement has been uneven. In international terms, there is a growing tension between the more affluent and less affluent nations in deciding what to do and who will pay for it. Overall, however, the increasing public and governmental recognition of the seriousness of environmental issues places these in the first rank of society's concerns.

National Industrial Policy

The questions are: Can the United States compete effectively in the international market place? Has it lost its competitive edge? What can be done to make the United States more economically effective and internationally competitive?

These are the problems that Richard D. Bingham addresses. He indicates that basically there are two schools of thought: the "preservationists" whose economic policies prevailed historically and whose position the Reagan and Bush administrations endorsed; and the "modernists," many of whose leading advocates hold positions of responsibility in the Clinton administration.

The preservationist would provide capital to industry through agencies modeled on the Reconstruction Finance Corporation, an approach that has worked in the past. There is a tendency to support old and perhaps less efficient industries and to depend on market forces to determine viability. The modernist would pursue more activist government interventions that would target industries for growth and focus resources on what is needed to compete in the future. The model is Japan. For example, the Japanese invested $122 million from the mid-1970s on in order to make a previously marginal computer industry a world leader. In comparison, the United States attempted to help its automobile industry fight the imports. The Reagan administration sought and gained voluntary imports on Japanese cars. The consequence was that the price of automobiles to U.S. consumers rose without perceivable gains in terms of the work force or market share. The United States invested $1.5 billion in the Chrysler bailout. Pension benefits were cut, the pay scale was lowered, eighteen plants were closed, and 27,000 workers lost their jobs. Perhaps such costs are justified. Still, bailouts such as the estimated $150 to $200 billion needed to rescue the Savings and Loan Associations lead many to question whether there might be a better way.

Bingham indicates that there is a national industrial policy of sorts. It emphasizes a piecemeal and functionally isolated approach to economic problem solving; the application of one plan to problem solving in all industries, regardless of relevance; a heavy defense outlay of modest benefit to the overall economy, a concentration of resources that will make for painful readjustments in the post–Cold War years; a commitment to free trade, an objective that if all nations accepted makes sense; local grants that represent a de facto industrial policy favoring urban development and real estate interests; a reliance on macro-economic fiscal and monetary policy to direct economic growth; and entrepreneurial, laissez-faire state-directed economic policies at the national level combined with more active, government-initiated tax and economic programs aimed at job growth at the state and local levels. There also has been a concern with technological development, although the investment in this is relatively minor.

Bingham recommends a national industrial policy intended to promote the goals of economic stability; human resource development; technological dominance; and capital accumulation. He makes a persuasive case, for example, that the American educational system is inferior to that of the United States' economic competitors and inadequate for the country's needs. The approach he advocates might just be worth a try. At a minimum, present economic conditions are going to force a serious rethinking of economic objectives and strategies, a process that is already underway.

Budget Policy

Budgetary priorities will be rethought in light of the collapse of the Soviet Union and world communism. In particular, defense spending will be cut severely; how and in what categories are yet to be decided. Also, should a "peace dividend" emerge, and there is no sign of it yet, decisions will have to be made as to how to allocate the funds. Such issues can be politically explosive. The American political system has entrenched interests that resist change. The Congress, in particular, appears responsive to constituent concerns that have a heavy investment in maintaining the status quo. Change will come, but it may well be slow, incremental, and politically expensive for both presidents and congresspeople alike. On the other hand, the collapse of communism may offer the opportunity for a fundamental recasting of budgetary commitments to meet postponed social needs and the demands of international economic competition.

These are the issues that Steven G. Koven addresses in assessing the budgetary implications of the new world order; the political factors that have shaped, and will continue to influence, budgetary decision making; and alternative budget strategies and philosophical approaches. Koven analyzes the consequences of the Reagan years' emphasis on supply-side economics: its redistribution of wealth; its increased funding of defense-related programs at the expense of those intended to service the concerns of society's most needy; the concentration on military rather than commercial research and development; and the heavy investment in defense-related high technology programs of limited social utility.

All of this is undergoing change. However, the transformation is neither as swift nor as basic as many have hoped. Budgetary commitments, as for example in certain types of military programs or employment, create dependencies. Politically, whatever the economic and international reality, and regardless of how dysfunctional these may appear in contemporary terms, they are difficult to change.

Kovens reviews these problems in depth and suggests three possible options for budgetary policy: an emphasis on debt reduction, the size of which constitutes a major barrier to long-term economic health; an increasing commitment to expanding social programs, a prospect that has limited political support at present; and the use of budgetary tools to increase international economic competitiveness. All three are desirable objectives; the three options, however, cannot receive equal attention. And, as Kovens demonstrates, any restructuring of budgetary priorities will take patience, political will, and social commitment.

Public Land Policy and National Security Needs

The post–Cold War tensions between a reduced military emphasis and peacetime commitments are encapsulated in the fight over public lands in the American west. The federal government owns a staggering one-third of land in the country, the overwhelming majority of which is in the western United States. Little realized, the Department of Defense controls, and uses for its own purposes, a valued proportion of this public land.

The Defense Department uses the land primarily for weapons testing and training purposes. The mandate to the federal government as part of this country's public lands policy is to hold the land in trust for the citizens of the United States. This policy does not apply to property under military control. Access to the areas is restricted and, unlike with other federal land, congressional mandates of multiple use management do not apply.

The Defense Department has resisted giving up rights to the land it controls. It maintains it is needed for its traditional military purposes of testing and that it may even be necessary to expand the areas under its jurisdiction. Many civilians disagree. Some would like to see U.S. resources utilized in economically profitable ways; others would like to have the land preserved in a natural state for future generations to enjoy. Both sides agree on one point: they would like the military to be forced to give up their claims. The dispute over the future use of this land has become a focal point of political controversy, one that helps to illustrate the difficulty in changing both missions and thinking frozen in a Cold War framework. Transitions do not come easily.

It is this controversy and its ramifications that R. McGreggor Cawley and Robert M. Lawrence explore. They review the history of public land management, from the earlier efforts at disposal to later battles between developers and preservationists. The public lands had been used mostly for resource development up until the passage of the Wilderness Act of 1964. This legislation allowed environmental concerns to influence decision making relevant to public land use. Eventually it was to result in a reversal of previous trends. Environmental interests replaced the interests of those who sought resource development as the major force in developing land policy.

In the battles over public land use, the military was not a factor until World War II. At that time the military expanded its control of public land from 3 million acres to approximately 25 million acres. At present, the Department of Defense has authority over 29 million acres of a federally owned 700 million acres. Seventy-five percent of the military holdings are in the Rocky Mountain and Pacific coast regions of the country. The land was turned to military use through administrative decree as needed for national security purposes, a clearly stipulated temporary condition. No congressional legislation was involved, and little public participation influenced the decisions made.

Cawley and Lawrence develop three case studies. The Engels Act of 1958, which attempted to place limits on military land procurement and set legislative procedures for such actions; the MX missile controversy; and the Military Lands Act of 1986, a product of the Reagan administration's emphasis on a defense buildup, which reasserted some military prerogatives in managing or acquiring further land (although several concessions were made to public concerns).

In the immediate aftermath of communism's decline (1979–1980), the military attempted to expand its control of public lands. Curiously, the war in the Persian Gulf illustrated the value of high technology weaponry and helped legitimize the military's claims. At the same time, and over a period of years, the Defense Department was involved in a prolonged negotiation over reductions in personnel and the closing of military bases. The fear among some is that the base closing will primarily be in the eastern and middle United States and have little affect on the western lands.

The future policy directions may lie in a cooperative approach to land management. The Department of Defense has indicated a concern with environmental protection (a "greening" of the Pentagon?) that, if followed, could allow for a common ground with environmentalists. The approach for the next decade or more may have already been established.

Social Welfare Policy

Gregory R. Weiher paints an unpromising picture of the prospects for fundamental change in social welfare policies for the immediate future. The

Reagan administration's hostility to social policy has been well documented. One by-product of its approach has been the increasing economic vulnerability of ever larger sectors of the American public. Unfortunately, the fiscal policies of the Reagan-Bush years, the defense buildup (in funding terms, at the direct expense of social welfare concerns); the accumulated national debt; the reductions of rates for personal and corporate higher income tax brackets; the increase in entitlement costs, primarily those benefitting the middle class and in social security and medicare payouts; the greater demand on the federal budget to meet the cost of pension programs for government and military retirees; and the generally poor performance of the economy all mitigate against concerns with social equity. Real income has declined. International economic competition has placed America at a disadvantage that the other essays in this volume indicate will be difficult to reverse. Manufacturing has declined, and the service sector of the economy has expanded, substituting low-paying jobs for high-wage ones. These developments, accelerated during the Reagan-Bush presidencies, will be with us for a long time to come.

One consequence has been a greater reliance on state-level social expenditures and service delivery, as both Weiher and Peter Gluck indicate, an uneasy foundation for social welfare policies.

The fall of communism may not bring the positive domestic results many had hoped for. As Weiher says, "monumental challenges" confront the United States at a point in time when many, if not most, citizens have little faith that the political or economic system can effectively move to meet them. The transference of social welfare functions to the states and the states' ability to administer them, introduced by Weiher, is explored in depth in the chapter by Peter R. Gluck.

Social Policy Delivery System

We end the volume with a look at intergovernmental delivery of human services in a period of retrenchment. How do service agencies compensate? What types of services and what clientele groups are the most adversely affected? These are the questions that Peter R. Gluck tries to answer while examining the impact of reduced social expenditures in the operations of public and not-for-profit agencies at the community level. The analysis is extensive, and it begins to address some of the basic concerns as to what takes place in times of funding cuts and service curtailment.

Changes in policy directions during the 1980s and reductions in social spending at the federal level led, in turn, to similar cutbacks by state and local governments unable to fill the void left by the federal withdrawal. The states faced difficult economic conditions themselves. More specifically, they suffered from reduced tax incomes in a shrinking economy at the time they were being forced to assume greater financial and administrative responsibilities for a broad range of social policies. The experience left the states wary of any changes in federal policy and, in particular, fearful that any expansion of social services by the Clinton administration will ultimately mean more pressure for increasing state taxes to fund the programs and more demands on the states to administer them. At the community level, there has been a period of retrenchment and adjustment in efforts to offer the same types of services but with reduced budgets and personnel.

Gluck reports on a study conducted in 1988 to ascertain the changes in impact and procedures the financial and policy cuts have made since 1980. The focus of the study was on public, mental health, and social service agencies in two economically depressed counties in Michigan that included the manufacturing center of Flint.

Since 1964, local groups have depended heavily on the federal government for funding. Jimmy Carter began to reverse the trend after his election in 1976, and Ronald Reagan set about in the 1980s to eliminate as much social spending as politically attainable. In addition, the national economy had been in recession, and the Frostbelt states of the Midwest and Northeast were particularly hard hit as their economies suffered with the transfer of jobs and industries to the Sunbelt states.

The Reagan administration's efforts to restrict social spending combined with the Deficit Reduction Act adopted by the Congress and the changes in tax policy championed by the Reagan administration acted to substantially decrease the funds available for social programs. President Clinton, in courting support for his initial budget, which did include some tax increases, agreed to implement further cuts in spending. Given international and economic conditions, significant increases in social support may not be possible for a considerable period of time.

While budgets are being cut and the economy stagnates, the demand for social services is increasing. With the closing of industrial plants in the Midwest and Northeast, a permanent underclass of citizens may be in the making.

The funding of programs is the most crucial aspect of their operations. As a consequence of political developments from the Progressive Era, the New Deal and the Great Society, local agencies have depended heavily on federal support. As this was reduced, they turned to private agencies, introduced fee requirements, and relied on United Way contributions, none adequate to meet the need. Reduced funding necessarily meant more-limited services were offered to fewer people. The greatest cut in funding was for programs serving the lowest income clientele.

Professional staffing decreased in the community agencies (a loss of about one in five of the professional staff) during the period covered by the study (1980–1987), forcing a greater reliance on part-time and lower level clerical personnel. The personnel changes differed in relation to the policy fields, with the severest reductions in the social agencies serving low income groups. On the other hand, personnel in public health programs slightly increased, and those in mental health agencies significantly increased. Not surprisingly, most agencies have limited the number of new clients they have taken on, preferring to serve the ones they already have as best they can. They have also attempted to increase the number of program services they can offer these clients. One consequence has been an increase in staff responsibilities and case loads. The community agencies have also attempted to implement management strategies to make themselves more cost effective, and they have more self-consciously attempted to reach out to local groups and public officials to build coalitions and increase support for their efforts.

Gluck reports two broad strategies in relation to funding retrenchments: a reactive approach that cuts programs but holds out the promise of changing patterns of policy and the increased availability of financing in the future, and a proactive stance that assumes that the decline in available money may be a long-run fact of life and that basic strategies must be enacted to deal with the condition. The latter approach, potentially a more realistic one, involves systematic planning to broaden the agency's revenue base, set priorities, target resources, improve organizational performance, and develop a political base of support. As Gluck points out, it remains to be seen whether such changes can assure the continued delivery of social services on the level of those previously funded by federal and state governments.

The changes in social policy in the last decade or so have been major. The problems the nation faces in adjusting to a post–Cold War social and economic order will be challenging, both in relation to how effectively the nation manages to compete internationally and how it chooses to allocate its resources and set its political priorities. The outcome of the debate that has begun is anything but predictable.

NOTES

1. For a somewhat different chronology, see Kudrle and Marmor, 1990, table 3.1, p. 83.

2. After losing the 1992 presidential race and before leaving office, Bush (who had himself been a target of investigators, although he had not been officially accused of knowledge of or participation in illegal activities) pardoned six people who had served in the Reagan administration and were involved in various aspects of the Iran-Contra affair. The action effectively ended the inquiry of the Special Prosecutor's office and any further efforts to secure court verdicts.

Charges of constitutional violations of office were to be raised again during the Bush presidency. These were over the illegal sale of arms and weapons technology to Iraq by the United States preceding the Persian Gulf war. The issues involved were poorly understood, and the accusations aroused little public or congressional interest and did not appear to hurt the administration. These were over the secret sale of arms and technology to Iraq by the United States preceding the Persian Gulf War. The case was complicated. Allegedly, the almost $5 billion transaction was financed through an Atlanta-based branch of a bank owned by the Italian government. The charge was that President Bush and his senior aids had attempted to cover up their activities after the invasion of Kuwait, an accusation similar to those made during the Watergate hearings involving the Nixon administration. Bank officials were tried in federal court, but both the Bush and Clinton Justice Departments concluded that there was no conspiracy on the part of the Bush administration and refused to prosecute further. The federal judge hearing the case was publicly skeptical. These actions, however, effectively terminated the investigation.

3. Much later it was revealed that the administration, in a disinformation strategy allegedly sanctioned by Caspar W. Weinberger, secretary of defense for the years 1981–1987, rigged tests and faked crucial data in support of the Star Wars program, intended it was said to mislead the Soviet Union but also used to gain support for the program in the Congress (Weiner, 1993).

4. For a defense of social program gains, see Schwartz, 1988, and Marmor, Mashaw, and Harvey, 1990.

5. These points reflect those Helco develops (1900, 399–400); see also Gough, 1979.

Policies on Aging in the Post–Cold War Era

ROBERT H. BINSTOCK

From the New Deal to the present public policies have substantially improved the well-being of older Americans. But as the twentieth century comes to a close in the post–Cold War era, policies on aging are approaching an important crossroads. There are still many urgent needs within the rapidly growing elderly population. Yet our political system may not respond to these needs. After many decades of creation and expansion of an "Old Age Welfare State,"[1] the present climate of American politics and public discourse is increasingly hostile to governmental programs benefiting older people.

A growing assumption that public benefits for aging persons are sufficient or, indeed, should be scaled down, was expressed effectively in an analysis of potential uses of a "peace dividend"—written when the cold War was coming to an end. A lengthy agenda of domestic policy initiatives that might be included in a "Post-Cold War Budget" was proposed, including: national health insurance for some 30 to 37 million uninsured persons; increased federal aid to education, including Head Start programs; establishment of a National Police Corps; rebuilding the nation's infrastructure of bridges and highways; expanding a program of supplemental food for women, infants, and children; and housing the homeless. But the only discussion of programs for older persons was as a source of financing for this list of initiatives:

> We could make no changes in Social Security or military pensions. Or we could make substantial savings that would be relatively painless to pensioners. . . .

> With the money saved through these reforms, we could end hunger in America.
> . . . Because Social Security and military pensions bulk so large in the budget,
> we could also begin to house the nation's homeless . . . on the money freed up by
> these two modest reforms. (Beatty, 1990, 81).

In the post–Cold War era, of course, public resources are perceived as scarce. The need to "reduce the deficit" of the federal government is a rhetorical mainstay of domestic politics. Spiralling health care costs are widely considered to be one of the major problems of our society.

The benefits provided to elderly persons through federal programs and the continuing growth of the older population are commonly viewed as contributing to or exacerbating each of these problems, and others as well. About 30 percent of the annual federal budget, or nearly $450 billion, is expended on benefits to older persons.[2] One-third of all American health care expenditures is on elderly people, or about $270 billion out of $809 billion in 1992 (Sonnefeld et al., 1991). The present 32 million Americans aged sixty-five and over, 12.5 percent of our population, is projected to more than double—to 69 million—by the middle of the next century. As early as the year 2030, fully 20 percent of Americans are expected to be aged sixty-five and over (Taeuber, 1990).

Accordingly, there is much anxiety about costs of governmental benefits to the aging, now and in the future. Already, a great many issues of domestic policy portray an artificially homogenized constituency of "the aged" as in conflict with other groupings of Americans, and as a growing and unsustainable burden that will undermine our national well-being.

How did this political milieu of hostility to older persons and policies on aging develop? In the context of present policies and their projected effects in the future, what are some of the urgent needs within the older population that could be helped through additional policies and policy reforms? What roles have the politics of older persons and old-age interest groups had in contributing to this situation, and how will they influence the future?

What is the outlook for post–Cold War policies? In the context of rapid population aging, with ever more older persons becoming eligible for public benefits, can the present level of expenditures on aging be economically and politically sustained in the long run? Will the Old Age Welfare State be dismantled as part of a redistribution of policy benefits among generations? Can programs on aging be reformed to achieve a more equitable distribution of benefits and burdens within the elderly population? Will old-age criteria remain viable as mechanisms for distributing public benefits?

The Evolution of Policies and Issues

Old people in the United States began to be perceived as a separate social category in the late decades of the nineteenth century, when common assumptions about older persons and their social roles did not fit in well with an increasingly industrialized world (see Achenbaum, 1978, 1985; Chudacoff, 1989; Haber, 1983; cf. Fischer, 1977). By the turn of the century old age was increasingly seen as a distinct phase of life identified by birthdays and the institution of retirement (Graebner, 1980).

An official boundary between adulthood and old age in the United States was first established by the New Deal's Social Security Act of 1935, enacted some quarter of a century after such public pension programs had been enacted in most of the industrial world (Hudson and Binstock, 1976). Even as early twentieth century laws regulating child labor and the age of sexual consent marked boundaries between childhood and adulthood, Social Security—by designating age sixty-five as an eligibility requirement for retirement benefits—publicly institutionalized an age norm for retirement, and set a major precedent for the notion that older Americans need help from government.

During the more than half a century since then American policies toward older persons have been adopted and amended in a number of different social, economic, and political contexts. The reasons why each policy was originally enacted and subsequently altered have been subject to widely variant interpretations (Achenbaum 1986; Binstock, et al., 1985; Campion, 1984; Cohen, 1983, 1985; David, 1985; Derthick, 1979; Estes, 1979; Graebner, 1980; Harris, 1966; Holtzman, 1963; Hudson and Binstock, 1976; Hudson and Strate, 1985; Iglehart, 1989; Jacobs, 1990; Light, 1985; Marmor, 1970; Marmor et al., 1990; Olson, 1982; Williamson, et al., 1982). But one feature common to them is that they have used old ages as sweeping, convenient markers for designating a category of American citizens as in need of governmental assistance.

1935 to 1978: Compassionate Ageism and the "Old Age Welfare State"

From the New Deal until the late 1970s, public policy issues concerning older Americans were framed by an underlying *ageism*— the attribution of the same characteristics, status, and just deserts to a heterogeneous group that has been artificially homogenized, packaged, labeled, and marketed as "the aged" (see Palmore, 1990).

The stereotypes of ageism—unlike those of racism and sexism—have not been wholly prejudicial to the well-being of their objects, the aged. Indeed, ageism has been expressed through a number of policies—such as Medicare health insurance and "senior citizen" discounts—that treat all older persons the same by providing them with benefits and protection simply on the basis of old age (Kutza, 1981).

Prior to the late 1970s the predominant stereotypes of older Americans were compassionate. Elderly persons tended to be seen as poor, frail, socially dependent, objects of discrimination, and above all "deserving." For more than forty years—dating from the Social Security Act of 1935—American society accepted the oversimplified notion that all older persons are essentially the same and all worthy of governmental assistance. The lowest levels of economic status, health, and functional capacities that could be found among older persons became familiar as common denominators (Neugarten 1970). As a leading gerontologist aptly summarized this ageism, in chastising professional reformers for fostering stereotypes of dependent older people:

> You are poor, lonely, weak, incompetent, ineffectual, and no longer terribly bright. You are sick, in need of better housing and transportation and nutrition, and we—the nonelderly and those elderly who align themselves with us and work with us—are finally going to turn our attention to you, the deserving elderly, and relieve your suffering. (Kalish, 1979, 398).

The American polity implemented this compassionate construct by adopting and financing major age-categorical benefit programs, and tax and price subsidies for which eligibility is not determined by need. Through the New Deal's Social Security, the Great Society's Medicare, and the Older Americans Act (an omnibus social service program), special tax exemptions and credits for being aged sixty-five or older, and a variety of other measures enacted during President Nixon's New Federalism, the elderly were exempted from the screenings that are applied to welfare applicants in order to determine whether they are worthy of public help.

During the 1960s and 1970s, just about every issue or problem affecting just some older persons that could be identified by advocates for the elderly became a governmental responsibility: nutritional, legal, supportive, and leisure services; housing; home repair; energy assistance; transportation; help in getting jobs; protection against being fired from jobs; public insurance for private pensions; special mental health programs; a separate National Institute on Aging; and on, and on, and on. By the late 1970s, if not earlier, American society had learned the catechism of compassionate ageism very well and had expressed it through a great many policies; a committee of the U.S. House of Representatives (1977), using loose criteria, was able to identify 134 programs benefiting the aging, overseen by forty-nine committees and subcommittees of Congress.

The Emergence of the Aged as Scapegoat

Since 1978, however, the long-standing compassionate stereotypes of older persons have been undergoing an extraordinary reversal. Older people have come to be portrayed as one of the more flourishing and powerful groups in American society and attacked as a burdensome responsibility. The immediate precipitating factor was a cash flow problem in the Social Security system that emerged within the larger context of a depressed economy during President Carter's administration (Estes, 1983; Light, 1985).

Two additional elements contributed importantly to this reversal of stereotypes. One element was tremendous growth in the amount and proportion of federal dollars expended on benefits to aging citizens, which had come to be more than one quarter of our annual budget and comparable in size to expenditures on national defense. Journalists (e.g., Samuelson, 1978) and academicians (e.g., Hudson, 1978) began to notice and publicize this phenomenon in the late 1970s. By 1982, an economist in the Office of Management and Budget had pointed up the comparison with the defense budget by reframing the classical trade-off metaphor of political economy from "guns vs. butter" to "guns vs. canes" (Torrey, 1982).

A second element in the reversal of the stereotypes of old age has been dramatic improvements in the aggregate status of older Americans, in large measure due to the impact of federal benefit programs. Social Security, for example, has helped to reduce the proportion of elderly persons in poverty from about 35 percent three decades ago (Clark, 1990) to 11.4 percent today (Radner, 1991). The success of such programs has improved the economic status of aged persons to the point where journalists and social commentators can now, with superficial accuracy describe older people, on average, as more prosperous than the general population.[3]

Throughout the 1980s and into the 1990s, the new stereotypes, readily observed in popular culture, have depicted older persons as prosperous, hedonistic, politically powerful, and selfish. For example, "Grays on the Go," a 1988 cover story in *Time*, was filled with pictures of senior surfers, senior swingers, and senior softball players. Older persons were portrayed as America's new elite—healthy, wealthy, powerful, and "staging history's biggest retirement party" (Gibbs, 1988).

A dominant theme in such accounts of older persons is that their selfishness is ruining the nation. The *New Republic* highlighted this motif early in 1988 with a drawing on the cover caricaturing older persons with the caption "greedy geezers." The table of contents "teaser" for the story that followed announced that "the real me generation isn't the yuppies, it's America's growing ranks of prosperous elderly" (Fairlie, 1988). This theme has been echoed widely in recent years, and the epithet "greedy geezers" has become a familiar adjective in journalistic accounts of federal budget politics (Salhoz, 1990). Early this year, *Fortune* declaimed that "the Tyranny of America's old" is "one of the most crucial issues facing U.S. society" (Smith, 1992).

In this unsympathetic climate of opinion, the aged have emerged as a scapegoat for an impressive list of American problems. Demographers and advocates for children have blamed the political power of elderly Americans for the plight of youngsters who have inadequate nutrition, health care, and education, and insufficiently supportive family environments (e.g., Preston, 1984). One children's advocate even proposed that parents receive an "extra vote" for each of their children, in order to combat older voters (Carballo, 1981). Former Secretary of Commerce Peter Peterson (1987) has suggested that a prerequisite for the United States to regain its stature as a first class power in the world economy is a sharp reduction in programs benefiting older Americans.

Widespread concerns about spiralling U.S. health care costs have been redirected, in part, from the health care providers, suppliers, administrators, and insurers—the parties that are responsible for setting the prices of care—to elderly persons for whom health care is provided, even though about two-thirds of the growth in health care costs are due to the general and health-sector-specific rates of inflation, and only 9 percent is attributable to population growth (Sonnefeld et al., 1991). A prominent biomedical ethicist, Daniel Callahan, has depicted health care costs for older persons as "a great fiscal black hole" that will absorb an unlimited amount of our national resources (1987, 17). He, and a number of other academicians and public figures, including politicians, have urged vigorously that American society set limits to health care for older people (see Binstock and Post, 1991).

In 1989 a distinguished "executive panel" of American leaders convened by the Ford Foundation designated older persons as the only group of citizens responsible for financing a broad range of social programs for persons of all ages. In a report entitled *The Common Good: Social Welfare and the American Future* the panel recommended a series of policies, costing a total of $29 billion (Ford Foundation, 1989). And how did the panel propose that this $29 billion be financed? Solely by taxation of Social Security benefits. In fact, every financing alternative considered in the report assumed that elderly people should be the exclusive financiers of the panel's package of recommendations for improving social welfare in our nation. Apparently, the Ford panel felt that the reasons for this assumption were self-evident; it did not even bother to justify its selections of these financing options, as opposed to others.

Equity as an "Intergenerational" Construct

These various problems for which elderly people have become a scapegoat have been thematically unified as issues of so-called "intergenerational equity," through the efforts of Americans for Generational Equity (AGE). Formed as an interest group in 1985, AGE had backing from the corporate sector as well as a handful of congressmen who led it, and it recruited some of the prominent "scapegoaters"—including demographer Preston and biomedical ethicist Callahan—to its board. According to its annual reports, most of AGE's funding came from insurance companies, health care corporations, banks, and other private sector businesses and organizations that are in competition with Medicare and Social Security (Quadagno, 1989).

AGE described itself as "a non-partisan non-profit coalition . . . dedicated to forging a coalition among all generations to protect the future of young Americans"; its main mission was "to promote greater public understanding of the trends arising from the aging of the U.S. population and to foster increased public support for policies that will serve the economic interests of all Americans in the next century" (*Generational Journal*, 1989).

Central to AGE's credo was the proposition that today's older people are locked in an intergenerational conflict with younger age cohorts regarding the distribution of public resources. AGE's basic view is that the large aggregate of public transfers of income and other benefits to today's cohorts of older persons, financed through unfairly burdensome taxes on the contemporary labor force, are unlikely to be available in the future as old age benefits (e.g., Social Security and Medicare) when the present cohort of workers, commonly termed the "baby boomers," becomes elderly retirees starting in the year 2010 and continuing through several decades (see Longman, 1987). The organization disseminated this viewpoint effectively from its Washington office through press releases, media interviews, and a quarterly publication, the *Generational Journal*, as well as through periodic conferences on such subjects as: "Children at Risk: Who Will Support an Aging Society?" and "Medicare and the Baby Boom Generation."

Although AGE faded from the scene in the early 1990s, its themes of intergenerational equity and conflict have been carried forward prominently by the Concord Coalition. This Washington-based organization, founded in 1993 by former U.S. Senators Paul Tsongas and Warren B. Rudman, proposes that entitlement payments, largely Social Security benefits, be scaled back in order to eliminate the federal deficit (Concord Coalition, 1993).

Moreover, the paradigm of intergenerational conflict has been adopted by the media and academics as routine perspectives for describing many social policy issues (Cook et al., in press). During the 1990 budget negotiations between the president and Congress, for example, a headline in the *Washington Post* (1990, 1) proclaimed: "Older Voters Drive Budget: Generational Divide Marks Budget Battle." The intergenerational themes have also gained currency in elite sectors of American society. The president of the prestigious American Association of Universities, for instance, has asserted: "[T]he shape of the domestic federal budget inescapably pits programs for the retired against every other social purpose dependent on federal funds, in the present and the future" (Rosenzweig, 1990, 6).

Present Policies and the Status of Older People

At the heart of debates concerning intergenerational equity are programs authorized by the Social Security Act. Initially legislated in 1935, Social Security was part of a larger New Deal effort at job creation and relief during an era when more than one quarter of the labor force was out of work.[4] It provided old age pensions to encourage older persons to leave or remain out of the labor force, as well as to provide income to elderly people.

Paradoxically, more recent federal legislation has been aimed at encouraging and permitting older workers to stay in the labor force. The Age Discrimination in Employment Act (ADEA) of 1967 authorized federal job training and placement programs for older workers and outlawed employment discrimination on the basis of age. Subsequent amendments to the ADEA in 1978 and 1986 outlawed mandatory retirement in almost all sectors of American employment. And a 1983 amendment to the Social Security Act increased the age at which workers, early in the twentieth-first century, will be eligible for old age retirement benefits.

Income Maintenance Policies

Among the great many adjustments made to Social Security since 1935, several are especially worth noting. The program was expanded to provide survivors' and dependent benefits in 1939 and disability benefits in 1956. In 1965, Medicare (providing comprehensive health insurance for persons age sixty-five and over and for disabled workers) and Medicaid (a federal grant-in-aid program providing health insurance for the poor) were added. Legislation in 1972 provided automatic cost-of-living adjustments (COLAs) for Social Security benefits by indexing them to inflation. And in 1983 the benefits of some Social Security recipients were made subject, for the first time, to taxation.

The Old Age Insurance (OAI) program of Social Security, providing cash benefits to 28.4 million retired workers and their dependents, is the largest income transfer program of the federal government. Due to the growth of the elderly population—as well as recurring liberalizations in the Social Security benefit formula prior to 1972, and the subsequent implementation of COLAs—OAI payments increased from under $1 billion in 1950 to $172 billion in 1990 (U.S. Social Security Admin., 1991, 132).

Eligibility for OAI benefits and the size of payments are based on an individual's history of participation in Social Security as a worker who has paid payroll taxes under the Federal Insurance Contributions Act and has reached the age of sixty-five (or ages sixty-two to sixty-four, for actuarially reduced benefits) and meets a retirement "earnings test" ($10,200 annually, in 1992) that is applied to determine if an individual is effectively retired. Monthly benefits for a retired worker average $603, and range from less than $200 to over $1,000 a month (U.S. Social Security Admin., 1991, 2). As indicated in table 2.1 OAI provides most of the income of lower-income elderly people (80 percent and 72 percent, respectively, for the lowest two quintiles), but less than one-tenth of income for the wealthiest 5 percent.

TABLE 2.1

Percent of Income of Aged Family Units, by Income Quintiles, from Different Sources of Income, 1989*

Income Quintile,	Percent of Income				
Lowest to Highest	Earnings	Social Security	Property	Pension	Other
1	2.0	80.0	4.1	3.1	10.8
2	6.1	72.3	8.8	7.1	5.7
3	11.2	55.5	14.9	15.4	3.0
4	18.9	37.2	21.6	19.7	2.6
5	32.1	15.9	33.2	17.1	1.7
Top 5 percent	35.8	8.9	40.2	13.6	1.5

Source: Tabulations from D. R. Radner, (1991), "Changes in the Income of Age Groups, 1984–89," *Social Security Bulletin*, 54(12):12.
*Income adjusted for size of family unit and age of head.

The poorest elderly people can also receive cash assistance through Supplemental Security Income (SSI), a federal program that, in 1974, replaced three types of state welfare programs: old age assistance (OAA), aid to the blind, and aid to the totally and permanently disabled. Persons age sixty-five and older are eligible for SSI if they meet both an asset and an income test. Individuals with assets of less than $2,000 and couples with assets of less than 3,000 are eligible (excluding such major assets as the value of one's home; household goods and personal effects valued up to $2,000; an automobile, up to $4,500; and life insurance with a face value of up to $1,500). SSI supplements the annual income of recipients up to a level (from all sources) of about $4,500 for an individual and $6,500 for a couple. Benefits are indexed to inflation. States are encouraged to supplement this floor, or are required to supplement it if it does not equal or exceed the level in the state's OAA welfare program that existed in 1973, just before SSI began.

Since SSI's inception in 1974, total federal and state payments to older recipients[5] have increased from $2.5 billion to $3.7 billion (U.S. Social Security Admin., 1991, 286). About 1.5 million aged persons received SSI payments in 1990; the average monthly benefit was $219 (pp. 285, 287). Studies indicate, however, that 40 to 60 percent of the aged who are eligible for SSI do not participate in the program, principally because they lack knowledge of it or because they are reluctant to participate in a means-tested welfare program (U.S. Senate, 1991, 125–27).

A relatively small number of low-income aged persons receive assistance from in-kind federal benefit programs that marginally improve their economic well-being. About 7 percent receive benefits under the block-grant

Low-Income Home Energy Assistance Program; 6 percent receive food stamps; 4 percent get public housing subsidies; and 2 percent have rental assistance (Schulz, 1988, 42).

The federal government, and state and local governments, also provide income to older persons through their employer-sponsored pension plans.[6] The Civil Service Retirement System (covering federal employees hired before 1984) and the Federal Employees Retirement System (covering employees hired from 1984 on) paid 2.2 million annuitants and cost $31 billion in 1990; about $20 billion is paid annually to 1.6 federal military retirees (U.S. Senate, 1991, 59, 65). Some 6,600 state and local government pension plans, paying 3.1 million retirees, have assets of $727 billion (p. 55).

Nearly 800,000 private pension plans, involving 58 million active workers and 8 million annuitants (Clark, 1990) are regulated by the federal government. The Employee Retirement Income Security Act (ERISA) of 1974 established a comprehensive set of minimum standards, financial safeguards, and disclosure requirements, all designed to help workers actually realize pension benefits that are promised to them. Moreover, when a private pension plan terminates with inadequate funds to pay benefits, the Pension Benefit Guarantee Corporation (PBGC), established by ERISA, guarantees the continued payment of benefits to retired workers and the future payment of benefits to workers who have a vested right to a pension. The PBGC is funded by annual insurance premiums required from all pension plans covered by ERISA.

Despite the impact of public income transfers and employer-sponsored pensions, a substantial percentage of older people are in difficult economic situations. Their status is reflected to some extent in tables 2.2 and 2.3, which show median and mean incomes by age groups, respectively. Family units headed by persons age sixty-five or older have a median income that is 31 percent less than units headed by persons under age sixty-five and a mean income that is 18 percent less.

A picture of economic distress within the elderly population emerges more clearly in table 2.4, where it can be seen that the older age groupings, and children and young adults, experience the most poverty. In 1990, the poverty threshold was an income of $6,268 for an elderly individual, and $7,905 for an elderly couple (U.S. Social Security Admin., 1991). Nearly 4 million persons, or 11.4 percent of the population age sixty-five and older, are classified as "below the poverty threshold." The proportion climbs to 27.2 percent, or about 9 million persons, when measured by the "near-poor" line (150 percent of the poverty threshold), which is frequently examined because of widespread criticism concerning the inadequacies of the poverty line as an appropriate measure (Ruggles, 1990). Those older people who fall between the poverty line and the near-poor line have been dubbed "the 'tweeners" (Smeeding, 1990) because, on the one hand, they are not poor enough to qualify for SSI, Medicaid, food stamps, and other means-tested public programs,

TABLE 2.2

Real Median Family Unit Income, by Age of Unit Head, and Average Annual Percentage Change in Real Median Income, 1984–89*
(in 1982 dollars)

Age of Unit Head	1984	1989	Average Annual Percentage Change
All ages	$13,330	$14,303	1.4
Under 65	14,116	15,303	1.6
65 or older	10,271	10,598	.6
20-24	8,505	9,030	1.2
25-29	13,067	13,443	.6
30-34	13,867	14,554	1.0
35-39	15,101	15,667	.7
40-44	15,738	17,519	2.2
45-49	17,356	19,475	2.3
50-54	17,662	19,980	2.5
55-59	16,803	17,965	1.3
60-64	14,097	15,761	2.3
65-69	12,509	13,241	1.1
70-74	10,574	11,479	1.7
75-79	9,143	9,306	.4
80-84	7,868	8,245	.9
85 or older	7,458	7,651	.5

Source: D. R. Radner, (1991), "Changes in the Income of Age Groups, 1984–89," *Social Security Bulletin*, 54(12):7.
*Income adjusted for size of family unit and age of head.

TABLE 2.3

Mean Incomes of Family Units, by Age of Unit Head, and Percentage Change in Mean Incomes, 1984–1989*
(in 1982 dollars)

Age of Unit Head	1984	1989	Percentage Change
All ages	$16,321	$17,687	8.4
Under 65	16,854	18,374	9.0
65 or older	14,185	14,991	5.7
Under 25	9,281	9,673	4.2
25-34	15,392	16,209	5.3
35-44	17,742	19,113	7.7
45-54	20,045	22,796	13.7
55-64	19,251	13,791	8.7
65-74	15,569	16,823	8.1
75 or older	12,133	12,459	2.7

Source: D. R. Radner, (1991), "Changes in the Income of Age Groups, 1984–89," *Social Security Bulletin*, 54(12):11–12.
*Income adjusted for size of family unit and age of head.

TABLE 2.4

Percentage of Persons Poor or Near Poor, by Age of Person, 1989

Age	Below Poverty Threshold	Below 150 Percent of Poverty Threshold
All ages	12.8	22.0
Under 65	13.0	21.1
65 or older	11.4	27.2
Under 5	22.6	33.9
5–9	20.3	31.2
10–14	18.1	28.2
15–19	15.6	25.0
20–24	14.8	24.7
25–29	11.3	20.0
30–34	10.8	18.4
35–39	8.9	15.2
40–44	7.2	13.1
45–49	7.2	12.2
50–54	7.7	13.0
55–59	9.7	16.2
60–64	9.5	17.4
65–69	8.2	20.2
70–74	9.6	24.7
75–79	13.5	32.7
80–84	16.7	36.8
85 or older	18.4	38.6

Source: D. R. Radner (1991), "Changes in the Income of Age Groups, 1984–89," *Social Security Bulletin*, 54(12):10.

but on the other hand they are not well enough off to be financially secure. These 'tweeners are highly vulnerable to unexpected high cost health care bills and sudden inflation in housing costs.

The subgroups of elderly people most heavily represented in low income categories are ethnic minorities, females, and the oldest among the aged. Among older persons living as "unrelated individuals," 63 percent of Black females and 61 pecent of Hispanic females live in poverty, compared with 22 percent of white females and 16 percent of white males (U.S. Senate, 1989, 29). And, as shown in table 2.4, the poverty rate for persons aged eighty-five and older is 18.4 percent, more than double the rate for persons aged sixty-five to sixty-nine.

Health and Social Service Policies

Although economists technically classify Medicare and Medicaid as income transfer policies, no income, of course, is directly transferred to older persons through these programs.[7] Nonetheless, the two health insurance programs are major components of the Old Age Welfare State. In 1992, Medicare spent $133 billion on health services and supplies for Medicare insurees (about 90 percent of whom are aged), and the federal Medicaid program spent about $34 billion on nursing homes and home health care for chronically ill and disabled poor elderly persons (Sonnefeld, et al., 1991, 25). Another $16 billion was spent on health care for older persons through other federal agencies and state and local governments, most of the latter—some $13 billion—on nursing homes that were reimbursed through state Medicaid funds.

Additional health and social services for older persons are provided through many other federal programs. Principal among these are the health and social care programs of the Department of Veterans Affairs, the Social Services Block Grant (Title XX of the Social Security Act), the Community Services Block Grant, and the Older Americans Act—a $1 billion grant-in-aid program that funds nutritional, legal, and transportation services, senior centers, and a broad range of supportive and outreach services including forty that are explicitly described in the statute, as well as ''any other services . . . necessary for the general welfare of older individuals'' (Older Americans Act, 1989, Sec. 321, a, 19).

At least eleven of the thirteen National Institutes of Health sponsor research and professional training on aging-related health issues, but one of them, the National Institute on Aging (NIA), has aging as its primary mission. Established in 1974, largely in response to lobbying efforts by professionals interested in aging (Lockett, 1983), its 1991 budget was about $325 million (U.S. Senate, 1991, 265). In addition, the National Institute of Mental Health has a special Mental Disorders of the Aging Research Branch.

Despite this armamentarium of governmental health insurance, health and social services, and biomedical research focused on aging, health care costs and health status continue to be problems for millions of elderly Americans. Older persons, themselves, finance 41 percent of their aggregate care. They pay 29 percent in direct out-of-pocket health care expenditures and pay an additional 4 percent in Medicare premiums and 8 percent in private insurance premiums (to cover expenses not reimbursed by governmental programs). These payments by older persons, like health care payments generally, have inflated substantially in recent years—more than tripling, for example, between 1977 and 1988. Perhaps of greater concern to older persons with limited or moderate incomes is the growth of out-of-pocket costs from under 13 percent of income to over 18 percent of income for the average elderly household during the same period (U.S. House of Representatives, 1989, 8).

Life expectancy at older ages has increased by several years over the past two decades, largely due to declines in mortality from heart disease and stroke (Manton, 1991). A woman aged sixty-five can be expected to live almost twenty years more, and one aged eighty-five will live, on average, over seven years; a man aged seventy-five is likely to live almost ten more years (National Center for Health Statistics, 1987a). But the prevalence of morbidity within the older population is increasing, largely because this group is becoming older, on average, within itself. Among older old-age groups the rates of disease and disability are much greater than the rates for the total group of persons aged sixty-five and over (Manton, 1991).

The distribution of age groups within the population aged sixty-five and older is changing markedly and will continue to do so. In 1980, for example, persons aged eighty-five and over—who have been termed the "oldest-old" (Suzman, et al., 1992)—constituted only 8.8 percent of the American older population; in 1990, they were 10.3 percent of that group, and in the year 2000, they will be over 13 percent. Similarly, in 1980 persons aged seventy-five and older—who have been termed the "old-old" (Neugarten, 1970)— constituted 39 percent of the older population; in 1990, they were 42 percent of it, and by 2000 they will be 48 percent (Taueber, 1990, 3). Viewed another way, by the end of this century, the median person in the sixty-five-plus age group will be just under seventy-five years of age.

Specific older age groupings within the age sixty-five and over population use substantially more health and social care than younger elderly persons. A few examples readily illustrate this point.

At present, persons aged sixty-five and older account for 40.5 percent of the days of care in "short-stay" (as opposed to chronic disease) hospitals in the United States. But within that aggregate, the age eighty-five and older grouping uses hospitals at a rate that is 123 percent higher than those aged sixty-five to seventy-four; persons aged seventy-five to eighty-four use hospitals at a 69 percent higher rate than the sixty-five to seventy-four years group (National Center for Health Statistics, 1987b).

Similarly, about 1 percent of Americans aged sixty-five to seventy-four years are in nursing homes; this compares with 6 percent of persons seventy-five to eighty-four years of age and 22 percent of persons aged eighty-five and older (Hing, 1987). The greater numbers of persons who soon will be in the older old-age categories is a major factor in projections that the current nursing home population of 1.5 million persons will increase to 2.0 million by the year 2000 and reach 4.6 million some forty years later (U.S. Senate, 1989).

The same pattern holds true among older persons who, because of functional limitations in their activities of daily living, need home health services

TABLE 2.5

Estimated Percent of Older Americans with Functional Limitations,[1] Living in the Community,[2] by Age Group

Age Category	Percent with Functional Limitations
65–69 years	7.7
70–74 years	9.7
75–79 years	13.7
80–85 years	19.1
85 years and over	26.6

Source: M. Gornick, J. N. Greenberg, P. W. Eggers, and A. Dobson (1985), "Twenty Years of Medicare and Medicaid: Covered Populations, Use of Benefits, and Program Expenditures," *Health Care Financing Review, Annual Supplement*, 22.
1. Limitations in activities of daily living (e.g., feeding, toileting, bathing, dressing, getting in and out of bed).
2. A residence other than a hospital, nursing home, or other health care institution in the United States.

from paid professionals or from their families or friends on an in-kind basis. Table 2.5 depicts the dramatic increases, by five year old-age intervals, in the percentage of older persons residing in the community who have limitations in activities of daily living (e.g., feeding, toileting, bathing, dressing, and getting in and out of bed). The proportion needing help rises from 7.7 percent in the sixty-five to sixty-nine year old category to 26.6 percent in the aged eighty-five and over group, with the largest percentage increase occurring between the seventy to seventy-four and seventy-five to seventy-nine year old categories. Even though about 85 percent of home care services are provided to older patients on an unpaid, informal basis by spouses, siblings, adult children, and broader kin networks (U. S. Senate, 1989), annual expenditures on home care for about 3 million elderly people are now more than $16 billion and are expected to double by the end of this decade. Yet, at present, about 40 percent of older Americans do not receive all of the help they need with activities of daily living that range from getting in and out of bed to getting around outside the home (Stone, et al., 1987).

The combined effects of high morbidity rates at older ages and the growing numbers and proportions of older people in their late seventies and eighties has generated considerable anxiety about the fiscal implications of an aging population. One projection suggests, for example, that Medicare costs for persons aged eighty-five and older may increase sixfold by the year 2040, as estimated in constant, inflation-adjusted dollars (Schneider and Guralnik, 1990).

The Politics of Aging and Their Impact on Policy

Media stereotypes concerning the politics of aging suggest that policies toward older people cannot be reformed—either to redistribute expenditures within programs for the elderly·or to reallocate them from old-age programs to other social goals. Older persons are frequently portrayed as a monolithic bloc of voters who promote and defend their self-interests successfully (e.g., Levy and Murnane, 1992). And old-age-based organizations are conventionally depicted as one of the most powerful constituencies in American politics.

In the fall of 1990, for example, when President Bush and congressional leaders agreed on a budget proposal that included changes in Social Security benefits and taxes, a *New York Times* reporter predicted a political explosion because: "America's older citizens are among the nation's most potent constituencies. They vote at higher rates than most other Americans. . . . In addition, their organizations, lead [sic] by the American Association of Retired Persons, swing great weight on Capitol Hill" (Oreskes, 1990, 12). A brief examination of the aging in American politics will indicate, however, that these nuggets of conventional wisdom are very oversimplified.

Political Attitudes

The attribute of old age has little impact on political attitudes and behavior. Numerous contemporary polls of political attitudes still support the general conclusion stated by Angus Campbell (1971) some two decades ago that

> because each age cohort includes people who differ profoundly in many important conditions of life it is not likely that any group will be very homogeneous in its attitudes. The evidence which national surveys provide us does in fact demonstrate that attitudinal differences between age groups are far less impressive than those within age groups. (P. 117)

A study by Day (1990), for instance, analyzed polls conducted from 1972 to 1986 by three different national opinion surveys to test for attitudinal differences between older, middle-aged, and younger adults with respect to policy areas that affect older persons most directly (e.g., Social Security and Medicare). Her analysis suggests that old age is not an important factor in shaping political attitudes and that there is no evidence of so-called intergenerational conflict to be found in comparing age group attitudes toward policy issues. She found that "older people are nearly indistinguishable from younger adults [both the middle-aged and younger categories] on most issues—including aging policy issues" (p. 47).

When Day examined the responses of older persons in subgroups defined by various combinations of socioeconomic characteristics and partisan attachments, she confirmed the findings of numerous studies that show clear relationships between such combinations and political attitudes among adults of all ages. For example, "Pluralities of people who were low-income, nonwhite, less educated, working-class, Democratic, or liberal favored increases in Social Security and Medicare, while pluralities of higher-income, white, well-educated, middle-class, Republican, or conservative people expressed satisfaction with current spending levels" (p. 53). This theme is echoed in National Opinion Research Center (NORC 1986–91) surveys of views of spending for Social Security. Among black older persons, a group that experiences a very high rate of poverty, 68.1 percent feel that we were spending "too little on Social Security." In contrast, only 43.8 percent of white older persons share this view.

Voting Behavior

Older persons do vote at much higher rates than most other Americans. The overall voting participation rate in the 1988 presidential election was 65.9 percent (NORC, 1986–91). The youngest age group—aged eighteen to twenty-nine—had the lowest rate of participation, just 44.8 percent; with each successive older age group the rate increased until it peaked in the age ranges of sixty to sixty-nine years (79.5 percent voting) and seventy to seventy-nine years (81.7 percent voting).

But older persons do not vote as a monolithic bloc, any more than middle-aged persons or younger persons do. Consequently, the aged are not a single-issue or several-issue voting constituency.

Table 2.6, showing the results of election exit polls in the last four presidential elections, should make clear that the votes of older persons usually distribute among candidates in about the same proportions as the votes of other age groupings of citizens. The 1992 election was unusual in that Bill Clinton fared much better among older voters than younger voters. Yet, it should be noted that the support of older people for George Bush was roughly the same as that of younger age groups and precisely the same as the overall average for Bush. Data from various polls suggest that the comparatively large plurality for Clinton among older voters—and their relatively low support for Ross Perot—might be explained by the relative reluctance of older people to accept Perot as a serious candidate. Although older voters tend to switch their allegiance among Democratic and Republican candidates in about the same patterns as most other voters, research has consistently shown that older persons have a greater attachment to traditional political institutions (see Hudson and Strate, 1985). A greater reluctance to support an Independent candidate such as Perot is consistent with this tendency. In 1980, when John Anderson was an Independent candidate, support for him was at levels of 11 percent and 8 per-

TABLE 2.6

Nationwide Vote Distribution, by Age Groups and Gender, in Elections for U.S. President, 1980, 1984, 1988, 1992

	1980			1984		1988		1992		
	Reagan	Carter	Anderson	Reagan	Mondale	Bush	Dukakis	Clinton	Bush	Perot
Percent of all Voters										
all ages	51%	41%	7%	59%	40%	53%	45%	43%	38%	19%
18–29 years old	43	44	11	59	40	52	47	44	34	22
30–44 years old	55	36	8	57	42	54	45	42	38	20
44–59 years old	55	39	5	60	40	57	42	41	40	19
60 years and older	54	41	4	60	40	50	49	50	38	12
Percent of Men										
all ages	55	36	7	62	37	57	41	41	38	21
18–29 years old	47	39	11	63	36	55	43	38	36	26
30–44 years old	59	31	4	61	38	58	40	39	38	22
44–59 years old	60	34	5	62	36	62	36	40	40	20
60 years and older	56	40	3	62	37	53	46	49	37	14
Percent of Women										
all ages	47	45	7	56	44	50	49	46	37	17
18–29 years old	39	49	10	55	45	49	50	48	33	19
30–44 years old	50	41	8	54	45	50	49	44	38	18
44–59 years old	50	44	5	57	42	52	48	43	40	17
60 years and older	52	43	4	58	42	48	52	51	39	10

Source: New York Times/CBS News Poll, "Portrait of the Electorate," *New York Times*, Nov. 5, 1992, p. B9.

cent among the younger age groups, but only 5 percent and 4 percent among the older age groups.

That older persons usually distribute their votes in the same fashion as younger persons should not be surprising. There is no sound reason to expect that an age cohort—constituted of all religions, ethnic groups, economic and social status, political attitudes, and every other characteristic in American society—would suddenly become homogenized in its political behavior when it reaches the "old age" category (Campbell and Strate, 1981; Hudson and Strate, 1985; cf. Cutler, 1977). As Heclo (1988) observes, " '[T]he elderly' is really a category created by policy analysts, pension officials, and mechanical models of interest group politics" (p. 393).

Moreover, the very assumption that mass groupings of the American citizenry, such as elderly people, vote primarily on the basis of self-interested responses to single issues is, in itself, problematic (Simon, 1985). To the extent that issues have an impact within a heterogeneous group such as older persons, self-interested responses to any single issue are likely to vary substantially. Even in the context of a state or local referendum that presents a specific issue for balloting—such as propositions to cap local property taxes or to finance public schools—the best available studies show that old age is not a statistically significant variable associated with the distribution of votes (Button and Rosenbaum, 1989; Chomitz, 1987).

But don't politicians behave as if older persons vote as a bloc in response to issues? Aren't they terrorized by so-called "senior power"? The answer is not so clear, judging from a case study of a successful presidential election campaign in which relatively negligible financial resources and efforts were expended on wooing older voters (Riemer and Binstock, 1978). It is certainly evident that no politician goes out of his or her way to offend aged constituents. On the other hand, there have been numerous cases in recent years, enumerated below, when Congress has enacted legislation that has adversely affected presumed old-age interests.

Old-Age Interest Groups

Early old-age based organizations—which emerged in the Great Depression—are probably better understood as social movements than interest groups in that they reflected a broad-based and time-bound discontent rather than expression of enduring interests and concerns associated with old age (Carlie, 1969; Holtzman, 1963; Messinger, 1955; Pinner, et al., 1959). Most notable of these were the Townsend Movement, a nationwide organization that campaigned for old-age pensions, and the McClain pension movement in California. At its peak in 1936, the Townsend Movement may have had as many as 1.5 million members, but it declined rapidly thereafter; the McLain organization reached a level of about 70,000 members during the 1950s and then withered after the death of its founder (Putnam, 1970). Holtzman (1963) suggested that the Townsend Movement may have accelerated the passage of Social Security in 1935, but a number of scholars and participants in the policy process at that time have tended to dismiss the organization's influence on the creation and adoption of the program (Altmeyer, 1968; Schlesinger, 1958; Witte, 1962).

Although there are literally hundreds of contemporary organizations that engage on an ad hoc basis in the politics of policies and programs affecting older persons, about fifty of them—often referred to as the "gray lobby" (Pratt, 1976)—are more or less exclusively preoccupied with national issues related to aging. As indicated in figure 2.1, some of them are mass membership organizations, and others have been organized to advocate for selected constituencies of older persons or for professional and trade interests associated with old age. About thirty of these have constituted themselves as a Leadership Council on Aging, which attempts to speak with one voice, but rarely does.

By far the largest of these aging-based organizations is the American Association of Retired Persons (AARP), which claims some 33 million members and has an annual budget of several hundred million dollars. Although AARP lobbies actively in national politics, its political activities appear to be less important as membership incentives than the material and associational incentives (see Clark and Wilson, 1961) provided through its investment funds, insurance programs, pharmaceutical discounts, publications, travel packages and discounts, local chapter educational and cultural programs, and a variety of other activities.[8]

Only limited political power is available to AARP and the other aging-based interest groups. As implied by the evidence from voting behavior, there is no indication that such organizations have been able to cohere or even to shift marginally the votes of older persons. In the 1980 presidential campaign, for example, the leaders of a number of major aging-based organizations vigorously endorsed President Carter in his bid for reelection. Nonetheless, a majority of older persons voted for his opponent, Ronald Reagan, and in roughly the same proportion as voters in younger age groupings.

Organized demands of older persons have had little to do with the enactment and amendment of the major old-age policies such as Social Security and Medicare. Rather, such actions have been largely attributable to the initiatives of public officials in the White House, Congress, and the bureaucracy who have focused on their own agendas for social and economic policy (on Social Security, see Derthick, 1979, and Light, 1985; on Medicare, see Cohen, 1985 and Iglehart, 1989). The impact of old-age-based interest groups has been largely confined to relatively minor policies that have distributed benefits to professionals and practitioners in the field of aging rather than directly to older persons themselves (Binstock, 1982; Binstock, et al., 1985; Estes, 1979; Fox, 1989; and Lockett, 1983).

FIGURE 2.1

National Old-Age Interest Groups, 1992 (Selected)

Mass Membership Organizations
American Association of Retired Persons
Gray Panthers
National Alliance of Senior Citizens
National Association for Older Persons
National Association of Retired Federal Employees
National Committee to Preserve Social Security and Medicare
National Council of Senior Citizens

Advocacy Organizations for Special Older Constituencies
Alzheimer's Association
Associacion Nacionale Pro Personas Mayores
Families U.S.A. Foundation (poor older persons)
National Caucus and Center on Black Aged
National Citizens Coalition for Nursing Home Reform
National Foundation for Long-Term Care
National Hispanic Council on Aging
National Indian Council on Aging
National Pacific/Asian Resource Center on Aging
Older Women's League

Professional and Trade Organizations
Alliance for Aging Research
American Association of Homes for the Aging
American Association for International Aging
American Federation for Aging Research
American Geriatrics Society
American Society on Aging
Association for Gerontology in Higher Education
Gerontological Society of America
National Academy of Social Insurance
National Association for Home Care
National Association of Area Agencies on Aging
National Association of Foster Grandparents
National Association of Meals Programs
National Association of Nutrition and Aging Services Programs
National Association of Retired Senior Volunteer Program (RSVP) Directors
National Association of Senior Living Industries
National Association of State Units on Aging
National Council on the Aging
National Senior Citizens Law Center

Some forms of power, however, are available to old-age interest groups. In the classic pattern of American interest group politics (Lowi, 1969), public officials find it both useful and incumbent upon them to invite such organizations to participate in policy activities. In this way public officials are provided with a ready means of having been "in touch" symbolically with millions of older persons, thereby legitimizing subsequent policy actions and inactions. A brief meeting with the leaders of AARP and other old-age organizations can enable an official to claim that he or she has obtained duly the represented views of a mass constituency.

The symbolic legitimacy that old-age organizations have for participating in interest group politics gives them several forms of power. First, they have easy informal access to public officials—members of Congress and their staffs, career bureaucrats and appointed officials—and occasionally to the White House. They can put forth their own proposals regarding Social Security, Medicare, nursing home regulations, and a variety of other matters and work to block the proposals of others. To be sure, their audiences or targets may be unresponsive in subsequent policy decisions. But access provides some measure of opportunity.

Second, their legitimacy enables them to obtain public platforms in the national media, congressional hearings, and in national conferences and commissions dealing with old age, health, and a variety of subjects relevant to policies affecting aging. From these platforms the old age organizations can initiate and frame issues for public debate and respond to issues raised by others.

A third form of power available to the old-age interest groups might be termed "the electoral bluff." Although these organizations have not demonstrated a capacity to swing a decisive bloc of older voters, incumbent members of Congress are hardly inclined to risk upsetting the existing distribution of votes that puts them and keeps them in office. Few politicians, of course, want to call the bluff of the aged or any other latent mass constituency if it is possible to avoid doing so. In fact, the image of "senior power" is frequently invoked by politicians when, for one reason or another, they desire an excuse for doing nothing or for not differentiating themselves from their colleagues and electoral opponents.

These forms of power, while minor when compared with the power available to organizations that are based upon major economic interests, may have some limited impact. Today, as policies affecting old age have become prominent on the agenda of domestic policy issues, the old-age interest organizations seem to have become one of what Heclo (1984) terms "anti-redistributive veto forces" in American politics. The limited power these organizations have available to them is being applied in a defensive effort to maintain the existing distribution of benefits and privileges among older persons, as well as among the many professional and practitioner interests that have emerged and flourished in relation to the growth of the elderly population.

Nonetheless, a number of public policy decisions that are conventionally perceived as adverse to the self-interest of older persons proved to be politically feasible in the 1980s. Medicare deductibles, co-payments, and Part B premiums have increased continuously. Old Age Insurance (OAI) benefits have been made subject to taxation. The legislated formula for cost-of-living adjustments (COLAs) to OAI benefits was rendered less generous. Five benefit and eligibility provisions of Social Security were narrowed, which had a direct adverse effect on OAI recipients. And the extra personal exemption that all persons sixty-five years of age and older had been receiving when they filed their federal income tax returns was eliminated.

The Case of the Catastrophic Coverage Act

The most recent major legislative actions on policy toward aging, the enactment of the Medicare Catastrophic Coverage Act (MCCA) in 1988 and its repeal in 1989, clearly illustrated that older persons are not a homogeneous monolith, either politically or in terms of self-interests. The MCCA, developed through the initiatives of public officials in the White House, Congress, and the bureaucracy, was the first major expansion of benefits to older persons in sixteen years. It provided insurance coverage for economically catastrophic hospital and physician bills, outpatient prescription drugs, and for some elements of long-term care. The White House and congressional leaders self-consciously determined that the program would be "self-financed," that is, paid for wholly by elderly people who are eligible for Medicare (Iglehart 1989). About one-third of the new benefits were to be financed through increased premiums paid by all Medicare Part B enrollees and two-thirds through a progressive, sharply escalating surtax levied on middle and higher income Medicare enrollees—about 40 percent of program participants.

AARP publicly endorsed this policy. But during a period of nearly two years between the introduction of the bill and its enactment as law, neither AARP nor members of Congress floated successful "trial balloons" to enable older Americans to understand what sorts of benefits they would receive through the new MCCA and who would pay for them. Consequently, when the proposal finally did become a law there was no popular constituency supporting it. But there was distinct opposition to it from those older persons who had to pay the most new taxes and who perceived that they already had private insurance coverage for the benefits provided through the new law (Crystal, 1990; Holstein and Minkler, 1991). They were a small numerical minority, yet they were dispersed through every congressional district. When they protested vociferously against the Act, Congress received no evidence of countervailing popular support for the new law, despite the fact that AARP lobbyists publicly endorsed retention of the MCCA.

When the House of Representatives voted overwhelmingly (360 to 66) to repeal the MCCA in 1989, its action was characterized in the press as "a stunning defeat for the American Association of Retired Persons, which had supported the expanded Medicare program and fought repeal" (Tolchin, 1989a). Representative Dan Rostenkowski, chairman of the House Ways and Means committee, explained the vote in a fashion that undercut the stereotype of older persons as a monolithic constituency. "Because we in this congress can't take the heat from the wealthy few," he lamented, "all principles are abandoned" (Tolchin, 1989a). Yet, when the Senate concurred in the repeal some seven weeks later, Rostenkowski resurrected the image of older people as a powerful monolith that is winning a battle between generations:

> One of the most unhappy results of our ongoing budget gridlock has been an uneven contest between the very young and the very old. The young have lost nearly every time. That partly because the old, however frail they may be, are sophisticated enough to use the political process to press their demands. . . . The sad story of the 1980s [was that] the old have gotten more while the young have gotten less. (Tolchin, 1989b)

Although Congressman Rostenkowski may have believed his characterization of congressional activity in the 1980s, the facts do not bear him out. There were no legislative choices or contests during the decade between the very young and the very old, and—due to the repeal of the Catastrophic Act— the old did not get more. But his willingness to characterize congressional activity in the 1980s in terms of intergenerational conflict reflects the trend through which this framework has become a conventional perspective for describing tradeoffs in health and social welfare polices.

The Outlook for Policies in the Post–Cold War Era

As we begin the post–Cold War era, the future of policies on aging is unclear. Looming in the background is the possibility that if present policies on aging are more or less maintained, the demographic trends of population aging will render them unsustainable midway through the first half of the twenty-first century. More immediately, the construct of intergenerational equity is in vogue, and it includes the perception that older Americans receive far more than their fair share of benefits. In the context of a perceived scarcity in public resources and a variety of domestic problems that might benefit from greater governmental expenditures, there is a growing sentiment for dismantling major policies on aging. At the same time, old-age interest groups have identified unfinished items on the agenda of the Old Age Welfare State, some of which have backing from congressional leaders. Most notable among these are proposals for the federal government to fund long-term care insurance that would reimburse nursing homes and in-home service providers for the care of victims of Alzheimer's disease and other chronic illnesses and diseases that are common among older persons.

Economic Consequences of Population Aging

A fundamental issue in considering policy on aging in the post–Cold War era is whether the present array of programs benefiting older people can be economically and politically maintained in the decades ahead. What will happen when the Baby Boom cohorts swell the ranks of older persons eligible for Social Security and Medicare (see Aaron, et al.; 1989; Light, 1988) and as the elderly population becomes older within itself, requiring higher rates of health care and social services?

A common approach for responding to this issue is to engage in "apocalyptic demography,"[9] that is, mapping the future by simply taking demographic projections of the growing numbers and proportions of older persons, and the swelling ranks of the old-old and oldest—old, and plugging them into a scenario in which it is assumed that the present array of public policies will remain unchanged. Although extrapolation is a relatively poor mode of prediction (see Bell, 1964), it is frequently used to sketch foreboding caricatures of the implications of population aging, such as one that has described the elderly population as "a new social threat" and a "demographic, economic, and medical avalanche . . . one that could ultimately (and perhaps already) do [sic] great harm" (Callahan, 1987, 20).

The principal anxiety, frequently expressed, is that "increasing dependency ratios"—a growth in the size of the retired "dependent" population—will make it impossible, economically, for our nation to sustain old-age benefits through the first half of the twenty-first century. If one looks at dependency ratios in isolation, using "working age" (ages twenty to sixty-four) as a proxy for labor force participation, and assumes that the bulk of old-age benefits need to be financed through FICA payroll taxes on workers (as they are now), there is some cause for concern. In the immediate future, while the Baby Boom cohort is still of working age, the dependency ratio will be relatively stable. Starting in 2010, as the Baby Boomers begin to retire, the proportion of our population that is of working age is projected to begin gradually declining from about 60 percent until it reaches 54 percent in 2035, and then remain stable after that (Palmer and Gould, 1986).

The 1983 amendments to Social Security are generating surpluses in the OASI trust fund (see table 2.7), designed to meet the benefits that will be due to Baby Boom retirees. Indeed, the current surpluses are so large that they have generated considerable controversy concerning their near-term impact on

TABLE 2.7

Surpluses and Deficits (−) in the Social Security Trust Funds, Fiscal Years 1971–1991 (in billions of dollars)

Year	Surplus or Deficit (−)	Year	Surplus or Deficit (−)
1971	3.0	1981	− 5.0
1972	3.1	1982	− 7.9
1973	0.5	1983	0.2
1974	1.8	1984	0.3
1975	2.0	1985	9.4
1976	− 3.2	1986	16.7
1977	− 3.9	1987	19.6
1978	− 4.3	1988	38.8
1979	− 2.0	1989	52.4
1980	− 1.1	1990	58.2
		1991	53.5

Source: Congressional Budget Office, U.S. Congress, *The Economic and Budget Outlook: Fiscal Years 1993–1997* (Washington, D.C.: U.S. Government Printing Office, 1992), p. 114.

the economy and their inclusion as revenues in annual reports and projections regarding the size of the federal deficit (Aaron, 1990; Gist, 1988).

Yet, Senator Daniel P. Moynihan's 1989 proposal to eliminate these reserves and return OASI to the status of a pay-as-you-go system illustrates that one can hardly assume that these surpluses will continue to accrue and remain intact (see Chen, 1990). As Heclo (1988) has observed, it is far more likely than not that the treasure in the OASI trust fund will be raided before it is time to draw it down for paying benefits to Baby Boom retirees.

Nonetheless, the outlook is not foreboding. Likely declines in child dependency will probably offset increases in elderly dependency (see Schulz, et al., 1991). Moreover, a focus on the ratio of retirees to workers does not adequately capture the range of macroeconomic elements that determine whether a society is economically capable of supporting dependents within it or the many different sources—including general revenues—through which government could fund such support. The productive capacity of an economy is a function of a variety of factors, at least including capital, natural resources, balance of trade, and technological innovation, as well as number of workers. Hence, issues involving productive capacity and number of workers are appropriately expressed in terms of "productivity per worker" (Committee on an Aging Society, 1986; Habib, 1990).

Understood in these broader terms, and freed from the assumption that benefits provided under the Social Security program must be financed wholly through a payroll tax levied on a worker-by-worker basis, the economic consequences of population aging do not appear dim. For a variety of reasons, demographic changes may contribute strongly to U.S. economic growth in the next century (see Palmer and Gould, 1986). In the last analysis, future benefits to the aging will not depend upon the proportion of retirees to workers, but on whether the American economy generates sufficient resources to be transferred and whether the political will to transfer them to older persons will be present.

Intergenerational Equity

Of more immediate concern are contemporary issues framed by the construct of intergenerational equity. The appeal that this construct has for advocates for children, the homeless, education, rebuilding the nation's infrastructure, combatting drug abuse, and other domestic concerns can be appreciated by examining table 2.8, which shows the distribution of federal outlays for fiscal year 1992. The proportion of gross federal outlays devoted to domestic discretionary spending is only 14.1 percent.[10] Nearly half of the budget goes for mandatory programs, and expenditures through Social Security's OAI (excluding survivors and disability insurance) and Medicare alone constitute 46 percent of the category (U.S. Congress, 1992, 56). If one adds in the portions of Medicaid, SSI, food stamps, and social service programs that provide benefits to older persons, over half of mandatory spending is on elderly people. And other mandatory programs that include older people, such as retirement and disability for federal civilian and military employees (excluding veterans benefits), bring the proportion of mandatory spending that is on benefits for the aging to about 60 percent. This perspective makes it easy to understand why proponents of various social causes view the old-age lobby as a prime competitor for a limited budgetary pie.

As the theme of intergenerational equity has swelled, some of the aging-based advocacy groups have undertaken projects and sponsored conferences to express intergenerational solidarity. One Washington-based foundation, with the mission of improving the lot of the elderly poor, has gone so far as to change its formal name to Families U.S.A. Foundation. The Gerontological Society of America, an organization of 7,000 academicians and professionals in the field of aging, produced a monograph arguing that public benefits to older persons also are of value to persons of all ages (Kingson, et al., 1986; also see Heclo, 1988). And about seventy Washington-based organizations have formed a coalition named Generations United, which advocates for causes of mutual concern such as greater funding for Title XX Social Service Block Grants.

Individual scholars have reacted in a variety of fashions. One approach has been to argue that issues of intergenerational equity be defused and dif-

TABLE 2.8

Federal Outlays, by Category, Fiscal Year 1992

Spending Category	In Billions of Dollars	As a Percentage of Gross Domestic Product
Defense Discretionary	313	5.4
International Discretionary	20	0.3
Domestic Discretionary	214	3.7
Mandatory Spending	708	12.1
Deposit Insurance	67	1.1
Net Interest	201	3.4
Gross Total	1,523	26.0
Offsetting Receipts	− 64	− 1.1
Desert Storm Contributions	− 5	− 0.1
Net Total	1,454	24.8

Source: Congressional Budget Office, U.S. Congress, *The Economic and Budget Outlook: Fiscal Years 1993-1997* (Washington, D.C.: U.S. Government Printing Office, 1992), p. 50.

fused through public policies providing benefits that can be shared by persons of all ages (Wisensale, 1988) and by "playing down" rather than "playing up" programs based on age (Neugarten and Neugarten, 1986). Another suggestion has been that old-age advocacy organizations form coalitions with advocacy groups based on interests other than old age (Kingson, 1988; Binstock, 1992). Still another approach has been to argue that the issues of intergenerational equity are spurious—masking issues of inequities among persons of all ages (Binstock, 1985).

The most commonly articulated approach in policy proposals for dealing with intergenerational equity has been to suggest that the age categories used to describe eligibility for old-age benefit programs be raised to older ages, thereby cutting substantially the number of aggregate "benefit years" for which the federal government would be obligated to fund entitlements. A rationale for this approach is that age sixty-five may have been a good marker for declining vigor and short life expectancy when Social Security was enacted in 1935, but an older old age would be a better marker today (see Chen, 1987). Thus, some have proposed that the age of eligibility for full OAI benefits, Medicare, services through the Older Americans Act, and other programs be raised to, perhaps, seventy (e.g., Torres-Gil, 1992) or seventy-five (e.g., Nelson, 1982). This approach would follow the precedent set by the 1983 amendment to Social Security which provides for the age of eligibility for full OAI benefits to increase gradually until it becomes age sixty-seven early in the next century.

A dramatic issue of intergenerational equity receiving attention in the early 1990s is whether health care should be rationed on the basis of old age, as a means of curbing the rapid growth of health care costs. A prime reason for this focus on old age within the broader context of health care cost-containment fever is that one-third of our annual national health care expenditures is on older people, in 1991, as an example, about $270 billion out of a total $809 billion (Sonnefeld, et al., 1991). Medicare, widely perceived as "the health program for the elderly," also tends to focus cost-containment attention on the aging. As the biggest single source of payment for health care, its large aggregate national costs are easily determined and readily viable. Moreover, changes in Medicare approaches to paying for care are a plausible strategy for implementing the more general goal of cost-containment, since this nationwide governmental program affects the financial incentives of most U.S. hospitals, nursing homes, physicians, and other health care providers and suppliers. In fact, the most far reaching cost-containment measures to date have been changes in reimbursement procedures under Medicare (Russell, 1989).

As early as 1983, economist Alan Greenspan, now chairman of the Federal Reserve Board, pointedly asked "whether it is worth it" to spend 30 percent of Medicare funds annually on just 5 to 6 percent of Medicare insurees who die within the year (Schulte, 1983).[11] The issue was broadened beyond Medicare in 1984 when Richard Lamm, then governor of Colorado, was widely quoted as stating that older persons "have a duty to die and get out of the way" (Slater, 1984). Although Lamm subsequently stated that he had been misquoted on this specific statement, he has been delivering the same message repeatedly since leaving office, in somewhat more delicately worded fashions (Lamm, 1987, 1989). In 1990, John Silber, the Democratic candidate for governor in Massachusetts, carried forth Lamm's torch by proclaiming, "When you've had a long life and you're ripe, then it's time to go" (Butterfield, 1990).

Throughout the late 1980s and early 1990s discussion of the notion that health care might be rationed on the basis of old age spread to a number of forums. Ethicists and philosophers have been generating principles of equity to undergird "justice between age groups" in the provision of health care, rather than, for instance, justice between rich and poor or justice among ethnic and racial subgroups (Daniels, 1988; Menzel, 1990). Conferences and books have explicitly addressed the issue with titles such as "Should Health Care Be Rationed by Age?" (Smeeding, et al., 1987).

Since 1987 this theme has received substantial popular attention with the publication of a book entitled *Setting Limits: Medical Goals in an Aging Society*, in which ethicist Daniel Callahan (1987) proposed that life-saving care be categorically denied to persons in their late seventies or older. *Setting Limits* received a great deal of national publicity, as it was reviewed in dozens of national magazines and newspapers and just about every relevant professional and scholarly journal and newsletter. Callahan has continued to present and defend his point of view in a subsequent book (Callahan, 1990) and in a number of articles (e.g., Callahan, 1989, 1992) and public forums throughout the country. His and other proposals for age-based rationing have come to be rather firmly embedded in public discourse concerning health care policies in the United States.

Putting aside the moral implications and political feasibility of such proposals, which are considerable (see Binstock and Post, 1991), they do not appear to be significant in terms of their potential impact on aggregate health care costs. Proponents of old-age-based rationing assume that their proposals will have a major role in reducing health care costs, but they have not identified the magnitude of savings that their schemes might achieve. But it is possible to construct an example.

About 3.5 percent of annual Medicare expenditures is on high-cost Medicare insurees who die within a year (Lubitz and Prihoda, 1984). In 1992, a policy that prospectively would have denied treatment to such high-cost patients would have saved $4.7 billion. Moreover, it is not easy to make highly reliable clinical distinctions between the 50 percent of such high-cost patients who survive and the 50 percent who die within a twelve-month period (McCall, 1984; Scitovsky, 1984). So some might propose denying treatment to all such high-cost patients, thereby saving a total of about $9 billion. Viewed in isolation, this is a substantial amount of money. But in the larger context, saving such an amount would have had a negligible effect on the overall situation, reducing national health care costs for the year from $809 billion to about $800 billion. It is doubtful that the American public, if reasonably well-informed about such a policy, would want to throw potential survivors and decedents into the same health care "wastebasket" for such an incremental change.

Intragenerational Equity

A very specific issue of health care costs—how to pay for Medicare—is increasingly prominent. The 1991 report of the Social Security Trustees estimated that, unless payroll tax rates for financing Medicare's Part A Health Insurance (HI) are increased, or other reforms in Medicare financing are enacted, HI costs will exceed tax revenues by 1995, and by 2005 the HI trust fund reserves will be exhausted and annual costs will exceed revenues by $66 billion (Ross, 1991). The Trustees 1992 report moved the date for exhaustion of the trust fund up to 2002 (Rosenblatt, 1992).

Policy responses to this problem may well be based on an approach involving some notion of *intra*generational equity, redistributing burdens among FICA taxpayers and/or among persons eligible for Medicare in accordance with their economic status. The wage and salary ceiling for the Medicare portion of the FICA payroll tax could be lifted substantially to include persons with very high incomes, following the precedent set when the Omnibus Reconciliation Act of 1990 raised that ceiling from $53,400 to $125,000 in earnings for the year 1991. Alternatively, or as complementary measures, higher rates of out-of-pocket deductibles and co-payments could be established for wealthier Medicare patients on a sliding-scale basis. And Medicare's Part B premiums for Supplementary Medical Insurance, which are now set at a flat rate, could be increased progressively for higher income program participants.[12]

Such measures to redistribute financial burdens among elderly program participants would simply be increments extending a ten-year trend through which Congress has reformed policies on aging to reflect the diverse economic situations of older persons. The Social Security Reform Act of 1983 began this trend by taxing one-half of the Social Security benefits of individuals with incomes exceeding $25,000 and of married couples with over $32,000. The Tax Reform Act of 1986, even as it eliminated the extra personal exemption that had been available to all persons sixty-five years and older when filing their federal income tax returns, provided new tax credits to very-low-income older persons on a sliding scale. The Older Americans Act programs of supportive and social services, for which all persons aged sixty and older are eligible, have been gradually targeted by Congress to low-income older persons (see Binstock, 1991). The Medicare Catastrophic Coverage Act of 1988 expressed this legislative approach in two respects, through its progressive taxation provisions and its requirement that Medicaid pay for the Part B premiums and cost-sharing expenses for Medicare enrollees who have incomes below the poverty line. (Although the former provision was repealed in 1989, the latter remains in effect.) And most recently, the Omnibus Budget Reconciliation Act of 1993 continued this decade-long trend by subjecting 85 percent of Social Security benefits to taxation for individuals earning over $34,000 and couples earning over 44,000.

A long-standing problem of intragenerational equity has been the status of very-low-income older persons, which has continued throughout the last three decades as the Old Age Welfare State has markedly improved the aggregate economic status of older persons. Proposals that would make OAI and SSI more effective in ameliorating conditions for the most economically vulnerable have been discussed for years (see, e.g., Cohen and Friedman, 1972; Commonwealth Fund Commission on Elderly People Living Alone, 1987; Leavitt and Schulz, 1988; Munnell, 1977; Pechman, et al., 1968; Ruggles, 1990). Innumerable legislative and administrative measures are feasible for decisively targeting the relatively small amounts of service resources available under Title III of the Older Americans Act (Binstock, et al., 1983). But, traditionally, such proposals have not been strongly supported by old-age interest groups (Binstock, 1972; Day, 1990). In the past few years there have been some signs of change. AARP has undertaken an ''outreach'' program, through which it attempts to encourage greater enrollment of older persons in SSI. And the Families U.S.A. Foundation, a small organization staffed by policy analysts and professional lobbyists, has emerged as an advocate for the elderly poor.

Ironically, the issue of intragenerational equity with which the old-age interest groups are presently most preoccupied is one of getting government to expand public benefits that are now available only to the elderly poor, so that they can become available to better-off older persons. A coalition called the Long-Term Care Campaign—which claims to represent nearly 140 national organizations and is spearheaded by AARP, the Alzheimer's Association, and the Families U.S.A. Foundation—is lobbying for legislation that would establish federal reimbursement for long-term care services provided in nursing homes and in residential environments, regardless of the patient's financial means (McConnel, 1990). At present, Medicaid reimbursement covers nursing home services and some elements of home care services for the poorest elderly patients. Medicare does not provide long-term care coverage at all.

The predominant, though not exclusive,[13] element of many older persons' interest in this potential new benefit is a fear of becoming poor through ''spending down,'' that is, depleting one's assets to pay for long-term care to the point where they are exhausted or sufficiently depleted for the patient to become eligible for Medicaid. This fear reflects a desire to protect estates, as well as the psychological intertwining of personal self-esteem with one's material worth and independence.

These concerns have led to the practice of ''asset transfer,'' the use of legal instruments (or informal, illegal measures) by persons who anticipate that they may need long-term care, in order to divert their financial assets from their own legal or visible control. Assets sheltered in this fashion will neither be depleted through paying for care nor counted in determining eligibility for Medicaid. The practice is of concern to both the federal government and state governments, of course, because of its undoubted impact on Medicaid expenditures on long-term care, expected to increase from $39 billion in 1992 to $79 billion by the year 2000 (Sonnefeld, et al., 1991, 17).

The extent of asset sheltering has not been conclusively identified, but it is obviously most prevalent among wealthier older persons who have assets sufficient to be worth sheltering. The number of attorneys specializing in this area, which they call Medicaid Estate Planning, has grown rapidly; and they have developed a substantial arsenal of strategies for exempting assets from administrative procedures that determine Medicaid eligibility (Burwell, 1991). One of these attorneys has written a best-selling book in which he calls asset sheltering ''avoiding the medicaid trap'' (Budish, 1989–90). Another way to put it would be: How to take advantage of a program for the poor without being poor.

The enactment of a federal long-term care insurance program would eliminate incentives for asset sheltering, but it would also cost a great deal of public money. Since 1989 a number of comprehensive long-term care bills have been introduced in Congress, with price tags ranging from $21 billion to $50 billion in projected expenditures for the first year, depending upon their varied details regarding specific populations eligible and technical provisions regarding the timing, nature, and extent of insurance coverage (U.S. Senate, 1991, 257–58). The latest such proposal was a provision for federal coverage of home- and community-based long-term care in the Health Security Act that President Clinton sent to Congress in the fall of 1993. The cost estimates for various approaches to public long-term care insurance, however, lead most analysts of congressional health policies and politics to believe that no major legislation on long-term care is likely to be enacted in the near future (Atkins, 1990).

If and when comprehensive long-term care emerges as a serious item on the legislative agenda, a number of difficult fundamental issues will need to be confronted, such as: What are the reasons why older people should not spend down their assets and income on long-term care? Should it be government's responsibility to take a more active role than at present in preserving economic status inequities from generation to generation by protecting estates so that they can be inherited? On what basis should some persons be taxed to preserve the inheritances of others? Politically satisfactory answers to such questions will be difficult to come by, even if the legislation being considered proposes to cover children and younger adults who need long-term care—including victims of AIDS—as well as the chronically-ill and disabled elderly (see Binstock, 1992).

Age or Need?

At the close of the 1970s, when the proportion of the budget spent on old-age benefits was being "discovered" and early signs of the intergenerational equity construct were emerging (Binstock, 1983), social psychologist Bernice Neugarten (1979) raised the issue of whether public policies toward older people should be structured on the basis of age or need. Her attention to this issue was due to her observations that societal age norms and the characteristics of older persons were changing: "[I]n a society in which age is becoming increasingly irrelevant as a predictor of life-style or as a predictor of need, policies and programs formulated on the basis of age are falling increasingly wide of the mark . . . income and health care and housing and other goods and services should be provided, not according to age, but according to relative need" (pp. 50-51).

Neugarten recognized the political complexities of designing, shifting to, administering, and sustaining massive public transfer programs based on the relative needs of individual citizens. So, in a subsequent book (Neugarten, 1982), she assembled a number of policy analysts and scholars to address these complexities. Among their efforts, particularly intriguing was an analysis laid out by Nelson (1982) employing three alternative models of policy towards aging: one based on age irrelevance, or the concept of "unitary adulthood"; a second based on attaining age seventy-five as the eligibility requirement for old-age benefit programs; and a third based on the idea of "veteranship," in which old age is conceived of as an "earned status."

In contrast to Neugarten's focus, contemporary interest in shifting from age to need as a basis for policy is primarily driven by budgetary concerns and is focused on substantially reducing benefits available through the Old Age Welfare State. Policy analysts (e.g., Hudson and Kingson, 1991; Marmor, et al., 1990) who have highlighted the extraordinary successes of Social Security's universal programs in insuring Americans against disability and also illness and poverty in old age have argued that a need-based approach would undermine the "social insurance" principle that has provided broad-based and enduring political support for American social welfare policies. But a recent proposal for constructing the "Next New Deal" with need-based policies (Howe and Longman, 1992) attempts to meet the challenge of maintaining political support. It would have all government benefits, including such benefits as farm subsidies and mortgage-interest deductions, as well as Social Security checks and tax exclusions for Part B Medicare premiums, proportioned to the individual recipient's economic need. But, at the same time, it would adjust benefits on a graduated scale and maintain at least a nominal benefit for everyone in order to preserve some vestige of "the quasi-contractual nature" of traditional social insurance programs.

Whatever courses policies on aging will take in the post–Cold War era, it is likely that they will involve complex mechanisms for balancing age and need as eligibility criteria for public benefits. Such mechanisms will be critical in determining whether issues of intragenerational equity within the older population are resolved. They will also serve to exacerbate or moderate concerns about intergenerational equity. And they will ultimately determine how well, in the longer-term, American society meets the economic, social, and political challenges of population aging.

NOTES

1. The term "Old Age Welfare State" was coined by Myles (1983).

2. This percentage is calculated on the basis of federal outlays, by category, estimated for fiscal year 1992 (U.S. Congress, 1992), as modified by more detailed

information from Sonnefeld, et al. (1991), U.S. Senate (1991), and U.S. Social Security Administration (1991).

3. As will become evident further on in this chapter, aggregate statistics on the economic status of older persons mask a substantial amount of economic deprivation experienced by subgroups within the older population; see Quinn (1987).

4. This exposition of the historical development of the Social Security Act draws on Schulz (1988).

5. These figures do not include payments to those older persons eligible for SSI because of blindness or disability.

6. Not all public and private pension annuitants, of course, are aged sixty-five or older. Many retire at younger ages, after qualifying for pensions by fulfilling a specified number of years of employment. For a discussion of the considerations in workers' decisions to retire, Quinn and Burkhauser (1990) and Schulz (1988).

7. The income value of these in-kind policies to older persons is imputed by assuming that they are worth the cost of purchasing insurance policies through the market that would provide equivalent health care coverage. For a discussion of how alternative imputed values of Medicare, Medicaid, and other in-kind transfers can be shown to reduce the rate of poverty among older persons, see Smeeding (1982).

8. For an extended description of AARP and other old-age organizations, see Pratt (1976); for a more up-to-date account, see Day (1990).

9. The term *apocalyptic demography* was initially used by Robertson (1991) to describe a political effect of a strategy engaged in by advocates for Alzheimer's disease research and services; the term is used in a broader sense here.

10. Some policy analysts would argue that Social Security and Medicare expenditures should not be included in calculating the percentage of the federal budget that is available for domestic or any other category of discretionary programs. Their reasoning is based on the fact that the revenues funding Social Security and much of Medicare are dedicated to the purpose of paying benefits under those programs, and therefore should not be included in the total pool of funds available for allocation between mandatory and discretionary spending purposes. From this perspective one would deduct from mandatory outlays all expenditures on OASDI and on Part A of Medicare, thereby reducing substantially the total pool available for spending choices and also increasing substantially the percentage of outlays on domestic discretionary programs.

11. A more accurate figure would be 28 percent of Medicare funds spent on 6 percent of Medicare patients who die within the year; see Scitovsky (1984).

12. Many other approaches can be taken, of course, to dealing with the revenue/ expenditure difficulties projected for Medicare. Heclo (1988) speculates that the surplus accrued in the OAI trust fund might be borrowed to fund Medicare. Taxes on OASI might be increased and the additional revenues dedicated to funding Medicare. Various limitations could be placed on Medicare coverage and reimbursements. For a comprehensive discussion of alternatives for reforming Medicare, see Blumenthal, et al. (1988).

13. For discussions of some of the other reasons why public long-term care insurance is regarded as desirable by its advocates, see Binstock, et al. (1992), especially chapters 1 and 11.

Annotated Bibliography

Aaron, Henry J., ed. ''Social Security and the Budget: Proceedings of the First Confer-
    ence of the National Academy of Social Insurance. Lanham, Md.: University
    Press of America, 1990. Views of economists and policy analysts regarding the
    fiscal and budgetary implications of the surpluses accumulating in the Social
    Security trust funds.
Binstock, Robert H., and Linda K. George, eds. *Handbook of Aging and the Social
    Sciences*, 3d ed. San Diego, Calif.: Academic Press, 1990. A compendium of
    aging-related research literature and research issues in public policy and the
    social sciences, including anthropology, demography, economics, health ser-
    vices research, political science, social psychology, and sociology.
Binstock, Robert H., and Stephen G. Post, eds. *Too Old for Health Care? Controver-
    sies in Medicine, Law, Economics, and Ethics*. Baltimore, Md.: Johns Hopkins
    University Press, 1991. An anthology of critical treatments of proposals for
    rationing the health care of older people; the topic is treated from the perspec-
    tives of economics, politics, law, medicine, health services research, philos-
    ophy, religion, and biomedical ethics.
Crystal, Stephen. *America's Old Age Crisis: Public Policy and the Two Worlds of
    Aging*. New York: Basic Books, 1982. An analysis of how policies on aging
    have simultaneously led to problems of *intra*generational equity and fostered
    perceptions of *inter*generational equity.
Day, Christine L. *What Older Americans Think: Interest Groups and Aging Policy*.
    Princeton, N.J.: Princeton University Press, 1990. A reasonably up-to-date
    description and analysis of the politics of old-age interest groups; includes a
    chapter analyzing opinion surveys (from 1972 to 1986) with respect to differ-
    ences among age groups in attitudes toward public policies.
Derthick, Martha. *Policymaking for Social Security*. Washington, D.C.: Brookings
    Institution, 1979. The classic analysis of the politics of Social Security policy
    from 1935 through the 1970s.
Marmor, Theodore R., Jerry L. Mashaw, and Philip L. Harvey. *America's Misunder-
    stood Welfare State: Persistent Myths, Enduring Realities*. New York: Basic
    Books, 1990. An up-to-date defense of Social Security, Medicare, and Ameri-
    can social welfare policies, generally, with recommendations for future policies.
Neugarten, Bernice L. *Age or Need? Public Policies for Older People*. Beverly Hills,
    Calif.: Sage, 1982. An anthology of thoughtful commentaries on the complexi-
    ties of balancing age and need as criteria for determining eligibility for public
    benefits.
Schulz, James H., Alan Borowski, and William H. Crown. *Economics of Population
    Aging: The ''Graying'' of Australia, Japan and the United States*. New York:
    Auburn House, 1991. An analysis of the demographic, economic, and policy
    factors involved in sustaining Social Security when the Baby Boomers retire in
    three industrial nations.
Torres-Gil, Fernando M. *The New Aging: Politics and Change in America*. New York:
    Auburn House, 1992. An analysis of the changing nature of the elderly popula-
    tion, and the implications of those changes for politics and policies affecting
    aging.

CHAPTER 3

Post–Cold War Health Policy

ROBERT H. BLANK

One of the most excruciating and frustrating set of policy issues to face policy-makers in the post–Cold War period is certain to be health care. The problems center on how to provide safe and effective health care for all citizens but, at the same time, constrain the burgeoning cost spiral. Although much of the burden of health care falls to the states, it is becoming increasingly clear that any effective resolution of these issues will require a concentrated national initiative. The U.S. government stands alone among Western democracies by not having a national health care system. It is unlikely, however, that an overhaul of the health system will come in the near future. Despite the urgent need for major reform, the political and economic climate is not favorable.

Historical Context

In order to understand the context of post–Cold War health policy, it is critical to examine major patterns during the Cold War period. The rapid expansion of biomedical technologies in the 1950s was fueled largely by the heightened support of medical research by the federal government during that decade. The expansion of the National Institute of Health funding led to technological breakthroughs and a new faith in medicine to cure ills. Central to this change was the development of the polio vaccines and the widening success of antibiotics to treat previously fatal infectious diseases. By the early 1960s, the belief in the technological fix was becoming well ingrained in the American psyche.

The major theme of quality of health care, largely defined by the rapid advances in technology, was supplemented during the 1960s and early 1970s by a growing concern over access to health care. Although biomedical innovations were giving the majority of the population a higher quality of care, and private insurance plans substantially expanded access to hospital care, significant numbers of persons failed to be served by the new medicine. Specifically, the elderly and poor were often unable to obtain adequate insurance coverage. In 1962, approximately 50 percent of all persons over age sixty-five had no insurance for hospital care (Brown, 1983, 260). Because of their greater need for hospital care, many elderly persons did not have access to health care services. Although accessibility was first addressed by the Hill-Burton Act of 1946, which attempted to deal with the problem by supporting state and local initiatives through matching funds to construct and modernize medical facilities, by the 1960s, the lack of access to the health care system became the major focal point for policy.

After initial interest in a national health insurance plan in the 1930s dissipated, and the welfare-linked Kerr-Mills program proved unsatisfactory, the compromise Medicare/Medicaid legislation became policy in 1965. Medicare was designed to provide health care coverage to those persons over sixty-five years of age, while Medicaid would provide coverage for the poor. Over the next decades Medicare would be expanded to cover endstage renal disease (1972) and other specific disease groups, thus diluting its original intention to guarantee access for the elderly. Also, because of the failure of Medicare to provide access for many elderly, Medicaid became largely a supplementary program for the poor elderly, so that by 1987 over 73 percent of Medicaid expenditures was going to Social Security recipients. Throughout the 1960s and 1970s, the emphasis on technological intervention that began in the 1950s shaped public expectations, now supplemented by the stated policy goal that all Americans should have access to this quality health care.

The highly optimistic assumptions espoused by policymakers in the 1960s that high quality health care could be provided to all citizens through government intervention began to sour during the 1970s. In part because of the heightened demand for ever more sophisticated, and costly, medical care and in part because of demographic changes, particularly an aging population, the costs of health care began to run out of control. Although initiatives to control health care costs began in the 1970s, by 1980 the primary emphasis in government policy had shifted from access to and quality of health care to cost containment. The 1980s clearly became the decade of cost containment, embodied most directly in the move, through the 1983 amendments to the Social Security Act, of Medicare away from fee for service reimbursement to predetermined diagnosis-related groups (DRGs). This legislation came in response to a Congressional Budget Office prediction that without major changes, the Hospital Insurance Trust Fund of Medicare could collapse by the end of the decade. With the DRG legislation, estimates were that the Fund would be solvent until 1994.

By the late 1980s, it became apparent that piecemeal efforts to contain costs had failed to resolve long-term health care problems. Although DRGs had some success in slowing the rates of increase in government health care funding, their major impact was to shift the burden of payment from the government to private parties. Furthermore, because Medicare reimbursement levels fell far below marketplace values, cost containment measures solidified the tiered system under which persons dependent on public funding receive less adequate care than those persons on private insurance plans. Access to quality care for a growing proportion of the population, including the estimated 37 million without insurance coverage is as elusive as it was in the early 1960s. Although those persons with good insurance plans or wealth have access to the best medical technology in the world, large numbers of persons do without even adequate primary care.

Policy Context

Post–Cold War health care policy options must be viewed within a crisis situation that has developed over the last several decades. Many seemingly unrelated demographic, social, and technological trends have combined to accentuate traditional dilemmas in medical policy making. The aging population, the proliferation of high-cost biomedical technologies designed primarily to extend life, conventional schemes of retroactive reimbursement by third-party payers, and the realization that health care costs are outstripping society's ability to pay all lead to pressures for expanded public action. Until now, however, public institutions have appeared both unable and unwilling to make the difficult decisions. Although major alterations in the health care system are essential in order to avert a breakdown, piecemeal ''solutions'' continue to be the political method of choice.

The constraints on economic resources already apparent are bound to be compounded by the confluence of the trends noted above. Even with current efforts to contain costs, health care expenditures in the United States increased from $387 billion in 1984 to an *estimated* $660 billion in the 1990s. After slowing for two years, the nation's health care spending resumed double-digit growth (10.4 percent) in 1988. At this rate, by the turn of the century, we will spend an estimated $2.0 trillion, representing 15 percent of the Gross National Product. This translates into a doubling of the nation's health care spending every seven years and an increase in per-person expenditures from $1,500 in 1984 to almost $7,000 by the year 2000. Moreover, annual health care costs in the United States are now over $2,500 per person; the comparative figure for Britain is $850 and for Japan is $1,000.

Further complications arise from the fact that the distribution of medical resources is skewed toward a very small proportion of the population. More and more medical resources have been concentrated on a relatively small number of patients in acute care settings. Substantial questions about the just distribution of scarce resources in a society are accentuated in the establishment of biomedical priorities. By 1980, the top 1 percent of users of medical care in the population accounted for 29 percent of all health care expenditures; the top 5 percent used 55 percent; and the top 10 percent used 70 percent. Patients with endstage renal disease, who represented less than .25 percent of all Medicare Part B beneficiaries, for example, accounted for over 9 percent of the total Medicare Part B expenditures (Evans, 1983, 2209).

Elderly persons are the leading users of hospital care and have the highest per capita expenditures for health care. In 1987 the cost to provide health care for elderly patients was $162 billion, or $5,360 per capita (Lonergan, 1991, 7). Ironically, because of medical improvements and technologies that prolong life, chronic disease requiring frequent medical care has become an increasing drain on scarce medical resources. Persons who in earlier times would have died of one illness are often kept alive to suffer long-term decline in quality of life. However, the demand for such intervention will continue to increase in an aging population. An estimated 11.4 percent of the U.S. population, or approximately 25.6 million people, are sixty-five years of age or older. By the year 2035, the elderly population will be more than double that size. Persons over eighty constitute about one-sixth of the total elderly, a proportion which is increasing in large part because of the intensive expenditure for medical care during that stage of life. Life expectancy at age seventy-five, for instance, increased by 2.2 years to 81.0 between 1965 and 1979. Because of the concurrence of multiple and often chronic conditions, the cost of prolonging life at older ages is usually higher than at younger ages, increasingly so since the introduction of antibiotics in the 1940s reduced the incidence of death from specific illnesses such as pneumonia (Ricardo-Campbell, 1982, 7). It is estimated that by the year 2000 the number of elderly aged eighty and over will increase by about 50 percent, and that by 2035 approximately one out of every ten Americans will be over eighty-five years of age. This aging population already has put a tremendous strain on the health care system to provide acute and, especially, chronic care facilities for a population which is heavily dependent on these services (Schneider and Guralnik, 1990). This fact led Callahan (1987) to make the controversial suggestion that we might consider setting limits on the use of life-prolonging technologies for the elderly.

The increased competition for scarce resources within the health care sector will necessitate resource allocation as well as rationing decisions (Blank, 1988; Callahan, 1990; Menzel, 1989). In turn, these actions are certain to exacerbate the social, ethical, and legal issues and intensify activity by affected individuals and groups. Although public officials might try to continue to avoid making the difficult decisions and attempt to resolve long-term problems with incremental solutions, they will soon be forced to become major participants in the explicit rationing of health care resources, because of the significant increase in the need for public funding support. One state, Oregon, has already proposed a strategy for reallocating health care expenditures from high technology rescue to primary care (Kitzhaber, 1991). Others are certain to follow as health care spending outstrips the financial means of most states to keep up with the increased demands.

Traditional Notions of Health Care in the United States

Health care in any country is the product of many cultural, social, and political factors. It is impossible to explain the reaction of a particular citizenry or its leaders to health issues without an understanding of this context. It is also unlikely that the United States can adopt without major alterations the health care system of any other country such as Canada (Evans, et al., 1989) no matter how attractive it might appear to some policymakers. Although it is not feasible here to examine the complex historical and cultural determinants, several factors are critical and largely define the unique context of medical decision making in the United States.

Observers of American society since Alexis de Tocqueville have commented on the uniqueness and the diversity of values among American citizens. American values have been seen alternately as products of heavy dependence on the liberal tradition or a fundamental consensus on the value of individual human life. As a society, we place much emphasis on individual autonomy, self-determination, personal privacy, and a shared belief in justice for all humans. Individuals in a liberal society are free to determine for themselves their preferred life-style and then, as long as they do not harm others, to live it even if it is self-destructive. Within this value context, even the suggestion that individuals have a responsibility to live a healthy life-style is often attacked as "victim blaming" and contrary to individual choice. The shift in the nature of disease—from infectious diseases that required major societal efforts to stem toward those linked to individual behavior, including the heavy use of medical resources by persons who smoke cigarettes, abuse alcohol and drugs, are sedentary or overweight, and are sexually promiscuous—challenges this value of life-style choice. McGinnis (1989), for instance, concludes that better control of fewer than ten risk factors could prevent between 40 and 70 percent of all premature deaths, one-third of all cases of acute disease, and two-thirds of all cases of chronic disease. This strategy, however, would require radical changes in the behavior of many persons.

In addition to placing a high priority on individual life-style choice, American society places heavy emphasis on individual rights to medical care. Furthermore, there has been a clear shift toward positive rights to health care which place on society the duty to provide the resources necessary to exercise those rights. This value is manifest in demands for government funding of organ transplants, catastrophic insurance, and national health insurance. Recent surveys indicate that upwards of 90 percent of the public feels that everyone has the right to get the best possible health care, even though there is little sympathy for raising taxes to pay for these positive rights (LORAN Commission, 1987).

American culture is also predisposed toward progress through technological means. Alexander Capron (1975, 123) suggests that this value extends to medical technology through a deep commitment to the belief that medicine will progress and give us ever greater powers over disease. A reinforcing value, according to Marc Lappé, is a "deep-seated aversion to chance in the Western psyche" (1972, 413). This desire for control is crucial to understanding our characteristic health care decisions. Presumably, equating the reduction of uncertainty with progress facilitates acceptance of a wide range of technologies. The result, unfortunately, has been an unrealistic dependence on technology to fix our health problems at the expense of nontechnological solutions. For instance, in their comparison of British and American doctors' views about technology, Miller and Miller (1986) conclude:

> British doctors are trained to be much more skeptical than their U.S. counterparts about the technological imperative—the notion that more sophisticated medical procedures are synonymous with better health care. In part this is because the British health establishment gives far greater credence to what good primary care can accomplish than do most U.S. doctors. In addition, however, British health professions and the population itself simply tend to cast a more critical eye on the promises of technology. (1986, 1385)

The emphasis on the individual's right to medical care is also reflected in the patient-physician relationship, which has been seen largely as a private one, beyond the public realm. Although in the aggregate we are willing to cut costs, when it comes to the individual patient, we have been ready to expend all resources without consideration of costs. There is a not-so-implicit assumption that every person has a right to unlimited expenditure on his or her behalf, despite the knowledge that in the aggregate this is unfeasible. The problem of unlimited individual claims in the context of limited societal resources produces the dilemma of health care today. As stated by Carl Schramm, "If society's task is to improve the health of the many, disproportionate spending on acute care for a small number of persons must come into question" (1984, 730).

However, the suggestion that we somehow limit medical expenditures on an individual in order to benefit the community contradicts the traditional patient-oriented mores of medicine. There are strong pressures for intensive intervention on an individual basis even in the last days of life; this, despite the enormous cost for very little return in terms of prolonging the patient's life. There is also a strong aversion by the U.S. medical community to serve as gatekeepers to the detriment of individual patients. Former Colorado Governor Richard Lamm's suggestion that terminal patients have a duty to refuse intensive and expensive medical intervention and to die was met with widespread criticism by the press, health professionals, and the public. Despite its cost-benefit logic and its attractiveness for the aggregate, Lamm's proposal directly challenged the tradition of not withholding care from a patient in need, whatever the cost.

In addition, by supporting this maximalist approach to medical care, we have created an intricate mechanism for minimizing the amount any single individual will pay for these benefits. Private health insurance allows individuals to protect themselves by spreading the risk of expensive medical treatment across many persons. The real cost of the services is thus obscured, because individuals seldom bear the costs directly or fully. This insulation of the individual patient from cost encourages the maximalist approach and supports the presumption that cost should not be a concern in the treatment of the patient. No matter how much is spent on the patient, a large part of the payment will usually be made by the amorphous third-party payer.

The belief that individuals have the right to unlimited medical care should they so choose it, the traditional acceptance of the maximalist approach by the medical community, and the insulation of the individual from feeling the cost of treatment, then, together have placed severe limits on the extent to which proscription of expensive and often ineffective intervention is possible. Arguments in favor of containing the costs of health care, while acceptable at the societal level, tend to be rejected when applied at the individual level. Although a large proportion of the population supports some type of cost containment in theory, traditional beliefs in the maximalist approach remain strong when their own health or that of their loved ones is at stake. It is little wonder that elected officials are unwilling to make allocation decisions that conflict with these strongly held values.

It has been suggested that no matter to what extent health care facilities are expanded, there will remain a steady pool of unmet demands. Additional manpower and money, then, are not the answer to the health care crisis. Instead of resolving the problems, this approach increases the demand for solutions to an ever-expanding range of technical medical problems. Although wealthier countries devote substantially higher proportions of their resources to health services than do poorer countries, demand for more services does not abate. Instead, the public comes to expect a level of medical care not imagined by persons in less affluent countries. Moreover, as more of these expectations are met, demand for expanded health services actually escalates. The rapid increase in the percent of GNP spent on medical care over the last three decades has had only a marginal impact on lowering overall mortality rates in the United States.

In a system where third-party reimbursement insulates much of the public from the real cost of meeting these higher expectations, it is not surprising that the public strongly supports increased development of medical technologies. William Schwartz comments, "However jaundiced the medical care experts have become about the excesses, inefficiencies, ineffectiveness, and irrelevance of much medical care, the fact is that the public does not share this perspective. Increased investment of medical care continues to be highly valued by the public" (1984, 24). Instead, the public demands more front-end insurance coverage to pay for high-cost medical care. As a society, we have come to expect the best that medical science can offer when it comes to care for ourselves or our loved ones. Although we complain about the high cost, when our health or life is at stake, we expect no expense to be spared. The preferred solution for many consumers is simply to shift the basis of payment to the government or private third-party payers. These demands clearly prevent any simple solution to the problems of health care.

Another concern of the American public which shapes demands for expansion of health expenditures is its obsession with prolonging life. Franz Ingelfinger concluded that too much money is spent to "convert Western octogenarians to nonagenarians" (1980, 143). The determinants of death are many, and to pour untold millions into defeating one merely shifts the opportunity to others. Saving an elderly person from one illness might very well expose that person to an even more debilitating disease. Although the quality of life of many persons at advanced ages is questionable and extensive technological intervention might prolong life only briefly, American society has an obsessive concern with avoiding death at all costs. Although there is considerable evidence that this value is changing rapidly (Weir, 1989), by far the most expensive year of life for most persons is their terminal year. Our system hesitates to withhold treatment, no matter how costly, if it extends life.

Moreover, as Norman Daniels (1986) argues, in the U.S. health care system, there are no assurances that beneficial treatments or procedures withheld from one patient will be put to better use elsewhere or that the resources will be used to meet the greater needs of other patients. It is especially difficult to justify saying no to a patient under these circumstances where the frequent result is that treatment is offered to even more marginal patients. Often physicians who personally realize that the aggressive treatment of a terminally ill patient is pointless continue to treat aggressively because of pressure from the patient's family, the fear of a malpractice suit, or simply because it is the path of least resistance within our value system. Yet, prolongation of life is bound to become even more expensive, because we are approaching an asymptote— we are reaching that point where no matter how much we spend on extending life span, the return, both in time gained and the quality of life, diminishes.

The situation is even more complex, however, because seldom does the public create the initial demand for more advanced technology. Instead, the initiative for medical research and development comes from the scientists themselves. The liver transplant, for instance, was never demanded by the public, not even by an interested segment of it. Instead, it was developed to meet a need perceived by the medical community that holds out promises that can be fulfilled only if new resources are made available. Once developed, however, media attention dramatizes medical innovation, and demand increases among both physicians and patients. As an innovation passes out of the experimental stage, consumers come to expect that it will become available for their benefit.

Public expectations may also be elevated unrealistically because of a tendency to oversell medical innovation and overestimate the capacities of new medical technologies for resolving health problems. Frequently, the initial response of the media is to report innovaions as medical "breakthroughs." Because most health care is routine and not newsworthy, the media naturally focus attention on techniques that can be easily dramatized. This is especially true in the United States, where the underlying "technological fix" mentality places tremendous emphasis on finding the cure for cancer, creating the bionic person, and, for many, discovering a technological fountain of youth. For instance, it was not until the promise of a quick vaccine or cure for AIDS proved illusory that prevention became a major theme. According to Franz Ingelfinger (1980), former editor of the *New England Journal of Medicine*, organized medicine is also to blame for the overselling of medicine because as a whole it has encouraged the belief in the omniscience, rather than the ignorance, of the medical profession. He also criticizes politicians who promise too much and voluntary health groups that suggest in their fund-raising campaigns that if only more money were thrown into the research mill, the major diseases would be contained. Despite the failure of medicine to deliver on many counts, as a whole the public continues to support the search for perfect solutions to health problems through technology.

Without doubt, these public expectations and perceptions of medicine have resulted in an overutilization of and reliance on technology in American medical practice. Patients demand access to the newest technologies because they are convinced of their value. Popular health-oriented magazines and television shows extol the virtues of medical innovations. Physicians have been trained in the technological imperative which holds that a technology should be used despite its cost if it offers any possibility of benefit. Whether to protect themselves from malpractice suits, to provide the most thorough workup for their patients, or to increase profits, many physicians would rather err heavily on the side of overusing diagnostic and therapeutic technologies. The heavy investment of medical providers in expensive diagnostic equipment much as computerized axial tomography (CAT) scanners and magnetic resonance imagers (MRIs), often merely to stay ahead of the competition, encourages their use even in situations where their benefit is marginal or nonexistent. Third-party retrospective reimbursement provides no disincentive against this overutilization of medical technology. Any limits on the allocation of medical technologies, then, must come from outside the health care system. The only agent with the power to effectuate such limits is the government. The reality of the post–Cold-War era, as opposed to the short-term euphoria in 1990, where it was assumed untold billions would be available for social programs, reiterates the need to make policy designed to set such limits. In light of the value context discussed here, the battle over health care policy is bound to be hard fought by the interests in favor of business as usual.

Reforming the Health Care System: Current Proposals for Averting Disaster

To date, the major initiatives in the 1990s have returned to the theme of "access" that served as the basis for the health care reforms of the 1960s. It is yet unclear how this "new" interest in access can be accommodated within the clear continuing need to contain costs. This section discusses some of the major proposals emerging from the post–Cold War policy context for salvaging the U.S. health care system. These proposals have been initiated by various public and private sources and represent, collectively, the views of experts across relevant fields.

The post–Cold War era already has witnessed a rash of proposals for reforming the U.S. health care system. Although there is a near consensus on the need for major alterations in the system, there remains critical disagreement over what form those alterations should take. In April 1990, the American College of Physicians called for a comprehensive health care reform that would include some form of national financing. Although the American Medical Association (AMA) has been vocally critical of such major changes, in May 1991, citing a worsening of the situation, all ten of the AMA scientific journals focused on the question of access and cost of health care in the United States. Over seventy proposals were published. At the state government level, a score of states have begun studies to investigate reform of health care. Led by Oregon, a growing number of states are even considering rationing plans that would have been unthinkable politically in the recent past.

Some proposals simply call for government initiatives to study this "enormous national problem." Davies and Felder (1990, 73) recommended that President Bush appoint a "blue-ribbon" commission to study the present system in depth and define alternative solutions. They argued that increased health care rationing in this decade is inevitable and that quick fixes, short-term solutions, and patchwork reform of the current system will create more severe problems for health care in the twenty-first century.

Other proposals focus on very specific goals. The American Academy of Pediatrics (AAP), for example, has developed a plan to provide access to health care for all children up to the age of twenty-two and for all pregnant women. Under this plan, the federal government would take the initiative and mandate a standard package of benefits that insurers must meet. All children and women who do not receive employer-based insurance would be covered by state-funded insurance. Benefits under this plan are divided into three groups: preventive care, primary and major medical care, and coordinated care (see Harvey, 1990, 1218, for a detailed list). Similarly, the Department of Health and Human Services (1990) issued a report to encourage every person to take responsibility for his or her own health. By creating a "climate of personal responsibility," the report concluded, three goals could be achieved: an increase in the span of healthy life; a reduction in the disparities in health care among various population groups; and access to preventive services for all Americans.

Many of the proposals take a broader approach to health care. Enthoven and Kronick's (1989) proposal calls for universal health insurance to promote quality and economy. Everyone not covered by existing insurance plans would be able to purchase affordable coverage through private employers or a "public sponsor." Enthoven and Kronick recognize the importance of the social context of health care.

> Such a plan must represent incremental, not radical, change; must respect the preferences of voters, patients, and providers; must avoid major disruption in satisfactory existing arrangements; must avoid creating major windfall gains or losses; must avoid large-scale income redistribution; and must not be inflationary. (1989, 94)

Without major alterations in public and provider expectations, it seems unlikely that this proposal could be effectual, despite the attractiveness of the above goals.

Among the many calls for a national program is that of Physicians for a National Health Program (Grumback, et al., 1991). It proposes covering all Americans under a publicly administered, tax financed national health program (NHP). One single public payer would replace the over fifteen hundred private and public insurers that now exist. This unitary administrative program, which has strong similarities to the Canadian system, would avowedly save tens of billions of dollars per year in administrative costs that presently account for an estimated 25 percent of health care costs in the United States. The funding package would augment existing government health care spending with earmarked health care taxes. The assumption of this group is that because these new taxes would replace employer-employee insurance premiums and substantial out-of-pocket expenditures, they "would not increase health costs of the average American."

The major focus of health policy initiatives so far in the 1990s centers on the paradox of American health care that, despite the fact that more can be done technologically to extend lives, tens of millions of citizens are uninsured and unable to afford the most basic preventive health services. The U.S. Census Bureau found that between 1986 and 1988, 63.6 million persons lacked coverage for at least one month—31.5 million lacked it during the final quarter of 1988 alone. Similarly, the Employee Benefit Research Institute reported that in 1988, 33.3 million Americans had no private insurance and were ineligible for public coverage (see Friedman, 1991, 2491). Although other estimates of the uninsured are somewhat lower, depending on how the uninsured are defined, the consensus seems to be in the 30 to 37 million range.

Pepper Commission

In September 1990, after a year of investigation and deliberation, the U.S. Bipartisan Commission on Comprehensive Health Care—the Pepper Commission—recommended actions to guarantee all Americans health care coverage in an efficient, effective system. The charge to the fifteen member commission (six from the Senate, six from the House, and three presidential appointees) was to develop recommendations for "workable and enactable" legislation to resolve the problems facing the health care system. In their report, *A Call for Action* (1990), the commission reached four fundamental conclusions:

1. Health insurance coverage must be universal, because only if everyone is adequately covered can we assure full access and bring to an end cost shifting and underservice to the uninsured.
2. Simply patching the current system cannot achieve universal coverage, because even if the government were to expand coverage to all the poor and subsidize private coverage for the near-poor, insurance coverage would remain too costly for about half of the currently uninsured.
3. Replacing the current system with government-run national health insurance is not practical. Shifting so many people and dollars from the private sector to the public sector is too disruptive to be politically feasible in the near future.
4. Expanding access and controlling costs must proceed hand in hand. To pursue one goal without the other is to further undermine a system already under serious stress.

In order to accomplish the goals of reform, the commission called for a combination of incentives and requirements that would guarantee all workers and their dependents insurance coverage through their jobs. The commission also recommended the replacement of Medicaid with a new federal program that would cover those persons who are not covered through the workplace and workers whose employers find public coverage more affordable. Furthermore, employers would be guaranteed affordable coverage through a complete overhaul of private insurance, tax credits for small employers, and the opportunity to purchase public coverage for their employees when preferable to small group private insurance. The commission would also create a minimum benefit standard for private and public plans that covers preventive and primary care services as well as catastrophic care. This plan would include cost sharing, subject to ability to pay. Finally, the commission called for a combination of public and private sector initiatives—including insurance reform, prospective payment for hospitals, a resource-based relative value scale for physicians, and reform of the medical malpractice system—in order to promote quality and efficiency and to contain costs.

In addition to addressing the issue of guaranteed job-based or public health insurance, the commission also proposed a plan to provide home and community-based care and nursing home care based on the level of a person's disability and ability to perform certain daily functions rather than on a person's age. Three months of nursing home coverage and four hundred hours of community-based care would be provided to everyone, with co-payments set at 20 percent of national average cost and subsidized for low income persons. Individuals would be financially responsible for nursing home care beyond the initial three months, but a plan financed by state and federal governments would take over once they had used up a set limit of their resources. It is interesting to note that this part of the plan won an 11 to 4 endorsement from the commission, while the insurance plan badly split the commission and was approved by a slim 8 to 7 vote.

Many of the members on the commission had their own plans and vehemently criticized the Rockefeller plan, which was eventually approved with modifications. One crucial area of contention was cost. The commission report estimated new federal spending after full implementation of the plan to be $66.2 billion per year. Of this, $23.4 billion would fund the new proposal for the uninsured, to be supplemented by new expenditures on employee health care of $20 billion per year by business. The long-term care recommendation would be phased in over a four-year period at a new federal cost of $42.8 billion, according to the report.

Immediately, these cost projections were attacked as unreasonable. Critics estimated that it would cost each American $750; that it contained no cost controls and no limits on what employers could do; that the financing of the plan was left unspecified; that long-term benefits were too broad; and that the commission's own cost projections were suspect. Daniel Callahan, director of the Hastings Center, was concerned by the commission's lack of specificity as to what constitutes the "minimum benefit package." How much and what kind of hospital care, diagnostic tests, and preventive services are to be guaranteed? According to Callahan (1991, 33), the "notorious shortcoming of this approach is evident: it opens the door to an unlimited range of benefits regardless of costs."

In contrast, Rockefeller (1991, 2510) argues that the plan is cost effective and would buy health coverage for all Americans for less than 2 percent more than current health expenditures. Individuals, he contends, would save an estimated $19 billion as employers and government would share in their insurance premiums and health care costs; state and local governments would save $7 billion in payments they now make; and employers who now offer health insurance to workers and dependents would save $13 billion, because they would no longer pay the costs of dependents who work for other firms and of uncompensated care.

In light of the huge budget deficits the government already faced in the 1990s, the cost issue was bound to emerge as the critical concern of Congress. Whatever the final legislative response, however, the Pepper Commission did articulate the problem of access to health care and did present a valuable starting point for public debate. It also provided the impetus for many other bodies to respond with plans of their own. Among the scores of proposals are: The Urban Institutes' "American Approach" (Holahan, et al., 1991); the Committee for National Health Insurance's "Health Security Partnership" (Fein, 1991); "The Physicians Who Care Plan" (Bronow, et al., 1991); The Enthoven/Kronick Plan (1991); the Heritage Foundation Plan (Butler, 1991); and Physicians for a National Health Program (Grumback, et al., 1991).

Health Access America

One of these plans, which was released at about the same time as the Pepper Commission report, was the American Medical Association's (AMA) "Health Access America." Health Access America (HAA) represents a major private initiative to deal with the health care crisis. (For a variation on HAA, see the discussion in Nutter et al., 1991, of the proposal of the Medical Schools' Section of the AMA). Using the policy development process of the AMA, the goal of HAA was to propose a plan to restructure the U.S. health care system that would ensure all Americans access to affordable, high-quality health care and moderate health cost increases. The proposal consisted of six fundamental principles and sixteen key recommendations. Many of the program's planks reflected existing AMA policy and were drawn from the over one hundred fifty principles developed in the Health Policy Agenda of the AMA and 172 other organizations in 1987 (AMA, 1987).

The AMA developed HAA primarily to emphasize the advantages of the American system and deflect pressures in favor of more extensive reform of the system. For instance, instead of replacing Medicaid, as the Pepper Commission recommended, HAA would expand Medicaid to provide "uniform adequate benefits" to all persons below the federal poverty level. In addition to expanding the pool of candidates for Medicaid, the range of benefits and the reimbursement levels would have to be raised substantially. HAA also calls for expanded long-term care financing through expansion of private sector coverage encouraged by tax incentives, with protection of personal assets and Medicaid coverage for those below the poverty level (Todd, et al., 1991, 2505). Medicare reform to avoid bankruptcy, catastrophic benefits to be funded through individual and employer tax contributions, and liability reform are crucial to the AMA plan.

Like the Pepper Commission, HAA would require employer provision of health insurance for all full-time employees and their dependents. It would create tax incentives and state risk pools to enable new and small businesses to afford such coverage. Unlike the Pepper Commission, which sets up a public fund for the uninsured, HAA recommends private insurance risk pools in all states, thus keeping the federal government out.

One major shortcoming of the Health Access America plan is the failure to provide any cost projections for its implementation. Although preliminary actuarial studies conducted by the AMA estimated the cost to the federal government of about $21 billion per year, the AMA's acting executive director, James Todd, said it is impossible to estimate a total price tag at this time, because it depends on what the American people wish to purchase in terms of health insurance and what the policymakers decide on the precise nature of the reforms and phasing they want to undertake (Todd, et al., 1991, 2506). Given the nature of HAA proposals, especially expansion of Medicaid, catastrophic coverage, and coverage for long-term care, it is not surprising the costs of this proposal have not been articulated.

Legislative Action

Although, to date, the Pepper Commission recommendations have gone unheeded, in the first of many congressional proposals Senate Democrats, in mid-1991, unveiled a plan designed to provide health insurance for all Americans and hold down spiraling health care costs. (For a description of another plan, "The USHealth Act," see Roybal, 1991). Under the leadership of Majority Leader George Mitchell, the plan was drafted over a two-year period. In line with the Pepper Commission, the Democratic plan would require employers to provide health insurance for all workers or pay a payroll tax of 6 to 8 percent to cover the uninsured. Owners of small businesses would have up to five years to provide coverage for their employees. Self-employed business owners could deduct all health insurance costs, and businesses with fewer than sixty employees would receive tax credits to buy insurance.

The plan would also establish a standard package of minimum benefits that every private insurance plan would have to meet, including hospitalization, doctors visits, diagnostic tests, preventive care, prenatal and well-child care, and mental health benefits. Waiting periods could not exceed thirty days and limits on preexisting conditions would be eliminated. Furthermore, again reflecting a proposal of the Pepper Commission, Medicaid would be replaced by a new federal-state program called AmeriCare. Workers enrolled in this new program would pay a share of the cost collected through a payroll tax, depending on their income. First-year costs of this program was estimated at $6 billion.

Finally, the Senate Democratic proposal projects savings of $78 billion over a five-year period, primarily by eliminating unnecessary medical procedures. To encourage this, it would set national treatment guidelines for physicians and promote the use of health maintenance organizations. A new federal agency would be created to set national health care spending targets and negotiate national hospital and physician rates. If all parties to the negotiations, including providers and consumers, agreed to the rates, they would become binding. The plan was a serious effort at working through an American version of an acceptable national health care insurance system, and it helped set the context for the debate over health care that took place in the 1992 presidential election campaign.

Various proposals to meet health care needs, including the adoption of a single-payer program based on the Canadian model, were put forward during the 1992 primaries and general election campaigns. In particular, Democratic presidential nominee Bill Clinton made health care reform one of his basic issues. Once elected, he placed his wife, Hillary Rodham Clinton, in charge of a task force to develop a national health care plan intended to embrace several, seemingly contradictory objectives and inclusive enough to achieve popular support and a congressional majority without alienating major health care constituencies. The plan's objectives included coverage for the estimated 37 million Americans without health care insurance; an overhaul and systemization of health care provider services under some type of government-mandated umbrella system; and a reduction in health care costs. The agenda is ambitious, and mobilizing support for basic change will be difficult. Nonetheless, the Clinton administration committed itself to introducing a comprehensive national health care program of a magnitude not attempted since Harry Truman's days.

Political Context: Making Difficult Decisions

Any health policy is the result of multiple pressures from providers and consumers as well as the constraints imposed by demographic factors and the structure of the government itself. Many of the unique problems encountered in the United States can be traced to the absence of any single locus of power for making health care decisions and the fragmented, decentralized policy process. Also, because of the immense strength of the health care community, any successful policy must have at least the tacit support of those being regulated. Moreover, because the population of the United States is large and diverse, any attempts to achieve a homogeneous pattern of allocation of health care resources will encounter severe difficulties.

The hard decisions that society faces in the post–Cold War decades must be made within this complex and often contradictory context. Although most of the proposals discussed above offer valuable suggestions for alleviating the health care crisis, particularly for increasing access to health care services, decisions made in the health care arena are unlikely to be founded on fully rational grounds. Health care is a very personal issue: what might be logical from an economic standpoint on the societal level frequently is unattractive from the emotional perspective of the individual. In addition to the irrational element of individuals' demands, powerful health groups naturally defend their own best interests, even if the overall results run counter to the long-term interests of society. Given these conditions, it is no surprise that most public officials do not see comprehensive alterations in the health care system as politically feasible, despite all the recent rhetoric and political maneuvering. No-win issues, such as allocating health care resources, are not amenable to dramatic or drastic political action.

As a result, the United States has, at least until now, largely avoided making the difficult decisions regarding the distribution of scarce medical resources. Most often the "solutions" have merely shifted costs from the individual to the government (or vice versa), or from one third-party agent to another. Aaron and Schwartz (1984), for instance, analyze the strategy of policymakers in the 1980s to rely on a shift toward prospective reimbursement schemes to solve health cost problems. Although giving the appearance of resolving the problem, these alterations only delayed the need to make even harder choices in the future. These interim shifts in the burden of payment failed to deal with the critical issues of establishing policy priorities and setting limits on the use of high-cost medical technologies, often of unproven effectiveness. To some extent, the Pepper Commission, Health Access America, the Senate Democrat Plan, and the other plans discussed here miss the point, because they do not recognize that no matter how we organize and fund the health care system, we cannot pay for the type of health care now expected by Americans. Unless policymakers are willing to take a stand and limit "extravagant health care," the financial burden on future generations will escalate dangerously.

Although most consumers have yet to experience directly the ramifications of the cost crisis in medicine, as expensive medical innovations continue to proliferate and public expectations rise, these problems will intensify to crisis proportions for all consumers. It is characteristic of our political system that we refrain from making hard choices in politically volatile areas until a crisis is obvious. Although this pattern is shortsighted, it is understandable, because most policy decisions are made in a very short time frame. Public officials are not reelected on the basis of their efforts to resolve future problems, no matter how legion. Therefore, it is not surprising that their attention is directed toward either effecting policies that are painless for their constituencies or dealing with unavoidable crisis issues.

In order to avoid a collapse of the health care system, vigorous action must be forthcoming on several fronts. Although it is essential to continue or even expand current efforts to establish procompetitive health delivery systems, regulate medical costs, develop a "resource-based relative value scale" for physicians' services (Hsiao, 1988), resolve the problem of the uninsured, and selectively reduce government support, lasting solutions necessitate major alterations in the basic public orientations toward medicine outlined earlier. We must rethink our social priorities and attempt to come to at least some broad agreement concerning what we as a society expect from the health care system.

Lasting solutions require policy choices at several levels. First, there must be a realistic appraisal of how much of society's resources we are willing to allocate to health care: 10 percent of the GNP? 12 percent? 15 percent? What priority does society place on medical care as opposed to education, housing, defense, leisure, and other areas described in this book? Once that appraisal is made, we must determine how these resources are to be allocated among the many competing categories of spending within health care. Do we wish to continue to place emphasis on sophisticated, but expensive, technologies designed to extend life, or should we shift emphasis to preventive medicine and primary care? Are we willing to continue to fund research on some diseases far in excess of the mortality or morbidity they are responsible for, while virtually ignoring research on other, perhaps less "glamorous," diseases? Finally, assuming we are unable to meet the health needs of all persons due to scarce resources (including money, technology, skilled personnel, blood, and organs), rationing decisions at the individual level are unavoidable. This will require educating the public about the limits of medicine, moderating public expectations concerning health care, and shifting our priorities toward preventive strategies within which the individual has an obligation to order his or her life to maximize health and minimize the need for expensive treatment.

Rationing Health Care

Rationing has always been a part of medical decision making. Figure 3.1 presents a spectrum of ways in which health care can be rationed. Whether

FIGURE 3.1

Forms of Rationing: A Continuum of Government Involvement

1	2	3	4	5	6	7
Physician Discretion	Competitive Marketplace	Insurance Marketplace	Socialized Insurance	Implicit Rationing	Explicit Rationing	Controlled Rationing

Form	Criteria Used	Effects on Health Care
1. Physician Discretion	Medical benefit to patient Medical risk to patient Social class or mental capacity	Reinforces technological imperative Increases costs with no constraint on major access points Reinforces differential access
2. Competitive Marketplace	Ability to pay	Creates tiered access system Leads to elaborate charity system
3. Insurance Marketplace	Ability to pay for insurance Group membership Employment	Encourages use of resources Escalates demand and costs of health care Spreads risk and thus expands access
4. Socialized Insurance (i.e., Medicaid)	Entitlement	Covers persons lacking adequate private insurance Increases role of government in medical decision making Increases cost to public Creates new tiered system of public versus private sector patients
5. Implicit Rationing	The queue Limited manpower and facilities Medical benefits to patient with consideration of social costs	Imposes shortage of some health care Increases role of government in regulation and budgeting Limits access to specialists Reinforces tiered system Shifts emphasis toward social benefits and costs
6. Explicit Rationing	Triage Medical benefit to patient with emphasis on social costs and benefits Strict allocation	Limits high-cost care with dubious benefits Makes peer review mandatory Imposes cost containment measures Imposes regulation of private as well as public sector Bureaucratizes rationing
7. Controlled Rationing	Equity in access to primary care Social benefit over specific patient benefits Cost to society	Eliminates private health care sector Fully bureaucratizes medical decision making Limits discretion of patient, physician, and other health providers Imposes strict regulation and control of all facets of medicine Eliminates tiered system

imposed by a market system, in which price determines who has and has not access, a triage system, where care is distributed on the basis of need defined largely by the medical community, or a queue system, in which time and the waiting process becomes the major rationing device, medical resources always have been distributed according to criteria that contain varying degrees of subjectivity. In almost all instances, rationing criteria are founded in a particular value context that results in an inequitable distribution of resources based on social as well as strictly medical considerations.

In addition to illustrating the range of rationing options for health care, figure 3.1 introduces yet another factor in defining the concept. Some forms of rationing infer or necessitate government involvement, either direct or indirect, while others fail to distinguish between private and public sector choices. This distinction, in fact, is very critical to a clarification of how current health care options differ from those in the past. Less explicit forms of rationing toward the left of the continuum are no longer sufficient to resolve health care dilemmas in this era. As a result, we are now witnessing a shift toward the right end of the spectrum, possibly culminating in a central role of the government in the rationing of increasingly scarce medical resources. Although explicit rationing under the authority of the government is but one form of rationing, there appear to be many forces that concurrently are moving American society in that direction. As summarized by David Mechanic (1977, 3):

> As people have learned to have high and more unrealistic expectations of medicine, demands for care for a variety of conditions, both major and minor, have accelerated. No nation that follows a sane public policy would facilitate the fulfillment of all perceptions of need that a demanding public might be willing to make. As in every other area of life, resources must be rationed.

Instead of focusing on whether some form of rationing is necessary, the post–Cold War debate more properly should be directed toward the extent to which the government and its agents should take a direct role in establishing rationing procedures and structure. Should the haphazard, inequitable, and often contradictory private rationing continue, or should the government accept responsibility for the allocation and use of medical resources and take active steps to design and implement a comprehensive rationing system? I argue here that the government has this responsibility and must soon act upon it if a health care crisis is to be averted.

Despite the strong antipathy toward the concept of rationing in the United States, the rationing of medical technologies will become more prevalent and ostensible. George Annas (1985, 188) is correct in suggesting that the customary approach to rationing medicine, where it is practiced by health care providers but not explicitly acknowledged, gives us the illusion that we do not have to make these choices, but it does so only at the cost of mass deception.

Moreover, this deception, in turn, has contributed to the misconception that as a society we can avoid explicit rationing decisions because we have managed to do so thus far. It is natural, when faced with such painful choices, to take solace in approaches that appear to free us from those decisions. It is becoming increasingly clear, however, that American society can no longer escape facing the problems of rationing. Although some persons remain content in the illusions of the customary approach, high technology medicine accompanied by the array of demographic and social trends discussed here make that impossible. Abrams and Wolf (1984) arrive at the same conclusion: "As we are forced to place limits on health care for financial reasons and reconcile competing claims to increasingly capable medical technology, we will face agonizing dilemmas with extraordinary political implications" (p. 631).

Although explicit rationing of medical resources is alien to a rights-oriented value system, there is no escape from making such decisions. In the absence of coordinated, consistent national criteria, rationing decisions will continue to be made on an ad hoc, reactive basis by a combination of public and private mechanisms including legislatures, courts, corporations, insurance companies, public relations firms, ethics committees, and physicians. The most appropriate question is not whether rationing ought to be done, but rather who should establish procedures that are fair and reasonable. To this end, a first order of business is to initiate a public dialogue over societal goals and priorities that includes consideration of the preferred agents for rationing medical resources. This initial enterprise could take the form of Lester Milbrath's (1986) Council for Long Range Societal Guidance, Abram and Wolf's (1984) temporary government committee, or other proposed mechanisms. Although direct government involvement in the deliberations of this group must be limited, the effort has to be initiated by the national government and must be viewed as legitimate and critical by public officials.

Although consensus on how medical resources ought to be distributed is unlikely, it is possible to reach general agreement on the procedures through which society will approach these problems. If we can agree that the decisional criteria are fair and understand that we are bound by them, specific applications, though difficult, might be perceived as unfortunate but not unfair. One of the reasons individuals and health providers tend to reject the notion of rationing or any attempt to withhold treatment is that there is no guarantee that the resources averted will be used fairly or even more efficiently. If one person forgoes a needed liver transplant, most likely someone else will have the transplant—someone perhaps who is less "deserving"—rather than the money being spent on something like prenatal care.

Any attempts to ration medicine by edict, particularly if they involve life-style changes, will fail in a society such as the United States, which stresses the predominance of individual rights over other societal priorities. Moreover, it is foolish to presume that moderation of the expectations, demands, and behavior of a public that has come to expect unlimited access to technological progress in medicine is an easy task. As noted by David Mechanic (1986, 215), even though it may be that the public has developed unrealistic expectations, it is "unlikely that the American population would support the rationing of expensive high technology in the fashion characterizing England's National Health Service." Moreover, because officeholders gain so little political credit for trying to convince people that they are largely responsible for their own health problems, one can hardly expect most elected officials to publicly advocate an explicit rationing policy. Elections and careers are lost, not won, on such issues. The difficulty of the issue, however, does not reduce the need and urgency of facing it.

A central element in any effort to ration medical resources in such a way as to be fair yet efficient is education designed to counter the technological imperative. Without a countervailing emphasis on the risks and dangers inherent in each proposed medical intervention, we are conditioned to embrace the technologies. Our failure to assess realistically the limits of medicine and the long-term consequences of high technology interventions, and to communicate this knowledge to the public, produces a situation where we have the intervention first and give it serious thought only after the fact. Public expectations must be revised to take into account the limits on what medical science can accomplish both for society and for the individual.

The government has a responsibility to educate the public both about the links between life-style choices and health and the need to moderate expectations. This educative approach must be accompanied by a significant shift at the allocation level toward preventive and primary health care programs that recently have received shrinking shares of the health care resources. This pursuit will be difficult, in part because of the momentum toward more profitable curative/rescue medicine and in part because of the strength of prevailing perceptions of health care. Unfortunately, the trend is continuing toward more emphasis on high-technology interventions at the exclusion of preventive education. Ongoing decisions by third-party payers, including the states and Medicare, to fund heart and liver transplants show that such a transformation is not imminent.

The most controversial aspect of rationing medicine is the advocacy of a shift toward individual responsibility for health status. Given the large proportion of health care expended on illnesses that are linked to life-style choice, however, any rationing policy, if it is to be effective, must place considerable emphasis on the ultimate responsibility of the individual not only for his or her own health but also for reducing the overall costs to society, both present and future.

Instilling a future-oriented perspective both for individual health and societal survival is critical. "There will be little meaning to political freedom of choice, if our society fails to prepare for predictable crises" (Milbrath,

1986, 33). Although the emphasis on life-style and individual responsibility for health does conflict with prevailing notions of free choice in a liberal society, failure to recognize and take action now, even at the expense of some freedom of choice, risks the loss of considerably more freedoms in the future. Collectively, the assumption that each individual has rights to unlimited medical resources is disastrous when resources are finite. Increasingly, these constraints on the use of medical resources will result in situations where the decision is made not to initiate life-saving treatment. Although such decisions have always been made, they were not perceived as the product of an explicit rationing policy.

The impending crisis in the allocation of large sums of money for the treatment of severely ill persons is inevitable because it is in direct competition with other health priorities. Thus, the question becomes not how much is a particular human life worth but what priority we put on that life versus another life or lives. Every decision we make to allocate large amounts of resources to save a life diverts those resources from other potentially life-saving treatments, albeit less dramatic ones. For instance, the decision to save the life of a disabled infant by aggressive medical intervention raises critical questions concerning long-term commitment of society to invest in substantial "downstream" resources needed to maximize the potential of that life. Until now, we have shown more interest in technologically "saving" the life than in the less ostensible, but more difficult, task of caring for those persons we have rescued. Before rushing into aggressive treatment of newborns with multiple gross malformations and severe prematurity, we must ask whether we have the willingness to expend the essential long-term resources to care for them. Similarly, before establishing policies that indiscriminantly fund major organ transplants, we must test our long-term commitment to the counseling and emotional aid that transplant patients require. We must ask the difficult questions of not only who should make the decision to rescue and on the basis of what criteria but also who pays the enormous costs, both tangible and intangible.

In summary, the explosion of medical technologies in this decade and the heightened conflict over the allocation of medical resources intensifies the need for a national dialogue over what the goals and priorities of society ought to be. The trade-offs inherent in any allocation of policies must be clarified if we are to appraise realistically the options available to us. Unfortunately, the choices we face increasingly are being constrained by the lack of adequate resources to utilize all the technologies needed to save the lives of all persons. Rationing these technologies, although not a popular option, is becoming a necessary one in the post–Cold War era.

All political decisions involve trade-offs when goods and services are distributed across a population. No matter what allocation scheme is used, some elements of society will benefit and others will be deprived. Philosophical debate has long been devoted to what criteria ought to be used to determine whether or not a particular policy is just or fair. Do we select those policies that maximize the good of the greatest number, help those who are least well off, or concentrate goods in a small elite on the assumption that somehow benefits might "trickle down" to those on the bottom? Since Plato first argued in *The Republic* that health resources should not be wasted on the sickly and unproductive, the distribution of these limited resources has been part of a public policy debate. Although historically the dominant policy in the United States has been to minimize direct government intervention in the allocation of health care resources, for reasons discussed here, this policy perspective is now in need of drastic revision leading to calls for major reform of the health care system.

Child Care Policy: Past, Present, and Future

JENNIFER MEZEY, MICHAEL L. MEZEY, AND
SUSAN GLUCK MEZEY

As the Cold War era drew to a close, the one major domestic policy initiative toward which both political parties seemed favorably disposed was child care. This rare consensus resulted in landmark legislation passed in 1990 providing significant federal funding for child care services. According to John Kingdon, a "focusing event," joining the problem, policy, and political "streams," can produce an environment for significant policy change (Kingdon, 1984). In the case of child care, the 1988 presidential election and the gender gap between George Bush and Michael Dukakis served as such an event. The child care problems faced by most American two-income families were magnified by the growing voting power of women, and this captured the attention of public policymakers. Various options were proposed and debated, and ultimately, the political climate produced by the budget summit of 1990 made national child care policy a reality.

However, as Kingdon points out, when "a political window" opens and action occurs, there is no guarantee that the problem that the policy addresses will be solved. Thus, as important as the 1990 legislation was, it constituted only a limited solution to the problem of child care. Funding was relatively modest; most of the money was directed at the poor and the working poor and was insufficient to meet fully the needs of even those targeted groups. Little in the legislation was aimed at helping middle-class families find safe, affordable child care services. This unfinished agenda combined with the growing number of women entering the job market means that child care will continue to be an issue into the 1990s. And because it raises fundamental questions about welfare policy and the role of women in society, it is an issue that is likely to become increasingly tendentious.

Framing the Issue

Child care raises questions about the boundary between the public and private spheres of human activity. Traditionally, children and their care have been at the heart of the family structure, located in the private sector beyond government control. Child care proposals raise the specter of removing child-rearing responsibility from the family to the state. On the other hand, governments at every level have consistently claimed a strong state interest in the welfare and protection of children. Head Start and, more generally, the nation's commitment to universal public education provides the most concrete demonstration of that interest.

Child care is also confounded by the controversy over the federal structure. Many of those arguing that protecting children is a public interest believe that state and local governments are the appropriate arenas in which to exercise that interest. Other policy areas that most directly affect the welfare of children—education, recreation, health, public safety—typically have been state rather than federal policy spheres. On the other hand, the trend during much of this century toward the nationalization of major policy questions combined with the broader revenue base of the federal government has helped place children's issues on the national agenda. Therefore, added to the question of whether there should be a government role in child care is the question of which level of government should have that role.

From a cultural perspective, the women's movement has made child care an issue for women as well as children. The culturally defined responsibility of women to bear, raise, and care for their children has been the primary impediment to their entry into the job market, to their career advancement, and, many would argue, to full gender equality. Proposals to improve the quality of child care services and make them more available thus challenge the patriarchal structure of American society by suggesting that mothers are not necessarily exclusively or even primarily responsible for child rearing.

Child care is also inextricably tied to questions of social class and race. Although families at every socio-economic level encounter difficulties obtaining quality child care services, the poor and the working poor have always been most in need of government subsidized child care because they are least able to afford its market price. This is why child care is typically phrased as a social welfare question. As such, child care could well be expected to attract more support than other welfare programs; of all the potential objects of welfare state expenditures, children, especially needy children, might well be the most sympathetic. But as a welfare issue, child care also has

had to carry the political liabilities that programs designed for the needy traditionally have had to bear. And, to the extent that such programs are aimed
exclusively at the "truly needy," they are likely to arouse the hostility of middle-class families, resentful that benefits they would like to have are unavailable to them. Finally, in the United States, welfare questions always implicate
issues of race, compounding even further the problem of gaining political support for effective child care policies.

Fiscally, child care proposals are never inexpensive. The fiscal environment created by the huge budget deficits and the antitax legacy of the Reagan
presidency means that proposals for new domestic spending will always be
suspect. Until the budgetary constraints imposed by the current high-deficit-
no-tax-increase mindset are loosened, it will be difficult for policymakers to
identify sources that can fund a comprehensive child care program.

History of Child Care

The first federal legislation dealing with child care was enacted during the
New Deal. With the passage of the Social Security Act, the federal government assumed a measure of responsibility for financial support of dependent
children by providing for children with deceased fathers through the Aid to
Dependent Children (ADC) program, which would later become Aid to Families with Dependent Children (AFDC). Also as part of the New Deal, the
Works Project Administration (WPA) created child care programs to provide
jobs for unemployed teachers (Goodman and Zigler, 1982). Although this limited WPA program enabled women with children to work, it was motivated
more by the economic crisis of the 1930s than by any recognition of a governmental responsibility to provide child care for working parents.

The first federal child care program that was designed explicitly to facilitate the entry of women into the work force was put into effect during World
War II, when the federal government opened child care centers to serve children whose mothers had taken jobs in the defense industry (Goodman and
Zigler, 1982). However, both the entrance of women into the work force and
the child care policies that made it possible were viewed as temporary, emergency wartime measures; once the war was over, the centers were closed, the
jobs were returned to the men, and the children, along with most of their
mothers, returned home.

After the war, child care virtually disappeared from the national policy
agenda for twenty years. It did not return until the Great Society and then primarily as a welfare measure to support and enhance the education of economically disadvantaged children. The most notable of these programs was Head
Start, designed to provide preschool training for children from low income
families. Although Head Start was targeted at a specific economic strata, it

made a more general and important contribution to the child care debate by legitimizing federal involvement in child care.

During the Nixon administration, opponents of the Great Society programs advocated the Family Assistance Plan (FAP) as an alternative to child care. FAP would have provided extra money to poor families with children to spend on child care or any other purpose they chose (*Congressional Quarterly Almanac*, 1971, 524). Congress defeated the Family Assistance Plan and later advanced the first comprehensive national child care policy, the Child Development Act (CDA) of 1971. Vetoed by President Nixon, CDA would have had the effect of expanding and generalizing Head Start by providing free day care along with health and nutritional services for the children of the poor and the working poor. Services also would have been available on a sliding scale fee basis to families with incomes above the poverty line (*New York Times*, June 14, 1991). Nixon vetoed the Act under pressure from the right wing of the Republican Party, some of whom saw it as another huge, expensive, and wasteful governmental program, while others viewed it as a sinister attempt by the state to assume responsibility for the care and raising of children.

Although the comprehensive approach to child care represented by the Child Development Act remained largely dormant until the late 1980s, the tax approach implied by FAP was resurrected in 1976 when Congress provided a tax credit, largely benefiting middle- and upper-income families, to defray the child care costs of working couples. The credit was nonrefundable and therefore inapplicable to poor people with no tax liability (Besharov and Tramontozzi, 1989). The latter group was helped by the refundable earned income tax credit that provided a form of negative income tax to the lowest paid workers with children. Unlike the child care deduction, the funds realized from the earned income tax credit did not have to be applied to child care (National Research Council, 1990, 212).

Child Care in the 1980s

Child care became a major policy issue in the late 1980s when over one hundred bills involving child care were introduced in the 100th Congress (Congressional Research Service, Dec. 19, 1988, 1). The most far-reaching of these, following the model of the Child Development Act, were designed to create a child care infrastructure, make child care more affordable and available, and improve its quality. Suddenly, policymakers of all political philosophies were interested in child care legislation.

In the spring of 1988, Democrats met at a resort in West Virginia to plan their party's agenda for the nineties. Among the subjects discussed was the political potential of family issues. The focus on child care was given extra urgency by the increasing number of women in the work force. By 1985, the labor force participation rate of married women with children under the age of eighteen was 61 percent; for single mothers it was 67.8 percent. For married women with children under two years old the rate was 54 percent, and for single women, it was 55.7 percent (Hayghe, 1986).

Families with children had also suffered disproportionately during the Reagan years, and poverty among children had increased. In 1987, more than one in five children were poor, and almost one in two black children were poor (Kammerman, 1989). The House Select Committee on Children, Youth, and Families reported that from 1979 to 1986 "the median-adjusted income for the bottom two-fifths of all families fell by 2 percent, while median adjusted income for the top two-fifths of all families rose 10 percent." The real median income of families with children had not increased during these years. The committee report concluded that "in 1987, 16.4 percent of all families with children were in poverty, up nearly 35 percent since 1979. Nearly one in every two female headed families with children lives in poverty compared to one in every twelve married couple families" (U.S. Congress, House Select Committee on Children, Youth, and Families, 1988, 3).

Notwithstanding the obvious need for child care for poor and working poor families, child care policy in the 1980s reflected Ronald Reagan's efforts at retrenchment of the welfare state. As in other areas of social welfare spending, funding was cut for most of the programs affecting low-income families. Funding for all federal child care programs increased from $4,048 million in 1977 to $6,170 million in 1988. However, the funding for tax credits for families earning more than $15,000 increased from $681 million in 1977 to $2,775 million in 1988. Therefore, the overall funding for child care for low-income families increased by only $28 million, compared to a $2,094 million increase in programs for middle- and upper-income families (General Accounting Office, 1989, 10).

The increase in the dependent child care tax credit mainly benefitted middle- and upper-income families by allowing them to take tax deductions of 20 to 30 percent of child care expenses, up to a maximum of $2,400 for one child and $4,800 for two or more. Because the credit could be claimed only by families above a certain threshold income level, it was of little help to the low-income working poor who paid no taxes (Kahn and Kammerman, 1987). Similarly, employer-provided child care support also primarily advantaged middle- and upper-income families.

The sole exception to this pattern was an increase in Head Start funds. However, even with these extra funds, Head Start did not serve anywhere near the number of needy children and parents in America. Thus, with few exceptions, the Reagan administration used the tax system to divert money for child care from the poor to the nonpoor. Focusing on demand, the administration paid little attention to the fact that the availability and quality of child care for all working families was inadequate.

The Late Reagan-Era Politics of Child Care

Despite a growing acknowledgment of the need for child care, the politics of child care during the late 1980s was still influenced by the nostalgic image of the family promoted by Ronald Reagan and the New Right, with the father as the breadwinner and the mother at home with the children. As Barbara Ehrenreich suggests, such a vision includes a "future in which . . . authority will be firmly vested in adults over children, in men over women, and in ancient sources of wisdom, such as the Bible, over modern science and 'humanism' " (Ehrenreich, 1987).

It was apparent that this perception of the ideal American family was at odds with reality. In 1987, against this backdrop, Senator Christopher Dodd (D-CT), working with a coalition of child welfare groups, educators, women's rights advocates, and labor unions (the Alliance for Better Child Care) introduced the Act for Better Child Care Services (known as ABC). Leading congressional Republicans also decided that shifting demographics in the last two decades compelled their involvement in the development of family policies. Indicative of this change was the conversion of Senator Orrin Hatch (R-UT), who had opposed child care in the past, arguing that families should raise their own children without governmental interference. But, in 1988, he and Representative Nancy Johnson (R-CT) introduced child care legislation, and in 1989 he would join forces with Dodd and become one of the prime sponsors of ABC.

The acquiescence of some Republicans in child care policy was motivated in large part by the 1988 presidential election and the gender gap that faced George Bush. According to *The Washington Post*, polls taken during the spring and summer of 1988 showed Bush trailing Michael Dukakis among female voters by 8 to 28 percentage points (*Washington Post*, July 25, 1988). Dukakis had already endorsed ABC in principle and had been involved in child care issues as governor of Massachusetts. At that time, Bush had no experience with child care and did not have a counterproposal. Finally, in a July 1988 speech to the National Federation of Business and Professional Women's Clubs, Bush unveiled a proposal that would make the earned income tax credit refundable, up to $1,000 per child, for people earning less than $10,000 a year. The money could be used to purchase child care or to allow a parent to stay at home with his or her children. Bush's plan also included incentives for private industry to establish day care centers, mandated child care facilities for federal employees, raised Head Start funding levels, and encouraged innovation by private centers (*Washington Post*, July 25, 1988). This tax credit portion strongly resembled the child care component of Nixon's Family Assistance Plan, which substituted cash payments for government services. The incentives for private businesses to provide child care was in the spirit of the privatization ethos of the Reagan era.

Senate Action—1988

Both the Speaker of the House, Thomas Foley (D-WA), and Senate Majority Leader, George Mitchell (D-ME), promised child care advocates that child care and other family issues would be a top priority in the 100th Congress. Hearings on various child care bills began in 1987, and on July 27, 1988, the Senate Committee on Labor and Human Resources reported out ABC. The bill allocated federal matching money to the states so that they could provide direct assistance to families and create a child care infrastructure. It also increased Head Start funds to allow Head Start to expand to an all-day, all-year program that would serve all eligible children.

Passage of ABC was intended to improve the quality and affordability and increase the availability of child care programs. To receive federal money, states were required to formulate a five-year plan, create an advisory committee, maintain or enhance licensing standards for child care facilities, and establish resource and referral agencies throughout the state. The authorization requirements were as follows: (1) 75 percent of the money had to be used for direct vouchers or grants to parents, with priority for low-income children; (2) 10 percent of these funds had to be used to expand Head Start or other part-day preschool programs to full-day programs; (3) up to 15 percent of the funds had to be used to improve resource and referral services, salaries, licensing procedures or other infrastructure areas; and (4) 10 percent of the funds could be used for administrative costs (U.S. Congress, Senate Committee on Labor and Human Resources, 1988, 54).

One of the more controversial parts of the bill was the creation of a National Advisory Committee charged with establishing minimum required standards for publicly assisted day care settings. Proponents argued that uniformity and regulation were necessary to ensure that children in child care were treated properly. Opponents of standards claimed that they would raise the price of child care services to prohibitive levels. During the Reagan years, federal standards were deemphasized in favor of policies that would enhance state autonomy in spending decisions. State officials had become increasingly resistant to mandatory federal standards governing program administration. They argued that states should be able to adopt their own standards to suit their own needs.

Child care was considered by the Senate in October 1988 in a legislative package that combined ABC with parental leave and anti–child pornography provisions. The strategy of combining these issues into one family bill was a calculated risk on the part of the Democratic leadership, who hoped to take advantage of the momentum created by the presidential candidates' professed support for family policies. The plan failed, however, when Republicans and some Democrats refused to support the Democratic initiative.

The Democratic leadership erred by ignoring the fact that each component of the bill had separate constituencies that could not be easily brought together. Business groups supported child care but balked at the family leave provisions in the package; conservatives favored the anti–child pornography measures but opposed federal standards for child care. Opposition also came from education groups such as the Parent-Teachers Association (PTA) and the National Education Association (NEA), who were concerned about the voucher and educational components of ABC; they feared that vouchers for child care could legitimize vouchers for elementary and secondary education. Further, the NEA was unwilling to support the bill if the funds could be used for sectarian purposes; when it looked as if the provisions preventing such use were being weakened, the NEA withdrew its support (*Washington Post*, Sept. 13, 1988). Ultimately, the bill died when its supporters failed to get enough votes to end debate.

The Post-Reagan Era

Senate Action—1989

The "New Right" lost its national spokesman when Ronald Reagan left office. With the election of George Bush, the Republican party and the country shifted its focus slightly. When Bush promised a "kinder, gentler nation," it seemed to signal a rhetorical movement toward a domestic policy that would meet the needs of all American families. However, this approach emphasized private sector initiative ("a thousand points of light") and no new taxes.

On June 15, 1989, Senator Mitchell introduced a substitute (S5) to the ABC bill that had been reported out of the Senate Labor and Human Resources Committee in 1988. The Mitchell substitute included a revised version of ABC, a tax provision applying to both child health care and child care, and an amendment that would allow federal funding for religious day care (*Congressional Record*, June 15, 1989, S6697).

Mitchell's bill, S5, was designed to gain the support of conservative Democrats and Senator Hatch by incorporating some of the provisions of the 1988 Hatch-Johnson proposal that had combined tax credits for employers who opened on-site child care centers with a child care block grant. Hatch-Johnson had also supported model standards that states could adapt to their particular circumstances (*Washington Post*, Feb. 8, 1988).

The funding formula for S5 was essentially the same as the 1988 version of ABC: (1) 70 percent of the money had to go to direct assistance to families; (2) 10 percent had to go to licensing, training, and resource and referral services; and (3) 12 percent of the money had to be spent on improving the quality of child care. S5 retained minimum standards provisions but weakened them with the phrase, "no standard recommended by the [National Advisory] Committee may be more rigorous than the strictest in that category which currently exists in any of the states.'' It also gave the states a one-year grace period for implementing the standards (U.S. Congress, Senate Committee on Labor and Human Resources, 1988, 25). These changes gained the support of many conservative Democrats and allayed the fears of the National Governor's Association that mandated federal standards would be excessive and intrusive.

Another controversial issue was the treatment of child care delivered in religious settings. Unlike ABC, S5 explicitly provided for parental vouchers for child care in religious settings while at the same time prohibiting child care centers from discriminating against employees on the basis of religion or denying admittance to children based on their religious creed. These provisions implied that child care that was expressly religious in nature could not be funded by the vouchers (U.S. Congress, Senate Committee on Labor ahd Human Resources, 1988).

The tax credit portion of S5 slightly increased the existing dependent care tax credit and made it refundable. At the insistence of Senate Finance Committee Chair Lloyd Bentsen (D-TX), S5 also created a new credit of up to $500 for health insurance premiums for families with children (*Congressional Quarterly Almanac*, 1989).

The Republicans countered by introducing a proposal calling for refundable tax credits and an increase in funding for existing child care block grants. This substitute, sponsored by Senate Minority Leader Robert Dole (R-KS) and Robert Packwood (R-OR), closely resembled President Bush's original 1988 proposal. Proponents claimed that, compared to the Democrats' bill, it would ''increase parental choice and decrease bureaucracy'' (*Washington Post*, June 16, 1988).

One June 23, 1989, after almost a week of debate, the Senate defeated the Dole-Packwood substitute by a 44–56 vote. Only two Democrats voted for the substitute, Kent Conrad (D-ND) and Sam Nunn (D-GA), and only three Republicans voted against it: John Chafee (R-RI), Orrin Hatch (R-UT), and James Jeffords (R-VT). The Senate then approved the Mitchell substitute, S5, by a vote of 63–37. This time, Nunn was the only Democrat to vote against it, while nine Republicans voted for it (see *Congressional Record*, June 22, 1989, S7176).[1]

House Action—1989

On June 27, 1989, the House Education and Labor Committee adopted a variation of ABC (HR3) introduced by the committee chair, Representative Augustus Hawkins (D-CA). HR3's grant approach and its church/state and model standards provisions were similar to those in S5. HR3 authorized $1.75 billion for improving the quality, affordability, and availability of child care. The money was divided in the following manner:

Title I: 25 percent for expanded Head Start services to include full-day and year-round programs and greater eligibility;

Title II: 25 percent for "Early Childhood Development and School-Related Child Care programs," including before- and after-school programs;

Title III: 35 percent for "Services to Infants, Toddlers, and Young Children," with 98 percent of the funds as direct subsidies to low- and moderate-income families. This section also made the secretary of Health and Human Services responsible for establishing a National Advisory Committee to formulate model standards;

Title IV: 15 percent for Coordinating Activities, including loans and grants to providers;

Title V: created a separate annual authorization of $25 million each year for FY1990 to FY1993 for a matching grant program to promote "Business Involvement in Meeting Employee Child Care Needs" (U.S. Congress, House Committee on Education and Labor, 1989, 35–36).

The House Ways and Means Committee reported out its version of HR3 on July 19, 1989, with no major changes in Titles I, II, or IV of HR3. In Title III, while retaining the National Advisory Committee on Child Care Standards, Ways and Means replaced the authorization for direct subsidies to low- and moderate-income families with an increase in the entitlements provided under the Social Services Block Grant to states. This change reflected a desire to locate a more secure form of funding for child care by establishing it as an entitlement. After replacing Title III, the committee then changed the authorization allocation to 35 percent for Title I, 35 percent for Title II, and 30 percent for Title IV. It also created a new Title VI that authorized $75 million to help states improve standards in child care delivery services (U.S. Congress, House Committee on Ways and Means, 1989, 28–29).

Ways and Means also increased funding for the earned income tax credit and made it refundable. For families with one child, the credit was increased from 14 percent of the family's first $6,500 to 17 percent, for two children, 21 percent, and for three or more children, 25 percent. Originally, the credit was reduced by 10 percent for every dollar in income that exceeded $10,240 and it would be completely phased out for those who earned more than $19,340. To balance the increase in the credit, the phase out was accelerated to 12 percent for families with one child, 15 percent for families with two children, and 18 percent for families with more than two children (*Congressional Quarterly Almanac*, 1989, 214).

The House leadership, desperately wanting a vote on child care, allowed the House membership to vote on the entitlement and authorization programs as one package. Before the package could be included in the Budget Reconciliation Act of 1989, the Ways and Means and Education and Labor factions joined forces to defeat substitute proposals by Representative Charles Stenholm (D-TX) and Representative Mickey Edwards (R-OK). The Stenholm bill, similar to the Ways and Means proposal, authorized less money and would have eliminated standards. The Edwards bill, which was the Bush administration's proposal, only increased the earned income tax credit for families with children (*Washington Post*, Sept. 27, 1989). The House approved the Education and Labor/Ways and Means package on October 5, 1989, rejecting the Stenholm and Edwards substitutes by votes of 195–230 and 140–285, respectively (*Congressional Record*, Oct. 5, 1989, D1135).

Conference—1989

In conference, an odd coalition emerged. Liberal Democrats George Miller (D-CA), from Education and Labor, and Thomas Downey (D-NY), from Ways and Means, joined with Republican Tom Tauke (R-IO), from Education and Labor, to support the Ways and Means Title XX block grant proposal. They argued that a secure entitlement was preferable to a risky authorization that would have to compete annually for appropriations with other domestic programs. They also believed the bill would be less likely to be vetoed by President Bush, who had repeatedly stated that he would not support the creation of an ABC grant for child care.

The Labor and Human Resources Committee and the Education and Labor Committee resolved their portion of the bill that included the categorical child care grants. But because the Ways and Means Committee and the Senate Finance Committee could not agree on the child care tax portions of the bill, child care was ultimately dropped from the Omnibus Budget Reconciliation Act of 1989. (*Congressional Quarterly Weekly Report*, Nov. 18, 1989, 3162).

The collapse of the child care bill provoked Marion Wright Edelman, president of the Children's Defense Fund, one of the founding and coordinating members of the ABC coalition, to release a letter indicting Downey and Miller for "engaging in a series of efforts . . . to sabotage ground-breaking child care legislation all year for petty jurisdictional and power reasons" (*Congressional Quarterly Weekly Report*, Nov. 18, 1989, 3162). She also said that if "the legislation is not enacted this year, the two of you will deserve the blame for this tragic and unnecessary outcome" (*Washington Post*, Nov. 20, 1989).

Responding to this attack, the House Ways and Means Subcommittee on Human Resources, chaired by Downey, issued a letter affirming its support for Downey and Miller and justified the decision to vote for the Tauke proposal. The letter accused Edelman of trying to "bully two members of Congress into supporting a policy with which they do not agree. Tom Downey and George Miller are no enemies of children or child care; you know that as well as we do" (*Washington Post*, Nov. 20, 1989).

House Action—1990

In the second session of the 101st Congress, the Democratic House leadership resolved the conflict between Education and Labor and Ways and Means. They arrived at a compromise that substituted Title XX funding for the ABC portions of HR3, increased funding for Head Start, provided grant money for before- and after-school programs, and required the states to formulate and implement child care standards in order to receive federal money. The leadership scheduled a House vote on the revamped HR3 for March 29,1990.

When the bill came up for a vote in the House, it competed with another amendment proposed by Stenholm, this time co-sponsored by Representative E. Clay Shaw (R-FL). Their proposal, which would have eliminated the school-based programs and phased out the dependent care tax credit for families with incomes over $90,000, (*Congressional Quarterly Weekly Report*, March 31, 1990, 948), was defeated by a vote of 195–225 (*Congressional Record*, March 29, 1990, H1336).

Two other important amendments were also defeated. The first, proposed by Representative David Price (D-NC), would have allowed states the option of offering vouchers to parents, as opposed to HR3's requirement of vouchers. The Price amendment was defeated by a vote of 182–243, (*Congressional Record*, March 29, 1990, H1312), with supporters arguing that it would increase state flexibility by allowing them to use a funding mechanism appropriate to their particular circumstances and opponents arguing that the amendment would restrict parental choice and give too much power to the states.

The second amendment, proposed by Representative Don Edwards (D-CA) of the House Judiciary Committee, would have allowed federal funds for church-based child care but would have prohibited funding for sectarian activities or for centers that engaged in discriminatory practices. The amendment's supporters argued that it would make HR3 constitutional. Its opponents characterized it as antireligious and claimed it would prevent parents from choosing religion-based child care. The debate on the House floor indicated that a majority of the House preferred not to take a position that could be construed as antireligious and implicitly delegated the responsibility for resolving the constitutional question to the courts. The amendment was defeated by a vote of 125–297 (*Congressional Record*, March 29, 1990, H1322).

Conference—1990

The 1990 House-Senate conference was more productive than the 1989 conference, in part because President Bush, under pressure to cooperate with Congress to produce a budget agreement, suddenly announced that he would accept a new child care grant program.

The finished product emerged on October 26, 1990. It was a combination of appropriations and entitlements authorizing $2.5 billion over three years to states. Seventy-five percent of the money had to be spent on providing child care services directly to families with incomes below 75 percent of the state median income or on increasing the availability or quality of child care. The states would have to spend approximately 20 percent on preschool programs or before- or after-school programs for school-age children; approximately 4 percent would have to go toward training or increasing the salaries of child care workers; states could spend the remaining 1.25 percent on either of these options (*Congressional Quarterly Weekly Report*, Oct. 27, 1990, 3605).

The tax committees agreed to create an earmarked entitlement within Title IV of the Social Security Act, the section for child welfare services, because the Senate Finance Committee continued to oppose Title XX funding (*Congressional Quarterly Weekly Report*, Nov. 3, 1990, 3722). The Title IV funds were to go to poor families with assets or income that made them ineligible for welfare. They authorized $1.5 billion over five years, with an additional $50 million per year to aid states in training child care workers and improving care standards (*Congressional Quarterly Weekly Report*, Oct. 27, 1990, 3606). There were also two increases in the earned income tax credit, the first, amounting to about $700 million over five years for parents with infants, and the second creating a child health insurance credit (*Congressional Quarterly Weekly Report*, Nov. 3, 1990, 3722).

Since 1987, child care legislation appeared doomed on several occasions yet survived and eventually became law. The following issues played a prominent role in the child care debate: ideological and generational differences among policymakers, parental choice, the method of funding, and the beneficiaries of the services.

Conflict among Ideologies

The child care debate in the 1980s can be seen as a battle among three ideologies: Great Society Democrats, the New Paradigm Republicans (and some Conservative Democrats), and the Class of 1974 Democrats. These philosophies differ significantly on the role and the size of government.

The Great Society faction, composed of people like Hawkins and Edelman, believed in an activist federal government with an affirmative responsibility to remedy social evils. The New Paradigm group called for an approach to government with less bureaucracy, more individual choice, and an environment for free market forces (*New York Times*, Dec. 7, 1990). This philosophy led them to favor less government at any level and minimal federal bureaucratic control over social programs. The Class of 1974 Democrats, or "Watergate babies," were "neoliberal" members of Congress who wished to "purge the Democratic party of its past: no more high-taxing, big-spending,

New Deal liberalism'' (Schneider, 1989, 35). Downey and Miller as members of the Class of 1974, offered technocratic, pragmatic approaches to domestic problems as opposed to the old-style interest group liberalism of the Great Society Democrats.

The original HR3 and ABC called for large expenditures, the building of a child care bureaucracy to oversee the program, and mandated federal standards and directions for state implementation. As such, it was a traditional Great Society approach to child care.

The New Paradigm Republicans envisioned tax credits as an ideal way to increase parental choice and minimize government interference. The federal government would play the role of a bank teller, collecting and dispensing money but having no part in decision making. However, Republicans eventually realized that tax credits alone would not address the issues of availability and quality of child care and supported increased money for the Title XX block grant as a way to preserve state autonomy.

Although Miller and Downey initially supported ABC, they ultimately abandoned it and moved closer to a New Paradigm approach because of President Bush's threat to veto any new grants. Downey and Miller did not believe child care supporters had the votes to override a veto of ABC or HR3 and so compromised to get a child care bill that Bush would sign. They argued that getting some form of child care legislation was more important than pleasing interest groups such as CDF and organized labor.

This willingness to compromise is consistent with Class of 1974 philosophy on the subject of government programs, an attitude expressed by Representative Les AuCoin (D-OR), who said, ''One of the marks of our class has been . . . a search for the best practical ideas in a number of ideological camps to put together something that works in a rapidly changing world'' (Schneider, 1989, 40).

Edelman's dispute with Downey and Miller represented the conflict between the Great Society and Class of 1974 philosophies. Downey characterized Edelman's attack on him as ''a battle between the liberals of the sixties and the liberals of the nineties, between uncompromising advocacy and willingness to recognize limits'' (*New York Times*, Jan. 5, 1990). He added that ''while Edelman and organized labor should be given credit for making child care a national issue, they have to realize that the era of the Great Society and the war on poverty is over'' (*Washington Post,* Nov. 20, 1989).

In the final legislation, the sixties liberals got the appropriations that they wanted because of Bush's political vulnerability. However, the nineties liberals were the true victors. The entitlement portion of the bill is much larger than the appropriations portion and most of the aid is direct rather than through grants. To placate Hawkins, the final legislation included some provisions for before- and after-school programs. However, Hawkins noted that ''the funding doesn't go as far as it should,'' and that available funding would serve only about 300,000 of the more than 10 million so-called latchkey children. "At that rate," he concluded, "we certainly aren't doing much for children" (*Congressional Quarterly Weekly Report*, Oct. 27, 1990, 3605).

Perhaps the approach of the new liberals is more in tune with the fiscal conservatism and distrust of government that became part of the policy landscape during the seventies. Although the "Watergate babies" tend to be progressive in their politics, they frequently engage in compromise and accommodation at the expense of ideology. Rather than address large social issues, they adopt narrow solutions that may partially solve a problem but do not address the fundamental structural inequalities in American society.

Parental Choice

In the context of child care, parental choice can be defined in two ways: the choice of parents to put their children in the kind of child care setting they desire and the choice about whether or not they wish to work outside the home.

For conservatives, the parental choice issue presumes that government programs tell people what to do, making them feel powerless and irresponsible. The New Paradigm Republicans, and some Democrats, argue that if the government simply gives people money, they can spend it as they want, and they will thereby be empowered. Thus, the choice issue appears to be a rallying cry for the preservation of private decision making and opposition to government activity at any level.

The demand for parental choice is also related to the public/private distinction in America's domestic policy. The tax credit/block grant approach treats the family as a private, decision-making entity that decides what is best for its children without government interference. Opponents of ABC and HR3 argued that these bills would restrict choice by allowing the federal government to control parent's options. Standards and licensing would drive up prices and force informal child care providers out of business, they claimed, compelling parents to place their children in centers against their wishes. The tax credit/block grant approach, they argued, would allow parents to maintain control over their choice of child care services. Parents could be trusted "to choose the most appropriate child care arrangements for their children, including care by relatives, friends, neighbors, and churches"; such arrangements would not be covered by HR3 (U.S. Congress, House Committee on Education and Labor, 1989, 64).

The HR3/ABC approach is premised on the view that children are a public good and the government has an interest in their education. For the most part, advocates of ABC/HR3 claimed their goal was to provide parents with the information and resources to make informed choices. Dodd charged that the New Paradigm view of parental choice does not take issues like affordability, availability, and quality into account:

Parental choice means more than giving families a few dollars each month. It means helping to increase the supply and the variety of local child care services for parents to choose from. Parental choice means minimum health and safety standards to help parents measure and improve program quality. Parental choice means better resource and referral networks to educate families about their child care options. (U.S. Congress, Senate Committee on Finance, 1988, 5)

Another aspect of parental choice concerns the proper role of religious child care. Opponents of ABC/HR3 argued that these approaches intruded on parents' religious freedom by restricting their ability to choose religion-based child care. A tax credit approach would allow individuals to use the money for such arrangements. The legislation initially proposed in 1987 did not include funding for religious day care. By 1990, funding for religious day care was allowed under limited conditions.

In testimony before the Education and Labor Committee, Barry Lynn, legislative counsel for the American Civil Liberties Union (ACLU), argued that federal child care money should not go to any religious organization unless there were no alternative sites and religious symbols were barred from the rooms (U.S. Congress, House Committee on Education and Labor, 1989, 398–408). He also urged a nondiscrimination policy for staff and students. These principles were represented in the rejected Edwards amendment.

The final component of parental choice involves the issue of whether or not public policy should encourage parents to stay home with their children or work outside the home. Proponents of the tax credit approach argued that parents should be able to use the money to supplement the income of one parent or to pay for child care. Although the concept of parental choice is usually presented in gender neutral terms, child care policy affects women disproportionately. Catharine MacKinnon's discussion of this subject applies as much to public policy as it does to law: women, she argues, are inherently unequal in society and cannot make the same choices as men because they are not similarly situated. The idea of gender neutrality in law and public policy treats women as individuals rather than members of a subordinated class and ignores the economic and social reality of gender in America (MacKinnon, 1989).

Both liberals and conservatives admit that some women do not have a choice, that to support their families they must work outside the home. However, many policymakers believe that if a woman does not "have to work," government should not pay for child care. Thus, phrasing the debate in terms of who has to work leads to child care as a means-tested welfare program rather than a universal entitlement. The concept of parental choice then becomes a code word for encouraging mothers to stay home. Senator Pete Wilson (R-CA) had supported the Dole substitute because he felt that ABC discriminated against the mother who chooses to stay at home. "We do wish to encourage women to make the choice to remain at home," he said, "if in fact they can by removing the discrimination of Federal law and providing them equal access to Federal assistance" (*Congressional Record*, June 21, 1989, 57057).

Zilla Eisenstein writes that "the priorities of patriarchy are to keep the choices limited for women so that their role as mothers remains primary" (Eisenstein, 1981). One of the ways that government limits choice for women is by providing economic incentives and social disincentives to their participation in the work force. Choices are not made in a vacuum; American society continues to structure women's choices about staying at home with their children through its attitudes and laws.

Appropriations versus Entitlements

As it turned out, the final legislation featured both funding mechanisms: entitlements and appropriations. Unlike entitlements, appropriations must compete with other programs for funding when they come before the appropriations committees, and the money appropriated is usually less than the amount allowed by the authorizing committee. Aaron Wildavsky compares Head Start, an appropriation, to AFDC, an entitlement, and finds that AFDC serves more of its eligible population than does Head Start. This is because entitlement programs must be attacked directly to alter spending, whereas programs supported by annual appropriations can be quietly underfunded. Thus, in his view, entitlements "can afford to be ordinary; programs funded by appropriations have to be extraordinary in order to do as well" (Wildavsky, 1988).

The promise of sure money and less political vulnerability is an attractive one, but there are hierarchies within entitlement programs as well. R. Kent Weaver identifies six types of entitlements: social insurance or income maintenance programs (e.g., Social Security); public assistance for low income people (e.g., AFDC); health entitlements (e.g., Medicare and Medicaid); federal retirement programs; unemployment insurance; and specialized programs. He concludes that entitlement programs with large, politically popular constituencies, such as Social Security and Medicare are more secure than entitlement programs for the poor, such as AFDC and Medicaid. During the welfare state retrenchment period of 1975–1984, the latter were cut more than the former (Weaver, 1985). Hawkins had supported the ABC/HR3 appropriations approach because he feared that child care would become a welfare entitlement program such as AFDC. As such it was likely to be custodial, with little or no emphasis on education. He argued that during the 1980s, while Title XX funding had decreased, the Education and Labor committee had successfully secured funding for programs for poor children, such as Head Start, through the appropriations process (*Congressional Quarterly Almanac*, 1989, 215).

In the end, both approaches were used. The entitlement portion, much larger than the authorization portion, directed its support at the working poor who did not qualify for welfare. The authorization portion gave states the option of either paying means-tested subsidies or increasing availability and quality for all families.

Beneficiaries

The issue that will determine the future of child care policy is its beneficiaries. If the debate is phrased in terms of children, child care should be fairly popular. However, child care is not perceived as being just for children because parents also benefit. Although the tax package provides money for training workers and improving standards, its major feature is relief for the poor and working poor. As with AFDC and Medicaid, programs with poor constituencies do not do as well in the budgetary process as those, such as Social Security, with large, middle-class constituencies.

Supporters of ABC/HR3 understood this issue. They argued that the tax credit/block grant approach focused only on low income people; ABC and HR3 built up an infrastructure and increased availability and quality, thus spreading the benefits. It is significant that child care was placed on the political agenda when middle-class women entered the work force and demanded it. Ironically, poor women have become the beneficiaries of this middle-class influence because they are the mothers whose labor force activity society condones.

Thus, if the goal is to provide all parents with choice and to create powerful constituencies for child care programs, child care should be a universal entitlement. However, this approach is not without its problems. It raises questions about whether it is fair and efficient to pay for child care for the middle class in order to ensure favorable political treatment. In times of budget constraint, is it right to divert resources from the poor to the nonpoor for political reasons? These questions reduce child care to a social welfare issue. But if one looks at child care as a way of securing women's rights, it is very important to make it a universal entitlement. Concluding the Senate debate on S5, Mitchell said the bill would promote "equal economic opportunity" for women by providing access to child care (*Congressional Record*, June 23, 1989, S7478).

By making child care a universal entitlement, the government would commit itself to equalizing the condition of women and men in the work force and society. The appropriation part of the bill tries to take into account the needs of middle- and upper-class women by improving the supply side of the child care equation. However, the funding for the before- and after-school programs, aimed at all children is very small. Also, no money is authorized for the resource and referral services needed by all parents. Additionally, there is no guarantee that the appropriations will match the authorizations.

The dangers of the means-tested approach in the final bill is that child care will be viewed as only for the poor and will become a stigmatized welfare program. If child care is to be accepted as an important developmental tool for all children and a vehicle for women's rights, it needs to be a universal entitlement.

Government child care policy sends a signal to many elements of American society. It tells women they are valued for something beyond their child-rearing abilities; it encourages the private sector to set up programs for their employees; it shows that America values its children and is committed to high quality care for them.

The Future

As one looks to the future, various policy options are available:

1. Retain the welfare approach to child care with whatever benefits there might be from the program accruing primarily to the poor. Because funding for programs aimed exclusively at the poor is never sufficient, this approach will ensure that, as is the case now with Head Start, some poor families will receive some child care help, that their child care services will be lower in quality than those available to the wealthy, and that funding will always be inadequate to meet the needs of all of those who are eligible for the program or who might benefit under more relaxed eligibility standards. It also will ensure relatively low levels of public support for child care as a predominantly white middle class comes to view such a program as simply one more subsidy to poor people among whom racial minorities are disproportionately represented.

2. Approach child care as a women's issue rather than as a welfare issue. Such an approach, which would view child care in the same terms as Social Security or, at the state level, public education, might well evoke greater political support because program benefits would be more widely spread. It is not a coincidence that Social Security is the one national welfare program that is generally immune from political attack. This is so largely because Social Security benefits are widely shared by all economic classes. Of course, such a universal approach doubtless will produce a more expensive program and in that sense runs counter to the prevailing consensus in Washington in favor of limited expenditures and a reduced role for the federal government. Just as significantly, such an approach will challenge the prevailing cultural premise that women should stay at home with their preschool aged children unless driven into the work force by extreme economic necessity.

3. Whether the narrow welfare approach or the more universal women's approach is selected, an additional issue is the training of child care workers and the standards for child care centers. Many have advocated licensing requirements for child care workers and facilities. If the federal government

established such standards or required states to establish such standards in order to qualify for federal funds, such actions, it is argued, would have a universal impact in the sense that the quality of all child care services would improve and all parents who use child care would be more confident about the quality of care that their children were receiving. On the other hand, without sufficient funding for either the welfare or the women's approach to child care services, upgraded training and higher standards might make child care less available to those at the bottom end of the socio-economic scale. Better trained child care workers will command higher salaries, and centers that adhere to higher standards will be more expensive to operate. The worst outcome for those without resources would be federally mandated quality control without the funds needed to assure general access to such upgraded facilities. Such has been the case with medical care. High standards for medical professionals and facilities has meant very high prices for medical services. Relatively meager funding for Medicaid and no funding at all for those ineligible for Medicaid has meant very poor health services or no health services for those with few resources while those with plentiful resources receive excellent health services.

NOTES

1. *Congressional Record*, Senate, June 22, 1989, S7176. In addition to Hatch, Jeffords, and Chafee, the other five Republicans were William Cohen (R-ME), Alfonse D'Amato (R-NY), Mark Hatfield (R-OR), John Heinz (R-PA), Nancy Kassebaum (R-KS), and Arlen Specter (R-PA).

Hunger Strategies for the Twenty-First Century: Developing Innovation in America's Domestic Food Assistance Policy

PETER A. MANNING

Throughout its history, the United States has been faced with a food paradox. On the one hand, a variety of factors (topography, climate, technology, the work force, etc.) created a farm economy leading to sufficient and, in some cases, burdensome surplus production of food. On the other hand, not everyone benefits from this abundance.

The 1930s became a testing period as circumstances forced new experimental solutions on existing nationwide problems. Starting in the 1960s, the debate over domestic food assistance policy became more intense. Food programs that initially had been set up to support the interests of the agricultural community became part of a series of "New Frontier" and "Great Society" programs to alleviate poverty in the United States. Interest by the White House and Capitol Hill increased media attention, and the publication of studies and reports about Third World–type hunger in America all combined to bring about greater public awareness.

With more attention came more money. Additional targeted support went to those special segments of the population who were at risk (e.g., low-income, school-age children without adequate breakfast; pregnant and lactating mothers; infants, preschoolers, children in nonprofit day care centers; school-age children in summer food programs). Support also increased in the

This chapter presents only the author's view and does not purport to express the official opinion of the U.S. Department of Agriculture or the U.S. government.

existing categorical aid program—the National School Lunch Program—with additional funds, technical assistance, and equipment purchases.[1]

As programs and benefit levels grew, so did the problems associated with them. Greater expenditure of funds led to more potential for misuse and thus a need for greater scrutiny. A proliferation of regulations and bureaucracies at various governmental levels took place in order to implement and account for these new programs. With the large expenditure of time, money, and effort at various levels of government over a period of sixty years, one might expect the problems of hunger and malnutrition to be resolved.

But any triumph in the war on domestic hunger appears premature. During the 1980s and into the 1990s, reports again surfaced about the extent of hunger and malnutrition in the United States. The problem goes beyond the traditional poor (i.e., the elderly, the infirm, and single-parent families). Emphasis now centers around additional classes of poor people (e.g., children, the newly unemployed, the underemployed, the homeless, farmers, etc.). Many of these poor individuals or families, like their counterparts in the 1930s, have never been dependent on governmental assistance or private charity until now.

The insights and conclusions derived from this chapter are intended to help those at all levels who plan, implement, and evaluate domestic food programs as well as those who want a better understanding of the strengths and weaknesses of the system. It examines four areas: defining hunger, monitoring hunger, administering hunger, and determining responsibilities to alleviate hunger. It ends with an examination of the potential for large scale versus incremental changes in these areas as part of a long-term developmental strategy. This chapter helps the reader draw conclusions—based on political and financial realities—regarding the conditions needed to bring about changes and improvements.

Background and Developments

In order to understand hunger and domestic food assistance policy in the United States, one must first look at the dichotomy that has developed over its dual base: part in agriculture and part in welfare. An examination of agriculture's role in food assistance policy is necessary for several reasons. First, domestic food programs had their origins within the agricultural system, not as a responsibility of health care or welfare. Second, at the federal level, they remain under the administration of agriculture officials. The impact of this from a policy, administrative, and fiscal standpoint has important implications for the programs' success.[2]

The American people have always had a strong bond to agriculture. Not only is it seen as providing the necessities of life; it is also seen as a positive moral force in American values and development. Although political and economic matters have taken the country well beyond this stylized image, it still persists and is used by the agriculture community to maintain—some would say manipulate—support beyond that community's numerical strength.

This was shown in the 1930s, as the Department of Agriculture (USDA) took on additional responsibilities. While specialized interest groups within the department became advocates for price controls, farm subsidies, increased regulatory responsibility, and targeted support (e.g., soil conservation, rural electrification), they were either existing components of the agricultural establishment or new constituents who fit within the traditional mode of agriculture. Those who were hungry, especially those outside the farm community, were not part of this entrenched system.

Gradually, this began to change. After World War II, the federal government's limited domestic food assistance efforts expanded to include targeted support. The National School Lunch Program and Special Milk Program helped enhance the diets of the school-age population. During this time, the commodity assistance program continued to provide noncategorical nutritional support through a monthy food package of surplus commodities to individuals and families in need. Administration of these programs continued to stay within the Department of Agriculture, even after the creation of the Department of Health, Education, and Welfare in 1956.

Minimal regulatory requirements, small caseloads, a great deal of state flexibility in the programs' management, and common agreement among the long-standing congressional committees that had responsibility for these programs ensured continued support for agricultural interests and minimal food assistance benefits for the poor. As long as these programs continued to remain a small, unpublicized portion of the annual agricultural appropriation, no one seemed to notice or care.

The number of bills to establish an improved food assistance program network grew dramatically during the 1950s, but no concrete action took place. At the state level, resources went toward providing a share of the Aid to Families with Dependent Children (AFDC) grants. In addition, funds supported state-sponsored general relief programs as well as state and locally run institutions for the handicapped and infirm. Hunger continued to be a dormant issue and certainly not the basis for a modified type of federal, state, and local cooperative effort.

There were several reasons for this. On the political front, the traditional long-term control of agricultural interests by conservative, Southern Democrats continued to be a force in the House of Representatives. This group not only represented its rural farm constituents well, but also had the additional benefit of maintaining power through Congress's agricultural committees. Specialized coalitions formed with the business interests they monitored—and sometimes represented—as well as with administrators within the Department of Agriculture (Lowi, 1979). The specialized interests did not include members of consumer, environmental, or welfare organizations.

These newer constituents had not yet organized to any great extent. Inflation and unemployment remained constant and low and therefore caused little political demand for protection or change. Middle-class consumers continued to enjoy an uninterrupted supply of reasonably priced food. Attitudes toward the poor continued to center around the temporary nature of their problems, the bad luck or divine providence afflicting them, or what others perceived as their own laziness. Studies that did exist to examine the problem of hunger were from the late 1930s and early 1940s.

Gradually, the system that benefitted from and perpetuated this tight network faced external changes, some of which were beyond its control. In the agricultural sector, demographic studies showed more people moving from rural to urban areas. At the same time as the number of farms continued to decline, foreclosures and out-migrations were offset by the increased agricultural productivity that came about from USDA's research efforts.

From a political standpoint, new coalitions were forming to challenge the existing interest groups in American agriculture. Outside forces would eventually coalesce and seek to be part of—as well as, in some instances, control of—the growing portion of the farm agenda that related to food assistance policy and consumer interests. Public advocacy groups formed, or grew, to support the poor and to monitor the government's operation.

The period of benign neglect was now giving way to an era of expansion in social policy. For example, the second Food Stamp Program developed as a nutritional supplement, as a boon to agricultural and food service industry interests, and as an income support to low-income consumers (U.S. Congress, 1977).[3] In the area of categorical support, increased spending came about for the existing school lunch program. Additional aid followed (subsidized milk, breakfasts, meals for pre–school-age children and for school-age children during the summer months, and food vouchers for pregnant/lactating mothers and their infants).

To accomplish these ambitious goals, costs initially grew at a moderate level, with the federal government assuming the major portion of the financial responsibility. Increased expectations then led to additional expenditure of program time and money. As other programs relating to health and welfare grew, they also provided, a "spin-off" effect that benefitted nutrition assistance. But positive accomplishments could not ensure continuing success.

Even with the increased public attention and funding, there were problems in resolving the issue of domestic hunger. Nutrition monitoring was difficult. Critics did not feel the government had a right or responsibility to monitor and possibly control the types of food recipients purchased. Even if monitoring could be completed, the results of improved nutrition would not be immediately evident from a clinical standpoint.

Program administration, trying to keep up with rapid growth, sometimes resulted in program inconsistencies. For example, in the Food Stamp Program, one portion of the regulations stressed outreach while another stressed containment. Regulations were also interpreted beyond their original intent. At one point, the Food Stamp Program provided assistance to college students, who by asserting they were single-family households could meet food stamp eligibility requirements even though they remained under their parents' support.

The specifics from the preceding paragraph related to another problem, that of accountability, examples of which might be trafficking in food stamps, poor service at the client level, or meals for children that did not meet requirements. Documentation of these problems appeared not only in government audits and studies but also in newspaper headlines and news media exposures.

A final problem related to the changing perceptions of the program. For example, the act authorizing the Food Stamp Program—the Food Stamp Act of 1964—stated that Congress intended to *supplement* the diet of low-income Americans, not totally *take over* what had originally been an individual or family responsibility. Gradually, this concept broadened, but not without raising concerns among program critics who felt these programs were going beyond their original intent. Program proponents said the programs worked as Congress envisioned they would, reaching the needy and providing a nutritional cushion, especially in times of economic recession and high unemployment. All of these factors, plus the increasing cost of the programs at the federal, state, and local levels, brought about more calls for change.

During the Reagan era, the argument over the federal government's responsibilities in welfare policy continued to increase. The president and Congress battled over the size of domestic policy spending. Part of the problem related to the increasing budget deficits. Another part related to the administration's increased emphasis on military spending at the expense of domestic program spending. As the Reagan policymakers carried on—even with the large voter mandate of the second term—a spirit of accommodation, brought on by political realities, tempered the early determination of the president's appointees. But, the problems of hunger, whether real or perceived, would not go away.

President Reagan's proposals for a "revolution" in the area of welfare policy actually turned out to be a skirmish, even though they did have an impact in several areas. The first was financial. The Omnibus Reconciliation Act of 1981 made cuts in government that directly affected entitlement programs. Included in this was the Food Stamp Program, which saw 1981 spending drop from $10.6 billion to $10.2 because of ninety-five separate legislative changes. For the first time since its inception, the largest food assistance program took a cut in its rate of growth.

The second was political. Food assistance, which in the 1960s and 1970s was a "sacred cow," was now extremely vulnerable to attack from critics' charges over unmet goals, as well as fraud, waste, and abuse. But despite these charges, programs were not dismantled as part of the president's New Federalism proposals to turn back welfare policy responsibility to states and localities. The Bush administration followed the course set by its predecessor.

While there have not been massive calls for administrative realignment and attacks on the funding base, food assistance programs are in a period of maturity and no growth. There are no major new funding or administrative initiatives. Increased attention and, in some cases, action is coming from the state and local levels and is directed towards refining existing policies. Efforts are also being undertaken by private sector and nonprofit organizations, but these are specialized efforts and not a massive realignment. Therefore, if domestic food assistance policy is in a mature stage in its development but the problems still exist or are, according to some, getting worse, the next stage should be to evaluate the circumstances and devise realistic alternatives.

Present Situation

The historical development presented in the previous section highlights the growth and leveling off of government support for domestic food assistance programs in America. Before the momentum, not only in a financial sense but also in a political sense, can be regenerated, there are several conditions that must be understood. One aspect relates food assistance policy to the overall social service environment. Food assistance policy faces old and new sources of competition for the taxpayers' dollars and the public's attention. When hunger became a "hot" social and political cause in the 1960s, it was a highly visible issue. This was a time when politicians and the voting public were willing to support initiation of new efforts and expansion of existing ones. In the early 1990s, and looking into the immediate future, existing sources of competition (e.g., health care, education, housing) are fighting for a portion of the fiscal pie which now may grow smaller. At the same time, new sources of competition (e.g., AIDS research and prevention, environmental concerns, rejuvenating the national infrastructure) compete for attention and money.

A second aspect relates to food programs becoming victims of their own success. The problems of poverty and malnutrition that were documented in the 1960s showed improvement in the 1970s. But as programs grew and successes were highlighted, so did expectations. In the 1980s—even during the economic boom—not everyone prospered, and additional classes of need grew (i.e., children, single-parent families). In some respects, the lofty goals of food assistance programs and the political rhetoric to eradicate hunger by a certain targeted deadline were unrealistic to begin with.

A third aspect of food assistance policy within the overall human service network is its top down approach in the policy setting agenda from the federal government. Since the 1930s and especially since the 1960s, it has been the federal government that has taken the initiative and the main financial responsibility. States and localities share part of the administrative burden and, in some instances, have spent additional local level resources to supplement programs. But in most instances, it is the federal government that has mandated action and funded initiatives. Proponents of this approach argue that it has been necessary, based on the states' and localities' traditional poor record of accomplishments. But leadership and responsibility must be shared if federal mandates have reached the limits of what they can accomplish.

In looking beyond the current constraints, there are options for change and refinement to the current level of food assistance policy. Some would argue for cutbacks to existing support mechanisms not only in a financial but also in an administrative sense, based on the perceived failings of the current system. Others would call for a massive fiscal and administrative assault to again work toward eradicating hunger in America. Still others would argue for a "do nothing" approach, based on the fact that even if programs are not fully funded, they provide an adequate safety net or supplement to other types of assistance.

Before accepting any of the positions presented above, policy planners and implementers need to examine specific parts of the problem. The following sections examine four potential areas as a starting point: defining hunger, monitoring hunger, administering hunger, and determining responsibilities to alleviate hunger.

Defining Hunger

From a clinical standpoint, hunger is defined as "the physiological need to eat" as opposed to appetite, which is "the desire to eat" (Whitney and Nunnelly, 1981, 283). The former is an "inborn instinct," while the latter is "a learned response to food." But this is only one narrow definition and it is not a sufficient one on which to base policy changes.

Another broader aspect is the economic definition of hunger. This is the inability to purchase and maintain a sufficient diet. But determining who has that inability is not always easy. In the early 1960s, at the outset of the War on Poverty, policymakers had little data about poverty, much less who was hungry. For example, the President's Council of Economic Advisors, in its 1964 annual report, stated that the elderly headed one-third of the nation's poor households (i.e., with $3,000 or less in annual income, regardless of family size). Two years later, the same organization reported to the President that children were the most numerous group of poor persons in America (43 percent of the total) and that the aged had been only 16 percent of the 1964 poor population. This example highlights the problems of inconsistent data and poor reporting. It characterizes initial efforts to define the economic impacts of poverty.

To take the poverty problem one step further and determine its impact on hunger and malnutrition, policy planners attempted to include food purchasing power in an official poverty index. Food cost statistics measured by the Department of Agriculture's Economy Food Diet were to be the basis. The Social Security Administration devised a way to measure poverty by pricing a minimal amount of goods and services. One-third of the amount went toward food purchases.

In attempting to quantify hunger, numerous problems arise. Hunger in the United States is different from its counterpart in Third World countries where such diseases as kwashiorkor and marasmus are clear signs of physical wasting. Extreme hunger of that type hardly occurs in modern-day America, but malnutrition can and does affect the quality and duration of life as well as the ability to learn. Therefore, this leads to a second step, developing mechanisms to monitor hunger.

Monitoring Hunger

Scientific methods do exist to determine nutritional status. When nutrients go into the body, the amount of intake can be calculated. After digestion and absorption into the bloodstream, the nutrient level of blood can be measured. Unused nutrients can also be measured through urine analysis. And if tissues of the body are able to store excess amounts of the nutrient, the storage of the nutrient can be measured. The use of dietary histories, clinical tests, physical exams, anthropomorphic measurements, and comparisons with similar subjects are methods to quantify the effects of hunger and malnutrition.

On an aggregate level, analysts have developed generalized statistics relating to hunger (i.e., decreases in nutrition-related diseases, increased-height statistics for children, longer life spans, and lowered infant mortality rates for children) as signs of progress. But developing this type of monitoring system on a mass basis may be expensive and does not always result in clear indications, whether on an individual or mass basis.

The issue of clarity is difficult to achieve when efforts to quantify hunger in America are constrained by other factors besides cost. Specialists in the field of nutrition science do not agree on specific standards. One example of this is the Dietary Guidelines for Americans. Published by the Department of Health and Human Services (DHHS) and USDA, they are used as an education tool, but stop short of recommending specific target levels. Therefore, if experts in the field of nutrition are unable to agree, laymen and women, especially when poorly informed, cannot be expected to know.

Even if an exact definition and minimum standards as well as a testing mechanism could be agreed upon, providing that information to the public is the next hurdle. Marketing efforts by the private sector may be in conflict with proper nutritional guidelines disseminated by government agencies. Sometimes the commercial message is targeted to those with the highest level of nutritional and financial risk. The problem may be compounded in the home by poor preparation and storage facilities or by higher prices at the local grocery store. At the individual level, the constraints may result from poor health, genetic factors, personality traits, and lack of ongoing access to nutrition education.

A final concern involves the timeliness of the data. While up-to-date information is available on the economic health of the United States (e.g., flash estimates of the data on the gross national product and a cost of living index), there is no comparable, monthly information on its nutritional health or the health status of specific segments of its citizens, from a geographic, age, income, and so on, perspective.

Government efforts to determine nutritional standards took on a greater urgency during the period of rapid growth in food assistance programs in the late 1960s. Congress directed the Department of Health, Education, and Welfare (HEW) to examine hunger and health-related problems in 1969. This resulted in the Ten State Nutrition Survey. Two years later, President Nixon directed HEW to set up the National Nutrition Surveillance Survey which would provide detailed insight into America's hunger and malnutrition. The objectives of this survey became incorporated into the first National Health and Nutrition Examination Survey, conducted from 1971 to 1974.

But while these efforts provided additional nutrition-oriented information, they did not resolve the ongoing debate for a continuous update on the nutritional and health status of the American public, much less those in poverty. In 1977, Congress directed USDA and DHHS to submit a comprehensive, nationwide nutrition monitoring system. But implementation plans dragged on; and by the election of Ronald Reagan, a plan was still not ready. Even though coalitions (i.e., professional, scientific, consumer, religious, etc.) formed to support the issue; even though the mechanisms to gather and evaluate data had improved; even though Congress made its intent known; and even though the President's 1984 Task Force on Hunger Policy recommended a form of nutrition monitoring, the concept still did not gather enough political strength to become enacted into law.

Government efforts thus far provide a starting point but not an ending point. While these efforts have been instrumental, but not necessarily definitive, in quantifying nutritional needs and the requirements of hunger and malnutrition, there may be other alternatives. Private and nonprofit sector efforts provide another option. Efforts by nongovernmental organizations to quantify hunger and to define nutritional risk have, in some instances, been useful mechanisms to support government efforts and, in some cases, have acted as a counterpoint to government policy. At other times, they point the way toward changing the direction of hunger policies.

A visible example of the former was a series of clinical surveys supported by the Field Foundation in the 1960s. Survey researchers went to low-income areas of the American South and Appalachia to quantify the extent and impact of hunger in rural areas. The study results were widely publicized throughout the news media and became the basis for influencing governmental hunger policy in the 1960s. Clinical evidence showed the shortcomings of the existing policies. When the Field Foundation researchers replicated their study in the same areas in 1979, they were able to report dramatic improvements in children's anemia and growth statistics (Kotz, 1979). The impact of government intervention was seen as the main variable, so much so that some claimed the hunger problem in America was on the way to being solved.

But the alleged "solution" was short lived. As program growth slackened, as economic conditions worsened, and as poverty became more visible in the 1980s, a growth industry developed over studies purporting to review the problem and resolve the issue. Some studies attempted to quantify the hunger problem. For example, in 1985, the Physicians' Task Force on Hunger reported that approximately 20 million Americans did not have access to sufficient resources to maintain proper nutrition. Other efforts tried to quantify the locations where hunger existed. Still other efforts sought to quantify the problem for certain segments of the nutritionally needy (e.g., the rural poor, children/infants, the elderly, the working poor, etc.). In addition there were a burgeoning number of state commissions and reports, as well as localized efforts, that highlighted the concerns at different levels.

Several general themes underline these efforts. They attempt to demonstrate to legislators and the general public that the initial gains made during the 1960s are no longer in place. Decreases in federal funding, inflation, high unemployment, and continued uncertainty over the federal government's role have all taken their toll. Specifically, they point to government rules and insensitivity as the cause of purported increases in hunger. They also provide an alternative to those who conclude enough is being done to resolve hunger and that initiatives from government and other sectors (e.g., corporate, nonprofit, and individual) must take on additional responsibility.

Critics of these studies, commissions, and reports blast their motives and methodology. They begin by questioning assumptions. They discredit "field work" that is ambiguous and incomplete. They dispute the alleged lack of success of governmental efforts and claims that increased public-sector financial support will resolve the problem. They highlight the findings of evaluators (e.g., the General Accounting Office) who contradict the results of some research efforts. They accuse their opponents of creating issues where none previously existed in order to make political statements. And most serious of all, they claim that their critics divert political energy away from more pressing needs or create the climate for a backlash which works against resolving the real aspects of the problem.

All of this provides lively reading and press coverage but does not resolve the problem of hunger. Nor does it always result in more innovative responses beyond the usual calls for increased federal spending. Controversy over nutrition monitoring has forced a change in direction in the way analysts examine hunger. The rudimentary clinical investigations that characterized research in the early part of the century are now being joined by economic, political, and social discussions and evaluations of the problem. But even the best analysis of the problem will not bring about change if programs are poorly administered.

Administering Hunger

A third problem area relates to the resources used to implement laws and policy directives relating to hunger. In the 1960s, guidance for a national hunger policy developed around executive orders from the executive branch, laws from the legislative branch, and policy guidance from the federal, state, and local bureaucracies. Court decisions supplemented the third area.

Gradually, all three levels of the federal government became more specific in their demands. In some instances, they wanted to improve and increase the benefits. In other instances, they wanted to curb abuses. In order to fulfill the policy mandates, existing bureaucratic systems grew and new ones formed. But while the initial focus was on program growth and the later focus was on program accountability, there was very little attention paid to monitoring program administration. Even as advocacy groups focused more public attention on hunger, the emphasis was usually on the need for more dollars and government resources, not on using existing resources more efficiently. There are several reasons why policy planners failed to stress the importance of administration in their planning efforts.

At the executive level, this sometimes resulted from mixed signals. For example, during the Nixon administration, the president's commitment to federal support of food assistance was shown through such visible means as a White House Conference on Hunger and the establishment of a federal agency to deal with the problem. But at the same time, as he expressed the federal commitment, the president also sought to shift the responsibility to the states and localities who had a poor or nonexistent record for administrative initiatives. This contradiction continued during the Ford administration but remained dormant under the Carter administration. President Reagan, on the other hand, provided very clear signals. From his viewpoint, over-regulation by the federal bureaucracy should be replaced by creativity at the local administrative level.

While the executive branch has not always been clear or realistic, neither has the legislative branch. For example, in strengthening the federal nature of the Food Stamp Program and increasing its complexity, Congress sometimes worked against itself and its stated goals. The Food Stamp Act of 1964 declared a national policy "to raise the levels of nutrition among low income households." Emphasis in the early years of the Food Stamp Program was on program growth, which meant increased federal spending. While trying to bring about change through spending and legislative fiat, legislators sometimes left out an important partner in the implementation process: local level administrators. States and localities, crucial elements in the delivery of service benefits, were not always able to keep up with the changes or did not have the necessary resources. Time frames were not always realistic. The results neither alleviated hunger nor improved the circumstances of the hungry.

In addition to being unclear, policy direction from top level policy administrators is sometimes conflicting. This results in another constraint to effective administration. Food assistance policy began as a market for agricultural products, expanded into a welfare focus and, in more recent efforts, is moving towards a health care focus.[4] Which of these should take precedence and to what degree as hunger policy matures? Setting up and maintaining a government administrative apparatus becomes even more challenging when the system is required to take on additional responsibilities beyond the hunger focus. As an example, federal and state food assistance administrators in the Food Stamp Program have, in the past, taken on responsibility to implement a workfare requirement, which traditionally has been a Department of Labor responsibility.

Administrative capabilities and levels of responsibility at the working level of the bureaucracy are an internal set of circumstances that can also impede the effective administration of hunger policy. Program administrators may be unwilling or unable to reach implementation goals. Besides the causes listed in the previous paragraphs, this may come about from inertia due to size, an unwillingness to accept change, or it may come from insufficient resources to solve the problem. In this set of circumstances, the problem moves from a policy issue to a managerial issue.

The managerial concerns are heightened as the bureaucracy changes in size to meet the potential or existing demand. Bureaucracies are now struggling to deal with down-sizing as the focus moves from growth to retrenchment. As they seek to restructure, the focus is less on policy mandates and more on effective operations (e.g., use of computers). It becomes more difficult to develop a constituency to pay for change in the current economic climate, even if funds go for more efficient administration and not program growth. Legislative and executive branch policymakers may not support long-term operational improvements with the same zeal they exhibit when supporting program growth. Nor will it come from the public, especially after hearing about instances of abuse from media sources. Therefore, a final step in examining the current hunger policy situation is to examine levels of responsibility.

Determining Responsibilities to Alleviate Hunger

Hunger, like other public policy issues, is also dependent on public understanding and support. Even if sufficient information is available, the food assistance program network still faces the broader issue raised by the political culture. In food assistance policy, this broadens the definition of hunger beyond the clinical and economic meanings that have already been presented. It means perceiving hunger in a political sense. The definition moves beyond the individual's role to note society's role in responding to hunger needs. An example of this definition might be: the absence of commitment, either by the public or private sector, to alleviate and eradicate causes of hunger and malnutrition within society.

Like the clinical and economic definitions, this definition is also subject to interpretation and confusion. Does society have a moral obligation to ensure the nutritional well-being of all of its citizens? Or of those who are ''hungry''? If so, how can this be accomplished, especially if the clinical and economic definitions are imprecise? The problem is compounded when limited resources are available, resources that must compete with other governmental agendas, both inside and outside the field of social welfare. Also, this definition is limited because it does not include the responsibility of the individual and the family (Mead, 1986). Nor does it speak to the nature and magnitude of the problem itself. Is the adult rational and responsible? For example, if drugs and alcohol intervene, no income is enough to ensure adequate nutrition. In that instance, poverty and malnutrition may be a symptom and not a cause of the problem.

Conservative policymakers, especially during the Reagan administration, raised this issue. Their point is that resources (i.e., food stamps, subsidized meals for school-age children) are available. Information on diet and proper nutrition is available to the entire population not only from government but also from private sector sources. In addition, supplemental medical care and nutritional assistance are available to the poor, the young, and the elderly and indirectly support the middle class as well. Therefore, they feel the government (preferably at the level closest to the general population), the private sector (through ''privatization''), the family, and the individual all have a co-responsibility.

Critics of this philosophy believe that it is unrealistic to call for decreased government involvement and increased privatization or self-help efforts. They contend the government has made a vast policy and financial commitment based on a documented and perceived need. They contend the financial returns would not be there if the public sector were not involved. To them, resources are insufficient and nutrition-related information may be misleading. Placing more responsibility on the low-income family or individual, who does not have the resources and is perhaps suffering from other problems, is not a realistic alternative. According to this line of reasoning, the public sector, in defining the political culture, has a moral obligation to help those in need. Therefore, hunger advocates call for increased government support of nutrition policies as an ethical and a practical response.

The perceptions of hunger are especially important because they reflect on the formation and implementation of a national hunger policy. The evidence concerning nutritional status of poor Americans continued to mount in the 1950s. When plans for a revised Food Stamp Program got under way in the 1960s, there was discussion and debate over developing and including nutritional-risk criteria. Instead, planners at USDA decided to develop a link between income and hunger in determining eligibility. Financial and resource limits again became the acceptable ways to define hunger. Nutrition criteria were only indirectly used in quantifying the eligibility criteria, as shown by the development and controversy surrounding USDA's Thrifty Food Plan.

From an administrative standpoint, this made some programs easier to control, if they were non-categorically based like food stamps. It also related to hunger's gaining momentum on the poverty agenda. But on the negative side, it aligned some food assistance efforts as poverty programs, not as health maintenance programs (such as WIC) or generic support (such as Social Security). The nutrition link was also deemphasized because the role of controlling food intake and diet was not regulated. In this way, no one's interests were threatened. The client could pick any food-related item even if its nutritional content was dubious. The agricultural community did not initially encounter limits on the products that were sold with stamps.[5] And retailers did not face the administrative hurdles at the check-out counter of sorting out noneligible food/nonfood items from acceptable nutritious items.

Even though it might have been opportune in the postwar period, a formal, national nutrition policy—which would include a monitoring component—still has not come about. Part of the answer can be traced to perceptions toward self-reliance and government support efforts that characterized America's development. A second part related to domestic activities to combat hunger that were already set up. Given these circumstances, the next step then becomes to develop mechanisms that will improve the existing hunger policy mechanisms.

Policy Options

The four areas presented in the previous section now become the focus to build toward future success. In some instances, the policy options have a clear focus that can be delineated by a short- or long-term focus or by an incremental or massive amount of change. In other instances, the policy options have a much broader focus and are the subject of intense debate.

Combining the Definition of Hunger and Its Monitoring

Policymakers, going back to the 1930s, wanted a clear definition of hunger. As the section on "Defining Hunger" has already shown, that is not an easy goal to accomplish. Clinical definitions, economic implications, and determining levels of responsibility complicate the issue. Information that correlates income to nutritional well-being, relates poor nutrition to health problems, and results in a system to monitor these on an ongoing basis has not been achieved.

A national prototype survey instrument resulting in timely information on at-risk portions of the population would go a long way to improve the situation of defining hunger and determining its extent. The benefits would be twofold. Comparable data would be developed at the local level to deal with local problems. This could then be aggregated at the regional and national level to produce data on food consumption and nutritional status. The process would resolve some of the confusion and inconsistency that characterizes the existing setup.

While this might be a noble goal, there are numerous questions that would need to be resolved. Even if sufficient funding were to be made available, important issues would need to be raised concerning the extent of monitoring. Should it just be related to the clinical aspects of hunger? For young children, growth measurements are inexpensive, easy, and sensitive indicators. For school-aged children, questionnaires, school performance, and participation in school food programs can provide insight. For adults, income and access to services can be measurements to monitor. Should these be correlated with economic considerations, both relating to the individual and to the government? Should the political variable (i.e., spending, outreach, administrative efforts) be included in the monitoring mechanism? The most recent national legislative proposals—none of which have made it beyond the committee process—deal with evaluating the clinical efforts. Even if passed, these proposals might not be sufficient to guarantee an adequate mechanism to exactly quantify hunger and result in more public and government support.

Therefore, supporters of hunger policy need to devise a two-part initiative. First, they must continue to demand government support in monitoring hunger, while understanding the limitations of federal efforts. This first option provides the direction for policy refinements, but it should not be the only barometer used to focus on changes. Second, hunger policy planners must look for additional creative ways, at other levels, which point to the direction for improvements.

The following example shows excellent accomplishments not only in its results, but also in its long-term potential. In 1986 a pilot project, funded in part by the Primerica Foundation and administered by the Connecticut Association for Human Services, selected a low-income neighborhood in New Haven, Connecticut, and developed a national prototype to identify hunger and nutritionally at-risk children. It is called the Community Childhood Hunger Identification Project (CCHIP) (Melmed, 1987).

Instead of reviewing the problem from a macro standpoint, the CCHIP surveyed a total of 403 families with 1,139 children. The detailed questions measured the extent and potential for hunger by gathering information on the following topics: "lack of resources to obtain food; food shortages in the household; changes in adult food intake; reliance on limited number of foods; changes in children's food intake; reported hunger; socio-demographic characteristics of the household; program usage; shopping habits; resources available to obtain food; and coping strategies when food is difficult to obtain" (Melmed, 1987). The CCHIP examined clinical, economic, and political aspects of the problem.

The benefits of this type of approach are numerous. Instead of dealing with the entire population, the strategy provides tangible, quantifiable evidence of a local problem. With this information, government officials and policy advocates were able to adopt specific interventions to meet local needs. In the case of the initial phase (i.e., the New Haven study) of the CCHIP project, the outcome resulted in the initiation of the School Breakfast Program in all of the city's elementary schools. Additional city and state funding went into the breakfast program. Private donations to existing food pantries also increased. The dimension and response to the problem became easier to handle when reviewed and acted upon from a local perspective.

On a broader scale, the CCHIP effort attracted additional corporate funding so that it could be refined and replicated. A field manual was prepared to plan the survey, develop the survey sample, train interviewers, and collect/analyze data. While the New Haven Mayor's Task Force on Hunger examined other low-income areas in that city, a national effort continued to examine the problem in other geographic locales.

The long-term implications of this type of monitoring approach are also important. The historical review of hunger policy in this chapter shows that while progress has been made from government intervention, all of the problems have not been solved. Quantifying hunger so organizations can develop a proper response is still a major issue. In this instance, a partnership of corporations and nonprofit interests works to resolve the policy concern. Using a bottom-up approach, CCHIP developed a combination of clinical and economic statistics at the local level to challenge those who claim hunger cannot be quantified in the United States.

In addition to quantifying hunger and pointing the way toward policy improvements, nutrition monitoring can also provide benefits in other, related areas. One specific is nutrition education, which can be refined to meet the needs of the hungry. The benefits go beyond recipients' improved use and storage of food resources to include their increased knowledge of health care issues and prevention information. Monitoring also works to resolve criticism of accountability since the education effort can include food purchasing practices.

On a general level, efforts such as CCHIP may be an additional resource to generate the political will necessary to sustain food assistance programs in a time of retrenchment. This should not be used to decrease government efforts, but to provide focus to these initiatives. Monitoring can strengthen the consensus between the program's two major policy constituents (i.e., agriculture and welfare) and building in the third (i.e., health care). It can strengthen the administrative focus between the federal, state, and local levels by highlighting improvements, as well as areas needing further research. And it can provide the general public with an additional accountability mechanism, through an improved format to judge the program's success.

Enhancing the Administrative Structure

If defining and monitoring hunger are imperative to bringing about constructive changes in the food assistance environment, administering programs effectively becomes another logical step. Except for study by academics and review by professional evaluators, this crucial policy area rarely receives public attention except when something goes drastically wrong.

The recommendations presented in the next several paragraphs focus on refinements at the federal level. This does not mean that economies and efficiencies should be limited to that level. Rather, because of the top down focus of hunger-related assistance in the post–World War II era, the federal bureaucracy becomes a logical first step toward improvements.[6]

The following ideas are divided into short-term and long-term implementation strategies. They also contain specific and generic recommendations for initiating change. And each is based on three goals: (1) improved effectiveness of the programs, resulting in better service to the client; (2) cost efficiency, resulting in higher administrative costs in some areas and lower costs in others; and (3) career impact on the civil service, which must accept and implement the change. Before presenting the specifics of the proposed organizational enhancements, it is important to define the existing organizational mechanism.

The current system has built up in the postwar era as Congress enacted programs or modified existing ones. The federal bureaucracy (i.e., the Food and Nutrition Service of the Department of Agriculture) works to fulfill their mandate through an administrative staff in Washington, seven regional offices, and a series of field offices (located in larger metropolitan areas or state capitals) throughout the country.[7] These offices interact with state level administrators, who in turn coordinate their activities with local-level counterparts.[8] In addition to the formal federal, state, and local administrative efforts, food assistance policy is implemented and monitored by advocacy groups and private sector efforts, but the overwhelming amount of resources and effort comes from the public sector (Manning, 1989). The geographic coverage of these efforts includes not only the fifty states and the District of Columbia but also the commonwealth and territorial entities in the Caribbean and the Pacific Basin.

The first specific short-term recommendation focuses on the headquarters level of the Food and Nutrition Service. While many internal areas might be streamlined, the following is an example of developing innovation. When food assistance programs were envisioned and initiated, there was a need for large policy development staffs to write regulations, prepare policy guidance, develop informational material, and monitor operations. As programs have matured in their growth cycles, the responsibilities of mandating direction from the federal level have slackened, but the large policy staffs remain.

Therefore, it becomes necessary to examine options to combine the regulatory writing staffs of various programs, the monitoring staffs, and the ongoing administrative support organizations into centralized units. The benefits of this approach would be administrative efficiencies, hopefully leading to cost reductions and more creativity, based on the employees' broader perspective. The negative aspects of this might entail opposition from career employees, especially those in middle management. But this could be resolved by initiating a gradual phase-in of this proposal (which would protect the grade structure of the existing employees), developing an enhanced grade structure (which could lead to better professional development), and promoting more personal job satisfaction (which would come about from more diversified job assignments and possibly greater levels of responsibility).

A second specific, short-term step might be to rethink and reorganize the concept of regional offices.[9] When programs were growing in the 1960s and 1970s as a result of the new initiatives and increased regulatory activity, the need for five—and eventually seven—regional centers made sense. Now that food assistance programs have moved from an initial implementation to a more mature implementation phase, regional and field office work loads need to be reexamined. One option is to return to the original structure of five regional offices. Another option is to decrease the number to three. At the same time, there could be a corresponding increase in the level of responsibility in the field locations. The goal would be twofold: to enhance the monitoring aspect of hunger policy and to enhance the support aspect at the local level.

The positive aspects of the approach are a more streamlined system of providing services and an eventual reduction in administration costs (staffing, travel, etc.) especially if the responsibilities of the field offices are broadened. As the layers of bureaucracy decreased, the corresponding goal of improving timeliness and quality of service at the client level would result.

The negative aspect of this approach relates to the short-term potential dislocation of the staff. As in any shifting of administrative responsibilities, program planners might build incentives through a "grandfather clause" to protect the grades of existing employees, promoting the potential for career enhancement in a more focused administrative structure, as well as the potential for greater personal satisfaction.

Because administrative structures are sometimes slow or hostile to change, especially after they have become entrenched, it is also important to recognize and deal with internal impediments as well as devising solutions. Skillful policy planners will incorporate several short-term, general changes as part of any overall reorganization effort. One involves staff incentives (mentioned earlier) to allay concerns and point the direction for future career development. The second involves union involvement to build understanding and resolve potential problems early on. Setting up a system to deal with internal concerns is imperative, since top level political appointees in an agency are temporary administrators, while career civil servants are permanent members of the team.

Overall, the Food and Nutrition Service has a positive record in employee development. To build on this, the agency might expand the use of Intergovernmental Personnel Act assignments and relate career promotion at certain higher levels to those who have multi-program experience from different geographic perspectives.[10] For those beginning in the organization, a generic entry level policy analyst position (replacing the current "Food Program Specialist" position) would require multi-program and geographic diversity as part of the employee's career development track. These types of efforts would build diversity to support the streamlined organizational structure.

The Food and Nutrition Service provides a useful laboratory for change for the ideas presented here, as well as other innovations. While it is part of the Department of Agriculture's structure, the agency is beyond the traditional agriculture establishment. Even though the FNS annual funding request takes up a major portion of the annual agricultural budget request, the agency's goals are not totally dependent upon support from old-line interests. Also, FNS is not part of the large Department of Health and Human Service bureaucracy, which might make the potential for innovation and change even more difficult to initiate.

Therefore, leaders within the system have an excellent opportunity to implement several far-reaching structural changes that could result in improved service to the client, enhanced administrative capabilities, and better use of existing financial resources. The long-term impacts of this relate directly to achieving an enhanced administrative structure and also to the fourth criterion for change presented earlier in this chapter: developing responsibilities. In assuming leadership through administrative reform, even if on an incremental basis, the federal government exercises the option to make programs better, not necessarily bigger. The achievements brought about might be used in other federal agencies, as well as state and local counterparts, which would directly support the client base in other areas of welfare reform. But the most important long-range impact of this might be to restore public confidence and lead to demands for more financial resources to alleviate hunger. In this way, the agencies that initiated change in the 1960s would again become leaders in taking on responsibility in the 1990s and beyond.

Building Areas of Responsibility

Earlier in this chapter, I presented the need to determine responsibilities in order to obtain improvements in the battle to alleviate hunger. During the 1960s and 1970s, that focus was never in doubt. While acknowledging problems, most theorists did not question the overall federal focus of the programs, and politicians were unwilling to forgo a source of power, despite the image problems that indirectly reflected back on them. Since the presidential elections of 1980 and 1984, that outlook has changed. During the 1980s, political analysts debated the validity of the federal government's responsibility while, at the same time, working to devise alternatives of their own. This debate over welfare policy reform, of which food assistance is a part, is one way to focus on the levels of responsibility.

One example of this new breed of political writers is Charles Murray, whose book, *Losing Ground American Social Policy, 1950–1980,* has been the subject of widespread debate (Murray, 1984). According to Murray, as welfare programs came into existence and then expanded, poor people no longer felt compelled to go out on their own or to improve their situations since the federal government had become their caretaker. The support provided beyond individual and family ties caused an abdication of personal responsibility. This was a rational response based on the lenient attitude of program administrators, educators, law enforcement officials, and others who worked with the poor. As programs grew, the constituency of advocates, along with supporters in Congress, demanded additional benefits without requiring corresponding accountability of the individual or at the program level. To bolster his theory, Murray examined welfare benefits during the 1970s and concluded that it did not pay for poor people to work.

The implications of this attack on federal responsibility in American social policy are important, because they coincided with the Reagan administration's plans for welfare reform in general and food assistance policy reforms in particular. Because of budget limitations, a continuing deficit, and disappointment over the accomplishments of welfare initiatives and reforms, Murray's proposals join with those of conservatives who wish to place food assistance policy on a more local level or beyond the public sector. And it has allowed conservative thinkers a chance to go on the offensive with their alternatives in a policy area that traditionally was a monopoly of liberal reformers. The counterattack is based on the premise that conservative alternatives are fairer to those in need and to those who pay the bills.

Critics of the Murray thesis and its conclusions take issue not only with his interpretation of statistics but also with his recommendations for changing the system. At the other extreme of this debate in determining policy options is one of the most supportive works on the overall impact of the social welfare programs, John E. Schwarz's *America's Hidden Success: A Reassessment of Twenty Years of Public Policy* (Schwarz, 1988). Schwarz also utilizes statistical evidence but concludes that governmental efforts were successful in reducing poverty while not reducing incentives and while keeping waste to a minimum. In the area of nutrition, he shows "the government's nutritional programs were almost fully effective in reducing flagrant malnutrition among Americans in locales of concentrated poverty across the nation" (Schwarz, 1988, 45). Schwarz argues that these improvements could not have been achieved only by private sector support, especially given demographic changes (i.e., the maturing of the "baby boomer" generation and more women entering the work force). To him, federal government responsibility in initiating new programs and expanding government has been (and continues to be) America's "hidden success."

Proponents of the Schwarz thesis call for continuing the federal focus of domestic food assistance. Part of the money would be used to expand program benefits, while other parts would expand areas where funding has been cut (e.g., outreach, nutrition education, special demonstration projects). But political will constrains the resources available for food assistance in relation to other social welfare issues and to competing government responsibilities. The potential for vast sums of additional funding for existing programs is as unrealistic as Charles Murray's call for a complete withdrawal to a local level focus.

While policy analysts argue about the validity of the welfare system, there are others searching for ways to improve it. Stuart Butler and Anna Kondratas in their book, *Out of the Poverty Trap: A Conservative Strategy for Welfare Reform*, follow the lead of Charles Murray in forming a conservative agenda where conservatives, until the 1980s, have rarely placed their emphasis (Butler and Kondratas, 1987). Their specific response is to rethink the process in several ways. For example, greater client control should be offered through the use of vouchers or direct cash payments. People in need will then be able to take control of their own circumstances. On a broader scale, they call for "welfare opportunity zones . . . to foster welfare policy experimentation" (Butler and Kondratas, 1987, 91-92, 238). For states with the least resources and greatest need, the authors propose "fiscal capacity grants" to supplement local efforts.

While conservatives are starting to set up their own agenda, liberals are building and refining the agenda where they have been predominant for a long period of time. David Ellwood represents a refined liberal position in his book, *Poor Support Poverty in the American Family* (Ellwood, 1988). While disagreeing with conservatives that the welfare system is the villain, he concurs that the system has not met expectations and is in need of massive change. Ellwood devises a broad framework—instead of a specific agenda—that is built around individual "autonomy, the work ethic, the primacy of the family and the desire for community" (Ellwood, 1988, 241). The outcome would be important in two dramatic ways. It would build the lives and the self-esteem of the poor themselves. And it would rebuild confidence among the general public that welfare support is accomplishing its goal. While not dealing specifically with food assistance policy, Ellwood's completed overhaul of the social service system would include food assistance support as part of a larger transitional welfare program.

It is interesting to note how the views of both conservative and liberal analysts converge. Both sides call for changes and, in some instances, radical realignments. Ellwood is certainly realistic when he points out that the bigger the proposed change, the less likely it is to be adopted. Both sides agree that the federal government cannot define all of the questions and does not have all of the answers. The result is a call for "empowerment" at the local level.

Perhaps the answer to this problem lies in redefining the federal government's responsibility and broadening it to include other entities. To accomplish this, the federal government could begin by providing more direction in monitoring hunger efforts, as highlighted earlier in this chapter. This, in turn, would help define the extent of the problem. A second step would be to focus on administrative improvements, also highlighted earlier in this chapter. This would give policymakers an opportunity to delineate their goals to employees, to other agencies, to the public, and to clients. It would signal the intention to continue improving efforts to combat hunger. In this way, defining hunger, monitoring hunger, and administering hunger all build to determine responsibility.

A final step would be to focus financial resources not toward existing programs but toward "hunger entrepreneurship" efforts (such as the CCHIP study). This does not negate the federal responsibility; it opens the federal government up to partnerships with the public and private sectors to determine new and additional refinements to improve ways to alleviate hunger. Building responsibility then becomes a joint effort. The long-term results of this will be creative new solutions for resolving hunger as well as increased public confidence and support for the ongoing battle.

Conclusions

After sixty years of growth, since the New Deal's politics, the American people are now being forced to confront what they want—and are willing to pay for—from government, whether it is at the federal, state, or local level. What is the appropriate role for state government, the federal government, localities, as well as the private sector? Beyond the ability to pay lies another question of equal importance. Who has the best capability to do the job? And what is the best utilization of resources?

The answers will be found not only in financial and personnel resources but also where the ideas and creativity lie. The theoretical and practical implications of this chapter will not solve the debate. They should, however, offer insight to those who are looking for alternatives and solutions.

In developing strategies for the 1990s and beyond, a more realistic alternative is to develop an incremental approach to problem solving. This is important for several reasons. As food assistance programs—like many of the War on Poverty counterparts—have grown, they have become more entrenched not only in the growth of budget but also in an administrative sense. A whole generation of federal, state, and local administrators has developed career and growth potential around the fortunes of these programs. Specialized interest groups also see their careers closely tied to these programs. As the historical portion of this chapter has shown, a whole body of regulations and policy guidance has been set up to ensure that the programs continue to operate. According to some, the placement of food assistance programs in the agriculture hierarchy, as opposed to a health care or social service orientation at the federal level, has been a blessing. Food assistance programs do not become minor line items in the human service budget agenda, and they provide agricultural interests with a greater link to the general public.

In rethinking the motives and operation of food assistance policy, there are several criteria that must be met. The first is development of a common ground to move beyond the current system. If a specific national consensus is not politically or economically possible—or necessarily desirable—the alternative is to devise a series of incremental strategies. This will set goals for improving nutrition for various at-risk portions of the population.

As a part of program flexibility to develop new options, there must also be administrative flexibility to refine existing ones. At the federal level, this involves a refocus in perspective. Flexibility involves change, and change does not always provide the expected or desired results. Therefore, while requiring accountability for the use of federal funds, federal administrators will have to accommodate a state's wish for increased flexibility. At the state level, flexibility entails additional responsibility. Part of the innovation may mean higher costs, which would now become a state burden. Another part would entail increased political and public scrutiny.

The final consideration—and the most important—is leadership. Leadership and innovation should not be relegated to just one government sector. Instead, it should be a partnership that shares ideas and offers flexibility, as highlighted throughout this chapter. In limited instances this is coming about. Some states continue to allocate their own resources to monitor hunger, supplement benefits, and develop a long-range strategy. Others have and are implementing new ways to combine and enhance the benefit distribution mechanism. These initial state-oriented activities are becoming models that shift goal setting and responsibility sharing burdens to create a "win-win" situation, not the current model whereby one government partner is subservient to the decisions of a "higher" authority.

There are two broader benefits from examining food assistance policy. One is the relationship to welfare reform. Food assistance is only one part of the social service support mechanism that also relates to other important topics, such as housing, jobs, income, and medical care. The current economic environment, the incremental nature of change occurring in welfare reform, and the coalescing of calls for change are dynamics in bringing about reforms in food assistance policy that also provide a focus for welfare initiatives.

And, finally, the ideas presented in this chapter also relate to the study of political science. The political scientist David Ricci, writing in the early 1980s when increased claims over hunger in America were being raised, attributed the "tragedy of political science" to its being limited in its contribution to understanding political problems or their solutions (Ricci, 1984). This chapter works to resolve Ricci's lament. It has provided the reader with an insight into the problems of domestic hunger and malnutrition. It has provided several alternatives for both the short and long term. The benefits will accrue from understanding not only hunger but, in a broader sense, the limits to and the potential of what the United States, as a society, can accomplish.

List of Acronyms

AFDC—Aid to Families with Dependent Children
CCHIP—Community Childhood Hunger Identification Project
DHHS—Department of Health and Human Services
FNS—Food and Nutrition Service
HEW—Department of Health, Education, and Welfare
USDA—United States Department of Agriculture
WIC—Special Supplemental Food Program for Women, Infants, and Children

NOTES

1. The terms "categorical" and "noncategorical" food assistance are used throughout this chapter. Categorical food assistance refers to those programs that target eligibility towards a specific segment of the population, such as school-age children, through the National School Lunch and School Breakfast programs. Noncategorical assistance provides broader support; for example, the Food Stamp Program is available to all low-income persons who meet the eligibility guidelines, not to just specific segments of the population.

2. The term "program" in this chapter—unless referring to a specific program—relates to the thirteen entities that make up the domestic food assistance network: the Food Stamp Program, the National School Lunch Program, the School Breakfast Program, the Special Milk Program, the Adult and Child Care Food Program, the Summer Food Service Program for Children, the Special Supplemental Food Program for Women, Infants, and Children (WIC), the Commodity Supplemental Food Program, the Food Distribution Program on Indian Reservations and the Trust Territories, the Nutrition Program for the Elderly, Commodity Distribution to Charitable Institutions, the Emergency Food Assistance Program, and the Nutrition Assistance Program (to Puerto Rico and the Northern Marianas).

3. An initial pilot Food Stamp Program took place from 1939 until 1943. A second pilot program, initiated in 1961, eventually became the program that exists today. One of the best resources on the historical development of this policy area is found in the "Appendix III: Staff Study—A History of the Food Stamp Program" in the Report on HR 7940, presented in the bibliography.

4. The National School Lunch Program, established in 1946, provides an example. Initially, the distribution was on an economic but nutrition-oriented consideration, because no reliable data existed to determine the number of children at-risk as well as the extent of their need. The welfare focus became more evident as lunches became subsidized. The health care focus is now becoming evident as efforts are being made to reduce the fat and sodium content of the food service, as well as to provide nutrition education efforts.

5. In 1977, the requirement to purchase food stamps was dropped. Limits still remain on certain nonfood items which grocers are not legally allowed to exchange for food coupons.

6. Others might argue that just the opposite—a bottom-up approach—is needed. But, the federal level has taken initiative in funding and program development, and hunger is now seen as a national issue.

7. The Food and Nutrition Service was established on August 8, 1969. The specific goals are "to provide needy people with access to a more nutritious diet, to improve the eating habits of the nation's children, and to stabilize farm prices through the distribution of surplus foods."

8. In food stamps, the relationship usually works down through the social welfare bureaucracy. In the Child Nutrition Programs, the relationship works through the education bureaucracy. In the Supplemental Food Program for Women, Infants, and Children, the relationship works through the health care bureaucracy.

9. The use of regional offices is a link—some would call it a buffer—between the policy-making and policy implementation levels. It is found in other federal agency organizational structures; for example, the Department of Health and Human Services utilizes ten regional offices.

10. This type of broadening experience might come at the state or local implementation level; it might be working with a social service, health care, or agriculture bureaucracy; and it might come from private sector, foundation, or academic experience.

CHAPTER 6

Housing: Out in the Cold in the Post–Cold War Era?

R. ALLEN HAYS

If you belong to a household whose income falls below the poverty level, you are very likely to find it difficult to obtain a decent place to live that is within your ability to pay for. You may be lucky enough to occupy a federally assisted unit, but, despite a large federal investment, this housing serves only one-quarter of low-income households. If you do not live in an assisted unit, you may occupy a physically adequate unit for which you pay over half your income; you may pay the same or less for a physically inadequate unit; you may live doubled-up with family or friends; or, in the worst case, you many wander from a shelter to a welfare hotel to the street as part of the approximately half million homeless.

One hesitates to call this a "housing crisis" only because the phrase has been overutilized to the point of neutralizing its impact. Yet, it is clearly a critical situation for the people involved, and it shows signs of getting worse.

Housing problems are not, of course, confined to the poor. Americans in the middle class and above are some of the best housed people in the world in terms of space and amenities. However, despite tax breaks and other subsidies, they have had to devote an increasing proportion of their resources to housing in recent years in order to maintain their standard of living. In many large cities, even in modest neighborhoods, house prices read like yacht prices, and most families are *not* in J. P. Morgan's enviable position of "not having to ask" the cost.

The purpose of this chapter is to explore future trends in U.S. housing policy. This implies two projections. One is to predict the direction which housing problems will take. The other is to predict what response government will make to these problems. Given the indeterminacy of social and political trends, both of these projections are virtually impossible to make accurately. However, one can explore present problems and policy responses, look at the decisions (and nondecisions) which have brought us where we are now, and suggest what future problems and decisions may flow from present circumstances.

In Part 1 of this chapter, I will outline recent trends in housing policy which have led us to our present situation. I will also discuss what may be called "nontrends," that is, things which did *not* happen despite the strong feelings of many in the housing policy community that they should have. In Part 2, I will discuss what future policy agenda has been laid out for us by our current situation.

Part 1: Housing Trends and Nontrends

Housing Market Trends

Since the private market is the main provider of housing in the United States, no discussion of public policy can take place outside the context of overall housing market trends. The "private" housing market is far from "laissez-faire," as government intervention occurs in almost all aspects of housing finance and production. Nevertheless, a look at private transactions gives us a sense of the overall dimensions of the problem.

The most publicized trend in housing markets since the late 1960s has been the relentless rise in the price of single family dwellings which are offered for sale. According to the Harvard Joint Center for Housing Studies, during the twelve year period from 1975 to 1987, the median price of a representative first home rose from $34,800 to $67,000. More revealing, however, are their data on the rise in home ownership costs relative to inflation. In 1967, the yearly after-tax, cash cost of owning a single family house was approximately $5,500 *in 1986 dollars*. By 1981, this had risen to just under $10,000. In the face of a market slowdown during the middle 1980s, this measure declined to $7,500 by 1987, but it still represented a 50 percent greater increase in house purchase costs than in the overall cost of living (Joint Center, 1988, 2).

Such an increase in real costs affects the first-time home buyer most severely, since he or she cannot reinvest capital gains from earlier home purchases. The Center calculates the cash cost burden for first-time home buyers by comparing incomes for those families in the traditional home-buying years with housing prices and finds that this burden has risen from 22.2 percent of

TABLE 6.1

Trends in Low-Income Housing Supply
1980–1989

	1980	1989
Poverty Income Level—Family of Four	$8,380	$12,673
Estimated Number of Renters Below Poverty Level	11,003,500	12,139,000
Affordable Rent at Poverty Level	$209	$316
Estimated Number of Units at or Below Affordable Rent	9,409,000	8,975,000

Source: U.S. Bureau of the Census and Department of Housing and Urban Development, *American Housing Survey*, 1980 and 1989.

income in 1967 to 32.4 percent in 1987. As a result, the rate of home ownership has declined, especially among low to moderate income families (Joint Center, 1988, 20).

A less publicized cost trend has been the increase in inflation-adjusted (real) rents. During the 1970s, as sales prices rose rapidly, contract rents (the cash rent paid to the landlord) stayed constant, or fell, as did gross rent (the contract rent plus utilities). This was due, in part, to declining demand from middle-income families, as many rushed into home ownership in order to jump on the inflation bandwagon. In 1981, however, real rents began to rise, despite relatively high vacancy rates. The national average in 1987 was $365, but rents in large cities were, of course, much higher.

A negative effect of constant or falling real rents during the 1970s was a low rate of rental housing construction. Unless subsidized by the federal government, rental housing was not an attractive investment, especially in relation to the many safer, higher yield alternatives available. Despite relative increases in rents during the 1980s, rental construction remained sluggish. Constructing various forms of owner-occupied dwellings remained the strategy of choice for builders.

Although increased costs for such a basic necessity have a negative effect at all income levels, their impact was especially severe on those at the lower end of the income scale. Table 6.1 measures this impact by comparing the supply of low-rent units with the number of persons in poverty in 1980 and 1990.

These data show a serious decline in available low cost units, despite the fact that they *understate* the severity of the problem in two respects. First, the median income for those in poverty is substantially below the "poverty line," and this gap has been growing. Thus, for most of the poor, their affordable rent level is much less than those given in table 6.1. Second, further analysis indicates that up to a third of the units at these rents are occupied by persons *above* the poverty line, thus making them unavailable to the poor. One may conclude, therefore, that these data are but a glimpse of a much larger problem.

The steady loss of affordable units has contributed greatly to the rise of homelessness. The debate over how to respond to homelessness has at times focused on whether or not dealing with immediate housing needs is a valid response or merely treats a symptom of deeper problems, such as mental illness or substance abuse. In commenting on the homeless literature, Wright (1989) suggests that while there are multiple individual causes of homelessness, the lack of affordable housing means that people who are vulnerable to extreme economic deprivation will more frequently suffer homelessness as a consequence of their overall plight. The situation is analogous to a game of musical chairs, in which an individual's probability of success depends on the ratio of chairs to players, as well as his or her agility in grabbing one of the available seats. Those who lose the "housing game" often (though not always) have severe personal problems, but the lower ratio of units to persons makes it inevitable that some households will end up without stable shelter.

Trends in Federal Housing Assistance

A discussion of recent trends in federal housing assistance must be placed in proper context by looking at the 1960s, when several new housing programs were initiated as part of the spurt of social legislation roughly labelled the "Great Society." The Housing Act of 1968 boosted funding for the public housing program, which involves public ownership and management of subsidized units and which had been the federal government's traditional approach to housing for the poor. However, the 1968 Act also created two new programs designed to promote private sector involvement in the provision of low income housing.

One, Section 236, was directed at investors and involved federal payment of the difference between the market interest rate for development financing and a flat 1 percent rate. The other, Section 235, directed a similar subsidy at low-income *purchasers* of homes. Between 1969 and 1973, production of assisted units under these programs and public housing rose to the highest levels since federal involvement began in the 1930s (Hays, 1985).

During the early 1970s, both public housing and the two newer programs generated controversy and criticism. Protracted legal battles over segregation, tenant strikes, and continued problems with maintenance (due, in part, to inadequate federal support) plagued public housing, and, though the program continued to provide decent housing for thousands of families, the demolition of the Pruitt-Igoe complex in St. Louis epitomized, for many decision makers, its shortcomings. The Section 236 program experienced numerous foreclosures, particularly among nonprofit sponsors, while Section 235 suffered from well-publicized scandals in which unscrupulous realtors took advantage of lax or corrupt FHA administrators to sell shoddy housing to low-income families (for a more detailed account, see Hays, 1985).

These problems provided the Nixon administration, which was already shifting rightward on domestic issues, a justification for declaring a moratorium on construction under these programs in January 1973. During this moratorium a study was produced, entitled *Housing in the Seventies*, which recommended a different approach to housing assistance for the poor, one based on cash allowances given directly to the households in need, rather than public ownership or construction subsidies (U.S. Department of Housing and Urban Development, 1976). This "housing allowance" concept was incorporated into the Housing and Community Development Act of 1974, which replaced Sections 235 and 236 with four related programs grouped under Section 8 of the new act.

The Section 8 New Construction, Substantial Rehabilitation, and Moderate Rehabilitation programs continued the tradition of what is now called "project based assistance" in that tenants were required to live in particular housing developments in order to receive assistance. Continued project based assistance under the public housing program was also funded. However, the Section 8 Existing Housing program allowed tenants to select existing units (including their current dwelling) which met minimum federal standards and to receive a subsidy for the difference between the Fair Market Rent (FMR) for comparable units in the area and 25 percent of their incomes. This was the first time this approach had been enacted on any substantial scale.

Under Section 8, the production of assisted units soared in the late 1970s, as it had earlier in the decade. These programs suffered some criticism but seemed to have resolved many of the problems of the earlier programs. Although Section 8 New Construction proved expensive and was soon heavily skewed toward the elderly, Section 8 Existing Housing proved to be a "bargain" in terms of subsidy costs, since the FMRs were much lower than on new units. Thus, what set these programs back on a downward course was not their own shortcomings but the economic problems of this period and the political changes which they produced.

The combination of high inflation and slow growth in the late 1970s helped elect Ronald Reagan in 1980, who promised to "get the government off our backs" and who criticized all federal efforts to aid the poor. Housing programs were particularly vulnerable to budget cuts because, unlike AFDC and food stamps, they were not "entitlement" programs which provided aid to all who were eligible. Though cuts were made in entitlements through eligibility changes, their funding was substantially preserved as part of the federal "safety net" of programs for the poor. In contrast, new funding for housing programs was cut almost 70 percent between 1981 and 1983 (Hays, 1990, 860).

The immediate impact of these cuts on low-income families was less drastic than it might have been. Units built in the 1970s were still under long-term subsidy contract, and there were thousands of previously funded units still in the construction pipeline during much of the 1980s. These, plus the small number of additional units which Congress funded over Reagan's protests, caused the total number of assisted units to keep growing during the 1980s, reaching 5.4 million units by 1988 (U.S. Congress, Budget Office, 1988, 37). However, the private market trends described above were shrinking the total supply of low cost units, and federal efforts were insufficient to address this problem. Moreover, by the end of the 1980s, the threat emerged that approximately 700,000 units assisted under earlier programs would become unavailable to low-income persons, due to the expiration of contracts between HUD and their owners.

The mix of unit types provided by federal programs also changed during the 1980s. Citing excessive per-unit costs, the Reagan administration pushed for the abolition of all new construction subsidy programs, except those directed at the elderly or handicapped, and Congress generally went along. A new program, housing vouchers, was also phased in. This was similar to the Section 8 Existing Housing program, except that tenants were allowed more flexibility in paying more or less than the Fair Market Rent (now called the payment standard) for their units. Voucher contracts were also for five years, rather than fifteen, thus tying up less budget authority for each unit approved and making the program appear cheaper. By the end of the decade, project-based new construction had become a minor part of the federal housing assistance effort (U.S. Congress, Budget Office, 1988).

The Bush administration was less doctrinaire in its approach to social programs than the Reagan administration, and Bush's appointment of former congressman Jack Kemp as secretary of HUD signaled a new interest in housing needs. Working with the Democratic Congress, Bush and Kemp hammered out the first comprehensive housing authorization legislation in over a decade, the Housing Act of 1990. Among other changes in housing programs, this act implemented Secretary Kemp's favored solution to the housing problems of the poor, home ownership. Following the lead of the Thatcher government in Great Britain, but on a much smaller scale, the new HOPE program encouraged public housing authorities to sell their units to their tenants at substantially discounted prices.

The extent of these new efforts was, however, severely curtailed by the huge budget deficits which were the legacy of the Reagan era. Even after Bush reversed his "no new taxes" pledge, new revenues went primarily for deficit reduction, not new program initiatives. In addition, the budget agreement of 1990 prevented defense/domestic tradeoffs, with the result that increases in one domestic program could occur only at the expense of others. Therefore, housing expenditures increased only marginally, and some new initiatives were funded by transfers of money from existing programs. Also, a significant proportion of new housing vouchers were allocated to units on which earlier subsidy contracts were expiring, thus providing no net addition to the supply of assisted units.

Local Housing Initiatives

As the flow of federal housing funds dried up during the 1980s, many localities were still deeply committed to solving their housing problems and began to search for ways to improve housing quality using their own resources. Two of the major watchwords of these efforts were *creative financing* and *community involvement*. Creative financing usually took advantage of the ability of the state and/or the locality to borrow funds at below-market rates, due to the federal tax exemption for bond interest. CDBG funds were also frequently utilized as a subsidy to lower project costs. The use of tax exempt bonds was curtailed by the Tax Reform Act of 1986, which put a tight per capita ceiling on the total amount which could be borrowed within any state for any purpose (housing, economic development, etc.). However, this was partially replaced by a new tax credit for low-income housing construction, and state and local governments continued to pursue various options to reduce financing costs.

Community involvement usually came in the form of local, nonprofit, community development corporations (CDCs), of which the principal purpose was housing development. These organizations had been a part of low-income housing production for many years, but they came into new prominence as federal subsidies to private, for-profit developers faded. CDCs were often based in a particular neighborhood and had a goal of upgrading the entire area, as well as individual housing units. They multiplied in many cities as virtually the only sources of new construction or substantial rehabilitation.

As Dreier and Keating (1990) point out, however, these local efforts occurred under severe resource constraints. Housing units are so expensive to build or rehabilitate that it costs far more than local tax bases can absorb to create enough standard units to meet most communities' needs. This is especially the case because the gap between the rents needed to support a project and the rents which very low-income people can afford is so large that very deep subsidies are required if they are to benefit from it. CDCs do an important service by providing modest priced housing to middle- and working-class persons, for whom the extremely high rents in large cities are burdensome. However, they often have to rely on the trickle of federal housing vouchers to assist the very poor.

Despite their shortcomings in terms of volume and depth of subsidy, CDCs are felt by many observers to have been a tremendous boon to housing policy beyond the actual units produced, because they have led to capacity building in housing administration at the local level. Their flexibility and responsiveness is seen as an improvement over the "bureaucratic" solution represented by public housing or the private management solution of Section 236 and Section 8. For this reason, CDCs were viewed as an important vehicle for renewed federal assistance by the drafters of the Housing Act of 1990 and were given a special set-aside in the new assistance programs which it created.

Housing Nontrends

The parameters of public policy-making are often more clearly defined by what does *not* happen than by what actually takes place. Therefore, it seems appropriate to discuss several potentially significant trends that failed to occur in housing policy in recent years. These items stand out in that, although they did not happen, they were widely discussed and debated within the housing policy community. Thus, these or similar ideas may have an impact on the future of housing policy.

Housing as an Entitlement. The first nontrend is the transformation of housing assistance into an entitlement, similar to food stamps, Aid to Families with Dependent Children, or Social Security. In an entitlement program, certain eligibility standards are set in the authorizing legislation, and a commitment is made to fund assistance to all eligible applicants. Although it is rare that all potentially eligible persons actually apply for such programs, those who do apply need not queue in long waiting lists until benefits are available. In contrast, in a nonentitlement program such as Section 8 housing, cities typically have waiting lists of eligible clients numbering in the hundreds or thousands, and waits of three years or more are the norm.

An entitlement represents a commitment on the part of society to meet a certain need, a commitment which is protected from the yearly vagaries of the appropriations process in Congress. Such expenditures are not, as some suggest, literally "uncontrollable." Congress can choose to reduce costs by altering the eligibility criteria in the authorizing act or can back out of the entitlement commitment altogether. Such actions are, however, much more difficult politically than simply adjusting annual appropriations. This is especially the case in programs such as Social Security, where large and well-organized program constituencies exist.

Determining exactly what proportion of the population in need is currently served by housing assistance is difficult, since so much depends on who is counted as eligible. Using the federal definition of "low income" as 80 percent of the median income, the Congressional Budget Office estimates that 25 percent of all households in this category (including single persons and groups of unrelated individuals as well as families) were served in 1988. However, federal programs have increasingly targeted only "very low income" persons, defined as those earning 50 percent of the median income or less. If only this group is counted as the eligible population, then approximately one-third are served (U.S. Congress, Budget Office, 1988, 53–54).

In trying to account for housing programs' lack of entitlement status, the factor of cost is clearly important. Costs per eligible recipient are generally higher to provide housing than to provide food or the minimal cash benefits which are dispensed through AFDC, especially if the assistance involves project-based construction of new units. The current yearly outlays needed to provide housing assistance to one-third of very-low-income households are in the range of $15 billion, which is comparable to outlays for food stamps for a much larger percentage of the eligible population. The Congressional Budget Office estimates that if housing assistance were to be made an entitlement, approximately 60 percent of the eligible population would participate. If most of this assistance were provided through vouchers, rather than new construction, outlays would rise by $11.1 billion per year (74 percent over the 1988 level (U.S. Congress, Budget Office, 1988, 105). Increases this size are not politically acceptable in the current budget climate.

Cost, however, is not a totally adequate explanation, since other programs with high costs per recipient (such as Medicaid) have retained their entitlement status. Another part of the explanation seems to be simply historical accident. AFDC and food stamps both started as small programs, restricted by eligibility or geography. Thus, their benefits became entitlements long before their client lists began to mushroom. (See, for example, Berry, 1984, on the growth of the food stamp program.) By the time the entitlement issue arose, housing assistance was already a large and expensive program, and this reduced the prospects of converting it into an entitlement.

Another possible reason why entitlement status for housing assistance was not pushed by housing advocates in the 1960s or early 1970s was that housing programs were growing, and entitlement status did not seem as important in an era when public policy decisions drove the budget, rather than vice versa. In the 1980s, budgetary politics dominated all aspects of domestic policy. During the complex maneuvering, and eventual stalemate, between Reagan and the largely Democratic Congress over the budget, entitlement programs acquired an almost mythical protected status. Congress went along with early eligibility changes (as part of the Omnibus Budget Reconciliation Act of 1981) which took hundreds of thousands off the food stamp and AFDC rolls, but it was unwilling to let the Reagan administration out of its "safety net" commitment beyond that. A tacit agreement evolved that deficit reduction would occur mostly in the "discretionary" portion of the budget, that is, that which was controlled by yearly appropriations, an agreement that was codified in the Gramm-Rudman-Hollings legislation in 1985. The fact that housing assistance programs were in this discretionary sector appears to account for the much more drastic cuts they received, as much as any unique features of these programs.

This somewhat detailed discussion of the "entitlement" issue is important to the present topic, because this goal continues to be espoused by housing advocates as the "ideal" status for such programs. In the current climate, it seems quixotic to pursue such a goal, but there may be a time when it is not so perceived. Of this, more in a later section.

Tax Subsidies to Middle- and Upper-Income Groups. A second nontrend of the last twenty years has been the absence of a serious challenge to the housing subsidies which are provided to middle- and upper-class home owners through the tax system. Most tax deductions for "necessities" are restricted either by an exclusion (i.e., as in the medical deduction, where only those expenses above 7.5 percent of gross income can be deducted) or a maximum (as in the child care deduction where no more than $2,000 per year may be deducted, regardless of expenses). In contrast, there are only the broadest of restrictions on the deductibility of home mortgage interest or property taxes. The home owner can deduct the interest on up to $1 million in indebtedness, and this deduction may include second homes, such as vacation cottages, as well as primary residences. In addition, the home owner is exempt from capital gains taxation on the sale of a home, with certain restrictions.

This deduction slipped unnoticed into the original act which established the income tax in 1913, after the 16th Amendment made such a tax constitutional (Grigsby, 1990). For many years, its revenue impact was inconsequential, due to low home ownership rates, low house prices, and low interest rates. In the mid-1970s, however, as all three of these became larger, the lost tax revenues from these deductions became substantial, even taking into account that many home owners take the standard deduction, thereby not benefitting directly from them. Cushing Dolbeare, writing for the Center on Budget and Policy Priorities, estimates that the revenue foregone from all special tax treatment of housing rose from $11.2 billion in 1976 to $53.9 billion in 1988, despite cuts in maximum rates for high tax brackets made during the 1980s (Center on Budget and Policy Priorities, 1989). Of this, nearly $40 billion is from the mortgage interest and property tax deductions, making these provisions one of the largest "tax expenditures" currently affecting the federal budget (U.S. Congress, Budget Office, 1988).

One is tempted to react emotionally to this situation, especially when one juxtaposes the image of rich people taking a tax deduction on their condos in Vail with the image of the homeless sleeping on heating grates, due to the lack of low-income housing assistance. Yet, even on a purely rational, economic basis, it is hard to justify the sweeping nature of the deduction as it exists now. It has often been defended as promoting home ownership, thereby encouraging various social virtues among the middle and working class, such as savings and property maintenance, and helping them acquire the only real asset most will ever own. If this is the rationale, then one would expect some sort of tax benefit with a progressive impact, such as a tax exemption rather than a deduction. Or, one would expect some ceiling on the deduction, such as exists for child care expenses. Since neither of these is in place, the deduction subsidizes housing the most for those who need it the least.

Henry Aaron, of the Brookings Institution, was one of the first economists to call attention to the regressive and economically questionable nature of this deduction in his 1971 book, *Shelter and Subsidies*. Other economists and housing activists have taken issue with it since then. Nevertheless, the political obstacles to addressing serious proposals to limit it are formidable, even in an era when Congress and the president frequently cast around desperately for measures to reduce the federal deficit. The main obstacle is, of course, the millions of taxpayers who would be affected. Even if a proposal were made that primarily affected the wealthy, interest groups could still raise fears that further cuts might be made in this "sacred cow."

The second is the fragile coalition which exists between organizations representing housing producers (such as the National Association of Home Builders) and organizations representing the housing needs of the poor. Over the years, producer opposition to low-income housing programs has been gradually neutralized, especially when housing assistance benefits them as well as the poor. As it stands, housing legislation can usually count on support, albeit at times lukewarm, from these powerful producer groups. However, if low-income housing advocates were to press this issue too hard, producers would see this as a direct threat to their livelihood, and the coalition could be seriously harmed. Moreover, even if the deduction were limited, there is no guarantee that the funds would be transferred to low-income housing, rather than simply used for deficit reduction. Thus, while advocates like Cushing Dolbeare continue to raise the issue, it is not as high on their agenda as is gaining more direct subsidies for the poor.

As with the entitlement issue, this nontrend will continue to loom in the background of the housing policy debate during the 1990s. If the major, bipartisan tax reform push of the mid-1980s could not dislodge this shibboleth, it is hard to imagine what constellation of political forces could succeed, yet the possibility should be kept in mind as the debate unfolds.

Housing and the Welfare System. A third trend which has not effectively materialized in the last twenty years has been the integration of housing assistance with the rest of the "welfare state." During this time, interest in "welfare reform" has ebbed and flowed periodically. During periods of intense scrutiny of the entire system, as in the early 1970s, late 1970s, and late 1980s, proposals for replacing the current system with a cash benefit such as the Negative Income Tax almost always receive considerable attention. This involves the "cashing out" (i.e., providing the cash equivalent) of "in-kind" benefits, such as food stamps, Medicaid, and housing assistance, benefits which are tied to a particular expenditure. Proponents of "cashing out" argue that a cash benefit is more efficient in that it allows the assisted family members to select the particular mix of goods and services *they* prefer, rather than being forced to "overconsume" an item in order to receive help.

The closest that any such proposal ever came to enactment was Nixon's Family Assistance Plan, which passed the House but was narrowly defeated in the Senate in 1971. Housing assistance was not included in the benefits "cashed out" under the Nixon proposal, but the liberal/conservative disagreement which derailed the FAP is the same one which has caused trouble in subsequent reincarnations of the idea, namely, disagreement over the size of the cash payment which should replace in-kind benefits. Liberals in Congress accused Nixon of trying to reduce the overall cost of welfare, by substituting a smaller cash benefit for more valuable in-kind benefits. Nixon argued that it was adequate (Lynn, 1980).

The deeper political dilemma behind this argument is, of course, that if all in-kind benefits were converted to a single cash benefit of equal value (assuming that they could be, which is doubtful in the case of health care), the total amount would very likely be politically unacceptable to a large segment of the public and Congress. The fact that the poverty level for a family of four is above $13,000 shows that even a minimum standard of living is very costly to maintain. Moreover, a study by this author found that public perceptions of assistance given for specific purposes, such as food or housing, were much more positive than their views of cash assistance programs (Hays, 1989). Middle-class citizens are not as willing as conservative economists to trust the poor to spend cash wisely.

In sum, the political prospects of any kind of cashing-out proposal remain slim for the foreseeable future, despite widespread dissatisfaction with the current welfare system. Nevertheless, there are three other trends which may encourage greater coordination of housing services with other services, short of a totally cash-based system. One is the increased attention to the interrelatedness of housing to other problems, which has arisen out of the problems of the homeless. Many of the homeless need not only shelter but also assistance with multiple problems, and programs for the homeless are beginning to bring together those who provide shelter with other service providers.

A second trend is an increased awareness that many lower income neighborhoods are experiencing a severe breakdown of the entire social fabric. Drugs, gangs, and violent death are but the most dramatic symptoms of this breakdown. When these kinds of antisocial behavior are rampant, the physical quality of one's dwelling seems a less important factor in the quality of life than physical safety while walking the streets. Therefore, housing agencies have become increasingly involved in attacking these problems. Many public housing projects now strive to be free of drug dealers through community resistance and tougher eviction measures. Dealing with crime and juvenile offenders no longer seems remote from the central concerns of housing administrators. Although the problems stimulating this trend are tragic, the holistic approach to the quality of life in low-income areas that they have stimulated is a positive development.

Finally, various kinds of social services, including housing, are being coordinated in a number of pilot programs to encourage upward mobility. In programs such as HUD's Operation Bootstrap, promising families sign "contracts" in which they receive preference for various kinds of aid in exchange for taking steps to pull themselves out of poverty, such as enrolling in college or job training programs. Whether or not these programs succeed in aiding large numbers of families, they at least overcome the traditional isolation of housing programs from other social welfare programs by increasing awareness that housing is part of a total bundle of services which must be treated as having a collective impact on clients.

Part 2: Future Trends

As is the case with any public policy, the future direction taken by housing policy depends on the interaction of the problem agenda and political forces unique to that policy area with the larger policy agenda and political configuration of forces that shape all policy choices. The preceding discussion of major problems in housing suggests how these problems might develop, absent any change in the current course of federal policy. Let us first examine trends in the problem itself, then the policy changes needed to respond to them, and finally the political conditions that will be more or less conducive to those changes.

Housing Supply and Costs

For low-income and very-low-income persons, current trends clearly point to a *worsening* of their housing situation in the future. The major negative impact will come from rising housing costs, rather than changes in physical conditions. Standard units will be available, but at costs which consume one-half or more of the income of these families. To pay these costs, other basic needs (e.g., nutrition or preventive health care) must often be sacrificed. Moreover, the size of this cost burden relative to income means that any significant income loss may result in the total loss of permanent shelter and entry into the netherworld of the homeless.

That housing cost, rather than physical quality, is the central housing problem of the poor speaks well of the United States' collective efforts to upgrade its housing stock over the last thirty years. Many new housing units have been built, many dilapidated units have been demolished, and housing codes have been gradually strengthened. Yet, the incomes of those at the bottom of the income distribution have not kept pace with the cost increases which these improvements (along with speculative pressures) have produced. Some commentators have suggested that we backtrack on physical quality standards in order to provide *some* form of increased shelter for the poor, but given the myriad of problems which substandard housing generates, this hardly seems a logical solution (MIT Center for Real Estate Development, 1988). The mismatch between incomes and housing costs is a problem which must be dealt with on its own terms, if one regards housing as a basic necessity which no person should lack.

Trends in the housing problems of the nonpoor are somewhat more complex. In large cities, particularly on the East and West coasts, the rapid inflation of single family house prices during the late 1970s and early 1980s drove up the proportions of income spent by middle-class families on housing and reduced home ownership rates by pricing first-time buyers out of the market. This inflation has subsided somewhat since the late 1980s as housing markets have softened, and, in many parts of the country (e.g., the Midwest), inflation has been much milder, leaving housing prices more within the range of middle income buyers. Thus, the impact on those of middle income or above has been very uneven—benefitting some through appreciation of assets, hardly affecting others, and curtailing others' housing chances quite severely.

These changes also have to be viewed in light of overall changes in income distribution. From 1979 to 1989, the share of aggregate household income earned by the top one-fifth of the income distribution increased from 43.0 percent to 46.8 percent, while the share of the middle 60 percent declined from 52.9 percent to 49.3 percent (U.S. Census, 1991). The top one-fifth includes not just the rich but the upper-middle class, who benefitted from growth in the upper end of the service economy plus Reagan era tax policies. These households have often substantially improved their housing, or, at the least, maintained quality if living in areas of high inflation. They also benefitted from a large share of the housing subsidies built into the tax code.

In contrast, the middle- and lower-middle class have seen growth in real incomes flatten out. For them, the burden of shelter costs has risen tremendously in areas of high inflation, and the prospect of home ownership has receded. In lower priced areas, it has been easier for them to hold their own, but attempts to improve their housing have brought higher costs. While they are not squeezed like the poor, housing is one of many areas in which their standard of living has not improved.

For the poor, cost and quality problems in housing are built into the economics of housing production. In the absence of government aid, it is difficult to imagine how the private market could ever produce housing which is affordable to those on the lower end of the income distribution. In contrast, for the middle- and upper-middle class, the affordability of housing varies with specific market trends and conditions. In looking to the immediate future, continued modest rates of price inflation coupled with lower interest rates may gradually alleviate cost burdens for middle income households, *if* incomes continue to rise. This outcome depends, in turn, on the overall performance of the economy in improving job prospects and incomes. Assessing these broader prospects is far beyond the scope of this chapter.

Housing Policies

The current level of federal commitment to housing assistance for low-income persons is, basically, the outcome of a tacit compromise between the Reagan administration and Congress. During the 1980s, Democrats in Congress accepted steep cutbacks in new commitments of units and the virtual elimination of new construction programs, while the Reagan administration accepted slower, but steady yearly additions of units to the assisted housing stock. The compromise also included modest funding for special programs to deal with the most visible manifestation of housing problems—homelessness. Despite greater flexibility and innovation, and despite new authorizing legislation, housing policy still flows within the basic contours of this compromise.

As has been shown, the assisted units generated by this current level of commitment serve only a fraction of the need. In light of the worsening situation for low-income households, a continuation of this level of commitment will result in unmet housing needs on a large scale during the 1990s. The expiration of contracts on existing subsidized units will exacerbate the situation, as a growing portion of the "new" units funded each year will be required to renew these old commitments. Special programs for temporary shelter and services will alleviate the suffering of the homeless but will not address the underlying housing problems which contribute to their plight. There will also be few resources to address the total quality of life in the neighborhoods in which low-income persons live.

To genuinely improve the situation requires that the goal of establishing housing assistance as an entitlement becomes central. Only by establishing decent housing as a universal subsistence right for those who cannot obtain it on their own will the level of effort expand to address the full need. If current estimates are correct, and a doubling of the current outlays of $15 billion will come close to accomplishing this, then the resources required are not massive in relation to a $1 trillion federal budget and a $5 trillion GNP.

The creation of a housing entitlement does *not* entail a return to a massive federal role in construction and management of assisted housing. The creation of new and rehabilitated units can be left to state and local governments or to nonprofits, provided vouchers are available to supply the deep subsidies needed for very low income residents. Federal new construction funds can still be reserved for special needs populations or for communities in which the housing supply is extremely tight.

In addition, the focus on funding individual housing needs which an entitlement implies does not mean that the complex web of community problems which can make even a physically sound neighborhood a social nightmare should be ignored. Housing benefits can be coordinated with other social welfare programs to encourage upward mobility by families. More social services such as child care and job training can be made accessible to residents of low-income housing, and security programs to control drug dealing and other crime can be expanded. Much can be accomplished in these areas with rather modest funding levels.

With regard to the housing needs of middle-income households, a large federal policy apparatus exists. This includes the direct regulation and assistance provided through FHA, VA, Fannie Mae, and Freddie Mac, as well as the massive indirect housing assistance provided through the tax code. Given the potential instability of capital flows in the absence of regulation, there is much to recommend a continued federal role in stabilizing mortgage markets and in providing modest assistance to buyers on the lower end of the middle-class market with FHA and VA loans.

The subsidies provided through the tax code are another matter. As noted above, they currently benefit the upper-middle class and the wealthy more than the middle class. If it is considered desirable to foster middle-class home ownership through tax deductions, then they should at least be targeted to those at the lower end of the middle class who have the most difficulty obtaining and maintaining their own homes. The elimination of the deduction on luxury second homes and the capping of the mortgage interest deduction at a level designed to concentrate the benefits in this more modest income group are rational and equitable tax provisions.

Prospects for Change

The current political climate in the United States is not conducive to large new federal commitments to meet basic human needs such as housing. The budget deficit removes much of the flexibility in federal spending choices. Large tax increases are politically impossible, and without them new federal initiatives add to the flow of red ink. Even the "dividend" from post–Cold War military cuts is not enough to change this basic fiscal situation. In addition, there are many competing demands for federal action in areas besides housing, of which health care is currently the most visible and expensive.

Public opinion polls repeatedly show popular majorities in favor of more government assistance to solve social problems such as health, housing, education, child care, and so on. However, there are also undercurrents of distrust towards recipients of such aid which undermine support for actual programs.

Perhaps more important in undermining middle-class support is the fact that the perpetually sluggish economy has not significantly raised the middle-class standard of living during the last decade. This intensifies resistance to redistribution of wealth or to any other public investments requiring additional taxes. Until this middle-class resistance weakens, a change in the political climate favorable to programs like low-income housing assistance is unlikely. Whether anything short of a major depression which places the middle class itself in need of government aid will alter this resistance is an imponderable question which will be left to others to debate.

Urban Policy in the Post–Cold War Era

DENNIS R. JUDD

The Rise and Fall of Urban Policy

From the 1930s to the 1980s, the New Deal coalition was able to provide effective support for urban policies designed to help the cities solve their pressing social and economic problems. Since the late 1970s this coalition has unravelled, and consequently the urban policies that it sponsored have been abandoned. These changes in domestic politics and policies are connected to some of the same international developments that have brought about an end to the Cold War. The transformation of the world economy has broken apart the urban hierarchy of the industrial age, encouraged regional population movements within the United States, accelerated investment and migration flows across national borders, and put pressure on cities to pursue policies that will allow them to successfully participate in the new international economy.

For several decades a set of "urban" policies encompassing housing, transportation, racial segregation, and economic development occupied the center of a public policy agenda built on the premise that the national government should influence the distribution of population and economic activity within the nation and that it should provide for the social welfare of citizens affected by processes of urban change. The recent justifications put forward for abandoning such policies are directly related to the assumption that governments cannot stand in the way of transformations brought about by a changing international economy. In this post–Cold War political climate, local strategies designed to secure assistance from the national government have been replaced almost entirely by efforts to promote local economic development. In this chapter, I break down the story I have summarized into its components, tracing (1) the evolution of the New Deal coalition; (2) the crafting and refining of urban policies; and (3) the political and economic pressures that forced the abandonment of traditional policies. Finally, I will comment on how urban policies are likely to evolve in the 1990s.

The Assumptions Driving Urban Policies

The foundation of America's urban policies was laid in the 1930s, though the edifice was constructed mainly in the decades following World War II. Two principal elements made national urban policy: the forging of a political coalition and the transformation of a new system of intergovernmental relations. These two elements were inextricably intertwined: mayors and other local officials, on whom Democrats with national political ambitions relied for getting out the vote in the cities, also became key links in the political communications and administrative machinery that came to constitute the intergovernmental grants system.

Urban policy, defined as a series of policies meant to deal with problems associated with the development of urban areas and particularly central cities, was essentially invented by the New Deal. These policies originally emerged more from political calculus than from conviction. Franklin Delano Roosevelt was not personally inclined to think much about the particular problems of cities; indeed, like so many of his contemporaries, he evinced a nostalgia for the nation's rural past and supported a back-to-the-land movement (Funigiello, 1978, xi–xii). His first public works program, and his favorite, was the Civilian Conservation Corps, which sent young people out to plant trees, maintain trails, stock fish, and do other good deeds in the countryside. Roosevelt felt that the program would improve the moral character of unemployed youth in the cities by exposing them to rural values (Leuchtenburg, 1963, 52). Rexford Tugwell, one of Roosevelt's closest advisors, confessed that "since my graduate-school days, I have always been able to excite myself more about the wrongs of farmers than those of urban workers" (Leuchtenberg, 1963, 35).

Roosevelt, however, relied on the urban working class for his electoral success. The big city vote was decisive in every one of FDR's four presidential campaigns. The nation's eleven largest cities provided 27.1 percent of his national vote plurality in 1932, and a much greater proportion of the votes in the industrial states (Eldersveld, 1949, 1200). Time after time, large pluralities in the big cities balanced out Republican pluralities in the suburbs and small towns—providing the margin of victory in key states with big blocks of electoral votes. Roosevelt would have been defeated in 1940, and he would also have lost in 1944 and 1948, without the overwhelming pluralities delivered in twelve big cities (Eldersveld, 1949, 1201).

These political facts of life did not themselves lead inevitably, or even easily, to policies specifically intended to help the cities. The New Deal accomplished a comprehensive farm policy of price supports, crop allotments, and federally guaranteed mortgages. In contrast, it produced its first program specifically for cities, the Wagner-Steagall Housing Act, in 1937. That program provided an important precedent for the Housing Act of 1949, which served as the linchpin program for the central cities up to the Great Society initiatives of the 1960s. In the context of the overall achievements of the New Deal, however, the 1937 legislation was a minor player. In light of the political importance of city voters to the New Deal, why were there not more and bigger programs targeted to cities?

Certainly one reason is that political actors at all levels were ambivalent about creating a direct relationship between the federal government and the cities. There was a huge amount of ideological resistance to the idea. In July 1931, the Socialist mayor of Milwaukee sent letters to one hundred mayors of the largest cities, feeling out his colleagues on the idea of organizing a conference to draft an appeal for a federal relief effort for unemployed in the cities. Several mayors criticized the suggestion on the ground that such assistance would amount to "an invasion of community rights" (Gelfand, 1975, 35). Receiving no reply from the mayors of New York City, Chicago, Philadelphia, and Detroit, he abandoned the attempt.

Within a year of that appeal, city officials began to reconsider their position, with consequences that would reverberate for several decades. In the spring of 1932, Frank Murphy, the mayor of Detroit, invited the mayors of the big cities to a conference. The mayors met in Detroit on June 1 and issued a call for federal assistance. What they requested was a federal role in unemployment relief; over the years they also learned to ask for federal aid for many other purposes.

There were few New Deal programs addressed to urban programs specifically because the Depression was a national crisis, and the problems in the cities tended to be no worse than elsewhere. The New Deal's first relief and recovery programs relied on the states for their administration. It did not take long, however, before federal officials began working directly with local officials. The three major public works programs for adults—the Public Works Administration, Civilian Works Administration, and Works Progress Administration—were administered by federal officials in cooperation with both state and local officials. In a few big cities, the welfare programs funded through the Social Security Act of 1935 flowed through the states nominally but actually went directly to welfare agencies run as components of local government.

Throughout the Depression years, local officials frequently went to Washington to testify about local problems and to meet with federal administrators. By 1934, a southern mayor observed, "Mayors are a familiar sight in

Washington these days. Whether we like it or not, the destinies of our cities are clearly tied in with national politics'' (Gelfand, 1975, 66). The institutional relationships that gave life to such an observation were put in place in the 1930s. The United States Conference of Mayors, formed in 1932, became a forum through which mayors met annually and communicated not only with one another but also with federal policymakers. The other lobby groups, such as the International City Management Association and the National Municipal League, were transformed by the Depression from organizations interested solely in the question of how to reform local government to groups that lobbied federal administrators, Congress, and the White House.

Because of the nature of the New Deal coalition, the electoral support for urban programs always was problematic. Indeed, Southern Democrats were generally hostile to urban legislation of any scope, in no small part because it was impossible to divorce racial from urban issues. The New Deal coalition could not have produced most of the urban legislation of the postwar era without substantial pressure from a well-organized urban lobby.

Urban Programs and the New Deal Coalition

The urban vote was crucial to John F. Kennedy's victory in the historically close election of 1960. Kennedy beat Nixon by 112,000 votes, a margin of less than one-tenth of one percent, but he carried twenty-seven out of the thirty-nine biggest cities (Mollenkopf, 1983, 83). In 1964, Lyndon Johnson won the presidential election by an unprecedented landslide, carrying 486 electoral college votes to Barry Goldwater's 53. Cities topped the national Democratic margins by 10 percent or more. The shape of the election was significant, even historic. While the cities were delivering huge margins to the Democratic ticket and nine out of ten blacks voted for Johnson, for the first time since the Civil War voters in the South began to desert the party. Goldwater received 87 percent of the popular vote in Mississippi, almost 70 percent in Alabama, and substantially more than 50 percent in Louisiana, Georgia, and South Carolina. Goldwater carried a majority of white votes in every former Confederate state except Texas (Bartley and Graham, 1975, 107). The shape of Johnson's landslide, as much as its magnitude, explains why the Great Society programs passed by the 89th Congress elected in 1964 were so distinctly oriented to the needs of urban constituencies in the North.

Except for the brief respite granted by the 1964 landslide (and, to some degree, the political atmosphere that existed in the aftermath of the Kennedy assassination), Northern Democrats never found it easy to reward their urban constituencies. Since the solid South also held a pivotal position in the party, time after time programs foundered on the divisions over race and ideology. Urban programs almost inevitably involved this question: would they be used to promote racial integration? Even aside from this anathema, few Southern congressmen shared the ideological predilections of their Northern brethren. Presidents Roosevelt, Truman, and Kennedy were constantly bedeviled by the presence of the congressional conservative coalition made up of Republicans and Southern Democrats.

Roosevelt would doubtlessly have pushed much further and faster with New Deal programs if his legislative majorities could have been fashioned without Southern congressional representatives. When President Truman proposed a civil rights bill in February 1948, Southern Democrats organized a states' rights conference to coordinate a strategy to mobilize opposition. During the nominating convention that year, an inspired speech by Minneapolis Mayor Hubert Humphrey helped win a vote to commit the convention to Truman's civil rights proposals. Most of the Southern delegates walked out, and within two weeks they formed the States' Rights party, which nominated South Carolina Governor Strom Thurmond for the presidency. Before the election, the Southerners drifted back into the fold, but they continued to oppose civil rights initiatives bitterly. Years later, Kennedy vacillated over civil rights until his hand was forced by the escalating violence against civil rights activists in the South. He thought, no doubt accurately, that if he moved too fast his entire legislative agenda would be torpedoed. When he came into office, Southerners chaired twelve of eighteen Senate committees and twelve of twenty-one House committees. Howard Smith, an avowed segregationist from Virginia, chaired the House Rules Committee.

Issues of race went beyond civil rights per se. Since urban proposals inevitably confronted the issue of race, Democratic presidents could rarely, if ever, propose urban programs without seeing them watered down or buried in some committee or bottled up in the Rules Committee. This fact of life is illustrated by the legislative infighting over the Housing Act of 1949. The elections of 1948 had returned Democratic leadership to both houses of Congress. In the battle over the bill (S.1070) in the Senate, Northern liberals who favored public housing were put to a test of fire. In a brilliant move, Senator John W. Bricker (R-OH) introduced an amendment prohibiting racial segregation in the public housing program. The squeeze was on. Such liberals as Hubert H. Humphrey and Paul Douglas determined the ultimate fate of the bill in the Senate by voting against the same provisions they had so recently advocated at the Democratic national convention. With a stipulation requiring racial integration, public housing could not have survived the opposition of Southern Democrats, and the liberals knew it.

At least public housing survived, although just barely (a margin of six votes in the House). Years later, when Kennedy was president, the racial issue delayed important urban legislation for years. In 1961 President Kennedy proposed a cabinet-level Department of Urban Affairs and Housing and promised to name Robert C. Weaver, whom he had earlier appointed as the head of the Housing and Home Finance Agency, as the first secretary. Republicans and

Southern Democrats united in opposition to the idea of a Negro serving as a cabinet member and killed the legislation. Every year thereafter presidents Kennedy and Johnson tried to gain approval for legislation to reorganize urban programs under one cabinet department. The 1964 landslide finally yielded the legislative majorities necessary, because several liberal Democrats won races in districts that were normally Republican. The Department of Housing and Urban Development came into existence in 1966, with Weaver as its head.

The coalition that provided support for the Great Society initiatives of 1966 to 1968 proved to be fragile and short-lived. The political base on which the social and urban programs rested was too narrow to survive the controversies that these programs engendered. Urban programs survived until the 1980s basically because Democratic majorities in the House and Senate were able to protect them, albeit in altered form in the Housing and Community Development Act of 1974, and—perhaps more importantly—because urban lobby groups maintained well-institutionalized relationships with Democratic office holders and federal administrators in Washington that outlasted the eroding electoral base.

The Intergovernmental Alliance

The alliance between local officials, Democratic presidents, liberal congressional representatives, and bureaucrats affected national and local politics. Democratic politicians entered into the arrangement in exchange for the delivery of city votes. In return, local officials expected favorable policy. The *institutionalization* of this relationship fundamentally shaped intergovernmental relations for at least three decades. The alliance changed politics and policy at every point in the intergovernmental system.

Especially in the 1960s, the lobbying capacity of local officials became elaborated to the point that local officials became direct participants in policymaking. Having served as a mayor became an important qualification for appointment. In the same way that the nuclear energy industry became embedded in the agency meant to regulate it and the lumber companies supplied administrators and advice to the Forest Service, local officials ceased being mere lobbyists for urban programs. They helped devise and administer them and, in the process, helped shape the federal policy process. The influence flowed both ways, however. Federal programs also transformed local politics.

The presence of federal programs shaped the contours of city politics from the 1950s to the early years of the 1980s to such an extent that it would be difficult, and pointless, to describe political coalitions in the big cities without reference to federal grants. Norman and Susan Fainstein have suggested that postwar central city regimes can be divided into three types: Directive (1950–1964), Concessionary (1965–1974), and Conserving (1975–1981) (Fainstein and Fainstein, 1986). The Directive regimes came together when aggressive mayors were able to forge a coalition of interests behind the cause of *federally financed* urban renewal. The Concessionary regimes, they assert, emerged when neighborhood groups were able to mobilize effective opposition to the renewal projects that, over and over, displaced people who lived in the path of the bulldozer, and when civil rights and community activists were able to lead broad movements demanding policies to reduce racial and economic inequality. Concessionary regimes were led by mayors and administrators *who used federal dollars* to provide a variety of social programs. Conserving regimes emerged in the mid-1970s, coincident with worsening fiscal problems brought on initially by the recession of the 1970s and made worse by the subsequent *cutbacks in federal grant-in-aid programs*. In each case, political coalitions and policies at the local level were shaped by the federal presence.

The concept of regimes is useful for describing the nature of political coalitions in local politics (Stone, 1989). Urban regimes are composed of both political and economic actors who constantly negotiate settlements among themselves and other claimants. The various participants in a regime possess necessary but not often sufficient resources for accomplishing their ends without the cooperation of others. For example, the two central partners in urban regimes, city hall and the downtown business elite, need to work together if any significant projects are to be undertaken. Local governments can provide the imprimatur of legitimacy because they claim to act in behalf of the public; they also can provide public subsidies, condemn land, and provide vital information and professional resources. Local business, for its part, controls most of the investment capital necessary for keeping the local economy healthy. Government and business occupy the center of urban regimes because they possess unique resources and because they have access to institutional power. There are, however, typically other regime participants; some of them, such as gays and feminists in San Francisco (for example) are able to gain a place at the table because they can cause significant trouble almost on cue if they are excluded (DeLeon, 1992).

Through the lens of the regime concept, the ways in which federal programs shaped local politics are readily apparent. In the 1950s, federal urban renewal funds provided an opportunity for a new breed of ambitious politician to seek to control city hall—because ample resources became available for building a political career by leading urban renewal. In cities all across the country, caretaker mayors were replaced by often younger, bright, aggressive types who sold urban voters a vision of civic renewal. They were able to bring local business elites, newspapers, and labor unions on board because they could realistically deliver federal dollars. Richard Lee of New Haven built his political career on just such a base:

> The mayor was building his political career on the success of redevelopment,
> [and] the Republicans could not damage him without attacking either redevelop-

ment or his role in it; but because everything in the redevelopment plan was endorsed by Republican [business] notables, to attack the mayor was to alienate established sources of Republican electoral and financial support. (Dahl, 1961, 134)

Without urban renewal funds, the only means of centralizing power in cities would have been through the revival or refurbishment of party machines.

Federally sponsored urban renewal and highway building provided the mechanism for the Directive regimes of the 1950s, but these programs eventually destabilized these same regimes. By the 1960s displacement was the main impetus for protest against City Hall. Of course, there also were other causes for unrest, the national civil rights movement being the principal one. It is important to note that the first important urban initiative of the 1960s, the War on Poverty, was dreamed up by young zealots in the Kennedy and then the Johnson administrations; they did not wait for a groundswell of demands from local officials. The Johnson administration, in particular, was extremely proactive in pushing a legislative agenda first and then lining up the political support after the fact (Levitan, 1969). As soon as local officials understood the new game, however, they became very skilled at securing the new federal dollars that became available.

The Concessionary regimes were keen to secure federal programs to appease militant black leaders. They often got more than they bargained for, however, partly because federal administrators were pursuing a political agenda that did not coincide with the idea of simply buying peace in the inner cities. Federal policymakers wanted to reform local politics as well. The early federal guidelines for the War on Poverty and the Model Cities programs called for the mobilization of the poor, or their leaders, so that they could gain a share of local political power. Often enough, city hall itself became the target. As Frances Piven and Richard Cloward so brilliantly pointed out in *Regulating the Poor*, the chief effect of the social programs of the Great Society was to lower discontent, enhance the political strength of black leaders, and coopt these leaders into national Democratic politics (1971, 274). Of course, local officials did not exactly appreciate the fact that such an agenda was being accomplished at their expense.

A panoply of new institutions sprang up in cities, many of them created specifically to receive federal funds: Community Action Programs to administer antipoverty grants; Model Cities Agencies; and nonprofit community and housing groups. The new institutions operated independently of and often at odds with city governments. The fact that so many programs became available so fast, to governmental and nongovernmental entities alike, meant that large volumes of federal money flowed into cities without anyone either at the national or local levels keeping track. To try to do so after the fact was a daunting task. In 1966, Oakland's mayor was praised by the chair of a Senate committee for the fact that his city had compiled a list of 140 programs and projects that received federal dollars in Oakland (Rich, 1991, 27). It is doubtful that any other mayor could have made such an accounting. Many of the programs had overlapping or parallel purposes, but that was only one of the problems. Each one of them required separate, often complex, application procedures. In trying to solve their social problems with the help of federal funds, cities were building whole bureaucracies whose sole function seemed to be filling out forms. In 1973, the mayor of Omaha, Nebraska, noted that a significant proportion of his city's employees' time was being spent providing the city's share of its ''in-kind'' matching contribution on federal grants. He was concerned that the pursuit of federal dollars was undermining the ability of the city to define its own priorities and activities. He asked, ''Are we going to wake up some morning and find that 25 percent of city employees are working on city business?'' (Wright, 1982, 59).

More than any other cause, perhaps, the mayors' steadfast resolve to regain control of federal programs revitalized the urban lobby. The ties to the Johnson administration were rebuilt and constantly maintained after 1966 with two objects in mind: the mayors wanted the flow of funds to continue—and they wanted those funds to flow through city hall. They got their wishes because the Johnson administration was extremely sensitive to any protest within the family that might endanger its overall legislative agenda. In June 1965, the United States Conference of Mayors adopted a resolution that urged the administration to ''assure the continuing control of local expenditures relative to this program be fiscally responsible to local officials'' (Greenstone and Peterson, 1968, 318). In October, President Johnson appointed Bernard L. Boutin, a former mayor of Laconia, New Hampshire, as the deputy director of the Office of Economic Opportunity. From that time forward the mayors had the ear of the administration. Two years later, in response to the mayors' complaints that the Model Cities program was being run without any coordination with City Hall, federal administrators quickly moved to give the mayors sign-off authority.

Even before the Republicans captured the White House in 1968, pressure was building to reform the grants-in-aid system. The way this reform impulse played itself out revealed a tension between Democratic liberals in Congress, who were ideologically committed to the idea that grants-in-aid should reflect a national effort to redress social and political inequalities, and the interests of local Democratic officials, who viewed grants as a way to manage their cities' problems. The disagreement was too fundamental to be papered over easily: it involved the fundamental question of whether the federal grants system was supposed to provoke change in local politics, or whether it was a way to strengthen local government as already constituted.

Reform as a Holding Action

As constructed by the Johnson administration, the federal grants-in-aid system could not be sustained for long, either politically or administratively. The edifice of social and urban programs rested on a narrow political base. Whereas the civil rights crusades of the early 1960s had created a mood of national consensus, after 1965 a conviction spread among middle-class suburbanites and blue-collar workers alike that blacks were receiving all of the benefits of federal activism. Riots in the cities stoked the backlash. In 1966, the Republicans gained four seats in the Senate, and in the House they raised their proportion of Republican membership from less than one-third to 43 percent. By the 1968 presidential campaign, the backlash had burst into full flame. George Wallace, running as a third-party candidate, made thinly veiled racist appeals for votes, complaining that the federal government was forcing people "to sell or lease your home or property to someone that they think you ought to lease it to" and "saying you folks don't know where to send your children to schools" (Page, 1978, 204–6). Nixon's campaign adroitly exploited racial stereotypes and antagonisms. One video spot depicted a policeman at a call box, followed by a rapid-fire collage of images—a bullet-shattered automobile window, a rifle and switch blade, a mugging, a drug sale, a youth gang fighting police, all interspersed with the faces of anxious Americans. Nixon's voiceover claimed that the crime rate was rising nine times faster than the national population. Another spot showed an anxious woman walking at night along a deserted street, the voiceover reciting statistics about muggings and robberies. In still another, scenes of urban riots carried a Nixon voiceover calling for "some honest talk about the problem of order" (McGinness, 1969).

The 1968 campaign was the first in which the Republicans successfully exploited the explosive issue of race to divide the constituencies of the Democratic party. In November, Hubert Humphrey carried only one southern state, Texas. Across the South, he carried only 31 percent of the vote, running behind both Nixon (34.5 percent) and Wallace (34.6 percent). The Republicans' racial strategy worked in the North, too. Middle-class suburban whites voted heavily Republican, and blue-collar union members supported Humphrey by a bare majority. The New Deal coalition was unravelling.

Under these circumstances, it is remarkable that social welfare spending actually rose sharply between Nixon's first election and the departure of Gerald Ford from the White House eight years later. Outlays for grants-in-aid to state and local governments increased from $20.3 billion in fiscal 1969 to $59 billion in fiscal 1976 (U.S. OMB, 1979, 276). Three factors were instrumental in facilitating such an expansion of grant programs under a Republican administration. The first two factors are closely related. First, Nixon was committed to administrative reform of the grants system. Second, he was forced to implement his reforms through the Democratic majorities that controlled both houses of Congress. To get the Democrats to go along with reform, he was willing to add more money to the system. A third factor was the institutionalized position of the urban lobby in the intergovernmental system. Even as the Democrats' electoral coalition began to come apart, the lobby groups continued to exert their influence. Years later, Ronald Reagan's budget director, David Stockman, specifically targeted the so-called "iron triangle" that linked local officials with federal administrators and congressional committees.

In February 1971, President Nixon proposed the consolidation of 129 categorical grants into six block grants that the administration labelled "special revenue sharing." The proposal was quite sweeping, since almost one-third of federal grants-in-aid would have been affected. Nixon's proposals were greeted with instant skepticism from congressional Democrats, who suspected that the block grant scheme was simply a ploy to cut overall spending for social welfare programs. They also objected to the idea, as proposed by Nixon, that special revenue sharing funds would be disbursed to states and localities with virtually no accountability to Congress—there would be no performance standards, few restrictions on eligible activities, and no reporting requirements (Conlan, 1988, 56).

Though Nixon's 1971 proposals fell flat, there was considerable currency in the basic idea that the grant-in-aid system needed reform. It is possible, as the Democrats suspected, that Nixon's original intent was both to reform the system and to reduce spending. The latter is difficult to judge, however, because the president assigned such a priority to reform that he was willing to increase spending significantly to persuade Congress to accomplish it. Two instances illustrate this fact particularly well. Even though Nixon failed to achieve consolidation of most grants programs (only two block grants were enacted, the Comprehensive Employment Training Act of 1973 and the Housing and Community Development Act of 1974, signed by President Ford after Nixon's resignation), he pushed for general revenue sharing anyway. The State and Local Fiscal Assistance Act of 1972 added $4.5 billion a year to federal spending without consolidating or cutting a single program.

The Community Development Act, which funded the Community Development Block Grant (CDBG) program, provides a second revealing example of how reform got traded for higher spending. Seven major categorical programs were folded into the Community Development Block Grant created by the legislation: grants for water and sewerage systems, land acquisition, code enforcement, neighborhood facilities, urban renewal, and Model Cities. A key provision that ensured congressional approval was the "hold harmless" guarantee that no entitlement city would receive less total federal money over the first three years than it would have received from the separate programs. Total appropriations went up by about 20 percent.

All through the 1970s, the urban lobby flexed its muscles. Revenue sharing would never have passed without the coordinated lobby efforts of the Big Seven—the National League of Cities, the U.S. Conference of Mayors, the National Legislative Conference, the National Governors' Conference, the Council of State Governments, the National Association of Counties, and the International City Management Association. It is clear that Democratic congressional leaders were intent on killing the legislation outright or, at a minimum, delaying it until after the 1972 presidential election. With a national election only a year away, the Democratic legislative leadership and presidential aspirants were loath to give the Republican incumbent any type of victory. Democrats also tended to be ideologically opposed to less federal oversight over grant-in-aid programs. They argued that local governments lacked the vision and political will to run such programs to benefit minorities and the poor. There was also a good deal of skepticism about the basic competence of state and local governments. In a book published in the same year that revenue sharing passed, Michael D. Reagan summarized the argument cogently:

> Fiscal poverty and poverty of ideas often go together in state government, especially when the programs are designed to help the least affluent and influential of citizens. . . . Revenue sharing is a cop-out as regards the almost universally admitted inadequacies of state and local government structure and financial systems. (1972, 130–31)

The groups that made up the Big Seven disagreed over how to allocate the money—but not over whether it should be forthcoming. A clash between the congressional wing of the party and state and local officials was more or less inevitable. Its intensity scared some of the participants, as shown by the heated exchange that broke out in a private meeting between the House leadership and the U.S. Conference of Mayors' Legislative Action Committee in March 1971:

> As one of those in attendance recalls it, New York's Mayor John V. Lindsay had just gotten up to speak, when Majority Leader Hale Boggs (D-La.) suddenly slammed his fist on the desk and shouted: "You don't need to make any points. Revenue sharing is dead. I'll see that it never passes. So let's get on to something else." Flabbergasted, Lindsay slid back into his seat. There was a moment of embarrassed silence and then a rolling southern drawl rang out from the back of the room. "Hale," said New Orleans Mayor Moon Landrieu, "that's the rudest treatment I have ever witnessed, and I think you better talk about revenue sharing and you better listen. Because, Hale, if you don't start thinking about helping the cities, I want you to know that you'll never be welcome in the city of New Orleans again." Now it was Boggs' turn to be flabbergasted. (*Newsweek*, 1971, 94)

It wasn't long before the Democratic leadership reconsidered its opposition.

In what turned out to be its swan song, the urban lobby was instrumental in securing amendments to the CDBG program in 1977. The representatives of distressed cities were upset over the fact that the 1974 CDBG allocation formula discriminated against them. A study by the Illinois Bureau of the Budget showed that the formula inadvertently, but nevertheless dramatically, discriminated against distressed cites, because it relied significantly on a city's population in figuring the allocation of money. Since the industrial cities in the North were rapidly losing population, it followed that they stood to lose CDBG money over time to the rapidly growing cities of the Sunbelt. The other components of the formula, the level of poverty and extent of overcrowded housing, did not necessarily favor the older cities either. The scheduled reallocations were significant. By 1980, Newark would lose more than 52 percent of its CDBG allocation; Philadelphia, almost 45 percent; Detroit, 22 percent; and Rochester, New York, almost 70 percent. The money lost to these cities would flow to such cities as Dallas, which would see its allocation rise by 549 percent by 1980, Fort Lauderdale, which would receive a 436 percent increase, and Phoenix, with its anticipated 727 percent increase.

The urban lobby won the bitter fight that broke out over a new allocation formula. It was its last significant victory. The Northeast-Midwest Congressional Coalition in the House lined up behind a new formula based on a calculation of a city's population *loss*, poverty rate, and the proportion of the housing stock built before 1939. The formula followed closely one developed at the Brookings Institution designed expressly to maximally benefit distressed cities. Southern and Western congressional leaders expressed in unusually bitter terms their dismay at this manner of making policy. The Southern Growth Policies Board waged a vociferous public campaign against the amendment.

The compromises struck to get the amendment passed illustrated, once again, that reform, 1970s style, usually came with a price tag attached. This time the trade-offs were made necessary by the increasingly sharp regional tensions within Congress rather than by a partisan struggle between the president and Congress. To make the new allocation formula palatable to Sunbelt representatives and lobby groups, the increased entitlements to the older industrial cities came from a $1 billion per year addition to appropriations. This made it possible to guarantee that the Sunbelt cities would not suffer any actual cuts. This still left the problem that the Sunbelt cities would have to forgo their scheduled increases in future years guaranteed by the old formula. To solve this sticky problem, Congress introduced a "dual formula" into the amendments, so that a city could select between the original 1974 formula or the new one, depending on which of the two brought the most money. All these compromises brought enough unity to the Democratic majorities in Congress to make possible the passage of the CDBG amendments and last major urban initiative of the 1970s (and 1980s), the Urban Development Action Grants (UDAG) Program.

The policy-making environment of the 1970s was, in many ways, quite perverse. A significant amount of money was committed to urban programs purely because of political compromises. The philosophical premises and national objectives of these programs seemed to get lost amidst the political battles that, in the first instance, pitted the president against Congress and the urban lobby against congressional majorities, and in the second, region against region. How different from the policy-making environment of the mid 1960s! By Ronald Reagan's election, the urban lobby had lost the political punch necessary even to negotiate artful compromises.

The Dissolution of Urban Policy

In a press conference held in October 1981, President Reagan suggested that the residents of cities where unemployment was high should "vote with their feet" and move to more prosperous areas of the country (*New York Times*, 1981). His remark provoked an instant controversy, but it was consistent with recommendations offered in 1980 by a group appointed by President Carter, the Presidential Commission on a National Agenda for the 1980s:

> The economy of the United States, like that of many of the older industrial societies, has for years now been undergoing a critical transition from being geographically-based to being deconcentrated, decentralized, and service-based. In the process, many cities of the old industrial heartland . . . are losing their status as thriving industrial capitals. . . . The historical dominance of more central cities will be diminished as certain production, residential, commercial, and cultural functions disperse to places beyond them. (President's Commission, 1980a, 66–67)

The commission recommended that the federal government let this process of decay in some areas and growth in others take its natural course. "Cities are not permanent," noted the commission; they adapt and change in response to economic and social forces. The adaptation should be facilitated, not altered:

> To attempt to restrict or reverse the processes of change—for whatever noble intentions—is to deny the benefits that the future may hold for us as a nation. (President's Commission, 1980a, 66)
>
> Ultimately, the federal government's concern for national economic vitality should take precedence over the competition for advantage among communities and regions. (President's Commission, 1980b, 4)

The commission acknowledged that some people might be left behind in this economic transformation, "consigned to become a nearly permanent urban underclass" (President's Commission, 1980a, 69). However, said the commission, attempts to compensate the victims of change were misguided:

> Where the federal government steps in to try to alter these dynamics, it generates a flood of demands that may sap the initiative of urban governments because of the expectation of continuing support. There must be a better way. (President's Commission, 1980a, 70)

One of these "better ways" was to provide retraining and relocation assistance so people could move when necessary: "The principal purpose of such programs would be to increase people's mobility by helping them acquire the necessary skills to ensure their continuing relevance to a changing economy" (President's Commission, 1980a, 70).

The recommendations by Carter's commission and in the policies subsequently pursued by the Reagan administration constituted a revolutionary sea change in philosophy: for the first time since national urban policy emerged in the 1930s, the judgment was being made that individual cities were not valuable cultural, social, or economic entities *except to the degree* to which they contributed to a healthy national economy. Three University of Delaware researchers characterized the new policies as "a form of Social Darwinism applied to cities as it has been previously applied, with pernicious consequences, to individuals and social classes" (Barnekov, Rich, and Warren, 1981, 3). Cities would survive if they managed to regenerate their local economies. Otherwise, they would be allowed to wither away.

The Reagan administration set about to sharply reduce federal urban aid, proclaiming that "the private market is more efficient than federal program administrators in allocating dollars" (U.S. HUD, 1982, 2, 23). In line with its ideology and its political base in suburbs and the Sunbelt, the administration sought to withdraw from urban policy and restore state control over the urban programs that remained. In Reagan's view, federal urban programs improperly finance

> activities that logically and traditionally have been the responsibilities of state and local governments. . . . Individuals, firms, and state and local governments, properly unfettered, will make better decisions than the federal government acting for them. . . . It is state governments that are in the best position to encourage metropolitan-wide solutions to problems that spill over political boundaries . . . and to tackle the economic, financial, and social problems that affect the well-being of the state as it competes with others to attract and retain residents and businesses. (U.S. HUD, 1982, 54–57)

The administration intended to devolve the "maximum feasible responsibility for urban matters to the states and through them to their local governments." Cities were instructed to improve their ability to compete in a struggle for survival in which "state and local governments will find it is in their interests to concentrate on increasing their attractiveness to potential investors, residents, and visitors" (U.S. HUD, 1982, 14). Thus, urban policy was built on the assumption that free enterprise would provide a bounty of jobs, incomes, and neighborhood renewal, and that such local prosperity would make federal programs unnecessary.

Reagan moved rapidly to reduce or eliminate all urban policies that tried to help distressed cities. The Community Development Block Grants (CDBG) and Urban Development Action Grants (UDAG) programs won a reprieve from being drastically reduced in the 1983 budget and so did revenue sharing. Budget Director David Stockman wanted to kill these programs altogether; he had previously attempted to write them out of the budget in 1981. But the administration, bending to the weakened but still viable urban lobby—represented principally by governors and mayors, quite a few of them Republican—backed off. The urban lobby groups came away relieved, even though budget cuts were in store.

The administration's success in forcing budget cuts on a Democrat controlled Congress can be explained by reference to two factors. First, the administration succeeded in focusing the public debate over domestic policy on tax cuts and economic growth. Tax cuts became an irresistible political cause for both Democrats and Republicans in 1981. Second, a changing political calculus had, by the 1980s, severely weakened the political influence of city voters and their representatives. For decades, people had been moving to the Sunbelt and to the suburbs. These constituencies had little interest in urban programs.

The Federal Retreat

On February 18, 1981, President Reagan proposed a massive tax cut to stimulate the economy. This package, projected to reduce federal revenues by $54 billion in 1982 alone, called for a 10 percent reduction each year for three years for all individual taxpayers, plus accelerated depreciation of capital assets and other liberalized tax write-offs for corporations. Congress was at first cool to the idea, but it soon became apparent to Democratic lawmakers that they could improve their own reelection prospects if they offered "improvements" that would be appealing to corporate campaign contributors and to individual constituents. By the time individual legislators had outbid one another to satisfy their own political constituencies, the revenue losses from the package promised to be so staggering that some White House advisors wanted to kill the bill. Reagan, however, still favored it, and he lobbied for it very hard, even going on television to appeal for expressions of popular approval (Conlan, 1988, 137).

Reagan signed the Economic Recovery Tax Act of 1981 on August 13, asserting that it was "a turnaround of almost a half a century of . . . excessive growth in government bureaucracy, government spending, government taxing (Conlan, 1988, 125). In its final version, the act reduced individual tax rates by 25 percent over three years and, in addition, reduced business tax liability by at least $50 billion. The revenue losses to the federal treasury were huge. In just the first two years $128 billion in revenue was lost to the treasury, and the total losses by 1987 amounted to more than $1 trillion (Conlan, 1988, 138). Throughout the 1980s and into the 1990s, the 1981 tax cuts in combination with increased expenditures for defense accounted for virtually the entirety of the huge budget deficits that dominated debates about domestic policy throughout the 1980s and into the 1990s.

The Tax Reform Act of 1986 further reduced federal revenues and sharply limited the capacity of governments at all levels to collect increased revenues in step with improvements in the economy. The 1986 legislation was sold as a fundamental "reform" of the tax code. Most Americans had the impression that the main purpose was to simplify a maddeningly complex tax system. This promise was never fulfilled. Instead, Congress collapsed the several tax rates in the code, which increased as a taxpayer's income went up, to three basic rates: 15 percent, 28 percent, and 32 percent. The tax rates were indexed to inflation, so that over time taxpayers could not drift into a higher tax bracket unless their incomes rose faster than the inflation rate. There were two dramatic effects. First, the new law almost eliminated the feature of the tax code that had historically allowed the federal government to collect increased taxes whenever incomes went up, either in real terms or through inflation. This change had the effect of institutionalizing the tax cuts adopted in 1981 by making it difficult for federal revenues to rise, even in a good economy, to reduce budget deficits. Only cuts in expenditures or increases in tax rates or new taxes could accomplish that.

Another effect of the Tax Reform Act was that tax rates fell only modestly or not at all for most taxpayers, but were drastically reduced for the rich. In subsequent years, the constant talk about rising deficits, the savings and loan scandal, and a general perception that taxes hit the middle class more than anyone else, helped fuel a tax revolt. George Bush won the presidency in 1988 partly with his promise to "read my lips, no new taxes." The political atmosphere for increased federal government spending on pressing social problems such as education, housing, health, and welfare was thoroughly poisoned.

Overall domestic spending during the Reagan years rose, both in actual and in constant dollars, though at a sharply reduced rate from previous decades. While many programs beneficial to the middle class were protected from cuts, those for the poor were hit hard. In February 1981, President Reagan told Congress that a "social safety net of programs" would remain in place for "those who through no fault of their own must depend on the rest of us" (Levitan and Johnson, 1984, 155). Budget Director David Stockman later admitted that this promise was a mere "political ploy" to build support for program reductions (Levitan and Johnson, 1984, 155).

Broad entitlement programs with middle-class recipients, such as the old-age and survivors' benefits funded through the Social Security Act of 1935 as well as veterans' benefits and Medicare, were affected only marginally. In contrast, deep cuts and new eligibility restrictions were imposed in public assistance programs for the poor. Medicaid, which was available through the states to welfare recipients, was reduced through tighter eligibility requirements. Enrollment in AFDC (Aid to Families with Dependent Children) fell by half a million recipients; a million people lost food stamps. It became harder to get unemployment benefits; whereas three-fourths of the unemployed received benefits during the recession of 1975, only 45 percent were able to qualify during the 1982–83 recession (Robertson and Judd, 1989, 233).

Since older cities had a disproportionate share of people in poverty, reductions in social programs hit them particularly hard. The capacity of states and localities to make up for federal cuts was severely curtailed by the fact that federal grants-in-aid to local governments were reduced even more sharply than programs for individuals. From 1982 to 1987 grants-in-aid to states and localities fell sharply. These were the first reductions of consequence for grants-in-aid since the 1940s.

As shown in table 7-1, from 1980 to 1984 grant programs fell by more than 14 percent and by an additional 3.5 percent from 1985 to 1987. The 1981 budget act reduced spending for categorical grants by 30 percent over a three-year period. In 1982, Reagan persuaded Congress to consolidate seventy-six categorical grants into nine block grants in health, social services, education, and community development. In the process, funding was reduced by 20 percent. Previously, many of these grants went directly to local governments. Now all of them went to the states, to be distributed as they saw fit. Because the states tended to spread funds broadly across a great many jurisdictions and give little priority to distressed communities, the cities were "one of the clearest losers of federal funds" under these block grants (Peterson, et al., 1986, 21). A 1982 study by the Joint Economic Committee of the Senate showed that distressed cities were losing a larger absolute amount and a higher percentage of federal aid than cities that were better off (Joint Economic Committee, 1982, 6). Cities whose economies were already in trouble before the cuts were being compelled to endure the highest proportional reductions in federal assistance.

Major urban programs were drastically reduced, and some were eliminated in the 1980s (see table 7.2). Overall spending dropped from $6.1 billion in fiscal year 1981 to $5.2 billion in fiscal year 1984. The $5.2 billion spent for

TABLE 7.1

Growth Rates in Federal Aid Spending, Selected Fiscal Years 1955–1987

Fiscal Year	Current Dollars		1972 Dollars	
	Amount (in billions)	Percent Change	Amount (in billions)	Percent Change
1955	3.2	—	5.6	—
1959	6.5	103	10.0	79
1960	7.0	—	10.8	—
1964	10.1	44	14.7	36
1965	10.9	—	15.5	—
1969	20.3	86	24.2	56
1970	24.0	—	27.0	—
1974	43.4	82	37.9	40
1975	49.8	—	39.2	—
1979	82.9	66	48.1	23
1980	91.5	10.4	48.2	0.2
1981	94.8	3.6	46.1	−4.4
1982	88.2	−7.0	40.4	−12.4
1983	92.5	4.9	40.7	0.7
1984	97.6	5.5	41.3	1.5
1980–1984	—	6.6	—	−14.2
1985	105.8	8.6	43.1	4.4
1986	112.4	6.1	44.5	3.0
1987	108.4	−3.6	41.7	−6.3
1985–1987	—	2.4	—	−3.5

Sources: Based on U.S. Advisory Commission on Intergovernmental Relations, *Significant Features of Fiscal Federalism, 1985–86*, M-146 (Washington, D.C.: U.S. Government Printing Office, 1986), p. 19; U.S. Office of Management and Budget, *Budget of the United States Government, Historical Tables, Fiscal Year 1989* (Washington, D.C.: U.S. Government Printing Office, 1990), table 12.1.

fiscal year 1984–85 amounted to a drop in spending of almost 20 percent, when inflation is taken into account. By the 1988 budget year, money for urban programs was cut to $3.6 billion—a further reduction of more than 40 percent, when the effects of inflation are considered. In fiscal year 1986 the revenue sharing program ended, and for the first time since the early 1960s, a majority of general-purpose governments in the United States received no direct federal assistance whatsoever.

Other budget cuts also affected the cities. Most subsidies for the construction of public housing were eliminated. Only 10,000 new units a year were authorized after 1983, compared with the 111,600 new or rehabilitated units authorized for 1981 alone (Aaron, et al., 1982, 119). Urban mass transit grants were reduced 28 percent from 1981 to 1983 and were cut another 20

TABLE 7.2

Federal Outlays for Urban and Regional Programs to State and Local Governments, Fiscal Years 1981–1988 (in billions of dollars)

	FY 1981	FY 1984	FY 1987 (est.)	FY 1988 (est.)
Community Development Block Grants	4.0	3.8	3.1	2.6
Urban Development Action Grants	0.4	0.5	0.4	0.3
Economic Development Administration and Appalachian Regional Commission	0.7	0.5	0.3	0.2
Other Community and Regional Development	1.0	0.4	0.7	0.4
Total	6.1	5.2	4.5	3.6

Source: U.S. Office of Management and Budget, *Budget of the United States Government, Historical Tables, Fiscal Year 1987* (Washington, D.C.: U.S. Government Printing Office, 1986), table 12.3.

percent by 1986. The programs of the Comprehensive Employment and Training Act (CETA) were eliminated entirely after the 1983 budget. The countercyclical urban aid programs initiated under President Carter ended early in the Reagan years.

Reducing the Capacity of State and Local Governments

President Nixon had conceived his New Federalism as a device to improve the management of federal programs. Block grants were described as mechanisms for streamlining and simplifying the grant-in-aid system and also for giving local governments more flexibility in spending federal dollars. The Reagan administration had something different in mind when it proposed reforms in the intergovernmental aid system. With his block grants, Reagan was trying to take, in his words, ''a step toward total withdrawal of the federal government from education, health and social services programs which . . . are properly the responsibility of state and local governments.'' Block grants, in other words, were a device not for administrative reform but for a political revolution that would, Reagan hoped, result in the national government eventually abandoning the responsibilities it had assumed in the New Deal years and in the 1960s and 1970s.

In his State of the Union address of January 27, 1982, President Reagan unveiled a revolutionary ''New Federalism'' intended, he said, to return power to states and communities. The president outlined a ten-year program for turning over to the states $47 billion in federal programs, all to be accomplished by 1991. In fiscal year 1984, Aid to Families with Dependent Children and Food Stamps, at a combined cost of $16.5 billion, would be turned over to the states. As a "bribe," the federal government would in turn assume all costs of the Medicaid program, which could save the states a combined $19.1 billion per year. From fiscal year 1984 through fiscal 1988 the states would go through a voluntary transition period, assuming responsibility for up to forty-three grant programs, including the CDBG, UDAG, and other urban programs. To help them pay for these programs, a trust fund would be established, composed of federal excise taxes on gasoline, tobacco, alcohol, and telephones, plus part of the federal "excess profits" tax on oil. After fiscal 1988 the trust fund would be phased out over four years, leaving the states with full responsibility to fund and administer the programs, if they saw fit.

David Cohen, the former president of Common Cause, noted that about half of the state legislatures did not have the staff and expertise that were needed for the types of programs they were being asked to assume. Based on all prior experiences, the states would not be responsive to the needs of cities. A 1982 Conference of Mayors report stated: "The history of city-state relations has too often been one of neglect of city needs by the state" (*New York Times*, 1982). A former Atlanta mayor pointed out that "at best, there are only four states—Massachusetts, Michigan, Minnesota, and California—that have shown responsibility on urban issues. The other forty-six have shown either neglect or downright hostility" (*New York Times*, 1982).

Decentralization of programs would have resulted in fewer programs, not a replacement of the federal effort. This was the result that Reagan actually wanted. Decentralization was a Trojan horse to reduce the scope of government not only at the national but also at state and local levels. He thought that citizen pressure at these lower levels of government would prevent those governments from funding programs as the federal government had: "When tax increases are proposed in state assemblies and city councils," he said, "the average citizen is better able to resist and to make his influence felt" (Conlan, 1988, 224).

Congress soundly rejected Reagan's New Federalism. Important features of the 1986 Tax Reform Act, however, were designed expressly to make it more difficult for states and localities to support activist government. When the tax rates were reduced to three levels in the federal code, with a 32 percent cap on the highest rate, most states similarly revised their state income laws; this change was irresistible since many state tax forms had, in the past, been modeled on the federal forms. Thus, many states almost automatically reduced their taxes when the federal government did. In addition, as originally proposed, the 1986 act would have eliminated (1) the federal deduction for state and local taxes paid and (2) any taxpayer exclusion of interest earned on tax-exempt municipal bonds. The first feature would have resulted in huge pressures on state and local governments to lower tax levels—and simultaneously would have increased federal tax revenues (which would, presumably, be used to reduce federal budget deficits and finance the arms build-up). The second feature would have radically reduced the capacity of state and local governments to sell tax-exempt bonds, which had been used, since before the 1930s, to build roads and bridges, schools, airports, water and sewer facilities, and other public infrastructure.

State and local officials furiously lobbied for the removal of these two features. They succeeded at saving the deduction for local property taxes, but the taxpayer deductions for state and local sales and personal property taxes were eliminated, which increased federal revenues by $17·billion over a five-year period (Conlan, 1988, 147). Additionally, a state-by-state cap was imposed on the volume and purposes of tax-exempt municipal bonds. By the early 1990s, the effects of federal cutbacks and tax code changes had reverberated throughout the intergovernmental system. State and local governments found themselves deep in debt, forcing them to slash funding for schools, higher education, and other programs.

Urban Enterprise Zones

Even against the background of program cuts, it would be inaccurate to say that the Reagan administration had no urban policy. Indeed, it went to some pains to make its policy clear: cities were instructed to cut taxes and offer tax abatements and other incentives to spur local economic growth. The one specific federal program proposed to help cities do this was urban enterprise zones. In June 1980, two New York representatives, Jack Kemp, a conservative Republican who later served as President Bush's secretary of housing and urban development, and Robert Garcia, a liberal Democrat from New York City, introduced the Urban Jobs and Enterprise Zone Act into Congress. A year later they introduced modified legislation.

The 1980 bill proposed to cut property taxes in designated zones by 20 percent over a four-year period, to allow depreciation of business property over a three-year period (as compared to five years in the federal tax code), to eliminate federal capital gains taxes, to lower corporate taxes, and to reduce employer social security tax contributions. All of this was designed to encourage businesses to locate in depressed urban areas. In 1981 the proposed legislation was amended to require a state and local commitment to lower tax levels. It also dropped the accelerated depreciation allowance and the Social Security tax reduction. As a substitute, businesses in the zones were to be allowed up to $1,500 in tax credits for each of their employees.

Deregulation provisions were included in both bills. In the 1981 bill, participating cities would be required to waive and relax various building codes, zoning requirements, and other regulations—the specific package to be proposed by each city. The administration pushed for a waiver of federal minimum wage laws, but Garcia adamantly opposed this recommendation.

Beginning in the fall of 1981, Secretary of Commerce Malcolm Baldridge chaired a study group composed mostly of HUD and Treasury staff members, with the purpose of modifying the Kemp-Garcia bill. The administration's own proposal, announced by President Reagan on March 23, 1982, proposed the creation of twenty-five zones a year for three years. Businesses in these zones would have 75 percent or more of their corporate income tax forgiven, would pay no capital gains tax, and would pay no tariffs or duties in areas also designated by the federal government as "free trade zones." Employees in the zones would be given tax credits. No relief from minimum wage laws would be granted. The proposal also required states and localities to reduce regulations and support privatization or contracting out of some municipal services.

Enterprise zones hardly constituted a comprehensive new urban policy. First, relatively few zones were proposed—after three years, seventy-five in all. The total cost to the Treasury was estimated to be $310 million in the first year, to peak at $930 million after four years. Perhaps even more significant, the incentives offered to businesses in the zones were actually rather inconsequential. According to Rochelle Stansfield of the *National Journal*, "federal taxes are far down the list of factors involved about where to locate." The tax relief promised in the zones proposal was expected to help "at the margins" (Stansfield, 1982, 359). Further, the enterprise zones would not generate additional business volume for the nation; they would only redistribute businesses from one location to another. The president's proposal, it seemed, was more symbolic than substantial.

President Reagan promised to push for passage of urban enterprise zones legislation during the special session of Congress in November and December of 1982. In the press of other business, however, the legislation was not even discussed. Finally, on March 7, 1983, the president sent his Urban Enterprise Zone Act to Congress, claiming that the legislation was a sharp departure from past policy:

> Enterprise zones are a fresh approach for promoting economic growth in the inner cities. The old approach relied on heavy government subsidies and central planning. A prime example was the model cities program in the 1960s, which concentrated government programs, subsidies and regulations in distressed urban areas. The enterprise zone approach is to remove government barriers, bring individuals to create, produce and earn their own wages and profits. (White House, 1983)

In spite of the president's rhetorical claims, the legislation was not a "fresh approach," but a logical progression from past policies, Democratic as well as Republican, that had long stressed the role of government in subsidizing private investment. Through the Reagan years the enterprise zones idea surfaced from time to time but was never pushed very hard by the administration. After George Bush's election as president in 1988, the idea continued to receive an occasional public relations nudge from the president or HUD, but it never rose to the level of being seriously proposed as a consequential part of the president's legislative agenda.

Even the Los Angeles rebellion of late April and early May 1992, failed to provide sufficient stimulus for a new round of urban programs. Within days proposals were wending their way through Congress, and President Bush, after a week of befuddlement, gave his backing to the idea of an urban aid package. But all of the proposals got lost in a quagmire of election-year politics.

Though President Bush initially responded to the rioting with a law-and-order statement, within a few days the White House felt pressured to promise a positive response to help the riot's victims. Both Democrats and Republicans rushed to pass urban aid legislation. For the first time in fifteen years it appeared that the national government might embark on an intiative to help the cities. On June 18, the House and Senate passed a $1.3 billion urban aid package. Among other provisions, it earmarked $500 million for 360,000 youth jobs in seventy-five distressed cities and $328 million for new Small Business Administration loans in Los Angeles and Chicago (which had just experienced a devastating flood in its central business district). Congressional leaders promised action on an urban enterprise zones proposal being developed by the White House. The programs would have created seventy-five urban and twenty-five rural zones and cost the Treasury about $2.5 billion over five years in tax breaks for businesses in the zones.

After a host of amendments, the Senate version contained liberalized (tax free) retirement accounts for upper-income people, as well as a repeal of luxury taxes on expensive yachts, furs, jewels, and planes (Democrats backed this amendment as lustily as did some Republicans). It was estimated that of the $30 billion that the Senate version would cost over five years, only $6 billion would go to depressed areas in cities (Krauss, 1992, A20). In addition to the various tax measures (a few business taxes were slightly increased), the estimated number of enterprise zones went up to as many as 125. Federal funds would be spread so thinly that the money could have little potential impact.

The revised legislation passed the House again, finally, on October 6 and the Senate on October 8. It was clear that the memories of voters were short; the pressure on the federal government to produce legislation had weakened considerably since summer. Congress adjourned on October 10. President Bush exercised a pocket veto. He could hardly do otherwise; he had trapped himself by his "no new taxes" pledge even as he was being pounded by Bill Clinton for doing nothing on the domestic front.

Why Urban Policy Has Changed

Abandoning urban policy made political sense for the Republicans. Party leaders have long sought to capitalize on white disaffection from Democratic civil rights and antipoverty policies. Reagan took advantage of this sentiment in 1980 and 1984. Jimmy Carter and Walter Mondale carried the vote of large cities (over 500,000 population) by substantial margins, while Reagan won slightly more than a third of the big city vote in each election. Reagan, however, carried the suburban and small city vote by a margin of 53 percent to 37 percent in 1980, and 57 to 42 percent in 1984. Since only 12 percent of the 1984 vote was cast in large cities, while 55 percent was cast in the suburbs and the small cities, the Republican advantage was devastatingly effective (Pomper, 1985, 68–69). To illustrate, Mondale carried 65 percent of 173,000 votes in the city of St. Louis in 1984, while Reagan carried 64 percent of 308,000 votes in suburban St. Louis County (State of Missouri 1986). Coupled with the antitax core of Reagan support, the administration had strong incentives to abandon forms of urban revitalization that required federal activism or intrusions on suburban autonomy.

Mayors are aware of their rapid decline in influence in both political parties. On February 28 and March 1, 1987, the National Municipal League met in Washington, D.C., to try to amplify their influence in the 1988 presidential election. They established an "Election '80 Task Force," designed to force candidates to promise programs important to local governments ("Mayors Plot," 1987, 12A). Their efforts were in vain. Even in the Democratic party, the political influence of central cities has melted away. In 1968 the Democrats used the word "city" twenty-three times in their party platform adopted at the presidential nominating convention. It did not appear even once in the 1988 platform. The substitute term, clearly a recognition of the power of the suburbs, was "hometown America."

As cities have lost population, they also have lost their influence in the White House and in Congress. In 1952, for example, voters in New York City cast 48 percent of their state's share of the presidential vote. By 1988 the city's share of the state vote had fallen to 31 percent. This has been the experience for other cities as well: Chicago's share of the presidential vote in Illinois dropped from 41 percent in 1952 to 23 percent in 1988; for St. Louis the city's share of Missouri's vote fell from 20 percent to 7 percent. Presidents of both parties, therefore, do not now pay as much attention as they once did to city voters or to urban issues. A similar development has occurred in Congress. The number of senators and representatives elected mainly by city voters has declined sharply over the past thirty years. Cities will lose influence even more after the redistricting that will occur as a result of the 1990 census.

The 1990 census revealed that during the 1980s the Sunbelt and suburbs continued to grow at a much faster rate than did the central cities. As of the

1990 census, 48 percent of Americans lived in suburbs, and a majority of all votes cast in the 1992 presidential election were suburban. The number of states with suburban majorities increased from three in 1980 to 14 in 1990. The influence of cities in state legislatures, in Congress, and in presidential politics has eroded to the point that central cities, on their own, can influence policies outside their borders very little. In the 1988 election, for example, George Bush could have carried almost all of the Northern industrial states without a single vote from the big cities in those states.

Congressional redistricting in 1992, which was required because of the results of the 1990 census, weakened the political voice of cities still further. Within the Frostbelt states, the suburbs commanded majorities in even more congressional districts. And in 1992, fifteen congressional seats were reapportioned to the South and West from Northern states.

Unlike Ronald Reagan, Bush as president did not have an actively hostile relationship with urban leaders. Urban issues were simply absent from his agenda. At the 1988 GOP convention, rural, but not urban, development rated a subcommittee in the platform debates. The omission of an "urban" focus in the platform, in effect, was made official by this language, "Urban America is center stage in our country's future. That is why we address its problems and potential throughout this platform, rather than limiting our concern to a particular section."

Under Bush and Secretary of Housing and Urban Development Jack Kemp, a federal initiative began to create seventy enterprise zones. Five bills to create such zones were introduced into Congress during 1989 (as a New York congressman, Kemp had introduced a bill himself in 1981). These zones would have cost the federal treasury about $1 billion a year in lost revenues. By the end of their tenure in office, however, the proposal for enterprise zones had achieved little.

Scandals involving subsidized housing programs administered during the Reagan administration derailed any new urban legislation that might have been put forward in the early 1990s. Former HUD Secretary Samuel Pierce refused to testify before Congress about his role in interceding to award HUD subsidies to housing projects financed by powerful Republican contributors. Hearings revealed that Republican "consultants," including former Secretary of the Interior James Watt, received $6 million in fees to help procure HUD housing grants.

In a proposal made in late 1990, the Bush administration offered to give $22 billion in block grants over to the states, with no strings attached. Urban leaders expressed opposition to the idea of giving the states the authority to distribute CDBG, mass transit, and other funds; they believed, in general, that the states would not be responsive to the needs of distressed cities. Indeed, the financial condition of states in the early 1990s made it more unlikely than ever that they can be responsive to cities. The recession of the early 1990s hit state budgets particularly hard. By 1992, two-thirds of the states were dealing with massive deficits and were sharply reducing expenditures on basic education and social services programs.

During the 1992 campaign, Clinton promised big city mayors a $20 billion a year infrastructure investment program that would link the physical revitalization of the cities to national economic revitalization (Ayres, 1992). In the wake of the Los Angeles riots of late April–early May 1992, he supported aid to the cities. In April 1993, Congress defeated a modest package of urban aid. An urban program was salvaged, however, when the administration incorporated "empowerment zones" into the Omnibus Budget Reconciliation Act of 1993, which passed the House by two votes and the Senate by a vice-presidential tie-breaker. This legislation will make $3.5 billion available for enterprise and empowerment zones in seventy-two urban and thirty-three rural communities. In March 1994, the selection process was going forward.

The passage of a modest urban program demonstrates that some urban programs can still be gotten through Congress, despite the decades-long movement to the suburbs and the Sunbelt. The fact, remains, however, that because cities do not implement national programs, as they do in Europe, they can be abandoned when it is politically advantageous for politicians to ignore them.

Constraints and Policy Options

The United States went much further than other countries in abandoning urban policy, but its retreat from policies designed to shore up declining regions and cities was not unique. In the decade of the 1980s governments everywhere began to reduce welfare state expenditures. Urban policy was one component of this trend. Central governments reduced their support for cities or reduced their share of public provision that passed through local governments in the United States, Canada, Great Britain, France, Denmark, Spain, Mexico, Brazil, Argentina, and elsewhere (Preteceille 1990, 27–59; Pickvance and Preteceille, 1991; Judd and Parkinson, 1990). In restructuring national-local relationships, these nations were responding to comparable pressures, which still prevail. It is, therefore, unrealistic to expect urban policy to be revived in the United States in its previous form.

From the end of World War II to about the mid-1970s, international trade, capital investment, and labor migration patterns contributed to rapid economic growth in the Western industrial nations. In Europe and in North America, older urban areas (if not always the center cities) that had prospered in the industrial age experienced a revival based on a new boom in manufacturing. The rebuilding of war-ravaged economies, heavy expenditures (especially in the United States) on armaments, the building of integrated financial and trade networks that linked the economies of the developed nations more closely, the availability of low-cost energy from several key oil-producing countries, and the flow of raw materials from so-called "developing" nations all helped to sustain a period of economic growth for the Western industrial nations and their urban areas. Generous social welfare policies and spatially specific policies for regions and cities that seemed to lag behind were seen as necessary to sustain productivity. Whether adopted under the rubric of Keynesian economics or some other generic label, such policies were regarded as important tools of economic management and balanced national development.

In the 1970s the relationships that had underwritten economic growth in the Western nations began to unravel. Conventionally, the recession and stagflation of that decade is traced to the oil embargo of 1973 and the attendant ratcheting up of oil prices over the next few years. However, deeper, structural forces were at work. The globalization of investment and production hit manufacturing sectors in the developed countries hard, as corporations sought to drive down the costs of production by moving manufacturing and assembly operations to places with low labor costs. The devastating impact on communities in the United States was well documented by the economists Barry Bluestone and Bennett Harrison in their aptly titled book *The Deindustrialization of America* (1982).

Global corporations developed the ability to shift productive enterprises and investment capital rapidly from place to place. Conglomerate corporations mushroomed in size and administrative capacity. The merger mania of the 1980s contributed to this dexterity; firms learned that they could break labor unions and pit one community, or region, or country against another by producing similar products in several locations and by acquiring competitors and diversifying products and services (Bluestone and Harrison, 1982). The job descriptions of corporate managers required them to constantly calculate profit margins for different divisions and products and to constantly monitor environmental regulations, transportation advantages, labor market characteristics, tax levels, and governmental policies. Many multi-national corporations ceased to identify with any particular place or even with their original charter countries (Barnet, 1974). The "efficiency" of one location compared to another became the single touchstone for corporate investment decisions. As a consequence, patterns of investment within the industrial nations changed very rapidly. The semiconductor, textile, clothing, and shoe industries relocated mostly outside the developed nations to low-cost labor sites in Third World countries or export platforms. Auto, steel, chemical, rubber, and other heavy industries dispersed their operations around the globe. New plants using more efficient technologies were built in regions within the core countries or in the developing countries in direct competition with the plants located in the old industrial regions (Glickman, 1987, 66–86).

Manufacturing regions and urban areas in North America and in Europe fell into rapid, even abrupt decline or collapse. In most of the developed countries manufacturing employment fell absolutely and as a proportion of the labor force. By the early to mid-1980s the declines in manufacturing jobs were partially compensated for by gains in service-sector jobs, but those jobs were not necessarily, or even generally, located in the same regions or urban areas that suffered severe job losses in manufacturing. Indeed, service-sector growth tended to take place disproportionately in new regions—the Sunbelt in the United States, the "sunrise" region in the south of England, southern West Germany.

Faced with local economic crisis, older cities and regions that had relied on industrial production or resource extraction responded, initially, in a predictable fashion: they sought favorable national policies. In all of the Western democracies it was assumed that central governments should intervene to protect declining regions and cities. Previous economic, social, and urban policies were built upon the assumption that national economic vitality and the success of key industries—which happened to be located in urban areas— were intricately linked. Until the 1980s the Western industrial nations attempted to insulate their national economies and declining regions and localities from the effects of the new world economy. These policies took the form in Great Britain, West Germany, and France (for instance) of subsidies to declining industries and targeted aid to cities and regions. In the United States, as we have seen, countercyclical legislation was adopted during the Carter administration, and though it was never adopted, the National Development Bank, proposed in 1978 would have made loans and grants available to areas with economic problems.

In the first half of the decade of the 1980s a policy revolution swept through the nations of North America and Western Europe. Adjustment rather than resistance to global economic change became the guiding principle for national policies. In the United States, President Reagan sought to dismantle all forms of urban policy. Soon after Margaret Thatcher and the Conservatives took power in Britain in 1979, the central government sought to curb spending by local authorities. Within a few years, the government had abolished regional authorities, and through city action teams, task forces, enterprise zones, free ports, urban development grants, urban regeneration grants, and urban development corporations it tried to force cities to focus on strategies of local economic development rather than on public planning, housing, and service provision. Though dominated by Labour councils, cities throughout the country were fully committed to such strategies by the late 1980s, if not sooner (Judd and Parkinson, 1990). Canada, France, and West Germany also changed policy to encourage local governments to become entrepreneurial (Judd and Parkinson 1990; Pickvance and Preteceille, 1991).

Against this background, it is clear that the old urban policies are not going to be revived. In light of the new political calculus mentioned earlier, this is an especially safe prediction for the United States. What, then, are the policy options available to cities in the 1990s?

First, cities are in the process of learning from their mistakes and refining strategies of economic development. For the first few years, states and cities seemed determined to simply give away the store to move the merchandise. Sunbelt states promised low taxes, few regulations, and cheap labor, all elements of a "good business climate" (Smith, Ready, and Judd, 1985). Cities copied this formula as far as they were able, freely bestowing tax abatements and rollbacks, sales tax exemptions, and other gimmicks in a "beggar thy neighbor" competition with other cities. Though such desperate, and even mindless, competition clearly continues, at least some public officials have become more sophisticated, realizing that high quality services, competent government employees, an educated, skilled work force, good infrastructure, and even a clean and safe natural environment might be as important as the cheapest possible playing field in keeping and luring business (Eisenger, 1988). Thus, cities use CDBG grant dollars, proceeds from tax increment financing, revenue bonds, and manpower training assistance in an attempt to promote economic growth without starving the public sector. The literature describing such techniques was sparse only a decade ago, but is now voluminous. The *Economic Development Quarterly* and other journals and newsletters are specifically devoted to research and information on economic development, and unlike the early 1980s, developers and promoters no longer completely dominate the field.

Some public officials have also rediscovered a basic truth: business may be an important constituency, but it is not the only one that politicians must answer to. Other constituencies must be attended to, a point made by Todd Swanstrom in his distinction between economic and political logic (Swanstrom, 1989). Politicians and public officials must be mindful not only that they must maintain an electoral constituency, but also that the public sector itself is an important employer and service provider. Some cities, most notably Boston, have learned to use linkage policies to extract public revenues or commitments from developers in exchange for approval of development projects (Smith, 1988, 93–109).

A second set of policy options is available in the 1990s. Though it is clear that urban policies, if defined as policies targeted specifically to older central cities, are defunct, urban policies more broadly defined are almost certain to be enacted over the next few years. For at least two decades the suburbs have been urbanizing, in the sense that problems once associated with older central cities have become characteristic of many suburbs. A great many social problems are not peculiar to central cities or even to families in poverty. Crime, drug use, family violence, child abuse, poor performance in schools, high rates of teenage pregnancy, the AIDS epidemic, inadequate access to health care—many of these problems are more prevalent in poor families, but they have also become widespread in middle-class suburban families. As the 1992 presidential election showed, there is a rising demand for governmental attention to such problems. The urban programs of the past will find a partial substitute in "cross-cutting" programs that treat social problems wherever they are found. Problems peculiar to poor people in central cities—most notably, homelessness—will no doubt continue to be neglected in comparison to problems that cut across social, ethnic, and racial groups. The retreat from social programs that began in the 1980s, however, may have provoked a reaction that will force government to confirm that it has responsibilities to ensure a minimum level of health and welfare for its citizens. If the "urban" component of this equation has been lost, it is because most citizens, whether they live in central cities or not, are now urban.

Urban Development Policies in a Globalizing Economy: Creating Competitive Advantage in the Post–Cold War Era

JACK N. BEHRMAN AND DENNIS A. RONDINELLI

The dramatic political and economic changes accompanying the end of the Cold War will not only transform the relationships among nations but also restructure interactions among cities in a global economy. The unforeseen political events that brought the end of the Cold War have focused public attention on the international affairs of nation-states, masking the enormous challenges facing governments and businesses in American cities. But the need for all countries to open their economies to international trade and investment in the post–Cold War period will diminish the economic influence of nation-states and increase the importance of cities and metropolitan areas as centers of international economic operations. Globalization of the world economy will require cities to adapt their development policies to the requirements of international competition.

The world economy is being restructured not only by political changes but also by the increasing geographic mobility of all factors of production. This mobility will change the location of productive activities as well as the direction and volume of flows of trade and investment among cities. The unanticipated opening of Eastern Europe and the demise of the Soviet Union, for example, and the slow but inevitable transformation from centrally planned to market economies in China, the Baltics and Balkans, and other socialist countries are creating new opportunities for trade and investment. These changes will continue to intensify the competition among cities around the world to attract and efficiently use capital, labor, and technology.

The opening of the world economy and the expansion of cross-border transactions not only will make nation-states more interdependent but also will require more cities to expand trade and attract foreign direct investment (FDI). Because FDI will be needed to create additional capacity to export and import, it will be sought more vigorously by cities than by national governments and will increase the competition among urban areas in attracting transnational corporations (TNCs), especially in high technology industries.

Over the past decade, improvements in telecommunications, air transport, and information technology have made distance to suppliers and markets—the traditional criteria for selecting business locations—less critical for transnational corporations than such factors as the supply of human skills, quality of education, community safety, quality of arts and recreation, and a clean environment (Behrman and Rondinelli, 1992). Thus, the most competitive cities in the post–Cold War era will be those with strong economic vitality and with cultures that support competent and well-trained labor forces, provide a good quality of life, and promote the innovation, creativity, and flexibility that will allow local economies to restructure and adapt to rapidly changing international conditions. The ability of the American economy to thrive and grow in the post–Cold War period will depend on the ability of its cities to adjust to complex social and economic changes and to reshape their cultures in creative and innovative ways to meet new global conditions. The ability of American cities to restructure their economies and adapt to changing needs depends significantly on their ability to energize their *cultural* resources in purposeful ways.[1]

Even before the collapse of communism in Eastern Europe it was clear that the increasing geographic mobility of factors of production was altering the structure and the location of employment, the use of technologies, the patterns of trade and investment, and the economic opportunities in cities (National Academy of Sciences, 1973, 1985). Metropolitan areas were already in keen competition to attract clean, high-technology industries. For older cities, this global restructuring accompanied the shift from heavy manufacturing or smokestack industries to "knowledge" industries and a rapid expansion of the service sector. New York, Boston, Washington, D.C., Los Angeles, San Francisco, and Atlanta had already become international information centers, tied in a network of communications and of financial, commercial, and supplier-vendor relations. Although these changes have increased the flexibility of cities in accommodating diverse types of industries and services, they have also made them more vulnerable to frequent and spontaneous shifts in the location of transnational activities.

Globalization of the world economy in the post–Cold War period will require cities to make significant cultural changes, to develop a sense of purpose and direction, and to create a sense of community and a quality of life that will attract the managers, scientists, technicians, and white-collar workers that form the backbone of international knowledge industries.

Globalization will thus alter not only growth rates in various cities but also the structure of their economies. Urban areas that are inward-looking will offer different opportunities than those stimulated by foreign direct investment or by exports. FDI will flow to those cities that openly seek it and that create a physical environment, a quality of life, and a sense of community in which transnational management and labor can flourish. This will require cities to expand their transport and communications infrastructure as speed becomes a more crucial factor in competition and to improve their educational systems as more career opportunities open in transnational companies. Cities will have to diversify their recreational, artistic, and cultural facilities and improve their health programs and concepts of health maintenance to respond to culturally diverse life-styles of the labor force. Attitudes toward the concept of community itself will have to shift to encompass the more open society required to attract foreign investors. Such shifts will be needed to prepare urban residents for a greater understanding of the extent to which the world is tied together in opportunities and problems that are becoming more common to all nations and peoples.

To meet the challenges of an open world economy, new policy initiatives will have to be taken in American cities to form internationally oriented communities centered around institutions promoting creativity in the physical sciences, technology, the arts, and the social sciences. In the future, the competitive cities will be those that can adapt their cultures to become part of a new international urban network with economic and cross-cultural ties.

This chapter describes the forces globalizing the world economy in the post–Cold War era, the implications for urban economic and cultural development, and the cultural changes that will be required for cities to increase their economic vitality and competitiveness.

Forces of Globalization in the Post–Cold War Economy

Three major forces are pressing relentlessly for globalization of the world economy: the first is the inexorable integration of nations economically; the second is the inevitable disintegration of nations politically, as military force recedes as the primary means of maintaining cohesion; the third is the spread of similar patterns of consumption and life-styles around the world (Behrman, 1984; Berhman and Rondinelli, 1992).

Economic Integration

American foreign policies have sought freer trade, payments, and investment across national borders since the end of World War II (Behrman and Grosse, 1990). But more extensive integration to achieve the benefits of common markets has been limited to regional economic associations. The pressures for integration have been reinforced during the past two decades by developments in technology and information exchange, by changes in market structures, by the emergence of transnational corporations, and by changing security and defense policies. These forces have led to, and have been reinforced by, increasing international mobility of factors of production; changes in the nature and scope of economic conflict, competition, and cooperation; and shifting attitudes of both TNCs and governments concerning business. All of these forces have created new modes of economic integration.

1. Technology Development. Technology—reflected in new production techniques, products, communication, transportation, and energy sources—has been a major force in opening and expanding markets. New technologies both enhance mobility and create new varieties of products. They also change the relative costs of production and distribution and the comparative advantages of corporations and cities. In so doing, they increase the gains from trade. The process of technological change continues to enhance specialization, leading to stronger economic linkages and further integration.

New technologies create information and make having it more important. By accelerating the flow of information they further stimulate technological development. The techniques of information flow permit rapid exchange of data across national borders, making collaborators and competitors abroad aware of new processes and products.[2] The mere flow of information, therefore, increases the similarity of behavior on the part of citizens of countries having access to it and thereby intensifies competition. Continually enhanced technology is affecting and accelerating all other aspects of global economic integration.

2. Global Market Expansion. Two aspects of market development also signal economic integration. The first is the need for increasing market size to reach economies of scale and specialization; the second is the growing similarity of tastes and demands for a variety of consumer and industrial products. The size of markets is both a stimulus and a constraint to economic growth. Small national markets mean that countries will remain relatively poor. Therefore, small countries can expand only by penetrating markets abroad. This strategy has worked well for countries like Japan, South Korea, New Zealand, Taiwan, Hong Kong, Thailand, Singapore, and the Netherlands. In the past, countries with large national markets have been able to grow more efficiently and rapidly through internal production and consumption, relying less on international trade.

However, since 1960, even the United States has increased its reliance on international trade; as a percentage of GNP, exports and imports more than doubled from 8 percent to nearly 20 percent (U.S. Dept. of Commerce, 1990). During this period GNP increased more than ten times in money terms and nearly three times in real terms. The expansion of markets through international trade has been recognized in the United States and Europe as a stimulus to growth even for large countries, an observation that has not entirely escaped the leaders of China and Eastern European countries. Thus, both small and large countries are seeking ways to serve foreign markets in order to accelerate economic growth.

3. Spread of Transnational Corporations. TNCs have spread throughout the world not only from the United States but also from Europe, Japan, the Asian newly industrializing countries (NICs), and even some developing countries. The United Nations (1989) estimates that in the mid-1980s, TNCs directly employed at least 65 million people in the more developed countries alone. The numbers employed by TNCs in less developed countries are more difficult to estimate, but affiliates of TNCs are found in virtually every large city in the world—where they produce, transfer technology, sell, trade, or provide numerous financial and other services. Foreign affiliates are tied to their headquarters company in a variety of ways that integrate their activities with other affiliates of the TNC and among the cities in which they are located.

4. Emergence of Corporate Strategic Alliances. The proliferation of intercorporate networks has led to a type of specialization among TNCs that is substantially different from that of trading. Each party to the alliance or network brings a particular talent that is merged with that of the others to produce a new technology, product, or service or to provide a similar one at less cost or higher quality. Manufacturing networks tie together various stages of production in plants located in cities around the world. The final assembly of the Ford Escort automobile in Halewood, England, and Saarlouis, Germany, for example, draws on components produced in fifteen countries—tires, paints, and hardware from the Netherlands; fan belts from Denmark; radiator and heater hoses from Austria; starters, alternators, and bearings from Japan; glass, valves, and hydraulic tappets from the United States; cylinder heads, carburetors, and defroster grills from Italy; and clutch release bearings, steering shafts, and joints from France (Dicken, 1986). These stages are linked by technology agreements, contracts, joint ventures, or direct ownership. In addition, a variety of services are attached to the process—including advertising, storage, transport, and financing.

Similar linkages exist in the sectors of electronics, aircraft, and chemicals. At any stage, an affiliate can be located in one of many cities, depending on national capabilities and incentives, market opportunities, infrastructure, and transport networks. These networks shift the type of employment and the income opportunities, thereby altering the patterns of living in each city.

5. Internationalization of Financial Institutions. Financial institutions are also moving rapidly to internationalize their operations, thereby contributing to global economic integration. Citibank, for example, operates in London, Paris, Frankfort, Mexico City, Sao Paulo, Rome, Hong Kong, Warsaw, Prague, and other major cities. Nomura Securities, the largest in Tokyo, also operates in New York and other major financial centers. Large brokerage houses and banks in major cities are dealing around the clock in securities markets and foreign exchange. In the future, not only will financial entities in many countries of the world be owned by a single TNC but also independent entities will be linked through information flows, research, brokerage agencies, underwriting, minority ownerships, and special collaborative agreements. Capital markets are increasingly linked through the flow of information and data. As more information is available to final investors, the competition for security assets in each of the major stockmarkets will become worldwide. At present, full integration is constrained only by legal obstacles and different regulatory practices by national governments.

The linkage of economies through the flow of goods and capital means that national economic growth in one country is tied to that in others, altering the ability of each to act independently in providing higher levels of employment, in shifting the nature of employment, or in relocating economic activity among countries and cities. These in turn will cause changes in the location of economic activities among cities and the life-styles of the people involved.

Disintegration of Nations with the Weakening of Military Force

The decline of importance in the geographic size of nations in maintaining security and the reluctance to use military force as the primary means of maintaining political unity are giving rise to pervasive efforts to redraw political boundaries at the margins—as has occurred in Yugoslavia, the Soviet republics, and South Asia. The increasing integration of the world economy means a virtual elimination of debates over autarchy, national self-sufficiency, and economic independence. The only question remaining is how far and in what ways nations will be interdependent. As the process of economic integration continues it will undoubtedly generate tensions and potential conflicts. Cultural differences will be exacerbated, raising continuing desires for political separation and autonomy. However, the recognition among the major powers that nuclear war is "unthinkable" and that disarmament is feasible is limiting military conflicts to minor incursions.

As the world economy becomes more open and military force becomes less acceptable, *national* governments will become less significant in international relations. It appears, for example, that with the rapid changes taking place in Eastern Europe, in the Western European economic market, the former Soviet Union, the Koreas, South Africa, and China, events are by-passing national governments. Washington, for instance, is no longer in a position, nor does the federal government have the funds, to influence the direction of policies in most of those regions. Indeed, U.S. policy is criticized in Europe for being one that "uses other people's money." The U.S. government can change Japanese trade policies only marginally, can influence economic relationships in the emerging European common market only peripherally, and has limited power to affect Chinese economic or political decisions. Despite frequent displays of U.S. and Soviet military force during the 1980s, they were effective only in influencing events temporarily in some weak, poor, or dependent states—Afghanistan, Grenada, Panama, Lithuania, or Estonia. Neither the United States in Vietnam nor the Soviet Union in Afghanistan was able to impose its will through military might alone. The coalition opposing Iraq in the 1991 Gulf War felt constrained not to destroy entirely Saddam Hussein's regime.

The major forces defining the new political boundaries will be ethnic and economic. The efforts of ethnic groups to redefine their political affiliations will form new states—something that has already happened in Yugoslavia, the Soviet Union, Southeast Asia, Eastern Europe, and portions of the Middle East, and is continually threatening to occur in Belgium, India, Pakistan, Sri Lanka, and even in Canada. Such changes will require new intergovernmental agreements. In the process, conflicts will arise and new forms of cooperation will be required to prevent the conflicts from being destructive. But mechanisms of economic integration are likely to be a primary means of re-forming political alliances: the emergence of the European Common Market and the United States' push for free trade agreements with Canada and Mexico portend a pattern of economic and political realignment that will be followed by other nations as well (Behrman, 1984). Discussions on integration of Asian Pacific Rim countries, for example, have recently become more serious.

Spread of Similar Patterns of Consumption and Life-Styles

Changing life-styles emulating those of the West are increasingly seen in the acceptance of Western clothes, popular music, movies, television shows, fast-food outlets, the spread of western style shopping malls, and the desire for Western appliances and luxury goods. Television networks such as CNN and the BBC link major portions of the globe, providing the latest news and exposing people to Western values and life-styles.

The ability to make similar products through the diffusion of technologies and the flow of information about products have increased the similarities in demand for consumer and industrial goods. No capital goods producer wishes to be uncompetitive because of the use of less advanced equipment; consequently, the transfer of technology has accelerated. Increasingly, capital equipment is becoming standardized around the world, but so are consumer goods such as jeans and telephones. Designs may be somewhat different, but their quality and use is virtually the same. A variety of products—ranging from pens and pencils to dictating equipment, stereos, VCRs, and even automobiles—are becoming international products. Significant differences remain, but the increasing similarities in tastes and demand mean a continuing globalization of markets.

In sum, but for differences of scale and extent, all countries will have to open up significantly to trade and investment in the post–Cold War era in order to participate in economic growth. The singular reason is that no national economy will find its internal market large enough to elicit the variety and scale of production necessary to be competitive. All will need to be a part of the open world economy in order to compete and grow successfully, and this increasing integration will set new cross-cultural trends.

Implications of Globalization for Cities

The forces of global economic integration will affect cities in at least three fundamental ways. First, while creating greater national interdependence, they promote the decentralization of decision-making in a system of internationally linked urban centers. Second, in this process of decentralization, international industries are forming core sectors that will play a more powerful role in the economies of cities and metropolitan areas. Third, the combination of economic decentralization and core sector dominance will require cities that wish to remain competitive to adapt their cultures to attract and accommodate the types of international economic activities they desire.

Decentralization of Transnational Economic Activities

The waning of national government interference in economic interactions will mean that substantial decision-making authority will move to the city and metropolitan levels. This shift is already reflected in the new arrangements being made directly between local governments and transnational corporations. Local governments at both the state and municipal levels in the United States, for example, have taken new initiatives to attract transnational companies, usually with little or no coordination with national government agencies. The State of Arkansas and the City of Little Rock have negotiated agreements with Japan's Ministry of International Trade and Industry (MITI) to spend more than $100 million to increase trade between companies in Arkansas and Asian countries. The Japanese External Trade Organization (JETRO) has assigned an advisor in Little Rock to work with local companies and Asian trading firms. Similarly, negotiations between the City of Memphis, the State of Tennessee, and Japan's Sharp Corporation have resulted in the relocation of Sharp's manufacturing facilities from Malaysia to Memphis (Raia, 1991). Prolonged negotiations of the State of Michigan and its City of Flat Rock with the Mazda automobile company of Japan resulted in state officials developing a complex incentive package, investments in infrastructure improvements, job training programs, and nearly $50 million in loans, while the municipality provided $87 million in property tax abatements to attract the Mazda plant (Bachelor, 1991). Municipal governments seeking to enhance local opportunities and employment are frequently more open to foreign investments than national government agencies, which tend to have protectionist mentalities (Behrman and Grosse, 1990).

This decentralization of power and authority to cities and metropolitan areas will be reinforced by a fundamental feature of an integrating world economy: the fact that the increasing mobility of capital, labor, management, and technology is largely uncontrollable by national governments unless they wish to isolate themselves from the globalization process. The classical economic argument for free trade among nations was that *factors of production* would *not* move across national borders and that to achieve efficiency it was necessary to have free movement of *products*. But over the past few decades, not only have capital and labor (which were supposedly immobile) moved among countries, so too have technology, management, managerial skills, and even labor and land. Capital has been mobile for centuries, of course, but the scale of the transfer has significantly increased with the expansion of foreign *direct* investment, which also involves the transfer of ownership, control, and management. Workers move on their own or are transferred through contracts for large projects in foreign countries. Managers are rotated among international branches and divisions and contract their services, and technology is transferred under licenses and joint ventures or to wholly-owned affiliates.

The mobility of production factors will make production capabilities in cities around the world more similar as nations attract or lose competitive advantages. Whether or not cities gain or lose economically depends upon government policies and the ability of business and political leaders to recognize the value, and to direct effectively the use, of their resources. To the extent that factor mobility narrows comparative advantages, the structure of production worldwide becomes more similar; or, at least, it becomes feasible to produce almost any item in a number of different locations. In the future, income differences among cities will be based on the productivity of labor and management in using similar production factors. Greater progress will occur in those cities that can attract the high value-added industrial and service sectors. Income differences will be a reflection of government policies and cultures.

Increasing Importance of Core Sectors in the Urban Economy

Cities must prepare for and adjust to the changes brought by the increasing mobility of transnational industries. The core industrial and service sectors bring greater contributions to local development by establishing related services and production. It behooves cities to find ways of attracting them. The electronics and semiconductor industries, for example, emerged in the early 1960s to become the core sectors of the economy of Hong Kong in the 1970s and early 1980s, just as they had in the Silicon Valley of California. In Hong Kong these industries accounted for a substantial portion of the foreign direct investment and for more than 60 percent of the employment in the foreign-owned sector. Over time, as labor costs increased in Hong Kong and assembly elements moved out to lower cost Southeast Asian cities, the core sector transformed Hong Kong from a specialized assembly location to an international semiconductor and electronics marketing and distribution center (Henderson, 1989). Transport machinery and automobile production played similar roles as the core industries of Aichi Prefecture, dominating the economies of Nagoya and Toyota City in Japan, as did electrical machinery industries as the core sector of the city of Kawasaki (Fujita and Hill, 1989).

Core industries are structurally autonomous—that is, they can organize virtually as they see fit and can spin off specialized activities as joint ventures. They are oligopolistic in that a few major companies dominate the sector. They attract suppliers and vendors who seek to gain a competitive advantage through geographic proximity. The Japanese practice of "just-in-time" inventory control, for example, requires close physical proximity among related manufacturing and service firms to permit quick response to changing production volumes.

The manufacturing and service complex that surrounds core industries and the sizable employment they generate makes cities increasingly dependent on them. No city can grow large with only supplier-vendor enterprises; some core industry is necessary *or* services (such as finance) must agglomerate with similar and complementary activities for overall efficiency.

The need for core industries or agglomerated services requires cities to develop a physical and economic environment and a quality of life that will attract managers and professional employees of TNCs and retain them. Many American cities, however, have lost major corporate offices because of adverse changes in their economic and physical environments: poor education, escalating housing costs, traffic snarls, congestion, and rising crime rates (Rondinelli and Behrman, 1991). San Francisco, for example, remains a leading city in terms of new business start-ups, but at the same time 8 percent of existing city businesses expect to move out within two years in order to expand. Corporate expansion is taking place on the northern and southern tips of the Bay Area rather than within the city. Dallas, on the other hand, has begun to attract more corporate headquarters as a result of the slow growth in the early 1980s that made available relatively inexpensive office space, skilled labor, and housing. The city is close to transnational shipping routes and, therefore, accessible to national and international markets. In both instances, conscious policy decisions about their future development are required in order for the cities to adapt effectively to the changing environment.

The Necessity of Cultural Adaptation

The movements of production factors under foreign ownership and control will alter the economic structures and life-styles of cities involved in international transactions more profoundly than growing similarities in consumption patterns. And with the increasing dominance of economic influence over military force in international relations, the direction of growth in any country can be guided only through *economic, commercial, and cultural* forces. National governments are not likely to be the most effective sources of any of them. Therefore, cities will inevitably become more important centers of change.

As noted earlier, the major force for change is technology, which is generating new industries and new products, opening new markets, eliciting new locations for production, and giving rise to mobile industries that are able to relocate fairly quickly among cities in response to changes in market and production conditions. New and more mobile technologies will require new types of infrastructure in cities and also require cities to develop or attract new kinds of economic activity.

At the same time, the spread of cultures across national boundaries is altering life-styles, social patterns, and politics and thereby the roles of cities. The ability to adjust to cultural changes will partly determine the readiness of cities to compete in the global economy of the twenty-first century. The cross-cultural movement of ideas carries with it a wider appreciation of values underlying particular life-styles, work, and progress in other countries. Moreover, values in many countries are changing with the modes of production (new technologies and products) and also with a wider appreciation of alternative opportunities.

As urban areas become more economically dependent on core industries, the owners of those industries acquire substantial political power in the city. When a foreign enterprise achieves such power, additional tensions are created. Cross-cultural understanding becomes essential in cities with foreign-owned companies in core industries. The work force and commercial services will adjust to this "domination" by a foreign core company, but some communities within the city will have more difficulty. Because cities cannot afford to lose their mobile core industries without replacing them, they will need to develop policies to attract the "right" foreign companies and provide appropriate infrastructure and services for them. They can hold those they now have only by offering the types of support these core sectors need. However, since movement of sectors responds to lower costs (and incomes), it will be more advantageous to let lower value-added sectors go and replace them with higher value-added sectors—as the Japanese have learned well.

The Cultural Imperatives of Globalization

It is an American trait to believe that all major aspects of American culture are strong and enduring, preparing America for unending progress. Underlying most Americans' orientation is the frontier mentality from which their culture evolved. Formed by a history of persistent success in meeting frontier challenges, American culture lacks a sense of tragedy—a sequence of events with an undesired end *despite* good intentions and energetic actions. Positivism among Americans leads to a belief that technical expertise coupled with ample resources will inevitably bring progress, as was the case for nearly three decades after World War II, a period during which American cities flourished by producing goods primarily for domestic markets that were rarely threatened by foreign imports. But during the 1980s, several nations caught up with American technology and have continued to keep pace or surpass it in an increasing number of sectors (National Academy of Sciences, 1985). American cultural orientations that supported and drove urban economic growth— those that welcomed innovation, adaptation, and change as exciting challenges—have themselves changed in ways that appear to weaken the capacity of Americans to restructure their urban economies to compete in national and international markets. The technological frontier is no longer, and is not likely again to be, uniquely American. This means that many American cultural assumptions are no longer valid and that, indeed, some of the cultural changes taking place in U.S. cities will be dysfunctional in the future.

Cultural Trends and American Cities

The culture of many American cities is being shaped by demographic and social trends that are not conducive to the necessary economic restructuring. The litany of problems has become all too familiar: the population of many cities is aging, the growth of the productive labor force is declining, the expanding underclass that is concentrated in the cores of American cities is ill-prepared educationally and psychologically for productive work and technological change, and the geographic mobility that allowed cities to attract diverse groups that periodically reshaped their cultures is slowing appreciably with the aging of their populations (Sternlieb and Hughes, 1987).

Many cities are facing a rapid decline in the growth of households; traditional families are being replaced by single female-headed families, a large proportion of whom are poor, and by nonfamily groups. About 55 percent of the children living in female-headed families were living in poverty in 1987, and one-fifth of all children in the United states lived in families whose incomes were below the poverty line (Bennett and Bloom, 1990). Only about 11 percent of the American population lived in conventional family configurations of a husband, wife, and two children in the late 1980s. The values, motivation, and discipline that middle-class families traditionally passed to their children have not been taken up and extended by other urban institutions. An alarming number of minority children in cities are growing up in poverty, without skills, and with little preparation for higher education. Equally serious is the declining work ethic in many American cities that yields low productivity and efficiency. In a recent poll, 60 percent of the chief executives of leading American companies said that the quality of the U.S. work force has either grown worse or not improved substantially over the past decade (Erdman, 1990).

A more critical problem for transnational companies attempting to operate in many large American cities is the low level of literacy and numeracy among those entering the work force. Nearly 76 percent of leading corporate executives claim that public education systems actually worsen the quality of the U.S. work force and more than 90 percent say that their companies must spend substantially more now on educating their employees because the public schools do not provide an education that meets their needs.

The public school systems of too many American cities have fallen far behind their Japanese and European counterparts in preparing American children in math and science. Few graduates of American schools have a fundamental knowledge of their own culture, much less the cultures, languages, and geography of their economic competitors. Studies by the U.S. Department of Education during the late 1980s of a sample of twenty-one- to twenty-five-year-olds found that nearly half could not locate information in a news article, 79 percent could not interpret a bus schedule, and 62 percent could not correctly determine change due from a two-item restaurant meal (Bennett and Bloom, 1990).

The ravages of the illegal drug trade have destroyed many black families and inner-city communities. The social cohesion and security of neighborhoods have all but disappeared in both center cities and the suburbs. As a result of these factors, American cities are today among the most violent and crime-ridden in the world. The central cities of most metropolitan areas, especially in the North and Northeast, have lost both population and employment-generating industries to the suburbs. The resulting fragmentation and segregation of communities within metropolitan areas has also fragmented and segmented the local polity that helps guide and facilitate urban economic development.

The immediate gratification, consumer-oriented culture that has emerged in many American cities has weakened the commitment of their residents to making the large financial investments needed to reinvigorate public institutions, especially the schools, and to maintain and reconstruct the physical infrastructure on which private companies depend for efficient operation.

The Congressional Budget Office has estimated a shortfall of $53 billion and the Congressional Joint Economic Committee $64 billion annually in investment needed for public infrastructure (transportation systems, water, wastewater, and drainage facilities) in the United States. Reductions in the proportion of GNP invested in infrastructure repair and maintenance during the past decade will create strong financial demands during the next decade to replace roads, bridges, and water systems in American cities (Gakenheimer, 1989).

The impacts of these adverse urban cultural conditions already manifest themselves in the American economy. Economists note that downward mobility is a reality for a large number of Americans in many parts of the country. The gap between the richest and the poorest segments of the American population has been growing. Between 1978 and 1987, the richest 20 percent of the population became 13 percent richer, while the poorest quintile became 8 percent poorer. The number of people who worked full time, year around, but received incomes below the poverty level increased by 43 percent during the ten-year period (Newman, 1988). The number of working poor rose from 6 million in the 1970s to more than 9 million during the 1980s. Many lived in cities with stagnant or declining economies that could only displace the shrinking number of manufacturing jobs with low-paying service sector jobs (Levitan and Shapiro, 1987).

These trends imply that cities that develop a sense of purpose, show flexibility in response to changes, foster cultures that promote and sustain innovation and adaptation, and find ways of guiding and accelerating their development will offer strong opportunities for investment in the coming decade. Those that cannot mobilize their cultural energies, adapt to their economic and natural environments, and use their resources in purposeful ways will stagnate or decline.

The Policy Implications for American Cities

Having lost its economic and technological hegemony, and having to rely on collaboration with other countries even for effective military action, the United States now faces a much more complex and diverse world than its leaders envisioned after World War II. It is highly unlikely that American cities will escape cultural shifts while the rest of the world is enduring them. On the contrary, American cities face significant changes in traditional life-styles in order to adjust to changing economic and technological needs. For example, they can no longer neglect the development of their more talented young people in the name of equality of opportunity, and they must find better ways of combining efficiency in production with quality in service. At the same time they will have to find new ways of achieving greater equity in the distribution of incomes and wealth. They must find new ways to mitigate or eliminate their proclivity to violence, corruption, power for personal gain, and excessive consumerism—all of which drain resources from efforts to promote more equitable and sustainable growth. They must develop those cultural traits that make them more open to ideas from elsewhere around the world and encourage a greater sense of individual responsibility to enhance personal as well as community growth.

Those cities that recognize the need for such changes and can mobilize their resources to implement them will progress the fastest and will be the best prospects for investment during the 1990s.

Balancing Urban Development: Work, Action and Contemplation

In the future, the dynamic cities will be those that ''get it right'' in perceiving, projecting, and guiding change—by observing trends in the city and in the larger international environment, developing a vision of improvement, and taking appropriate action. The vision must be that of achieving and maintaining a *balance* in urban development among the three major aspects of life—work, contemplation, and action—reflected in the economic, intellectual-spiritual, and socio-political environment of the community.

Transnational corporations are increasingly seeking cities with strong work ethics and skilled labor resources in which to locate or expand their operations. *Fortune* magazine's 1990 ratings of American cities with the best working conditions, for example, pointed out that companies value urban areas with a large available labor force that has advanced skills and a strong work ethic (Sellers, 1990). *Fortune* chose Salt Lake City, Minneapolis-St. Paul, Atlanta, Sacramento, Austin, Columbus, Dallas-Fort Worth, Phoenix, Oklahoma City, and Jacksonville, Florida, as the best labor markets in 1990. Both domestic and foreign firms considered the disciplined, hard-working, and loyal work force in Salt Lake City, Sacramento, and Minneapolis-St. Paul a principal factor in increasing their productivity and efficiency, permitting more rapid adjustment to changing market demands.

Although a productive and efficient work force will remain a critical feature of internationally competitive cities, action and contemplation are increasingly valued as well. One of the qualities often cited in *World Trade* magazine's selection of the top ten urban locations for international companies, for example, is the ability of local groups to work together to attract new investment (Graff, 1990). In its 1990 rankings, Atlanta was praised for the cooperative action of city government and business leaders in seeking investment by international corporations and in being designated as the site of the 1996 Summer Olympics. Seattle was praised for its Office of International Affairs, which coordinates fourteen sister-city programs, provides government and businesses with international trade, cultural, and political information, and works with the Chamber of Commerce and a dozen other internationally oriented business and civic associations in maintaining international relations that attract new businesses. Tucson's International Trade Office in Asia was also cited as an example of community action that provided extensive help for foreign companies interested in locating in the city.

In an international high-technology economy, the cities that develop their intellectual, artistic and educational institutions to provide a higher quality of life will also become more attractive to TNCs. *Fortune* noted that Minneapolis-St. Paul is a popular location for technology-oriented companies because of its environment of cleanliness and safety and because of the educational quality of its schools and universities. Businesses are also attracted to Minneapolis-St. Paul because of its rich resources in the arts, music, education, and recreation and are willing to support financially a higher quality of life. In ranking Salt Lake City first in labor market conditions, *Fortune* pointed out that Utah had the highest literacy rate in the United States and that because so many of Salt Lake City's residents had participated in Mormon missions overseas they were better educated in foreign languages than people in most other American cities (Sellers and Michels, 1990). Austin, Columbus, Baltimore, and the research triangle (Raleigh-Durham-Chapel Hill) of North Carolina have become more attractive because their universities provide a steady supply of well-educated and technically trained people who can meet the needs of international companies.

Cultural Mandates for Cities

As we noted earlier, a city needs three activities to perpetuate its growth and maintain its economic vitality: wealth gained through *work*; security and stability gained through political and social *action;* and personal development through education, innovation, and adaptation arising from and leading to *contemplation*. Each of these requires a distinct institutional structure. But many American cities now find themselves without effective institutional means of providing either physical or economic protection. Nor are city governments any longer the providers of a "culturally oriented" education or one aimed at personal development in all dimensions—physical, emotional, intellectual, and spiritual. The economies of many cities are becoming less able to offer economic security in the form of full employment; nor does wealth generation support the contemplative aspects of urban culture, especially in the form of quality education.

Because cities remain the primary locations for wealth generation, they must seek new ways to integrate the three aspects of culture—work, action, and contemplation—in order to ensure that they remain creative and economically vital places in the future. Emerging trends indicate that, in order to compete effectively, cities will have to develop a stronger work ethic, be able to mobilize resources quickly to restructure their economies for both import replacement and export production, and develop a well-trained, innovative, and adaptable work force. To do this effectively requires greater cooperative action, socially and politically, with more participatory decision making. This must be accomplished by expanding opportunities for individual development. All three aspects of culture are integrally related to each other and to the future potentials of a city.

The cities with the best investment potential during the 1990s will be those that take the following actions:

1. Implement Educational Reform. No city has been or will be internationally competitive that does not develop its contemplative and educational institutions and create an environment for scientific, philosophic, artistic, and spiritual pursuits. The international competitiveness of American cities is judged by *World Trade*, for example, on "the quality of the intellectual infrastructure that companies require to compete in the global marketplace"— including the general performance of local schools, availability of curricula emphasizing foreign language skills, world history, and geography, and the availability of public, private and academic R&D centers that can assist international companies (Raia, 1991).

For most American cities, substantial changes must be made in educational policies. Clearly, the educational system in cities must be reformed not only to teach the basics of literacy and numeracy but also to allow students to attain greater competency in math, science, and liberal arts at the primary and secondary levels. U.S. schools must do a far better job in teaching English, foreign languages, and comparative cultures. Beyond that, they must teach in a way that fosters innovation and creativity. Both secondary and higher educational institutions must focus much more on students *learning how to learn*; a knowledge of the process of learning will be far more important to students in the future than the information acquired during their formal education. A strong grasp of fundamentals is needed in a process of teaching that creates the capacity for life-long learning, a task that few American schools now address adequately.

In the future, companies will be looking for a work force that is not only technically trained but also skilled in managing rapidly changing businesses and able to adapt. Reich (1991, 37) points out that three types of skills are becoming more essential in high value businesses where "profits derive not from scale and volume but from an ongoing discovery of connections between the solutions to problems and the identification of new needs." To remain economically vital and competitive, he asserts, cities must develop in their labor force the *"problem-solving skills* required to put things together in unique ways . . . and *problem-identifying skills* required to help customers understand their needs and how those needs can best be met by customized products." In addition, competitive businesses need entrepreneurial managers with *strategic broker skills* who "understand enough about specific technologies and markets to see the potential for a new product, raise whatever money is necessary to launch the project, and assemble the right personnel to solve and identify problems." Yet, even graduate business school programs in the United States rarely go much beyond the problem-solving skills.

2. *Adopt Entrepreneurial Strategies for Economic Development.* Increasing evidence suggests that a culture that promotes innovation, creativity, flexibility, and adaptability will be essential to keep American cities economically vital during the next decade. Economic development policies that have focused only on replacing declining industries by providing incentives to attract others (choosing "winners" and "losers") or on correcting market failures have not been highly successful, especially in attracting high-tech industries. Cities are more likely to be successful by shifting to "entrepreneurial" policies. These policies develop an environment that attracts and supports technologically based manufacturing and services, encourage the creation of new locally initiated or "incubated" economic activities by the private sector, and remove unnecessary or overly restrictive barriers to the creation or expansion of small- and medium-scale enterprise (Clark and Gaile, 1989).

Such entrepreneurship is necessary in transforming the economies of cities through import replacement and export promotion (Jacobs, 1984). Recent studies of regional economic growth and decline in the United States confirm that entrepreneurial functions are the most critical factors affecting regional economic change (Suarez-Villa, 1989). Entrepreneurs make new investments, link markets together, coordinate production, plan strategically, and develop inventions, all functions that are critical to sustaining a city's economy. And they will become an even stronger source of international competitiveness in the future.

In order to sustain economic vitality, governments and civic organizations must give much more attention to the creation and expansion of local small- and medium-scale businesses. Small enterprises are a significant source of job creation. Indeed, the majority of new jobs created in the United States are in firms with less than one hundred employees. Although studies have found that jobs in small businesses initially offer lower wages and benefits, those jobs are generally of higher quality—allowing more creativity, autonomy, and individual responsibility as well as generating a higher level of job satisfaction—than those in large corporations (Zipp, 1991). Cities that are generating large numbers of high quality jobs are more likely to develop the type of economic infrastructure and labor force that is more flexible and creative in adjusting to economic changes.

3. *Improve Quality of Life and Environmental Conditions.* Metropolitan areas seeking to create an environment for attracting and sustaining high-tech

industries and services must give much more attention to cultural changes that promote a higher quality of life. Although the narrower site- and location-specific criteria traditionally used by manufacturing industries are still important, recent studies conclude that "a good deal of evidence gathered over the last fifteen years from several regions of the U.S. suggests that least-cost location criteria may now have given way to QOL [quality of life] considerations in industrial location preferences" (Hart, et al., 1989).

High-technology plants located in communities ranking low on the "livability scale" have greater difficulty attracting technical and managerial personnel or moving them from other plants in the company (Rees, 1986). Studies of the location preferences of high technology firms in the Southeast have found that the livability and education factors were the most important locational criteria, followed by local transportation and infrastructure availability (Malizia, 1985).

4. Promote Leadership and Civic Action. To attract and sustain technology-based manufacturing and services, the culture of a metropolitan area must promote a common civic perspective in the public and private sectors and a positive attitude about the region's comparative advantages. The U.S. Office of Technology Assessment (1984, 8) contends that successful regions and cities must develop a culture that "nurtures leaders, both public and private, who combine an established track record for innovation with a broad view of their community's resources and promise."

A culture that encourages and supports action, in the form of cooperation among the public, private, and civic sectors to anticipate and adapt to change, is also crucial for continued economic vitality. And, in view of the pervasive incursions of technology in all aspects of life, it will require not only cooperation but contemplation infused with ethical considerations to achieve acceptable solutions. In nearly every city that has successfully restructured its economy, changes came through concerted action and civic commitment. The restructuring of metropolitan Pittsburgh's economy, for example, was the result of leadership and close cooperation among business executives, local and state government officials, and university executives in the area. Although they were formed and often acted independently, many of the groups had overlapping memberships that ensured widespread cooperation (Ahlbrandt and Weaver, 1987).

5. Explore New Forms of Metropolitan Governance. In order for urban regions to maintain their economic vitality, they must be able to create the institutions that allow leadership to emerge and that facilitate cooperation among business, public, and educational organizations throughout metropolitan areas. The increasing intra- and intermetropolitan interaction that is necessary to restructure regional economies implies the need for new forms of governance that encompass entire metropolitan areas and reduce the segmentation and competition among communities.

Cities must find new ways of enhancing the development and acceptance of individual responsibility through each aspect of culture and in the processes of social ordering and community decision making. This will involve a shift from hierarchical decision making structures to more participatory forms; and from participatory decision making to greater individual responsibility.

6. Enhance Community Security. Another crucial aspect of a community's quality of life is physical security. Economically vital cities must develop neighborhood and community solidarity to ensure greater physical security and reduce crime and violence. More effective law enforcement must be supplemented by the promotion of community arts, recreation, and social functions that can help forge stronger community ties and reduce the incidence of conflict. Policies that strengthen neighborhood and community identity and interaction and that encourage individual and household responsibility for crime prevention can also contribute to a higher quality of life.

7. Maintain and Expand Urban Infrastructure. Economically vital and competitive metropolitan areas must have modern and efficient physical infrastructure—roads, bridges, highways, energy systems, telecommunications, and airport and air cargo facilities. Improving air cargo facilities will be especially important for cities with large numbers of companies involved in international business transactions and for cities attempting to attract transnational companies using just-in-time manufacturing and inventory control methods and firms that must make frequent small shipments to overseas markets (Kasarda, 1991). The increasing importance of air freight, which already accounts for one-third of the value of U.S. export products, will make air cargo facilities essential for American cities that wish to be part of the emerging global urban network linking Europe, the Asian Pacific Rim, and Latin America.

States and cities will have to assume a greater role in physical facility expansion and maintenance in the face of declining federal and overall expenditures. Total spending on infrastructure in the United States has steadily declined from 4 percent of GNP in the 1960s to 2 percent in the 1980s; federal government expenditures declined from 0.97 percent in 1970 to 0.75 percent in 1990 at a time when governments in Japan and Western Europe have invested heavily in "smart roads," high speed trains, national information networks, and air cargo systems (Reich, 1991).

The most attractive cities for international investment during the 1990s will be those that give increasing attention to infrastructure that makes business operations more efficient within the metropolitan area and allows businesses to operate more effectively in an international economy.

8. *Rehabilitate the Urban Underclass.* Government, business, and civic organizations must give greater attention to bringing the expanding urban underclass into the productive work force. Reducing the demand for drugs and rehabilitating drug users will be essential first steps. As Anthony Downs (1991) has pointed out, the drug culture greatly complicates efforts to change the attitudes, behavior, and motivations of the underclass in American cities because it attracts potentially entrepreneurial persons, destroys motivation and the work ethic among young males, and perpetuates addiction among young mothers, thereby assuring a new generation of damaged children. The answer is through cultural and personal development—an objective that should be given the highest priority in any event.

In the face of increasing labor shortages, cities must find new ways of quickly training the urban underclass, especially women who are heads of households, for skilled jobs through vocational education; of providing early childhood care and "head-start" education for poor preschool children; and of changing welfare policies that reduce or eliminate incentives for the poor to work and maintain family living arrangements.

In sum, the cities that will be most attractive as locations for transnational activities will be those that provide not only least-cost conditions for TNCs to operate effectively but also a quality of life that will satisfy their managers and employees. Competition among cities will increase the pressures for cultural change. It will require cities to adopt cultures that foster a sense of community and purpose and to offer attractive physical and social conditions for international companies.

Conclusions

In the post–Cold War global economy, cities will progress toward economic development only by creating a stronger competitive position and a better quality of life. The goals of urban economic development policy must focus on improving three aspects of culture—work, contemplation, and action—that are integrally related to each other and to strengthening the competitive position of the city in a technology-driven global economy. Emerging trends indicate that, in order to compete effectively, cities will have to develop a strong work ethic, be able to mobilize resources quickly to increase trade and attract foreign direct investment, and develop a well-trained, innovative, and adaptable work force. To attract and sustain technology-based manufacturing and services, the culture of a city must promote a common civic perspective in the public and private sectors and a positive attitude about the city's comparative advantages. This will require greater cooperation among business, government, and civic leaders, more participatory decision making, and the creation of new opportunities for individual development. In a global economy, improvements in telecommunications, air transport, and information technology have made distance to suppliers and markets far less important than human skill factors, quality of education, community safety, quality of arts and recreation, and a clean environment in attracting high-tech professionals.

In the post–Cold War era, the cities that grow economically will do so because they develop purpose and identity, which will come more from *values* than from the modes of production or location advantages (Lodge and Vogel, 1987). Identity is similar to spirit and commitment in that one strives to maintain that identity even in the face of adversity. Thus, location and work are seldom adequate to define a community; *shared values* form the real foundation.

The challenge to international cities is fundamentally one of creating a "mind-change" that places the city in a global setting. It is the growing perception of a common purpose or common bonds necessary to achieve *any* purpose that constitutes the emerging global "mind change" (Harmon, 1988). Such a shift affects all other aspects of urban life, changing priorities, altering life-styles, and redirecting the structure and nature of communities. It leads to a greater appreciation of the need for unity with diversity. Urban development policies in the post–Cold War era will have to focus increasingly on creating the international mind-change that will allow American cities to attract foreign direct investment and on developing the prerequisites for competitiveness to engage in international trade in a rapidly globalizing world economy.

NOTES

1. In this sense, Mumford (1938, 492) defined the culture of cities as the "cultivation of each human being's fullest capacities as a sentient, feeling, thinking, acting personality," leading to "the disciplined seizure and use of energy toward the economic satisfaction of man's wants."

2. The problems of internationalizing in a basically "informationless" society are shown in the study by Shapiro, Behrman, Fisher, and Powell (1991).

CHAPTER 9

Post–Cold War Education in the United States: The American OPEC

BARRY KEATING AND MARYANN KEATING

Survey of Current Relevant Developments in the Educational Arena

In the early 1980s, the secretary of education created a commission to examine the quality of education in the United States and to make a report to him. The reason for the creation of a commission was a widespread popular feeling that we were in deep trouble. The report given to the secretary was the well-known *A Nation at Risk* document (National Commission on Excellence in Education, 1983). The report coined the phrase "a rising tide of mediocrity" to describe the nature of American education; it was unabashed in its criticism of our educational attainments.

The "risk" referenced in the title of the document referred to the possibility that America was quickly becoming a Third World country in terms of its educational attainment. Our international standing in economic markets and laboratories was compared with our international standing in education; the comparison did not favor the United States. The commission used many indicators to explain their sharp rhetoric. On nineteen academic achievement tests covering the decade ending in 1981 American students scored last seven times and were never first or second. Average achievement in high schools at the time of the report was lower than when Sputnik was launched twenty-six years previously. The College Board's Scholastic Aptitude Test (SAT) had shown a monotonic decline since 1963, and both the number and proportion of students demonstrating superior achievement (with scores of 650 or above) had declined. Tested achievement of college graduates was also lower for the decade, while remedial math courses in public four-year colleges increased by 72 percent.

A tone of frustration was evident in the document. There was no evidence that Americans were becoming better off educationally than they had been in the past. The system seemed to be in freefall.

The report cited several studies of attitudes of the American public about education; the public recognized the value of quality education. The public had "no patience" with "superfluous high school offerings" and undemanding courses. Three-quarters of those questioned believed that all high school students should take four years of mathematics, English, history and science. The public attitudes far exceeded the strictest of high school graduation requirements and even exceeded most of the admissions requirements for all but a handful of colleges and universities. Why was there such a dichotomy between what the public (who paid for the education) wanted and what they were getting?

The *Nation at Risk* report described the reason as "disturbing inadequacies in the way the educational process itself is often conducted." It provided a set of recommendations which covered public, private, and parochial schools alike. The recommendations covered four topics:

a. Content Recommendations—more English, science, social studies, computer science, and math.
b. Standards Recommendations—harsher grading, higher college admission requirements, more rigorous textbooks, and new instructional materials.
c. Time Recommendations—seven-hour schools days, 220-day school years, more homework, and stricter attendance policies.
d. Teaching Recommendations—higher standards for teachers, higher salaries for teachers, full-year contracts for teachers, and "career ladders" for teachers.

There were two major economic changes taking place in the period before and shortly after the *Nation at Risk* report. First, federal funding of schools increased remarkably during the decade of the 1960s; a much slower growth continued into the 1970s, followed by a small decline in the 1980s. The current expenditures on education (elementary and secondary) amount to about 4 percent of GNP.

The second major change was the steady shift in the source of the financial support for education. For the last twenty-five years, the states have steadily increased support for education, while local revenues have declined. The amount of government support for private schools is inconsequential.

Some ten years after the "Nation at Risk" report, a second study has again changed the manner in which researchers are viewing schools. This is the Brookings Institution study done by John Chubb and Terry Moe, titled *Politics, Markets, and America's Schools* (1990). The Chubb and Moe study lamented the fact that all previous research on the educational process took for granted the institutional framework within which problems have been identified and reforms have been suggested. Educational research, according to Chubb and Moe, has taken the democratic public school delivery system for granted and limited research to suggesting "fixes" for the current system. Few studies have taken the wider environment of education, including all of private education, seriously. This is where Chubb and Moe have changed the recent direction of research and discussion. The alternatives to democratic public schools are being carefully examined and compared. In this new line of research even the form of the delivery system is a variable.

In the next section of this chapter we examine the issues originally examined in *Nation at Risk*, and in the final section, we examine the most important concerns covered by Chubb and Moe in their more recent work.

The Educational Production Function

Any production process involves collecting various inputs at the production site and combining them in such a way as to yield the desired finished product or service. Some of the inputs may be relatively fixed in supply: the buildings or equipment available. The other inputs may be varied and, as different quantities are used, the level of output may be expected to vary. The relationship between the various amounts of inputs used in the production process and the level of output is called a production function.

Production functions in economics are expressed as mathematical relationships between a combination of inputs and the best output which can be generated from those inputs with the existing level of technology. Production functions change as the technology used in the production process changes. It is usually assumed that the decision maker has complete knowledge of the production function, that is, for any given combination of inputs a particular output may be predicted.

Most studies done by economists of the educational process are analyses of educational production functions, that is, they are studies examining the relationship between different inputs into and outcomes of the educational process. The studies are most often statistical estimations of the production function as opposed to experiments like those run in most other social sciences.

Textbook explanations of production functions consider only the most rudimentary of situations: a company producing a single product using only labor and capital. The mathematical form of the production function is assumed, and the prices of each of the inputs are assumed to be known. The student is then faced with the problem of how to combine inputs efficiently to produce a given output at least cost. Even the simplest specification of production can be a powerful decision tool telling the decision maker the correct combinations of inputs to use to achieve the desired result, and estimates of production functions are widely used in many industries as a basis for decision making.

The production function studies done on the education process, however, run into a number of problems. The form of the production function itself is usually unknown to the researcher. The "output" of the process is difficult to define, and there are quite likely multiple outputs. Multiple outputs to a single productive process complicate analysis. Measurements of both the outputs and the inputs are imperfect. The one thing that is certain about educational production functions is that they are frequently used to justify public policy or "educational reform" (Hanushek, 1986).

The Concept of Efficiency

To examine the way in which inputs can be used efficiently in a production process, the researcher must examine various combinations of inputs that can be used to produce the outputs. The particular combination of inputs into the production process such that one output cannot be increased without decreasing another output is called *technical efficiency*. The inputs would be inefficiently allocated if reallocating them causes more of one or both services to be produced. With more than one output, technical efficiency is important because it means that inputs are allocated in the production of all services so that production costs are minimized. It is this concept of technical efficiency which we are using in this section of the chapter.

A second, but not less important, type of efficiency is discussed later; that type of efficiency is called *economic efficiency*, or output efficiency. Even if a system is producing services at minimum cost with technical efficiency, it must also produce services in combinations that match people's willingness to pay for them. Meeting this condition is economic efficiency.

Aggregate Data Show Limited Relationship Between Inputs and Performance

The earliest of the education production studies in the economics literature is the "Coleman Report", which most people identify with justifying school bussing in the 1960s (Coleman, et al., 1966). Coleman, a sociologist at the University of Chicago, completed what was actually a study of the educational production function for the U.S. Office of Education (as it was then called). The results were quite unexpected and caused Coleman to be both harassed and vilified as well as awarded academic prizes for his efforts.

First, Coleman found that the facilities and resources devoted to the educational process were not distributed unevenly by race; black and white children in the same region and setting commanded almost identical sets of resources. The only significant difference in resources distribution were not by race but as a result of different distributions across the country.

Secondly, he found that even if the facilities and resources had been unevenly distributed, it would not have mattered much. The outputs were quite unrelated to the differences in resources allocated to the various schools. Those resources allocated by school boards, per-pupil expenditures, age of textbooks, and so on were unrelated to effectiveness. Coleman later explained that this finding was really not at all surprising considering that Soviet schools, which operate under state management much like our own, also showed inputs almost entirely unrelated to outputs (1991). One single input stood out, however, in the 1966 study as having a significant effect on student performance: if the teacher scored well on a vocabulary test, this was related to student verbal achievement (note carefully that teachers' degrees, teachers' salaries, and teachers' experience were all in the "unrelated to student performance" category).

A final result of the Coleman production study was that black children performed far better in schools with student bodies made up primarily of middle-class students. While school resources themselves mattered little, the group with which students took classes did make a difference. This final result was touted almost exclusively as the reason for school busing in the years after 1966. Surprisingly, school busing to achieve racial equality was also promoted as a means of achieving equality of resources even though Coleman had carefully explained that the resources were not allocated by race and that even if they had been, it would have mattered little.

Coleman believes little was said about the significant result concerning a teacher's vocabulary test score because the likely outcome of critically examining that result would have been to change the racial composition of the teaching force. Coleman recognized that the role modeling provided by black teachers would lead to an opposite conclusion but argued that the empirical evidence implied that "a major source of the inequality of educational opportunity for black students was the fact that they were being taught by black teachers" who "were generally less well prepared than were white teachers."

Other researchers as well have echoed Coleman's results by providing studies which show little or no effect on student performance caused by differences in schools (Hanushek and Kain, 1972). Hanushek reports that production function studies of the educational process are met with a great deal of skepticism by professional educators, probably because the results show gross inefficiencies in the use of resources by those same educators. The results are startling when looked at in the aggregate: over many years and throughout hundreds of studies the evidence on the effect of various educational inputs is remarkably clear. The results shown here indicate the effects estimated from various studies on educational output (Bowles and Levin, 1968; Cain and Watts, 1970; Hanushek, 1986).

Input	Result
class size	of 112 estimates, only 9 showed smaller classes as more effective
teacher salaries	of 60 estimates, only 9 indicate a positive effect
teacher education	of 106 estimates, only 6 indicated a positive effect
teacher experience	of 109 studies, only 33 indicated a positive effect
expenditures per pupil	of 65 studies, only 13 indicated a positive effect
family background	very important in almost all studies

The output measures used in almost all of these studies are by their very nature proxies for what we see as the real outcomes to an educational process; the proxies are needed because varying quantities of a homogeneous output (such as the output of microwave ovens at General Electric) are not easily translated into an educational equivalent. The education process is a service which transforms an individual in some meaningful manner, but what manner the change takes and how and when to measure that change are imperfectly approximated at best in empirical research.

The inescapable conclusion, however, is that over twenty years of study have shown American schools to be *technically inefficient*. Furthermore, the attributes of the system most often singled out for change and reform are not even related to educational outcomes. The conclusion of technical inefficiency should not come as a surprise to economists since almost all the studies covered only public schools which are organized as monopolies with virtually no competition. These schools are also not-for-profit institutions and so do not have the normal incentives to minimize costs.

Measurements quantified most often by economists are SAT scores, attendance rates, continuation in higher education (or dropout rates), or any other easily quantifiable outcome. These are often not the actual outcomes a researcher might want to measure, but they are the outcomes which are visible and generally available. In this sense, then, they stand as imperfect proxies for the educational outcomes we would like to measure.

A Critique of the Educational Production Tests: Measuring the Outputs

The most common measure of output used in educational production functions is some type of test score. Note carefully that any test score is probably a proxy at best for what we might really want to measure. We might, for instance, be interested in whether a particular education process allows a student to become a better consumer or a more productive member of the labor force. Test scores, we presume, are somewhat related to these traits, but the actual linkage is probably weak and far from automatic. We also have the problem that post-school outcomes (the ones we are really interested in) cannot be well measured by observing an individual's schooling. Researchers, however, still use cross-sectional analysis of test scores with current inputs in order to predict future (i.e., post-school) performance.

An example of one such study would be the one performed by Summers and Wolfe (1977) on Philadelphia public school children. The model used was quite simple; Summers and Wolfe assumed that output would be measured by a standardized test score. The particular test they used was the Iowa Test of Basic Skills (Composite). They assumed that the performance on this test depended upon various input factors:

> "Test Score" is a function of:
>   Income, Race, Sex, IQ, Unexcused Absences, Lateness, Rating of Teacher's College, Teacher's Experience, National Teacher Exam Score, Class Size, School Size, School Library Size, Percentage of Blacks Enrolled, Percentage of High Achievers Enrolled, Percentage of Low Achievers Enrolled, Number of Disruptive Incidents.

Educators and parents seem to believe that standardized test scores are very important and quite predictive of future outcomes. Nevertheless, considerable uncertainty exists about the actual relationships between test scores and various school characteristics (such as those listed above) as inputs.

As far as economists are concerned, the most serious problem with using a formulation like the one above is specification error. Specification error is the name given to the problem encountered when a test does not include all of the "correct" independent variables in a test of the relationship.

Consider that in the Summers and Wolfe formulation above there were other important determinants of a student's test score which did not appear in their equation. For instance, assume that the color of a person's hair was an important determinant of how well an individual scored on standardized tests. Since this variable does not appear in the Summers-Wolfe formulation, an economist would say that the analysis suffers from specification error.

The real problem is that if hair color really is related to test scores and if it is left out of the test, all the results of the empirical test will now be incorrect to some degree. Could the errors be large enough to cause serious misinterpretation? Yes, the errors could very easily cause some variables to appear unimportant when in fact they may be the most important determinants of improved test scores.

Almost all tests of achievement, no matter how informative, suffer from a problem of specification error, yet a tool exists for correcting the error and improving our results.

The Value-Added Approach

Almost all tests of educational performance have been conducted as "level" tests, that is, they use information from only one period. Summers and Wolfe, for instance, used 1970–71 pupil files for their study (1977). All the variables used were contemporaneous. In theoretical production functions, however, we are always interested in the value added by a particular process. What we really want to know is if this particular year of schooling, in this particular school, and with this particular teacher has "added" anything to the students' abilities. Of course, any particular student brought with him or her to this school year a set of talents which were obtained elsewhere; what we want to know is if any addition to these talents has taken place as a result of this year's experiences.

This value-added form of test will be a bit more difficult to employ, since it assumes that we have some knowledge of the student covering a range of time, rather than information covering only a single level or an instant. We could easily use standardized test scores for a value-added test, since we often have information on the same students for a number of years. This still leaves us with the problem of choosing the correct inputs to include in our tests, but even the value-added approach does not solve the problem of using an incorrect research format.

The Educational Market

An economic system may produce services at minimum cost with technical efficiency, but it must also produce services in combinations that match people's willingness to pay for them. Meeting this condition is called *economic efficiency*. Even if our schools were technically efficient using resources in the correct combinations and amounts, they could still be failing to produce the outcomes that the customers want; hence the schools would be economically inefficient.

What would your reaction be to the following press release?

> The president today signed legislation creating a nationwide chain of government owned and operated cafeterias. Meals at the cafeterias will be free to anyone who enters, and will be prepared following a menu approved by the Food and Drug Administration, state boards of nutrition, and locally elected nutrition boards. The cafeterias will be funded by a new tax on people's homes. *The tax*

must be paid regardless of whether a taxpayer ever enters a cafeteria or eats a
single meal in one.

Asked whether the new plan was fair to people who eat most of their meals at home, the president replied, "People who don't eat at the cafeterias should have to pay for the privilege of eating somewhere else. We shouldn't subsidize their decisions to be antisocial or to choose a diet that is different from what locally elected officials say is best."

If people don't like what is being served in the cafeterias, the president said, "they should run for election to their local nutrition board and work to improve the system, not abandon it." The president also predicted that the cost of food would go down since there would no longer be "wasteful competition" among restaurants and grocery stores. (Bast and Wittman, 1991, 24)

The proposed government cafeterias could very well be quite technically efficient in the sense that they could utilize resources in correct combinations and amounts to produce at least cost, and yet they would be quite inefficient in a very different sense. A large portion of the public might be quite upset at the thought of being forced to pay for cafeteria services which they don't want to use. Many Americans would also likely rather have a choice of restaurants if they were going to eat out, and few people would agree to paying for the cafeterias if they never expected to use them.

Are America's schools like these cafeterias? The similarities are stunning. Americans pay for public schools whether or not they ever expect to use them; these schools are nominally under the direction of locally elected or appointed boards; the only recourse to grievances against these schools is through a political system. Yet, due to changes in funding, the costs of affecting political change are prohibitive.

American public schools today have all the characteristics of cartel arrangements. There are only a few schools in any market area, and those schools are all members of a collusive agreement which provides protection against the entry of new schools and allocates a certain portion of the market to each school (whether or not the school deserves it). Any cartel which is well enforced includes member agreements to limit production in order to drive up price.

Most cartels nonetheless are very weak and soon disintegrate. This is a fortunate outcome for consumers and comes about because cartel members are prone to cheat on one another. History is full of short-lived cartel arrangements.

But some cartels are very long lasting. The reason for this is that some cartels have been able to use easily enforceable agreements among their members. The best way to get cheap and effective enforcement is to have the government sanction a cartel and its purposes; this is what has happened to America's schools.

Years ago, public schools were run as a local monopoly and financed on a local level through property taxes. If a parent was displeased with the schooling, it was often possible to "vote with one's feet" and move to a neighboring school system which might be run more in keeping with a parent's ideal view. Today, however, voting with your feet does little good; school districts across the United States have formed giant cartels by using the government to enforce the agreements.

Traditionally, in the United States, the constituency of a school was limited to the local level. We are not using the term constituency here to simply mean the number of students enrolled, but rather to mean the size of the group from which funding is obtained (and through which control is exercised). A subtle change has taken place over the last twenty years or so with respect to school funding (and control). School districts began to consolidate and merge. In 1945 there were 100,000 separate school districts, but by 1990 there were fewer than 16,000. In addition, 1978–79 revenue from state sources began to exceed the revenue from local sources nationwide. While the relative roles of the private and public schools have not changed substantially over the past decade, the role of state funding of the public schools have changed appreciably. Has this had any effect on the schools? We believe it has had a measurable and undesirable effect, but an effect that is explainable.

How does this change in funding affect school performance? Consider a set of parents who are upset because the local school district raises property taxes (or reduces the quality of education). There will be an incentive for these parents to "vote with their feet" and move to a neighboring school district-because they perceive that their children can get just as good an education at lower cost.

But what if all the school districts within a very wide area have signed a collusive agreement in which they concur that all the districts will raise taxes at the same time? Voting with your feet becomes an ineffective response. The parents are stuck, and the school board knows it.

So, raising property taxes (or reducing the quality of education) becomes difficult for one school district to do, but it becomes quite easy if many districts have an arrangement. This is precisely what American school districts have done; the state governments (and the federal government to an increasing extent) have acted as cartel enforcers for the local school districts.

By funding the largest portion of schooling with state taxes and then allocating the funds to the various school districts, the local districts have a mechanism to prevent cheating by cartel members. The system works even better if the state government can set not only the financing levels but also the educational standards for the entire state. In this way the individual school districts cannot even cheat by changing the quality of education. Individual school districts also have little or no incentive to offer a curriculum any different than any other member of the cartel. For parents, this means a loss in the variety of schools available; few schools will attempt to distinguish themselves by producing better outcomes in a manner any different from any other member of the cartel. If the state also insures that no significant funds are allowed to flow to any potential competitors (such as private schools), the cartel is iron-clad in its ability to control the industry.

Formidable as the state and local government's role is in legally enforcing the cartel, it also provides one other important function for cartel members—it acts as the formulator of public opinion. The state government (and federal government to some extent) often form coalitions with the teachers' unions and the school boards to promote state mandated educational spending and policies. The reason for this coalition is obvious when you consider that the National Education Association (the teachers' largest union) is the most powerful lobbying organization in the United States (far more powerful than even the American Medical Association or the National Association of Manufacturers). It is not uncommon to see parents' groups which are protesting the poor quality of education being chastised by state officials, union leaders, and local school officials, all speaking with a single (cartel-like) voice.

The effect of this coalition in forming public opinion about education in America should not be overlooked. This cartel operates the public schools like a defunct Eastern European country: the outcomes get worse with each passing year, but the officials tell us that things are actually getting better and that true success is just around the corner if only we will allocate a bit more money to fund the last few necessary programs. Can there be any doubt that the "American OPEC" is now as hopelessly bankrupt as were Czechoslovakia and East Germany in 1990?

The only solution for the problems of post–Cold War Eastern Europe was the complete dissolution of the monopolistic economies and the construction of free markets in both labor and goods. Can there be any other solution to our own cartel?

The Private Schools

One subject we have touched on only lightly has been any analysis of the few private schools we do have in the United States. They are few and far between and their budgets are minuscule compared to the government schools, but perhaps there is a lesson to be learned from them. The research by Chubb and Moe (1990) has sought out the data from these private institutions simply because they are uncontrolled by democratic politics, but are instead subject to the strictest of all masters: the free market.

Because the private schools are uncontrolled by democratic politics, they, like all firms operating in free markets, determine their own goals, standards, and methods. Each private school becomes a reflection of the controlling interest in the institution, which is sometimes parochial and sometimes not. Since most of these institutions sell their product (that is, at least a large portion of their funding comes from service rendered), they are quite sensitive to their local constituency.

Roman Catholic schools are very sensitive to the parish board and the diocese, while nonparochial private schools are quite sensitive to their governing boards (almost certainly made up of concerned parents of students or recent graduates). In each of these types of schools parents can "vote with their feet" much more easily than with a public system; it takes little effort to stop paying one school's bills and enroll Johnny and Becky in another school. If the quality of schooling changes or if the tuition increases abruptly, parents are free to move at any time.

Parents may also choose to keep their children in a private school even when that school changes for the worse and hope to bring about an improvement through parental effort. Parents working with a private school have a much better chance of this happening than parents subject to the democratic politics of the public system. After all, if your tuition payment leaves with your child, the school managers will pay a bit more attention to your voiced opinions.

Don't mistake the private system, however, for one in which parents pull children out on a whim and move them around like pieces on a chessboard among the various schools. There is actually very little movement among private schools. The reason is that the system itself promotes harmony by allowing parents to choose, in the first place, a school likely to meet their own idealistic vision of what a school should be like. Since most private schools have clearly defined missions, especially the religious ones, a self-selection takes place between parents and private schools which promotes a harmony in the system.

Chubb and Moe used a database of over 60,000 students to determine what private schools were like and how their outcomes were different from public institutions. They studied both elite private schools (judged as elite by performance in the National Merit Scholarship competition) and Roman Catholic schools (characterized by their shared institutional context). The single question they sought to answer was "Are private schools more likely to possess the characteristics widely believed to produce effectiveness?" What did they find?

Most private schools have a governing board, but few have any accompanying administrative apparatus. One New York City educator related to us that the central (nonteaching) staff of the public system included more than 4,000 administrators. When asked how many central administrators the Roman Catholic system had, he phoned their offices. The Roman Catholic schools have one-ninth the enrollment of the NYC public schools. The nun who answered was unsure of exactly how many people were employed there. When our friend pressed her for an estimate she replied "well now, let's see . . . one, two, three . . ."; she could count only thirty.

The proliferation of administrators in public systems is not confined to only New York City; the New Orleans public system has 660 central office employees and 83,000 students, but the competing Roman Catholic system, with 53,000 students, has a scant sixteen central office employees. Bruce Cooper of Fordham reports that of all the funds spent by schools systems, over 50 percent are used in the classroom in Roman Catholic systems nationwide. Less than a third of the funds spent in the New York City public school system ever reach the classroom ($1,972 out of $6,107 spent per pupil). Most of these nonclassroom funds go to non-teaching administrators.

Even the numbers of administrators fail to tell the real differences between public and private school systems. Greeley (1977) found in a study of the two systems that the Roman Catholic hierarchy actually had very little role at all in governing their schools. There was far greater autonomy for the individual school and the individual principal in the Roman Catholic schools. According to Chubb and Moe (1990), private schools better manage and control their curriculum and the quality of the educational opportunities they offer.

Private schools also have some degree of control over who enrolls, while public schools are not able to select students. Public schools are then saddled with more narrow goals than private schools—goals such as basic literacy. But even after allowing for economic and social backgrounds, the evidence is clear that private schools outperform the democratic political schools (Lanier, 1982; Schultz, 1983; O'Connor, 1986; Flanigan, 1991).

The private schools determine their own goals and have a clearer picture of what those goals are; they are more oriented by academic excellence and personal growth. The homework policies in the private schools are stricter. Private schools have more stringent graduation requirements; their students take more mathematics, science, history, and foreign language than their public counterparts. Private school principals have much greater autonomy than public school administrators to hire and fire faculty to weed out undesirable teachers and retain and reward the best educators.

The Importance of Incentives in Education

An essential characteristic of a free market system is its reliance on the profit incentive to produce competitive results. Without this incentive, the system has no driving force. Are there any incentives for a democratic political school system to do well in educating young people? No doubt there are many educators who want desperately to do a good job in the public system. But there are few, if any, rewards for performing well. When a school's resources are guaranteed, it cannot be allowed to continue on as before or change direction at its own choosing merely because the principal and faculty would like to do so. Because it is not the school (i.e., the principal and the faculty) that makes the gains or suffers the loss due to their actions, the choices about what to do must be made for them by those who control the funds. These days the funds are increasingly controlled by state and federal authorities far distant from the individual classrooms.

The problem of adequate incentives which arises here is commonly discussed as if it were a problem mainly of the willingness of people to do their best. But this, although important, is not the whole, nor even the most important, aspect of the problem. It is not merely that if we want schools to do their best we must make it worthwhile for them. What is more important is that they must be given some readily intelligible yardstick by which to measure the social importance of the different things they might choose to do. Even with the best will in the world it would be impossible for anyone to choose between various alternatives if the advantages they offered him or her stood in no relation to their usefulness to society. Economists have for some time recognized that it is not likely people will give their best for long periods of time unless their own interests are directly involved. In all institutions some external pressure is needed if they are to give their best (Hayek, 1944).

Incentives may be either positive or negative, and presumably they are formulated to reflect ''society's'' choice. Much of the criticism of ''incompetent educators'' and ''inadequate schools'' implicitly assumes that the bureaucracy is pursuing an assigned goal but simply failing to achieve it due to lack of effort or ability. In reality, the public school bureaucracy may be responding quite rationally to the incentives facing it. The only real protection of the public interest built into the public school system incentive structure are the legal penalties for blatantly illegal conduct, such as mistreatment of minors or taking bribes. But grossly illegal acts are seldom exposed, and ''throwing the rascals out'' is often the tactic taken when parents are upset with educational results.

What is needed is a restructuring of the incentives facing the system. The only way to do that is to allow some entry into and exit from the system; in other words, there must be alternatives or potential alternatives for the parents to choose between. New schools, whether public or private, should be free to enter and leave the educational market. The funding of education should take the position of funding students, not schools. Students would take their funding with them wherever they went.

Existing schools would face the threat of losing students and funding if enrollments dropped and would face the opportunity of more students and greater funding if enrollments climbed. The incentives would be clear to cut wasteful spending and to respond to parents' desires before new schools decided to enter the market. And it would be a market; with free entry and exit of schools, parents would face real alternatives to monopoly education.

Efficient schools, as judged by the customers, would gain enrollment and survive, while schools that did not perform well would lose students and suffer lower budgets. Perhaps choice is a panacea for our educational ills.

CHAPTER 10

Environmental Policy: Problems and Prospects in the New Age

SHELDON KAMIENIECKI, ANTHONY KANDEL, AND LOUIS SCHUBERT

The environmental movement is having a growing impact on American and international politics, and there is little evidence to suggest that this momentum will slow in the near future. Nationally, surveys indicate a sharp rise in public concern over environmental problems and government action concerning them (Mitchell, 1990). Feeling intense pressure from various quarters, policymakers are enacting stringent regulations concerning air pollution, the handling of toxic and hazardous materials, and natural resource conservation, including wildlife protection. Internationally, a sense of urgency about the deteriorating condition of the earth's ecological system is sweeping the capitals of foreign governments, and nations are now working together that have never worked together before.

Several factors account for these trends in American and international environmental politics. Rapid industrialization and economic growth have increased the number, seriousness, and scope of pollution problems. Regardless of where people reside, threats to the environment and health are experienced by nearly everyone. Often, these problems are transnational and require binational or even multinational cooperation to solve them. As a result, policymakers have become increasingly aware of the vulnerability of the ecosystem and of the immediate need to take bilateral or multilateral action.

Apprehension about pollution can also be traced to the cumulative impact of major news stories and events in recent years. The chemical accident at Bhopal, India, the release of radiation from the fire at the Chernobyl nuclear power plant, the huge oil spill from the *Exxon Valdez* in Prince William Sound in Alaska, and the release of oil into the Persian Gulf and the burning of Kuwait's oil wells during the war with Iraq were widely covered by the technologically advanced communications media. Porter and Brown (1991) further point out that additional scientific data on environmental problems have led to increased awareness and concern about the present condition of the earth's ecosystem. Compared to ten years ago, for example, scientists have a much better understanding of the causes and effects of global warming and the thinning of the ozone layer.

To a large extent, the withering of superpower competition in the early 1990s has redirected attention away from strictly military issues and toward national and international environmental problems. The United States and other countries are redefining and expanding their definition of national security to include natural resource issues (Schubert and Kamieniecki, 1991). Like peace and arms control, truly international cooperation is required to protect the global environment. Additional social learning and value transformation must first occur before effective cooperation at the international level is possible.

This chapter analyzes American policies in three major areas: air-pollution abatement, the handling of toxic and hazardous substances, and natural resource conservation. The study examines how public policy developed in each of these areas and where government efforts are most likely to focus during the post–Cold War period. Toward the latter part of the chapter, the discussion turns to international environmental issues. The interplay between economic and political forces shaping public policy is highlighted throughout the study.

Toxic and Hazardous Waste Management

Toxic and hazardous waste has grown from an unknown enemy into one of the most serious environmental problems presently facing the United States (Cohen and Kamieniecki, 1991; Kraft and Vig, 1990; Lester and Bowman, 1983). The steady growth of generated waste, coupled with increasing awareness of the dire threat posed to both human health and the environment, has pushed the issue high on the political agenda. Although Congress and the Environmental Protection Agency (EPA) have enacted numerous laws and regulations to control toxic waste, industrial waste generators of such waste have generally been uncooperative, despite evidence of the economic and environmental benefits of waste reduction and recycling.

Of all environmental problems, toxic and hazardous waste has been the least abated and remains the most serious threat today (Kraft and Vig, 1990). For decades, toxic waste has been carelessly disposed of in lagoons, ponds, landfills, injection wells, and rivers and lakes. The result has been widespread contamination of the environment, as polluted liquid waste has seeped into groundwater and entered the food chain. The EPA has stated that 90 percent of waste ponds will contaminate the groundwater and has added that "most land disposal units . . . will eventually leak" (CBO, 1985, 3). This pollution is long lasting, as the lack of exposure to sun or air prevents evaporation, and some heavy metals remain toxic permanently (Block, 1985). Thirty percent of the nation's groundwater is now contaminated, and 50 million Americans, mostly in rural areas, are at risk (Postel, 1987).

Since 1945, the United States has increased its synthetic chemical production by fifteen times and has tripled its pesticide use in the last twenty years (Postel, 1987). This has led to a vast increase in chemical waste. The 1988 EPA estimate was 264 million tons, and growing at 1 percent a year, although this amount could be much higher. The Office of Technology Assessment (OTA), a research arm of Congress, has estimated the 1988 waste at 560 million metric tons. The cost of handling this waste totals approximately $70 billion a year, with government picking up one-third of the cost (Schneider, 1988).

Illegal storage of toxic waste, the disposal of liquid toxic substances in landfills, and "midnight" dumping are a serious threat to the environment. Such actions were a concern as early as the 1960s. The criminal prosecution of these activities must be a priority, as the regulation of waste generators through fines is not totally effective.

Old, abandoned toxic waste sites, such as Love Canal and Valley of the Drums, have become infamous. There are presently over 30,000 abandoned toxic waste sites, and the OTA predicts that at least 10,000 of these will require clean up. This number has continued to grow, however, and recent figures reported by a research team at the University of Tennessee estimated the probable cost of clean up to be $750 billion over thirty years, with the possibility of reaching $1.7 trillion (Abramson, 1991). The time period from site identification to the end of abatement ranges from nine to twelve years, and with over 1,200 sites on the EPA'S National Priority List (NPL), the time and resources required are staggering.

The Legislative History

In 1971, the Council on Environmental Quality (CEQ) concluded, "It is clear that current laws are inadequate to control the actual and potential dangers of toxic substances" (Comptroller General, 1980, 3). Laws controlling air or water pollution and insecticide use were helpful, but they were not comprehensive enough to allow the federal government to attack effectively the toxic threat. Therefore, in 1976, toxic and hazardous waste was regulated directly. Congress passed a pair of laws, the Toxic Substances Control Act (TSCA) (PL 94-469) and the Resource Conservation and Recovery Act

(RCRA) (PL 94-580), which initiated a policy of control over the production, generation, transportation, and disposal of harmful chemicals and waste (or from "cradle to grave").

TSCA allowed the EPA to test any chemical suspected to be dangerous and bill the manufacturer for the cost. EPA demands for information have proven difficult, as the chemical companies have fought investigation and have been unwilling to provide necessary data (Rosenbaum, 1991). The EPA also gained more control over the marketing and distribution of chemicals, mandating tests of chemical effects on the environment and forcing industry to keep records of the tests. Finally, TSCA established an interagency testing commission, comprised of representatives from eight federal agencies, which was to recommend substances for testing to the EPA.

RCRA was passed with the intent of protecting public health and the environment and promoting the reuse and recycling of toxic and hazardous waste. The first goal was accomplished to a limited degree, while the latter failed miserably. The law mandated operating permits for facilities which treat, store, or dispose of hazardous waste, defined hazardous wastes by several characteristics, including toxicity, and named some four hundred substances specifically. These definitions were vague, however, and many toxic materials were not included (for example, exemptions were granted for oil and mining waste) (CBO, 1985). The law stipulated that each state's program be at least as stringent as the EPA's, although several states have gone further in restricting substances (e.g., California). Finally, the legislation allowed for citizens to sue a company or the EPA for violations, and provided money for the states to administer and enforce the law. The ineffectiveness of RCRA, due to loopholes and lax enforcement, is evidenced by the fact that few companies have any incentive to recycle and that 45 RCRA-regulated sites have since been deemed polluted enough to qualify for federal Superfund clean-up money (CBO, 1985).

In 1984, RCRA was amended by the Hazardous and Solid Waste Amendments Act (HSWA) (PL 98-616). The intent of this act was to provide that "whenever feasible, the generation of hazardous waste is to be reduced or eliminated as expeditiously as possible" (Postel, 1987). The House-Senate Conference Committee added, "Land disposal should be used only as a last resort" (*Congressional Record*, 1984, 717). It was hoped that these two goals would be complementary, with the reduced use of landfills expected to spur efforts at waste reduction and recycling. Hazardous waste disposal at landfills was severely restricted, and waste injections directly into drinking water sources was prohibited. Double lining was required for landfills, and underground storage tanks (e.g., at gasoline stations) and small quantity generators (e.g., paint and body shops and dry cleaning stores) were also regulated (Cohen and Kamieniecki, 1991). The legislation was weakened by exemptions. The double lining was not required for six years, and even after that the requirement could be waived if EPA ruled that no alternative was possible or that the toxic waste could not migrate (CBO, 1985). Despite stricter regulations on waste streams, the EPA granted numerous exemptions, some of them permanent (Magnuson, 1985). The new restrictions raised the cost of operating landfills, forcing many sites out of business. As landfill space becomes increasingly scarce, this legislation could come under fire from small quantity generators desperate for somewhere to dump their waste.

In 1978, the horrors at Love Canal were widely covered by the media, and for the first time the nation learned of the serious threat posed by old, abandoned toxic waste sites. As a result of growing public concern, Congress passed the 1980 Comprehensive Environmental Response Compensation and Liability Act, or Superfund (PL 96-510). This legislation authorized raising $1.6 billion, mostly from taxes on chemical feedstocks, to be used for a five year plan for emergency and remedial cleanup of abandoned toxic waste dumps and a postclosure liability fund (Ingersoll and Brockbank, 1986). The law also sought to regulate spills and provided for emergency cleanup at the owner's expense. Failure to report a spill could result in a $10,000 fine, waste generators whose inaction forced government cleanup could be fined triple damages, and a partial polluter could be hit with the full abatement costs (Keene, 1985).

Superfund has been racked by politics and slow implementation (Cohen and Kamieniecki, 1991; Rosenbaum, 1991). A victim compensation clause was omitted from the final draft of the bill, and included was a clause which mandated that one site from each state must be included on the NPL (Davis and Lester, 1988; Harthill, 1984). Cleanup was widely criticized, as the EPA often moved wastes from one site to a RCRA-approved site, which meant in all likelihood the same waste would eventually be abated again. By 1985, only six NPL sites had been abated, and it appeared that even these had not been properly cleaned. At one site on the Susquehanna River, where cleanup had been completed, the first heavy rain after completion brought 100,000 gallons of toxic wastes to the surface. Similarly, in Baltimore, a site had been declared abated after one foot of topsoil was removed, despite evidence that poisons existed as deep as fifteen feet (Satchell, 1989).

In 1986, as Superfund was due to expire, Congress passed the Superfund Amendments and Reauthorization Act (SARA) (PL 99-499), which appropriated an additional $8.5 billion through 1991. Despite the additional funding, Superfund cleanup has been riddled with corruption and inflated prices. By the end of 1989 the NPL list had 1,224 sites, with only 43 finished and 250 begun (Abelson, 1989). Congress, in criticism of the EPA's tendency toward temporary abatement practices, dictated ''remedial actions in which treatment which permanently . . . reduces the volume, toxicity, and mobility of the hazardous contaminants are to be preferred'' (Wolf, 1989, 42). It seems clear that the

EPA has failed not only this objective but also in creating and following a long-term, goal-oriented plan of action.

The Bureaucracy

The EPA, since its establishment in 1970, has been too slow in responding to the nation's serious toxic waste problem because of politics. Normally, the political agenda of the administration will affect the actions of those in the bureaucracy, and this has been the case in toxic waste policy-making. In 1979, Hugh Kaufman, manager of the EPA Hazardous Waste Assessment Program, claimed that the White House wanted to dismiss the toxic waste problem and portray the costs of cleanup as exorbitant. Ronald Reagan's EPA administrator, Anne Gorsuch Burford, abolished the office of enforcement and ignored Congress when it urged the hiring of more toxic waste site investigators (Block, 1985). During the early 1980s, 40 percent or less of allotted Superfund money was spent yearly, and the number of cases referred to the Justice Department dropped dramatically (Block, 1985). The EPA suspended regulations requiring toxic waste generators to file reports because it was "not efficient," suspended a ban on toxic barrels in landfills, and extended the deadline which mandated that industry implement the "best available technology" in toxic waste management to 1988. There were reports of secret meetings between EPA officials and industry personnel, during which industry officials were assured of lax regulation (Rosenbaum, 1991). Finally, evidence exists that Burford and Rita Lavelle, an assistant administrator at EPA and the director of the Superfund program, used Superfund money for strictly political purposes, holding reported meetings with several White House officials to select sites for the dispersement of grants as well as for the withholding of funds. Such behavior did not escape the eye of the House Energy Committee, which noted that Burford and Lavelle "disregarded the public health and the environment by adopting a 'go slow' approach to the cleanup of toxic waste" (O'Donnell, 1984, 27).

Although both women were eventually forced from office, and Lavelle was sent to jail, the EPA has not shown dramatic change under new leadership. A congressional study of EPA monitoring of toxic contamination of groundwater found the work "inaccurate, incomplete, and unreliable" (Magnuson, 1985). A 1988 OTA study of the EPA's toxic waste program was also highly critical, finding a lack of leadership and central guidance, little shared information, a preference for containment of waste over abatement, young, scared, and ill-trained personnel, too few suits filed, too much negotiation with industry, an overemphasis on cost, and Superfund money being spent six times more than private monies in toxic waste cleanups (Wolf, 1989).

In general, the twelve years encompassing the Reagan and Bush presidencies were difficult ones for environmentalists. The EPA administrator under Bush, William Reilly, formerly a spokesperson for environmental concerns, did reverse the Reagan administration's policy of exempting certain municipal landfills from receiving Superfund money (thus placing the burden on the states). All sites became eligible for funding as needed (Steinzor, 1989). The Superfund itself remained severely underfunded, a condition the Clinton administration with its environmentally aware vice president, Al Gore, committed themselves to changing.

Other initiatives of the Bush administration were less welcome. The administration fought congressional efforts to force the federal government to comply with RCRA landfill requirements (*CQ Weekly Report*, 1989). Particularly disturbing was the government's policy of ignoring toxic waste regulations at federal sites, including those controlled by the departments of Defense and Energy. "National Sacrifice Zones" were proposed by Bush appointees in the Energy Department and by no less than the head of the toxic waste cleanup in the Department of Defense (Satchell, 1989). Such areas constitute vast land spaces set aside for the storage of waste, fenced-off and forgotten. No effort would be made to clean or decontaminate them.

The precedent is a dangerous one. Wide tracts of land could eventually be consigned to such status. Thousands of acres could fall victim to such a fate, touted as an economically efficient approach to waste management. Such proposals consequently have a certain political attractiveness to officials operating under severe budget constraints. The challenge is to find alternatives that better protect both the environment and the public's health and do so at reasonable cost.

Finally in this context, unworkable congressional mandates have exacerbated bureaucratic difficulties. SARA, for example, required those using underground storage tanks (regulated under HSWA) to carry liability insurance, yet insurance companies have been unwilling to write such policies (Cohen and Kamieniecki, 1991; Kamieniecki and Cohen, 1990). As a result, EPA has been unable to enforce this requirement, thereby increasing the likelihood that the federal government will have to pay for the abatement of future leaks and spills.

Choices and Solutions

The four alternatives for dealing with toxic waste, listed in a least to most preferable order, are disposal, treatment, recycling, and reduction. Unfortunately, to date, the last two options have been under employed, while treatment has suffered due to closures of several facilities. Long the short-term cheapest and easiest method, disposal is still the most common way of dealing with toxic and hazardous waste.

As restrictions shut down many sites, disposal has become more difficult. Several states do not have any capacity for disposal and are finding it

TABLE 10.1

Hazardous Waste Generated, Pounds per Capita, 1990

States Generating the Least Waste		States Generating the Most Waste	
South Dakota	3	Tennessee	13,932
Idaho	4	Georgia	12,498
North Dakota	9	West Virginia	2,476
Alaska	10	Virginia	8,769
New Mexico	12	Louisiana	6,097
Maine	12	Pennsylvania	5,278
Hawaii	14	Texas	4,731
Oregon	23	Kentucky	4,110
Rhode Island	24	Alabama	3,685
Missouri	27	South Carolina	3,180

increasingly difficult to locate other sites for their toxic waste. Historically, less affluent nations have accepted toxic waste in exchange for much needed hard currency. Africa, long providing a place for toxic waste disposal, is shutting the door to the poisonous imports. Thus, in 1987, the United States exported only 100,000 tons, less than one-tenth of 1 percent of its total output (Lief, 1988). Within the United States, several states have traditionally shipped toxic waste to the South, where it has been more welcome. In 1989, however, both South Carolina and Alabama stated that no further toxic waste shipments would be accepted from states which have no in-state disposal capacity (*New York Times*, 1989). Although a federal appeals court overturned the Alabama law one year later, it appears that the trend of the future is for nations and states to move towards a less conciliatory stand on accepting toxic waste. This is especially important in light of the huge differences among the states in regard to the amount of hazardous waste generated (see table 10.1).

As the number of disposal sites declines, incineration is receiving increased attention as an alternative treatment method. There has been strong public opposition to treatment facilities, as the NIMBY (Not in My Backyard) syndrome has spread. State and local governments play a limited role in treatment since no public facilities exist. With the cost of cleanup estimated at ten to one hundred times that of treatment at the source (CBO, 1985), an incentive exists for the government to become involved. Whereas private companies might treat only those toxic wastes which would be profitable, a public facility would treat all types. The government could fund a loan subsidy program for new facilities to replace older plants as they shut down, as well as becoming involved in a state-owned venture. The fact remains that toxic waste will never disappear. Should there be a dearth of such treatment plants, the highly dangerous illegal dumping could increase. Public education should be sponsored, and if necessary, states must invoke eminent domain laws to site a facility.

Recycling of solid waste (e.g., aluminum cans) is becoming increasingly common throughout the country, especially as garbage landfills begin to overflow. Unfortunately, this is not the case for toxic waste. The EPA has found that only 4 percent of toxic and hazardous waste is recycled. The federal government estimates that 80 percent of the amount of solvents in waste streams can be recycled (Postel, 1987). Waste exchange between industries is one possibility, as one company's waste could be another's gold mine. Transportation costs, lack of information, and fear of disclosing trade secrets, however, have led to slow advances in this area, but private companies specializing in waste matchmaking could spur an increase in such activity. "Bottle bills" have been adopted in several states with great success, and perhaps a similar deposit/refund program for toxic and hazardous substances might be adopted in states that generate considerable waste. This would reward industries that find ways to reuse their waste, while adding a financial burden to those who are inefficient or are dumping illegally.

The most economically efficient and environmentally effective method of dealing with toxic waste is waste reduction. The federal government has done very little to promote reduction, but a combination of state initiatives and industrial success provides hope for the future. In 1988, the EPA requested only $400,000 to study hazardous waste reduction, a mere .03 percent of its budget. The initiative of state governments has been mixed; although thirty-five states have some reduction program, the average budget is only $150,000 per year, enough for only two full-time employees (Dolin, 1988). In addition, a 1989 survey of twenty-one states found that only four planned to have toxic waste reduction play a major role in future waste management (Gold, 1989). One positive note is the opening of a waste reduction center in North Carolina under the auspices of the EPA, the Tennessee Valley Authority, and eight southern states. This idea of regional cooperation is promising, especially since several states, when submitting twenty-year plans for waste management to the EPA in 1989, chose not to present individual plans, instead opting for participation in regional programs (Gold, 1989).

Finally, many small companies are suffering from a lack of information and capital to implement effective hazardous and toxic waste control plans and therefore require government help. Loans for process modification and a central information bank would be cost effective and reduce waste from small quantity generators. Regulations which presently reward only treatment of generated waste could be altered to benefit those who reduce their output through tax relief or loans for program expansion. With space running low at disposal sites and treatment technology still emerging, reduction is the most sensible option.

Technology, Enforcement, and the Future

Developing technology offers new options for controlling toxic waste. One New Jersey firm is creating a nontoxic chemical mix which can immobilize toxic waste, thus preventing migration. Batelle Laboratories is developing a method to electrify contaminated soil at 4000 degrees F, melting the earth and destroying toxic waste in the process (*Futurist*, 1987). There is also research being done on chemical dismantling (i.e., leaving substances harmless) and bioengineered organisms which can eat toxic wastes.

Agriculture, a major source of toxic waste, can work toward reduction by using new methods. Integrated Pest Management (IPM) stresses the use of small amounts of pesticides in concert with natural predators. This has been used on up to 8 percent of the nation's cropland and has proved to both save money and reduce environmental damage (Postel, 1987). Overreliance on pesticides can be reduced, but the information and technology must be made available to the nation's farmers.

The government must combine stricter operational measures with better enforcement to insure that the toxic pollution problem does not exacerbate in the post–Cold War era. Although the need for new treatment facilities is apparent, the EPA must maintain strict licensing not only to insure that the facilities are properly managed but also to keep a close watch on the ratio of waste produced to the capacity of the operating plants. If too many waste-producing plants are built, existing toxic waste disposal sites might fill up quickly, creating an incentive for some industries to avoid environmentally sound abatement procedures. Enforcement, which has been the greatest weakness of the EPA, must become far more efficient and effective.

There have been many proposals for increased enforcement at the federal, state, and local levels. Los Angeles, for example, has a task force which has jailed several corporate offenders for industrial accidents (O'Donnell, 1984). Some states have raised penalties for illegal dumping; Pennsylvania increased the punishment from a $300 fine to one year in jail and/or a $500,000 fine (Block, 1985). A 1986 California referendum, which passed by a two-to-one margin, restricts the discharge of chemicals causing cancer and places the burden of proof in court on the offending industry. A 1988 Connecticut law forces payment for environmental damage and has gone so far as to place a price on every fish killed in a water pollution accident (Carpenter, 1989). At the federal level, the government has been aided by the courts, which have continually upheld strict liability under Superfund. EPA fines for illegal activity, however, must be increased; Weyerhauser, of which former EPA Administrator William Ruckleshaus is now the CEO, admitted in a paper filed with the Securities and Exchange Commission (SEC) regarding EPA fines, "the company does not believe that such amounts are likely to be . . . detrimental to the company's business" (Sibbison, 1989, 524). Business must have a strong incentive to act legally, not small fines which are less than the cost for disposing of waste properly.

Some have suggested using the RICO law, which allows prosecution for racketeering if two or more laws are broken, with sentences ranging up to twenty years (Block, 1985). In addition, property can be confiscated; the potential loss of a factory would certainly be encouragement to behave legally. There have also been several cases in New York and Illinois where business owners have been indicted for murder when employees have died of toxic fumes or accidents. This policy could be broadened to include polluters, who could be tried for the murder or attempted murder of thousands of people who drink contaminated water.

As already mentioned, the increase in the amount of hazardous and toxic waste generated in the United States and abroad is the direct result of rapid, uncontrolled industrial growth. This growth has also led to a considerable decline in the nation's air quality over the last forty years, seriously endangering the environment and public health in several metropolitan areas. The next section analyzes present and future trends in government efforts to improve air quality.

Air Pollution

Whether obscuring a beautiful ocean sunset in Los Angeles, a majestic Denver mountain panorama, or the view over the Grand Canyon, the ugly brown haze of smog has become perhaps the preeminent symbol of the excesses of an industrial society. Stress on economic growth and the power of the business sector have created a general acceptance among both elites and the masses of the inevitability of air pollution in an advanced industrial society. As the costs of air pollution have become more obvious, however, the public has become increasingly unwilling to grant industrial polluters carte blanche when it comes to spewing smoke into the atmosphere. Many citizens are less willing to alter their personal behavior and are more willing to support controls on industry. One study conducted for the Southern California Air Quality Management District (SCAQMD) in 1988 found that numerous people would oppose air pollution regulation which significantly affected personal driving patterns (Kamieniecki and Ferrall, 1991). This attitude is characteristic of the difficulties prevalent over three decades of working toward a national goal of clean air.

The Nature of the Problem

The loss of aesthetic beauty is perhaps the most benign aspect of the air pollution problem. Toxins emitted into the air from smokestacks, incinerators, exhaust pipes, and other sources damage the natural environment, private property, and public health. Various gases, especially carbon dioxide, contribute to global warming, which may have recently resulted in several of the warmest years on record in certain parts of the United States. Predictions for the future include the possibility that desertification could spread in the United States, and another dust bowl era could occur within fifty years (Caplan, 1990). Moreover, toxic air pollutants damage the outside of buildings and homes. Sulfur dioxide emissions, a product of fossil fuel use, leads to acid precipitation, which damages crops, lakes, rivers, and forests in the Northeast and Canada.

In addition to being a threat to property and the environment, air pollution is extremely harmful to human health. Carbon monoxide impairs the central nervous system, nitrogen dioxide can weaken the lungs, especially in children, and particulates often carry carcinogenic agents (Mann, 1990). Ozone, which is harmful at ground level, causes irritation to the eyes and respiratory system, as well as severe headaches. Moreover, asthma, bronchitis, and emphysema are believed to be linked with long-term exposure to smog. The reduction of air pollution serves several aims: preservation of the environment, improved public health, and even economic benefit.

Attacking the Problem

The first serious effort by the federal government to tackle the air pollution problem was the passage of the Clean Air Act in 1970 (PL 91-604). Until 1970, federal government action on air pollution was largely noncoercive and incremental, stressing research and the responsibility of the states. Spurred by the environmental movement of the late 1960s, Congress initiated the era of modern environmental legislation by attacking the nation's air-pollution problems.

The Clean Air Act established national air-quality standards, partially in order to alleviate fears that states would compete for business by lowering emission restrictions. The legislation also capped certain emissions for stationary sources as well as for motor vehicles, and it required each state to have a state implementation plan (SIP) to meet federal guidelines by 1975. The act was weakened by a clause which allowed the EPA administrator to grant extensions, which has occurred several times and has delayed full implementation of the law. This legislation created the "command-and-control" method of environmental regulation, which meant that the federal government set standards and then enforced them with various coercive tools, such as fines or litigation.

As Downs' (1972) "issue attention cycle" theory would predict, the environmental movement began to experience a slowdown soon after the passage of the Clean Air Act, as other issues, especially the energy crisis brought on by the Arab oil embargo of 1973, moved to prominence. Deadlines for meeting motor vehicle requirements were postponed, and SIP deadlines were extended, as few areas of the country had attained any of the national air-quality standards. In 1977 the Clean Air Act was amended (PL 95-95). Congress formulated the Prevention of Significant Deterioration (PSD) Program, which wrote into law a doctrine created by a federal district court five years earlier in the case of *Sierra Club v. Ruckleshaus* (Melnick, 1983). The PSD Program mandated that areas with clean air could allow only very slight increases in pollution levels. This protection for national parks and other rural areas was applauded by environmentalists, but earned the ire of developers and energy interests. The program also increased state flexibility, as the classification of airsheds into three types was largely determined by state governments.

During the 1980s, the Reagan administration's goals of increasing economic growth and reducing governmental regulation prevented Congress from passing new clean-air legislation. By the late 1980s, the combination of George Mitchell (of acid rain victim Maine) replacing Robert Byrd (of coal producing West Virginia) as Senate majority leader and the willingness of President Bush to support new clean-air legislation facilitated the passage of the 1990 Clean Air Act Amendments (PL 101-549) (Kamieniecki and Ferrall, 1991). The most recent additions to the act, after thirteen years of legislative stalemate, have taken into consideration increased knowledge and scientific data concerning the air pollution threat. The 1990 legislation mandates that areas which have not attained EPA levels in ozone or carbon monoxide take certain steps toward reduction. Requirements are outlined for cleaner burning fuels, tailpipe emissions, and the reduction of toxic air pollutants and ozone destroying CFCs. The issue of acid precipitation was also addressed by requiring utilities to reduce emissions of sulfur dioxide.

Perhaps the most revolutionary initiative is the development of marketable pollution permits. Utilities which reduce emissions below permitted levels, by such actions as installing smokestack scrubbers, can defray the costs of pollution control by selling permits to another polluter who has exceeded the allowable limit. This plan follows in the footsteps of earlier EPA attempts to provide flexibility and economic incentives in air-pollution reduction, such as the "bubble" concept, which allows a plant to be flexible in cutting emissions from several sources as long as the total output of the plant meets required standards. These steps away from direct "command-and-control" regulation have long been considered by business and some environmentalists as being more efficient and effective. The SCAQMD in southern California agreed in 1992 to develop and implement a marketable pollution permit plan (Kamieniecki and Ferrall, 1992).

Promise and Performance

As the country moves into the mid-1990s, there is reason for both hope and despair when evaluating the nation's air-quality effort. The EPA has reported that the smoggiest cities in the United States had seen a 10 percent

FIGURE 10.1

Metropolitan Areas Violating EPA Ozone Standard

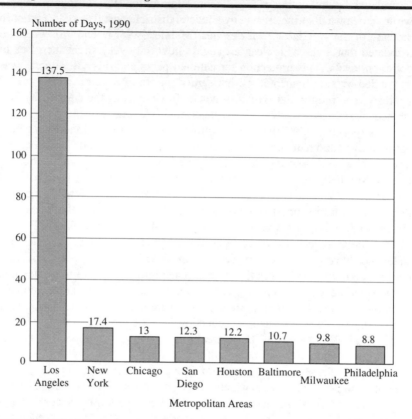

Number of Days, 1990

drop in air pollution during the 1980s, and that 10 million fewer Americans are breathing unhealthful air (Stammer, 1991). As figure 10.1 shows, although the Los Angeles metropolitan area has particularly high levels of ozone (the main ingredient of smog), ozone levels in other major cities are much lower than those in Los Angeles. The northeastern states also have serious air-pollution problems when one takes into account the large percentages of people who live in areas which violate federal ozone standards (see table 10.2).

The EPA appears to be dedicated to implementing the regulations under the 1990 Clean Air Act and pursuing the goal of clean air by the year 2010. Moreover, Congress passed a transportation bill in 1992, which added to the job-creating highway buildup program desired by the president and gave the states for the first time great flexibility in deciding whether to spend federal dollars on mass transit systems. The allocation of $151 billion over six years could spur new public works projects in mass transportation, perhaps deemphasizing the automobile as the primary form of transportation in urban areas.

Encouraging signs again exist at the state and local level. Over the last five years, for example, the state of Colorado and the city of Denver have taken several steps which have resulted in significant improvement of the air quality in the Denver metropolitan area. Measures such as improved automobile inspection, mass transit subsidization, limits on wood-burning stoves and fireplaces, and compulsory changes in gasoline composition have resulted in reducing the number of days of noncompliance with federal carbon monoxide levels from eighty in 1984 to just four in 1990 (Harris, 1991). In November 1991 the California State Air Resources Board, fighting off intense lobbying by oil companies, adopted regulations mandating that all gasoline sold in the state be 30 percent cleaner by 1996. This is part of a larger, comprehensive twenty-year plan adopted by California in 1989 to improve its air quality (Kamieniecki and Fer-

TABLE 10.2

Percent of State Populations Breathing Air Violating Federal Standards for Ozone, 1990

Alaska	0.0	Wisconsin	40.7
Colorado	0.0	Georgia	41.9
Hawaii	0.0	North Carolina	44.1
Idaho	0.0	Indiana	46.2
Iowa	0.0	Kentucky	48.5
Minnesota	0.0	Texas	49.4
Montana	0.0	Florida	51.5
Nebraska	0.0	Tennessee	53.0
Nevada	0.0	Missouri	55.0
New Mexico	0.0	Michigan	59.2
North Dakota	0.0	Virginia	60.6
South Dakota	0.0	Utah	62.6
Wyoming	0.0	Maine	65.6
Arkansas	2.1	Illinois	69.0
Mississippi	2.4	New Hampshire	72.0
Washington	2.4	Ohio	76.5
Vermont	3.3	New York	77.6
Oklahoma	11.1	Pennsylvania	84.6
Louisiana	17.8	Maryland	88.7
Oregon	21.4	California	91.8
Kansas	23.4	Connecticut	100.0
West Virginia	28.5	Delaware	100.0
Arizona	28.7	Massachusetts	100.0
South Carolina	32.3	New Jersey	100.0
Alabama	32.7	Rhode Island	100.0

rall, 1991, 1992). Although such programs are valuable steps forward, many environmentalists claim that present efforts are too few and too limited in the face of the monumental task of achieving clean air (Kandel, 1992).

In addition to governmental initiatives, the battle for clean air could gain a new ally from formerly hostile ranks in the near future. As the business of developing advanced pollution control strategies (e.g., cleaner burning fuels) and equipment grows, a split will likely develop within industry in general. Lobbyists for companies dependent on clean-air regulations to stimulate their sales are very likely to join with environmentalists to urge legislators to clamp down on polluters. Previously large polluting firms that have switched to cleaner burning fuels or have adopted the most technologically advanced equipment might also join environmentalists.

Problems and Possibilities

Despite the noted possibilities and improvements, serious air-pollution problems could plague the nation for years to come. Both technology and politics present obstacles to cleaner air. For example, several of the requirements in the 1990 Clean Air Act Amendments depend on technologies that have yet to be developed. Although the 1970 Clean Air Act was the impetus behind the development of the catalytic converter, there are no guarantees that research will give birth to needed technology within a given time period. Several of the alternatives being considered as substitutes for gasoline might, in the long run, prove to be equally problematic. Methanol emits fewer hydrocarbons than gasoline, but does emit formaldehyde, which is a known carcinogen; thus, one danger merely replaces another. Ethanol is derived from grain, yet it is possible that the energy expended to grow the grain could cause more pollution than that which is saved by the process. Industry would say that these examples point to the need for further scientific research before additional public policies are implemented. A 1991 study by the National Academy of Sciences concluded that the health dangers of many pollutants have been underestimated, thus resulting in misdirected public policy. For instance, the lack of strong regulation of nitrogen oxides, originally thought to be less serious than other pollutants, has resulted in less protection of public health (Stammer and Pasternak, 1991).

Politically, air-quality protection is often a victim of ideological and economic infighting. Throughout the 1980s, Representative John Dingell of Detroit and Senator Robert Byrd of coal-mining West Virginia, both Democrats, fought clean-air legislation. Although growing public concern over environmental quality in the late 1980s allowed for compromise, powerful legislators representing wealthy special interests are certain to create roadblocks to more stringent legislation in the future.

The White House has also been obstructionist. Under President George Bush, the Council on Competitiveness was created to insure that regulations were not overly detrimental to business interests. The EPA's proposed regulations for implementing the 1990 Clean Air Act, after being sent to the White House, were returned by the Council because they were thought to be too burdensome on industry. Instead, the Council recommended over one hundred proposals for weakening the regulations (Ross, 1991). The Council came under fire for keeping few written records, refusing to appear before Congress, and having members with direct conflicts of interest working on policy.

At the local level, cities can follow the lead of Denver and take strong steps to reduce pollution from all sources. Encouragement of mass transit systems and stiff regulation of stationary polluting sources can result in drastic reductions in unhealthful air. Urban greening programs should also be supported. One NASA study found that one green plant every 100 square feet can reduce indoor toxic air pollution by 87 percent (Reinhardt, 1991). A concerted effort to plant trees and bushes, especially those which are known to be resistant to smog, would help to improve air quality. In the long run, cities must be innovators in altering the personal behavior of citizens toward less-polluting life-styles. Otherwise, uncontrolled economic and population growth will offset gains in air quality.

According to Lester (1990), Reagan's budget cuts in many areas during the 1980s stimulated policy innovation by state governments. Such innovation will be crucial in the battle against air pollution during the post–Cold War period. State legislators can employ fiscal incentives to encourage pollution reduction, such as the proposal by California Senator Gary Hart to waive sales taxes on low-polluting vehicles while charging double for the purchase of inefficient models. Fees based on the amount of miles driven could work to encourage less driving, while charges calculated by tailpipe emissions could encourage the development and purchases of automobiles which use cleaner burning fuels. The states will need to work with cities to develop strategies for the behavior modification necessary to reduce pollution from population sources, while at the same time standing firm on requirements that industry use the most advanced technology to reduce emissions. These goals can be more easily achieved if the state acts as a partner with industry rather than as an adversary, offering information and technical assistance to help achieve the desired aim of cleaner air.

The federal government must serve in a leadership role if an issue with such transboundary qualities as air pollution is to be effectively addressed. Funding for research into hydrogen and solar electric automobiles, which are both clean burning and emission free, was slashed by Reagan and should be increased immediately. Development of such fuels not only is environmentally sound but also would serve to reduce dependence on foreign sources of energy. Washington must take an active role to alleviate domestic industry's conservative tendencies and encourage changes in research and implementation of air-pollution control technology (e.g., scrubber technology). The United States must become a world leader in fighting pollution, not a recalcitrant observer. Europe has been urging the United States for years to agree to make significant reductions in carbon dioxide emissions, which contribute to global warming, but both the Reagan and Bush administrations showed little willingness to cooperate, citing concerns over excessive burdens on business. While the Clinton administration shares some of these concerns, it has proven more willing to explore alternatives and to take the lead in negotiating international standards in these areas. Over the long run, energy consumption must be reduced through alterations in life-styles and increased efficiency that directly translate into improved air quality and can have an immediate and positive impact on air-pollution control efforts and the "greenhouse effect."

The Clinton administration has indicated its intention to rethink national policies and to introduce an "environmentally friendly" era. Its early efforts, however, were overshadowed by its policy initiatives in other areas and a generally slow and cautious, if promising, approach to policy implementation relevant to the environment.

Natural Resource and Wildlife Protection

The United States is a nation endowed with a variety of natural resources rivaled by few other countries. The colonists who came to America faced a great wilderness and responded with awe and respect as they built farms and homes out of the vast land before them. The intimate relationship between Americans and America has been one of conflicting desires to preserve the beautiful spacious skies and majestic mountains on the one hand, and to conquer the wilds and develop the nation on the other. This same contradiction in values and desires that early Americans faced remains with us today in the battle between conservation and development.

A central issue of natural resource and wildlife protection in the United States today is the trade-off of long-term preservation for immediate economic benefit (Kamieniecki, Cahn, and Goss, 1991). Which should hold precedence, the needs of the nation at the present or the rights of future generations? Americans, especially the last few generations, have been driven by the notion of immediate gain and quarterly profit, without regard for long-term consequences. The issue of natural resource and wildlife policy is framed by the ecological consciousness of the American people, which includes both deep reverence for nature as well as the Judeo-Christian mandate to go forth and conquer the environment. The outcome of this philosophical debate will determine the integrity of the natural environment for centuries to come.

The protection of American wildlife and natural resources is a public policy issue because, among other things, vast tracts of land are owned and managed by the federal government. While most property in the United States is privately owned, almost all of it was once federal land, which was subsequently privatized through programs such as the Homestead Act of 1862. Today, the federal government still owns roughly 677 million of the 2.313 billion acres of American territory, or about 29 percent. Of this, 320 million acres are National Resource Lands administered by the Bureau of Land Management of the Department of the Interior, 89 million acres are National Wildlife Refuges under the Fish and Wildlife Service, also at Interior, 80 million acres belong to the National Parks System run by Interior's National Parks Service, and 188 million acres of national forests are under the aegis of the Department of Agriculture's Forest Service (Miller, 1988). The 1976 Federal Land Policy and Management Act (PL 94-579) ended the traditional policy of transferring federal land to private ownership. The use, management, and protection of over a quarter of the area of the United States are guided by the natural resource and wildlife policies enacted and enforced by the federal government. What is done with public land is the single largest issue relating to the protection of America's natural heritage (Baden and Lueck, 1986; Dennis and Simmons, 1986; Rosenbaum, 1991).

Policies Protecting Wildlife and Natural Resources

The protection of the natural resources of the United States began in earnest with the establishment of Yellowstone National Park in 1872 when conservation was placed on the government agenda (Caulfield, 1989). From the conservationist movement of the late nineteenth and early twentieth centuries to the present, there has been public support and pressure for the federal government to care for the land that it holds in the national trust. This demand has been translated into law and policy by the government. The period since the enactment of the 1969 National Environmental Policy Act (NEPA) has seen a heightened awareness of the fragility of the nation's ecosystems, the beginning of the modern environmental movement, and a correspondingly active era of policy creation.

Building on a history of nature conservation and the momentum after the first Earth Day in 1970, the United States began a comprehensive program of natural resource and wilderness protection policy in regard to managing federally owned land. Several landmark pieces of legislation were crafted to build on already existing laws such as the 1964 Wilderness Act (PL 88-577). The 1973 Endangered Species Act (PL 93-205) expanded wildlife protection to include threatened as well as endangered species and provided a federal grant program to fund such efforts by the United States Fish and Wildlife Service (Tobin, 1990). In 1976, the Federal Land Policy and Management Act (PL 94-579) called for the Bureau of Land Management to administer public land with the goal of enhancing long-term benefits. Also in 1976, the National Forest

Management Act (PL 94-588) gave statutory permanence to the national forest system and decreed tougher standards for resource utilization by restricting timber harvesting to protect soil and watersheds and by limiting clear cutting. Significant due to the sheer area of relatively pristine land involved, the Alaska National Interest Lands Conservation Act of 1980 (PL 96-487) set aside 102 million acres of public land as national wilderness, wildlife refuges, and parks. A strong movement toward the preservation of natural America was thus occurring.

Policy, however, is not always a forward moving process, as the retrenchments in the commitment to environmental protection under the Reagan administration demonstrate. As discussed earlier, Reagan's philosophy of reducing federal "interference" with business and the desire to "get government off the backs of the people" created policies favoring developmental interests over those of environmental protection. The administrative dismantling of environmental regulation was performed by personnel originally chosen for their well known probusiness and prodevelopment sentiments (e.g., Anne Gorsuch Burford). The individual responsible for the most damage to the public lands was Secretary of the Interior James Watt. Formerly a lawyer for western development interests, Watt was chosen to push a program of permitting greater access to natural resources for mining, energy, and lumbering interests, particularly in the western states that formed the backbone of Reagan's electoral coalition.

Watt became the national representative of a growing political movement known as the Sagebrush Rebellion, which sought greater control over the use of federal resources (McCurdy, 1986). The central tenet of the Sagebrush Rebellion was the reestablishment of the discontinued federal practice of privatizing public lands or, at minimum, the transferral of ownership to the states where developers had considerably more political control. Through his position as secretary of the Department of the Interior, and therefore also overseer of the Bureau of Land Management, the Park Service, and the Fish and Wildlife Service, James Watt facilitated the granting of logging rights in national forests. The regulations created by the 1977 Surface Mining Control and Reclamation Act (PL 95-87) were weakened through lax enforcement on strip mining activities. Watt also aggressively moved to grant off-shore drilling permits to the oil industry for the outer continental shelf area to enhance the already considerable revenue the federal government derived from such permits. This ran counter to environmental clauses in the 1978 Amendments to the Outer Continental Shelf Land Act of 1953 and the 1972 Coastal Zone Management Act. Long-term ecosystem protection of the American natural heritage took a back seat to Watt's prodevelopment agenda.

With the reversal of commitment to the protection of natural resources and wildlife, the motivating force for continued preservation switched from the federal government to nongovernmental organizations (NGOs), certain states, and the judicial system. The granting of off-shore oil leases, for example, was blocked by a coalition of the Natural Resources Defense Council (NRDC) and the State of California in the courts. The strip mining of coal in Wyoming and other states was blocked by a lawsuit filed by the International Wildlife Federation, forcing Environmental Impact Statements (EISs) to be prepared on all such operations. While specific cases are numerous, the general trend of continuing public support for the protection of America's natural resources is apparent, whatever the policies are of those in charge.

Present and Future Concerns

The conflict between development and preservation continues into the present. The Bush administration (although George Bush proclaimed himself to be an "environmental president") was philosophically also predisposed to the probusiness perspective, although it did demonstrate a political awareness of the sensitivity of the environmental issue. The Department of the Interior continued many ecologically dubious policies, such as subsidized cattle ranching and increased access to national forests for logging interests, but it avoided the flagrant antagonism of conservation groups that characterized James Watt's tenure.

In contrast, Bill Clinton's secretary of the interior, Bruce Babbitt, has won support among environmental advocates and has proven more politically adept at balancing the interests of preservationists and developers.

The maturation of the environmental movement and public concern for the limited and shrinking American wild areas and natural resources are providing increased support for preservation over development, or accepting the need for some degree of resource exploitation, the enlightened management of development. Increased scientific knowledge of ecology has brought with it a better understanding of the complexity of the issue, creating new challenges for natural resource and wildlife policy.

As the economy and population of the United States continues to expand and the world's finite stock of resources dwindles, there will be increasing pressure to use the natural resources on federal land.[1] Part of the mandate of public land management is to provide for such use, but with the caveat of allowing for long-term effects. With growing public controversy over traditional resource extraction methods, those industries are developing "enlightened" management schemes. With care and expense, strip-mined land can be restored to a rough approximation of its original state. Selective harvesting, which permits the continued integrity of the indigenous ecosystem, can allow lumbering to go on without the devastation of clear cutting. Enhanced understanding of the biological principles of nature can allow Americans to live in harmony with their natural world.

At the same time, new issues are arising. Growing demand for the amenities of the National Park System are creating chronic overcrowding, pollution, and deterioration of the places people travel to, to see America's natural beauty. Reservations are now needed to visit many of the nation's more popular parks, such as Yellowstone or Yosemite. The management of public access is becoming a major issue for the Park Service.

Wildlife protection is being redefined as the preservation of biodiversity, which is growing in importance as a policy issue (Tobin, 1990). The genetic pool of plants and animals inhabiting public lands is a priceless and irreplaceable national resource. Until recently, for example, the Pacific yew tree was discarded as an unwanted by-product of the clear cutting of federal forests; its bark is now used in cancer research. With much concern about the biodiversity of the tropical rainforest, it must be remembered that the United States also is home to a vast number of species. The Endangered Species Act of 1973 was reauthorized and expanded in 1988 (PL 100-478) to include a larger number of species, additional funds for administration and state grants, and required monitoring by the Fish and Wildlife Service of species that are candidates for listing. The 1988 bill extended the 1973 legislation through fiscal 1992, when it came up for review (or repeal). The political debate focuses on the issue of economic growth versus species protection, a confrontation that takes place in the context of a troubled economy. The value of protecting such species as the Northern spotted owl, the sockeye salmon, and certain threatened predator species at the risk of weakening a local economy are in the forefront. The 1990s will see biodiversity continue to grow as a major economic, political, and ecological issue.

Like all things ecological, the issues at hand are part of a larger web of interconnectivity. Population growth and (sub)urbanization create demand for access pressures on national parks and wilderness areas, as well as increased consumer demand for the end products based on the raw materials taken from federal land. An overall plan for long-term growth and development is needed. Much of the controversy over federal land use involves oil, natural gas, and coal development in ecologically sensitive areas. After initial efforts in the 1970s, attempts to create a national energy policy have all but disappeared. Even after a war with tens of thousands of casualties fought over oil in the Middle East, America continues its addiction to fossil fuels whose extraction and use are environmentally harmful.

As the United States and the world rapidly reach the limits to growth first discussed by Thomas Malthus almost two hundred years ago, it becomes apparent that the development-oriented economic system under which the planet operates must redefine itself to become sustainable in the long term. The problem is the reconciliation of the enlightenment promise of eternal growth and development and the diminishing resources available to provide for such expansion. Modern ecological writers, such as Lester Milbrath

(1989), address the issue of continuing to provide the system and its adherents with better standards of living while not undermining the natural system that makes human economic life possible. By addressing the more holistic questions of America's economic and ecological future and better defining what our relationship to our natural surroundings will be, environmental policies, such as natural resource conservation and wildlife protection, can be created for the long term.

International Environmental Issues

Ever since the day when an American astronaut peered out of his space vessel to see the small, blue Earth in the distance, the people of the United States and the world have had a visual image of the fragility and the delicate beauty of the planet they inhabit. The earth is a biosphere where all parts of the web of life are bound to all others, and where damage to one portion is a loss to the planet as a whole. The interconnectivity of all components of the world that is such a popular topic when discussing politics or economics is based on the biological rule that Barry Commoner (1971) called the Law of Ecology: Everything is connected to everything else. No politics or policy ever takes place in a vacuum; environmental politics and policy is necessarily global by its nature.

International environmental issues take a variety of forms, but for the sake of convenience we will place them into a two level typology. As table 10.3 shows, the simple category (Type I) can be defined as the international versions of the types of issues previously discussed: air pollution, toxic and hazardous waste disposal, and natural resource conservation. Each of these is predominantly addressed at the local and national level of policy-making, but can frequently expand beyond national frontiers to involve other national governments. Much of the internationalization of this type of environmental issue results from the increasing integration of each nation and region into the global political economy. Environmental issues will become international as this process advances (Kamieniecki, 1991, 1993).

The second type of environmental issues (Type II) are those that are inherently global in scope. Problems like ozone depletion and global warming threaten almost everyone everywhere on the planet. Just as the consequences are widely distributed, so are the causes for this category of environmental problems, necessitating a global response to policy-making and problem solving.

In Type I international environmental issues, either the cause or effect of an ecologically degrading action is found in a different political sovereignty. In a simple case, such as the acid rain problem between the United States and Canada, pollution is created in one nation and then crosses the border so that its effects are felt in another country (sulfur dioxide emissions from the Ohio Valley migrate to Canada and those from southern Ontario pollute the north-

TABLE 10.3

Typology of International Environmental Issues

Dimensions	Type I	Type II
Scale	bi-, multinational	global
Scope	crosses borders; affects two or more nations	affects all nations
Distribution of Causes	point, narrow	highly dispersed
Distribution of Effects	local, regional	global
Solutions	traditional diplomacy; international law	new diplomacy; global policy
Level of Uncertainty	low	high
Role of Sovereignty	solved through nation state	sovereignty transcended
Issues	acid rain, water/air pollution, toxic waste, natural resource conservation	ozone depletion, global warming

eastern United States). Relatively well-defined point sources of the environmentally offensive act can be determined, establishing legal responsibility for damages. Here, as in northern Europe, diplomatic negotiation can take place under a level of scientific certainty as to the causes and effects of the specific problem under discussion. (Hence, the efforts of the Reagan administration to deny this footing to Canadian negotiators until the end.) In this subgroup of simple environmental issues, the path to solution is through legal and diplomatic channels, as has been the case with international negotiations for the reduction of acid rain.

A second subgroup of Type I environmental issues is the kind of environmental problem that arises through the inconsistent application of environmental regulation across international boundaries. As previously mentioned, a great deal of toxic waste that is politically difficult to store in the United States or Europe is dumped in less affluent nations which are economically restrained from rigorous environmental protection. Commonly, the income derived from providing toxic storage exceeds the perceived cost of living with contaminated land, at least in the short term. Thus, hundreds of enterprises have been locating along the manufacturing belt on the Mexico side of the American-Mexican border to avoid tougher United States environmental regulations, resulting in locally unhealthy conditions. The necessity to comply with governmental regulations is part of the cost of doing business anywhere, and the United States promotes the export of environmentally degrading economic activity by not requiring imported goods to be manufactured under the same standards as

American goods. The American regulatory system encourages "dirty" production to continue abroad and avoid legal retribution by relocating. If those goods produced abroad had the long-term costs of environmental degradation factored into their production costs, they would be comparatively less competitive. The export of waste and polluting activities is a result of regulatory policies and trade policies that do not hold foreign nations to the high environmental standards to which the United States and other Western nations hold themselves.

As discussed in the previous section, the political importance of the protection of wildlife and biodiversity is couched in terms of pragmatism and the short-term needs of developing economies. There is a rough correlation between economic well-being and the ability to "afford" environmental regulation of business activity. The United States is a world leader in international wildlife protection, having been chief sponsor of several international endangered species protection agreements, the movement to ban commercial whaling, and, most recently, the restriction of drift-net fishing which kills dolphins and other marine life. In the area of deforestation, the United States leads in the development and application of forest management techniques and has encouraged the use of debt-for-nature swaps. The United States has functioned as a world leader and positive role model on this issue, exhibiting an understanding of the need for economic development but balancing it with natural resource conservation. More action along these lines is firmly recommended.

A Type II international environmental issue is a complex issue that exists on a global scale and in which policy actions or inactions affect the entire planet. Unlike the above mentioned "simple" issues, traditional political and diplomatic structures and lessons cannot be applied to environmental problems such as global warming or ozone depletion (Benedick, 1991). The causes of these problems are human economic activity, especially industrialization and development (Porter and Brown, 1991). While the specific causes and sites of pollution activity are myriad, the possible end effects are spread over most of the earth's surface.

The complexity of these issues is compounded by several other characteristics besides scale. First among these is scientific uncertainty. Both global warming and ozone depletion have much scientific research and an establishment of causality already behind them, although total certainty has remained elusive. In the political negotiations surrounding the two, those who oppose taking action consistently cite uncertainty as the basis for inaction (Benedick, 1991). Considering the characteristic high costs of a Type II problem, such an approach may appear justifiable unless one remembers that astronomical costs are not only in reference to the cost of action, but even more to inaction. Simply stated, these issues are an evaluation of the benefits for economic development and expansion on the one hand, and the possibility of serious harm to humans on the other hand. Policy thus becomes a modern Pascal's wager.

Ozone depletion refers to the destruction of the ozone layer in the atmosphere which functions to protect life from harmful ultraviolet (UV) solar radiation. Rapidly growing scientific evidence links the thinning and in some places outright disappearance of the ozone layer with increased death due to skin cancer, blindness due to cataracts, and injury to the human immune system. The cause of ozone destruction is the use of chemical compounds such as chlorofluorocarbons (CFCs), hydrochlorofluorocarbons (HCFCs), and others in industrial and consumer products and processes. These chemicals rise in the atmosphere where they bond with the atmospheric ozone (O_3), causing it to lose its protective characteristics.

Since the discovery of a hole in the ozone layer over the Antarctic, scientists have found the problem to be considerably more widespread. In 1991, it was observed that the ozone had thinned to a level dangerous for human health even over the temperate latitudes where most people live. Conservative projections of death and illness resulting from unfiltered UV radiation run into the hundreds of millions. The world political community responded quickly to this threat to its citizens. In a 1985 convention in Vienna, many nations decided to cooperate internationally and research ozone depletion, to monitor the ozone layer, and to exchange information freely on the issue. The resulting evidence led to the 1987 Montreal Protocol which called for the gradual phasing out of CFCs and other chemicals and controls on their usage. Scientific information about the potential danger has continued to grow. Thus, at a 1990 London conference, a large number of nations agreed to limit more chemicals, completely phase out others on an accelerated schedule, and to assist less affluent nations with technical and financial aid.

The quick action on ozone depletion was made possible by increased scientific evidence and the availability of substitute chemicals to replace those at fault. In the United States, a major push came from chemical companies with the technological capability to find these substitutes. The American government has been a leader on this issue, and it has supported economic assistance to less affluent nations to prevent further ozone damage.

Global warming refers to the trapping of solar heat between the earth's surface and atmospheric carbon dioxide and other gases. The neighboring planet Venus has a runaway greenhouse effect in its atmosphere, giving it surface temperatures of over 500 degrees F. Since the advent of industrialization, human activity has raised the amount of carbon dioxide (CO_2) in the atmosphere by over 25 percent and the amount of methane by over 100 percent. More than any other issue, the global warming debate is driven by scientific uncertainty. The vast majority of the scientific community is willing to recognize an association between CO_2 and global temperature, but direct causation and likely consequences are argued without consensus.

As noted earlier in the chapter, the primary contributors to global warming are the emissions from the burning of fossil fuel. In simple terms, to stop global warming an entirely new source of cheap, transportable energy would be required. The economic stakes are extremely high. Recognizing a potential problem, the United Nations established an Intergovernmental Panel on Climate Change (IPCC), which meets regularly to coordinate international and national efforts to deal with the issue. Of the industrialized world, the United States has generally been the odd man out, calling only for more research, for which it now budgets over $1 billion, and no action until something conclusive has been established. Here again, the United States has abandoned its leadership role. IPCC gatherings produce calls for reduction of carbon dioxide emissions, cooperation on research, and assistance to developing nations to find energy alternatives.

Global warming is a relatively new issue. Nonetheless, the IPCC's research has concluded that it is reaching crisis proportions and that immediate action is needed. The United States is moving slowly to join its allies and the rest of the world in working to stop the potential destruction of the environment and hence its ability to sustain life. In early 1992, the United States offered $75 million, not a large sum in the scale of things but a beginning, to less affluent nations to help them reduce the emission of gases that lead to global warming. A much anticipated United Nations' conference in Brazil on the future of the environment held in 1992 and intended to establish new international cooperative efforts on this and other environmental matters, including ozone depletion, proved disappointing.

The new world order of the post–Cold War period is one characterized by increasing global interdependence, the continued erosion of national sovereignty to international concerns, and a sense of cohabitating a small world with limited resources and a fragile ecosystem. Whether environmental issues merely cross borders between adjacent nations or are the immediate concern of the entire globe, it is clear that the problems of one nation, even one as large as the United States, are too difficult to deal with on a unilateral basis.

Conclusion

It is clear that both the United States and the international community face serious environmental problems in the post–Cold War era. Although this chapter focused primarily on America, the problems are far more acute in other parts of the world. This is particularly true for air pollution, the management of toxic and hazardous materials, and the conservation of natural resources. Regardless of the problem or the nation, it appears that the dramatic interplay between political and economic interests has helped shape previous policy (or lack thereof) and will continue to influence government action in the years ahead.

While this chapter has been quite critical of American environmental policy, there have been a few successes that are worth noting. Unlike most countries, the United States does an excellent job of controlling sewage discharges. The development of advanced sewage-treatment technologies and the construction of a large number of treatment plants have helped to minimize contamination of water and soil. In addition, the United States spends more money on pollution-control research and equipment than any other country. Both the public and private sectors are quite active in this area. Perhaps most noteworthy, the United States has adopted more environmental laws and regulations than any other nation in the world. (Admittedly, lax enforcement and lenient penalties have hurt America's pollution-control effort in the past.)

As this chapter has suggested, however, the United States has a mixed record at the international level. With the possible exception of the ozone depletion issue, national policymakers have been slow to embrace international agreements intended to conserve the earth's natural resources and protect the global environment. In particular, the United States has refused to ratify the Law of the Sea Treaty and to adopt strict controls on the emission of "greenhouse" gases. Economic interests will likely remain influential in these areas in the future, and whether additional scientific data and concomitant public pressure will be able to over power such interests is uncertain.

Perhaps the major obstacle to achieving international agreements on global environmental issues is the growing gap between less affluent and wealthy nations, and the strong conviction on the part of many leaders that economic growth will improve the material standard of living and quality of life of their nations. The advanced industrialized nations are deeply concerned about maintaining their economic well-being and have demonstrated resistance on occasion to conserve natural resources. Politics aside, the finite nature of natural resources and the vulnerability of the earth's ecosystem make it virtually impossible for every nation to achieve the kind of economic growth the West has experienced since World War Two. Those who recognize this have therefore begun to call for the establishment of sustainable societies as an alternative to unmanaged and uncontrolled economic and population growth (e.g., Milbrath, 1989).

Any international effort to establish sustainable societies must seriously address the economic, political, and environmental problems of the majority of the world's nations. Air and water pollution, toxic and hazardous waste disposal, the rapid destruction of rain forests, and the extinction of certain species of wildlife are among the major environmental problems that are not being effectively addressed. Clearly, the economic and political conditions commonly present in most less affluent nations severely hinder efforts to conserve natural resources and abate pollution in those nations. Dictators and authoritarian governments do not tolerate public protests against their policies, and they often resort to force to prevent them from occurring. The poor economic conditions and heavy debt load in many less affluent countries place a great deal of pressure on leaders to sell off their nation's natural resources quickly in return for hard currency. While some leaders recognize the vulnerability of the global ecosystem, most reject calls by Westerners to limit their economic growth. In many cases less affluent nations are controlled by a single family or a small group of wealthy landowners who see little benefit in conserving their country's natural resources for possible future use.

It is unrealistic to expect less affluent countries to adopt the radical political and economic reforms being called for by the West. The most effective strategy, at least in the short run, is for Western nations and international organizations to provide the necessary (and less controversial) scientific and technical expertise needed to encourage both economic investment and environmental protection. Future economic assistance, regardless of the source, must also contain stipulations for the conservation of natural resources. No doubt, the pressure for economic development in less affluent nations poses the toughest challenge for the environmental movement in the 1990s and beyond. While environmentalists have been rather successful in influencing the agendas and policies of the United States and other Western nations, they are likely to achieve fewer victories in other countries.

NOTE

1. See the discussion in chapter 11 by R. McGreggor Cawley and Robert M. Lawrence, ''National Security Policy and Federal Lands Policy, or, The Greening of the Pentagon'' in this volume.

CHAPTER 11

National Security Policy and Federal Lands Policy, or, The Greening of the Pentagon

R. McGREGGOR CAWLEY AND ROBERT M. LAWRENCE

Lands under the administration of the Department of Defense (DOD) are part of the overall federal estate—the roughly one-third of the nation's land base owned by the federal government. As such, they are technically public lands, ostensibly held in trust for the citizens of the United States. Yet, as this ominous warning posted prominently around the perimeter of a Strategic Air Command Minuteman III launch facility clearly demonstrates, DOD lands are not particularly "public" (Day, 1983).

WARNING

RESTRICTED AREA

IT IS UNLAWFUL TO ENTER THIS
AREA WITHOUT PERMISSION OF THE
INSTALLATION COMMANDER.
WHILE ON THIS INSTALLATION
ALL PERSONNEL AND PROPERTY
UNDER THEIR CONTROL
ARE SUBJECT TO SEARCH.

USE OF DEADLY FORCE

AUTHORIZED.

Nuclear weapons installations, like this Minuteman III facility, are an extreme example, of course, but public access to all DOD lands is generally restricted by national security concerns as well as by their use for personnel training and the testing of weapons systems.

At one level, limited public access to DOD lands is not necessarily problematic. DOD lands are a relatively small portion of the federal estate—roughly 30 million acres out of 700 million acres. Moreover, unlike other portions of the federal estate, DOD lands do not carry a congressional mandate for public access. Thus, DOD lands represent a special type of public land use, categorically different than the lands administered by the Forest Service, Bureau of Land Management, National Park Service, and other federal land management agencies.

Given the unique character of military lands, it is perhaps not surprising that the issue has received only passing notice in the literature on federal lands policy. However, efforts by DOD to expand its landholdings, primarily in the western United States, during the post–World War II era have provoked considerable public opposition. At the same time, DOD's national security mission has not made military lands immune from the demands created by the wave of environmental policy enacted throughout the 1970s. Viewed in this light, we believe that the lack of attention to military lands is an omission which needs to be corrected.

One task of this chapter, then, is to offer a preliminary investigation of DOD's efforts to fulfill its national security mission against a political backdrop of public resistance and mandates requiring environmentally responsible land management. A second, and more intriguing, task is to pursue the argument that a political alliance between the military establishment and the environmental community represents a practical and plausible development in future federal lands policy negotiations. Accomplishing these tasks requires several steps.

We begin with a general description of the military lands which reveals an underlying paradox. On the one hand, military use of federal lands is, by definition, environmentally disruptive; but on the other hand, there are large portions of the military estate that look very much like nature preserves. Because the military is able to restrict public access, the military lands provide areas where indigenous flora and fauna can exist largely free from human intrusions. It is this aspect of the military lands which raises the possibility of a coalition between DOD and environmentalists.

Although an alliance between the military and environmentalists offers certain advantages in a contemporary context, it is not a development anticipated by history. In the next section of the chapter we sketch out a brief history of the military's experiences in the federal lands policy arena. Examining four case studies of conflict over the military lands reveals a dialogue revolving around some recurring themes. DOD consistently defended its expansion efforts on the basis that modern military technologies require increasing amounts of space. Opponents of military expansion were equally consistent in raising complaints about the extent to which military acquisition closed off large portions of the federal estate to traditional uses. More important, the opposition camp was populated by environmental groups and commodity user groups—interests that are traditionally antagonists in federal lands policy disputes.

However, as we will see in the final section of the chapter, there is reason for believing that history may not be an accurate gage of future developments in the federal lands policy arena. For example, the consequences of the Persian Gulf war, combined with evidence of DOD's growing commitment to environmental protection, have given DOD an enhanced bargaining position. In short, these factors raise the possibility that previous arguments between the military and environmentalists may give way as both sides come to recognize that by forging a coalition they could create a mutually beneficial and politically powerful force in federal lands policy.

The Military Lands

At present, DOD controls 29 million acres of the federal estate,[1] with roughly 21 million acres of that land under the administration of the air force, army, and navy (table 11.1). By way of comparison, this is an area larger than half the state of Minnesota. More important, the majority of these military lands are located in the twelve states comprising the Rocky Mountain and Pacific regions of the United States (table 11.2). The prevalence of military lands in the West can be explained by three factors. First, about 90 percent of the total federal estate is located in the American West. Indeed, as table 11.3 demonstrates, significant portions of these twelve states are owned by the federal government.

Second, the arid climate and consequently low agricultural productivity potential for much of this land make it an ideal setting for modern military requirements. For example, the training of pilots can take advantage of the

TABLE 11.1

Department of Defense Landholdings

Department	Total Holdings (acres)
Corps of Engineers	8,362,063
Air Force	7,919,301
Army	10,494,412
Navy	2,277,996
Defense Total	29,053,772

Source: U.S. Department of Interior, Bureau of Land Management, *Public Lands Statistics, 1984* (Washington, D.C.: U.S. Government Printing Office, 1984), pp. 32–33.

TABLE 11.2

Military Lands in the West (Acres)

	Air Force	Army	Navy
Alaska	109,317	1,617,973	65,988
Arizona	2,538,638	959,173	718
California	241,617	890,599	1,526,197
Colorado	26,083	117,933	—
Idaho	110,986	1,892	—
Montana	4,577	1,610	—
Nevada	2,903,513	155,528	39,855
New Mexico	119,077	2,404,284	1
Oregon	174	17,609	234
Utah	921,149	865,127	1,021
Washington	2,807	384,545	58,673
Wyoming	6,091	9,464	—
Western Total	7,029,029	7,539,737	1,692,687
Percent of Total Holdings	89	72	74

Source: U.S. Department of Interior, Bureau of Land Management, *Public Land Statistics, 1984* (Washington, D.C.: U.S. Government Printing Office, 1984), pp. 32–35.

TABLE 11.3

Total Federal Landholdings in the West

	Federal Land (acres)	Percent of State
Alaska	318,328,000	87
Arizona	31,304,000	43
California	46,465,000	46
Colorado	24,045,000	36
Idaho	33,716,000	64
Montana	28,456,000	31
Nevada	59,790,000	85
New Mexico	24,342,000	43
Oregon	29,971,000	49
Utah	33,535,000	64
Washington	12,480,000	29
Wyoming	30,878,000	49

Source: U.S. Department of Commerce, Bureau of Census, *Statistical Abstract of the U.S., 1990* (Washington, D.C.: U.S. Government Printing Office, 1990), p. 197.

greater number of good weather days in the West, and particularly in the Southwest. More important, the destruction caused by weapons tests, both nuclear and conventional, were viewed in the past as less harmful to the "barren" landscapes of the West than anywhere else in the United States.

Third, the wide expanse of land and low population density of the West provided a key component of the federal government's strategy at the beginning of the nuclear confrontation with the Soviet Union. Locating most of the land based strategic nuclear delivery systems, like the B-52 intercontinental range jet bombers and Intercontinental Range Ballistic Missiles (ICBMs), in the West offered a way to minimize collateral damage to civilian and industrial assets in the event of either a first strike or retaliatory attacks by the USSR. It might also be noted that this policy was tantamount to designating the West as a "national sacrifice area" in the event of nuclear war.

But even without war, military use of federal lands has adverse consequences. Indeed, unlike other civilian and government entities, the military has a mission to engage in the intentional, unavoidable, and politically sanctioned destruction of the environment. For example, the appropriately named *Jornada del Muerto* (Journey of Death) plain in New Mexico provided an ideal location for detonation of an implosion assembly dubbed "Fat Man"—the first nuclear weapon ever tested. Other environmental assaults carried out by the military include explosions caused by conventional bombs, missiles, and artillery shells on firing and bombing ranges in Idaho, and the surface disturbances created by the tracks of multi-ton armored vehicles on the semi-desert terrain of Camp Irwin in California or the prairie grasslands of Camp Carson, Colorado.

These activities are legally permitted for several reasons. First, most of the bombing and gunnery ranges, training grounds for armored vehicles, and rocket test sites predate environmental regulations. Second, existing ordnance, such as bombs, rockets and artillery shells, do not come under the authority of existing environmental regulations until either they have become a "waste product" requiring disposal and cleanup or they have created an impact upon the environment which could require restoration efforts. Third, although military lands must meet the same environmental regulations as other federal lands, many environmental laws contain provisions which suspend their application during emergency situations.

For example, the National Environmental Policy Act of 1969 (NEPA) requires all government agencies to conduct an Environmental Impact Study (EIS) before undertaking any major actions on federal lands. However, DOD regulations implementing NEPA suspend the need for an EIS in emergency "actions that must be taken to promote the national defense" (32 CFR 214.6). To date, this provision has been invoked only once—shortly after the Iraqi invasion of Kuwait in August 1990 (Schneider, 1991, A14).

And yet, the portrait of military lands as simply "environmental waste-land" is far from accurate. There are thousands of acres of military lands in the United States which are not subject to any kind of use and hence are in reality kept as a kind of nature preserve. For example, Frances E. Warren Air Force Base in Wyoming is home for the most destructive strategic nuclear weapon in the U.S. arsenal—the MX or Peacekeeper ICBM. The missiles themselves are positioned underground in steel and concrete silos inside barbed wire enclo-sures, scattered as few-acre enclaves across the rolling plains of eastern Wyo-ming, northeastern Colorado, and western Nebraska. The support functions for the missiles—barracks, married personnel quarters, mess halls, adminis-trative and maintenance buildings—occupy very little space on the 6,000 acre main base near Cheyenne, Wyoming. Thus, a majority of the base is upland prairie kept in a relatively pristine fashion. It is a place where various indige-nous fauna and flora are allowed to live out their life cycles with only minimal direct human impact, as demonstrated by flourishing herds of deer and ante-lope. In fact, the Colorado butterfly plant, an endangered species, appears to be making a comeback in the area.

And Warren Air Force base is only one example. The 1987 edition of *Environmental Quality*, an annual report on the nation's environment, con-tains selected cases drawn from military establishments in California, Colo-rado, Florida, Texas, and Washington intended to demonstrate the extent to which DOD "is committed to protecting the environment, while at the same time accomplishing its primary task of defending the nation" (U.S. Council on Environmental Quality, 1988, 155–57). What begins to take shape, then, is the possibility that military use of federal lands may be more supportive of environmental goals than commonly assumed.

Viewed in this light, we believe there is a basis for arguing that an alli-ance between the military establishment and the environmental community would offer a mutually beneficial and politically powerful coalition in the fed-eral lands policy arena. On the one hand, testing and training requirements for modern military technologies have created a pressing need for expansion in DOD's landholdings. Support from the environmental community, in turn, would help assure success for DOD's land acquisition efforts. On the other hand, DOD's apparent commitment to environmentally responsible land man-agement, in combination with its ability to restrict public access to military lands, would help the environmental community advance its goal of greater utilization of the federal estate for environmental preservation purposes.

While a coalition between environmentalists and the military offers cer-tain advantages in a contemporary context, it is not a development anticipated by the history of federal lands policy. Throughout the post–World War II era, federal lands interests concerned with environmental preservation (Sierra Club, Wilderness Society, etc.) have generally joined with commodity use interests (ranchers, mining companies, timber companies, etc.) in voicing protests against military acquisition and use of the federal estate. It is to a brief account of that history that we now turn.

The Military and Federal Lands Policy

Although the military's presence in federal lands policy can be traced back to the early days of the republic, it has attracted little attention from federal lands policy scholars. For example, the only extended discussion of military related issues in the federal lands policy literature centers on the topic of the "Military Bounty Lands" (Hibbard, 1924; Robbins, 1942; Dana, 1956; Gates, 1968; Dana and Fairfax, 1980). From the Revolutionary War to 1855, the national government offered grants of free land both to entice people into military service and to reward service rendered. While not a federal lands policy per se, the need to fulfill these bounty claims fed into the matrix of justifications for territorial expansion carried out by the United States during the nineteenth century. It might also be noted that the federal government frequently employed military force to accomplish its goal of territorial expansion.

Other connections between the military and federal lands policy are worth noting here. In 1817, the secretary of the navy was charged with protecting the nation's supply of live oak and red cedar trees in order to provide wood for ship building and maintenance. Subsequently, Congress appropriated $10,000 for the navy's acquisition of land in Florida to be used as a live oak tree plantation. Unfortunately, this early attempt at federal forest management was a failure, and the lands were eventually returned to the public domain (Gates, 1968, 533–34). On a more positive note, from 1886 to 1916, the U.S. Army was given the task of protecting the nation's national parks (Ise, 1961, 44–45). The army relinquished its duty when the National Park Service was created, but a lasting reminder of the army's role is the military style uniforms, especially the "cavalry" hats, still worn by park rangers.

Despite these early examples, the military's involvement in federal lands policy prior to World War II remained small for two primary reasons. First, as late as 1937, the military controlled a mere 3 million acres out of a federal estate containing over 700 million acres. Second, military land transactions (acquisitions and disposals) were generally handled through administrative actions linked to national security concerns. As such, there was little opportunity for public participation, let alone public criticism.

However, from the termination of World War II to the present, military lands have been the focus of increasing political conflict. It is the post–World War II era, then, with which we are particularly concerned. More specifically, four confrontations help reveal the underlying patterns of the conflict over military use of federal lands. The first confrontation occurred in the mid 1950s, when Representative Clair Engel (D-CA), then chairman of the House Interior and Insular Affairs Committee, convened hearings on the military lands. In most important respects, these hearings established the basic themes that have animated arguments over the military lands in the post–World War II era.

The remaining confrontations took place in the late 1970s and throughout the 1980s. One centered on the controversial, and ultimately unsuccessful, proposal for locating the "race track" MX ICBM basing mode in Nevada and Utah. The next was a relatively quiet move by DOD in the mid 1980s which increased its landholdings by roughly 7.1 million acres. And finally, in 1989 DOD attempted to secure an additional 4.5 million acres. Because of the dramatic changes in the threat posed by communism in general, and by the Soviet Union in particular, this last confrontation sparked a more visible public outcry, leading DOD to suspend its efforts pending a reevaluation of its acquisition program.

The Engel Hearings, 1956–1957

As noted above, the total military estate in 1937 was only 3 million acres. However, with the outbreak of World War II, the military inaugurated its first major land expansion, and by the end of the war in 1945, the Pentagon (the Department of Defense was not created until 1947) controlled roughly 25 million acres. All the withdrawals of land from the public domain during this time were conducted as administrative actions sanctioned by a presidential declaration of unlimited national emergency. Importantly, most of the withdrawals of land from other federal agencies were *temporary* actions, carrying the expressed intent to return the appropriated lands to their original status within six months after the end of the emergency declaration.

But the Cold War with the Soviet Union soon replaced the hot war with the Axis nations (Germany, Japan, Italy), and most of the land acquired during World War II remained under military control. Moreover, from January 1, 1954, to June 30, 1955, the recently created Department of Defense expanded its landholdings by an additional 4.1 million acres and had applied for another 8.7 million acres. The military's expansion plans raised concerns, particularly in the western United States, leading House Interior and Insular Affairs Committee Chairman Clair Engel (D-CA) to convene hearings on the military lands. Although numerous concerns were expressed at these hearings, most of the dialogue centered on three key issues (U.S. Congress, 1956, 1957).

First, while recognizing the needs created by national emergencies (war), opponents saw no justification for military expansion in the relative peace of the mid 1950s. Indeed, at the time of the Engle hearings, the Second World War and the Korean War had been successfully concluded, and the Cold War was in its formative stages. In response, DOD argued that post–World War II weapons systems—both conventional and nuclear—required considerable space for testing and training. Thus, the expansion efforts represented an important component of DOD's broader mission to maintain the nation's military readiness.

A second issue, and the one generating most discussion, was the extent to which military lands were restricted to public access. The mid 1950s were a time of increasing public demand for both the commodity resources (timber, forage, minerals, etc.) and recreational resources provided by the western federal lands. And though this demand created tension among traditional public land users, the military's ability to restrict public access was perceived as a common threat to all interests. In fact, at one point in the hearing record, the Interior Committee noted that the effort to limit military expansion had "received unprecedented support . . . from official State agencies of 39 states, from all major conservation groups, [and] from numerous local groups, organizations and individuals" (U.S. Congress, 1957, 288).

Although admitting that some areas would have to be closed to the public for safety and national security reasons, DOD attempted to minimize the issue by demonstrating its efforts to carry out wildlife management and to encourage hunting and fishing on the military lands. The effort was less than successful as opponents, especially state game and wildlife agencies, submitted an impressive array of evidence which suggested that military lands were run largely as private game reserves for military personnel, frequently in open violation of state hunting and fishing laws.

The third, and most important, issue was the military's apparent violation of the land acquisition process. In 1910, Congress enacted the General Withdrawal Act (36 Stat. 2247) which granted the president authority to make temporary withdrawals from public domain lands. This act provided the legal justification for military acquisitions during World War II. However, eleven years after the war, the military still had not released those withdrawn lands, a situation which led Engel and other members of the Interior Committee to conclude that Congress needed to adopt a more active posture in the military land acquisition process.

The eventual outcome of this controversy was the Engel Act of 1958 (43 USC 155-58). The key principle established by this act was that DOD withdrawals of areas in excess of 5,000 acres required an act of Congress, with the attendant public hearings, except in time of war or presidentially declared national emergencies. Withdrawals of 5,000 acres or less remained an administrative action. In addition, the military was required to assess the potential impact withdrawals would have on "conservation, utilization, and development of mineral resources, timber, and other material resources, grazing resources, fish and wildlife resources, water resources, and scenic, wilderness, and recreation, and other values" (43 USC 157).

In short, the Engel Act brought to a close the earlier era in which military land transactions were conducted without public scrutiny. As such, it also made clear that future military acquisition plans would have to meet the test of public acceptance. And as the next confrontation suggests, securing public acceptance represented a formidable task for the military.

The MX ICBM Controversy

Two sets of events interacted to form the backdrop for the MX controversy. On the one hand, the increasing sophistication of the strategic nuclear arms competition between the United States and the USSR raised new theoretical and technical defense problems. On the other hand, the emergence of the environmental movement, and consequent body of environmental policy, placed new constraints on federal lands activities deemed to have adverse environmental impacts.

The roots of the MX controversy can be traced to the early 1970s. At that time, DOD officials voiced concern that the modernization of the Soviet ICBM forces—greater accuracy from larger, and eventually multiple, warheads—would increasingly place at risk U.S. defense systems. In essence, it appeared that the Soviets were developing a first-strike disarming capability which would enable the USSR to hit U.S. land-based forces with little warning, and thus substantially reduce the ability of the United States to retaliate in a second strike. The problem, then, was that the deterrent value of U.S. strategic forces would be undermined, perhaps freeing the Soviets for all kinds of devilment in Europe, including the potential for some kind of nuclear blackmail against the United States. Since a diplomatic solution to this problem was not evident at that time (this was years before the Strategic Arms Reduction Talks [START] negotiations and the 1991 demise of the Soviet Union), DOD sought a technical response.

That solution finally emerged from the nation's military laboratories and testing ranges in the form of a new ICBM, the Missile Experimental, hence MX. This ICBM carried ten "accurate multiple individually targeted re-entry vehicles" (MIRVs), each containing a thermonuclear warhead. There was one remaining problem with the MX—how to base the missiles so they would not be vulnerable to a first strike by the USSR. After a number of alternative basing modes were evaluated, the Carter administration, which had inherited the MX from earlier administrations, announced its choice. It was a high tech variation of the old "shell game" dubbed the "race trace," or "multiple protective shelter" deployment mode.

The government's more elegant shell game to protect MX ICBMs was to create a mobile basing system in which the MX missiles would move clandestinely among a larger number of shelters. Ostensively, this system would fool Soviet reconnaissance, making it virtually impossible to target the missiles. So it was that in 1979 the Carter administration announced its intent to pursue basing of the MX in the Great Basin region of Nevada and Utah.

Although the MX "race track" deployment mode offered a seemingly plausible solution to the nation's national defense needs, it also contained the potential for massive environmental disruption. The specifics of the initial proposal called for rotating 200 missiles among 4,600 shelters in a 40,000 square mile area. Constructing this system required some 10,000 miles of service roads, 20,000 workers and their families, and would have consumed 190 million gallons of water over a twenty year period (Holland and Hoover, 1985, 101–2). In short, the MX proposal clearly fit the definition of a major federal action and, therefore, had to meet the requirements of the National Environmental Policy Act of 1969 (NEPA).

This situation, in itself, was not problematic. Following the enactment of NEPA, DOD promulgated regulations declaring its intent to "act with care to insure to the maximum extent possible that, in carrying out its mission of providing for national defense, it does so in a manner consistent with national environmental policies" (32 CFR 214.4). These regulations also prescribed the procedures DOD would follow in preparing Environmental Impact Statements (EIS) required by NEPA. And in the case of the MX proposal, the Air Force prepared two EISs (U.S. Department of the Air Force, 1978, 1980).

What created the problem was that these statements largely confirmed that the MX "race track" proposal would create massive disruptions on both the physical and social environments of the Great Basin area. Moreover, since part of the EIS process requires public review, these statements provided MX opponents with ample ammunition. Thus, the military found itself embroiled in yet another federal lands confrontation.

In most important respects, the MX controversy generated a dialogue strikingly similar to the Engel hearings. Virtually every traditional public land interest group opposed the proposal. As Paul Culhane (1987, 97) noted: "In my research, I discovered only one standard public lands constituency that favored the MX." The exception was the chamber of commerce for Clark County, Nevada, which viewed the MX project as a potential "boom" for the local economy, not unlike how a community might have greeted a federal works project in the 1930s. Every other public lands constituency viewed the MX proposal as an activity that would close off large areas of the federal estate to traditional uses, either as a result of military restrictions or through the destruction of the fragile desert ecosystems (U.S. Congress, 1980, 1981).

The air force defended the proposal on three grounds. First, the MX represented a vital component of the nation's national security strategy. Second, while acknowledging that the construction phase would be disruptive, the air force offered assurances that the area would eventually be restored. Finally, the air force pointed out that only small portions of the deployment area would be restricted for security reasons, and thus most of the Great Basin would eventually be reopened to public access. As part of its overall campaign, the air force produced a compelling twenty-minute color movie for public viewing. The movie remains a classic example of DOD public relations—a combination of the need to defend against the Soviet threat and calming reassurances that defense needs were compatible with environmental values and the traditional uses of western federal lands.

An interesting facet of the initial MX controversy is that it occurred in the context of a major conflict over federal lands policy dubbed the "Sagebrush Rebellion." Among the many issues at dispute in the Sagebrush Rebellion was open confrontation between commodity user groups and environmentalists over the character of existing and future federal land management policies. Nevertheless, the MX proposal caused these groups to set aside their other differences and form a common chorus in protest against the air force. Whether or not this broad-based public outcry would have been effective in blocking the "race track" proposal remains debatable. However, it did demonstrate that the claim of national security provided DOD little shelter in the turbulence of western federal lands policy matters.

In the end, the MX controversy was resolved at the ballot box when Ronald Reagan defeated Jimmy Carter in the 1980 presidential election. Concerned about the enormous cost of the "race track" proposal, the Reagan administration opted for deployment of MX (renamed Peacekeeper) missiles in retrofitted Minuteman III silos. Since these were existing silos, there was no need for additional land. Moreover, the construction activity required to enlarge and reinforce the silos created very little environmental disturbance. In consequence, the only significant opposition to the Reagan administration's plan came from peace groups which argued that the Peacekeepers would have potentially destablizing effects for U.S.-USSR arms control relations.

But Reagan's election also marked a new era of support for the military establishment. A key principle of the Reagan administration's national security posture was that the Soviet Union constituted an "Evil Empire," and to be successful, the United States needed to be able to bargain from a position of strength. Alleging that the Carter years had weakened the nation's military establishment, Reagan pledged to revitalize national defense. The administration's commitment to strengthening the military suggested that DOD might be in a better bargaining position in the federal lands policy arena. A test of this possibility came in the controversy over the Military Lands Act of 1986.

The Military Lands Act

Although generating far less national attention than earlier episodes, this controversy exhibited familiar patterns. The primary dispute centered on the air force's attempt to secure an 89,000 acre area (Groom Mountain) adjacent to Nellis Air Force Bombing Range in Nevada. Originally, the air force had tried to close the area administratively. That effort created public opposition and brought the issue before Congress. In 1984, Congress authorized a temporary withdrawal of the area pending the findings of an EIS. In 1985, Representative Beverly Byron (D-MD) included the Nellis area in an omnibus bill covering military land withdrawals in four western states—Nevada, Arizona, New Mexico, and Alaska.

The ensuing congressional hearings followed a now standard script. For example, Charles Callison, representing the Nevada Outdoor Recreation Council and the Natural Resources Defense Council, argued that the "history of military reservations in the West shows that the armed services always asked for more land than they really need" (U.S. Congress, 1986a, 309).[2] Ruth Robbins, wife of a Nevada rancher and co-founder of the Mothers Against Military Arrogance (MAMA), expressed a similar, albeit more pointed, sentiment:

> The Federal Government wants to withdraw so much of Nevada's public lands for defense or in the name of national security purposes without the consideration of who really owns this land. We the people do, whether it be the public or private lands. It is our wilderness, our wildlife, and our personal lives that are being affected. Quite frankly, we think that the military . . . should be embarrassed by their arrogant attitudes concerning the American citizen. (U.S. Congress, 1986b, 50)

The military completed the dialogue parallel by arguing that the withdrawals were necessary for training and testing of equipment in the context of the continued threat from the Soviet Union. Moreover, the military provided assurances that, wherever possible, it would cooperate with other federal agencies in protecting environmental values and allowing traditional use activities. And on November 6, 1986, DOD prevailed when the Military Lands Act (PL 99-606) became law.

While authorizing the military's requests, the act also limited the duration of the withdrawals to fifteen years, and required preparation of an EIS no later than twelve years after the enactment date to assess the need for continuation of the withdrawals. In addition, the secretary of the appropriate military branch was authorized to limit public access upon a determination that such closure was necessary for military operations, public safety, or for reasons of national security. However, management responsibility for open areas was given to the Department of Interior, following the principles defined in the Federal Land Policy and Management Act (43 USC 1701, et seq.). Though generally a victory for the military, the act also reflected ongoing concerns expressed by opponents of military land use.

As noted above, DOD's success in this confrontation was, at least in part, a result of the Reagan administration's commitment to strengthening the nation's military establishment. Yet, by the end of his second term, Reagan had conceded that the Cold War was drawing to an end. Indeed, the United

States and the Soviet Union had negotiated the Intermediate Nuclear Forces Treaty and started to jointly destroy their respective intermediate range ballistic missiles (Pershings and SS-20s). And then, in the fall of 1989, Americans sat enthralled before their TV sets, watching the end of the Soviet empire in Eastern Europe. Against this background, DOD embarked on yet another expansion move.

The 1989–1990 Expansion Effort

The primary issue at dispute in this controversy was DOD's request to renew its control over 1.5 million acres and expand its holdings by an additional 3.2 million acres in the states of California, Colorado, Idaho, Montana, Nevada, Utah, and Washington. There were also some peripheral issues. For example, the Mississippi National Guard sought to acquire 32,000 acres in the DeSota National Forest. These requests, in the context of changing international situations, set the stage for a confrontation nearly identical to the Engel Hearings of the mid 1950s.

In this case, the congressional point man was Representative Bruce Vento (D-MN), chair of the Subcommittee on National Parks and Public Lands of the House Interior Committee. And in a statement which could have been made by Engel thirty years earlier, Vento opened hearings on the military lands by observing:

> Federal lands do make a significant contribution to our military readiness and to our national defense effort. At the same time, expansion of these military uses will inevitably have an impact on the resources and values of these lands. . . . It is important for us to take the initiative in this subcommittee to get a better understanding . . . on how the present proposed military operations on Federal lands affect . . . wildlife, recreation, range quality, and watershed and how they will affect public access to enjoy and utilize these lands. (U.S. Congress, 1990, 7)

Vento went on to note that the "fast-paced activities in Eastern Europe, and on the world scene generally," raised question about whether or not military use needed to be "reduced or altered because of changing national priorities."

Not surprisingly, the dialogue during these hearings followed familiar patterns. Robert Stone, DOD deputy secretary for installations, explained that the requests reflected changing training and testing requirements. As examples of this change, Stone noted:

> Cruise missiles we test today over vast amounts of land didn't exist 10 years ago. Aerial maneuvers used to cover 5 miles. Now they cover 40 miles. In the future they will cover 80 miles. Army units, like mechanized infantry battalions, used to need 4,000 acres to train. Now they need 80,000. (U.S. Congress, 1990,11)

Yet, in meeting these needs, DOD remained committed to a policy of "being a good neighbor" by permitting public use "when it is compatible with military operations, planning for environmental concerns, safeguarding endangered species, and using airspace properly" (U.S. Congress, 1990, 15).

And once again, the military encountered broad-based public opposition. National environmental groups (Wilderness Society, National Wildlife Federation) joined commodity user groups (National Cattleman's Association, American Mining Conference) in voicing concern about military use of federal lands. Moreover, the controversy spawned an impressive array of local opposition expressed by citizen groups such as Citizen Alert in Nevada, Skyguard in Nevada and Utah, Idaho Is Too Great to Bomb Coalition, Alliance for Rural Montana, and a Kansas group calling itself Preserve Rural America.

Interestingly enough, this controversy ended abruptly in September 1990 when then Deputy Defense Secretary Donald J. Atwood announced a moratorium on all DOD proposals to add more than 1,000 acres to existing military lands. "As we reshape our forces and close or realign bases," Atwood explained, "the department must insure that we propose the acquisition of land only where there is a clearly demonstrated need" (Egan, 1990, 1), a development which led Representative Vento to exclaim, "The big land grab just backfired" (Egan, 1990,1).

It could be that the military's disengagement represented a victory for the opponents of military acquisitions. However, other events, not directly related to the military land issue, raise the possibility of a different interpretation of this controversy. It is to those events that we now turn.

The Military, Federal Lands Policy, and the Future

As noted earlier, this brief journey through the history of the military's experiences in the federal lands policy arena does not immediately suggest the basis for a coalition between DOD and environmentalists. In fact, it seems to point in the opposite direction. After over thirty years of conflict, environmentalists appear no more sympathetic now to DOD's requests than they were during the Engel hearings. Nevertheless, the history of military lands conflict makes two points clear.

First, and most obvious, the ability of DOD to acquire federal lands is directly related to the credibility of its justification for the use of those lands. Second, and perhaps less obvious, DOD has made rather surprising efforts to develop its image as an environmentally responsible land management agency. Viewed in this light, it is our contention that several recent developments have considerably improved the military's posture in the federal lands policy arena.

In March of 1990, during the height of DOD's most recent expansion effort, the White House released a document entitled, *National Security Strat-*

egy of the United States. Under the title, ''Trends in Weaponry,'' this report noted:

> Modern battlefields are characterized by an unprecedented lethality. The greater precision, range, and destructiveness of conventional weapons now extend war across a wider geographical area, and make it much more rapid and intense. (U.S. White House, 1990, 6)

This statement offers collaboration for DOD's claim that modern weapons need greater space for training and testing purposes. Further, the strategy document linked concerns about modern weapons with a new development on the international scene—Third World conflicts.

On the one hand, the report warned that the ''erosion of U.S.-Soviet bipolarity could permit and in some ways encourage the growth'' of Third World conflicts (White House, 1990, 6).

It also warned that the spread of ''global weapons production'' served to make modern weapon systems ''increasingly available to smaller powers'' (p. 6). At the juncture of these concerns, then, was the possibility that ''highly destructive regional wars'' would increasingly pose a threat to U.S. interests. The Iraqi invasion of Kuwait in the fall of 1990, and the subsequent Persian Gulf war, affirmed the White House's predictions.

One of the consequences of the six-week air war and four day ground war in the Persian Gulf was a dramatically heightened public awareness of the spectacular weapons possessed by the U.S. military. Indeed, the American public was given documented evidence of the effectiveness of U.S. weapons throughout daily televised coverage of the war. Another, and related, consequence is greater appreciation of the arid West's utility for training U.S. personnel. The desert training center at Camp Irwin, California, for example, helped prepare American ground troops for the conditions they encountered in the Persian Gulf. And the Barry M. Goldwater Air Force Range in southwestern Arizona provided an ideal training site for air force, navy, and marine pilots who conducted the air war in Iraq. In short, Operation Desert Storm gave the military a credible justification for federal land use.

At the same time, other events pointed to a concerted effort by the U.S. military establishment to cultivate a commitment to environmental protection efforts. In June 1990, Sam Nunn (D-GA), the powerful chairman of the Senate Armed Services Committee, delivered a major address on new environmental priorities for DOD. The primary thrust of his remarks was that as the Soviet threat receded, the nation should recognize environmental destruction as a ''growing national threat'' (Shabecoff, 1990, 1). Joined by fellow Armed Services Committee members Jeff Bingham (D-NM), James Exon (D-NE), Al Gore (D-TN), and Tim Wirth (D-CO), Nunn called for the creation of a Strategic Environmental Research Program in DOD. In essence, this program would use military equipment (airplanes, satellites, submarines, ships to collect environmentally relevant information, which could then be analyzed in DOD research laboratories as part of the broader effort to develop logical responses to global environmental problems.

While grafting "environmental defense" onto DOD's mission was an intriguing proposal, there were reasons for suspecting that it might have been motivated by concerns other than environmental protection. As the *New York Times* noted editorially, "[Nunn's] new [environmental] interests may not be entirely unconnected to his old interest in safeguarding military spending" ("Painting the Pentagon Green," 1990, A16). Nevertheless, the editorial went on to concede that the proposal was worth considering on its merits. Moreover, since the proposal's sponsors were all Democrats, there was also room for suspecting that it emerged from partisan maneuvering.

Yet, in September 1990, DOD sponsored a forum in the nation's capital as part of its newly established Defense and Environment Initiative. This event represented the first formal discussion of military and environment issues in a context other than arguments during congressional hearings. In his address to the forum, Dick Cheney (1990, 1), secretary of defense in the Bush administration, suggested:

> Environmental responsibility sustains life on Earth, enriches society and the conditions of life, and expands opportunities for the future. Within the federal government, I want the Defense Department to be the federal leader in agency environmental compliance and protection.

Cheney went on to note that in DOD "more than 5,000 people make a full-time commitment to protecting the environment" (p. 2). DOD's commitment to environmental protection, therefore, appeared to be a phenomenon that transcended partisan boundaries.

Although the outbreak of the Persian Gulf war diverted attention from these initiatives, there are some examples which demonstrate that DOD has already embarked on a new environmental path. For instance, the Pinon Canyon Maneuver Site, located 150 miles southeast of Fort Carson, Colorado, has been used as an armored vehicle and tank training area since 1985. Recognizing the destructive character of its use, the army instituted several management practices intended to help maintain the overall environmental quality of the area. The army's primary management regime is a variant of the traditional soil conservation technique called "rest-rotation." More specifically, after an area in the sixty-mile-long installation is used for training, it is blocked off, reseeded, and fertilized, and then left undisturbed for two years. This approach allows damaged areas to recover without interfering with the army's training exercises.

In addition, during high precipitation months—April, May, and June—when vehicle training would be particularly damaging, the area is used for dismounted training, which excludes the use of heavy tracked vehicles such as the MI-Al tank. Finally, at the center of the installation, along the Purgatorie River, is a 16,000 acre site containing Indian pictographs and dinosaur tracks. To insure these artifacts are preserved, the area is being transferred to the U.S. Forest Service for management purposes.

To date, the army's efforts at Pinon Canyon have received little attention. But in a recent film produced by the National Audubon Society entitled, "The New Range Wars," the army received unexpected, albeit indirect, praise from the environmental community. Primarily an environmentalist broadside depicting the alleged environmental destruction caused by domestic livestock grazing, at one point in the film the audience is shown tank maneuvers as the narrator explains that tank training at Pinon Canyon creates less environmental disruption than grazing. It would be stretching the point, of course, to imply that the Audubon Society prefers tank training to grazing on the federal lands. On the other hand, it does demonstrate that a political coalition between environmentalists and the military is more plausible than commonly assumed.

Another example involves the U.S. Army Corps of Engineers. Historically, the corps' mission to dam and channel western rivers has made it the target of overt environmental hostility (Morgan, 1971; Clarke and McCool, 1985; Reisner, 1986). However, in the fall of 1991, the corps inaugurated an Environmental Compliance Assessment System. Administered by the Toxic and Hazardous Materials Agency within the corps, this program is designed to develop solutions for past and present environmental problems at military installations. It is possible to envision the corps developing an "environmental response team" capable of resolving a wide array of environmental problems in the United States, and even in the successor states to the former Soviet Union and Eastern Europe, where the neglect of the environment is substantially greater than in the United States.

What begins to take shape, then, is the possibility that the U.S. military establishment is experiencing something of a "green revolution." Whether this phenomenon results from an authentic commitment to environmental protection or is merely a ploy to protect defense budgets is ultimately beside the point. If the military remains committed to this green revolution, it will become an important component of the broader effort to restore and preserve the national, indeed international, environment. This point brings us, in turn, back to the issue of military lands.

Rather than a victory for opponents of military expansion, DOD's disengagement from the 1989–90 acquisition move might have been a "strategic retreat." Stated differently, recognizing that the demise of the Cold War undermined it's expansion justification, DOD opted to withdraw and regroup.

Such an interpretation is clearly implied by the deputy defense secretary's comments cited above.

Initially, the focus of the regrouping effort was to emphasize DOD's commitment to environmental concerns as a way to allay concerns about the military use of federal lands. However, with the developments in the Persian Gulf came dramatic new support for the military cause, as DOD prepares for participation in what may be a series of United Nation peacekeeping missions around the world.

But whatever the interpretation for the 1989–90 controversy's outcome, the more important point is that the military is in a favorable bargaining position for the rest of this century. It has a credible and persuasive justification for the use of federal lands as sites for non-nuclear testing and training; and it has begun developing some rather impressive environmental credentials. Thus, DOD could become a formidable player in the federal lands policy arena.

If environmentalists come to understand that the goal of emphasizing environmental preservation on the federal estate is in fact being accomplished by DOD on the military lands, then they might find common ground with the military establishment. Indeed, recent reports suggest that commodity user groups have mobilized a rather effective counteroffensive against environmentalists (Alexander, 1991). In consequence, environmentalists might view an alliance with the military as a way to improve their posture against their traditional opponents. In short, some startling political coalitions may be struck in the federal lands policy arena. And yet, such a development may not be so startling after all. If nothing else, the rapid changes in the international political arena serve as a potent reminder that history may no longer be a reliable predictor for future events.

NOTES

1. We are using the best available *published* data here.
2. It might be noted that Callison also testified against military acquisition of federal lands during the Engel hearings.

NIP in the Nineties and Beyond: Post–Cold War National Industrial Policy

RICHARD D. BINGHAM

It has been clear since before the end of the Cold War that international competition in the 1990s will largely be defined in economic and not military terms. For the past decade scholars and policymakers have been concerned with America's industrial productivity. The question has been asked: *Can America Compete?* (Lawrence, 1984). This issue of U.S. competitiveness has received extraordinary attention in recent years (for example, Cohen and Zysman, 1987; Dertouzos, et al., 1989; Galbraith, 1989) and has led to a renewed interest in industrial policy. For if the United States is in fact losing its competitive advantage, it may well find itself sliding toward second-rate economic status. Those who see the United States in such a slide but believe that it can be corrected have been calling for a new industrial policy for the nation. Others believe that the only good industrial policy is no industrial policy (McKenzie, 1985). All would agree, however, that industrial policy is an important national issue.

This chapter will focus attention on national industrial policy issues. It begins with a summary of the debate over national industrial policy which occurred in the early and mid-1980s, describes the major components of national industrial policy under the Reagan and Bush presidencies, and concludes with some thoughts on a new national industrial policy.

The Debate

During the first half of the decade of the 1980s, there was serious public debate over what has traditionally been defined as national industrial policy. Economist R. D. Norton (1986) characterized this debate as between the "preservationists" and the "modernizers."[1] Both groups characterized the U.S. economy as being in deep trouble with productivity stagnating and manufacturing jobs drifting offshore.

The preservationists' position was best exemplified by the editors of *Business Week* (1981), sociologist Amitai Etzioni (1983), and banker Felix Rohatyn (1983). Their strategy was essentially one of fighting market forces and preserving U.S. industries. *Business Week* (*America's Restructured Economy*, 1981), for example, believed that market forces would continue to weaken manufacturing in the North by steering funds (and investments) into the energy and high-tech sectors in the South and West. *Business Week* advocated new government policy to stimulate investment and to target this investment where it was needed.

Rohatyn also tells us that "market forces are destroying our basic industries, possibly permanently, but these market forces are by no means free" (1983, 14). Rohatyn proposed a new Reconstruction Finance Corporation (RFC) to provide capital to industries in exchange for concessions from management, labor, and so on, which would lead to industry rationalization. The structure and functions Rohatyn proposed were modeled after the Municipal Assistance Corporation (MAC), which constructed New York's fiscal reorganization in the 1970s. Rohatyn headed MAC.

The modernizers' position is exemplified by Lester Thurow (1980) and Robert Reich (1983). Thurow advocated a redistribution of resources from "sunset" to "sunrise" industries, while Reich called for policies to speed the shift of capital and labor into high value-added activities.

But this industrial policy debate—the preservationists and modernizers—was short-lived. It made it only to the Reagan-Mondale election. Norton (1986, 1) noted that "Industrial policy has turned out to be an idea with a brief career." Even Reich observed that "industrial policy is one of those rare ideas that has moved swiftly from obscurity to meaninglessness without any intervening period of coherence" (1984, 32). And yet Reich argues that the United States does have an industrial policy, although it exists in piecemeal form.

The reason our industrial policy takes such a fractured form is that the dominant paradigm concerning the role of government in society prohibits corporatist activities. George Lodge (1990) identifies two ideological paradigms concerning the role of government—individualistic and communitarian. In an individualistic society, government is limited and is separate from business. It intervenes in the affairs of business only when questions of national health and safety are involved. Its role is to keep the marketplace open so that competition among firms is as vigorous and as free as possible.

In a communitarian society government is authoritarian. Its function is to define the needs of society and to see to it that those needs are met.

Among the developed capitalistic nations of the world the United States is probably the most individualistic and Japan the most communitarian (Lodge, 1990, 15–16). Thus, Japan believed that it was "a function of the state . . . to induce, guide, and accelerate the structural changes needed for long-term growth. Japanese industrial policy thus involves a commitment to long-term planning and programming of the nation's economy" (Johnson, 1982, 28). In Japan this long-term planning and programming has historically been the responsibility of the Ministry of International Trade and Industry (MITI) (although today the Ministry of Finance is playing a larger role in shaping Japan's economy). In other words, MITI was expected to select industries in which growth and technical progress were comparatively high and to develop policies to promote this growth (Lodge, 1990, 19). The case of microchip development illustrates the Japanese approach.

By the mid-1970s the Japanese had developed a small computer industry, but it was well behind the world leaders. The industry was composed of two groups—the Electronic Industry Promotion Association, composed of seventy-odd relatively small companies, and the five mainframe manufacturers, Hitachi, Fujitsu, Toshiba, NEC, and Mitsubishi. Concern with IBM's domination of the Japanese market led industry and MITI leaders to develop a plan to bolster Japan's computer industry by developing a more powerful microchip. In 1976, the Very Large-Scale Integrated Circuit Technology Research Association (VLSI/TRA) was formed for this purpose. Its members included the five mainframe manufacturers. It was MITI's job to ensure that the major firms participated and to force them to cooperate. VLSI/TRA was given four years to accomplish its mission. It was governed by a board of directors with the chairmanship rotating annually among the company presidents. However, the executive director of VLSI/TRA was a widely respected former MITI official. The association consisted of six labs which were funded on a fifty-fifty basis by MITI and the member firms. Researchers were on loan from the five member firms and were mandated to bring the research results back to their parent firms. The parent firms paid the researchers' salaries while they were on assignment. It is reported that the researchers were not the companies' best but were clearly competent.

The results of this effort stunned the world. When VLSI/TRA closed its doors in 1980, it had developed a 256K RAM chip—a far cry from the 64K chip with which it had begun. It also had applied for 1,000 patents in VLSI processing technology. VLSI/TRA ended up costing the Japanese government $112 million in direct subsidies and more in tax breaks (Lodge, 1990, 76–77).

Lodge credits the success of VLSI/TRA to the following:

(1) It had clear objectives, which were understood and shared by all participants.
(2) There were a sense of urgency, if not crisis. The timing was right.
(3) Deadlines were set.

(4) The key players—the Big Five—were involved.
(5) There was at least a year of advance preparation and planning.
(6) It attracted competent and strongly motivated personnel. (1990, 77)

This is a far cry from the way in which industrial policy is made in the United States. Industrial policy in the United States is fractionalized. Its components are neither coherent nor connected.

National Industrial Policy

There are undoubtedly many ways to describe the fractionalized components of U.S. policy. The following elements are suggested here: functional problem solving, global steering, defense spending, free(er) trade, real estate/downtown development, industrial growth as a state responsibility, and technology-based development.

Functional Problem Solving

The term "functional problem solving" has been used to describe a major component of U.S. industrial policy (Jarboe, 1985, 200–204). This approach views every industrial problem in isolation from all others. It is standard practice to define a problem facing a specific firm or industry and then take the appropriate governmental action to alleviate it. The functional problem-solving approach is illustrated by three government actions: protecting the auto industry, saving the Chrysler Corporation, and the savings and loan bailout.

Voluntary Export Restraints. From 1978 to 1981, the U.S. auto industry had been lobbying for protection from Japanese imports. In February 1981, one month after Ronald Reagan had taken office, reports indicated that the Japanese had captured nearly 25 percent of the U.S. auto market. At that point Senator John Danforth of Missouri introduced legislation requiring a reduction in Japanese imports to 1.6 million cars a year. His intent was to spur the Reagan administration into action. The strategy worked. After considering a nuinber of alternatives, the administration decided that the restraint must come from the Japanese themselves. There would be no formal trade action, no bilateral discussions, no formal quota—the administration would simply signal the Japanese that they must restrain their auto shipments.

The Japanese were not pleased with the American move. They wanted the U.S. government to make specific demands. But as the Danforth bill moved through Congress, the Japanese position softened. On April 30, 1981, MITI announced that it would limit auto exports to the United States to 1.68 million units and that the future growth of Japanese imports would be limited to 16.5 percent of the market expansion.

The consequences of the voluntary restraint agreement were immediate. It let U.S. automakers raise prices without losing sales. By the third year of the restraints American consumers were estimated to be paying as much as $5 billion a year in higher prices for cars than they would have paid without the quota (Reich and Donahue, 1985, 244–45).

The Chrysler Bailout. The Chrysler bailout provides a fascinating example of functional problem solving at its best (Reich and Donahue, 1985). In December 1979, President Jimmy Carter signed the Chrysler Loan Guarantee of 1979 into law. Final agreement was reached on the terms of the bailout after many months of haggling between the administration, Congress, the Chrysler Corporation, its banks, the United Auto Workers, and a host of other interested parties (like suppliers). Under the terms of the agreement the government would guarantee up to $1.5 billion in Chrysler debt—if the other parties specified in the act reached accommodation.

The act required concessions from eight sources before the loan guarantee kicked in:

1. Unionized workers have to agree to concessions of $462.5 million (including a $203 million concession in an earlier UAW-Chrysler contract);
2. Nonunionized workers would have to give up $125 million;
3. U.S. banks and other creditors would contribute $500 million (80 percent in new loans and 20 percent in concessions to outstanding debt);
4. Foreign creditors would contribute $150 million in new loans;
5. Chrysler would be required to sell off $300 million in assets;
6. State and local governments would contribute $250 million;
7. Suppliers and dealers would contribute $180 million; and
8. Chrysler would have to sell $50 million in new stock.

The whole deal was administered by a Loan Guarantee Board headed by the secretary of the treasury and included the chair of the Federal Reserve and the comptroller general. The secretaries of labor and transportation were nonvoting members. The board hired a staff which was responsible for day-to-day administration.

The terms worked out with the various parties were extremely complex. Here are the terms of the plan approved by the board:

Lenders would extend the maturity date on $154 million in loans, forgive $181 million in interest, and defer $345 million in interest (this totals $680 million—a figure Chrysler had been using—but the government valued the package at $642 million). After 1983, Chrysler would have the option—if its cash flow improved and the K-car sold well—of giving the banks an equivalent value in preferred stock instead of paying deferred interest. Union employees would sacrifice $462.5 million and nonunion benefits would be cut by $125 million. In addition, $418 million in pension fund deferrals would be valued at $342 million (given Pension Benefit Guarantee Corporation claims). The board counted $628 million in asset sales based on "reasonable assurances" of $171 million from real estate sales, $250 million for a chunk of Chrysler Financial, and $100 million as an asset sale for the stock-secured loan from Peugeot, plus $106 million from subsidiaries in Brazil, Argentina, and Australia. Michigan lent Chrysler $150 million, and Delaware and Indiana were listed for loans of $5 million and $32 million. Canada would contribute $170 million in loan guarantees after 1982. Finally, the $78 million in convertible debentures sold to dealers and suppliers counted as $63 million, for a total private aid package of $2.6 billion. (Reich and Donahue, 1985, 185)

Even then, the situation was constantly changing. By the end of 1980, the situation at Chrysler was even worse than predicted, and the Loan Guarantee Board had to force more concessions. These included a wage freeze agreement with the UAW. Workers gave up a COLA of $1.15 an hour. When this was added to the original cuts, it meant that the typical Chrysler worker was giving up about $14,500 over the life of the union contract.

The Chrysler rescue worked. But was the bailout the best response the public could have asked for? There is no telling. But the costs were painful. Between 1979 and 1984 Chrysler cut about 27,000 hourly workers from its workforce and closed eighteen of its plants. Former Treasury Secretary G. William Miller called the bailout "just a professional reorganization outside of bankruptcy" (Reich and Donahue, 1985, 295).

The Savings and Loan Bailout. Functional problem solving had traditionally been applied to manufacturing industries, but that is not the case today—not with the savings and loan bailout. The costs of the bailout are estimated to be between $159 billion and $203 billion. This comes to $641 to $819 per person in the United States. Something between 58 and 61 percent of the bailout costs will come from personal income tax payments.

Outside of the costs to the taxpayers, the bailout will have a number of ramifications. First, commercial and residential properties in the Southwest and New England have been dumped on the market at highly discounted prices. This has tilted development toward the Southwest for the near future. Second, this devalued surplus real estate has damaged solvent thrifts and commercial banks by curtailing new construction and thus reducing the demand for new mortgages. Third, the crisis has made the S&Ls skittish about making new loans. Fourth, banks and thrifts are forcing developers to put more equity in speculative projects—thus dampening development. Fifth, the bank mergers and closings have created a noticeable drop in employment in the banking industry. And finally, the experience of the S&L debacle will undoubtedly ensure that the federal government will steer clear of any new expenditure programs that will encourage construction or any other development activities (Hill, 1990).

Instrument-Specific Industrial Policy. One of the problems with functional problem solving is that it tends to become instrument-specific (Jarboe, 1985, 201–3. Here the focus shifts from the industry to the instrument. Once a specific problem is solved using a specific instrument, the instrument is given special status and is thought to be able to solve all other problems as they emerge. Jarboe equates this with the law of the hammer: "Give a child a hammer and suddenly everything resembles a nail" (1985, 201). In other words, the tool is used simply because it is available.

The operation of the law of the hammer is clearly illustrated by the Reagan administration's fascination with voluntary trade restraint agreements. The auto quotas initiated in 1981 were understandable and were probably unavoidable—but then the law of the hammer took over. The auto restraints were followed by new restraints on heavyweight motorcycles, textiles, and a network of voluntary restraint agreements on carbon steel aimed at limiting imports to 20.2 percent of domestic production (Destler, 1986, 148). And all of this from a president who was essentially a free trader.

Global Steering

The second major component of our industrial policy is global steering. Global steering was first used to describe industrial policy during the Johnson administration. It is

> the exclusive use of macroeconomic instruments for industrial policy purposes. Global steering is a modified laissez-faire system where the government manages the macroeconomy through fiscal and monetary policies. Each individual industry takes care of itself. (Jarboe, 1985, 203)

The Reagan administration's underlying philosophy regarding industrial policy was that federal efforts at promoting economic growth and international trade could best be achieved by generally leaving businesses and individuals free to conduct their affairs as they saw fit (Hudgins and McKenzie, 1989, 34). Global steering served that venue.

Robert Lawrence's *Can America Compete?* is one of the best-reasoned arguments for global steering. Lawrence holds that macroeconomic policies, rather than microeconomic measures such as selective industrial policies (e.g., functional problem solving), are the appropriate policy tools for guiding the country's growth. He argues that the debate about selective industrial policies (the preservationists and the modernizers mentioned earlier) is a debate not about how to increase employment or U.S. competitiveness, but about how to best allocate resources. And in his view, government is not an efficient allocator of resources.

> A move toward greater government participation in resource allocation is . . . unlikely to enhance efficiency given the U.S. political system and administrative traditions. Without a broad national consensus about the necessity for such programs, there can be no continuity in their implementation. Some proponents of selective industrial policies believe that the conditional provision of government aid and trade protection could speed up the pace of domestic adjustment. But it is questionable whether the government has the knowledge and monitoring capabilities to set such conditions. It is also questionable whether government aid could be confined to troubled industries that provide a plan to restore their international competitiveness. Previous efforts to aid depressed regions and cities have been diffused into relatively ineffective programs with numerous recipients receiving token assistance. (Lawrence, 1984, 12)

Defense Spending

Defense spending must also be seen as a major component of our national industrial policy. In FY 1986, the federal government spent $53.1 billion on research and development (R&D) activities and facilities—two-thirds of which was spent by the Defense Department. Between 1976 and 1986, defense-related R&D grew at an annual rate of 13.4 percent, while nondefense R&D grew at only 4.5 percent. This is 1.5 percent (annually) below the rate of inflation (Penner, 1988, 81). And this is only research and development.

When the totality of defense spending is examined, its impact is enormous. For 1992 national defense outlays were $295 billion, although with the projected defense cuts they will be down to $289 billion by 1995.

Another way of looking at the same phenomenon is in terms of employment. There are more than 1.3 million servicemen and women stationed at military installations in the United States. Another million civilian employees work for the Department of Defense. But this is small potatoes when compared to the 3.4 million civilian employees working for defense-related contractors. Thus, almost 5 percent of the workforce in the United States is directly dependent on the military (Whitehead, 1991).

During the past half-century, defense contracting has produced a new economic map of the United States. Ann Markusen et al. (1991) call it America's gunbelt. The gunbelt runs "from the state of Washington through California to the desert states of the Southwest, on through Texas and the Great Plains, across to Florida, and discontinuously up the East Coast to New England" (p. 6). The heart of the gunbelt is Los Angeles.

The rise of the gunbelt has worked as a kind of "underground regional policy." During World War II and the Korean War, the Midwest and Mid-

Atlantic states were the homes to most defense contractors. In 1952, the Midwest and Mid-Atlantic states had 57 percent of the prime defense contracts. By 1984, that 57 percent had fallen to a mere 21 percent. On the other hand, gunbelt prime contracts—in Census Bureau terms New England, South Atlantic, East and West South Central, Mountain and Pacific division—increased from 38 to almost 70 percent (Markusen, et al., 1991).

Nowhere is this more evident than in Los Angeles. Los Angeles County is America's manufacturing center, with 860,000 manufacturing jobs—300,000 more than its closest rival, Chicago. If the four neighboring counties are added in, the total comes to 1.2 million jobs. And much of this is defense-related. Aerospace and high-technology firms employed about 400,000 people in the five-county area in 1991 ("Can LA Still Make It?" 1991).

But if defense spending works as a kind of regional policy, what will happen to the gunbelt if the projected cuts in the defense budget do come about? Philip Vincent, an economist with the First Interstate Bank, believes that one in six aerospace jobs in the Los Angeles area will be lost by 1995. But, he believes that the economy can absorb that easily ("Can LA Still Make It?" 1991, 59).

What about the rest of the gunbelt? David Whitehead (1991) recently examined the potential impact of both military base closings and proposed defense cuts on employment on a state-by-state basis. In terms of net employment, only 12,900 military and 7,742 civilian workers nationwide are expected to be affected by base closings. California will be hardest hit, losing 17,324 jobs. But with more than 204,000 active-duty military personnel and more than 130,000 DOD civilian workers, California is losing only 5 percent of its direct military employment due to base closings. Furthermore, this represents a very small part of the total employment picture in California—only one-tenth of 1 percent.

With regard to prime contractor workers, Whitehead believes that most states have enjoyed sufficient economic growth to absorb potentially displaced private-sector defense workers into the work force in a reasonable time frame. The exceptions are Virginia, Colorado, Massachusetts, Connecticut, and Missouri. These states have been more dependent on defense spending than the rest, and they also showed less employment growth than other states. There may be hard times ahead for parts of the gunbelt.

Free(er) Trade

A fourth component of U.S. industrial policy consists of efforts to promote an international system of freer trade. We benefit from international trade for the same reasons that we benefit from a division of labor in our own society. If individuals and groups produce their products with the greatest efficiency, people can obtain a far greater quantity of goods at lower prices than if they produced these goods themselves.

The Reagan, Bush and early Clinton administrations have all pursued policies that reduce trade barriers and open markets. In recent years many of these negotiations have been on a bilateral basis. The U.S.-Canada Free Trade Agreement passed in 1988 and the U.S.-Mexico Free Trade Agreement are two examples.

Promotion of freer trade policies is clearly a major component of our industrial policy. It will not be discussed here at length.[2] It is sufficient at this point to say that the arguments against protectionism and continuing efforts toward freer trade are compelling. When standardized products are produced and sold in competitive markets, no country can gain at the expense of others by subsidizing its exports. Export subsidies transfer income from the country granting the subsidies to consumers in the importing nations. The implication of this is that a country maximizes its national income by pursuing a policy of free trade no matter what the policies of its trading partners (Stone, 1988, 119).

Real Estate/Downtown Development

One component of national industrial policy was targeting economic assistance to distressed places. The implementation of the policy was carried out in the very traditional way that most other federal domestic initiatives are implemented—through grants-in-aid to states and localities.

The Urban Development Action Grant (UDAG) program, while only one of nearly seventy federal programs that dealt with economic development during the Carter years, provides an example of how targeted industrial policy worked. UDAG's principal focus was on the problems of disinvestment and employment and population declines that many of the nation's central cities were experiencing. Participation in the UDAG program was limited to communities that qualified as "distressed" cities (and to "pockets of poverty" in cities which were not distressed). While UDAG was a targeted program, targeting for economic development purposes was not a new concept. Several EDA programs and the Anti-Recession Fiscal Assistance program were earlier examples of targeted economic development aid. About half of the larger (50,000 or more population) cities were UDAG-eligible. UDAG awards were made on a competitive project basis. Project requirements included:

> (1) firm financial commitments from public and private participants; (2) a minimum leveraging ratio of $2.50 in private funds to $1.00 in UDAG funds; (3) the "but for" prerequisite that requires no substitution of UDAG funds for local funds, certification that the project would not proceed but for the UDAG, and that the UDAG is the least amount necessary to make the project feasible; (4) a substantial impact on the physical and economic development of the city or urban county; (5) the proposed activities are likely to be completed in a timely

fashion; and (6) evidence that the applicant has a satisfactory performance record in carrying out housing and community development programs (Rich, 1992, 151).

The UDAG program began in 1978 and operated for about 12 years. Over its lifetime UDAG awarded $4.6 billion to finance some three thousand projects. UDAG funds generated more than $30 billion in private investment, much of which might not have occurred "but for" UDAG.

Targeting distressed communities through project grants created a de facto industrial policy with geographic and sectoral implications. Most of the UDAG funds were targeted to the most distressed cities; and since most of the distressed cities (as measured by UDAG criteria) are in the Northeast and Midwest, most of the UDAG money went to cities in the Northeast and Midwest (71.8 percent). Furthermore, most of this money went to downtown commercial projects. These projects were office buildings, retail trade, and/or hotels (Rich, 1992).

Thus, this component of the de facto industrial policy of the 1970s and early 1980s was targeted sectoral growth. And the target of that growth was downtown redevelopment through offices, hotels, and retail space. The ultimate outcome was, of course, the creation of an enormous number of service sector jobs.

UDAG, however, was only one component of targeted support for the real estate sector. During the late 1970s and 1980s, Congress changed a number of the rules governing banks and passed changes to the tax laws that encouraged investment in real estate. In 1978, rules that govern the conduct of large investors like insurance companies were changed to liberalize the amount of funds which could be invested in real estate. Then, the Economic Recovery Act of 1981 shortened the period of depreciation of commercial and industrial real estate from thirty-five to seventeen years. And the Garn–St. Germain bill allowed thrifts to increase their holdings in real estate, eliminated margin requirements, and encouraged lending institutions to take risky ownership positions in their projects.

All of this succeeded dramatically. During the 1980s, an incredible 12.5 billion square feet of commercial real estate space was built—between one-third and two-fifths of the total space available today. All of this construction was financed with over $1 trillion in debt (as we know, much of that debt went bad) (Vaughan and Hill, 1991, ch. 3).

Industrial Growth as a State Responsibility

The emphasis on industrial growth as a state responsibility is predicated on the belief that the states have major, if not exclusive, responsibilities for building the foundations on which an economy can grow. These foundations include:

> (1) a capable and motivated work force; (2) sound physical infrastructure; (3) well-managed natural resources; (4) universities and other research institutions involved in the development, dissemination, and application of knowledge and technology; (5) an effective system of regulation, and capital and technical assistance; (6) an appealing quality of life; (7) sound fiscal policy with respect to tax rates and debt management. (Haider, 1986, 464)

Peter Eisinger (1988) refers to the emergence of state and local governments as major partners in industrial development as the rise of the entrepreneurial state. The entrepreneurial state seeks to identify market opportunities on behalf of private actors whose activities may serve public ends. It is based on the concept that jobs are a public good. The states see themselves as "company formers"—stimulating new private business formation. State and local governments promote growth by lowering production costs through subsidies of capital and through low taxes, by stimulating new business formation and expansion, and by assisting the private sector to identify market opportunities. This is far cry from the laissez-faire policies of the national government.

> At the national level during the years in which the entrepreneurial state took shape, the critical ideas were deregulation, privatization, the free market, voluntarism, and the supply-side macroeconomic doctrine. Yet the entrepreneurial state is based on a strategy of intervention, guidance, and initiative in the economy. The fifty states and many of their communities are in the process of fashioning, with varying degrees of vigor and coherence, separate little industrial policies, self-conscious attempts to foster selected industries judged to provide comparative local advantage or to be critical to the local economic future. (Eisinger, 1988, 6)

As an aside, industrial policy in the United States illustrates a useful point about American federalism. "It illustrates the versatility of a federal arrangement that permits governments at the two different levels to pursue quite different (though not necessarily conflicting) courses of policy" (Eisinger, 1988, 6).

State industrial policy—or economic development policy, as it is commonly referred to—is shaped by a framework which has been fairly constant over the years. The elements of this framework include public-private partnership, decentralization, an absence of planning, the primacy of capital, and pragmatism (Eisinger, 1988, 21–33).

The idea of public-private partnerships is central to any industrial policy. The states believe that some social goals can best be achieved by the private sector supported by the public sector. Partnerships are justified on the grounds that private investment cannot or will not take place without public inducements.

Decentralization means that development tasks are the responsibilities of state governments, local governments, quasi-public organizations such as industrial development corporations, and private entities such as chambers of commerce. The consequences of decentralization are interjurisdictional competition and policy variety. Interjurisdictional competition occurs as states compete with states and cities compete with cities for job-creating investment. This in turn leads to a wide variety of policies as those governments look for the most effective ways to attract business.

In the economic development field, businesses are seen as targets of opportunity. Targets of opportunity do not lend themselves to planning. In addition, Americans have traditionally been hostile to economic planning of any kind. Both of these situations have made economic development planning very difficult.

The focus of most industrial development efforts has been on capital. Capital, not labor, is key. The primary development goal of governments has been to encourage and subsidize the investment of private capital.

Finally, Americans are pragmatic. They continue to search for whatever works best. Neither ideology nor theory constrains the inventiveness of efforts to encourage business investment.

Technology-Based Development

Technology-based development is the final component of U.S. industrial policy. It is mentioned last because it is not very significant in terms of emphasis or dollars. However, it is perhaps the most interesting policy component because it is a movement in the direction of traditional industrial policy. It is best illustrated by the emergence of Sematech.

In 1984, Congress passed the National Cooperative Research Act, which allowed corporations to band together to conduct joint research while exempting them from antitrust prosecution. In 1985, the United States began the process of developing a research association akin to Japan's VLSI/TRA discussed earlier.

In December 1985, the deputy undersecretary of defense for research and engineering established a task force of the Defense Science Board (DSB) to assess the importance of recent trends in the semiconductor industry. In February 1987, the task force issued its report. It concluded that U.S. leadership in commercial volume semiconductor production was in jeopardy.

> Since "the existence of a healthy U.S. semiconductor industry was critical to the national defense," the task force recommended that "DOD . . . encourage and actively support with contract funding [approximately $200 million per year] the

establishment of a U.S. Semiconductor Manufacturing Institute formed as a consortium of U.S. manufacturers.'' (Lodge, 1990, 82)

The Semiconductor Industry Association (SIA) proposed Sematech immediately following the DSB report and began lobbying Washington for the funds. Sematech was to be a cooperative venture to concentrate on manufacturing process know-how. Its original fourteen founders included many of the industry giants such as IBM, AT&T, Digital Equipment Corporation, and National Semiconductor.

As it turned out, Sematech was not the success that had been hoped for. In December 1988, Sematech member Texas Instruments announced plans to enter a joint venture with Hitachi to share the costs of developing a 16-megabyte chip to be used in high-definition TV (made in Japan). In April 1989, the world's leading producer of chip-making equipment, Perkins-Elmer, announced that it was abandoning the business because of Japanese competition. Finally, Monsanto, the last remaining merchant producer of silicon wafers and a major supplier to Sematech, announced that it was selling its wafer production facility to a German firm, Heuls AG (Lodge, 1990, 87–88).

Summary

The seven elements discussed above constitute the de facto industrial policy of the United States. The single most important element is global steering—the macromanagement of the economy to produce economic growth. The other rational component of the current policy is the promotion of free trade. Other actions of the federal government are also components of NIP, but they are not part of an overall strategy. They are defense spending, the promotion of real estate and downtown development, and the devolution of economic development responsibilities to the states. The on-again-off-again fascination with a technology policy, however, is a slight movement toward what one traditionally thinks of when discussing industrial policy.

But is this enough? Will this de facto NIP be adequate for the challenges of the twenty-first century? It is unlikely, because a fractionalized industrial policy causes a misallocation of resources, and in an ever-more-competitive world it is a misallocation the United States can ill afford. First, by its very nature functional problem solving is preservationist. Functional problem solving works to solve industrial problems. And these industrial problems are the difficulties being experienced by declining but politically powerful industries. So functional problem solving protects noncompetitive industries.

Second, relying on the spillover from defense spending as a component of industrial policy has a number of negative consequences. Sematech was founded for defense-related purposes and operated with funding and guidance from the Department of Defense. In order that a consortium like Sematech be successful its products and patents must have wide commercial application. The narrow focus of defense needs significantly reduces commercial potential. Of course, this also illustrates a related but wider problem—the massive spending of government R&D money for defense purposes means that government-sponsored R&D is concentrated in areas that have few commerical applications.

Finally, the promotion of real estate and downtown development and the devolution of economic development activities to the states leads to a shuffling of economic resources. But at what cost? Has this harmed the overall competitive position of the nation?

Toward a New National Industrial Policy

The United States should never again find itself losing ground economically to the rest of the world. To remain competitive it should consider an industrial policy based upon four cornerstones: economic stability, human resources, technological dominance, and capital accumulation.

Economic Stability

The most important component of a national industrial policy is economic stability. The federal government must continue the fiscal and monetary policies of the past decade aimed at keeping inflation low, interest rates down, and exchange rates stable. Individuals, companies, and nations can hardly be concerned with long-term industrial growth (or their own futures) without a stable economy. Sound fiscal and monetary policy can promote this stability.

Human Capital

Beyond economic stability, the most important industrial initiative is the investment in human capital. A well-educated, flexible labor force is the most valuable asset an economy can have.

> A key conceptual issue involves the relationship between investment and the pace of technological change. Is new investment necessary to exploit new knowledge, or can it be exploited by rearranging the existing capital stock and labor force? If new investment is necessary, the return to policies that stimulate investment will be very much higher than if it is not. Exactly the same questions can be raised with regard to investments in human capital that also may be necessary to use new knowledge. (Penner, 1988, 76–77)

But is the American educational system providing what it needs to provide?

Problems in the Schools

In late April 1983, the National Commission on Excellence in Education released a much-heralded but disturbing report, *A Nation at Risk*, on the status of education in America. The commission concluded:

> Our nation is at risk. Our once unchallenged preeminence in commerce, industry, science, and technological innovation is being overtaken by competitors throughout the world. . . . The educational foundations of our society are presently being eroded by a rising tide of mediocrity that threatens our very future as a nation and a people. (National Commission on Excellence in Education, 1983, 1)

Some alarming trends in our educational system were identified. For example:

- International comparisons of student achievement, completed a decade ago, reveal that on nineteen academic tests American students were never first or second and, in a comparison with other industrialized nations, were last seven times.
- Some 23 million American adults are functionally illiterate by the simplest tests of everyday reading, writing, and comprehension.
- About 13 percent of all seventeen-year-olds in the United States can be considered functionally illiterate. Functional illiteracy among minority youth may run as high as 40 percent.
- Average achievement of high school students on most standardized tests is now lower than it was twenty-six years ago when Sputnik was launched.
- Over half the population of gifted students do not match their tested ability with comparable achievement in school.
- The College Board's Scholastic Aptitude Tests (SAT) demonstrate a virtually unbroken decline from 1963 to 1980. Average verbal scores fell over 50 points, and average mathematics scores dropped nearly 40 points.
- College Board achievement tests also reveal consistent declines in recent years in such subjects as physics and English.
- Both the number and proportion of students demonstrating superior achievement on the SAT's (i.e., those with scores of 650 or higher) have also dramatically declined.
- Many seventeen-year-olds do not possess the "higher order" intellectual skills that we should expect of them. Nearly 40 percent cannot draw inferences from written material; only one-fifth can write a persuasive essay; and only one-third can solve a mathematics problem requiring several steps.

- There was a steady decline in science achievement scores of U.S. seventeen-year-olds as measured by national assessments of science in 1969, 1973, and 1977.

The commission lays the blame for these startling statistics squarely on the shoulders of our system of public education. It concluded that the declines in educational performance are the result of inadequacies of the educational process itself. The specific inadequacies of secondary school curricula and requirements include:

- Secondary-school curricula have been homogenized, diluted, and diffused to the point that they no longer have a central purpose. In effect, we have a cafeteria-style curriculum in which the appetizers and desserts can easily be mistaken for the main courses. Students have migrated from vocational and college-preparatory programs to ''general track'' courses in large numbers. The proportion of students taking a general program of study has increased from 12 percent in 1964 to 42 percent in 1979.
- This curricular smorgasbord, combined with extensive student choice, explains a great deal about where we find ourselves today. We offer intermediate algebra, but only 31 percent of our recent high-school graduates complete it; we offer French I, but only 13 percent complete it; and we offer geography, but only 16 percent complete it. Calculus is available in schools enrolling about 60 percent of all students, but only 6 percent of all students complete it.
- Twenty-five percent of the credits earned by general-track high-school students are in physical and health education, work experience outside the school, remedial English and mathematics, and personal service and development courses, such as training for adulthood and marriage.
- The amount of homework for high-school seniors has decreased (two-thirds report less than one hour a night) and grades have risen as average student achievement has been declining.
- A 1980 state-by-state survey of high school diploma requirements reveals that only eight states require high schools to offer foreign language instruction, but none requires students to take the courses. Thirty-five states require only one year of mathematics, and thirty-six require only one year of science for a diploma.
- In thirteen states, 50 percent or more of the units required for high-school graduation may be electives chosen by the student. Given this freedom to choose the substance of half or more of their education, many students opt for less-demanding personal-service courses, such as ''bachelor living.''

- "Minimum competency" examinations (now required in thirty-seven states) fall short of what is needed, as the "minimum" tends to become the "maximum," thus lowering educational standards for all.

The commission also complained that American students spend much less time in the classroom than students in other nations, that the time spent is used ineffectively, and that teachers are frequently drawn from the bottom quarter of graduating college students and are not qualified in the subject matter they are required to teach.

A decade and more after the publication of *A Nation at Risk*, it does not look as though things have changed very much. In 1991, the average score on the verbal section of the Scholastic Aptitude Test (SAT) fell to an all-time low, while the average mathematics score declined for the first time in a decade. In 1969, verbal scores averaged 464—today they are 422. In 1969, math scores were 493—today they average 474. And this occurred in spite of the fact that real spending on public education rose by one-third over the past eleven years.

What can be done? As a beginning, the federal government needs to establish minimum competency standards for secondary schools, mandate a lengthening of the school year, and ensure access to higher education for all qualified youth who wish to pursue education beyond the secondary level.[3]

The Department of Education should develop a national competency test to be given to all secondary school students annually. The need for such a test rests on the assumption that there are measurable minimum competencies necessary for survival in the modern world. Parents will be able to judge the "survivability" of their children beyond the inflated grade reports they now receive from many of our failing school systems. National competency testing will also promote accountability. Parents will be able to judge the effectiveness of schools and school systems based on a comparison of test scores.

In spite of the logic for such tests, powerful interests oppose them. They say that teachers would "teach the test" instead of concentrating on real learning. They say that such tests would lead to a nationalization of the curriculum. And they argue that any such tests would be culturally biased.

But similar tests already exist and are given to millions of young people every year—the SATs and ACTs. It is just that they are not given to all students. A national competency test is simply an extension of a system which already exists. The arguments against such a test are simply not compelling.

The federal government should also encourage or mandate a lengthening of the school year. American children spend far fewer days in the classroom than do their European or Asian counterparts. Most public school children in the United States spend only about 180 days in the classroom. And lengthy summer vacations lead to forgetting what has been learned. Three unusual church-sponsored schools for inner-city youth are lighting the way. Children at the Cornerstone Schools in Detroit attend class 240 days a year (Japanese children attend 243 days of school). Furthermore, parents can choose whether to let children take a one-month vacation during the summer. Why must public school children always end up the losers?

Finally, all young people should be given the opportunity to attend college or technical school on a full-time basis should they so desire. For the individual student this means removing financial considerations from the equation. All qualified youths should receive federal junior college or college scholarships in an amount necessary to cover tuition at moderately priced state or local institutions. College scholarships might be in the range of $2,500 per year, while junior college scholarships might be $1,300. Scholarships would only be for full-time students who maintain an acceptable grade-point average and would be paid directly to the educational institution. This is the only way we will have a work force ready for the twenty-first century.

Technological Dominance

Technological dominance should be the third cornerstone of a national industrial policy. The United States must be in a position of world leadership in the development of important new technologies. To attain this leadership position, the United States should promote the development of several new "Sematechs" but more in the mold of the Japanese VLSI/TRA. It is possible to learn from the experience of Sematech.

It will be necessary to build these new research associations slowly. Perhaps one or two research associations should be established as a national experiment in technology development—there should be no more than five. Each research association might have three to five laboratories located in major areas of agglomeration.

Each research association should be a nonprofit corporation with a life span restricted to five years, including a front-end year for planning. The association would be funded by both government and industry. Government funding might be in the neighborhood of $300-$400 million per year. The association would have a specified research agenda, and its research results should be potentially useful in a wide range of *commercial* products (as opposed to defense). The association should be directly overseen by an assistant secretary of the Department of Commerce. The executive director of the association would be appointed by the secretary of commerce. The scientists involved would be from both the private and public sectors, and patents and discoveries would belong to all participants.

There is some evidence that such an approach might work, although experiments to date have been on a very small scale. In particular there are the National Science Foundation's University-Industry Cooperative Research Centers. A typical center is engineering based and consists of collaborative research involving a multidisciplinary team that can include both university and industry engineers. While the centers have not been formally evaluated in terms of their ability to contribute to national competitiveness or industrial innovation, preliminary indications are that the consequences have been significant (Roessner, 1989, 13).

The first question to be asked, of course, is: What research would be singled out for such special treatment? Charles Stone, an economist with the Federal Communications Commission, summarizes the traditional arguments against any form of ''modernist'' industrial policy:

> Whether couched as competitiveness, industrial policy, or infant industry protection, their main argument is that there are some industries that are so important to promoting economic growth but so vulnerable to failure, especially in the early stages of new-product development, that they should receive targeted government support in the form of tariffs or subsidies until they have grown large enough and strong enough to survive on their own without that targeted support.
>
> The main objections that have been raised against the adoption of strategic trade policies center on the enormous difficulty of translating the theoretical case for intervention into practical policies that do more good than harm. First, . . . it is difficult to identify clear, practical instances in which the theoretical conditions under which intervention would be appropriate apply. Second, the decision about what industries to target requires considerable guesswork about unknowable future developments, and the cost of guessing wrong can be quite high because resources that would otherwise have been more profitably employed have been diverted into the target industry. The private market, too, is vulnerable to misforecasting the future, so the question becomes whether the potential myopia of myriad decision makers in the private market is more of a problem than the risk that a government remote from the action will put all of its eggs in the wrong basket. Finally, and perhaps most important, decisions about what industries to target will almost inevitably become political decisions rather than economic decisions, increasing the likelihood that criteria other than those that underlie the case for intervention will be applied. (Stone, 1988, 124–25)

But, even those who question whether government can act competently in supporting industrial research believe some targeting is necessary. Economist Paul Krugman, for example, concedes that:

> If we must have a targeted industrial policy, it would probably be best to target the high technology industries, which have both important dynamic scale economies and important externalities. But we have no assurance that this is actually the right policy. (1983, 138)

But surely the task of selecting one or two significant areas of research is not so difficult? In 1986, two IBM scientists announced the discovery of new materials that carry an electric current without resistance at the relatively high temperature of −288 degrees Fahrenheit (absolute 0 is −459.67 degrees

Fahrenheit). This set off a race among the industrialized nations to find other materials which would carry electricity with little resistance at even higher temperatures (Lodge, 1990, 98). The implications of this are enormous. Surely most thinking individuals see the enormous potential payoff for society if superconductivity can be achieved at near room temperature?

A second recommendation, and one that has also been experimented with on a limited basis, is "magnet infrastructure." A major attraction of magnet infrastructure is that it makes sophisticated equipment available, rented on a time-share basis, thereby allowing small firms to defray high fixed costs. One example of this type of institution, funded by the federal government, is now in place at the Illinois Institute of Technology. Frank Young, director of the Food and Drug Administration, explains the rationale:

> In the United States, we've done a very unusual thing, relative to other parts of the industrial world, by making our investment in fermentation pilot plants and scale-up plants before the product is actually ready for production. Typically, the product arrives when the plant is a minimum of four years out of date, in some cases as much as eight. By making fermentation technology available to industry and university scientists through our consortium, on what amounts to a turn-key rental basis, we'll help companies delay their investment in state-of-the-art technology until their products have actually proved themselves in later-stage clinical trials. This should save enormous amounts of money.
>
> Instrumentation in molecular biology becomes obsolete in something like two-and-a-half years. If each of us—academia, industry, and government—buys state-of-the-art equipment and underutilizes it through its brief period of high performance, we're in effect lowering the productivity of capital in the nation. The FDA's initiative is a capital-sparing strategy. (Blakely and Nishikawa, 1992)

Capital Accumulation

During the 1980s the United States experienced what can only be considered mediocre economic performance. Productivity advances were disappointing, the household savings rate declined, and workers' real hourly incomes were barely advanced.

Supply side economics was going to be a savior. The tax cuts of the early 1980s were supposed to generate new private savings and foster a new era of growth. Instead, household savings as a percentage of gross domestic product fell precipitously in the United States, as it did in other developed countries. Household savings in the United States were well below that of other industrialized nations.

The United States became a debtor nation internationally in 1985. The federal deficit, of course, contributed to this circumstance. But the major reason the United States is a debtor nation is that gross domestic savings have not kept pace with gross domestic investment. Since 1985, net savings from abroad have financed from 15 to 20 percent of gross fixed capital formation and from 33 to 45 percent of gross investment in producers' durable goods.

The problem is that people in the United States have not been saving enough to sustain even a mediocre economic performance—we have been forced to rely on foreign savings to finance a rather anemic rate of domestic capital formation. In itself, there is nothing wrong with a nation relying on foreign financing to achieve growth per se.

> But common sense tells us that there is something wrong when a very wealthy nation—one that has for four decades been the world's leading industrial and economic power—must rely on foreign capital simply to achieve mediocre results. . . . The net result is a nation that is in danger of losing its credibility abroad and its vitality at home. (Graham, 1991, 142)

To maintain world leadership, the United States must be better than mediocre. And to be better than mediocre, the United States must be able to finance its industrial structure. Since the tax cuts of the 1980s did not provide an incentive to save, a new approach must be taken. It may be time to stop taxing savings altogether.

The objective of maintaining industrial competitiveness is a worthy one. And the policies of the past seem to have served us well. But can we expect to remain competitive in the future? Perhaps so, but it will be more likely if industrial policy is viewed as evolving and not static—if it changes as changes are needed.

The Japanese auto industry has shown how a little tinkering around the edges can lead to enormous productivity gains. The policies suggested above are hardly revolutionary—but they are evolutionary. They are worth a try.

NOTES

The author wishes to thank Cal Clark for helpful comments on an earlier version of this chapter.

1. The appendix to R. D. Norton's (1986) industrial policy article in the *Journal of Economic Literature* provides an excellent summary of the debate.

2. See Yong S. Lee, "U.S. Trade Policy in the Post–Cold War Era: A Search for New Direction," in W. Crotty, ed., *Post–Cold War Policy: The International Context* (Chicago: Nelson-Hall, 1994).

3. For one approach, see Barry Keating and Maryann Keating, "Post–Cold War Education in the United States: The American OPEC," in W. Crotty, ed., *Post–Cold War Policy: The Social and Domestic Context* (Chicago: Nelson-Hall, 1994).

Budgetary Policy in the Post–Cold War Era

STEVEN G. KOVEN

The 1990s appear to represent a rare window of opportunity for policy choice. The sudden perception that the "evil bear" is no longer a threat to American security combined with the perception that the United States is slipping as an economic power create a necessary, however, not necessarily sufficient, environment for major policy redirection. Free from the albatross of defender of the free world and protector from an expanding Communist menace, the United States can forge new priorities and pathways in the post–Cold War era. Choices made today will, in turn, influence the quality of life in America well into the next century. This chapter will explore the perceived demise of the Communist threat, budgetary implications of the new world environment, political influences on budgeting, and alternative budget scenarios. The intent of the chapter is to stimulate thinking about budgetary policy in a period of time that may offer more opportunity for change than any period since the end of World War II.

Demise of the Communist Threat

As a singular date for marking the "end of the Cold War," November 9, 1989, is commonly cited. This date represents the day the Berlin Wall which had divided East and West for twenty-eight years came down. The Berlin Wall was said to stand as a symbol not only of a divided city but also of a divided Europe and a divided world. Western leaders customarily made pilgrimages to the wall in order to express their commitment to freedom in the struggle between East and West.

East Germany was not alone in dismantling once-feared symbols of Soviet power. A succession of events in Hungary, Czechoslovakia, Poland, and Romania quickly transformed Eastern Europe. These events were all part of the mosaic which clearly identified hatred of the Soviet Union and the repudiation of communism as an ideological wave of the future.

Perhaps the precipitating event that opened the floodgates of change was Hungary's dismantling of the barbed-wire fence along the Austria-Hungary border. ''Tourists'' from East Germany flocked to Hungary, where they were able to pass into Austria and then travel to West Germany. Automobiles (representing years of labor) were simply abandoned at the Hungarian border as people dashed to freedom to live under a new system.

Reasons for the fall of Communist influence abound. Internal division within the Soviet Union is cited as one explanation for the inability of the Soviets to retain influence in Eastern Europe. Internally, the Soviet Union confronted independence movements in many of its republics. On December 9, 1991, the Soviet Union's three Slavic republics of Russia, Byelorussia, and the Ukraine forged a new alliance, declaring the government of Mikhail Gorbachev dead. A few days later, five more Soviet republics agreed to join in a new alliance, threatening the relevance of the old system.

The rush to establish new arrangements between republics of the former Union of Soviet Socialist Republics underscores ethnic and economic divisions. Governmental fragmentation is likely to enhance the perception in the United States that the old world order can be put to rest and that a new era has emerged. The defection of the Ukraine as well as Russia from the central state government greatly fragments the central government of the Soviet Union. The Ukraine accounted for more than 65 percent of the USSR's sugar production, 30 percent of its grain, and 25 percent of its meat in 1991. Ethnic Ukrainians also accounted for more than 40 percent of the Soviet officer corps and were invited ''home'' to help form a 450,000 strong Ukrainian army (Freeland and Corwin, 1991, 69).

The failed coup within the Soviet Union further indicated that hardliners were no longer in power. Some equated the failed coup as a final attempt to make a dead horse run by flogging it. The dead horse metaphor refers to the Soviet economic system, which has proven itself incapable of delivering the quality and quantity of consumer goods demanded by citizens of the state. Crops rotting in the field, a transportation system in disarray, near-empty food shelves, long waits in order to obtain the barest of necessities, a currency lacking international value, ethnic hatred, and appeals for a massive bailout from the West all signify the bankruptcy of a system that once evoked mixtures of both fear and admiration.

Economic failure of the Communist system is cited as a second rationale for the decline of the Soviet empire. An ideological system that once promised to bury the West appears to be in tatters. A few factors are commonly cited in order to explain the sudden turn of events. First, the goal of equality is said to discourage initiative, hard work, risk taking and innovation—the cornerstones of free market, capitalist systems. If equality of outcome is more or less guaranteed for all but a few high-level officials, choosing leisure (even consumption of large quantities of vodka) over work can be viewed as a rational choice. One can ask why work long hours when the fruits of labor are shared and there is very little to buy anyway?

Second, a system based upon production (regardless of consumer demand) is also likely to lead to poor quality products. Quotas are established by bureaucrats who may be out of touch with consumer desires. Anecdotal accounts of millions of left-foot shoes and no right-foot shoes coming out of factories are heard. When high quality goods are available, they might find their way into the black market. In the extreme, production based output can lead to a "Law of Reduction of Value." A Sovietologist in Moscow is quoted as claiming that the Soviet Union actually was the first society that based its economy on efforts which subtracted value from inputs. He cited a factory in the provinces that made steel ingots which were worth less than the cost of the raw materials involved in their production. This state of affairs is due to the fact that there is no market for steel ingots. Since there is no real market for the product, the ingots were loaded into wheelbarrows and sent to the factory entrance where they were manufactured all over again. The ultimate conclusion after observing this phenomenon is that while production adds value under capitalism, it subtracts value in a mature socialist economy (O'Sullivan, 1991, 28).

Ethnic divisions and a flawed economic system do not represent the universe of explanations for the sudden demise of Soviet influence. Empire overreach, suppression of individual spirit through restrictions on speech and exercise of religion, the military buildup under Ronald Reagan, poor discipline in the Soviet military as a result of the war in Afghanistan, and other factors are competing and complementary explanations for the demise of the Communist empire. A combination of numerous factors probably contributed to the collapse of communism in the late 1980s and early 1990s. More important than the cause of the collapse, however, is the perception of disarray in the Soviet Union and the implications of such a perception on U.S. defense posture.

A general consensus seems to have emerged within the United States that the Cold War is over. The ill-fated coup of August 1991 appeared to further undermine the position of "hard-liners" in the Soviet Union and enhance the posture of forces for democratization and change.

Events in the Soviet Union even forced organizations such as Stanford University's Hoover Institute on War, Revolution, and Peace to reevaluate their mission. The Hoover Institute maintained since 1919 a mission to "demonstrate the evils of the doctrines of Karl Marx." The notion that the dimension of the Soviet threat had been significantly reduced was also expounded by former CIA Director William Webster. In testimony before the House Armed Services Committee, Webster stated that the political changes in the Soviet Union and its former allies could not be reversed. Webster argued that even if Gorbachev was overthrown by hard-liners inclined to reverse the decline in Soviet military power, there was "little chance that Soviet hegemony could be restored in Eastern Europe." Webster stated that "a successor regime would face the same types of economic and political pressures that President Gorbachev has and would probably continue to pursue arms control agreements with the West" (*Congressional Quarterly*, 1990b).

In 1993, an influential British publication declared that Russia was "stumbling toward stability," and "neither dictatorship nor disintegration is now a plausible outcome." It was believed that a lowering of the inflation rate would lay the basis for real economic stability, democracy, and growth (*Economist*, 1993, 15).

Events in the Soviet Union seem to have created the perception that a new era in East-West relations has dawned. While the Soviet Union still possesses 30,000 nuclear weapons and appears to be more unstable than ever, with the bloody storming of Parliament and extreme nationalist Vladimir Zhirinovsky gaining a surprising 22 percent of the popular vote, a generally accepted view of the media and political elites is that the Cold War has become a historical artifact. The post–Cold War environment, devoid of the stimulus of rising military expenditures, in turn allows for nonincremental and innovative budgetary behavior.

Budgetary Implications of a New Environment

It is logical to infer that withdrawal of Soviet troops from Eastern Europe and the perception of general fragmentation within the Soviet Union should allow for major reductions in U.S. defense spending. Plans to reduce the U.S. military presence in Europe have already been proposed. Strategies to counter Soviet tank invasions across West Germany are now obsolete. A reduction in defense spending is today perceived to be prudent. From the rational budgetary perspective, therefore, the revised assessments of the "Soviet threat" should directly translate into lower levels of defense spending.

Recent U.S. defense budgets reflect the view that the post–Cold War era has ameliorated the need for a continued defense buildup. In the 1992 budget presented to Congress, George Bush turned out to be the first president to request an actual cut in defense spending authority in more than twenty years.

The budget requested $295.2 billion in outlays, an actual decline of 1.2 percent (*Congressional Quarterly*, 1991a). The final bill signed by Bush on December 6, 1991, provided for $291 billion in spending. Under the plan, defense requests for fiscal 1992 and 1993 would continue a step-by-step retrenchment. By fiscal year 1995 defense spending was projected to decline to inflation-adjusted 1980 spending levels. Defense outlays were projected to account for 3.6 percent of gross national product by 1997, the lowest level since the 1930s. The long-range plan would also slice (by 1995, one-fourth or 61.5 million) the number of service members on active duty. Significant cuts were proposed for the number of combat units and in weapons procurement (*Congressional Quarterly*, 1991a, 345).

The Clinton presidency probably will hasten the reduction in national defense spending. This is revealed when comparing future defense spending projections of the last Bush budget with projections made in the early years of the Clinton administration (Koven, 1994, 9).

Defense spending projections reflect the assessment that the Soviets' ability to project power beyond their borders would continue to decline, either as part of a broad strategy of improving relations with the West, or because of the continued economic collapse within the Soviet Union. Consistent with this assessment, the following reductions were proposed: active duty army divisions to decline from eighteen to twelve; navy ships from 545 to 451; and air force fighter wings from twenty-four to fifteen. The Clinton administration was to attempt even further reductions.

Proposed cuts in military personnel were to be equally shared across the three branches of the service. Army and air force personnel were slated to bear the brunt of reductions. Table 13.1 describes the distribution of personnel cuts between the branches of the military.

TABLE 13.1

Distribution of Military Personnel Cuts

Active Military	1987	1995	Percent Change
Army	781,000	536,000	−31
Navy	587,000	510,000	−13
Marine Corps	199,000	171,000	−14
Air Force	607,000	437,000	−28
Total active	2,170,000	1,650,000	−24
Selected reserves	1,150,000	906,000	−21
Civilians	1,130,000	940,000	−17

Source: Basic data, U.S. Department of Defense.

TABLE 13.2

Defense Budget Authority, Fiscal Years 1990–1994 (in millions of dollars)

Department of Defense	1990 actual	1991 est.	1992 est.	1993 est.	1994 est.	Percent change
Personnel	$78,876	$79,021	$78,017	$77,513	$76,474	−3
Operations and Maintenance	88,309	86,019	84,452	84,666	84,642	−5
Procurement	81,376	64,099	63,404	66,721	68,775	−16
Construction and Housing	8,273	8,291	8,148	7,268	11,039	+3
Subtotal, Defense	292,999	272,953	278,282	277,895	278,224	−5

Source: *Budget of the U.S. Government, 1991.*

The proposed plan would reduce navy personnel by only 13 percent while cutting air force and army personnel by 28 percent and 31 percent, respectively. Reductions in reserves (projected to decline by 21 percent in 1995) were also proposed. A strategy of priority setting was also set in regard to aggregate military spending. Projected reductions in spending were targeted in the area of procurement. This strategy is consistent with the view that the surest method of cutting defense spending was to terminate or curtail production of expensive weapons systems. Table 13.2 describes the distribution of cuts among Defense Department functions for the fiscal years 1990 through 1994.

Different strategies may be used to reduce defense spending. Presidents tend to advocate shutting down the production of existing weapons such as the F-15, F-16, and F-14D fighters, the Apache helicopter, and the M-1 tank in order to increase spending on the development of future technologies. Congress, on the other hand, prefers to formulate plans which would protect existing systems.

Deeper reductions in defense spending have been proposed by some politicians who advocate reducing military expenditures in order to fund tax cuts (Molotsky, 1991). Iowa Senator Tom Harkin has called for reordering priorities. Harkin's proposal to halve military spending by the end of the century was adopted by others such as economist Robert Heilbroner, who contended that military spending cuts of one-third or as much as one-half were not unrealistic. William Kaufmann of the Brookings Institution developed a plan for a $146.8 billion defense budget by the year 2001. A noted rush to "break open the Pentagon candy jar" accelerated with the failure of the August coup in the Soviet Union (Norman, 1991).

Drastic reductions in defense spending may have a short-term destabilizing impact on the American economy. The long-term impact of reduced defense spending, however, may be positive. As philosopher Adam Smith stated in *The Wealth of Nations*:

> The whole army and navy, are unproductive labourers. They are the servants of the public, and are maintained by a part of the annual produce of the industry of other people. Their service, how honorable, how useful, or how necessary soever, produces nothing for which an equal quantity of services can afterwards be procured. (Smith, 1937, 315)

Paul Kennedy, author of the best-selling book *The Rise and Fall of the Great Powers*, also expressed his concern over the long-term implications of U.S. defense spending:

> If the United States continues to invest a massive amount of its R&D activities into military-related production while the Japanese and West Germans concentrate upon commercial R&D; and if the Pentagon's spending drains off the majority of the country's scientists and engineers from the design and production of goods for the world market while similar personnel in other countries are primarily engaged in bringing out better products for the civilian consumer, then it seems inevitable that the American share of world manufacturing will steadily decline, and also likely that its economic growth rates will be slower than in those countries dedicated to the marketplace and less eager to channel resources into defense. (Kennedy, 1987, 532)

The impact of reductions in defense spending, however, will be determined by the political environment in the United States. Exogenous forces such as turmoil in the Soviet Union exert pressure on the budget, yet such pressures should not be perceived as the primary determinant of budget outputs. Key (1940) and Wildavsky (1961) have long recognized that budgets in democratic societies such as the United States reflect pressure group conflict to a greater extent than they reflect "objective" assessments of need. Politics, therefore, acts as an essential intervening variable in defining budget outputs of a polity.

Exogenous Forces 1 Domestic Interpretation 1 Budget Outputs

A cursory investigation of actions in America's pluralistic society is helpful in order to predict the budgetary outcomes of post–Cold War policy. It is likely that domestic interpretations or "spins" on events as well as the political clout of domestic actors with vested interests will play a larger role in determining U.S. budget outputs than events in the Soviet Union.

Political Influences on Budgeting

It appears evident to many analysts that the needs of military spending are less pressing today, yet it is also apparent that budgeting involves negotiation, protection of vested interests, and pork barrel spending. In a democracy such as the United States, lobbyists, public interest representatives, and others are expected to compete in the budgetary process. It has been documented that while internal politics helps to define outputs, budgets are also subject to external shocks such as events in the Soviet Union (Ott and Ott, 1965).

An alternative to the rational perspective in budgeting maintains that outputs are responsive to the political environment wherein they are shaped (Wildavsky, 1964; Wanat, 1976; Koven, 1988; Rubin, 1990). From this perspective, pork barrel, constituent service, representative's seniority, prevailing political ideology, the media, bureaucratic considerations, and other factors are as important or more important in determining budget outputs than external shocks such as the termination of Cold War hostilities.

Although events in the Soviet Union seem to sound a clarion call for drastic reductions in defense spending, vested interests are expected to resist proposed defense cuts. A number of strategies conceivably can be pursued by anti-defense-cut advocates. First, defense spending advocates can attempt to shift the foci of defense concern away from bipolar, strategic issues to fears over regional instability. The Persian Gulf war offers an excellent example of such a scenario, which can be used to justify increased spending. Instability in the Soviet Union represents another rhetorical ploy to justify spending. Finally, the purely pork barrel rationale of protecting jobs also may influence the budgetary debate. Protecting constituents who would be adversely affected by reductions in defense spending has been a preoccupation of a number of congressional representatives in the late 1980s and early 1990s.

The efforts of Georgia Democrat George Darden and New York Democrat Thomas Downey are illustrative of typical attempts by vested interests to politicize the budgetary process. Both Darden and Downey made heroic attempts to save weapons systems vital to their constituents. In terms of outcome, the efforts of Downey were more successful than those of Darden, yet both managed to increase their popularity through their efforts to save weapons systems which were important to the economic bases of constituents. Actions of both congressional representatives reflect how politics intrudes into the sometimes technical domain of weapons procurement. In 1987, Darden made an impassioned floor speech in support of the Lockheed-built C-5 military transport plane. The air force ultimately was successful in replacing the C-5 (built in Darden's district of Marietta, Georgia) with the C-17 to be built by McDonnell Douglas in California. Marietta, Georgia, lost approximately 10,000 to 20,000 employees at the Lockheed plant. However, Darden was rewarded at the polls for his defense of the C-5. In the next (1988) election, he received 65 percent of the vote in a district overwhelmingly carried by Republican presidential candidate, George Bush. Darden had been regarded by Republicans as vulnerable in his two previous elections (1984 and 1986).

Similarly, Thomas Downey was at the forefront of the 1989 fight to avoid cancellation of the F-14 fighter airplane produced by Long Island's largest single employer, Grumman. Downey and other New Yorkers in Congress were successful in securing funding for eighteen new F-14 aircraft. The limited victory gave Grumman three additional years before they had to shut down production lines. Downey's popularity soared as a result of his efforts, and he was lionized in the Long Island media for his defense of local interests (*Congressional Quarterly*, 1990a). Subsequently, Downey and other New York delegates were able to further extend promises of government funding for the F-14, an aircraft that had been slated for termination.

The alternative concerns can be illustrated. The Bush administration advocated eliminating expensive weapons systems. Congress, led by then chair of the House Armed Services Committee, and later secretary of defense in the Clinton administration, Les Aspin, proposed shifting procurement funds from existing hardware into future research and development. The congressional plan also would keep more funding in existing weapons systems as well as maintain higher force levels for the National Guard and reserves. It would cut funding for projects such as stealth technology and (SDI) strategic defense initiatives, programs long advocated by the Reagan and Bush administrations.

Political feasibility appeared to support the congressional determination to maintain the status quo, or something as close to it as possible. In a key 1991 vote, more than 20 percent of the House Republicans, many from districts negatively impacted by the cut-back plans, including representatives from New York, Pennsylvania, and Texas, voted with Democrats to avoid basic changes in direction or funding for defense programs (*Congressional Quarterly*, 1991b).

Base closings proved to be another contentious political issue associated with the defense budget. The Congress rejected the initial list of bases to be closed. As proposed by a Republican administration, the vast majority of bases to be terminated were located in districts represented by Democratic legislators. Subsequently, a new procedure was established in an attempt to achieve greater political neutrality that carried over into the Clinton administration.

A list of base closings was drawn up by the military and reviewed by a special commission headed by former New Jersey Representative James Courter. In order to reduce the role of politics in the decision-making process, the list was to be accepted or rejected as a package by Congress. Politics undoubtedly played a role in the decision-making process since the 377 bases slated for cuts were concentrated in 209 congressional districts. Assuming that all representatives voted parochial interests, the plan still established a working majority of votes in the 435 congressional districts.

Political sentiment for shifting the burden of defense to other nations also grew in the early 1990s. Representatives such as Patricia Schroeder of Colorado, Byron Dorgan of North Dakota, and Charles Schumer of New York called for U. S. allies to pay a larger share of defense costs. House members contended that the need for the U. S. dominance of Western defense spending was a relic of an earlier era. They argued that nations such as Japan and Germany no longer needed the U. S. defense subsidy. These nations have surpassed the United States in various indicators of economic growth, productivity, and prosperity. Schumer maintained that U. S. tax money should be spent at home before it is spent protecting relatively prosperous nations such as Japan and Germany:

> Every dollar that we spend on a troop in Japan is not spent educating our children, on building our infrastructure or improving the health of our citizens or improving the kind of factories that we have. (*Congressional Quarterly*, 1991b)

Shifting U. S. tax money away from the defense of Europe and Japan and forcing other nations to pay a larger share of the costs has obvious political advantages. ''Wealthy allies'' who do not share in the costs of defending freedom are a convenient scapegoat for the inability of the United States to pay for politically desirable but militarily useless bases or expensive new weapons systems.

The political debate over the size of the defense budget appears to have been won by the advocates of downsizing. Recent budgets represent real reductions in defense spending and a sensitivity to the new political realities. As the size of the total defense budget shrinks, it is expected that the debate over the distribution of the budget will intensify. The distributional debate focuses on protecting established bases and production lines (status quo) versus investing in exotic new technologies. Resolution of this political debate will to a large extent determine defense spending priorities.

It is contended in this chapter that both external international forces and internal political factors will exert pressures on the allocation of scarce resources. The dissolution of the empire and poor levels of economic growth in the Soviet Union reflect an alteration from the old Cold War environment. As previously stated, however, exogenous factors are filtered through the highly politicized context of domestic politics. How political conflict between interest groups in the American pluralistic setting is resolved should therefore largely determine budgetary outcomes. A number of outcomes are possible. Three scenarios have been chosen for detailed discussion.

Alternative Budgetary Scenarios

The end to the Cold War lends itself to ''arm chair quarterbacking'' as analysts try to predict the future. A strong case can be made for reducing defense expenditures, given the new realities of the post–Cold War era. The wisdom of investing massive research and engineering time into "cutting edge" defense hardware is questionable. Billions of dollars can be spent developing military technologies that will only be stolen or diffused throughout the world community through, for example, scientific conferences. Since monopoly ownership of technological advances in weaponry is not guaranteed in perpetuity, the danger of propelling a wasteful and unnecessary arms race exists if the United States rushes to implement new generations of weapons. Analysts maintain that money saved from the military budget could be used for more pressing domestic needs, which include: deficit reduction, social equity, and economic competitiveness.

Deficit Reduction

The assumption that a sizable "peace dividend" will be redistributed to a list of worthy programs remains somewhat tenuous. It is possible that the "peace dividend" will be much smaller than projected. Political considerations may preclude sustained cuts in defense spending. Defense overruns on expensive technologies, "discovery" of new threats, or efforts of local representatives to save jobs are the likely candidates to attempt to negate projected defense savings. If significant defense savings actually are realized, they may not be directed to other programs but may be utilized for deficit reduction.

Targeting defense savings to the deficit appeals to many analysts who are fearful of the long-term effects of the size of the government debt. Economists cite a number of reasons to be wary of budget deficits. One such negative effect is the potential for inflation. The experience of Germany in the period following World War I suggests that excessive debt can lead to currency debasement. Borrower nations benefit if loans are repaid through the printing of money. Another effect of deficit spending is that of "crowding out." Since deficits increase the demand for available funds (savings), deficits will tend to drive up interest rates. Increases in interest rates will have a negative effect on the economy through downward pressure on purchases of large ticket goods such as automobiles and housing. Budget deficits if they attract foreign money (as they have in the United States) will also tend to enhance the value of the dollar, which will have the effect of reducing the demand for U.S. exports. Budget deficits also exacerbate income inequities in that tax dollars taken from middle- and working-class families pay the net interest that is transferred to upper-income bondholders. Finally, external debt (not owed to American citizens) can be injurious to the health of the American economy since wealth is transferred away from the taxing reach of the U.S. government (Koven, 1991, 18).

A growing sentiment exists that deficits have contributed to the evisceration of the American tradition of an upwardly mobile society. Donald Kettl (1992) contends that it is probably an exaggeration to suggest that an eroding

TABLE 13.3

Trends in Federal Debt Held by the Public (dollars in billions)

Year	Current Dollars	1982 Dollars	Debt as Percent of GNP	Interest as Percent of Outlays
1980	709	837	26.6	10.6
1981	785	842	26.3	12.0
1982	919	919	29.3	13.6
1983	1,131	1,085	34.0	13.8
1984	1,300	1,202	35.3	15.7
1985	1,499	1,344	37.9	16.2
1986	1,734	1,516	41.5	16.1
1987	1,888	1,600	42.7	16.0
1988	2,050	1,686	42.9	16.2
1989	2,190	1,728	42.7	16.5
1990	2,410	1,829	44.6	16.2

Source: *Budget of the U.S. Government, 1991*, p. 218.

standard of living and declining wages directly stem from deficits, yet deficits are said to be a major contributor to economic problems. Kettl maintains that:

> Curing the problems, furthermore, is impossible without higher national savings, and increasing savings is very difficult when the deficit is high. The overwhelming consensus of economists and financial analysts is that persistent deficits of the size the federal government ran in the 1980s are dangerous, perhaps not in the next few years but certainly in the next century and for the coming generation. (1992, 35)

The high level of deficit spending in the United States suggests that the public sector has not been successful in putting its economic house in order. Table 13.3 describes total federal debt between 1980 and 1990. The data indicate that total federal debt held by the public has more than tripled since 1980. Debt as a percent of gross national product also grew from 26.6 percent in 1980 to 48.4 percent in 1990. Interest as a percent of total outlays grew from 10.6 percent in 1980 to 16.2 percent in 1990. Especially troubling to economists is the large growth of debt relative to the growth of gross national product. This phenomenon indicates that debt comprises a growing burden on the economy.

An inability to balance the federal budget will have negative repercussions on the health of the American economy. The repercussions will arise from the negative externalities of deficits such as higher interest rates, "crowding out" of private borrowers, redistribution of wealth, and transferring money out of the country. A number of analysts have directly placed blame on the Pentagon for deficits which are said to have contributed to systemic economic problems such as high interest rates, which in turn have buoyed the dollar and propelled large trade deficits. Political scientist David Calleo traced the roots of America's budget deficit to the Kennedy and Johnson administrations (Kapstein, 1992, 44). Deficits accelerated significantly during the Reagan and Bush periods.

The Bush administration attributed the deficit it encountered to the troubles of the banking community and thrift industry and the recession. The administration, however, projected that a small surplus could be generated by 1996. This would result from resolution of the thrift crisis, economic expansion, and spending constraints instituted by the Omnibus Budget Reconciliation Act of 1990 (*Budget of the U.S. Government, 1991*, 284). In the past, however, "rosy scenarios" such as these have not come to fruition. Most recently, the Omnibus Budget Reconciliation Act of 1990 was purported to be the "solution" which would close the gap between revenues and expenditures. The persistence of deficits nevertheless prevailed. The durability of deficits suggests that politicians lack the will to either cut spending or increase taxes necessary to balance the federal budget. The first major battle of the Clinton administration, won narrowly in both houses of the Congress, was to provide for some tax increases with the additional funds to be directed to debt reduction.

The Clinton budget, which was passed by Congress in August of 1993, purported to reduce the deficit by an estimated $469 billion over a period of five years. This would be accomplished by almost $241 billion in additional taxes and $255 billion in spending cuts.

Social Equity

A second scenario could be the shifting of spending from defense-related priorities to social welfare programs. The viability of this type of reprioritization, however, is highly dependent upon political factors which act as an intervening variable in the interpretation of budgetary needs.

This type of "fairness" is a relative thing. To date, it has included imposing restrictions on entitlements received by upper-income recipients and measures aimed at controlling the amount of payments to "non-needy" recipients. These include reducing farm subsidies to individuals with high levels of nonfarm income, reducing Medicare subsidies for individuals with high incomes, and restructuring higher education assistance and school lunch subsidies to better target the needy.

The intent of George Bush's "fairness" measures did not deal with "safety net" issues of protecting the bottom strata of society. Rather, the intent was to limit the amount of tax money being transferred from working people through taxes to higher income recipients of entitlement programs. The 1992 budget estimates projected that reductions in mandatory entitlement programs (from cuts to higher income recipients) would amount to $47 billion over a five-year period. The $47 billion savings were in addition to the $100 billion reduction (over five years) enacted in the Omnibus Reconciliation Act of 1990 (*Budget of the U.S. Government, 1991*, 13).

"Fairness" in taxation is also a volatile political issue, as the efforts to enact Clinton's first tax bill showed. The tax revolt of California's Proposition 13 reflected popular discontent with property tax rates. The rhetoric of supply-side economics, the dominant economic ideology of the Reagan years, suggested that progressive income taxes were counterproductive in that they constrained economic growth. It was contended that investment and risk taking would be impaired by such an "unfair" system.

Some of these assumptions can be examined. An analysis of federal revenues between 1980 and 1990 indicates that only some of the economic goals of the Reagan administration were achieved. Total revenues (as a percent of gross national product) declined from a high of 20.1 percent in 1981 to a low of 18.1 percent in 1984, rising to 19.2 percent in 1988 (Koven, 1991). Expenditures, however, were not checked by the Reagan administration. The growth of expenditures, therefore, is given credit for producing the high levels of deficits and total debt that plague the nation today.

"Success" was achieved in the 1980s in terms of redistributing the burden of taxation. Tax breaks aimed at corporations and higher income individuals produced a noticeable effect. The impact of shifting the burden of taxation away from income taxes toward Social Security taxes is shown in table 13.4.

TABLE 13.4

Government Revenue by Source, 1980 and 1990 (in billions of dollars)

Source	1980	1990	Dollar Change	Percent Change
Individual income taxes	244	467	223	91
Corporate income taxes	65	94	29	45
Social Security insurance taxes and contributions	161	380	219	136
Excise taxes	24	35	9	38
Estate and gift taxes	6	12	6	100
Customs duties	7	17	10	142
Miscellaneous	13	27	14	108
Total Receipts	520	1,031	511	98

Source: *Budget of the U.S. Government, 1982, 1992*.

It is apparent that some shifting in the distribution of the tax burden occurred between 1980 and 1990. Growth of the regressive Social Security payroll tax outpaced growth in the other two major sources of taxation, corporate and individual income taxes. Social insurance contributions increased by 136 percent in the decade of the 1980s, while individual income tax receipts and corporate income tax receipts grew by 91 and 45 percent, respectively.

Personal income taxes as a proportion of total receipts also declined (from 47 percent to 45 percent) in the decade of the 1980s. Corporate income taxes declined from 13 percent of total receipt to 9 percent, while social insurance contributions (payroll taxes) increased their relative share of total receipts from 31 percent to 37 percent. Such a reprioritization away from the more progressive forms of income taxation toward the more regressive payroll taxes is consistent with Reaganite supply-side philosophies of providing greater incentives to investors. The payroll tax is perceived to be regressive since it is not levied on income above a certain level. Higher income earners, as a result, are taxed a smaller percentage of their income. Lowering income taxes and shifting the burden of taxation to payroll taxes benefits upper income groups.

Kevin Phillips (1990) documented the shift in tax burden that occurred after 1977. According to Phillips, the *proportion* of taxes paid by wealthy increased yet their tax *burden* decreased. This is explained by the sharp rise in incomes of upper-bracket groups relative to other groups:

> Families below the top decile, disproportionately burdened by Social Security and excise increases and rewarded less by any income tax reductions, wound up paying higher effective rates. The richest families, meanwhile, paid lower rates, largely because of the sharp reduction applicable to nonsalary income (capital gains, interest, dividends and rents. (1990, 82)

It is evident that tax policies contributed to the redistribution of income toward upper income groups, as was advocated by proponents of supply-side economics. A review of spending priorities also is instructive in terms of understanding "fairness." Table 13.5 describes growth of spending in nineteen expenditure categories of the federal budget.

Spending increases in national defense ($163 billion), Social Security ($132 billion), net interest ($119 billion), Medicare ($63 billion), as well as commerce and housing credit ($59 billion) accounted for much of the $672 billion increase in expenditures between 1980 and 1990. The large increase in commerce and housing credit expenditures is largely attributed to the $46.5 billion outlay in 1990 for the Resolution Trust Corporation. The bailout of the thrift industry, however, was perceived by the Bush administration to be a temporary phenomenon. Whether or not pledges to maintain the integrity of the thrift and bank industries turn into larger expenditures depends to a great

TABLE 13.5

Budget Outlays by Function, 1980 and 1990 (in billions of dollars)

Function	1980 (actual)	1990 (actual)	Dollar Change	Percent Change
National defense	136	299	163	120
International affairs	11	14	3	27
General science, space and technology	6	14	8	133
Energy	6	2	(4)	(67)
Natural resources and environment	14	17	3	21
Agriculture	5	12	7	140
Commerce and housing credit	8	67	59	738
Transportation	21	30	9	43
Community and regional development	10	9	(1)	(10)
Education, training, employment, and social services	31	39	8	26
Health	23	58	35	152
Medicare	35	98	63	180
Income security	76	147	71	93
Social Security	117	249	132	113
Veterans benefits	21	29	8	38

extent on factors such as the health of the real estate market and the overall vibrancy of the American economy.

Growth of spending diverged greatly between functional categories. A number of functions grew at a slow pace in the 1980s, while some such as energy and community and regional development declined in actual dollars. Categories of spending which grew in the 1980s at a much slower rate than the national average of 116 percent included: international affairs (27 percent), natural resources and environment (21 percent), transportation (43 percent), education, training, employment and social services (26 percent), and veterans' benefits (38 percent). It is apparent that categories of spending targeted to lower income groups (such as community and regional development) did not grow as robustly as categories of spending linked to "middle-class" entitlements or "mandatories" such as net interest.

Lobbying efforts on the part of the elderly no doubt influenced decisions on the part of congressional representatives to continue robust funding of Social Security and Medicare programs. The rescission of the 1989 catastrophic-care legislation (providing for higher payments from higher income elderly) is indicative of the difficulty in trying to instill "fairness" in powerful voting groups in American society.

Fairness certainly became an issue as the decade of the 1980s ended, but by no means was it the only issue of concern. Phillips (1990, 221) claimed that dangers posed by "greed and insufficient concern for America as a community went beyond the issue of fairness and, by threatening the ability of the United States to maintain its economic position in the world, created an unusual meeting ground for national self-interest and reform." The concern over American economic competitiveness is real and represents a third alternative in terms of budget reprioritization.

Economic Competitiveness

A corollary to the decline of the Soviet Union was the perception that the economic health of the United States was being threatened by rivals such as Japan and Germany. In light of the current attention paid to American competitiveness and the relative decline in the American standard of living, it is conceivable that the vacuum left by the decline of the Soviet Union will quickly be replaced by the bogeyman of Japan as a threat to American prosperity. In such a scenario, defense policy spending is replaced by "industrial policy" spending, connoting some sort of partnership between government and business allied in an effort to preserve American prosperity.[1] From this perspective, the end of the Cold War era did not arrive with Soviet cooperation in the Persian Gulf war or with the fall of the Berlin Wall but will end when events such as the growing market share of Toyotas and the purchase of Rockefeller Center by Japanese investors become the true focus of attention.

For the World War II generation, acceptance of Japan and Germany as "new enemies" may be less problematic than for the Cold War generation. Unlike the Soviet Union, neither Japan nor Germany represents ideologies antagonistic to capitalism. American anxieties do not seem to be a reflection of fundamentally different mind sets but rather seem to reflect the view that the United States is less able to compete and succeed in the world marketplace.

Industrial policy appears to spring from the perspective that the United States is losing or has lost comparative advantages in a number of key industries. Industrial policy is a response to the observation that American leadership in major industries such as steel, autos, electronics, and microprocessors has eroded. An expanded role for government in the private sector, however, is antithetical to the laissez-faire philosophy expounded, at least rhetorically, by the Reagan administration. American industries nevertheless are likely to call for government action if it becomes increasingly apparent that they are unable to compete against foreign competitors.

American devotion to the philosophy of laissez-faire is a major impediment to creating an industrial policy. Detractors of industrial policy claim that political allocation of resources will be less efficient than market forces. Supporters of government intervention, however, make the case that as American competitiveness lags, as the economy falters, and as dependence on foreign capital grows, the case against laissez-faire philosophies grows stronger. One such supporter of intervention stated:

> Today American public philosophy is at one of its periodic great divides. We can pursue the laissez-faire solution: balance the federal budget, continue the process of reducing taxes and regulatory constraints on business, and continue to try to sell this philosophy to the rest of the world. We can continue lowering wages paid to American workers, to compete on the basis of cheap labor because we no longer compete by working smarter. We can continue to pretend that other countries don't intervene in their markets, that there is no effective difference between Japanese, U. S., and European industries. If we follow that route, we will gradually become a poorer and less affluent country. Or we can get on with the great challenge of building institutions that reconcile a dynamic private economy with a decent and viable society. (Kuttner, 1991, 287)

Conclusions

The end of the Cold War calls for a period of both retrospection and introspection. Certainly the Cold War exacted costs and demanded sacrifice. Wars in Korea and Vietnam demanded the ultimate sacrifice of many and remain as vivid reminders of the costs of war. As a combat veteran of the war in Vietnam, I am especially sensitive to the human costs exacted during the Cold War era. Friends and families of people whose names appear on the wall at the Vietnam Memorial in Washington, D. C., appear now to have the right to ask what the fruits of victory will be. Was the outcome worth the costs? Can families reconcile the sacrifice of loved ones lost in one manner or another? Is there truth to the aphorism that the Cold War is over and the winners were the Japanese and Germans? The motivations for the Cold War may remain an enigma, yet the outlines of future choices are beginning to crystalize.

The budgetary issue of the post–Cold War era ultimately is subsumed under the broader issue of forging a new direction for the nation now that the Cold War has been laid to rest. Alternative reactions are possible. As with the end of World War I, a return to "normalcy," greater isolation, and detachment from external problems of the world may be forthcoming. The perceived fall of the enemy would in this scenario call for a period of calm and contentment. Improvements in communication, transportation, and protection of American interests, however, may act to counter isolationist desires.

A number of budget scenarios have been discussed. One alternative focuses upon the opportunity to shift defense savings to social needs. Domestic problems of poverty, education, health care, the environment, crime, and drugs are deserving of attention. The issue of social equity was ignored in the Reagan era, while income inequalities grew. From a budgetary perspective, much of the massive defense buildup of the 1980s came at the expense of programs aimed at the needy. This group also bore a disproportionate share of the fighting in Vietnam. Values of justice and equity would suggest that the time to reprioritize attention in support of the needy may have arrived with the end of the Cold War. As previously stated, however, budgeting is largely defined by the political environment, and the poor are less able to project political influence than other groups. The new era may assist the poor only in the sense that they have the opportunity in a free nation to prosper in a free market system that they defended.

In a second scenario, "competitiveness" or economic nationalism may replace the expansion of Communist influence as a focus of American concern. Recession or slow recovery will exacerbate concerns over "level playing fields" and the ability of American producers to sell high value-added products. Protectionism and/or government-business cooperation may be promoted as economic policies in the post–Cold War era.

"Industrial policy" focusing upon American competitiveness also presents an opportunity for ambitious politicians seeking greater influence. Politicians may attempt to focus economic discontent on foreign nations who are perceived to be "unfair" competitors to the United States. "Scapegoating" of other nations can be appealing to populist politicians who attempt to mobilize alarm over the relative decline of American economic power. In such a scenario, the post–Cold War era may be marked by greater spending on developing linkages between business and government in order to enhance U. S. competitiveness.

Finally, it is conceivable that reduced defense spending will be employed in order to reduce deficits. Such a strategy can be interpreted as both prudent and economically advantageous. Deficits are debilitating if allowed to grow unchecked. Deficit growth in excess of growth in gross national product may limit investment in plants and equipment, which in turn acts to constrain productivity and reduce standards of living. Deficits also can transfer wealth from the United States if large proportions of the national debt are owned by foreign creditors.

The end of the Cold War ostensibly marks a triumph for freedom, democracy, and capitalism over the "evil empire," or totalitarian, Communist rule. Questions remain, however, as to future directions for the nation and the value of past sacrifices. If November 9, 1990, represented the fall of communism, then one cannot avoid asking questions such as: What are the spoils of victory? What are the future challenges to be confronted? And, How shall the nation's scarce resources be allocated to meet those challenges?

This chapter has attempted to raise fundamental questions as well as suggest future scenarios. It is contended that exogenous influences as well as internal political forces will shape future American budget priorities. The "spin" that issues take and the success of politicians in exploiting issues will, in all likelihood, determine which of numerous budgetary scenarios is likely to prevail. In retrospect, one can say that the end of the Cold War did not come about swiftly in a climax from storming the barricades, it came about incrementally after forty-five years of conflict. The implications of the end of the Cold War remain uncertain but will be defined in the immediate future.

NOTE

1. See Richard D. Bingham, ''NIP in the Nineties: Post–Cold War National Industrial Policy,'' in this volume.

Post–Cold War Social Welfare Policy: Limited Options

GREGORY R. WEIHER

Has the end of the Cold War had any direct implication for social welfare policy? This chapter will argue that it has not. At various times, the Cold War consumed resources that might otherwise have been used for social welfare programs. So, toward the end of the Johnson administration, the Cold-War-become-Hot-War—Vietnam—became so expensive that presidential support for social welfare programs diminished; and, at the beginning of the Reagan administration, a very conscious decision was made to fund defense at the expense of social welfare.

The natural expectation is that, should the end of the Cold War have any impact on social policy, it will be in the form of a "peace dividend"—in the one–super-power world. Reduced defense funding should free resources for social welfare programs. The peace dividend, however, appears illusory. The federal government is hemmed in by a staggering deficit, growing international uncertainties, a flock of serious domestic problems, and a nagging recession. Its policy options are limited by scarce resources as the number of challenges it faces grows. Since a peace dividend is unlikely to materialize, the title of this chapter is of mostly chronological, not analytical, significance.

The important influences on social welfare policy are, for the greater part, of older vintage than the end of the Cold War. The parameters of policy were set during the first year of the Reagan administration and reinforced by secular economic trends and policy developments. Perhaps the most important single determinant of present and future policy was the 1981 Omnibus Budget

Reconciliation Act (OBRA). Long-term and short-term shifts in the economy have increased the economic fragility of those in lower income and wealth brackets at the same time that they have restricted the resources available to federal and state governments. The result is an unpalatable combination of circumstances—a growing economically vulnerable population and a government with very few social welfare policy options.

These straitened circumstances come at a time when social welfare policy innovation may be most required. The great majority of future entrants into the labor market will be immigrants, members of minority groups, and women. Furthermore, the nature of international economic competition dictates that national productivity and standards of living will depend not upon our elite colleges but upon the acquisition of human capital by the bottom 50 percent of the work force. The United States has been least able to augment the human capital of these very groups from which most new workers will come.

This chapter begins with a summary of developments in the eighties which have influenced current social welfare programs. Next is a review of recent figures on poverty as well as other data which reveal the economic vulnerability of a large portion of the American public. The current policy status of the American states, which have become increasingly responsible for program design, delivery of services, and social welfare financing, is then discussed. Finally, there is a discussion of the need for renewed attention to social welfare policy based upon its confluence with human capital investment policy in the nineties.

The Omnibus Budget Reconciliation Act

In their very useful reader on Reagan administration policy initiatives, Palmer and Sawhill (1984) offer the following summary:

> First, the tax cuts and the defense buildup took precedence over balancing the budget. Second, reducing inflation took precedence over moderating the recession.
>
> Third, it turned out that there was not enough fat in the domestic side of the federal budget to avoid reducing benefits and services. The deepest cuts were proposed for grants to state and local governments and for programs serving the poor. Little was done to reduce rapidly rising expenditures for Social Security, Medicare, government employee pensions, and other predominantly middle-class programs that have been the chief source of growth in the federal budget since the 1950s.
>
> Fourth, the tax cuts were designed with economic growth not equity in mind. . . . Consequently, rates were cut across the board, providing the greatest benefits to higher-income families.

The budget strategies of the Reagan administration have been discussed in detail elsewhere (Palmer and Sawhill, 1984; Phillips, 1990). Nevertheless, certain of the provisions of OBRA explain a great deal of the current situation in social welfare policy. The enduring consequences of OBRA have been:

- A diversion of resources away from social welfare purposes at the federal and state levels.[1]
- The creation of an immense, intractable budget deficit with substantial debt-maintenance requirements.
- A de facto devolution of social welfare policy-making and funding responsibilities to the American states.

Reduced Commitment to Social Welfare

Bawden and Palmer (1984) judged that Reagan administration cuts would result in social welfare expenditures in 1985 that were about 10 percent less than they otherwise would have been. This reduction was half what President Reagan originally requested. The average, of course, hides much larger expenditure cuts in particular programs. For instance, Unemployment Insurance was cut by 17.4 percent; Aid to Families with Dependent Children (AFDC) was cut by 14.3 percent; the Food Stamp program was cut by 13.8 percent; Child Nutrition expenditures were cut by 28 percent; Housing Assistance was cut by 11.4 percent, representing a halt of funding for any new housing construction; the Social Services Block Grant was cut 23.5 percent; the Community Services Block Grant was cut 37.1 percent; General Employment and Training expenditures were cut 38.6 percent; Public Service Employment was eliminated; and the Work Incentive Program (WIN) was cut 35.1 percent.

The chief means by which the Reagan administration reduced social welfare expenditures was by reducing the number of people eligible for welfare programs (Bawden and Palmer, 1984). A principal group targeted for removal from the welfare rolls was the "working poor," or "near poor." Prior to the passage of OBRA, AFDC recipients benefitted from the "thirty and one-third rule," which provided that they could keep some portion of earned income without losing comparable benefit amounts. OBRA reduced to four months out of the year the time during which the thirty-and-one-third benefit could be claimed. It also required that the value of food stamps as well as housing allowances be counted as income for purposes of means-testing. Palmer and Sawhill report that reducing eligibility for AFDC in this fashion caused 400,000 to 500,000 families to be removed from the rolls and resulted in reduced AFDC benefits for another 300,000 families (1984, 364). These reductions had repercussions for other welfare programs. For instance, Medicaid eligibility was often awarded with eligibility for AFDC; the loss of the latter meant a loss of Medicaid coverage also.

The Deficit

OBRA budgetary decisions resulted in an unprecedented growth of the federal deficit. Though spending for intergovernmental and welfare programs was greatly reduced, spending for defense increased. Real defense spending increased by 7 percent per year and increased from 26 percent of federal spending to 32 percent when President Reagan took office. Federal spending as a share of GNP increased from 23.5 percent in 1981, Reagan's first year, to 24.1 percent in 1985 (Palmer and Sawhill, 1984, 9). Concomitant with these budget shifts was an overall cut in federal taxes.

Because of their greater concern for inflation than for the possibility of a recession (Palmer and Sawhill, 1984; Sawhill and Stone, 1984), the Reagan administration and the Federal Reserve followed a policy of fiscal conservatism. This policy produced the recession of 1981–82, which, because of reduced revenues and greater demand for social welfare services, contributed to the federal deficit.

The combined result of these budgetary and fiscal policies was little moderation in federal expenditure and a substantial reduction in federal revenue. In the first four years of the Reagan administration, the total deficit reached unprecedented size, nearly doubling from $800 billion to $1.5 trillion. Though there have been subsequent attempts to pare away this record deficit, none have been successful.[2] In 1991, the federal budget deficit was $268.7 billion. The 1992 projection was $350 to $400 billion ("Budget Outlook," 1992; Pianin, 1992). The total federal deficit for 1990 (estimated) was $3.11 trillion. The annual service on this debt is $186 billion—almost 17 percent of total federal government expenditures (U.S. Bureau of Economic Analysis, 1991, 13).

Reductions in Intergovernmental Transfers

The Reagan administration had a philosophical commitment to reforming intergovernmental relations in the United States. One priority was the devolution of government programs from the federal level to the states and localities, thereby shifting responsibility to units more accessible to citizens. A second priority was to "clarify" intergovernmental relations, making some programs clearly the responsibility of national government, while other responsibilities would be firmly lodged with the states. A third priority was to eliminate the federal impetus for program growth at the state level. Reagan felt that state policy agendas were distorted, including programs that would not exist if they were not propped up by federal money.

Formal devolution of programs, under which the states would have been responsible for food stamps and AFDC and the federal government would have taken over Medicaid, found no support among the states (G. Peterson, 1984). There was considerable *informal* devolution of responsibilties to the states, however. The result was greater freedom and greater responsibility for state policymakers.

Informal devolution was accomplished by reducing intergovernmental transfers. States were presented with greater policy latitude once the lure of federal dollars was withdrawn and were free to continue endangered programs out of their own funds, and hence to change them as they saw fit. The abdication of the federal government from certain state policy areas left the field open to the states; they had only to find their own sources of funding.

Intergovernmental programs were among those most deeply cut in 1981. Transfers to state and local governments were reduced by 13.1 percent from the levels that would have prevailed had no cuts been imposed (G. Peterson, 1984). The heaviest cuts were sustained in direct grants to local and state governments, as opposed to grants such as Medicaid which go to individuals. From 1978 to 1983, federal grants to governments were reduced by 36.3 percent in constant dollars (G. Peterson, 1984). As a percentage of the total federal budget, intergovernmental grants declined by 32.8 percent over the same period (G. Peterson, 1984). Where outright cuts were not imposed, Reagan sought to limit state expenditures by reducing the federal match. In some cases, caps were placed on federal funds available for matching, while in others the ratio of federal to state dollars was reduced (G. Peterson, 1984).

Additionally, the Reagan administration lifted a number of requirements and simplified the grant structure, providing more policy-making latitude to the states. Seventy-six categorical grants were consolidated into block grants. Furthermore, many of the federal standards for programs funded by the new block grants were relaxed, allowing the states to choose cheaper alternatives (G. Peterson, 1984). Of particular interest in this area was the provision that states could enroll AFDC recipients in a work program in return for their benefits (Schiller and Brasher, 1990: G. Peterson, 1984).

During the eighties, the relative social welfare (SW) burden of the states has increased (table 14.1). State and local social welfare expenditures have grown as a percentage of GNP, while the federal percentage has declined. The same is true of relative percentages of total government SW spending, with the state and local percentage increasing from 38.5 percent to 40.9 percent.

Informal devolution to the states of policy implementation and funding responsibilities has had the net effect of making them more important policy actors. With the withdrawal of the carrot—federal funding—and the stick—federal regulation—the states have become freer to explore their policy options (Bowman and Kearney, 1986). In some areas, such as economic development, states have become quite active (Bowman and Kearney, 1986). Social welfare policy is another area of considerable state innovation. Indeed, much of the Family Support Act of 1988 is modeled on existing programs in the states.

TABLE 14.1

Social Welfare Expenditures

	Percent of Expenditures		Percent of GNP	
	Federal	State/Local	Federal	State/Local
1980	61.5	38.5	11.2	7.1
1985	61.4	38.6	11.4	7.2
1987	59.5	40.4	11.2	7.6
1988	59.1	40.9	10.9	7.6

Source: U.S. Bureau of the Census, *Statistical Abstract of the United States, 1991*, 111th ed. (Washington, D.C.: U.S. Government Printing Office, 1991).

As a result, however, the slack in state resources has been eliminated. Many states reacted to reductions in social welfare expenditures and federal transfers by increasing their own funding of programs (G. Peterson, 1984). In ensuing years, states have had to meet additional demands upon their resources in areas such as corrections and education. Funding of Medicare alone has exerted tremendous pressure on state budgets (Lemov, 1991). Collectively, these circumstances have meant that state revenue systems were already under considerable strain heading into the recession of the early nineties.

The Poor and Near-Poor: Current Circumstances

The eighties were not kind to those near the bottom of the income distribution in the United States. The recession of 1981–82 combined with reductions in welfare expenditures sent the poverty rate to over 15 percent of the population—the highest level since the mid-sixties (table 14.2). In the early 1980s, the pretransfer poverty rate approached 20 percent, its highest observed level (Sawhill, 1988). Although the recession gave way to the longest sustained expansion of the U.S. economy, the relief for poor Americans was only partial—the poverty rate remained a couple of points higher through the decade than it had been in the seventies. In 1990, the official poverty rate was 13.5 percent (Social Security Administration, 1991). American children have been at particular risk in this period (Edelman, 1991). One in five American children (20.5 percent) now lives in poverty (Social Security Administration, 1991, 121).

Part of this increase in poverty is certainly due to the Reagan administration policy initiatives discussed previously. As might be expected, reduced social welfare expenditure results in fewer people being lifted above the official poverty line. Indeed, the effectiveness of the U.S. social welfare system in lifting citizens out of poverty, never great in comparison to the systems of comparable nations, decreased markedly in the 1980s (Smeeding, 1992; Cutler and Katz, 1992).

The official poverty rate alone does not adequately portray the magnitude of the income shift that occurred during the eighties. A separate but related issue is earnings/income inequality. Fluctuations in the official poverty rate should be evaluated in the context of these developments.

There has been a long-term trend of increasing inequality in the distribution of income and wealth in the United States. This trend has been noted for the eighties (Phillips, 1990), but can also be traced through a considerable preceding period (Thurow, 1980; Ryscavage and Henle, 1990; W. Peterson, 1991; Sawhill, 1988; Cutler and Katz, 1992). Prior to the eighties, this increase was glacial. Furthermore, its effects were cushioned by increases in transfers to low-income Americans (Thurow, 1980; Sawhill, 1988). In the eighties the increase in income inequality accelerated, however (Ryscavage and Henle, 1990; W. Peterson, 1991).

The increase in income for those at the top of the distribution was dramatic—the top 1 percent enjoyed an increase of 49.8 percent in income, while the income of the top 5 percent increased by 23.4 percent from 1977 to 1988. As the top 10 percent of families saw their incomes increase by 16.5 percent, however, the bottom 10 percent suffered a decrease of 14.8 percent. Fully 80 percent of families experienced decreased income. Only the top 20 percent saw their incomes increase (W. Peterson, 1991).

Perhaps the most frequently cited cause of the decline in income for most households is the shift in the U.S. economy away from manufacturing and toward the provision of services. Service sector jobs, on average, are less well-paid than manufacturing jobs (Ryscavage and Henle, 1990). The types of ser-

TABLE 14.2

Official Poverty Rate by Year

Year	Number (in millions)	Percent
1959	39.5	22.4
1970	25.3	12.6
1975	25.9	12.3
1980	29.3	13.0
1985	33.1	14.0
1988	31.7	13.0
1989	31.5	12.8
1990	33.6	13.5

Source: Social Security Administration, *Social Security Bulletin: Annual Statistical Supplement, 1991* (Washington, D.C.: U.S. Government Printing Office, 1991).

vice jobs that laid-off factory workers are likely to find—in retail trade, for instance—are particularly poorly paid. Most newly created jobs in the United States are in the service sector (Plunkert, 1990). Over half of the new jobs created in the 1980s (50.4 percent) paid annual wages below the poverty level (W. Peterson, 1991). This trend has prompted Schwarz (1990) to note that hard work at a steady job (if one can be found) is no longer a guarantee of economic security.

Poverty was a greater problem in the 1980s than it was in the late 1960s and 1970s. But the official poverty rate occurs in a context of growing economic vulnerability for Americans in low and moderate income brackets. Good jobs—ones which pay nonpoverty wages and provide benefits—are harder to find. The jobs which are being created are so poorly paid that those who take them are in a perpetual state of economic marginality. A comfortable standard of living is available only to those who are on the opposite side of a widening income chasm.[3]

Lagging Productivity

As one observer notes, "productivity is the key to an improved standard of material life—if there is any single proposition upon which all economists can agree, this is probably it" (W. Peterson, 1991). Productivity generates economic surpluses, and from such surpluses the transfers that comprise social welfare programs must be taken.

The United States enjoyed healthy gains in productivity in the post–World War II period up to the early seventies. At that point, however, growth in productivity nearly halted (Packer, 1991; W. Peterson, 1991; Thurow, 1980). Between 1948 and 1973, U.S. economic productivity increased at the rate of 2.51 percent per year. Since that time productivity increases have hovered around 1 percent, dipping to about 0.83 percent through the recession of 1981–82 and rebounding slightly to 1.28 percent afterward.

Such productivity increases do not support a very rapid increase in the standard of living. They are even more troubling when compared to the productivity gains of our international competitors. In the same period that U.S. productivity began to flag, West Germany experienced increases in productivity of almost 4 percent per year, and Japan's increases were about 5 percent (Thurow, 1980). Recent productivity increases from the emerging industrial economies of the Pacific Rim are equally impressive. Our competitors are amassing wealth at a much faster rate than we are.

As our productivity has stagnated, so has our standard of living. There has been *negative* growth in real weekly income in the United States since 1973 (-1.22 percent annually, 1973–1990). The average real weekly income of a worker in 1990 was 19.1 percent lower than it had been in 1973. Median family income over the same period increased by only 0.04 percent yearly (W.

Peterson, 1991; see also Thurow, 1992). There was no absolute decline in this statistic primarily because of an increase in dual-worker families and the number of hours worked.

The numbers of economically marginal Americans are increasing due to growing inequality in the distribution of income and wealth and to an economy that is creating many jobs that support only a poverty level standard of living. Simultaneously, lagging productivity is generating smaller surpluses from which to provide a safety net for this growing population. Complicating this picture further is the fact of high consumer and public debt in the United States. Consumer debt and the federal deficit lay prior claim to the small surpluses that the economy is creating (Rauch, 1992). Social Welfare is, at an optimistic best, second in line.

The Family Support Act of 1988

In many ways, the Family Support Act (FSA) of 1988 is an extension of the 1981 Omnibus Budget Reconciliation Act. The FSA relies heavily on the states for policy design, financing, and implementation. More specifically, the impetus toward workfare in OBRA, which permitted states to require AFDC recipients to enroll in a job program, is strengthened in the Family Support Act.

A number of states capitalized on the workfare provision in OBRA by making job training and search a condition of assistance. Twenty-six states experimented with some form of workfare between 1981 and 1987 (Schiller and Brasher, 1990); programs in California, Massachusetts, and Florida have been cited for their effectiveness.

The success of some of these state workfare programs, as well as the receptiveness to welfare reform manifested by the states, persuaded Congress to pass the FSA. Many of the lessons learned at the state level were incorporated into the legislation. Heavy emphasis on workfare provisions is retained. Beneficiaries are provided family support that permits them to enroll in job training and search for jobs. The penalties for working are reduced. At the same time, the intention of FSA is to leave particulars of design and implementation to the states, permitting them to choose the arrangements that they think will work best.

There are a number of good discussions of the basic provisions of the FSA (Riggins, 1991; Barnhart, 1991; Sylvester, 1991; Rovner, 1991). Its centerpiece is the Job Opportunity and Basic Skills (JOBS) program.

A key provision of JOBS is the integration of diverse services through a case management approach. The social worker analyzes the needs of a particular recipient and then arranges the combination of services that will enable that recipient to find employment. The array of services includes training, education, job search assistance, counseling of various kinds, transportation, medical care, and child care in addition to the financial support, in-kind transfers, and services provided through AFDC and related programs.

FSA requires states to enroll 20 percent of AFDC cases in the JOBS program by 1995. AFDC recipients must participate in JOBS unless they are single parents with children three years old or less or are caring for a disabled family member. Recipients can be compelled to participate in the program for up to twenty hours a week. Minor parents may be required to live with an adult in order to receive benefits. States must spend a majority of JOBS funds on young, custodial parents with less than a high-school education and upon households with protracted AFDC dependence. States also must participate in the AFDC-UP (unemployed parent) program, which provides benefits to two-parent families in which the primary wage-earner is unemployed. (The provision of benefits to two-parent families was optional for states prior to the passage of the FSA.)

When individuals withdraw from AFDC to take employment, their child care and medical benefits continue for up to one year. This provision is intended to reduce employment disincentives.

In 1989, Congress provided $600 million to fund the provisions of the FSA and $800 million in 1990. One billion dollars was allotted for 1991, 1992, and 1993. The total provision is $4.4 billion, though the inability of states to fund their programs fully is expected to reduce actual expenditures to about $3.3 billion (Riggins, 1991).

There has been a conscious attempt to preserve some latitude for the states in designing and implementing their own JOBS programs, and many demonstration projects are being tried by the states (Romig, 1991). Some of the principal features of AFDC remain in place, however. Benefits still vary considerably from state to state, and penalties to recipients in the form of lost benefits for taking a job are still substantial (Gold, 1991).

Problems with the FSA

The Family Support Act emulates OBRA by shifting great responsibility for social welfare policy to the states. Funding for these reforms is capped at the annual totals previously discussed. The matching ratio is 90 percent for expenditures for direct welfare services, and matches for each state are capped at the amount of that state's 1987 Work Incentive Program (WIN) federal expenditure (Riggins, 1991). These amounts are not overly generous given the high cost of the case management approach (Rovner, 1991), or the increased expenditure burden states face in extending AFDC benefits to two-parent families or finding day-care capacity to meet the increased demand. Thus far, however, the problem has not been federal funding limitations because the states have failed to generate enough money to procure the full federal match.

Fiscal Conditions in the States

The American states are in their worst financial condition since 1983 (Hutchison and Zimmerman, 1991; Snell, 1991; Eckl, 1991). The revenue crises of 1991 and 1992 were, at least in part, the culmination of the shift of policy prerogatives and responsibilities to the states that began with the Omnibus Budget Reconciliation Act of 1991. Deep budget cuts in social welfare programs and intergovernmental transfers, the areas in which OBRA realized its greatest savings, have forced states to reconcile conflicting pressures between service demands and funding shortfalls. In many cases, in the wake of federal funding curtailments, states have financed programs from their own revenues (G. Peterson, 1984). Doing so has inevitably increased pressures on state revenue systems.

In ensuing years, Congress has continued this load shedding by multiplying federal mandates on the states. Congress, of course, faces its own pressures in the form of the deficit. Gramm-Rudman-Hollings requires a "pay-as-you-go" approach to new programs. Funding must be identified up front, or other programs have to be sacrificed to free support for the program being proposed (Fabricius, 1991a, 1991b). Rather than negotiate this dangerous path, representatives pursue program objectives by mandating implementation and financing responsibilities to the states—"federally imposed mandates on the states offer congressional leaders a way to take credit for popular programs without incurring any additional costs" (Fabricius, 1991a, 28). The Budget Reconciliation Act of 1991 alone imposes $15 billion in additional expenditures on the states over five years (Fabricius, 1991a).

Additional claims upon state resources have come from the growing service expectations of state residents. Few states have escaped the public outcry for more prisons. Expenditures on corrections continue to grow at twice the rate of growth in state revenues (Snell, 1991). Indeed, expenditures for Medicaid, education, and corrections are all growing faster than state budgets (Romig, 1991). In the late eighties and early nineties, twenty-four states passed major reforms of public education, the majority of which call for substantial increases in educational expenditures (Office of the Texas Comptroller of Public Accounts, 1991). Social welfare has been one of the fastest growing areas of state expenditure. FSA mandates increases in a number of areas, such as the AFDC-UP program, for which the states are not compensated. Medicaid is the fastest growing area of expenditure for most states (Lemov, 1991). New York has experienced 20 percent annual growth in Medicaid expenditures—a new burden of $800 million to $900 million yearly (Snell, 1991, 15). Medicaid now accounts for over 10 percent of state expenditures (Snell, 1991). Finally, the recession of the early nineties has caused AFDC enrollment to increase to 4.42 million (Hutchison and Zimmerman, 1991; the previous record was 3.8 million enrollees in 1981—Perales, 1991). Claims for Unemployment Insurance, AFDC, and Public Assistance are all up, while tax revenues are down.

State financial data give some indication of the level of fiscal distress the states are experiencing. Thirty states were faced with budget shortfalls of at least 1 percent in fiscal year 1991. The average potential deficit was 5.18 percent (Snell, 1991). These are only potential deficits, of course, because most states are prohibited from deficit spending. They have to deal with budget shortfalls by cutting expenditures, increasing taxes, or appropriating general fund reserves. In FY 1991, twenty-eight states had already cut their budgets or were planning to (Snell, 1991). Tax increases for FY 1992 for all states amounted to $16.2 billion, the largest dollar increase ever (Eckl, 1991). This followed upon tax increases by 24 states in FY 1990 (Snell, 1991). Political realities limit the possibility of returning to this particular well in the near future. State budget reserves have been drawn down in recent years to such a degree that they will not be sufficient to cover shortfalls. In 1991, state balances stood at their lowest historical point—1.9 percent of expenditures (Eckl, 1991). It is generally considered sound budgetary strategy for states to maintain reserves of at least 5 percent of expenditures.

This is the budgetary and economic context in which states are attempting to implement the Family Support Act of 1988. The large majority of states have been unable to fund their own programs completely and hence have not been able to claim the full federal match. Of the $150 million allotted for the JOBS program in 1989, states could claim only $69.1 million (46 percent) (Romig, 1991). In 1990, only 67 percent of the $800 million federal allotment was claimed, and it was anticipated that only 56 percent of the $1 billion allocated for FY 1991 would be used (Rovner, 1991). Collectively, it is expected that the states will fall $1.1 billion short of claiming the full federal allotment for the JOBS Program through 1994 (Riggins, 1991).

In fact, in the wake of the passage of FSA, it is an open question whether overall state social welfare effort should be characterized as a renaissance or a retrenchment. While states have been struggling to comply with FSA mandates, they have been cutting efforts elsewhere. Large cuts have been proposed for public assistance (Sylvester, 1992), the social welfare program that states offer out of their own revenues to citizens that cannot qualify for federal programs. Ohio and Massachusetts cut public assistance, and Governor Engler of Michigan proposed its outright elimination. A number of other states have proposed substantial public assistance cuts (Sylvester, 1991).

States have also been trying to find ways of limiting their AFDC liability at the same time that they comply with JOBS program provisions by strictly monitoring AFDC eligibility and cutting nonmandatory programs. Many states, Wisconsin being the most visible, have tried to restrict AFDC eligibility to state residents (Romig, 1991). Maine proposed to cut AFDC spending by $1.7 million, thus removing 1,500 recipients from the rolls and reducing benefits to another 2,500 (Romig, 1991). These measures include reduced spending for day care. Pennsylvania considered eliminating medical programs that are not specifically mandated by FSA (Romig, 1991).

In all, states have been compensating for federal mandates and increasing expenditures for corrections, education, and medicare by either reducing AFDC efforts outright or by not maintaining real levels of expenditure. State welfare spending in real dollars has fallen 50 percent during the late seventies and the eighties (Romig, 1991). While sixteen states increased AFDC spending by 10 percent in 1990, another nine states reported reduced expenditures (Romig, 1991).

Perhaps the most telling assessment of the Family Support Act at both the state and federal levels comes from the Congressional Budget Office. It estimated that of the 3 million families on the AFDC rolls in 1989, FSA will remove only 50,000 by 1994 (Schwarz, 1990).

Other Problems

Even if states were to claim all of the federally allocated matching funds for JOBS, expenditures would probably be too small to materially affect poverty levels. Observers have noted the contradictory purposes of the FSA (Burtless, 1992; Sanger, 1990). It attempts to increase simultaneously the disposable income of nonwelfare households and the income of welfare recipients by moving the latter into private sector jobs. The expenditures required, however, to make chronic welfare recipients economically self-dependent cannot be supported without taking a large bite from nonwelfare income (see the discussion of the human capital deficit of the chronically poor in the next section). The FSA attempts to address the problem, but it does not contemplate anything approaching this level of expenditure.

Furthermore, the capacity to provide day care in the amounts envisioned by the FSA has not been identified (Sanger, 1990). And welfare recipients still pay a high penalty in lost services for the income they gain from private sector jobs. Continuing medical services and child care for one year is helpful but probably is not sufficient time for the newly (and in many cases, marginally) employed to augment their incomes to compensate for these delayed costs.

Social Welfare and Human Capital

At the state and federal levels, severe constraints limit social welfare policy options. The federal deficit stands as a serious negative assumption facing any new policy proposal. The states are in their worst fiscal crisis in a decade. They have not been able to generate sufficient funding for social welfare to claim federal funds already in place. Thus, they have not been able to fully capitalize on opportunities for innovation in the Family Support Act, and many are seeking ways to reduce their social welfare commitments.

Additional constraints are posed by long-term deficiencies in productivity, declining real income, and historic levels of consumer debt. The country is not generating wealth as quickly as it once did or as quickly as newer industrial powers in Europe and Asia. It is by now a commonplace to note that in the decade of the eighties, the United States went from being the world's greatest creditor nation to being its greatest debtor nation (Thurow, 1992). One reasonable way of interpreting the eighties is to see it as a decade in which the United States made a last attempt to avoid the fact that it was no longer generating sufficient wealth to support its life-style. It continued to consume more goods from foreign countries than it shipped abroad; to consume more government services than it was willing to pay for; and to indulge in levels of private consumption that precluded internationally competitive rates of private investment out of its own wealth. Future social welfare needs cannot be financed by absorbing slack in the system, because all of the slack was used in the eighties.

Are these constraints worrisome? If current social welfare efforts are adequate, then there is no problem. Only if new requirements are placed on the social welfare system, or if some deficiency in present service levels is found, need such constraints be of concern.

Events in Los Angeles and other American cities following the Rodney King verdict raise a serious question about the sufficiency of current social welfare programs. The American social welfare philosophy has always seen programs as a means of supplementing the livelihood of those who are *temporarily* outside the economic mainstream. Evidence indicates, however, that central city minority citizens are *permanent* economic outsiders, with infant mortality rates higher than many Third World nations, structural unemployment in double digits, and incomes that are both lower than those of whites and decreasing in relative terms (Urban Institute, 1992a).

The Family Support Act attempts to address this isolation of the economically disadvantaged by including programs for increasing their human capital and providing support during the transition period when they are gaining skills and entering the job force. Unfortunately, these programs are widely recognized as being small in scale compared to the human capital needs of the minority poor (Sanger, 1990). Sanger addresses the shortfalls in human capital that are typical of welfare recipients:

> Welfare recipients, even those with some education and work experience, have very poor basic skill competencies—or those skills that employers say they need for even low level positions. Basic Skills Assessment tests that were given to a national sample of WIN registrants to determine their qualifications for various occupations show a wide range of basic skills competency. Comparing these test results to the findings of a survey of employers who were asked about minimum

job requirements necessary for 83 occupations, researchers found striking evidence that a large portion of the AFDC population lack critical skills to do even menial jobs. . . . Over one quarter of the registrants did not have sufficient math competency levels required for even the lowest level jobs, as determined by employers (this category includes street cleaner, file clerk I, crossing guard, window cleaner, kitchen helper, food assembler).

These findings were further confirmed by testing done in the Philadelphia Saturation Work Program. . . . Results indicated that over 80 percent of those tested were reading between the 4th and 7th grade levels and 12 percent were reading below the 4th grade level. In math, 63 percent tested below the 4th grade level. (1990, 671)

It is doubtful that the federal and state governments will be willing to invest the resources required to overcome the skills deficits of the urban poor.

Realization of legislative goals will require considerably more investment in employment and training than recent experience suggests states are likely to undertake on their own. Federal budget commitments and target participation rates do not suggest that a significant new investment in intensive interventions is likely to occur. (Sanger, 1990, 671)

These considerations make human capital investment a critical concern for existing social welfare policy; but it will be an even more important concern in the future (Hornbeck and Salamon, 1991). Arnold Packer (1991) speaks of a "demographic imperative" for human capital investment that arises from the changing composition of the American population. Anglos are a shrinking proportion of the population because of differential fertility rates and rates of immigration (both legal and illegal). In the 1980s, of 9 million immigrants, only about 750,000 were from Europe or Canada. The remainder came predominantly from Asia (44 percent) or Latin America (40 percent; Urban Institute, 1992b, 16-17). As the Urban Institute notes, "the U.S. population has changed from a predominantly white population with a black minority to a multi-cultural, multi-ethnic society" (1992b, 17).

One result of this demographic change is that about 85 percent of new entrants into the labor force in the next fifteen to twenty years will be women, immigrants, or members of minority groups (obviously some will be all three; Packer, 1991). These are precisely the groups that have been least successful in acquiring human capital in the United States. All three fall disproportionately within the poverty population. The shifting composition of the population, then, implies both growing pressure on the social welfare system and extraordinary challenges for human capital investment. There is a further implication of increasing overlap between the two policy areas.

The productivity of the economy and the American standard of living will increasingly be dependent upon workers who have traditionally been outside the economic and social mainstream. The challenge will be to create policies which overcome class and race barriers and enhance the skills of these new workers. This will require not only an educational system that is more effective and inclusive than it has been in the past but also the provision of a sufficient standard of living to made education effective. Students who lack shelter, nutrition, and health care are unlikely to apply themselves to learning the technologies that will translate into future economic survival.

Increased international economic competition has caused human capital to be a critical consideration for several reasons. One is simply that competing in high-tech industries requires highly accomplished workers. Furthermore, because the emphasis in this competition is on *process* innovation rather than *product* innovation, success will depend more on the bottom 50 percent of the work force—"If the bottom 50 percent cannot learn what must be learned, new high-tech processes cannot be employed" (Thurow, 1992, 52).

The historical record is not encouraging.

> If sustainable competitive advantage swirls around workforce skills, Anglo-Saxon firms have a problem. Human-resource management is not traditionally seen as central to the competitive survival of the firm in America or Great Britain. Skill acquisition is an individual responsibility, and business firms exist to beat wages down. Labor is simply another factor of production to be hired—rented at the lowest possible cost—much as one buys raw materials or equipment. (Thurow, 1992, 53-54)

This is the challenge that the social welfare system is facing. The way in which Americans think of "welfare" policy will likely have to become broader. The Family Support Act is an encouraging move in that direction, with its provision for educational and training services, counseling, child care, and health needs in addition to income support. Clearly, however, FSA is a very small effort compared to what will probably be needed before too long. The combined welfare/human capital requirements of large segments of the population that are currently excluded or alienated from economic centers must be addressed in much more comprehensive fashion. However, given the constraints now facing policymakers, a broadening of social welfare programs and definitions may not be a feasible option.

Conclusions

This is a particularly important time for social welfare policy—though not necessarily because of the temporal coincidence of the end of the Cold War. The disintegration of the Soviet Union and concomitant reduction in international military tensions is not expected to have a large direct effect on social welfare policy-making. Absent the materialization of the peace dividend, welfare programs will probably not change greatly as a result of the destruction of the Berlin Wall or the ouster of the Communists in Romania.

A number of other long-term secular changes *do* have tremendous implications for social welfare policy, however. Among these are:

- Increasing international economic competition
- Depressed domestic economic productivity
- Declining real income and increased income inequality
- Reduction in manufactures and increasing reliance on services
- Increasing numbers of minority and immigrant citizens
- Growing federal deficits
- Increasing policy demands upon state public resources

We might also add to this list what appear to be growing racial tensions and growing disgust on the part of the American people with government and politics. Even without these additional items, however, one senses a widespread perception that things in the United States are changing, as well as a conviction that it may not be for the better. Monumental challenges loom on the horizon, and Americans are not sure that their political and economic institutions are addressing them. There is a disapproval of politics in general, a growing support for term limitations, disgust with the Congress, a lack of confidence in the schools, a fear of AIDS, crime, and drug culture, a lack of faith in savings and loans and oversight of the financial system, and a lack of confidence in the economy, which, in spite of repeated predictions to the contrary by politicians and government economists, cannot seem to extricate itself from the recession of the early nineties. Dealing with these conditions is a weary Congress that feels that it has "done welfare reform" (Sylvester, 1991, 55). In such an environment, one wonders if the social welfare system can adapt to the new demands that are apt to be made upon it in the post–Cold War era.

Postscript: Clinton Administrative Initiatives

President Clinton has made the pledge to "end welfare as we know it," making welfare reform equal in priority to the reform of health care and reducing crime. This pronouncement is surely calculated to achieve maximum dramatic effect. The reality is likely to be less dramatic.

The pillars of the Clinton strategy are as follows:

- A two-year limitation on the period during which an individual can receive AFDC benefits
- Redoubled government efforts to insure the payment of child support

- Enhancement of the supports—child care, health care, counseling, transportation, education, and training—that enable welfare recipients to find and keep jobs
- Increased earned income tax credits (EITC) for low income people

Taking these proposals singly, child-support enforcement can hardly be expected to end welfare as we know it, and enhanced support for job-acquisition efforts *is* welfare as we know it in the Family Support Act of 1988. Similarly, earned income tax credits have recently been increased in the Budget Reconciliation Act of 1990. The only really new proposal here is for a two-year limitation on individual AFDC benefits.

This proposal is clearly aimed at the dependent poor, since those who stay on the AFDC rolls for less than two years will not be affected. It is questionable that a two-year limit, however satisfying it may sound to conservatives, will actually mean that the indigent and unemployed will be turned out into the streets at the end of their eligibility. One imagines a video of single mothers housing their children in abandoned cars on winter nights. Any administration would be hard put to hold the line on a policy the brunt of which was borne by such innocents.

A more plausible alternative is that those who are not employed at the end of two years will be transferred into a public jobs program. Such a program could be expensive and would incur the criticism that public employment is only a nominal end to welfare dependence, particularly if large percentages of the dependent poor wind up there.

What the two-year limit really does is increase the pressure for the JOBS program to move the AFDC dependent into the private economy. If JOBS is not successful, then it is unlikely that the two-year limit will result in an end to welfare as we know it. Even though JOBS may be expanded by the Clinton administration, it faces the same problems it did in its FSA incarnation. The states are still having problems qualifying for their full federal match. The experience and education deficits of the dependent poor make it hard to transform them into a highly employable work force. And the economic marginality of increasing numbers of Americans—the percentage of the population comprised of the working poor increased from 12 percent in 1979 to 18 percent in 1992 (Cloward and Piven, 1993)—raises questions that entry level employment alone will lift the dependent poor out of poverty. If not, then large numbers of the long-term poor are likely to remain on public support, whether it is called AFDC or public employment.

NOTES

1. As a percentage of gross national product, total expenditures for social welfare have not declined from 1980 through 1988 (18.4%—18.5%) (U.S. Bureau of the

Census, 1991, 355). There *is* an overall reduction compared to the seventies—total governmental social welfare expenditures represented 19.0% of GNP in 1975. This decline, however, begins during the Carter administration and cannot be exclusively attributed to OBRA.

A qualification to this trend in the eighties should be mentioned. The consistency of this percentage hides a shift in the allocation of social welfare expenditures by function. Over this same period of time, expenditures on health and medical care as a percentage of social welfare expenditures increased seven points (20.4%—27.8%) (U.S. Bureau of the Census, 1991, 356). In order to accommodate this increase in resources dedicated to health care, the proportion of total resources going to other purposes—education, veterans programs, medical services other than Medicare and Medicaid, and the "Other Social Welfare" category, including child welfare and child nutrition—has had to shrink.

In other words, social welfare expenditures have been a constant percentage of GNP in the eighties largely because of dramatic increases in costs in the health programs where governments have little discretion over expenditures—Medicaid and Medicare. Ever greater expenditures are needed to maintain constant levels of service. Given that social welfare expenditures as a proportion of GNP *have not* increased over the same period, a proportionate shift toward Medicare and Medicaid means a reduction in the proportion of GNP dedicated to providing services in other areas—and an overall decrease in welfare services.

The diversion of resources away from social welfare can also be seen in another historical series. The annual percentage change in social welfare expenditures per capita has decreased markedly in the eighties. The increase from 1959 to 1960 (1988 constant dollars) in per capita social welfare expenditures was 4.1%. From 1969 to 1970, it was 6.5%. From 1979 to 1980, it was 4.2%. But from 1984 to 1985, 1986 to 1987, and 1987 to 1988, it was 1.9%, 2.0%, and 1.3%, respectively (U.S. Bureau of the Census, 1991, 356). For 1985 to 1986, 1986 to 1987, and 1987 to 1988, the increases in the overall size of the federal deficit were 16.7%, 10.6%, and 10.9%. Increases in federal spending for the same years were 4.6%, 1.4%, and 6.0%. Increases in federal defense spending for these three years were 8.2%, 3.1%, and 3.0% (U.S. Bureau of the Census, 1991, 318).

2. The point will be made later in this chapter that budget deficits of this magnitude severely restrict the policy options open to the federal government in meeting social welfare needs. In fairness, it should be recognized that consumer debt is at least as great a limiting factor as public debt. While public debt limits the expenditure options of government, consumer debt limits its revenue options. A population that is heavily in debt is likely to present political dangers to government officials who suggest increased levies for social welfare expenditures. Both consumer debt and public debt make prior claims on economic surpluses, thus restricting what can be hoped for in the area of social welfare. John Schwarz (1988, 87–89) notes, in this regard, that consumer debt has increased apace with public debt in the last three decades (see also Thurow, 1992, 263–64). Rauch (1992) points out that total debt, private and public, now comprises almost 190% of the U.S. annual gross national product.

3. I have not mentioned demographic developments in this discussion of a growing economically vulnerable population, though they are of real concern. The

baby-boom generation is approaching retirement age. As many observers have noted (Packer, 1991), the ranks of those taking Social Security will be swollen, while the number of those productively employed in the economy will shrink. This will place increased demands upon the incomes of workers, making their lot more economically precarious; or, it will result in reduced benefits for the elderly. In either case, some portion of the population, in the absence of dramatic productivity gains, is likely to see its economic status decline.

Intergovernmental Delivery of Human Services: Retrenchment and Compensation

PETER R. GLUCK

The focus of this chapter is on the analysis of public and nonprofit agencies at the community level that rely on federal and state revenues to deliver human services. Community-based human services agencies face the dilemma of having to serve more clients with less resources from federal and state governments. This circumstance results from the convergence of many factors. These include changes in national policy direction as well as national, state, and regional economic conditions.

To continue serving clients, human services agencies have had to experiment with policy options in efforts to manage the effects of retrenchment. These include tactical decisions affecting the use of existing resources and strategic planning as to the management of resources and organizational capacity.

Drawing upon a national study designed and conducted by the Urban Institute, a survey of human services agencies was conducted to ascertain changes in funding, client/service levels, and management practices from 1980 to 1987, a period of sharply curtailed federal and, in turn, state governmental funding for domestic programs (Millar and DeVita, 1986; DeVita and Altschuler, 1987). The survey focused on public and nonprofit agencies that provide social services at the local level. The programs studied include those providing mental health and public health care. The study was conducted in Flint and Genesee counties, Michigan, areas particularly hard hit by both the funding cutbacks and a series of economic recessions. The latter have resulted in substantial unemployment, and the area as a whole epitomizes the problems of the frostbelt states, presently undergoing severe economic problems. Of the sixty-six agencies included in the study, fifty-seven (86.4 percent) completed and returned the surveys.

The length and detail of the survey instrument and the uneven pattern of agency record keeping produced some inconsistencies in the depth and scope of the data. For example, some agencies do not maintain records at the program level. Rather, they aggregate and report data for the agency as a whole. At the program level, the small number of agencies in the analysis limits the findings to a description of characteristics, trends, or conditions. Other agencies lack automated record-keeping capability and do not maintain their agency database for more than three years. Consequently, these agencies were unable to provide data going back to 1980.

Notwithstanding these limitations, the agencies surveyed constitute virtually all of the public and nonprofit agencies in the geographic area of the study. In this sense, the research is more a survey than a sample of the universe. The findings are believed to represent an accurate description of the conditions of retrenchment and management responses to it.

Policy Developments in the Intergovernmental Delivery of Human Services

Since 1964, the human services have relied heavily on the federal government for funding. In 1976, the Carter administration began to reconsider the policy of ever-increasing support for human services. By 1980, a number of developments converged to precipitate an important change in policy direction. First, the national economy was in recession. Second, some state and regional economies, particularly in the industrialized Northeast and Midwest, were in the throes of what some economists and public officials considered a depression. Third, the election of Ronald Reagan brought to the presidency a relentless, outspoken, and effective advocate of reduced federal funding for domestic programs, increased military and defense expenditures, and lowered taxes.

From 1981 on, the Reagan administration succeeded in reducing federal budget support for a wide range of domestic programs. The budget and tax cuts of the first Reagan administration were only the beginning of a long and continuing series of changes in policy direction affecting human services. The Gramm-Rudman-Hollings Deficit Reduction Act also became an effective tool for limiting both domestic and nondomestic federal expenditures. Tax reform in the second Reagan administration played an important role in reducing the revenues available for domestic programs. The long-range deficit reduction pact agreed to in the Bush administration between the president and congressional leaders made it even more difficult to increase federal outlays for human services. The agreement mandated that revenue, either from new taxes or existing sources, needed to be identified and set aside before any expansion in domestic programs could be attempted. And the budget act signed by President Clinton, hailed as his first major legislative victory, was won at the price of promises to find further spending cuts. The result is that increased social spending in the immediate future is unlikely.

This scenario has been played out primarily during the administrations of two conservative Republican presidents. Still, there are those in the political and policy arenas who believe that the policy direction taken in the human services transcends the electoral fortunes of the major political parties and their candidates. The importance of budget and trade deficits as political and economic issues suggests little likelihood of significant increases in federal budgetary support for domestic human services programs. Furthermore, the 1979–1982 and more recent recessions illustrate how state and local governments look to human services for cutbacks when faced with the need to meet constitutional or statutory requirements for a balanced budget (Agranoff, ed., 1983; Bresnick, 1983; Checkoway, ed., 1986; Booth and Higgins, 1984).

While these developments have been occurring, the need for services and the client levels of agencies have been increasing. These agencies are expected to serve more clients at a time when the effects of national, state, and regional funding cuts have taken their toll. Economic conditions and the resulting increase in unemployment have served to strengthen the demand for a wide spectrum of public assistance programs. Communities in the industrial Northeast and Midwest which have relied on manufacturing have been especially hard hit. Plant closings and job elimination have combined to create a large and perhaps permanent underclass of jobless and underemployed workers. These individuals, many of whom once earned high wages and had substantial fringe benefits in industries such as automobile manufacturing, find themselves on indefinite (and permanent) layoff status. Many attempt to work minimum wage jobs in the service sector which offer few, if any, fringe benefits such as health care. It is this at-risk population that has swelled client levels in the human services at the same time that federal and state funding has been curtailed.

Dimensions of Retrenchment

First, we look at some key characteristics of the agencies that provide human services. The data in table 15.1 indicates that most human services agencies are private nonprofit or public organizations. This is especially true of social services and public health agencies (table 15.1, part A). Private for-profit organizations have become more numerous in the field of mental health as a result of changes in third-party reimbursement. More than a quarter of the agencies (28 percent) in the study have existed for no more than the past ten years. The age of these agencies coincides with the last recession in 1978. About another third of the agencies appear to be products of the War on Poverty undertaken in the mid-1960s.

Most agencies provide a limited number of services. More than 60 percent operate three or fewer programs and almost all of them describe their primary function as direct service (table 15.1, part B). However, the majority of

TABLE 15.1

Characteristics and Functions of Social Service Agencies

A. Basic Characteristics of Human Services Agencies

	Number	Percent
Type		
Private nonprofit	39	68
Public	14	25
Private for-profit	4	7
Total	57	100
Age		
10 years old or less	16	28
11 to 24 years old	20	35
25 years old or more	20	35
Missing	1	2
Total	57	100
Number of Programs		
3 or less	35	61
4 to 6	11	19
7 to 9	4	7
10 or more	7	13
Total	57	100

B. Primary and Secondary Functions of Human Services Agencies

	Primary		Secondary	
	Number	Percent	Number	Percent
Direct Service	51	89	8	5
Information/Referral	4	7	41	25
Public Education	1	2	45	27
Advocacy	—	—	42	26
Research/Planning	—	—	18	11
Other	1	2	10	6
Totals	57	100	164	100

human services agencies also undertake a variety of secondary functions including information/referrals, public education, and advocacy.

In many metropolitan areas, private funding for human services often comes from community-wide fund-raising drives conducted by organizations such as the United Way. About half of the agencies in this study are currently affiliated with and receive operating funds from the annual United Way campaign. Of those agencies that are not currently affiliated with United Way, just over 20 percent have been in the past.

Agencies participating in the study were asked to provide information on funding, staffing, and client/service levels from 1980 through 1987. With this information, it was possible to examine levels and uses of agency resources from the perspective of either a single year or longitudinally.

Funding

Funding may be the most important organizational resource. Without it, other necessities of service delivery, including personnel, equipment, facilities, and the like, cannot be acquired. Consequently, changes in the level of funding have a direct and immediate impact on an agency's capacity to serve its clientele.

Historically, human services agencies have relied on public more than private sources of funding. The origins of this reliance probably date to the Progressive Era and were reinforced and accelerated first by the New Deal in the 1930s and then by the Great Society initiatives of the 1960s. Beginning in the latter part of the 1970s, domestic programs began to experience a decline in funding from public sources. This was especially true at the federal level.

The data in figure 15.1 show the changes that have occurred in funding levels from different sources for the period 1980–1987. Federal and state governments provided 90 percent of total funds for human services agencies in all but one (1987) of the years for which data are reported. In the years 1980–83, federal and state dollars accounted for almost all of the total funding. In 1983 and 1984, this figure declined. Following two years of relative stability in the level of funding from federal and state governments, the last year covered by the study witnessed a decline below 90 percent for the first time in the decade.

It is worth noting that federal funding ranged from 50.5 percent (1981) to 46.9 percent (1987). The other major source of public funding, state government, has ranged between 46.1 percent (1980) and 42.6 percent (1987).

In an attempt to replace lost dollars from federal and state governments, services agencies have sought to increase their financial contributions from other, nongovernment sources. Funding from fees, for example, has increased continually since 1983. Over the seven year period, fee income for human services agencies has grown, although it remains a relatively small proportion of the total budgets. Funding from United Way has also become a more important source of revenues for agencies. These organizations reported receiving 3.2 percent of their operating support from United Way in the last year of the study. By contrast, in 1981 United Way provided just less than 1 percent of agency dollars.

Service agencies have met with modest success in seeking to offset the loss of federal and state dollars. However, increases from nongovernmental sources such as third-party payments and private fund-raising drives such as those by the United Way have proven inadequate in compensating for lost fed-

FIGURE 15.1

Sources of Funding for Human Services Agencies

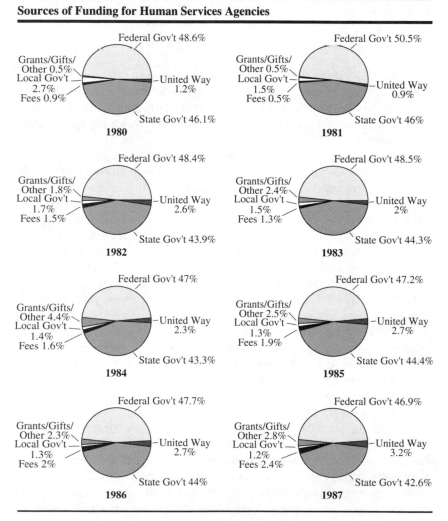

1980 — Federal Gov't 48.6%, Grants/Gifts/Other 0.5%, Local Gov't 2.7%, Fees 0.9%, United Way 1.2%, State Gov't 46.1%

1981 — Federal Gov't 50.5%, Grants/Gifts/Other 0.5%, Local Gov't 1.5%, Fees 0.5%, United Way 0.9%, State Gov't 46%

1982 — Federal Gov't 48.4%, Grants/Gifts/Other 1.8%, Local Gov't 1.7%, Fees 1.5%, United Way 2.6%, State Gov't 43.9%

1983 — Federal Gov't 48.5%, Grants/Gifts/Other 2.4%, Local Gov't 1.5%, Fees 1.3%, United Way 2%, State Gov't 44.3%

1984 — Federal Gov't 47%, Grants/Gifts/Other 4.4%, Local Gov't 1.4%, Fees 1.6%, United Way 2.3%, State Gov't 43.3%

1985 — Federal Gov't 47.2%, Grants/Gifts/Other 2.5%, Local Gov't 1.3%, Fees 1.9%, United Way 2.7%, State Gov't 44.4%

1986 — Federal Gov't 47.7%, Grants/Gifts/Other 2.3%, Local Gov't 1.3%, Fees 2%, United Way 2.7%, State Gov't 44%

1987 — Federal Gov't 46.9%, Grants/Gifts/Other 2.8%, Local Gov't 1.2%, Fees 2.4%, United Way 3.2%, State Gov't 42.6%

FIGURE 15.2

Total Funding of all Agencies

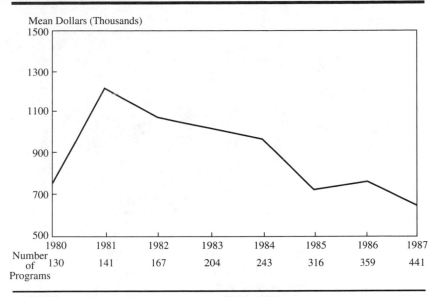

Mean Dollars (Thousands)

	1980	1981	1982	1983	1984	1985	1986	1987
Number of Programs	130	141	167	204	243	316	359	441

eral and state dollars. The services and programs provided for clients have suffered.

The trend in total funding reveals an uneven pattern. Total agency funding increased considerably between 1980 and 1981, then declined gradually for three years, declined substantially between 1984 and 1985, then increased slightly and declined again between 1986 and 1987. During the period, total funding went down approximately 50 percent, from a high of about $1.25 million to a low of about $650,000 (figure 15.2).

The data also show considerable change in the funding from all sources. For example, each level of government was providing less funding at the end of the eight-year period than at the beginning (figure 15.3). Financing from the federal government was uneven, although the total dollars were about the same in 1987 as in 1980. State government dollars showed less variability, and the totals were also about the same at the start of the decade as at its end.

Revenues from fees paid by clients, third-party payers, and Medicaid showed a net and, in some cases, dramatic increase. Client-paid and third-party paid fees more than doubled from the first to the last year studied, and Medicaid fees more than tripled. It is tempting to view Medicaid reimbursements as a variation of federal support. The effort of the federal government to limit payments under Medicaid suggests that this may be its view also.

FIGURE 15.3

A. Trends in Social Service Agency Funding

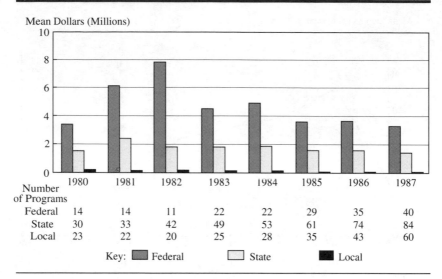

Mean Dollars (Millions)

Number of Programs	1980	1981	1982	1983	1984	1985	1986	1987
Federal	14	14	11	22	22	29	35	40
State	30	33	42	49	53	61	74	84
Local	23	22	20	25	28	35	43	60

Key: ■ Federal   □ State   ■ Local

B. Trends in Social Service Agency Funding

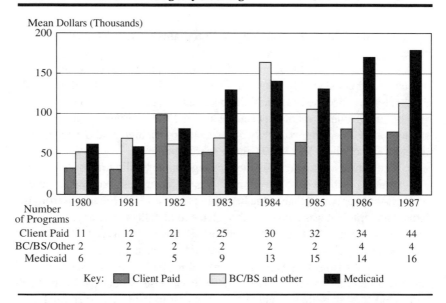

Mean Dollars (Thousands)

Number of Programs	1980	1981	1982	1983	1984	1985	1986	1987
Client Paid	11	12	21	25	30	32	34	44
BC/BS/Other	2	2	2	2	2	2	4	4
Medicaid	6	7	5	9	13	15	14	16

Key: ■ Client Paid   □ BC/BS and other   ■ Medicaid

(continued next page)

FIGURE 15.3 (CONTINUED)

C. Trends in Social Service Agency Funding

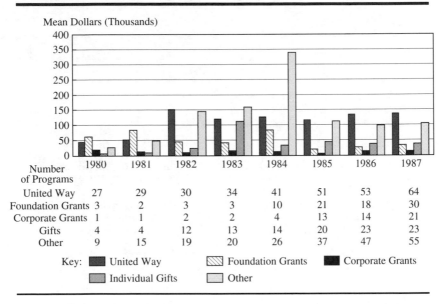

Mean Dollars (Thousands)

Number of Programs	1980	1981	1982	1983	1984	1985	1986	1987
United Way	27	29	30	34	41	51	53	64
Foundation Grants	3	2	3	3	10	21	18	30
Corporate Grants	1	1	2	2	4	13	14	21
Gifts	4	4	12	13	14	20	23	23
Other	9	15	19	20	26	37	47	55

Key: ■ United Way   ▧ Foundation Grants   ■ Corporate Grants
     ▨ Individual Gifts   ▢ Other

Funding from all other nongovernment sources including United Way, corporate and foundation grants, gifts, and other income, is shown in figure 15.3, part C. The data indicate that United Way's support more than tripled between 1980 and 1987.

At the program level, social services experienced the greatest decline in funding, while public health and mental health programs have each realized net increases. The trend of declining funding for social services was gradual but consistent during the period. Public and mental health programs, on the other hand, fared better (figure 15.4).

Programs serving low-income clients experienced the most sustained and the steepest decline in funding. From 1980 to 1983, these programs rode a funding roller coaster. They then went through four consecutive years of decreasing funds. Over the eight years, programs serving low income clients experienced a 75 percent decrease in their total funds.

Programs serving other client groups, including children, adults, and combinations of these, experienced a steady and gradual increase in funding. The pattern of funding for programs benefitting the elderly was uneven. In each of the first two odd-numbered years (1981 and 1983), programs serving the elderly increased their funding from the preceding year. In 1984, the programs received twice the level of funding they had in 1983. Then, for the next

FIGURE 15.4

Trend in Agency Funding by Program

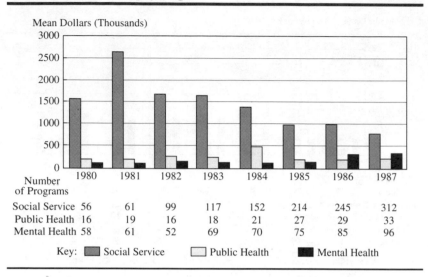

Mean Dollars (Thousands)

Number of Programs	1980	1981	1982	1983	1984	1985	1986	1987
Social Service	56	61	99	117	152	214	245	312
Public Health	16	19	16	18	21	27	29	33
Mental Health	58	61	52	69	70	75	85	96

Key: ▨ Social Service   ☐ Public Health   ■ Mental Health

two years, funds for programs serving the elderly declined to almost two-thirds the 1984 level, and then, between 1986 and 1987, funding for these programs about doubled.

Staffing

Professional and clerical staff are a critical resource in human services agencies. Since the bulk of an agency's budget is used to pay support compensation, changes in funding should be reflected in staffing levels. For all agencies in the study there is a loss of 0.5 FTE (full time equivalent) professional staff positions in eight years. However, this tells only part of the retrenchment picture. During the period, professional staffing levels fluctuated from almost 9.0 FTE (1982) to about 7.0 FTE (1987). Clerical staffing also fluctuated considerably, although it was higher at the end of the study period (3.0 FTE in 1987) than the beginning (approximately 2.5 FTE in 1980).

Agencies compensated for the reduction in full-time professionals by making greater use of part-time staff. Full-time staff declined by slightly more than 10 percent from 1980–1987, while the use of part-time staff increased.

Staffing reductions hit social service programs severely. Notwithstanding a modest increase between 1982 and 1983, social services experienced a steady and gradual decline in staffing on the magnitude of almost 20 percent between 1980–1987. Public health programs, on the other hand, experienced a substantial and steady increase. Staffing levels in public health programs increased by more than 50 percent from 1981 to 1987. The most dramatic and uneven staffing levels occurred in mental health programs. Agencies delivering mental health services increased staffing levels almost threefold, from 3.0 FTE in 1980 to 8.0 FTE in 1987.

Retrenchment of agency staff declined the most severely among professional personnel in social services agencies. These agencies began the decade with 9.0 FTE positions. By 1987, there was a 50 percent decline. Mental health agencies, on the other hand, increased their staffs by almost 300 percent. And professional staffing of public health programs went from 5.0 FTE to just over 8.0 FTE. Levels for clerical staffing increased in all three types of agencies and most dramatically for those in the field of mental health.

Staffing levels increased in agencies that serve children, adults, the elderly, and low-income clients. The work force in agencies that serve more than one client group declined.

An examination of staffing levels for professional and clerical positions shows some change for programs targeted to different client groups. For example, professional staffing declined most dramatically—from about 18.0 FTE to about 12.0 FTE—in agencies serving low-income clients. Most other agencies experienced a more modest decrease in professional staff or remained relatively stable. In one case, that of agencies serving multiple client groups, there was an increase in the professional staff levels from about 4.0 FTE to 6.0 FTE.

There was a net increase overall in the number of clerical positions with considerable variation for agencies different client groups. The pattern of increase is uneven for agencies serving low-income clients and only gradual improves in those serving the elderly. The greatest magnitude of increase affected agencies serving adult clients.

Client/Service Levels

The clients of human services agencies are defined in a variety of ways. Age, income, gender, and physical or emotional conditions are a few of the most common ways clients are categorized.

The agencies participating in the study were asked to use 1985 as a benchmark to describe changes in their clientele. Five different groups—children and youth, the elderly, the unemployed, low income, and the emotionally/mentally disabled constituted more than half the agencies' clients prior to 1984. Three of those groups—children and youth, the unemployed, and low income—were served in greater numbers by the same agencies after 1985. Furthermore, low income, unemployed, children, and youth are reported as requiring more services by roughly one-half of the agencies that survived. It should be noted that only a small percentage of agencies report admitting new client groups after

1985. Agencies appear to be focusing on meeting the needs of their traditional client groups. These client groups have expanded in numbers, and the local agencies are attempting to provide a broader range of services.

Program level data are of limited use because there is considerable variation in the way agencies maintain such records. Some agencies record these data for the agency as a whole, while others disaggregate their service data to the program level. Notwithstanding these difficulties, three measures—duplicated clients, families per month, and unduplicated clients—can be used to illustrate what has happened to agency service levels. While unduplicated clients have increased modestly, both duplicated clients and the number of families served per month have more than doubled.

Dimensions of Compensation

When organizations are faced with declining resources and increased demand from clients, they must retrench. The role of management in a period of retrenchment is to find ways to compensate for declining resources.

The managers of human services agencies were asked to describe the practices they initiated with respect to services, funding, operations/management, and external relations since 1985 to cope with declining resources and the increasing demands for services. They were also asked to describe the barriers they perceived to block the effective management of retrenchment (Brager and Holloway, 1978; Lynn, 1980; Perlmutter, ed., 1984).

Services

Management practices in the area of services suggest that agencies recognize the need to find ways to continue serving clients despite the strain on resources (table 15.3). More than four-fifths of the agencies reported that they provided more services than before 1985, while almost three-quarters said that they have prioritized the services they provide. Managers also described a number of initiatives taken to reduce the level of client demand by changing the availability of services, cancelling or delaying new services, stretching out response times, and allowing waiting lists to increase.

A comparison of the practices taken by managers in private nonprofit and public agencies suggests a similar pattern of response to retrenchment. Managers in both private nonprofit and public agencies indicate that efforts at a broader range of services is the most common response. A higher proportion of the managers in public agencies reported taking this approach, while more of the private nonprofit agencies attempted to prioritize their services. It is likely that this difference in responses reflects the statutory mandates under which public agencies operate and the greater latitude generally enjoyed by private nonprofit organizations.

TABLE 15.2 CLIENTS SERVED BY SOCIAL SERVICE AGENCIES

A. Clients Served by All Agencies (N = 57)

Client Groups	Agencies serving before 1985		Agencies reporting greater numbers since 1985		Agencies reporting more services since 1985		Agencies reporting new groups since 1985	
	Number	Percent	Number	Percent	Number	Percent	Number	Percent
Children and youth	40	70.2	30	52.6	28	49.1	4	7.0
Elderly	37	64.9	22	38.6	23	40.4	1	1.8
Unemployed	40	70.2	35	61.4	31	54.4	2	3.6
Low income	45	78.9	39	68.4	32	56.1	4	7.0
Emotionally impaired; Mentally ill	33	57.9	21	36.8	19	33.3	5	8.8
Developmentally disabled	23	40.4	15	26.3	17	29.8	3	5.3
Substance abusers	27	47.4	20	35.1	18	31.6	4	7.0
Refugees	9	15.8	5	8.8	5	8.8	2	3.6
Other	15	26.3	9	15.8	8	14.0	5	8.8

B. Clients Served by Private Nonprofit Agencies (N = 39)

Client Groups	Agencies serving before 1985		Agencies reporting greater numbers since 1985		Agencies reporting more services since 1985		Agencies reporting new groups since 1985	
	Number	Percent	Number	Percent	Number	Percent	Number	Percent
Children and youth	28	71.8	20	51.3	17	43.6	3	7.7
Elderly	26	66.7	13	33.3	15	38.5	1	2.6
Unemployed	29	74.4	25	64.1	23	59.0	1	2.6
Low income	33	84.6	29	74.4	25	64.1	2	5.2
Emotionally impaired; Mentally ill	26	66.7	15	38.5	14	35.9	2	5.2
Developmentally disabled	19	48.7	10	25.6	14	35.9	1	2.6
Substance abusers	18	46.2	11	28.2	11	28.2	2	5.2
Refugees	4	2.6	3	7.7	3	7.7	2	5.2
Other	12	30.8	7	17.9	6	15.4	2	5.2

(continued next page)

C. Clients Served by Public Agencies (N = 14)

Client Groups	Agencies serving before 1985		Agencies reporting greater numbers since 1985		Agencies reporting more services since 1985		Agencies reporting new groups since 1985	
	Number	Percent	Number	Percent	Number	Percent	Number	Percent
Children and youth	9	64.3	7	50.0	8	57.1	0	0
Elderly	9	64.3	8	57.1	6	42.9	0	0
Unemployed	9	64.3	7	50.0	6	42.9	1	7.1
Low income	10	71.4	7	50.0	5	35.7	2	14.3
Emotionally impaired; Mentally ill	6	42.9	4	28.6	4	28.6	3	21.4
Developmentally disabled	4	28.6	5	35.7	3	21.4	2	14.3
Substance abusers	7	50.0	6	42.9	5	35.7	2	14.3
Refugees	5	35.7	2	14.3	2	14.3	0	0
Other	3	21.4	2	14.3	2	14.3	2	14.3

TABLE 15.3

Management Practices in Social Service Agencies: Services

	All Agencies (N = 57)		Private Nonprofit Agencies (N = 39)		Public Agencies (N = 14)	
	Number	Percent	Number	Percent	Number	Percent
Increased services	48	84.2	31	79.5	13	92.9
Prioritized services	40	70.2	28	71.8	9	64.3
Changed availability of services	31	54.4	20	51.3	7	50.0
Cancelled or delayed new services	20	35.1	14	35.9	4	28.6
Allowed response time to grow	19	33.3	12	30.8	7	50.0
Allowed the waiting list to grow	16	28.1	10	25.6	6	42.9
Agency has revised eligibility to:						
make services more restrictive	14	24.6	10	25.6	4	28.6
make services less restrictive	19	33.3	11	28.2	7	50.0
Eliminated services or programs	11	19.3	6	15.4	5	35.7
Limited services by reduction of						
cases, scope of services, etc.	10	17.5	4	10.3	6	42.9
Reduced maximum dollar amount						
or value of assistance						
provided	8	14.0	2	5.1	5	35.7

Funding

In addition to compensating for declining federal and state support by changing services, managers have taken a number of actions with respect to funding (table 15.4). The service agencies continue to press for additional funding from public sources despite the fact that such appeals have failed to produce significant results. However, almost three-quarters of the managers reported seeking additional funding from current public sources, presumably two of the same sources—federal and state governments—that have decreased the dollars appropriated for human services. The same proportion of agency managers indicated that they sought additional funding from nonpublic sources such as foundations, corporations, and community-wide fund-raising campaigns. More than two-thirds of agencies identify initiatives that seek funding from new public sources and just under two-thirds identify initiatives that seek funding from new nongovernmental sources. More than half of the agencies reported initiating their own fund-raising efforts.

Comparing private nonprofit and public agencies with respect to funding, it is notable that such actions were initiated by a greater proportion of public agencies. For example, all public agencies indicated that they continued to seek additional funding from current public sources, while 72 percent of private non-

TABLE 15.4

Management Financial Practices in Social Service Agencies

	All Agencies (N = 57)		Private Nonprofit Agencies (N = 39)		Public Agencies (N = 14)	
	Number	Percent	Number	Percent	Number	Percent
Sought additional funding:						
from current public sources	42	73.7	28	71.8	14	100.0
from current nonpublic sources	42	73.7	30	76.9	12	85.7
Sought new funding:						
from public sources	39	68.4	26	66.6	12	85.7
from nonpublic sources	35	61.4	24	61.5	11	78.6
Increased agency-based fund-raising	32	56.1	24	61.5	7	50.0
Reduced expenditures:						
for administrative overhead	29	50.9	21	53.8	6	42.9
for direct programs or services	19	33.3	12	30.8	6	42.9
Developed new markets through subcontracts with other agencies	25	43.9	13	33.3	11	78.6
Increased fees to clients	17	29.8	13	33.3	2	14.3
Draw on reserves	15	26.3	8	20.5	6	42.9
Developed separate for-profit operations	8	14.4	6	15.4	1	7.1
Shifted emphasis on funding:						
from federal to state government	8	14.0	4	10.3	4	28.6
from one type of grant to another	16	28.1	9	23.1	7	50.0
Initiated fees	6	10.5	3	7.7	3	21.4
Other	2	3.5	2	5.1	0	0
Renegotiated employee contracts	1	1.8	0	0	1	7.1

profit agencies reported taking this action. Perhaps more surprising is the fact that 85 percent of public agencies indicated they sought additional funding from current nonpublic sources, while 77 percent of private nonprofit agencies had taken this action. And with regard to new funding, public agencies again reported making more extensive efforts than private nonprofit agencies.

Staffing

Data from agencies concerning the use of staff to compensate for reduced resources involves a variety of practices (table 15.5). A significant proportion of agencies expanded the responsibilities of the staff. More than two-thirds increased the caseload of direct service-providing staff. And just over half increased the use of volunteers to serve clients.

There appear to be few significant differences in the use of staff by public and private nonprofit agencies in managing retrenchment. Both types of agencies expanded staff responsibilities and increased caseloads in nearly equal proportions. However, a greater percentage of public agencies increased the use of volunteers both to serve clients and to provide clerical support. In addition, a larger percentage of public agencies reassigned staff to different programs.

Operations/Management

Agencies have taken a wide range of initiatives in their internal operations/management to compensate for reduced funding. Five different management practices were reported by more than half of all the agencies (table 15.6). The priority of actions differed. Public agencies attempted four of the five management initiatives in greater percentages than private agencies. Only one management practice—increased management discretion—was taken by more private than public agencies.

TABLE 15.5

Management Staffing Practices in Social Service Agencies

	All Agencies (N = 57)		Private Nonprofit Agencies (N = 39)		Public Agencies (N = 14)	
	Number	Percent	Number	Percent	Number	Percent
Expanded responsibilities of staff	42	73.7	31	79.5	10	71.4
Increased caseload for direct staff	39	68.4	27	69.2	11	78.6
Increased use of volunteers:						
to provide service to clients	30	52.6	20	51.3	10	71.4
to provide clerical support	21	36.8	13	33.3	8	57.1
Reduced size of staff that provides:						
direct services	20	35.1	12	30.8	7	50.0
clerical support	12	21.1	9	23.1	3	21.4
Reduced the staff through:						
job sharing, increased use of part-time employees, reduction of hours	23	40.4	16	41.0	5	35.7
planned layoffs	10	17.5	6	15.4	3	21.4
planned attrition	6	10.5	4	10.3	2	14.3
Reassigned staff to different programs	23	40.4	15	38.5	8	57.1
Other	3	5.3	3	7.7	0	0

TABLE 15.6

Operations/Management Practices in Social Service Agencies

	All Agencies (N = 57)		Private Nonprofit Agencies (N = 39)		Public Agencies (N = 14)	
	Number	Percent	Number	Percent	Number	Percent
Initiated efforts to improve staff morale	42	73.7	27	69.2	11	78.6
Initiated a review of priorities	39	68.4	25	64.1	10	71.4
Held management training programs to increase efficiency	35	61.4	20	51.3	11	78.6
Initiated cooperative planning with other agencies	33	57.9	21	53.8	10	71.4
Increased management discretion for greater flexibility in assignments, etc.	31	54.4	22	56.4	7	50.0
Shared facilities with other agencies	24	42.1	16	41.0	8	57.1
Merged selected service functions or procedures with other agencies	13	22.8	11	28.2	2	14.3
Shared administrative functions	8	14.0	6	15.4	2	14.3
Merged with other agencies	5	8.8	5	12.8	0	0
Other	0	0	2	5.1	1	7.1

External Relations

Agencies have recognized the need to promote their services and client needs. This is evident from the data in table 15.7. With near unanimity, agency managers placed greater emphasis on public relations campaigns and on coalition building within the community. A greater percentage of public than private nonprofit agencies took these two actions with respect to external relations.

Barriers to Effective Management

Restrictions from a variety of sources pose the most serious barriers to managing retrenchment. These include: federal and state agencies that impose limitations and eligibility criteria on the use of their funds; agency policies and procedures; and the limits placed by nongovernmental funding

TABLE 15.7

Management External Relations Practices in Social Service Agencies

	All Agencies (N = 57)		Private Nonprofit Agencies (N = 39)		Public Agencies (N = 14)	
	Number	Percent	Number	Percent	Number	Percent
Increased public awareness of agency mission; the need for services	48	84.2	31	79.5	13	92.9
Participated in coalitions with other agencies to coordinate services, programs, etc.	47	82.5	31	79.5	13	92.9
Participated in coalitions with other agencies to increase lobbying efforts	30	52.6	21	53.8	8	57.1
Hired a staff person to increase public or government relations efforts	8	14.0	5	12.8	1	7.1
Other	0	0	0	0	1	7.1

TABLE 15.8

Barriers to Effective Management in Social Service Agencies

	All Agencies (N = 57)		Private Nonprofit Agencies (N = 39)		Public Agencies (N = 14)	
	Number	Percent	Number	Percent	Number	Percent
Restrictions established by:						
state agencies	17	29.8	12	30.8	6	42.9
federal agencies	15	26.3	9	23.1	4	28.6
other funding sources	12	21.1	9	23.1	2	14.3
foundations	3	5.3	2	5.1	1	7.1
Agency policies and procedures	12	21.1	6	15.4	5	35.7
Poor staff morale	10	17.5	2	5.1	7	50.0
Lack of support or resistance from agency board of directors	7	12.3	5	12.8	2	14.3
Provisions of employee contracts	3	5.3	1	2.6	2	14.3
Other	1	1.8	1	2.6	0	0

sources such as corporations and community-based campaigns on the use of their contributions.

Table 15.8 indicates the differences between public and private nonprofit agencies in response to such limitations. While both types of agencies suffered from such restrictions, poor staff morale was identified as more of a problem in public agencies. Furthermore, agency policies and procedures were of much greater concern in public than private nonprofit agencies.

Policy Options: Alternative Approaches to Compensation

Human services agencies appear to have two alternatives to compensate for reduced public support of services and clients. One alternative is essentially reactive. It consists of making tactical decisions concerning the allocation of resources. Since resources are appropriated annually by almost all funding sources, public and nongovernmental alike, an agency's tactical decisions are constrained by its annual budget, and the decisions taken one year may not be the same ones taken the following year.

The second alternative is essentially proactive. It consists of strategic planning and the management of resources and organizational capacity. Unlike the tactical approach, which deals with the declining resources on an annual basis and at least implies that things may get better the next year, strategic planning and management accepts declining resources as a continuing and, perhaps, permanent condition. As a result, the strategic planning and management approach is long-range and comprehensive. The two approaches to compensate for declining resources are not mutually exclusive. On the contrary, most agencies combine elements from both.

Tactical Decisions

The reactive approach to managing retrenchment is best captured by the concept of cutback management. In essence, cutback management consists of specific steps taken to reduce the costs of providing services to clients. It is a discrete response to the resources allocated for a particular fiscal year. There may not be any continuity between tactical decisions made one year and those made the next, though the literature on incremental budgeting suggests the opposite.

Cutback management seeks to make an agency more efficient with respect to the relationship between resources and services, but it cannot pay attention to efficiency and effectiveness at the same time. Rather, human service managers appear to recognize that reducing operating costs and increasing workloads are likely to occur at the expense of the quality and effectiveness of services. Tactical decisions taken to reduce the strain on an agency's annual resources include reducing operating costs, decreasing client levels, and augmenting revenues.

A common tactical decision in cutback management is to reduce operating costs by laying off or rearranging staff assignments. In one agency, for example, the administrative staff was reduced in size, and administrators were asked to assume a service delivery role in addition to their supervisory responsibilities. In other instances, expenditures for direct care staff were reduced by shifting responsibilities to para-professionals and volunteers. Still another option involved increasing the workload of direct care staff and authorizing overtime in lieu of hiring additional personnel.

The use of flex-time or shared time can lower operating costs and have a positive effect on productivity. In one particular case, two full-time direct care positions were reduced to .60 FTE. Since the individuals involved supported the change, there were benefits for both the agency and staff. Other agencies reported the use of job sharing and various part-time arrangements to reduce personnel costs.

Agencies' employees expressed a willingness to trade higher pay for more work. One agency manager described combining clerical, bookkeeping, and office management responsibilities into a single position. Another upgraded salaries, which made it possible to hire better qualified applicants capable of assuming greater responsibility. In another instance, an agency cut an administrative position and assigned its duties to a remaining position with compatible responsibilities.

Public agencies at the community level are also impacted by statutory limits and appropriations enacted at the state or federal levels. One public agency described a hiring freeze imposed by the parent agency at the state level. At the local level, the freeze forced the agency to operate with fewer staff than authorized in the budget.

Another common technique of cutback management is to shift the effects of retrenchment to clients. Many agencies reported changing eligibility criteria to make it more difficult for clients to qualify for services. Sometimes this was done to maintain control over the length of the agency's waiting list. At other times its purpose was to cut down on the frequency with which clients received services. For example, one agency reported changing admission criteria to keep "rotating door" clients from coming in too frequently; another reviewed client eligibility to "put the clamp on competition."

Proof of eligibility is another way of maintaining control over client levels. A number of agencies that use income as a criterion of eligibility reported instituting verification procedures. Discouraging referrals from other agencies or allowing waiting lists to grow were other tactical measures taken to compensate for reduced revenues.

A unique approach was taken by an agency that added a work component to client requirements. In this case, clients were required to perform ten hours of service in order to receive assistance.

Tactical decisions also included various measures to increase revenues by instituting or increasing fees paid by clients. Despite the fact that the target population for human services generally has a limited capacity to pay, many agencies began instituting fees. One initiated an approach to broaden its fee base that combined charging a fee for services with liberalized screening that interpreted eligibility criteria more broadly than in the past. The consequence of this effort was to increase the number of clients who paid for the agency's services.

Fee income can be generated in other ways as well. In some cases, fees were instituted for clients who had previously received services at no charge. In other instances, employees who received services as part of the agency's benefit program were required to pay for those services.

Strategic Planning and Management

The proactive approach to managing retrenchment emphasizes systematic planning concerning the management of resources and the organization's performance capacity within a multi-year time frame. Strategic decisions identify and weigh the internal and external factors affecting an agency, set priorities, and implement a plan of action to achieve identifiable objectives. Strategic planning and management initiatives include broadening the agency's revenue base, setting priorities and targeting resources, improving organizational capacity, and seeking a broader political base.

There is widespread recognition that funding for human services has relied too heavily on federal and state governments. Furthermore, agencies realize that there is a limited capacity for growth in revenues from these two sources. Consequently, most agencies are engaged in strategic planning to broaden their revenue base.

Many reported initiating major endowment development programs. The commitment to endowment and fund-raising programs is reflected in the steps agencies implemented to improve their prospects of success. Some contracted for development and public relations services. Others designated and created a position for grant writing. Others approached philanthropies and corporate sponsors for support.

Agencies generally recognize that resources are no longer sufficient to support the wide range of services they provide. Rather, it has become necessary to set priorities and concentrate resources on the limited number of services that an agency is best able to offer.

Priority setting and targeting resources are accomplished in a variety of ways. Some agencies instituted a "triage" approach in which clients are evaluated for the severity of needs and aid is provided on the basis of degree of need. Other agencies discouraged referrals of clients who could be served elsewhere.

The most widespread form of prioritizing and targeting is found in redefining the agency mission and clarifying its identity. This effort serves as the basis for achieving a balance between programs and organizational capacity. In some cases, the redefinition and clarification of the agency's mission resulted in decisions to eliminate programs or to delay services. A number of agencies reported that decreased funding and staff led to the decision to postpone the implementation of specialized programs.

Retrenchment has adversely affected organizational capacity and performance in a number of ways. Agencies reported a widespread perception among employees that they were overworked, underpaid, and unrecognized for the importance of their efforts. For their part, agency directors reported declining productivity, higher staff turnover, more sick leave, and difficulty in recruiting new personnel. Low wages and other restrictions on compensation only partly explain the difficulty agencies encountered trying to replace staff.

Agencies have initiated a number of strategic measures to improve and develop organizational capacity. There is an increasing movement toward a more generalist approach to staff recruitment and job responsibility. In lieu of staff with specialized knowledge and skills, organizations are emphasizing the importance of broad-based knowledge and abilities that enable an individual to participate in a wide range of functions and activities. Second, more effective utilization of staff requires increased attention to training and development for direct care staff, supervisors, and managers. This includes increasing supervisory review and a greater use of performance-based evaluation. Third, agencies have expressed support for using participatory management that includes staff in decision making and increases communication. Agencies are coming to view the involvement of staff in decision making as a part of each person's job function. Additionally, there is evidence in the agency surveys that an informed and involved staff perceives itself to be more effective and more valued by the organization. Finally, a greater organizational capacity is developed by paying closer attention to the composition and role of the board of directors. Especially among private nonprofit agencies, the value of a working board cannot be overstated. Many agencies reported that their boards have become more active in setting goals, policy, and priorities. In addition, the selection and appointment of new members to the board involves looking for persons with particular expertise in such critical areas as fund-raising.

Cultivating support for the human services through networking, coalition building, and increased visibility and presence in the community is another approach of strategic planning and management. Most agencies encourage their professional staff to be involved in the community, and some even give "comp time" for it.

Building political support through networking, coalition building, and lobbying is a widely used approach that agencies believe offers long-term benefits. Agencies recognize the importance of this approach on a horizontal as well as vertical plane. Many agencies reported participation in lobbying activities in the state capitol and, occasionally, in Washington, D.C., by holding a "Legislative Day."

The importance of networking and coalition building is not limited to public and political support. Many agencies recognize that limited resources require reducing the duplication and overlap of services between providers. Consequently, greater attention is paid to case management to serve clients, to monitoring progress through the human services system, and to avoiding duplication. Formal working agreements including information and referral systems are often used to achieve such ends.

Human services agencies compensate for reduced funding from state and federal governments by employing a combination of tactical and strategic decisions. Tactical decisions have enabled agencies to compensate for the constraints of the annual budget. It remains to be seen whether strategic planning and management will enable human services to find alternatives to the reliance on state and federal funding that can assure the continued delivery of services without adversely affecting their organizational capacity to serve clients.

Conclusion

However one looks at the situation, it has been and will likely continue to involve a period of contraction and retrenchment in the availability and delivery of social services. The Reagan-Bush era targeted social welfare policies for major funding cuts and a minimalization of services, geared in particular to affect the less politically active (the poor, the elderly, children).

This reductionist approach has had a ripple effect. Without federal dollars and in a time of economic recession (seen more as a depression in many of the frostbelt states such as Michigan that have been losing jobs and industries to the sunbelt and foreign countries), state governments have substantially cut back on their contributions to implementing social programs. The combination of difficult times economically and a lessened availability of domestic programs has resulted in more people eligible for, and in need of, social services at a point where these programs have been severely underfunded.

The Reagan-Bush era, with its deemphasis of the government's social responsibilities, is a distinctive period in the history of welfare policy and federal-state intergovernmental relationships in the United States. The New Deal shifted the burden for domestic programs to the federal government and significantly expanded the government's commitment to supply needed support services to the American public.

For four decades or more (up to the early 1980s), the federal government's role as the major funder and provider in these areas went unchallenged. Lyndon Johnson's "Great Society" in the mid-1960s expanded the national government's responsibilities in such areas as education, preschooling (Head

Start), nutrition, community-based welfare, health (Medicare and Medicaid), housing, the environment, poverty, and in a range of other concerns (civil rights, for example). The Nixon administration chose a different path, emphasizing its "New Federalism" with money given—whenever possible in the form of unrestricted block grants—to the states, to prioritize and administer at their discretion. The Carter administration began the deemphasis of domestic programs, placing more emphasis on budgetary concerns and program costs. It was an approach that was to hurt Carter. The president lost support within his own party and eventually faced a challenge in the 1980 presidential pre-nomination race.

The Carter administration efforts to stabilize and reduce domestic program costs set the stage for the Reagan presidency, which engaged in a full-scale retrenchment and fundamental redesign of the federal government's role as a provider of social services (see the discussions and references cited in MacManus, 1991; Weber, 1991; and Sabatier, 1991).

There is little evidence to indicate that the recent trends will be reversed in the foreseeable future. The Clinton administration has placed an emphasis on workfare proposals and a selective redistribution (rather than an expansion) of funds, emphasizing, for example, work training and job re-entry programs over continued subsistance care.

The consequence has been a continuing series of adjustments at the local level to make do with less. All social service agencies, whether public or private, have suffered from the cutbacks, although some policy areas (mental health is the significant illustration) have fared better than others. The major differences among social agencies involve their approach to retrenchment. Even here the similarities are more apparent than the differences. There is a limit to the alternatives available to an organization. Basically, all rejected new clients, increased the workload and responsibilities of the professional (and part-time and clerical) staff, reworked eligibility requirements, charged user fees, and pursued more aggressive fund-raising and political coalition-building strategies within their local communities. The payoffs did not appear great. The emphasis necessarily was on organizational survival rather than comprehensive service delivery.

The basic differences among the agencies, and there were significant overlaps in these regards as well, were in the nature of short- and long-run decision making. Some chose to emphasize tactical adjustments based on a premise (spoken or unspoken) that the hard times would pass (the reactive position). Other agency decision-makers chose to take a strategic, proactive stance. Basically, they accepted the situation, believed fundamental improvement was unlikely, and sought ways to help the organization adjust and survive in a changed political environment.

The cuts in social program budgeting by the federal and state governments did have major consequences for local agencies, the availability and comprehensiveness of the programs they could offer, and the clientele they normally would have served. In this regard, it is useful to take the study one step further: What happens to those eligible under previous standards for social services but unable to claim such program support in the contemporary context? The guess is that the consequences in terms of health, life-style, unemployment or underemployment, economic opportunity, and family stability are significant. What is clear is that when the government reduces its commitment to social policies, the impact, as this study indicates, is both real and substantial.

Contributors

Jack N. Behrman is Luther Hodges Distinguished Professor Emeritus at the Kenan-Flagler Business School of the University of North Carolina at Chapel Hill and director of MBA Enterprise Corps at the Kenan Institute of Private Enterprise. He has served as Assistant Secretary of Commerce for Domestic and International Business in both the Kennedy and Johnson administrations.

Richard D. Bingham is a professor of public administration and urban studies and a Senior Research Scholar at the Urban Center of Cleveland State University. He has written extensively on economic development, national industrial policy, and international trade.

Robert H. Binstock is the Henry R. Luce Professor of Aging, Health, and Society at Case Western University and served as the director of the White House Task Force on Older Americans. He is one of the foremost authorities on aging in the United States. Through his extensive publications and service on governmental and foundation commissions, he has had a significant impact on policy concerns relevant to older Americans.

Robert H. Blank is a professor of political science at the University of Canterbury and served previously as associate director of the Program for Biosocial Research at Northern Illinois University. He has received a number of professional recognitions and has published numerous studies in the area of health policy, geriatric and reproductive technology.

R. McGreggor Cawley is a professor of political science at the University of Wyoming. He teaches and publishes in the areas of public land policy, environmental concerns, federal-state relations, and the policy-making process.

William Crotty is a professor of political science at Northwestern University and a former president of the Policy Studies Organization.

Peter R. Gluck is a professor of political science at the University of Michigan–Flint. His areas of interest and professional work include federal-state intergovernmental relations, policy processes, organizational decision making, and public administration.

R. Allen Hays is a professor of political science at Iowa State University. He has conducted numerous studies and published research reports, including a principal analysis of public housing policy, relating to the development of federal housing programs and their impact.

Dennis R. Judd is a professor of political science at the University of Missouri, St. Louis, and has served as director of its Center for Metropolitan Studies. His areas of concern and many publications focus on urban politics, policy processes, and the development of social policy in the United States.

Anthony Kandel is a graduate student in political science at the University of Southern California.

Sheldon Kamieniecki is a professor of political science and vice chair of the Department of Political Science at the University of Southern California. He has researched and written extensively on environmental and ecosystem concerns in the United States and in an international comparative context, and he directs a program in these studies at the University of Southern California.

Barry Keating is Jesse H. Jones Professor of Business Economics and chair of the Department of Finance and Business Economics in the College of Business Administration at the University of Notre Dame. He has published extensively on international and United States economic policy, economic decision making, organizational management, and social service delivery systems.

Maryann Keating is a professor of economics at Gosten College, with a particular interest in international macroeconomics, nonprofit firms, the female labor force, and comparative trade. In these areas, among others, she has published a number of books and professional papers.

Steven G. Koven is a professor of political science at Iowa State University and has served in the Department of Health, Education and Welfare and the Department of Commerce. He has written on budgetary and social policy and political economy.

Robert M. Lawrence is a professor of political science at Colorado State University and a visiting professor of political science at the University of Colorado. He has written on environmental, defense, and national security, and arms control policies in the United States and in an international comparative context, and he has been a consultant to the Rand Corporation and other organizations.

Peter A. Manning has taught at both Northeastern University and Bentley College and has won professional recognition for his more than twenty years of work in food and nutrition with the Department of Agriculture and for his research on hunger and food policies in the United States.

Jennifer Mezey is a graduate student at the John F. Kennedy School of Public Policy at Harvard University.

Michael L. Mezey is a political science professor and associate dean of the College of Arts and Sciences at DePaul University. He has published in the areas of comparative legislatures and policy-making processes in the United States, Europe, and Asia.

Susan Gluck Mezey is a professor of political science at Loyola University of Chicago and has served as an advisor to the Department of Health and Human Services. Her areas of interest focus on ethics, gender representation, and the impact of the courts in applying policy.

Dennis A. Rondinelli is professor of international business at the Kenan-Flagler Business School at the University of North Carolina, Chapel Hill, and director of the International Private Enterprise Development Research Center at the Kenan Institute of Private Enterprise. He has served as an advisor to the World Bank, the U.S. Agency for International Development, the Asian Development Bank, and the United Nations.

Louis Schubert is a graduate student in political science at the University of Southern California.

Gregory R. Weiher is a professor of political science at the University of Houston and director of its Center for Public Policy. He has researched and written on a broad range of social policies, assessing their development and their impact.

References

Chapter 1: The Role of the State in a Post–Cold War Society

Aaron, Henry J. ed. 1990. *Setting National Priorities: Policy for the Nineties*. Washington, D.C.: Brookings Institution.

———. 1991. *Serious and Unstable Condition: Financing America's Health Care*. Washington, D.C.: Brookings Institution.

Aaron, Henry J., and Charles L. Schultze, eds. 1992. *Setting Domestic Priorities: What Can Government Do?* Washington, D.C.: Brookings Institution.

Abramson, Paul R., John H. Aldrich, and David W. Rhode. 1982. *Change and Continuity in the 1980 Election*. Washington, D.C.: Congressional Quarterly Press.

———. 1986. *Change and Continuity in the 1984 Election*. Washington, D.C.: Congressional Quarterly Press.

Andrews, Edmund L. 1993. "Swords to Plowshares: The Bureaucratic Snags." *New York Times*, Feb. 16, C1.

Anderson, Kristi. 1979. *The Creation of a Democratic Majority, 1928–1936*. Chicago: University of Chicago Press.

Associated Press. 1992a. "For Poor Children, A Bad Decade." *Chicago Tribune*, July 8, p. 5.

———. 1992b. "Census Shows Further Deterioration of U.S. Families." *Chicago Tribune*, July 17, p. 3.

———. 1993. "Aspin: Base Closings to be Fair." *Chicago Tribune*, March 8, p. 3.

Barr, Nicholas. 1993. *The Economics of the Welfare State*. Stanford, Calif.: Stanford University Press.

Berkowitz, Edward O. 1991. *America's Welfare State: From Roosevelt to Reagan*. Baltimore, Md.: Johns Hopkins University Press.

Berkowitz, Edward O., and Kim McQuaid. 1992. *Creating the Welfare State: The Political Economy of Twentieth-Century Reform*, rev. ed. Lawrence: University Press of Kansas.

Berman, Larry, 1990. "The Legacy of the Reagan Years." In L. Berman, ed. *Looking Back on the Reagan Years*, pp. 3–17. Baltimore, Md.: Johns Hopkins University Press.

———, ed. 1990. *Looking Back on the Reagan Presidency*. Baltimore, Md.: Johns Hopkins University Press.

Berman, Larry; and Bruce W. Jentleson. 1991. "Bush and the Post–Cold War World: New Challenges for American Leadership." In Colin Campbell and Bert A. Rockman, eds., *The Bush Presidency: First Appraisals*. Chatham, N.J.: Chatham House.

Block, Fred, Richard A. Cloward, Barbara Ehrenreich, and Francis F. Piven. 1987. *The Mean Season: The Attack on the Welfare State*. New York: Random House.

Blumenthal, Sidney, and Thomas B. Edsall, eds. 1988. *The Reagan Legacy*. New York: Pantheon.

Burnham, Walter D. 1970. *Critical Elections and the Mainsprings of American Politics*. New York: Norton.

Burt, Martha R., and Karen J. Pittman. 1985. *Testing the Social Safety Net: The Impact of Changes in Support Programs during the Reagan Administration*. Washington, D.C.: Urban Institute Press.

Campbell, Colin, and Bert A. Rockman, eds. 1991. *The Bush Presidency: First Appraisals*. Chatham, N.J.: Chatham House.

Cannon, Lou. 1982. *Reagan*. New York: Putnam's.

Clinton, Bill, and Al Gore. 1992. *Putting People First: How We Can All Change America*. New York: Times Books.

Cook, Fay L., and Edith J. Barrett. 1992. *Support for the Welfare State*. New York: Columbia University Press.

Crotty, William, ed. 1993. *America's Choice: The Election of 1992*. Guilford, Conn. Dushkin.

DeParle. 1992. "Incomes in Young Families Drop 32% in 17 Years Study Finds." *New York Times*, April 15.

Destler, I. M. 1988. "Reagan and the World: An 'Awesome Stubbornness.' " In Charles O. Jones, ed., *The Reagan Legacy: Promise and Performance*, pp. 241–61. Chatham, N.J.: Chatham House.

Draper, Theodore. 1991. *A Very Thin Line: The Iran-Contra Affairs*. New York: Hill and Wang.

Dugger, Ronnie. 1983. *On Reagan: The Man and His Presidency*. New York: McGraw-Hill.

Edelman, Marian W. 1992. "Children." In Mark Green, ed., *Changing America: Blueprints for the New Administration*, pp. 431–42. New York: Newmarket Press.

Esping-Andersen, Gosta. 1985. *Politics Against Markets*. Princeton, N.J.: Princeton University Press.

———. 1990. *The Three Worlds of Welfare Capitalism*. Princeton, N.J.: Princeton University Press.

Evans, David. 1993a. "Joint Chiefs Outline Defense Cuts." *Chicago Tribune*, Feb. 13, p. 1.

———. 1993b. "Joint Chiefs' Report Sidesteps Tough Issues." *Chicago Tribune*, Feb. 14, p. 8.

Feldman, Stanley, and John Zaller. 1992. "The Political Culture of Ambivalence: Ideological Responses to the Welfare State." *American Journal of Political Science*, 36 (1) (Feb.): 268–307.

Flora, Peter, and Arnold J. Heidenheimer, eds. 1990. *The Development of Welfare States in Europe and America*. New Brunswick, N.J.: Transaction.

Goldsmith, William G., and Edward J. Blakeley. 1992. *Separate Societies: Poverty and Inequality in U.S. Cities*. Philadelphia, Penn.: Temple University Press.

Gough, Ian. 1979. *The Political Economy of the Welfare State*. London: Macmillan.

Green, Mark, ed. 1992. *Changing America: Blueprints for the New Administration*. New York: Newmarket Press.

Greenhouse, Steven. 1992. "A Foreign Notion for Washington: U.S. Needs Higher Taxes." *New York Times*, Nov. 29, p. 2E.

Gueron, Judith M., and Edward Pauly. 1991. *From Welfare to Work*. New York: Russell Sage Foundation.

Gutman, Amy, ed. 1988. *Democracy and the Welfare State*. Princeton, N.J.: Princeton University Press.

Hacker, Andrew. 1992. *Two Nations: Black and White, Separate, Hostile, Unequal*. New York: Ballantine.

Helco, Hugh. 1990. "Toward a New Welfare State." In Peter Flora and Arnold J. Heidenheimer, eds., *The Development of Welfare States in Europe and America*, pp. 383–406. New Brunswick, N. J.: Transaction.

Helco, Hugh, and Henrik Madsen. 1987. *Policy and Politics in Sweden: Principled Pragmatism*. Philadelphia, Penn.: Temple University Press.

Howe, Irving, ed. 1982. *Beyond the Welfare State*. New York: Shocken Books.

Ignatius, David. 1988. "Reagan's Foreign Policy and the Rejection of Diplomacy." In Sidney Blumenthal and Thomas Byrne Edsall, eds., *The Reagan Legacy*, pp. 173–212. New York: Pantheon.

Jencks, Christopher, and Paul E. Peterson, eds. 1991. *The Urban Underclass*. Washington, D.C.: Brookings Institution.

Johnson, Haynes. 1991. *Sleepwalking Through History: America in the Reagan Years*. New York: Anchor.

Johnson, Kirk. 1993. "A State's Strategy for Economic Recovery: Innovation, Sacrifice and Hope." *New York Times*, Feb. 11, p. A12.

Jones, Catherine. 1985. *Patterns of Social Policy: An Introduction to Comparative Analysis*. London: Tavistock.

Jones, Charles O., ed. 1988. *The Reagan Legacy*. Chatham, N. J.: Chatham House.

Jouzatis, Carol. 1993. "Clinton Acts to Soften Blow of Defense Cuts." *Chicago Tribune*, March 12, p. 1.

Katz, Michael B. 1986. *In the Shadow of the Poorhouse: A Social History of Welfare in America*. New York: Basic Books.

———. 1989. *The Undeserving Poor: From the War on Poverty to the War on Welfare*. New York: Pantheon.

Kelley, E. W. 1987. *Policy and Politics in the United States: The Limits of Localism*. Philadelphia, Penn.: Temple University Press.

Kelley, Stanley, Jr. 1988. "Democracy and the New Deal Party System." In Amy Gutman, ed., *Democracy and the Welfare State*, pp. 185–205. Princeton, N. J.: Princeton University Press.

Kohl, Jurgen. 1990. "Trends and Problems in Postwar Public Expenditure Development in Western Europe and North America." In Peter Flora and Arnold J. Heidenheimer, eds., *The Development of Welfare States in Europe and America*, pp. 307–44. New Brunswick, N. J.: Transaction.

Korb, Lawrence J. 1990. "The 1991 Defense Budget." In Henry J. Aaron, ed., *Setting National Priorities: Policy for the Nineties*, pp. 111–43. Washington, D.C.: Brookings Institution.

Kozol, Jonathan. 1992. *Savage Inequalities: Children in America's Schools*. New York: HarperPerennial.

Kudrle, Robert T., and Theodore J. Marmor. 1990. "The Development of the Welfare State in North America." In Peter Flora and Arnold J. Heidenheimer, eds., *The Development of Welfare States in Europe and America*, pp. 81–121. New Brunswick, N. J.: Transaction.

Lehmann-Haupt, Christopher. 1993. "Middle-Class Rage, Past and Future." *New York Times*, Feb. 1, p. B2.

Lieber, Robert J. 1990. "The Middle East." In Larry Berman, ed., *Looking Back on the Reagan Presidency*, pp. 50–70. Baltimore, Md.: Johns Hopkins University Press.

Lubove, Roy. 1986. *The Struggle for Social Security, 1900–1935*. Pittsburgh, Penn.: University of Pittsburgh Press.

Marmor, Theodore R., and Michael S. Barr. 1992. "Health." In Mark Green, ed., *Changing America: Blueprints for the New Administration*, pp. 399–414. New York: Newmarket Press.

Marmor, Theodore R., Jerry L. Mashaw, and Philip L. Harvey. 1990. *America's Misunderstood Welfare State: Persistent Myths, Enduring Realities*. New York: Basic Books.

Marshall, T. H. 1964. *Class, Citizenship, and Social Development*. New York: Doubleday.

————. 1977. *Social Policy in the Twentieth Century*. London: Hutchinson.

Marshall, T. H., and Tom Bottomore. 1992. *Citizenship and Social Class*. London: Pluto Press.

Marshall, Will, and Martin Schram, eds. 1993. *Mandate for Change*. New York: Berkeley Books.

McClosky, Herbert, and John Zaller. 1984. *The American Ethos: Public Attitudes Toward Capitalism and Democracy*. Cambridge, Mass.: Harvard University Press.

McElvane, Robert S. 1984. *The Great Depression: America, 1929–1941*. New York: Times Books.

McIntyre, Robert S. 1992. "Tax Policy." In Mark Green, ed., *Changing America. Blueprints for the New Administration*, pp. 29–45. New York: Newmarket Press.

Meyer, Jack A., and Marilyn Moon. 1988. "Health Care Spending on Children and the Elderly." In John L. Palmer, Timothy Smeeding, and Barbara Boyle Torrey, eds., *The Vulnerable*, pp. 171–200. Washington, D.C.: Urban Institute Press.

Meyer, Karl E. 1993. " 'Socialized Medicine' Resistance." *New York Times*, Aug. 2, p. A10.

Mills, Gregory B. 1984. "The Budget: A Failure of Discipline." In John L. Palmer and Isabel V. Sawhill, eds., *The Reagan Record: An Assessment of America's Changing Domestic Priorities*, pp. 107–39. Cambridge, Mass.: Ballinger.

Moon, Marilyn, and Isabel V. Sawhill. 1984. "Family Incomes: Gainers and Losers." In John L. Palmer and Isabel V. Sawhill, eds., *The Reagan Record: An Assessment of America's Changing Domestic Priorities*, pp. 317–46. Cambridge, Mass.: Ballinger.

Murray, Charles. 1984. *Losing Ground: American Social Policy, 1950–1980*. New York: Basic Books.

Myles, John. 1988. "Postwar Capitalism and the Extension of Social Security into a Retirement Wage." Margaret Weir, Ann S. Orloff, and Theda Skocpol, eds., *The Politics of Social Policy in the United States*, pp. 265–84. Princeton, N. J.: Princeton University Press.

Nasar, Sylvia. 1993. "Supply Side Goes by the Wayside." *New York Times*, Feb. 20, p. 13.

Okin, Susan M. 1981. "Liberty and Welfare: Some Issues in Human Rights Theory." In J. Roland Pennock and John W. Chapman, eds., *Human Rights (NOMOS Series XXIII)*, pp. 230–55. Albany: New York University Press.

Orloff, Ann S. 1988. "The Political Origins of America's Belated Welfare State." In Margaret Weir, Ann S. Orloff, and Theda Skocpol, eds., *The Politics of Social Policy in the United States*, pp. 37–80. Princeton, N. J.: Princeton University Press.

Palmer, John L., and Isabel V. Sawhill, eds. 1984. *The Reagan Record: An Assessment of America's Changing Domestic Priorities*. Cambridge, Mass.: Ballinger.

Palmer, John L., Isabel V. Sawhill, Timothy Smeeding, and Barbara B. Torrey, eds. 1988. *The Vulnerable*. Washington, D.C.: Urban Institute Press.

Pastor, Robert A. 1990. "The Centrality of Central America." In Larry Berman, ed., *Looking Back on the Reagan Presidency*, pp. 33–49. Baltimore, Md.: Johns Hopkins University Press.

Pear, Robert. 1992. "Social Programs Grow, But Largely by Neglect." *New York Times*, Aug. 2, p. 1.

————. 1993. "Clear Break: Clinton's Bold Plan Sets Social Policy His Way." *New York Times*, Feb. 21, sec. 4, p. 1.

Peckman, Joseph A., and Michael S. McPherson, eds. 1992. *Fulfilling America's Promise: Social Policy for the 1990s*. Ithaca, N.Y.: Cornell University Press.

Peterson, Paul E., and Mark Rom. 1988. "Lower Taxes, More Spending, and Budget Deficits." In Charles O. Jones, ed., *The Reagan Legacy: Promise and Performance*, pp. 213–40. Chatham, N. J.: Chatham House.

Petrocik, John R. 1981. *Party Coalitions: Realignment and the Decline of the New Deal Party System*. Chicago: University of Chicago Press.

Phillips, Kevin. 1969. *The Emerging Republican Majority*. New York: Arlington House.

———. 1991. *The Politics of Rich and Poor*. New York: HarperPerennial.

———. 1993. *Boiling Point: Republicans, Democrats and the Decline of Middle-Class Prosperity*. New York: Random House.

Pierson, Christopher. 1991. *Beyond the Welfare State? The New Political Economy of Welfare*. University Park: Pennsylvania State University Press.

Piven, Frances F. and Richard A. Cloward. 1971. *Regulating the Poor: The Functions of Public Welfare*. New York: Vintage Books.

———. 1985. *The New Class War: Reagan's Attack on the Welfare State and Its Consequences*. New York: Pantheon Books.

Prokesch, Steven. 1993. "Companies Struggle to Adjust as U.S. Cuts Military Budget." *New York Times*, Feb. 2, p. A1.

Rawls, John. 1971. *A Theory of Justice*. Cambridge, Mass.: Harvard University Press.

———. 1993. *Political Liberalism*. New York: Columbia University Press.

Reinhardt, Uwe E. 1992. "American Health Care at the Crossroads." In Joseph A. Peckman and Michael S. McPherson, eds., *Fulfilling America's Promise: Social Policies for the 1990s*, pp. 50–84. Ithaca, N.Y.: Cornell University Press.

Rice, Condoleeza. 1990. "U.S.-Soviet Relations." In Larry Berman, ed., *Looking Back on the Reagan Presidency*, pp. 71–89. Baltimore, Md.: Johns Hopkins University Press.

Ringen, Stein. 1989. *The Possibility of Politics: A Study in the Political Economy of the Welfare State*. Oxford: Clarendon Press.

Risen, James. 1992. "Fed Says Rich Got Richer under Reagan." *Chicago Sun-Times*, Jan. 7, p. 6.

Robertson, David B., and Dennis R. Judd. 1989. *The Development of American Public Policy: The Structure of Policy Restraint*. Glenview, Ill.: Scott, Foresman.

Rogin, Michael. 1987. *Ronald Reagan, the Movie: And Other Episodes in Political Demonology*. Berkeley: University of California Press.

Rosner, Jeremy D. 1993. "A Progressive Plan for Affordable, Universal Health Care." In Will Marshall and Martin Schram, eds., *Mandate for Change*, pp. 107–28. New York: Berkeley Books.

Rossi, Peter H. 1989. *Down and Out in America: The Origins of Homelessness*. Chicago: University of Chicago Press.

Rueschemeyer, Dietrich, Evelyne H. Stephens, and John D. Stephens, eds. 1992. *Capitalist Development and Democracy*. Chicago: University of Chicago Press.

Salamon, Lester M., and Michael S. Lund, eds. 1984. *The Reagan Presidency and the Governing of America*. Washington, D.C.: Urban Institute Press.

Schick, Allen. 1984. "The Budget as an Instrument of Presidential Policy." In Lester M. Salamon and Michael S. Lund, eds., *The Reagan Presidency and the Governing of America*, pp. 91–125. Washington, D.C.: Urban Institute Press.

Schultze, Charles L. 1990. "The Federal Budget and the Nation's Economic Health." In Henry J. Aaron, ed., *Setting National Priorities: Policy for the Nineties*, pp. 19–63. Washington, D.C.: Brookings Institution.

Schwartz, John E. 1988. *America's Hidden Success: A Reassessment of Public Policy from Kennedy to Reagan*, rev. ed. New York: Norton.

Shapiro, Robert J. 1993. "Enterprise Economics and the Federal Budget." In Will Marshall and Martin Schram, eds., *Mandate for Change*, pp. 21–50. New York: Berkeley Books.

Skocpol, Theda. 1988. "The Limits of the New Deal System and the Roots of Contemporary Welfare Dilemmas." In Margaret Weir, Ann S. Orloff, and Theda Skocpol, eds., *The Politics of Social Policy in the United States*, pp. 293–311. Princeton, N. J.: Princeton University Press.

———. 1991. "Targeting Within Universalism: Politically Viable Policies to Combat Poverty in the United States." In Christopher Jencks and Paul E. Peterson, eds., *The Urban Underclass*, pp. 411–36. Washington, D.C.: Brookings Institution.

———. 1992. *Protecting Soldiers and Mothers: The Political Origins of Social Policy in the United States*. Cambridge, Mass.: Harvard University Press.

Stein, Charles. 1993. "Counter-Revolution." *Boston Sunday Globe*, Feb. 21, p. 69.

Stephens, John D. 1979. *The Transition from Capitalism to Socialism*. Urbana: University of Illinois Press.

Stockman, David A. 1987. *The Triumph of Politics: The Inside Story of the Reagan Revolution*. New York: Avon.

Sundquist, James L. 1983. *Dynamics of the Party System*. Washington: D.C.: Brookings Institution.

Tilton, Tim. 1991. *The Political Theory of Swedish Social Democracy: Through the Welfare State to Socialism*. Oxford: Clarendon Press.

Weatherford, M. Stephen and Lorraine M. McDonnell. 1990. "Ideology and Economic Policy." In Larry Berman, ed., *Looking Back on the Reagan Presidency*, pp. 122–55. Baltimore, Md.: Johns Hopkins University Press.

Weiner, Tim. 1993. "Lies and Rigged Star Wars Test Fooled the Kremlin and Congress." *New York Times*, Aug. 18, p. A1.

Weir, Margaret, Ann S. Orloff and Theda Skocpol, eds. 1988. *The Politics of Social Policy in the United States*. Princeton, N. J.: Princeton University Press.

Wolfe, Alan. 1989. *Whose Keeper? Social Science and Moral Obligation*. Berkeley: University of California Press.

Chapter 2: Policies on Aging in the Post–Cold War Era

Aaron, H. J., ed. 1990. *Social Security and the Budget: Proceedings of the First Conference of the National Academy of Social Insurance*. Lanham, Md.: University Press of America.

Aaron, H. J., B. P. Bosworth, and G. Burtless. 1989. *Can America Afford to Grow Old? Paying for Social Security*. Washington, D.C.: Brookings Institution.

Achenbaum, W. A. 1978. *Old Age in the New Land: The American Experience Since 1790*. Baltimore, Md.: Johns Hopkins University Press.

———. 1985. "Societal Perceptions of the Aging and the Aged." In R. H. Binstock and E. Shanas, eds., *Handbook of Aging and the Social Sciences, Second Edition*, pp. 129–48. New York: Van Nostrand Reinhold.

———. 1986. *Social Security: Visions and Revisions*. New York: Cambridge University Press.

Altmeyer, A. J. 1968. *The Formative Years of Social Security*. Madison: University of Wisconsin Press.

Atkins, G. L. 1990. "The Politics of Financing Long-Term Care." *Generations,* 14(2):19–22.

Beatty, J. 1990. "A Post–Cold War Budget." *Atlantic Monthly*, 256(2):74–82.

Bell, D. 1964. "Twelve Modes of Prediction—A Preliminary Sorting of Approaches in the Social Sciences." *Daedalus*, 93:845–80.

Binstock, R. H. 1972. "Interest Group Liberalism and the Politics of Aging." *Gerontologist*, 12:265–80.

———. 1983. "The Aged as Scapegoat." *Gerontologist*, 23:136–43.

———. 1985. "The Oldest-Old: A Fresh Perspective or Compassionate Ageism Revisited?" *Milbank Memorial Fund Quarterly/Health and Society*, 63:420–51.

———. 1991. "From the Great Society to the Aging Society—25 Years of the Older Americans Act." *Generations*, 15(3):11–18.

———. 1992. "Aging, Disability, and Long-Term Care: The Politics of Common Ground." *Generations*, 16(1):83–88.

Binstock, R. H., J. Grigsby, and T. D. Leavitt. 1983. *Policy Options for "Targeting" to the Economically Needy under Title III of the Older Americans Act*. Waltham, Mass.: Policy Center On Aging, Heller School, Brandeis University.

Binstock, R. H., M. A. Levin, and R. H. Weatherley. 1985. "Political Dilemmas of Social Intervention." In R. H. Binstock and E. Shanas, eds., *Handbook of Aging and the Social Sciences*, 2d ed., pp. 589–618. New York: Van Nostrand Reinhold.

Binstock, R. H., and S. G. Post, eds. 1991. *Too Old for Health Care? Controversies in Medicine, Law, Economics, and Ethics*. Baltimore, Md.: Johns Hopkins University Press.

Binstock, R. H., S. G. Post, and P. J. Whitehouse, eds. 1992. *Dementia and Aging: Ethics, Values, and Policy Choices*. Baltimore, Md.: Johns Hopkins University Press.

Blumenthal, D., M. Schlesinger, and P. B. Drumheller. 1988. *Renewing the Promise: Medicare and Its Reform*. New York: Oxford University Press.

Budish, A. 1989–90. *Avoiding the Medicaid Trap: How to Beat the Catastrophic Cost of Nursing Homes*. New York: Henry Holt.

Burwell, B. 1991. *Middle-Class Welfare: Medicaid Estate Planning for Long-Term Care Coverage*. Lexington, Mass.: SysteMetrics/McGraw-Hill.

Butterfield, F. 1990. "Silber Taps Public's Anger to Run a Strong Race in Massachusetts." *New York Times*, July 27, p. A6.

Button, J. W., and W. A. Rosenbaum. 1989. "Seeing Gray: School Bond Issues and the Aging in Florida." *Research on Aging*, 11(2):158–73.

Callahan, D. 1987. *Setting Limits: Medical Goals in an Aging Society*. New York: Simon and Schuster.

———. 1989. "Rationing Health Care: Will It Be Necessary? Can It Be Done Without Age or Disability Discrimination?" *Issues in Law and Medicine*, 5(3):353–66.

———. 1990. *What Kind of Life? The Limits of Medical Progress*. New York: Simon and Schuster.

———. 1992. "Caring for People with Dementia: Justice and Public Policy." In R. H. Binstock, S. G. Post, and P. J. Whitehouse, eds., *Dementia and Aging: Ethics, Values, and Policy Choices*, pp. 141–52. Baltimore, Md.: Johns Hopkins University Press.

Campbell, A. 1971. "Politics through the Life Cycle." *Gerontologist*, 2(2):112–17.

Campbell, J. C., and J. M. Strate. 1981. "Are Old People Conservative?" *Gerontologist*, 21:580–91.

Campion, F. D. 1984. *The AMA and U.S. Health Policy Since 1940*. Chicago: Chicago Review Press.

Carballo, M. 1981. "Extra Votes for Parents?" *Boston Globe*, Dec. 17, p. 35.

Carlie, M. K. 1969. "The Politics of Age: Interest Group or Social Movement?" *Gerontologist*, 9:259–63.

Chen, Y.-P. 1987. "Making Assets Out of Tomorrow's Elderly." *Gerontologist*, 27:410–16.

———. 1990. "Time to Restructure Social Security." *Gerontologist*, 30:422–24.

Chudacoff, H. P. 1989. *How Old Are You? Age Consciousness in American Culture*. Princeton, N. J.: Princeton University Press.

Chomitz, K. M. 1987. "Demographic Influences on Local Public Education Expenditure: A Review of Econometric Evidence." In Committee on Population, Commission on Behavioral and Social Sciences Education, National Research Council, *Demographic Change and the Well-Being of Children and the Elderly*, pp. 45–53. Washington, D.C.: National Academy Press.

Clark, R. L. 1990. "Income Maintenance Policies in the United States." In R. H. Binstock and L. K. George, eds., *Handbook of Aging and the Social Sciences,* 3d ed., pp. 382–88. San Diego, Calif.: Academic Press.

Clark, P. B., and J. Q. Wilson. 1961. "Incentive Systems: A Theory of Organizations." *Administrative Science Quarterly*, 6:219–66.

Cohen, W. J. 1983. "The Bipartisan Solution, Securing Social Security." *New Leader*, 66:5–8.

———. 1985. "Reflections on the Enactment of Medicare and Medicaid." *Health Care Financing Review*, Annual Supplement, pp. 3–11.

Cohen, W. J., and M. Friedman. 1972. *Social Security: Universal or Selective?* Washington, D.C.: American Enterprise Institute.

Committee on an Aging Society, Institute of Medicine and National Research Council. 1986. *America's Aging: Productive Roles in an Older Society*. Washington, D.C.: National Academy Press.

Commonwealth Fund Commission on Elderly People Living Alone. 1987. *Old, Alone and Poor: A Plan for Reducing Poverty among Elderly People Living Alone*. Baltimore, Md.: Commonwealth Fund Commission on Elderly People Living Alone.

Concord Coalition. 1993. *The Zero Deficit Plan: A Plan for Eliminating the Federal Budget Deficit by the Year 2000*. Washington, D.C.: The Concord Coalition.

Cook, F. L., V. W. Marshall, J. G. Marshall, and J. E. Kaufman. In press. "Intergenerational Equity and the Politics of Income Security for the Old." In V. L. Greene and T. R. Marmor, *Economic Security, Intergenerational Justice: A Look at North America*. Washington, D.C.: Urban Institute Press.

Crystal, S. 1990. "Health Economics, Old-Age Politics, and the Catastrophic Medicare Debate." *Journal of Gerontological Social Work*, 15(3/4):21–31.

Cutler, N. E. 1977. "Demographic, Social-Psychological, and Political Factors in the Politics of Aging: A Foundation for Research in 'Political Gerontology.' " *American Political Science Review*, 71:1011–25.

Daniels, N. 1988. *Am I My Parents' Keeper? An Essay on Justice Between the Young and the Old*. New York: Oxford University Press.

David, S. I. 1985. *With Dignity, the Search For Medicare and Medicaid*. Westport, Conn.: Greenwood Press.

Day, C. L. 1990. *What Older Americans Think: Interest Groups and Aging Policy*. Princeton, N. J.: Princeton University Press.

Derthick, M. 1979. *Policymaking for Social Security*. Washington, D.C.: Brookings Institution.

Estes, C. L. 1979. *The Aging Enterprise*. San Francisco, Calif.: Jossey-Bass.

———. 1983. "Social Security: The Social Construction of a Crisis." *Milbank Memorial Fund Quarterly/Health and Society*, 61:445–61.

Fairlie, H. 1988. "Talkin' 'bout My Generation." *New Republic*, 198(13):19–22.

Fischer, D. H. 1977. *Growing Old in America*. New York: Oxford University Press.

Ford Foundation, Project on Social Welfare and the American Future, Executive Panel. 1989. *The Common Good: Social Welfare and the American Future*. New York, N. Y.: Ford Foundation.

Fox, P. 1989. "From Senility to Alzheimer's Disease: The Rise of the Alzheimer's Disease Movement." *Milbank Quarterly*, 67:58–102.

Generational Journal. 1989. Untitled statement of organizational purpose and tax status of Americans for Generational Equity, 1(4):unnumbered page following 103.

Gibbs, N. R. 1988. "Grays on the Go." *Time*, 131 (8):66–75.

Gist, J. R., ed. 1988. *Social Security and Economic Well-Being across Generations*. Washington, D.C.: American Association of Retired Persons.

Graebner, W. 1980. *A History of Retirement: The Meanings and Functions of an American Institution, 1885–1978.* New Haven, Conn.: Yale University Press.

Haber, C. 1983. *Beyond Sixty-Five: The Dilemma of Old Age in America's Past.* Cambridge, U.K.: Cambridge University Press.

Habib, J. 1990. "The Economy and the Aged." In R. H. Binstock and L. K. George, eds., *Handbook of Aging and the Social Sciences*, pp. 328–45. San Diego, Calif.: Academic Press.

Harris, R. 1966. *A Sacred Trust.* New York: American Library.

Heclo, H. 1984. "The Political Foundations of Anti-Poverty Policy." *IRP Conference Paper on Poverty and Policy: Retrospect and Prospects*, pp. 6–8. Madison, Wis.: Institute for Research on Poverty.

———. 1988. "Generational Politics." In J. L. Palmer, T. Smeeding, and B. B. Torrey, eds., *The Vulnerable*, pp. 381–411. Washington, D.C.: Urban Institute Press.

Hing, E. 1987. *Use of Nursing Homes by the Elderly: Preliminary Data from the 1985 National Nursing Home Survey.* Advance Data no. 135. Hyattsville, Md.: National Center for Health Statistics, U.S. Department of Health and Human Services.

Holstein, M., and M. Minkler. 1991. "The Short Life and Painful Death of the Medicare Catastrophic Coverage Act." In M. Minkler and C. Estes, eds., *Critical Perspectives on Aging: The Political and Moral Economy of Growing Old*, pp. 189–208. Amityville, N. Y.: Baywood.

Holtzman, A. 1963. *The Townsend Movement: A Political Study.* New York: Bookman.

Howe, N., and Longman, P. 1992. "The Next New Deal." *Atlantic Monthly*, 269(4):88–99.

Hudson, R. B., and E. R. Kingson. 1991. "Inclusive and Fair: The Case for Universality in Social Programs." *Generations* 15(3):51–56.

Hudson, R. B., and J. Strate. 1985. "Aging and Political Systems." In R. H. Binstock and E. Shanas, eds., *Handbook of Aging and the Social Sciences*, 2d ed., pp. 554–85. New York: Van Nostrand Reinhold.

Hudson, R. H. 1978. "The 'Graying' of the Federal Budget and Its Consequences for Old Age Policy." *Gerontologist*, 18:428–40.

Hudson, R. H., and R. H. Binstock. 1976. "Political Systems and Aging." In R. H. Binstock and E. Shanas, eds., *Handbook of Aging and the Social Sciences*, pp. 369–400. New York: Van Nostrand Reinhold.

Iglehart, J. K. 1989. "Medicare's New Benefits: 'Catastrophic' Health Insurance." *New England Journal of Medicine*, 320:329–36.

Jacobs, B. 1990. Aging in Politics. In R. H. Binstock and L. K. George, eds., *Handbook of Aging and the Social Sciences*, pp. 349–61. San Diego, Calif.: Academic Press.

Kalish, R. A. 1979. "The New Ageism and the Failure Models: A Polemic." *Gerontologist*, 19:398–407.

Kingson, E. R. 1988. "Generational Equity: An Unexpected Opportunity to Broaden the Politics of Aging." *Gerontologist*, 28:765–72.

Kingson, E. R., B. A. Hirshorn, and J. M. Cornman. 1986. *Ties That Bind: The Interdependence of Generations.* Washington, D.C.: Seven Locks Press.

Kutza, E. A. 1981. *The Benefits of Old Age.* Chicago: University of Chicago Press.

Lamm, R. D. 1987. "A Debate: Medicare in 2020." In *Medicare Reform and the Baby Boom Generation*, edited proceedings of the second annual conference of Americans for Generational Equity, April 30–May 1, 1987, pp. 77–88. Washington, D.C.: Americans for Generational Equity.

———. 1989. "Columbus and Copernicus: New Wine in Old Wineskins." *Mount Sinai Journal of Medicine*, 56(1):1–10.

Leavitt, T. D., and J. H. Schulz. 1988. *The Role of the Asset Test in Program Eligibility and Participation: The Case of SSI.* Waltham, Mass.: Policy Center on Aging, Heller School, Brandeis University.

Levy, F., and R. J. Murnane. 1992. "Orphans of the Ballot Box." *New York Times*, Feb. 6, p. A15.

Light, P. C. 1985. *Artful Work: The Politics of Social Security Reform*. New York: Random House.

———. 1988. *Baby Boomers*. New York: Norton.

Lockett, A. 1983. *Aging, Politics, and Research: Setting the Federal Agenda for Research on Aging*. New York: Springer.

Longman, P. 1987. *Born to Pay: The New Politics of Aging in America*. Boston: Houghton Mifflin.

Lowi, T. H. 1969. *The End of Liberalism*. New York: Norton.

Lubitz, J., and R. Prihoda. 1984. "The Use and Costs of Medicare Services in the Last Two Years of Life." *Health Care Financing Review*, 5(3):117–31.

Manton, K. G. 1991. "The Dynamics of Population Aging: Demography and Policy Analysis." *Milbank Quarterly*, 69:309–38.

Marmor, T. R. 1970. *The Politics of Medicare*. London: Routledge and Kegan Paul.

Marmor, T. R., J. L. Mashaw, and P. L. Harvey. 1990. *America's Misunderstood Welfare State: Persistent Myths, Enduring Realities*. New York: Basic Books.

McCall, N. 1984. "Utilization and Costs of Medicare Services by Beneficiaries in Their Last Year of Life." *Medical Care*, 22:329–42.

McConnell, S. 1990. "Who Cares about Long-Term Care?" *Generations*, 14(2):15–18.

Menzel, P. T. 1990. *Strong Medicine: The Ethical Rationing of Health Care*. New York, N.Y.: Oxford University Press.

Messinger, S. L. 1955. "Organizational Transformation: A Case Study of a Declining Social Movement." *American Sociological Review*, 20:3–10.

Munnell, A. H. 1977. *The Future of Social Security*. Washington, D.C.: Brookings Institution.

Myles, J. F. 1983. "Conflict, Crisis, and the Future of Old Age Security. *Milbank Memorial Fund Quarterly/Health and Society*, 61:462–72.

National Center for Health Statistics. 1987a. *Health United States, 1986*. Publication no. (PHS) 87–1232. Hyattsville, Md.: U.S. Department of Health and Human Services.

———. 1987b. *Current Estimates from the National Health Interview Survey, United States, 1986*. Series 10, no. 164. Hyattsville, Md.: U.S. Department of Health and Human Services.

National Opinion Research Center (NORC), University of Chicago. 1986–1991. Data provided by the Roper Center, University of Connecticut, Storrs, Conn.

Nelson, D. W. 1982. "Alternative Images of Old Age as the Bases for Policy." In B. L. Neugarten, ed., *Age or Need?: Public Policies for Older People*, pp. 131–69. Beverly Hills, Calif.: Sage.

Neugarten, B. L. 1970. "The Old and the Young in Modern Societies." *American Behavioral Scientist*, 14:13–24.

———. 1979. "Policy for the 1980s: Age or Need Entitlement?" In P. Hubbard, ed., *Aging: Agenda for the Eighties*, pp. 48–52. Washington, D.C.: Government Research Corp.

———, ed. 1982. *Age or Need? Public Policies for Older People*. Beverly Hills, Calif.: Sage.

Neugarten, B. L., and D. A. Neugarten. 1986. "Age in the Aging Society." *Daedalus*, 115(1):31–49.

Older Americans Act. 1989. *The Older Americans Act of 1965, As Amended Through December 31, 1988*. Prepared for the Subcommittee on Human Resources of the Committee on Education of the House of Representatives (Serial No. 101–A) and for the Special Committee on Aging of the United States (Serial No. 101–B). Washington, D.C.: U.S. Government Printing Office.

Olson, L. K. 1982. *The Political Economy of Aging: The State, Private Power and Social Welfare*. New York: Columbia University Press.

Oreskes, M. 1990. "Social Security: A Tinderbox Both Parties Handle Gingerly." *New York Times* Sept. 28, p. 12.

Palmer, J. L., and S. G. Gould. 1986. "The Economic Consequences of an Aging Society." *Daedalus*, 115(1):295–323.

Palmore, E. B. 1990. *Ageism: Negative and Positive.* New York: Springer.

Pechman, J. A., H. J. Aaron, and M. K. Taussig. 1968. *Social Security: Perspectives for Reform.* Washington, D.C.: Brookings Institution.

Peterson, P. 1987. "The Morning After." *Atlantic*, 260(4):43–69.

Pinner, F. A., P. Jacobs, and P. Selznick. 1959. *Old Age and Political Behavior.* Berkeley: University of California Press.

Pratt, H. J. 1976. *The Gray Lobby.* Chicago: University of Chicago Press.

Preston, S. H. 1984. "Children and the Elderly in the U.S." *Scientific American*, 251(6):44–49.

Putnam, J. K. 1970. *Old Age Politics in California: From Richardson to Reagan.* Stanford, Calif.: Stanford University Press.

Quadagno, J. 1989. "Generational Equity and the Politics of the Welfare State." *Politics and Society*, 17(3):353–76.

Quinn, J. F. 1987. "The Economic Status of the Elderly: Beware of the Mean." *Review of Income and Wealth*, March, pp. 63–82.

Quinn, J. F., and R. V. Burkhauser. 1990. "Work and Retirement." In R. H. Binstock and L. K. George, eds., *Handbook of Aging and the Social Sciences,* 3d. ed., pp. 307–27. San Diego, Calif.: Academic Press.

Radner, D. B. 1991. "Changes in the Income of Age Groups, 1984–1989." *Social Security Bulletin*, 54(12):2–18.

Riemer, Y., and R. H. Binstock. 1978. "Campaigning for the 'Senior Vote': A Case Study of Carter's 1976 Campaign." *Gerontologist*, 18:517–24.

Robertson, A. 1991. "The Politics of Alzheimer's Disease: A Case Study in Apocalyptic Demography." In M. Minkler and C. L. Estes, eds., *Critical Perspectives on Aging: The Political and Moral Economy of Growing Old*, pp. 135–50. Amityville, N.Y.: Baywood.

Rosenblatt, R. A. 1992. "Medicare Is Going Broke: Hospital Trust Fund to Run Out in 2002." *Plain Dealer*, April 3, p. 1.

Rosenzweig, R. M. 1990. Address to the President's Opening Session, 43rd Annual Scientific Meeting, Gerontological Society of America. Boston, Mass., Nov. 16.

Ross, S. G. 1991. The Financial Status of the Social Security and Medicare Programs. Paper presented at the annual meeting of the Gerontological Society of America, San Francisco, Calif., Nov. 23.

Ruggles, P. 1990. *Drawing the Line: Alternative Poverty Measures and Their Implications for Public Policy.* Washington, D.C.: Urban Institute Press.

Russell, L. B. 1989. *Medicare's New Hospital Payment System: Is It Working?* Washington, D.C.: Brookings Institution.

Salholz, E. 1990. "Blaming the Voters: Hapless Budgeteers Single Out 'Greedy Geezers.' " *Newsweek*, Oct. 29, p. 36.

Samuelson, R. J. 1978. "Aging America: Who Will Shoulder the Growing Burden?" *National Journal*, 10:1712–17.

Schlesinger, A., Jr. 1958. *The Politics of Upheaval.* Boston, Mass.: Houghton Mifflin.

Schneider, E. L., and J. M. Guralnik. 1990. "The Aging of America: Impact on Health Care Costs." *Journal of the American Medical Association*, 263:2335–40.

Schulte, J. 1983. "Terminal Patients Delete Medicare, Greenspan Says." *Dallas Morning News*, April 26, p. 1.

Schulz, J. H. 1988. *The Economics of Aging,* 4th ed. Dover, Mass.: Auburn House.

Schulz, J. H., A. Borowski, and W. H. Crown. 1991. *Economics of Population Aging: The "Graying" of Australia, Japan and the United States.* New York: Auburn House.

Scitovsky, A. A. 1984. " 'The High Cost of Dying': What Do the Data Show?'' *Milbank Memorial Fund Quarterly/Health and Society*, 62:591–608.

Simon, H. A. 1985. "Human Nature in Politics: The Dialogue of Psychology with Political Science." *American Political Science Review*, 79:293–304.

Slater, W. 1984. "Latest Lamm Remark Angers the Elderly." *Arizona Daily Star*, March 29, p. 1.

Smeeding, T. M. 1982. *Alternative Methods for Valuing Selected In-Kind Transfer Benefits and Measuring Their Effect on Poverty.* Technical Paper No. 50. Washington, D.C.: U.S. Bureau of the Census.

Smeeding, T. M. 1990. "Economic Status of the Elderly." In R. H. Binstock and L. K. George, eds., *Handbook of Aging and the Social Sciences,* 3d. ed., pp. 362–81. San Diego, Calif.: Academic Press.

Smeeding, T. M., M. P. Battin, L. P. Francis, and B. M. Landesman, eds. 1987. *Should Medical Care Be Rationed by Age?* Totowa, N.J.: Rowman and Littlefield.

Smith, L. 1992. "The Tyranny of America's Old." *Fortune*, 125(1):68–72.

Sonnefeld, S. T., D. R. Waldo, J. A. Lemieux, and D. R. McKusick. 1991. "Projections of National Health Expenditures through the Year 2000." *Health Care Financing Review*, 13(1):1–27.

Stone, R., G. L. Cafferata, and J. Sangl. 1987. "Caregivers of the Frail Elderly: A National Profile." *Gerontologist*, 27:616–26.

Suzman, R., D. Willis, and K. Manton, eds. 1992. *The Oldest Old.* New York: Oxford University Press.

Taeuber, C. 1990. "Diversity: The Dramatic Reality." In S. A. Bass, E. A. Kutza, and F. M. Torres-Gil, eds., *Diversity in Aging: Challenges Facing Planners and Policymakers in the 1990s,* pp. 1–45. Glenview, Ill.: Scott, Foresman.

Tolchin, M. 1989a. "House Acts to Kill '88 Medicare Plan of Extra Benefits." *New York Times*, Nov. 5, p. 1.

———. 1989b. "Lawmakers Tell the Elderly: 'Next Year' on Health Care." *New York Times*, Nov. 23, p. 10Y.

Torres-Gil, F. M. 1992. *The New Aging: Politics and Change in America.* New York: Auburn House.

Torrey, B. B. 1982. "Guns Vs. Canes: The Fiscal Implications of an Aging Population." *American Economics Association Papers and Proceedings*, 72:309–13.

U.S. Congress, Congressional Budget Office. 1992. *The Economic and Budget Outlook: Fiscal Years 1993–1997.* Washington, D.C.: U.S. Government Printing Office.

U.S. House of Representatives, Select Committee on Aging. 1977. *Federal Responsibility to the Elderly: Executive Programs and Legislative Jurisdiction.* Washington, D.C.: U.S. Government Printing Office.

———. 1989. *Health Care Costs for America's Elderly, 1977–1988.* Washington, D.C.: U.S. Government Printing Office.

U.S. Senate, Special Committee on Aging. 1989. *Aging America: Trends and Projections.* Washington, D.C.: U.S. Government Printing Office.

———. 1991. *Developments in Aging: 1990,* vol. 1. Washington, D.C.: U.S. Government Printing Office.

U.S. Social Security Administration. 1991. *Social Security Bulletin, Annual Statistical Supplement, 1991.* Washington, D.C.: U.S. Department of Health and Human Services.

Washington Post. 1990. "Older Voters Drive Budget: Generational Divide Marks Budget Battle." Oct. 15, p. 1.

Williamson, J. B., L. Evans, and L. A. Powell. 1982. *The Politics of Aging: Power and Policy.* Springfield, Ill.: Charles C. Thomas.

Wisensale, S. K. 1988. "Generational Equity and Intergenerational Policies." *Gerontologist*, 28:773–78.

Witte, E. 1962. *The Development of the Social Security Act*. Madison: University of Wisconsin Press.

Chapter 3: Post–Cold War Health Policy

Aaron, Henry J., and William B. Schwartz. 1984. *The Painful Prescription: Rationing Hospital Care*. Washington, D.C.: Brookings Institution.

Abram, Morris B., and Susan M. Wolf. 1984. "Public Involvement in Medical Ethics: A Model for Government Action." *New England Journal of Medicine*, 310(10):627–32.

American Medical Association. 1987. *Health Policy Agenda for the American People*. Chicago: American Medical Association.

———. 1990. *Health Access America: The AMA Proposal to Improve Access to Affordable, Quality Health Care*. Chicago: American Medical Association.

Annas, George J. 1985. "The Prostitute, the Playboy, and the Poet: Rationing Schemes for Organ Transplantation." *American Journal of Public Health*, 75(2):187–89.

Blank, Robert H. 1988. *Rationing Medicine*. New York: Columbia University Press.

Blendon, Robert J., and Jennifer N. Edwards. 1991. "Caring for the Uninsured: Choices for Reform." *Journal of the American Medical Association*, 265(19):2563–65.

Bronow, Ronald S., Robert A. Beltran, Stephen C. Cohen, et al. 1991. "The Physicians Who Care Plan: Preserving Quality and Equitability in American Medicine." *Journal of the American Medical Association*, 265(19):2511–15.

Brown, E. Richard. 1983. "The Rationing of Hospital Care." In President's Commission for the Study of Ethical Problems in Medicine and Biomedical and Behavioral Research, *Securing Access to Health Care*, vol. 3. Washington, D.C.: U.S. Government Printing Office.

Butler, S. M. 1991. "A Tax Reform Strategy to Deal with the Uninsured." *Journal of the American Medical Association*, 265(19):2541–44.

Callahan, Daniel. 1987. *Setting Limits: Medical Goals in an Aging Society*. New York: Simon and Schuster.

———. 1990. *What Kind of Life: The Limits of Medical Progress*. New York: Simon and Schuster.

———. 1991. "Medical Futility, Medical Necessity." *Hastings Center Report*, 21(4):30–35.

A Call for Action: Final Report of the Pepper Commission. 1990. Washington, D.C.: U.S. Government Printing Office.

Capron, Alexander M. 1975. "Legal Issues in Fetal Diagnosis and Abortion." In Charles Birch and Paul Abrecht, eds., *Genetics and the Quality of Life*. Sydney: Pergamon Press.

Daniels, Norman. 1986. "Why Saying No to Patients in the United States Is So Hard: Cost Containment, Justice, and Provider Autonomy." *New England Journal of Medicine*, 314(21):1380–83.

Davies, Nicholas E., and Louis H. Felder. 1990. "Applying Brakes to the Runaway American Health Care System." *Journal of the American Medical Association*, 263(1):73–76.

Department of Health and Human Services. 1990. *Healthy People 2000: National Health Promotion and Disease Prevention Objectives*. Washington, D.C.: Department of Health and Human Services.

Enthoven, Alain, and Richard Kronick. 1989. "A Consumer-Choice Health Plan for the 1990s: Universal Health Insurance in a System Designed to Promote Quality and Economy" (2 parts). *New England Journal of Medicine*, 320(1):29–37; and 320(2):94–101.

Evans, Robert G., Jonathan Lomas, Morris L. Barer, et al. 1989. "Controlling Health Expenditures—The Canadian Reality." *New England Journal of Medicine*, 320(9):571–77.

Evans, Roger W. 1983. "Health Care Technology and the Inevitability of Resource Allocation and Rationing Decisions: Part II." *Journal of the American Medical Association*, 249(6):2208–19.

Fein, Rashi. 1991. "The Health Security Partnership: A Federal-State Universal Insurance and Cost-Containment Program." *Journal of the American Medical Association*, 265(19):2555–58.

Friedman, Emily. 1991. "The Uninsured: From Dilemma to Crisis." *Journal of the American Medical Association*, 265(19):2491–95.

Grumbach, Kevin, Thomas Bodenheimer, David U. Himmelstein, and Steffie Woolhandler. 1991. "Liberal Benefits, Conservative Spending: The Physicians for a National Health Program Proposal." *Journal of the American Medical Association* 265(19):2549–54.

Harvey, Birt. 1990. "A Proposal to Provide Health Insurance to All Children and All Pregnant Women." *New England Journal of Medicine*, 323(17):1216–20.

Holahan, John, Marilyn Moon, W. Pete Welch, and Stephen Zuckerman. 1991. "An American Approach to Health System Reform." *Journal of the American Medical Association*, 265(19):2537–40.

Hsiao, William C. 1988. "Resource-Based Relative Values: An Overview." *Journal of the American Medical Association*, 260(16):2347–53.

Ingelfinger, Franz J. 1980. "Medicine: Meritorious or Meretricious." In Philip H. Abelson, ed., *Health Care: Regulation, Economics, Ethics, Practice*. Washington, D.C.: American Association for the Advancement of Science.

Kitzhaber, John. 1991. "A Healthier Approach to Health Care." In Robert H. Blank and Andrea Bonnicksen, eds., *Emerging Issues in Biomedical Policy*, vol. 1. New York: Columbia University Press.

Lappé, Marc. 1972. "Moral Obligations and the Fallacies of 'Genetic Control.' " *Theological Studies*, 33:411–27.

Lee, Philip R., Paul B. Ginsburg, Lauren B. LeRoy, and Glenn T. Hammons. 1990. "The Physician's Payment Review Commission Report to Congress—1989." In Philip R. Lee and Carroll L. Estes, eds., *The Nation's Health*. Boston, Mass.: Jones and Bartlett.

Levit, Katharine R., Helen C. Lazenby, Suzanne W. Letsch, and Cathy A. Cowan. 1991. "National Health Care Spending, 1989." *Health Affairs*, Spring, pp. 117–30.

Lonergan, Edmund T., ed. 1991. *Extending Life, Enhancing Life*. Washington, D.C.: National Academy Press.

LORAN Commission. 1987. *Making Difficult Health Care Decisions*. Cambridge, Mass.: Harvard Community Health Plan.

Lundberg, George D. 1991. "National Health Care Reform: An Aura of Inevitability Is Upon Us." *Journal of the American Medical Association*, 265(14):2566–67.

McGinnis, J. Michael. 1989. "National Priorities in Disease Prevention." *Issues in Science and Technology*, Winter, pp. 46–52.

Mechanic, David. 1977. "The Growth of Medical Technology and Bureaucracy: Implications for Medical Care." *Milbank Memorial Fund Quarterly*, 55 (Winter):61–78.

———. 1986. *From Advocacy to Allocation: The Evolving American Health Care System*. New York: Free Press.

Menzel, Paul. 1989. *Strong Medicine*. New York: Oxford University Press.

Milbrath, Lester W. 1986. "A Governance Structure Designed to Help a Society Learn How to Become Sustainable." Paper presented at American Political Science Assoc. meeting, Washington, D.C., Aug. 30.

Miller, Francis H., and Graham A. H. Miller. 1986. "The Painful Prescription: A Procrustean Perspective." *New England Journal of Medicine*, 314(21):1383–85.

Nutter, Donald O., Charles M. Helms, Michael E. Whitcomb, and W. Donald Weston. 1991. "Restructuring Health Care in the United States." *Journal of the American Medical Association*, 265(19):2516–20.

Physician Payment Review Commission. 1990. "1988 Annual Report to Congress." In Philip R. Lee and Carroll L. Estes, eds., *The Nation's Health*. Boston, Mass.: Jones and Bartlett.

Ricardo-Campbell, Rita. 1982. *The Economics and Politics of Health Care*. Chapel Hill: University of North Carolina Press.

Rockefeller, John D., IV. 1991. "The Pepper Commission's Blueprint for Health Care Reform." *Journal of the American Medical Association*, 265(19):2507–10.

Roybal, Edward R. 1991. "The USHealth Act: Comprehensive Reform for a Caring America." *Journal of the American Medical Association*, 265(19):2545–48.

Schneider, Edward L., and Jack M. Guralnik. 1990. "The Aging of America: Impact on Health Care Costs." *Journal of the American Medical Association*, 263(17):2335–40.

Schramm, Carl J. 1984. "Can We Solve the Hospital-Cost Problem in Our Democracy?" *New England Journal of Medicine*, 311(11):729–32.

Schwartz, William B. 1984. "The Most Painful Prescription." *Newsweek*, Nov. 12, p. 24.

Shortell, Stephen M., and Walter J. McNerney. 1990. "Criteria and Guidelines for Reforming the U.S. Health Care System." *New England Journal of Medicine*, 322(7):463–68.

Todd, James S., Steven V. Seekins, John A. Krichbaum, and Lynn K. Harvey. 1991. "Health Access America—Strengthening the U.S. Health Care System." *Journal of the American Medical Association*, 265(19):2503–06.

Weir, Robert F. 1989. *Abating Treatment with Critically Ill Patients*. New York: Oxford University Press.

Chapter 4: Child Care Policy: Past, Present, and Future

Besharov, Douglas J., and Paul N. Tramontozzi. 1989. "Federal Child Care Assistance: A Growing Middle Class Entitlement." *Journal of Policy Analysis*, 8:31.

Congressional Quarterly Almanac. 1971. Washington, D.C.: Congressional Quarterly, Inc.

——————. 1989. Washington, D.C.: Congressional Quarterly, Inc.

Congressional Quarterly Weekly Report. Nov. 18, 1989; March 29 and 31, Oct. 27, Nov. 3, 1990. Washington, D.C.: Congressional Quarterly, Inc.

Congressional Record. June 15, 21, 22, 23, Oct. 5, 1989, March 25 and 29, 1990. Washington, D.C.: U.S. Government Printing Office.

Congressional Research Service. 1988. *Child Day Care: Patterns of Use Among Families With Preschool Children*. Report 88–762 EPW. Washington, D.C.: Congressional Research Service.

Ehrenreich, Barbara. 1987. "The New Right Attack on Social Welfare." In Fred Block, Richard Cloward, Francis F. Piven, and Barbara Ehrenreich, eds., *The Mean Season*. New York: Random House.

Eisenstein, Zilla. 1981. *The Radical Future of Liberal Feminism*. New York: Longman.

General Accounting Office (GAO). 1989. *Child Care: Government Funding Sources, Coordination, and Service Availability*. HRD-90-26-BR. Washington, D.C.: U.S. Government Accounting Office.

Goodman, Jody, and Edward F. Zigler. 1982. In Edward W. Gordon and Edward F. Zigler, eds., *Day Care: Scientific and Social Policy Issues*. Dover, Mass.: Auburn House.

Hayghe, Howard. 1986. "Rise in Mothers' Labor Force Activity Includes Those with Infants." *Monthly Labor Review*.

Kahn, Alfred J., and Sheila B. Kammerman. 1987. *Child Care: Facing the Hard Choices*. Dover, Mass.: Auburn House.

Kammerman, Sheila. 1989. "Toward a Child Policy Decade." *Child Welfare*, 68 (July/Aug.):378.

Kingdon, John W. 1984. *Agendas, Alternatives, and Public Policies*. New York: HarperCollins.

MacKinnon, Catharine. 1989. *Toward a Feminist Theory of the State*. Cambridge, Mass.: Harvard University Press.

National Research Council. 1990. *Who Cares for America's Children*. Washington, D.C.: National Academy Press.

New York Times. Jan. 5, Dec. 7, 1990; June 14, 1991.

Schneider, William. 1989. "JFK's Children: The Class of '74.' " *Atlantic Monthly*, March, p. 35.

U.S. Congress, House Committee on Education and Labor. 1989. *Early Childhood Education and Development Act of 1989: Report to Accompany HR3*. Washington, D.C.: U.S. Government Printing Office.

U.S. Congress, House Committee on Ways and Means. 1989. *Early Childhood Education and Development Act of 1989: Report to Accompany HR3*. Washington, D.C.: U.S. Government Printing Office.

U.S. Congress, House Select Committee on Children, Youth, and Families. 1988. *Children and Families: Key Trends in the 1980s: A Staff Report*. Washington, D.C.: U.S. Government Printing Office.

U.S. Congress, Senate Committee on Finance. 1988. *Child Care Welfare Programs and Tax Credit Proposals*. Washington, D.C.: U.S. Government Printing Office.

U.S. Congress, Senate Committee on Labor and Human Resources. 1988. *Act for Better Child Care Services of 1988: Report to Accompany S1885*. Washington, D.C.: U.S. Government Printing Office.

Washington Post. Feb. 8, June 16, July 25, Sept. 13, 1988; Sept. 27, Nov. 20, 1989.

Weaver, R. Kent. 1985. "Controlling Entitlements." In John Chubb and Paul Peterson, eds., *New Directions in American Politics*. Washington, D.C.: Brookings Institution.

Wildavasky, Aaron. 1988. *The New Politics of the Budgetary Process*. Glenview, Ill.: Scott, Foresman.

Chapter 5: Hunger Strategies for the Twenty-First Century

Butler, Stuart, and S. Anna Kondratas. 1987. *Out of the Poverty Trap: A Conservative Strategy for Welfare Reform*. New York: The Free Press.

Ellwood, David T. 1988. *Poor Support Poverty in the American Family*. New York: Basic Books.

Kotz, Nick. 1979. *Hunger in America: The Federal Response*. New York: Field Foundation.

Lowi, Theodore J. 1979. *The End of Liberalism: The Second Republic of the United States*, 2d ed. New York: Norton.

Manning, Peter A. 1989. "Dealing with Hunger: Corporate Involvement and Food Assistance Policy." In James E. Post, ed., *Research in Corporate Social Performance and Policy*. Greenwich, Conn.: JAI Press.

Mead, Lawrence. 1986. *Beyond Entitlement: The Social Obligations to Citizenship*. New York: Free Press.

Melmed, Matthew. 1987. *Community Childhood Hunger Identification Project*. Hartford, Conn.: Connecticut Association for Human Services.

Murray, Charles. 1984. *Losing Ground: American Social Policy 1950–1980*. New York: Basic Books.

Ricci, Donald M. 1984. *The Tragedy of Political Science Politics, Scholarship, and Democracy*. New Haven, Conn.: Yale University Press.

Schwarz, John E. 1988. *America's Hidden Success: A Reassessment of Twenty Years of Public Policy*. New York: Norton.

U.S. Congress, Committee of the Whole House. 1977. *Food Stamp Act of 1977 Report Together with Supplemental Views, Dissenting Views, Minority Views, Additional Views on H.R. 7940*. H. Prt. 95–464, 95th Cong., 1st sess.

Whitney, Eleanor B., and Eva M. Nunnelly. 1981. *Understanding Nutrition*. St. Paul, Minn.: West.

Chapter 6: Housing: Out in the Cold in the Post–Cold War Era?

Berry, Jeffrey M. 1984. *Feeding Hungry People: Rulemaking in the Food Stamp Program*. New Brunswick, N.J.: Rutgers University Press.

Center on Budget and Policy Priorities and Low Income Housing Information Service. 1989. *A Place to Call Home: The Crisis in Housing for the Poor*. Washington, D.C.: CBPPLIHIS.

Dreier, Peter, and W. Dennis Keating. 1990. "The Limits of Localism: Progressive Housing Policies in Boston, 1984–1989." *Urban Affairs Quarterly*, 26(2):191–216.

Grigsby, William G. 1990. "Housing Finance and Subsidies in the United States." *Urban Studies*, 27(6):831–45.

Hays, R. Allen. 1985. *The Federal Government and Urban Housing. Ideology and Change in Public Policy*. Albany, NY: State University of New York Press.

_____. 1989. "Housing and the Future of the American Welfare State." *Built Environment*, 14(3/4):177–90.

_____. 1990. "The President, Congress, and the Formation of Housing Policy: A Reexamination of Redistributive Policy-Making." *Policy Studies Journal*, 18(4):847–70.

Joint Center for Housing Studies of Harvard University. 1988. *The State of the Nation's Housing*. Cambridge, Mass.: Harvard University Press.

Lynn, Lawrence. 1980. *Designing Public Policy: A Casebook on the Role of Policy Analysis*. Santa Monica, Calif.: Goodyear.

MIT Center for Real Estate Development. 1988. *The Homebuilding Industry: What Will It Take to Produce More Affordable Housing?* Cambridge, Mass.: MIT Center.

U.S. Bureau of the Census. 1991. *Money Income of Households, Families and Persons in the United States: 1988 and 1989*. Washington, D.C.: U.S. Government Printing Office.

U.S. Bureau of the Census and Department of Housing and Urban Development. 1990. *American Housing Survey for the United States in 1987*. Washington, D.C.: U.S. Government Printing Office.

U.S. Congress, Congressional Budget Office. 1988. *Current Housing Problems and Possible Federal Responses*. Washington, D.C.: U.S. Government Printing Office.

U.S. Department of Housing and Urban Development. 1976. *Housing in the Seventies: A Report on the National Policy Review*. Washington, D.C.: U.S. Government Printing Office.

Wright, James D. 1989. *Address Unknown: The Homeless in America*. New York: Aldine De Gruyter.

Chapter 7: Urban Policy in the Post–Cold War Era

Aaron, Henry J., et al. 1982. "Nondefense Programs." In Joseph A. Pechman, ed., *Setting National Priorities: The 1983 Budget*. Washington, D.C.: Brookings Institution.

Ayres, D. Drummond. 1992. "Mayors Applaud Clinton's Promise to Remake American Economy." *New York Times*, June 23.

Barnekov, Timothy K., Daniel Rich, and Robert Warren. 1981. "The New Privatism, Federalism, and the Future of Urban Governance: National Urban Policy in the 1980s." *Journal of Urban Affairs*, 3.

Barnet, Richard. 1974. *Global Reach: The Power of the Multinational Corporations*. New York: Simon and Schuster.

Bartley, Numan V., and Hugh D. Graham. 1975. *Southern Politics and the New Reconstruction*. Baltimore, Md.: Johns Hopkins University Press.

Bluestone, Barry, and Bennett Harrison. 1982. *The Deindustrialization of America: Plant Closings, Community Abandonment, and the Dismantling of Basic Industry*. New York: Basic Books.

Conlan, Timothy. 1988. *New Federalism: Intergovernmental Reform from Nixon to Reagan.* Washington, D.C.: Brookings Institution.

Dahl, Robert A. 1961. *Who Governs?: Democracy and Power in an American City.* New Haven, Conn.: Yale University Press.

DeLeon, Richard E. 1992. *The Urban AntiRegime: Progressive Politics in San Francisco.* Lawrence: University Press of Kansas.

Eisenger, Peter K. 1988. *The Rise of the Entrepreneurial State.* Madison: University of Wisconsin.

Eldersveld, Samuel J. 1949. "The Influence of Metropolitan Party Pluralities in Presidential Elections Since 1920: A Study of Twelve Key Cities." *American Political Science Review*, 43.

Funigiello, Philip J. 1978. *The Challenge to Urban Liberalism: Federal-City Relations during World War II.* Knoxville: University of Tennessee Press.

Fainstein, Susan S., and Norman I. Fainstein. 1986. "Economic Change, National Policy, and the System of Cities" and "Regime Strategies, Communal Resistance, and Economic Forces." In Susan S. Fainstein, Norman I. Fainstein, Richard C. Hill, Dennis Judd, Michael P. Smith, eds., *Restructuring the City: The Political Economy of Urban Development*, rev. ed. New York: Longman.

Gelfand, Mark I. 1975. *A Nation of Cities: The Federal Government and Urban America, 1933–1965.* New York: Oxford University Press.

Glickman, Norman J. 1987. "Cities and the International Division of Labor." In Michael Peter Smith and Joe R. Feagin, eds., *The Capitalist City.* Cambridge, Mass.: Basil Blackwell.

Greenstone, J. David, and Paul E. Peterson. 1968. "Reformers, Machines, and the War on Poverty." In James Q. Wilson, ed., *City Politics and Public Policy.* New York: Wiley.

Joint Economic Committee, U.S. Senate. 1982. "Emergency Interim Survey: Fiscal Condition of Forty-eight Large Cities." Washington, D.C.: U.S. Government Printing Office.

Judd, Dennis, and Michael Parkinson, ed. 1990. *Leadership and Urban Regeneration: Cities in North America and Europe.* Newbury Park, Calif.: Sage.

Krauss, Clifford. 1992a. "Congress Passes Aid to Cities." *New York Times*, June 9.

————. 1992b. "For Cities: Some Christmas Tree." *New York Times*, Oct. 3, p. 22.

Leuchtenberg, William E. 1963. *Franklin D. Roosevelt and the New Deal, 1932–1940.* New York: Harper and Row.

Levitan, Sar. A. 1969. *The Great Society's Poor Law: A New Approach to Poverty.* Baltimore, Md.: Johns Hopkins University Press.

Levitan, Sar A., and Clifford M. Johnson. 1984. *Beyond the Safety Net: Reviving the Promise of Opportunity in America.* Cambridge, Mass.: Ballinger.

Logan, John R., and Todd Swanstrom, eds. 1990. *Beyond the City Limits: Urban Policy and Economic Restructuring in Comparative Perspective.* Philadelphia, Penn.: Temple University Press.

"Mayors Plot to Regain Influence." 1987. *St. Louis Post Dispatch*, March 2.

McGinniss, Joseph. 1969. *The Selling of the President 1968.* New York: Trident Press.

Missouri, State of. 1986. *Official Manual, 1985–1986.* Jefferson City: State of Missouri.

Mollenkopf, John. 1983. *The Contested City.* Princeton, N. J.: Princeton University Press.

Newsweek. May 24, 1971.

New York Times. Oct. 23, 1981, and Jan. 21, 1982.

Page, Benjamin I. 1978. *Choices and Echoes in Presidential Elections.* Chicago: University of Chicago Press.

Peterson, George E. et al. 1986. *The Reagan Block Grants: What Have We Learned?* Washington, D.C.: Urban Institute.

Pickvance, Chris, and Edmond Preteceille, eds. 1991. *State Restructuring and Local Power: A Comparative Perspective.* London and New York: Pinter.

Piven, Frances F., and Richard A. Cloward, 1971. *Regulating the Poor: The Functions of Public Welfare*. New York: Pantheon.

Pomper, Gerald. 1985. "The Presidential Election." In Gerald Pomper, ed., *The Election of 1984: Reports and Interpretations*. Chatham, N. J.: Chatham House.

President's Commission for a National Agenda for the Eighties. 1980a. *A National Agenda for the Eighties*. Washington, D.C.: U.S. Government Printing Office.

_____. 1980b. *Urban America in the Eighties: Perspectives and Prospects*. Washington, D.C.: U.S. Government Printing Office.

Preteceille, Edmond. 1990. In John R. Logan and Todd Swanstrom, eds., *Beyond the City Limits: Urban Policy and Economic Restructuring in Comparative Perspective*. Philadelphia, Penn.: Temple University Press.

Reagan, Michael. 1972. *The New Federalism*. New York: Oxford University Press.

Rich, Michael J. 1991. *National Goals and Local Choices: Distributing Federal Aid to the Poor*. Unpublished manuscript.

Robertson, David B., and Dennis R. Judd. 1989. *The Development of American Public Policy: The Structure of Policy Restraint*. Glenview, Ill.: Scott, Foresman.

Scammon, Richard. 1955. *American Votes*. Washington, D.C.: Elections Research Center, Congressional Quarterly.

Smith, Michael P. 1988. "The Use of Linked Development Policies in U.S. Cities." In Michael Parkinson, Bernard Foley and Dennis Judd, eds., *Regenerating the Cities*. Manchester, U. K.: Manchester University Press.

Smith, Michael P., Randy L. Ready, and Dennis R. Judd. 1985. "Capital Flight, Tax Incentives and the Marginalization of American States and Localities." In Dennis R. Judd, ed., *Public Policy across States and Communities*. Greenwich, Conn.: JAI Press.

Stansfield, Rochelle L. 1982. "New Federalism: A Neatly Wrapped Package with Explosives Inside." *National Journal: The Weekly on Politics and Government*, Feb. 27.

Stone, Clarence N. 1989. *Regime Politics: Governing Atlanta 1946–1988*. Lawrence: University Press of Kansas.

Swanstrom, Todd. 1989. "Semisovereign Cities: The Politics of Urban Development." *Polity*, 21:83–110.

U.S. Department of Housing and Urban Development. 1982. *The President's National Urban Policy Report*. Washington, D.C.: U.S. Government Printing Office.

U.S. Office of Management and Budget. 1979. *Special Analysis, Budget of the United States Government*. Washington, D.C.: U.S. Government Printing Office.

White House Press Release. 1983 (March 7).

Wright, Dell S. 1982. *Understanding Intergovernmental Relations*, 2d ed. Monterey, Calif.: Brooks/Cole.

Chapter 8: Urban Development Policies in a Globalizing Economy

Ahlbrandt, Roger S., Jr., and Clyde Weaver. 1987. "Public-Private Institutions and Advanced Technology Development in Southwestern Pennsylvania." *Journal of the American Planning Association*, 53:449–59.

Bachelor, Lynn W. 1991. "Michigan, Mazda and the Factory of the Future." *Economic Development Quarterly*, 5:114–25.

Behrman, Jack N. 1984. *Industrial Policies, International Restructuring and Transnationals*. Lexington, Mass.: Lexington Books.

Berhman, Jack N., and Robert E. Grosse. 1990. *International Business and Governments: Issues and Institutions*. Columbia: University of South Carolina Press.

Behrman, Jack N., and Dennis A. Rondinelli. 1993. "The Cultural Imperatives of Globalization: Urban Economic Growth in the 21st Century." *Economic Development Quarterly*, 6.

Bennett, Neil G., and David E. Bloom. 1990. "Plotting Our Destiny: Interpreting Our Demographic Trajectory." *Journal of the American Planning Association*, 56:135–40.

Clark, Susan E., and Gary L. Gaile. 1989. "Moving Toward Entrepreneurial Economic Development Policies: Opportunities and Barriers." *Policy Studies Journal*, 17:574–98.

Dicken, Peter. 1986. *Global Shift: Industrial Change in a Turbulent World*. London: Harper and Row.

Downs, Anthony. 1991. "Obstacles in the Future of U.S. Cities." *Journal of American Institute of Planners*, 57:13–15.

Erdman, Andrew. 1990. "How to Make Workers Better." *Fortune,* Oct. 22, pp. 75–77.

Fujita Kuniko, and Richard C. Hill. 1989. "Global Production and Regional 'Hollowing Out' in Japan." In Michael P. Smith, ed., *Pacific Rim Cities in the World Economy*, pp. 200–203. New Brunswick, N.J.: Transaction.

Gakenheimer, Ralph. 1989. "Infrastructure Shortfall: The Institutional Problems." *Journal of the American Planning Association*, 55:14–23.

Graff, Don. 1990. "Hotspots: North America's 10 Best Cities for International Companies." *World Trade*, Aug.-Sept., pp. 72–78.

Harmon, Willis W. 1988. *Global Mind Change: The Promise of the Last Years of the Twentieth Century*. Indianapolis, Ind.: Knowledge Systems.

Hart, S. L., D. R. Denison, and D. A. Henderson. 1989. "A Contingency Approach to Firm Location: The Influence of Industrial Sector and Level of Technology." *Policy Studies Journal*, 17:599–623.

Henderson, Jeffrey. 1989. "The Political Economy of Technological Transformation in Hong Kong." In Michael P. Smith, ed., *Pacific Rim Cities in the World Economy*, pp. 102–55. New Brunswick, N.J.: Transaction.

Jacobs, Jane, 1984. *Cities and the Wealth of Nations: Principles of Economic Life*. New York: Random House.

Kasarda, John D. 1991. "Global Air Cargo-Industrial Complexes as Development Tools." *Economic Development Quarterly*, 5:187–96.

Levitan, Sar, and Isaac Shapiro. 1987. *Working But Poor: America's Contradiction*. Baltimore, Md.: Johns Hopkins University Press.

Lodge, George C., and Ezra F. Vogel, eds. 1987. *Ideology and National Competitiveness: An Analysis of Nine Countries*. Boston: Harvard Business School Press.

Malizia, Emil. 1985. "The Locational Attractiveness of the Southeast to High Technology Manufacturers." In Dale Whittington, ed., *High Hopes for High Technology*, pp. 173–90. Chapel Hill: University of North Carolina Press.

Mumford, Lewis. 1938. *The Culture of Cities*. New York: Harcourt, Brace and World.

National Academy of Sciences. 1973. *Meeting the Challenge of Industrialization*. Washington, D.C.: National Academy of Sciences/National Academy of Engineering.

——————. 1985. *The Competitive Status of U.S. Industry*. Washington, D.C.: National Academy Press.

Newman, Katherine S. 1988. *Falling from Grace: The Experience of Downward Mobility in the American Middle Class*. New York: Free Press.

Raia, Patricia. 1991. "The USA's 10 Best Cities for International Companies." *World Trade*, Dec., pp. 46–48.

Rees, John, ed. 1986. *Technology, Regions and Policy*. Totowa, N.J.: Rowan and Littlefield.

Reich, Robert B. 1991. "The Real Economy." *Atlantic Monthly*, Feb., pp. 35–52.

Rondinelli, Dennis A., and Jack N. Behrman. 1991. "Where Will High-Tech Industries Invest in the 1990s?" *Business in the Contemporary World*, 3:29–39.

Sellers, Patricia. 1990. "The Best Cities for Business." *Fortune*, Oct. 22, pp. 48–51.

Sellers, Patricia and Antony J. Michels. 1990. "Fortune's Top Ten." *Fortune*, Oct. 22, pp. 58–72. (Quote at p. 58.)

Shapiro, James E., Jack N. Behrman, William A. Fisher, and Simon G. Powell. 1991. *Direct Investment and Joint Ventures in China*. Westport, Conn.: Quorum Books.

Sternlieb, George, and James W. Hughes. 1987. "The Demographic Long Wave: Population Trends and Economic Growth." *Economic Development Quarterly*, 1:307–22.

Suarez-Villa, Luis. 1989. *The Evolution of Regional Economies: Entrepreneurship and Macroeconomic Change*. New York: Praeger.

United Nations. 1989. *Transnational Corporations in World Development: Trends and Prospects*. ST/CTC/89. New York: U.N. Centre for Transnational Corporations.

U.S. Department of Commerce. 1990. *U.S. Foreign Trade Highlights 1990*. Washington: U.S. Department of Commerce.

U.S. Office of Technology Assessment. 1984. *Technology, Innovation and Regional Economic Development*. Washington, D.C.: U.S. Congress. (Quote at p. 8.)

Zipp, John F. 1991. "The Quality of Jobs in Small Business." *Economic Development Quarterly*, 5:9–22.

Chapter 9: Post–Cold War Education in the United States

Bast, Joseph, and Robert Wittman. 1991. *The Case for Educational Choice*. Chicago, Ill.: Heartland Institute.

Bowles, Samuel, and Henry M. Levin. Winter, 1968. "The Determinants of Scholastic Achievement—An appraisal of Some Recent Evidence." *Journal of Human Resources*, 3:3–24.

Cain, Glen G., and Harold W. Watts. 1970. "Problems in Making Policy Inferences from the Coleman Report." *American Sociological Review*, 35 (April):32–52.

Chubb, John E., and Terry M. Moe. 1988. "Politics, Markets, and the Organization of Schools." *American Political Science Review*, 82 (Dec.):1065–87.

————. 1990. *Politics, Markets, and America's Schools*. Washington, D.C.: Brookings Institution.

Coleman, James S. 1991. "A Quiet Threat to Academic Freedom." *National Review*, March 18, pp. 28–34.

———— et al. 1966. *Equality of Educational Opportunity*. Washington, D.C.: U.S. Government Printing Office.

Flanigan, Peter M. 1991. "A School System That Works." *Wall Street Journal*, Feb. 12.

Greeley, Andrew M. 1977. "Who Controls Catholic Education?" *Education and Urban Society*, 9:146–66.

Hanushek, Eric. 1986. "The Economics of Schooling: Production and Efficiency in Public Schools." *Journal of Economic Literature*, 24 (Sept.):1141–77.

Hanushek, Eric, and John F. Kain. 1972. "On the Value of 'Equality of Educational Opportunity' as a Guide to Public Policy." In Frederick Mosteller and Daniel P. Moynihan, eds., *On Equality of Educational Opportunity*, pp. 116–45. New York: Random House.

Hayek, Friedrich A. 1944. *The Road to Serfdom*. Chicago: University of Chicago Press.

Lanier, Alfredo S. 1982. "Let Us Now Praise Catholic Schools." *Chicago Magazine*, Oct., pp. 147–53.

National Commission on Excellence in Education. 1983. *A Nation at Risk: The Imperative for Educational Reform*. Washington, D.C.: U.S. Government Printing Office.

O'Connor, Rory. 1986. "The Bishop Who Stayed Home." *Cleveland Magazine*, Dec., pp. 127 ff.

Schultz, Danielle L. 1983. "America's Best Run Schools." *Washington Monthly*, Nov., pp. 52–53.

Summers, Anita A., and Barbara L. Wolfe. 1977. "Do Schools Make a Difference?" *American Economic Review*, 67 (Sept.):639–652.

Chapter 10: Environmental Policy: Problems and Prospects in the New Age

Abelson, Philip. 1989. "Cleaning Hazardous Waste Sites." *Science*, Dec. 1, p. 1097.

Abramson, Rudy. 1991. "U.S. Waste Cleanup Bill Put at $750 Billion." *Los Angeles Times*, Oct. 10, p. A.

Baden, John, and Dean Lueck. 1986. "Bringing Private Management to the Public Lands: Environmental and Economic Advantages." In Sheldon Kamieniecki, Robert O'Brien, and Michael Clarke, eds., *Controversies in Environmental Policy*. Albany: State University of New York Press.

Benedick, Richard. 1991. *Ozone Diplomacy*. Cambridge, Mass.: Harvard University Press.

Block, Alan. 1985. *Poisoning for Profit*. New York: Morrow.

Caplan, Ruth. 1990. *Our Earth, Ourselves*. New York: Bantam.

Carpenter, Betsy. 1989. "Superfund, Superflop." *US News and World Report*, Feb. 6, p. 47.

Caulfield, Henry. 1989. "The Conservation and Environmental Movements: An Historical Analysis." In James Lester, ed., *Environmental Politics and Policy: Theories and Evidence*. Durham, N.C.: Duke University Press.

Cohen, Steven, and Sheldon Kamieniecki. 1991. *Environmental Regulation Through Strategic Planning*. Boulder, Colo.: Westview.

Commoner, Barry. 1971. *The Closing Circle: Nature, Man, and Technology*. New York: Bantam.

Comptroller General. 1980. *Report to the Congress*. Washington D.C.

Congressional Budget Office (CBO). 1985. *Hazardous Waste Management*. Washington, D.C.: U.S. Government Printing Office.

Congressional Quarterly Weekly Report. July 22, 1989.

Congressional Record. Oct. 3, 1984.

Davis, Charles, and James Lester, eds. 1988. *Dimensions of Hazardous Waste Politics and Policy*. Westport, Conn.: Greenwood Press.

Dennis, William, and Randy Simmons. 1986. "From Illusion to Responsibility: Rethinking Regulation of Federal Public Lands." In Sheldon Kamieniecki, Robert O'Brien, and Michael Clarke, eds., *Controversies in Environmental Policy*. Albany: State University of New York Press.

Dolin, Eric. 1988. "Industry Going on a Waste-Watchers Diet." *Business Week*, Aug. 22, p. 94.

Downs, Anthony. 1972. "Up and Down with Ecology—The Issue-Attention Cycle." *Public Interest*, Spring.

Futurist. 1987. "Toxic Clean-Up." July 18.

Gold, Allan. 1989. "States' Deadlines Today on Toxic Waste Plans." *New York Times*, Oct. 17.

Harris, Ron. 1991. "Denver's Tough Approach to Pollution Is Breath of Fresh Air." *Los Angeles Times*, Oct. 2, p. A5.

Harthill, Machalann. 1984. *Hazardous Waste Management*. Boulder, Colo.: Westview.

Ingersoll, Thomas, and Bradley Brockbank. 1986. "The Role of Economic Incentives in Environmental Policy." In Sheldon Kamieniecki, Robert O'Brien, and Michael Clarke, eds., *Controversies in Environmental Policy*. Albany, N.Y.: State University of New York Press.

Kamieniecki, Sheldon. 1991. "Political Mobilization, Agenda Building, and International Environmental Policy." *Journal of International Affairs*, Winter.

—————. 1993. "Emerging Forces in Global Environmental Politics." In Sheldon Kamieniecki, ed., *Environmental Politics in the International Arena: Movements, Parties, Organizations, and Policy*. Albany, N.Y.: State University of New York Press.

Kamieniecki, Sheldon, Matthew Cahn, and Eugene Goss. 1991. "Western Governments and Environmental Policy." In Clive Thomas, ed., *Politics and Public Policy in the Contemporary American West*. Albuquerque: University of New Mexico Press.

Kamieniecki, Sheldon, and Steven Cohen. 1990. "Strategic Regulatory Planning in the Management of Hazardous Materials." *Policy and Politics*, July.

Kamieniecki, Sheldon, and Michael Ferrall. 1991. "Implementing Air Pollution Policy in California." *Publius*, Summer.

——————. 1992. "Implementing Clean-Air Policy in Southern California: Prospects and Potential Obstacles." Paper delivered at the Annual Meeting of the Western Political Science Ass'n, San Francisco, Calif., March 19–21.

Kandel, Anthony. 1985. Intergovernmental Relations and the Determinants of Environmental Policies in the American States. PhD diss., University of Southern California, Los Angeles.

Keene, J. 1985. "RCRA Facilities Face Hard Questions on Safety." *Chemical Week*, July 2, p. 44.

Kraft, Michael, and Norman Vig. 1990. "Environmental Policy from the Seventies to the Nineties: Continuity and Change." In Norman Vig and Michael Kraft, eds., *Environmental Policy in the 1990s*. Washington, D.C.: Congressional Quarterly Press.

Lester, James. 1990. "A New Federalism? Environmental Policy in the States." In Norman Vig and Michael Kraft, eds., *Environmental Policy in the 1990s*. Washington, D.C.: Congressional Quarterly Press.

Lester, James, and Ann O'M. Bowman, eds. 1983. *The Politics of Hazardous Waste Management*. Durham, N.C.: Duke University Press.

Lief, Louise. 1988. "Dirty Job, Sweet Profit." *US News and World Report*, Nov. 21, p. 54.

Magnuson, Ed. 1985. "A Problem That Cannot Be Buried." *Time*, Oct. 14, p. 76.

Mann, Eric. 1990. "LA's Smogbusters." *Nation*, Sept. 17, p. 257.

McCurdy, Howard. 1986. "Environmental Protection and the New Federalism: The Sagebrush Rebellion and Beyond." In Sheldon Kamieniecki, Robert O'Brien, and Michael Clarke, eds., *Controversies in Environmental Policy*. Albany: State University of New York Press.

Melnick, R. Shep. 1983. *Regulation and the Courts: The Case of the Clean Air Act*. Washington, D.C.: Brookings Institution.

Milbrath, Lester. 1989. *Envisioning a Sustainable Society: Learning Our Way Out*. Albany: State University of New York Press.

Miller, G. Tyler. 1988. *Environmental Science*. Belmont, Calif.: Wadsworth.

Mitchell, Robert. 1990. "Public Opinion and the Green Lobby: Poised for the 1990s?" In Norman Vig and Michael Kraft, eds., *Environmental Policy in the 1990s*. Washington, D.C.: Congressional Quarterly Press.

New York Times. Aug. 31, 1989.

O'Donnell, Frank. 1984. "No Time for Toxics." *Sierra*, Nov. 11, p. 25.

Porter, Gareth, and Janet Brown. 1991. *Global Environmental Politics*. Boulder, Colo.: Westview.

Postel, Sandra. 1987. *Defusing the Toxics Threat*. Worldwatch Paper #79.

Reinhardt, C. 1991. "Kiss of the Spider Plant: Cleaner Air." *Working Woman*, July, p. 54.

Rosenbaum, Walter. 1991. *Environmental Politics and Policy*. Washington, D.C.: Congressional Quarterly Press.

Ross, Michael. 1991. "Proposed Clean Air Rules Changes Spark Battle." *Los Angeles Times*, Nov. 11, p. A20.

Satchell, M. 1989. "Uncle Sam's Toxic Folly." *US News and World Report*, March 27, p. 20.

Schneider, C. 1988. "Hazardous Waste—The Bottom Line Is Prevention." *Issues in Science and Technology*, Summer.

Schubert, Louis, and Sheldon Kamieniecki. 1991. "Environmental Security and the Military." Paper delivered at the Western Regional Conference of the International Studies Ass'n, Los Angeles, Calif., Nov. 1–2.

Sibbison, Jim. 1989. "Revolving Door at the EPA." *Nation*, Nov. 6, p. 524.

Stammer, Larry. 1991. "Smoggiest Cities See Dip in Pollution." *Los Angeles Times*, Nov. 11.

Stammer, Larry, and Judy Pasternak. 1991. "Data Used in Smog War Challenged." *Los Angeles Times*, Dec. 14, p. A1.

Steinzor, Rena. 1989. "Reilly Reverses Deferral Policy." *Nation's Cities Weekly*, July 10, p. 1.

Tobin, Richard. 1990. *The Expendable Future: U.S. Politics and the Protection of Biological Diversity*. Durham, N.C.: Duke University Press.

Wolf, Douglas. 1989. "Superfund Implementation." *Environment*, Jan./Feb., p. 42.

Chapter 11: National Security Policy and Federal Lands Policy

Alexander, Charles P. 1992. "Gunning for the Greens." *Time*, Feb. 3. 50–52.

Cheney, Dick. 1990. "Remarks by the Secretary of Defense Dick Cheney at the Defense and Environment Initiative Forum." *Defense Issues*, 40:1–2.

Clarke, Jeane N., and Daniel McCool. 1985. *Staking Out the Terrain: Power Differentials among Natural Resource Management Agencies.* Albany: State University of New York Press.

Culhane, Paul J. 1981. *Public Land Politics: Interest Group Influence on the Forest Service and the Bureau of Land Management*. Baltimore, Md.: Johns Hopkins University Press.

————. 1987. "Heading 'Em Off at the Pass: MX and the Public Lands Subgovernments." In Phillip O. Foss, ed., *Federal Lands Policy*. New York: Greenwood.

Dana, Samuel T. 1956. *Forest and Range Policy*. New York: McGraw-Hill.

Dana, Samuel T., and Sally K. Fairfax. 1980. *Forest and Range Policy: Its Development in the United States*. New York: McGraw-Hill.

Day, Samuel H., Jr. 1983. "The Restless Ranchers of Missile Country." *Progressive*, 10:22–25.

Egan, Timothy. 1990. "Pentagon, Facing Opposition, Suspends Land Buying Plans." *New York Times*, Sept. 18.

Gates, Paul W. 1968. *History of Public Land Law Development*. Washington, D.C.: U.S. Government Printing Office.

Hays, Samuel P. 1975. *Conservation and the Gospel of Efficiency: The Progressive Conservation Movement, 1890–1920*. New York: Atheneum.

————. 1987. *Beauty, Health, and Permanence: Environmental Politics in the United States, 1955–1985*. Cambridge: Cambridge University Press.

Hibbard, Benjamin H. 1924. *History of Public Land Policies*. New York: McMillian.

Holland, Lauren H., and Robert A. Hoover. 1985. *The MX Decision: A New Direction in U.S. Weapons Procurement Policy?* Boulder, Colo.: Westview.

Ise, John. 1961. *Our National Park Policy: A Critical History*. Baltimore, Md.: Johns Hopkins University Press.

Morgan, Arthur E. 1971. *Dams and Other Disasters: A Century of the Army Corps of Engineers in Civil Works*. Boston, Mass.: Porter Sargent.

"Painting the Pentagon Green" (Editorial). 1990. *New York Times*, June 29.

Reisner, Marc. 1986. *Cadillac Desert: The American West and Its Disappearing Water*. New York: Viking Penguin.

Renner, Michael. 1991. "Assessing the Military's War on the Environment." In Lester R. Brown, ed., *State of the World 1991*. New York: Norton.

Robbins, Roy M. 1942. *Our Landed History: The Public Domain 1776–1936*. Princeton, N.J.: Princeton University Press.

Schneider, Keith. 1991. "Pentagon Wins Waiver of Environmental Rule." *New York Times*, Jan. 30.

Shabecoff, Phillip. 1990. "Senator Urges Military Resources Be Turned to Environmental Battle." *New York Times*, June 29.

U.S. Congress. 1956. House Committee on Interior and Insular Affairs. *Withdrawals and Utilization of the Public Lands of the United States. Hearings*. Washington, D.C.: U.S. Government Printing Office.

_____. 1957. House Committee on Interior and Insular Affairs. *Military Land Withdrawals. Hearings*. Washington, D.C.: U.S. Government Printing Office.

_____. 1980. House Subcommittee on Public Lands. *The MX Missile System. Oversight Hearings*. Washington, D.C.: U.S. Government Printing Office.

_____. 1981. House Subcommittee on Public Lands and National Parks. *The MX Missile System. Oversight Hearings*. Washington, D.C.: U.S. Government Printing Office.

_____. 1986a. House Committee on Interior and Insular Affairs. *Military Land Withdrawals. Hearings*. Washington, D.C.: U.S. Government Printing Office.

_____. 1986b. Senate Committee on Energy and Natural Resources. *Military Land Withdrawals. Hearings*. Washington, D.C.: U.S. Government Printing Office.

_____. 1990. House Subcommittee on National Parks and Public Lands. *Military Activities on Federal Lands. Hearings*. Washington, D.C.: U.S. Government Printing Office.

U.S. Council on Environmental Quality. 1988. *Environmental Quality: Annual Report 1987–88*. Washington, D.C.: U.S. Government Printing Office.

U.S. Department of the Air Force. 1978. *Final Environmental Impact Statement, MX: Milestone II*. Washington, D.C.: U.S. Government Printing Office.

_____. 1980. *Deployment Area Selection and Land Withdrawal Draft EIS*. Washington, D.C.: U.S. Government Printing Office.

White House. 1990. *National Security Strategy of the United States*. Washington, D.C.: U.S. Government Printing Office.

Chapter 12: NIP in the Nineties and Beyond

America's Restructured Economy. 1981. Special Issue. *Business Week*, June 1, pp. 55–100.

Bingham, Richard D., and David Hedge. 1991. *State and Local Government in a Changing Society*. New York: McGraw-Hill.

Blakely, Edward J. 1989. *Planning Local Economic Development: Theory and Practice*. Newbury Park, Calif.: Sage.

Blakely, Edward J., and Nancy Nishikawa. 1992. "Incubating High-Technology Firms: State Economic Development Strategies for Biotechnology." *Economic Development Quarterly*, 6 (Aug.):241–54.

Business Week. *The Reindustrialization of America*. 1983. New York: McGraw-Hill. (Based on a special issue of *Business Week*, June 30, 1980, pp. 55–146.)

"Can LA Still Make It?" 1991. *Economist*, July 27, pp. 59–60.

Cohen, Stephen S., and John Zysman. 1987. *Manufacturing Matters*. New York: Basic Books.

Dertouzos, Michael L., Richard K. Lester, Robert M. Solow, and the MIT Commission on Industrial Productivity. 1989. *Made in America: Regaining the Productive Edge*. Cambridge, Mass.: MIT Press.

Destler, I. M. 1986. *American Trade Politics: System under Stress*. Washington, D.C.: Institute for International Economics.

Eisinger, Peter K. 1988. *The Rise of the Entrepreneurial State: State and Local Economic Development Policy in the United States*. Madison: University of Wisconsin Press.

Etzioni, Amitai. 1983. *An Immodest Agenda: Rebuilding America before the Twenty-First Century*. New York: McGraw-Hill.

Fosler, R. Scott. 1988. *The New Economic Role of American States: Strategies in a Competitive World Economy*. New York: Oxford University Press.

Galbraith, James K. 1989. *Balancing Acts: Technology, Finance and the American Future*. New York: Basic Books.

Graham, Edward M. 1991. "Real and Imagined Dangers of U.S. Dependence on Foreign Capital." *Annals of the American Academy of Political and Social Science*, 516 (July):126–43.

Haider, D. 1986. "Economic Development: Changing Practices in a Changing U.S. Economy." *Environment and Planning: Government and Policy*, 4:451–469.

Hill, Edward W. 1990. "The Savings and Loan Bailout." *Economic Development Commentary*, 14 (Fall):18–26.

Hudgins, Edward L., and Richard B. McKenzie. 1989. "The Department of Commerce." In Stuart M. Butler, Michael Sanera, and W. Bruce Weinrod, eds., *Mandate for Leadership II: Continuing the Conservative Revolution*. Washington, D.C.: Heritage Foundation.

Jarboe, Kenan P. 1985. "A Reader's Guide to the Industrial Policy Debate." *California Management Review*, 27 (Summer): 198–219.

Johnson, Chalmers. 1982. *MITI and the Japanese Miracle: The Growth of Industrial Policy, 1925–1975*. Stanford, Calif.: Stanford University Press.

Judd, Dennis R., and Randall L. Ready. 1986. "Entrepreneurial Cities and the New Politics of Economic Development." In George E. Peterson and Carol W. Lewis, eds., *Reagan and the Cities*. Washington, D.C.: Brookings Institution.

Krugman, Paul R. 1983. "Targeted Industrial Policies: Theory and Evidence." In Federal Reserve Bank of Kansas City, *Industrial Change and Public Policy: A Symposium*. Sponsored by the Federal Reserve Bank of Kansas City.

Lawrence, Robert Z. 1984. *Can America Compete?* Washington, D.C.: Brookings Institution.

Lodge, George C. 1990. *Perestroika for America: Restructuring Business-Government Relations for World Competitiveness*. Boston, Mass.: Harvard Business School Press.

Markusen, Ann, Peter Hall, Scott Campbell, and Sabina Deitrick. 1991. "The Rise of the Gunbelt." *Northeast Midwest Economic Review*, June 17, pp. 5–9.

McKenzie, Richard B. 1985. *Competing Visions: The Political Conflict Over America's Economic Future*. Washington, D.C.: Cato Institute.

National Commission on Excellence in Education. 1983. *A Nation at Risk: The Imperative for Educational Reform*. Washington, D.C.: U.S. Government Printing Office.

Norton, R.D. 1986. "Industrial Policy and American Renewal." *Journal of Economic Literature*, 24 (March):1–40.

Penner, Rudolph G. 1988. "Economic Growth." In Isabel V. Sawhill, ed., *Challenge to Leadership: Economic and Social Issues for the Next Decade*. Washington, D.C.: Brookings Institution.

Porter, Michael E. 1980. *The Competitive Advantage of Nations*. New York: Free Press.

Reich, Robert. 1983. *The Next American Frontier*. New York: Penguin Books.

—————. "Small State, Big Lesson." *Boston Observer*, 3 (July):32.

Reich, Robert B., and John D. Donahue. 1985. *New Deals: The Chrysler Revival and the American System*. New York: Times Books.

Rich, Michael J. 1992. "UDAG, Economic Development and the Death and Life of American Cities." *Economic Development Quarterly*, 6 (May):150–72.

Roessner, J. David. 1989. *Federal Programs and Technology-based Regional Economic Development: The U.S. Experience*. Atlanta: Georgia Institute of Technology.

Rohatyn, Felix. 1983. *The Twenty-Year Century: Essays on Economics and Public Finance*. New York: Random House.

Stone, Charles F. 1988. "International Trade." In Isabel V. Sawhill, ed., *Challenge to Leadership: Economic and Social Issues for the Next Decade*, Washington, D.C.: Brookings Institution.

Thurow, Lester. 1980. *The Zero-Sum Society*. New York: Basic Books.

Vaughan, Roger, and Edward W. Hill. 1991. *Financial Futures: American Banking in the 1990s*. Washington, D.C.: Washington Post Books.

Whitehead, David D. 1991. "FYI: The Impact of Private-Sector Defense Cuts on Regions of the United States." *Economic Review* (Federal Reserve Bank of Atlanta), 76 (March/April): 30–41.

Chapter 13: Budgetary Policy in the Post–Cold War Era

Budget of the U.S. Government, Fiscal Year 1982. Washington, D.C.: U.S. Government Printing Office.
Budget of the U.S. Government Fiscal Year 1991. Washington, D.C.: U.S. Government Printing Office.
Budget of the U.S. Government Fiscal Year 1992. Washington, D.C.: U.S. Government Printing Office.
Congressional Quarterly. 1990a. Jan. 13, p. 87.
Congressional Quarterly. 1990b. March 10, p. 759.
Congressional Quarterly. 1991a. Feb. 9, p. 345.
Congressional Quarterly. 1991b. May 25, pp. 1382–84.
Economist, July 3, 1993, pp. 15–16.
Freeland, Chrystia, and Julie Corwin. 1991. "The Ukraine Votes for Independence." *U.S. News and World Report*, Dec. 2, pp. 67–69.
Kapstein, Ethan. 1992. *The Political Economy of National Security*. Columbia: University of South Carolina Press.
Kettl, Donald. 1992. *Deficit Politics Public Budgeting in Its Institutional and Historical Context*. New York: Macmillan.
Kennedy, Paul. 1987. *The Rise and Fall of the Great Powers*. New York: Vintage Books.
Key, V. O., Jr. 1940. "The Lack of Budgetary Theory." *American Political Science Review*, 34 (Dec.):1137–40.
Koven, Steven G. 1988. *Ideological Budgeting: The Influence of Political Philosophy on Public Policy*. New York: Praeger.
_____. 1991. "The U.S. Budget Deficit and the Economy." In F. Waldstein and P. Davies, eds., *Political Issues in America*. Manchester, U.K.: Manchester University Press.
_____. 1994. "Budget Policy." Presented at the annual meeting of the Midwestern Political Science Assoc., Chicago.
Kuttner, Robert. 1991. *The End of Laissez-Faire*. New York: Knopf.
Molotsky, Irvin. 1991. "Bentsen Calls for Tax Cuts and I.R.A.'s." *New York Times*, Oct. 21, p. C1.
Norman, Jane. 1991. "Breaking Open Pentagon's Jar of Candy." *Des Moines Register*, Nov. 10, p. 1.
O'Sullivan, John. 1991. "When Winter Comes." *National Review*, Oct. 21, pp. 28–29.
Ott, David J., and Attiat F. Ott. 1965. *Federal Budget Policy*. Washington, D.C.: Brookings Institution.
Phillips, Kevin. 1990. *The Politics of Rich and Poor*. New York: Random House.
Rubin, Irene S. 1990. *The Politics of Public Budgeting*. Chatham, N.J.: Chatham House.
Smith, Adam. 1937. *The Wealth of Nations*. New York: Modern Library.
Wanat, John. 1976. *Introduction to Budgeting*. North Scituate, Mass.: Duxbury Press.
Wildavsky, Aaron. 1961. "Political Implications of Budgetary Reform." *Public Administration Review*, 21 (Autumn):183–190.
_____. 1964. *The Politics of the Budgetary Process*. Boston, Mass.: Little, Brown.

Chapter 14: Post–Cold War Social Welfare Policy: Limited Options

Barnhart, Jo Anne B. 1991. "The Family Support Act: Public Assistance for the 1990's." *Intergovernmental Perspectives*, 17(2) (Spring):13–17.

Bawden, D. Lee, and John L. Palmer. 1984. "Social Policy: Challenging the Welfare State." In John L. Palmer and Isabel V. Sawhill, eds., *The Reagan Record*, pp. 177–216. Cambridge, Mass.: Ballinger.

Bowman, Anne O'M., and Richard C. Kearney. 1986. *The Resurgence of the States*. Englewood Cliffs, N. J.: Prentice-Hall.

"Budget Outlook." 1992. *Congressional Digest*, 71(5) (May):131.

Burtless, Gary. 1992. "When Work Doesn't Work." *Brookings Review*, 10(2) (Spring):26–29.

Cloward, Richard A., and Frances Fox Piven. 1993. "The Fraud of Workfare." *The Nation*, 256(20) (May 24):693–96.

Cutler, David M., and Lawrence F. Katz. 1992. "Untouched by the Rising Tide." *Brookings Review*, 10(1) (Winter):40–45.

Eckl, Corina. 1991. "Strapped States Face Hard Choices." *State Legislatures*, 17(11) (Nov.):20–22.

Edelman, Marian W. 1991. "Social Services." In David W. Hornbeck and Lester Salamon, eds., *Human Capital and America's Future: An Economic Strategy for the '90s*, pp. 269–96. Baltimore, Md.: Johns Hopkins University Press.

Fabricius, Martha. 1991a. "More Dictates from the Feds." *State Legislatures*, 17(2) (Feb.):28–33.

————. 1991b. "Mandate Stratagems." *State Legislatures*, 17(11) (Nov.):13.

Gold, Steven D. 1991. "Replacing an Impossible Dream." *State Legislatures*, 17(2) (Feb.):24–27.

Hornbeck, David W., and Lester M. Salamon, eds. 1991. *Human Capital and America's Future: An Economic Strategy for the '90s*. Baltimore, Md.: Johns Hopkins University Press.

Hutchison, Tony, and Christopher Zimmerman. 1991. "Making the Budget Fly." *State Legislatures*, 17 (11) (Nov.):16–19.

Lemov, Penelope. 1991. "Climbing Out of the Medicaid Trap." *Governing*, 5(1) (Oct.):49–53.

Office of the Texas Comptroller of Public Accounts. 1991. "School Daze: Finding the Right Equation." *Fiscal Notes*, 91(3) (March):1–7.

Packer, Arnold H. 1991. "The Demographic and Economic Imperatives." In David W. Hornbeck and Lester M. Salamon, eds., *Human Capital and America's Future: An Economic Strategy for the '90s*. pp. 43–68. Baltimore, Md.: Johns Hopkins University Press.

Palmer, John L., and Isabel V. Sawhill. 1984. "Overview." In John L. Palmer and Isabel V. Sawhill, eds., *The Reagan Record*, pp. 1–30. Cambridge, Mass.: Ballinger.

Perales, Cesar A. 1991. "Implementing JOBS Deserves a Chance." *Intergovernmental Perspective*, 17(2) (Spring):24–30.

Peterson, George E. 1984. "Federalism and the States: An Experiment in Decentralization." In John L. Palmer and Isabel V. Sawhill, eds., *The Reagan Record*, pp. 217–60. Cambridge, Mass.: Ballinger.

Peterson, Wallace C. 1991. "The Silent Depression." *Challenge*, 34(4) (July/Aug.):29–34.

Phillips, Kevin. 1990. *The Politics of Rich and Poor: Wealth and the American Electorate in the Reagan Aftermath*. New York: Random House.

Pianin, Eric. 1992. "Budget Amendment Faces Money Crunch." *Houston Chronicle*, May 22.

Plunkert, Lois M. 1990. "The 1980's: A Decade of Job Growth and Industry Shifts." *Monthly Labor Review*, 113(9) (Sept.):3–16.

Rauch, Jonathon. 1992. "The Long Good-Bye." *National Journal*, 24(8) (Feb. 22):438–41.

Riggins, Phillip E. 1991. "Welfare Reform in the Federal System." *Intergovernmental Perspectives*, 17(2) (Spring):7–12.

Romig, Candace L. 1991. "Welfare Reform: How Well Is It Working?" *Intergovernmental Perspectives* 17(2) (Spring):20–23.

Rovner, Julie. 1991. "Raising the Curtain on Welfare Reform." *Governing*, 4(4) (Jan.):19–22.

Ryscavage, Paul, and Peter Henle. 1990. "Earnings Inequality Accelerates in the 1980's." *Monthly Labor Review*, 113(12) (Dec.):3–16.

Sanger, Mary B. 1990. "The Inherent Contradiction of Welfare Reform." *Policy Studies Journal*, 18(3) (Spring):663–80.

Sawhill, Isabel V. 1988. "Poverty in the U.S.: Why Is It So Persistent?" *Journal of Economic Literature*, 26(3) (Sept.):1073–1119.

Sawhill, Isabel V., and Charles F. Stone. 1984. "The Economy: The Key to Success." In John L. Palmer and Isabel V. Sawhill, eds., *The Reagan Record*, pp. 69–106. Cambridge, Mass.: Ballinger.

Schiller, Bradley R., and C. Nielson Brasher. 1990. "Workfare in the 1980s: Successes and Limits." *Policy Studies Review*, 9(4) (Summer):665–80.

Schwarz, John E. 1988. *America's Hidden Success: A Reassessment of Public Policy from Kennedy to Reagan.* New York: Norton.

_____. 1990. "Welfare Liberalism, Social Policy, and Poverty in America." *Policy Studies Review*, 10(1) (Fall):127–39.

Smeeding, Timothy M. 1992. "Why the U.S. Antipoverty System Doesn't Work Very Well." *Challenge*, 35(1) (Jan./Feb.):30–35.

Snell, Ronald K. 1991. "Deep Weeds: Dismal Outlook for 1991." *State Legislatures*, 17(2) (Feb.):14–18.

Social Security Administration. 1991. *Annual Statistical Supplement, 1991.* Washington, D.C.: U.S. Government Printing Office.

Sylvester, Kathleen. 1991. "Welfare: The Hope and the Frustration." *Governing*, 5(2) (Nov.):50–55.

_____. 1992. "The War against the 'Able-Bodied Poor.' " *Governing*, 5(5) (Feb.):24–26.

Thurow, Lester C. 1980. *The Zero-Sum Society: Distribution and the Possibilities for Economic Change.* New York: Basic Books.

_____. 1992. *Head to Head: The Coming Economic Battle among Japan, Europe, and America.* New York: Morrow.

U.S. Bureau of the Census. 1991. *Statistical Abstract of the United States: 1991*, 111th ed. Washington, D.C.: U.S. Government Printing Office.

U.S. Bureau of Economic Analysis. 1991. *Survey of Current Business*, 71(5) (May):13.

Urban Institute. 1992a. "Contrasting Wage Gaps by Gender and Race." *Urban Institute Policy and Research Report*, 22(1) (Winter/Spring):7–8.

_____. 1992b. "Immigration and Race: Past and Future Trends." *Urban Institute Policy and Research Report*, 22(1) (Winter/Spring):16–17.

Chapter 15: Intergovernmental Delivery of Human Services

Agranoff, Robert, ed. 1983. *Human Services on a Limited Budget.* Washington, D.C.: International City Management Assn.

Booth, Alan, and Douglas Higgins. 1984. *Human Service Planning and Evaluation for Hard Times.* Springfield, Ill.: Charles C. Thomas.

Brager, George, and Stephen Holloway. 1978. *Changing Human Service Organizations: Politics and Practice.* New York: Free Press.

Bresnick, David A. 1983. *Managing the Human Services in Hard Times.* New York: Human Services Press.

Checkoway, Barry, ed. 1986. *Strategic Perspectives on Planning Practice.* Lexington, Mass.: Lexington Books.

DeVita, Carol J., and David M. Altschuler. 1987. *Flint Nonprofit Organizations: The Challenge of Retrenchment*. Washington, D.C.: Urban Institute.

Lynn, Lawrence E., Jr. 1980. *The State and Human Services: Organizational Change in a Political Context*. Cambridge, Mass.: MIT Press.

MacManus, Susan A. 1991. "Federalism and Intergovernmental Relations: The Centralization Versus Decentralization Debate." In William Crotty, ed., *Political Science: Looking to the Future*, vol. 4, pp. 203–54. Evanston, Ill.: Northwestern University Press.

Millar, Annie, and Carol J. DeVita. 1986. *The Flint Nonprofit Sector in a Time of Retrenchment*. Washington, D.C.: Urban Institute.

Perlmutter, Felice D., ed. 1984. *Human Services at Risk*. Lexington, Mass.: Lexington Books.

Sabatier, Paul A. 1991. "Public Policy: Toward Better Theories of the Policy Process." In William Crotty, ed., *Political Science: Looking to the Future*, vol. 2, pp. 265–92. Evanston, Ill.: Northwestern University Press.

Weber, Ronald E. 1991. "The Study of State and Local Politics: A Preliminary Exploration of Its Contributions to Empirical Political Theory." In William Crotty, ed., *Political Science: Looking to the Future*, vol. 4, pp. 255–85. Evanston, Ill.: Northwestern University Press.

Index

GOSHEN COLLEGE - GOOD LIBRARY

3 9310 01082068 4

AP